The Mongol Empire

THE EDINBURGH HISTORY OF THE ISLAMIC EMPIRES
Series Editor: Ian Richard Netton

Editorial Advisory Board

Professor C. E. Bosworth
Professor John L. Esposito
Professor Carole Hillenbrand
Professor David Morgan
Professor Andrew Rippin

Available or forthcoming titles

The Umayyad Empire
Andrew Marsham

The Abbasid Empire
Matthew Gordon

The Almoravid and Almohad Empires
Amira K. Bennison

The Seljuk Empire of Anatolia
Sara Yur Yildiz

The Great Seljuk Empire
A. C. S. Peacock

The Fatimid Empire
Michael Brett

The Mamluk Empire
Jo van Steenbergen and Patrick Wing

The Mongol Empire
Timothy May

The Ottoman Empire
Gokhan Çetinsaya

edinburghuniversitypress.com/series/ehie

The Mongol Empire

Timothy May

EDINBURGH
University Press

Edinburgh University Press is one of the leading university presses in the UK. We publish academic books and journals in our selected subject areas across the humanities and social sciences, combining cutting-edge scholarship with high editorial and production values to produce academic works of lasting importance. For more information visit our website: edinburghuniversitypress.com

© Timothy May, 2018

Edinburgh University Press Ltd
The Tun – Holyrood Road
12 (2f) Jackson's Entry
Edinburgh EH8 8PJ

Typeset in Adobe Garamond Pro by
Servis Filmsetting Ltd, Stockport, Cheshire

A CIP record for this book is available from the British Library

ISBN 978 0 7486 4237 3 (hardback)
ISBN 978 0 7486 4236 6 (paperback)
ISBN 978 1 4744 1740 2 (webready PDF)
ISBN 978 1 4744 1741 9 (epub)

The right of Timothy May to be identified as author of this work has been asserted in accordance with the Copyright, Designs and Patents Act 1988 and the Copyright and Related Rights Regulations 2003 (SI No. 2498).

Contents

List of Boxes	vi
List of Illustrations	vii
List of Abbreviations	x
Note on Transliteration, Conventions and Geographical Terminology	xviii
Acknowledgements	xix
Preface	xxi
1 Mongolia before the Mongol Empire	1
2 The Rise of Chinggis Khan and Unification of Mongolia	18
3 The Mongols outside Mongolia	44
4 The Institutions of the Empire	76
5 The Reign of Ogodei	94
6 The Reign of Guyuk and the Regents	122
7 Mongke and the Toluid Revolution	144
8 The Yuan Empire	181
9 The Ilkhanate	223
10 The Ogodeid and Chaghatayid Uluses	257
11 The Jochid Ulus or Golden Horde	280
12 Anxiety and Accommodation	315
13 Conclusion: End of the Chinggisids and the Rise of the Qarachu	336
Appendix I	354
Appendix II	358
Appendix III	365
Glossary	372
Bibliography	377
Index	399

Boxes

Chapter 1
Climatic Causes for the Mongol Empire? ... 3
The Church of the East or Nestorianism ... 12
Chapter 2
Alan Goa and the Parable of the Arrows ... 20
The Wedding Party ... 22
Chapter 3
Onggud Relations ... 51
Zhuds ... 54
Chapter 5
Food Preparation ... 102
Nerge Formation ... 110
Chapter 6
Ortoq ... 124
Gerege ... 129
Chapter 7
Yasa and *Yosun* ... 145
Chapter 8
Zhongwen Qingwu ... 183
Governor Polo? ... 191
Chapter 9
Qanat or *Karez* ... 227
Counterfeiting and Coin Clipping ... 240
What's in a Name? ... 248
Chapter 11
Colour Confusion ... 283
Sarai ... 288
Bubonic Plague ... 301

Illustrations

Figures

(Author photographs except where indicated)

1.1	Steppes of Mongolia	4
1.2	Bactrian (two-humped) camels	6
1.3	The Mongolian horse	7
2.1	Reconstructed *ger* on a wagon platform (Ovorkhangai, Mongolia)	21
2.2	Cangue, nineteenth century (National History Museum Ulaanbaatar, Mongolia)	27
2.3	The Orkhon River Valley (Mongolia)	29
2.4	Chinggis Khan monument (Tsonjin Boldog, Mongolia)	40
2.5	Modern depiction of a Mongol warrior (Tsonjin Boldog, Mongolia)	41
3.1	Sandy steppe land (Ovorkhangai aimag, Mongolia)	46
3.2	Camels with saddles (Ovorkhangai aimag, Mongolia)	49
3.3	Chinggis Khan advising his sons on his deathbed (0019400 The Granger Collection, New York)	66
3.4	Modern statue of Chinggis Khan (Ulaanbaatar, Mongolia)	67
4.1	Typical nomad's camp (Mongolia)	80
4.2	Thirteenth-century Mongol arrowheads (National History Museum, Ulaanbaatar, Mongolia)	81
4.3	The black tuq, the war standard of the Mongols (Mongolia)	82
5.1	Statue of Ogodei Khan (Ulaanbaatar, Mongolia)	96
5.2	Qarabalghasun (Orkhon River Valley, Mongolia)	100
5.3	Erdene Zuu at Qaraqorum (Kharkhorin, Mongolia)	101
5.4	The tortoise of Qaraqorum (Kharkhorin, Mongolia)	104
5.5	A *yam* station (Tov aimag, Mongolia)	105
5.6	Basilica of St Mary, Krakow, Poland (courtesy T. Christopher Jespersen)	114

5.7	Chinese woodcut depicting Subedei (0057609 The Granger Collection, New York)	116
6.1	Gold jewellery at Qaraqorum (Kharkhorin Museum, Kharkhorin, Mongolia)	129
6.2	Gilded *gerege* or *paiza* (National History Museum, Ulaanbaatar, Mongolia)	130
7.1	Tile work from Qaraqorum (Kharkhorin, Mongolia)	148
7.2	Rubruck's Tree (Tov aimag, Mongolia)	158
7.3	Narrow arrowheads for piercing armour (National History Museum, Ulaanbaatar, Mongolia)	162
7.4	Mongol archery (Ovorkhangai aimag, Mongolia)	163
7.5	The Mongol composite bow, unstrung (Ovorkhangai aimag, Mongolia)	164
8.1	Portrait of Khubilai Khan on silk (0024455 The Granger Collection, New York)	186
8.2	Statue of Marco Polo (Ulaanbaatar, Mongolia)	192
8.3	Statue of Khubilai Khan as lawgiver (Ulaanbaatar, Mongolia)	194
8.4	Yuan mace (Tower of London)	199
8.5	A *gerege* with Phagspa inscription (Kharkhorin Museum, Kharkhorin, Mongolia)	204
8.6	Copper mirror (Kharkhorin Museum, Kharkhorin, Mongolia)	210
9.1	A Mongol prince studying the Qur'ān (ART390847 illuminated manuscript page from *Jamia'at al-Tawarikh*, by Rashid al-Din, Iran)	243
9.2	Fourteenth-century Mongol chain mail (National History Museum, Ulaanbaatar, Mongolia)	249
10.1	The steppes and hills near Qaraqorum (Kharkhorin, Mongolia)	268
11.1	White jade *tamgha* (Kojima Jade)	294
11.2	Tukel's Phagspa seal (Kojima Jade)	294
12.1	Chinggis Khan lecturing the grandees of Bukhara (0110813 The Granger Collection, New York)	316
13.1	*Tamgha* in Phagspa script (Kharkhorin Museum, Mongolia)	345
13.2	Chinggis Khan pavilion (Ulaanbaatar, Mongolia)	350

Maps

1.1	Mongolia in the twelfth century	11
3.1	The Mongol Empire in 1216	56
3.2	The Mongol Empire at the time of Chinggis Khan's death	75
5.1	The Mongol Empire during the reign of Ogodei	121
7.1	The Mongol Empire during the reign of Mongke	168
7.2	The Mongol Empire in c. 1300	174

8.1	The Yuan Empire, 1279–1368	202
9.1	The Ilkhanate, 1256–1353	228
10.1	The Ogodeid and Chaghatayid Uluses	262
11.1	The Jochid Ulus	281

Tables

1	Genealogy of the Khans of the Yeke Monggol Ulus	359
2	Genealogy of the Yuan Emperors	360
3	Genealogy of the Ilkhans	361
4	Genealogy of the Ogodeids	362
5	Genealogy of the Chaghatayids	363
6	Genealogy of the Jochids	364

Abbreviations

Journals and Secondary works

AAC2	Larry V. Clark and Paul Alexander Draghi (eds), *Aspects of Altaic Civilization II: Proceedings of the XVIII PIAC, June 29–July 5, 1975* (Bloomington, 1978).
AAC3	Denis Sinor (ed.), *Aspects of Altaic Civilization III* (Bloomington, IN, 1990).
AEMA	*Archivum Eurasiae Medii Aevi*
AOASH	*Acta Orientalia Academiae Scientiarum Hungaricae*
AOH	*Acta Orientalia Hungarica*
BEFEO	*Bulletin de l'école française d'extrême-orient*
BLGK	Linda Komaroff (ed.), *Beyond the Legacy of Genghis Khan* (Leiden, 2006).
BSOAS	*Bulletin of the School of Oriental and African Studies*
CAJ	*Central Asiatic Journal*
CAS	*Central Asian Survey*
CDMP	Jurgen Tubach, Sophia G. Vashalomidze and Manfred Zimmer (eds), *Caucasus during the Mongol Period – Der Kaukasus in der Mongolenzeit* (Wiesbaden, 2012).
CEMA	Istvan Zimonyi and Osman Karatay (eds), *Central Eurasia in the Middle Ages: Studies in Honour of Peter B. Golden* (Wiesbaden, 2016)
CHCAR	*The Cambridge History of China*, Vol. 6, *Alien Regimes and Border States 907–1368*
CHCSD	*The Cambridge History of China*, Vol. 5, *The Sung Dynasty and its Precursors, 907–1279*.
CHEIA	*The Cambridge History of Early Inner Asia*
CHI	*The Cambridge History of Iran*
CHIA	*The Cambridge History of Inner Asia*

CHT	*The Cambridge History of Turkey*
CHW	*The Cambridge History of the World*
CMRS	*Cahiers du Monde russe et soviétique*
EI²	*Encyclopedia of Islam*, 2nd edition
EI³	*Encyclopedia of Islam*, 3rd edition
EM	*Études Mongole*
EMLCH	Volker Rybatzki, Alessandra Pozzi, Peter W. Geier and John R. Krueger (eds), *The Early Mongols, Language, Culture and History* (Bloomington, 2009)
EMME	Christopher P. Atwood, *Encyclopedia of Mongolia and the Mongol Empire* (New York, 2004).
HJAS	*Harvard Journal of Asiatic Studies*
HMEIR	*Harvard Middle Eastern and Islamic Review*
HUS	*Harvard Ukrainian Studies*
IA	*Inner Asia*
IHR	*The International History Review*
IJMES	*International Journal of Middle East Studies*
ITSOTK	*In the Service of the Khan: Eminent Personalities of the Early Mongol-Yüan Period*
JAH	*Journal of Asian History*
JAOS	*Journal of the American Oriental Society*
JESHO	*Journal of the Economic and Social History of the Orient*
JNES	*Journal of Near East Studies*
JRAS	*Journal of the Royal Asiatic Society*
JSAH	*Journal of Southeast Asian History*
JSAI	*Jerusalem Studies in Arabic and Islam*
JSYS	*Journal of Song-Yuan Studies*
JTS	*Journal of Turkish Studies*
LGK	Linda Komaroff and Stefano Carboni (eds), *The Legacy of Genghis Khan* (New York, 2003)
MEL	Reuven Amitai-Preiss and David O. Morgan (eds), *The Mongol Empire and Its Legacy* (Leiden, 2001).
MME	Bruno De Nicola and Charles Melville (eds), *The Mongol's Middle East: Continuity and Transformation in Ilkhanid Iran* (Leiden, 2016).
MS	*Mongolian Studies, the journal of the Mongolia Society*
MTO	Reuven Amitai and Michal Biran (eds), *Mongols, Turks, and Others: Eurasian Nomads and the Sedentary World* (Leiden, 2005)
NCHI	*The New Cambridge History of Islam*

PFEH	*Papers on Far Eastern History*
RHC	*Recueil des historiens des croisades*
SOM	Henry G. Schwarz (ed.), *Studies on Mongolia: Proceedings of the First North American Conference on Mongolian Studies* (Bellingham, WA, 1978)
TIWBME	James Muldoon (ed.), *Travellers, Intellectuals, and the World Beyond Medieval Europe* (Burlington, VT, 2010)
TP	*T'oung Pao*
UAJ	*Ural Altaische Jahrbucher*
WHC	*World History Connected*
WIAH	Nicola Di Cosmo (ed.), *Warfare in Inner Asian History* (500–1800) (Leiden, 2002)

Editions of Commonly Cited Texts

Abu Shamah	Abu Shamah, Shihab al-Din ʿAbd al-Rahman ibn Isma'il al-Shafi, *Tarajim rijal, al-qarnayn al-sadis wa'l-sabi al-ma'ruf bi-dhayl al-rawdatayn*, ed. Muhammad Kawthari (Cairo, 1947).
Benedict	Benedictus Polonus, 'Relatio Fr. Benedicti Poloni', in P. Anastasius Van Den Wyngaert, *Sinica Franciscana: Itinera et Relationes Fratrum Minorum Saeculi XIII et XIV* (Florence, 1929), 131–43.
Benedict/Dawson	Benedict the Pole, 'The Narrative of Brother Benedict the Pole', trans. Christopher Dawson, in Christopher Dawson, *Mission to Asia* (Toronto, 1980), 77–84.
BH1	Bar Hebraeus, *The Chronography of Gregory Abu'l-Faraj*, 2 vols, trans. Ernest A. Wallis Budge (Amsterdam, 1932).
BH2	Bar Hebraeus, *The Chronography of Gregory Abu'l Faraj*, 2 vols, trans. Ernest A. Wallis Budge (Piscataway, NJ, 2003).
Bridia	Bridia, C. de, *The Tatar Relation*, trans. George D. Painter, pp. 54–101, in R. A. Skelton, Thomas E. Marston and George D. Painter (eds), *The Vinland Map and the Tatar Relation* (New Haven, 1965).
CM	Matthew Paris, *Chronica Majora*, 7 vols, ed. Henry Richards Luard (Cambridge, 2012).
Dhahabi	Al-Dhahabi, *Kitab Duwal al-Islam* (Les Dynasties de L'Islam), trans. Arlette Negre (Damascus, 1979).

Dughlat/Thackston	Dughlat, Mirza Haydar, *Tarikh-i-Rashidi: A History of the Khans of Moghulistan* (Books 1 and 2), trans. Wheeler M. Thackston (London, 2012).
EL	*Ermonlinskaia Letopis'*, A. I. Tsepkov (ed.) (Riazan', 2000).
Grigor of Akanc	Grigor of Akanc, 'The History of the Nation of the Archers by Grigor of Akanc', ed. and trans. R. P. Blake and R. N. Frye, *HJAS* 12 (1949), 269–399.
GVC	Perfecky, George A. (ed. and trans.), *The Hypatian Codex II: The Galician-Volynian Chronicle* (München, 1973).
Hadid	al-Hadid, ᶜAbd al-Hamid ibn Hibat Allah Ibn Abi. *Sharh Nahj al Balaghah* (Beirut, 1963).
Hetoum	Hetoum, *A Lytell Cronycle*, trans. Richard Pynson, ed. Glenn Burger (Toronto, 1988).
He'tum	Het'um, 'The Journey of Het'um I, King of Little Armenia to the Court of the Great Khan Mongke', trans. John A. Boyle, *CAJ* 9 (1964), 175–89.
Historia de Morbo	Mussis, Gabriele de, 'Historia de Morbo', in Rosemary Horrox (ed. and trans.), *The Black Death* (Manchester, 1994).
IB1	Ibn Battuta, *Rihala Ibn Battuta* (Beirut, 1995).
IB2	Ibn Battutah, *The Travels of Ibn Battutah*, trans. H. A. R. Gibb, ed. Tim Mackintosh-Smith (London, 2002).
Ibn al-Athir	Ibn Al-Athir, *Al Kamil fi al-Ta'rikh*, Vol. XII (Beirut, 1979).
Ibn al-Athir/Richards	Ibn al-Athir, *The Chronicle of Ibn al-Athir for the Crusading Period from al-Kamil fi'l-ta'rikh, pt. 3: The Years 589–629/1193–1231: The Ayyubids after Saladin and the Mongol Menace*, trans. D. S. Richards (Burlington, VT, 2008).
IL	*Ipat'evskaia Letopis'*, ed. A. I. Tsepkov, Russkie Letopisi, Vol. 1 (Riazan', 2001).
JPC	Plano Carpini, Iohannes de, 'Ystoria Mongalorum', in P. Anastasius Van Den Wyngaert, *Sinica Franciscana: Itinera et Relationes Fratrum Minorum Saeculi XIII et XIV* (Florence, 1929), 27–130.
JPC/Dawson	Plano Carpini, John of, 'History of the Mongols', trans. A Nun of Stanbrook Abbey, in Christopher Dawson, *Mission to Asia* (Toronto, 1980), 3–72.

Juvaini/Boyle	Juvaini, ʿAla-ad-Din ʿAta-Malik, *The History of the World-Conqueror*, trans. J. A. Boyle (Seattle, 1997).
Juwayni/Qazvini	Juwayni, Ala-ad-Din ʿAta-Malik, *Ta'rikh-i-Jahan-Gusha*, 3 vols, ed. Mirza Muhammad Qazvini (Leiden, 1912–37).
Juzjani/Habibi	Juzjani, Minhaj Siraj, *Tabaqat-i-Nasiri*, ed. A. H. Habibi, Vol. 2 (Kabul, 1964–5).
Juzjani/Raverty	Juzjani, Minhaj Siraj, *Tabakat-i-Nasiri* (*a History of the Muhammedan Dynasties of Asia*), trans. Major H. G. Raverty (Kolkata, 2010).
KDRH	Peter B. Golden (ed.), *The King's Dictionary The Rasulid Hexaglot*, trans. Tibor Halasi-Kun, Peter B. Golden, Louis Ligeti and Edmund Schutz (Leiden, 2000).
Khwandamir	Khwandamir, *Habibu's-Siyar: The History of the Mongols and Genghis Khan*, trans. Wheeler M. Thackston (London: I. B. Tauris, 2012).
Kiracos	Kiracos de Gantzac, 'Histoire d'Armenie', in M. Brousset (trans.), *Deux Historiens Arméniens: Kiracos de Gantzax, XIII S., 'Histoire d'Arménie'; Oukhtanès D'Ourha, X S., 'Histoire en trois parties'* (St Petersburg, 1870).
Kirakos	Kirakos Gaandzakets'i, *History of the Armenians*, trans. Robert Bedrosian, http://rbedrosian.com/kgtoc.html.
LOE	Malcolm Barber and Keith Bates (eds and trans.), *Letters from the East: Crusaders, Pilgrims and Settlers in the 12th–13th Centuries* (Burlington, VT, 2010).
LPLS	*Letopis' Po Lavrentievskomu Spisku* (St Petersburg, 1872).
Maqrizi	Al-Maqrizi, Ahamd Ibn Ali, *Kitab al-Suluk li M'arifat fi Dul al-Muluk*, Ziyardah Muhammad Mustafi (ed.) (Cairo, 1956).
Maqrizi/Quatremere	Al-Maqrizi, Ahmad Ibn ʿAli. *Histoire des Sultans Mamlouks de L'Egypte*, trans. Etienne Quatremere (Paris, 1837, 1845).
Master Roger	Master Roger, 'Epistola in miserabile carmen super destructione Regni Hungarie per tartaros facta', trans. Janos M. Bak and Martin Rady, in Janos M. Bak, Martyn Rady and Laszlo Veszpremy (eds), *Anonymous and Master Roger* (Budapest, 2010), 132–227.

Matthew Paris	Matthew Paris, *English History*, 3 vols, trans. J. A. Giles (New York, 1968).
MDBL	Zhao Hong, *Meng-Da Bei-Lu (Polnoe opisanie Mongolo-Tatar)*, trans. N. Ts. Munkueva (Moscow, 1975).
MP1	Polo, Marco, *The Travels of Marco Polo*, trans. Henry Yule and Henri Cordier, ed. Morris Rosabi (New York, 2012).
MP/Cliff	Polo, Marco, *The Travels*, trans. Nigel Cliff (New York, 2015).
MP/Latham	Polo, Marco, *The Travels*, trans. R. E. Latham (New York, 1958).
MP/Marsden	Polo, Marco, *The Travels of Marco Polo*, trans. William Marsden (New York, 2001).
MP/YC	Polo, Marco, *The Travels*, trans. Henry Yule and Henri Cordier (New York, 1993).
Nasawi	Al-Nasawi, Muhammad ibn Ahmad, *Sirah al-Sultan Jalal al-Din Mankubirti* (Cairo, 1953).
Nasawi/Houdas	En-Nesawi, Mohammed, *Histoire du Sultan Djelal ed-din Mankobirti*, trans. O. Houdas (Paris, 1895).
Nikon	Zenkovsky, Serge A. (ed.), *The Nikonian Chronicle*, 5 vols, trans. Serge A. and Betty Jean Zenkovsky (Princeton, 1986).
Novgorod	Michell, Robert and Nevill Forbes (eds and trans.), *The Chronicle of Novgorod, 1016–1471* (London, 1914).
Nuwayri	Al-Nuwayri, Ahmad ibn ᶜAbd al-Wahhab. *Nihayat al-Arab Fi Funun al-Adab*, ed. Saʾid ᶜAshur. Cairo: Al-hayat al Misriyyat al-ᶜammat lil-kitab, 1975.
Odoric	B. Odoricus de Portu Naonis, 'Relatio de B. Odoricus de Portu Naonis', in P. Anastasius Van Den Wyngaert, *Sinica Franciscana: Itinera et Relationes Fratrum Minorum Saeculi XIII et XIV* (Florence, 1929), 381–495.
Odoric/Yule	Odoric of Pordenone, *The Travels of Friar Odoric*, trans. Henry Yule (Grand Rapids, MI, 2002).
RD/Karimi	Rashid al-Din, *Jami' al-tawarikh*, ed. B. Karimi (Tehran, 1983).
RD/Thackston1	Rashiduddin Fazlullah, *The Compendium of Chronicles*, trans. W. M. Thackston (Cambridge, MA, 1998).

RD/Thackston2	Rashiduddin Fazlullah, *Jami'u't-Tawarikh: Compendium of Chronicles*, Vol. 3, *Classical Writings of the Medieval Islamic World: Persian Histories of the Mongol Dynasties*, trans. Wheeler M. Thackston (London, 2012).
RS	Rabban Sawma, *The Monks of Kublai Khan, Emperor of China: Medieval Travels from China through Central Asia to Persia and Beyond*, trans. E. A. Wallis Budge, new introd. by David Morgan (London, 2014).
Rubruc	Rubruc, Guillelmus de, 'Itinerarium Willelmi de Rubruc', in P. Anastasius Van Den Wyngaert, *Sinica Franciscana: Itinera et Relationes Fratrum Minorum Saeculi XIII et XIV* (Florence, 1929), 145–332.
Rubruck/Dawson	Rubruck, William of, 'The Journey of William of Rubruck', trans. A Nun of Stanbrook Abbey, in Christopher Dawson (ed.), *Mission to Asia* (Toronto, 1980), 89–220.
Rubruck/Jackson	Rubruck, William of, *The Mission of Friar William of Rubruck*, trans. Peter Jackson (Indianapolis: Hackett, 2009).
SHM	Rachewiltz, Igor de (trans.), *The Secret History of the Mongols: A Mongolian Epic Chronicle of the Thirteenth Century*, 3 vols (Leiden, 2004 and 2013).
SWQZL	'Shengwu Qinzheng Lu (Bogda Bagatur Bey-e-Ber Tayilagsan Temdeglel)', in Asaraltu (ed.), *Bogda Bagatur Bey-e-Ber Tayilagsan Temdeglel* (Qayilar, PRC, 1985), 3–95.
Thomas of Spalato	Thomas of Spalato, *Istorija Archiepiskopov Salony i Splita*, trans. A. I. Solopov, ed. O. A. Akimova (Moscow, 1997).
Thomas of Split	Thomas of Split, *Historia Salonitanorum atque Spalatinorum pontificum*, ed. Olga Peric, trans. Damir Karbic, Mirjana Matijevic Sokol and James Ross Sweeney (Budapest, 2006).
Vardan	Vardan Arewelc'i, 'The Historical Compilation of Vardan Arewelc'i', trans. Robert W. Thomson, *Dumbarton Oaks Papers* 43 (1989), 125–226.
Vartan	Vartan, 'Les Mongols d'après les historiens arméniens: Extrait de l'histoire universelle de Vartan',

	ed. and trans. M. Ed Dulaurier, *Journal Asiatique* 13 (October–November 1860), 273–315.
Xi Youji	Chih-Ch'ang, Li, *The Travels of the Alchemist: The Journey of the Taoist Ch'ang Ch'un from China to the Hindukush at the Summons of Chingiz Khan*, trans. Arthur Waley (Westport, CT, 1976).
Yelu Chucai	Yeh-lu Ch'u-Ts'ai, 'The Hsi-yu Lu', trans. Igor de Rachewiltz, *Monumenta Serica* 21 (1962), 1–128.
YS 98	'*Yuan Shi* chapter 98', in Ch'i-ch'ing Hsiao, *The Military Establishment of the Yuan Dynasty* (Cambridge, MA, 1978), 72–91.
YS 99	'*Yuan Shi* chapter 99', in Ch'i-ch'ing Hsiao, *The Military Establishment of the Yuan Dynasty* (Cambridge, MA, 1978), 92–124.
YS 135	Richard Paul Currie (trans.), 'An Annotated Translation of the Biography of Togto Temur from the Yuan Shih', MA thesis, Department of Uralic and Altaic Studies, Indiana University, 1984.
YUS	Demchigdorzh, Ch. (trans.), *Yuan Ulsyn Sudar*, ed. B. Sumiyabaatar and J. Serjee (Ulaanbaatar, 2002).

Note on Transliteration, Conventions and Geographical Terminology

Anyone who studies the Mongol Empire experiences the unique challenge of working with names transliterated from at least half a dozen languages. While scholars have agreed on some standardisation, multiple systems abound. With both personal and geographical names, I have attempted to remain faithful to the names in terms of their pronunciation according to the language from which they originated. In some cases, more modern spellings have been used rather than the medieval spellings (e.g. Khubilai Khan instead of Qubilai Qan), simply for reasons of popular convention and ease of access. Diacriticals have been omitted as per the series guidelines. Scholars proficient in those languages will have little difficulty in deducing the terms in the original language.

Geographical terms refer to their medieval connotation; hence, references to Mongolia, Syria or China do not refer to the modern state, unless specifically noted. The same goes for other locations. In some instances, such as Afghanistan, a modern term is used for the sake of simplicity. Afghanistan as a concept did not exist in the thirteenth century, but the term still proves useful when discussing the region in general.

There are various translations of the *Secret History of the Mongols*. Igor de Rachewiltz's is considered the best and has copious notes, but Urgunge Onon's and Francis Cleaves' are also quite serviceable. Rather than the pages of all translations being cited, the section or paragraph is cited so that the reader can refer to any edition. See Igor de Rachewiltz (ed. and trans.), *Secret History of the Mongols*, 3 vols (Leiden, 2004, 2013); Urgunge Onon (ed. and trans.), *The Secret History of the Mongols: The Life and Times of Chinggis Khan* (London, 2001); and Francis W. Cleaves (ed. and trans.), *The Secret History of the Mongols* (Cambridge, MA, 1982).

Acknowledgements

It is hoped that this work not only meets the intended goals of the series, but will serve as an introduction to the Mongol Empire. Writing it was a challenging task and forced me to reconceptualise many ideas and reconsider my own understanding of events. For that alone, it was worth the effort.

No book is written alone, and a number of individuals who have been instrumental in this project must be recognised. First and foremost are the two individuals who recommended me to Edinburgh University Press for this series: Jack Weatherford and David Morgan. I will always be in David's debt for his mentoring, friendship, and conversation about the Mongol Empire. Also, I thank Peter Jackson and Thomas Allsen, whose works have always been inspirational. Their comments and support during the initial stages undoubtedly made this a much-improved book. Peter also read the entire manuscript and provided useful commentary throughout. His wisdom is always appreciated.

Nicola at Edinburgh University Press will forever have my gratitude for patience, as my deadline increasingly became a suggestion rather than a date. Ian Netton, as the editor of the series, also had the foresight to include the Mongols, often a black sheep in Islamic history, in a series on Islamic Empires.

I also thank Don Larson and Glen Pawelski of Mapping Specialists, who patiently created my maps; Art Resource and the Granger Collection for some of the images used here; Will Tomlinson of Kojima Jade for permitting me to use an image from their collection; and the numerous museums which permitted me to photograph items from their exhibits in Mongolia and the UK.

A number of people, colleagues and minions, have my gratitude for their comments on various chapters and pieces. Conversations with Bruno de Nicola and Anne Broadbridge about the Mongol queens were particularly fruitful, as well as several others on a variety of matters with Michael Hope, Reuven Amitai and Michal Biran. Paul D. Buell and Jeremy Black have always been reliable readers and critics. The same goes for Scott Levi and Charles Halperin. Three years' worth of students took my course on the Mongols and read earlier unedited drafts. Many provided useful comments and questions that helped refine the drafts. Robert Klemm always asked probing questions that forced me to elaborate and reconsider certain points. My research assistants, Minion William Zopff and the Redshirt Amy Collerton, both served well in their duties as reader, commenter and copy editors. The book is undoubtedly better thanks to these people. Despite all their assistance, any errors remain the fault of the author. I also thank Scott Jacobs for his support of my research and work.

The Royal Asiatic Society graciously permitted me to use sections of my 'Commercial Queens' article that appeared in the festschrift volume for David Morgan (*JRAS* 26 (2016)). Edinburgh University Press has kindly permitted me to use sections of my chapter from *Violence in Islamic Thought from the Mongols to European Imperialism*.

Finally, my departmental colleagues, librarians and family have long endured my constant ramblings and rants about the Mongol Empire. To my colleagues and to His Deanliness Christopher Jespersen (who also provided the photograph of the Basilica of St Mary's in Krakow), I offer thanks for respecting my 'writing time'. The staff and faculty of the UNG library have always been of great assistance. New Glarus' Brewing Company's Spotted Cow ale and the music of Ritchie Blackmore (in all forms) are constant inspiration. To my wife and children, thank you for putting up with me and letting me write, even when we'd all rather do something else. Finally, to my cat Leia: it is better if you sit on my lap and not on the keyboard when I write at home. We do not have to have this discussion every time.

Preface

First and foremost, this volume is a narrative history of the Mongol Empire, not only of the unified empire or *Yeke Monggol Ulus*, but also of the post-dissolution period. I attempt to approach the Mongol Empire as I have done since I first began my study of the Mongol Empire as an undergraduate at The College of William & Mary – from the perception of the Mongols. As the Mongols ruled the largest contiguous empire in history, we must understand how they viewed their actions and interests. As so few sources actually come from the Mongols themselves, we will never possess a perfect understanding, but it remains a worthwhile effort.

This volume is also part of a series on Islamic Empires. At first glance, this may seem a devilish ploy as many Muslims viewed the Mongols (as did many others) as a punishment from God for their sins and as infidels of the worst sort. Nonetheless, three Islamic empires emerged from the post-dissolution Mongol state. This transformation was slow and not always obvious to those dwelling in those states.

I endeavour to capture the anxiety that existed in the Islamic world as well as investigate how accommodation to Mongol rule took place. I analyse Mongol relations and interactions with Muslims: not only how the Mongols viewed Muslims, but how the Muslims engaged with the Mongols. In doing so, I hope to explore how the *Yeke Monggol Ulus*, created by a man of no particular religion, was transformed into a number of Islamic empires.

Most of the companion volumes in The Edinburgh History of Islamic Empires series require no explanation of what is meant by that name. The Ottomans, Fatimids and Seljuks were Muslims before they established their empires. The Mongols (as in so many instances) are the exception. Thus, by 'Islamic Empire' I mean a poly-ethnic and multicultural state that possesses a Muslim ruler and uses Islamic institutions, including but not limited to the use of *shariʿa*. Additionally, its neighbours must view it as an Islamic state. While themes of conversion will be addressed, the discussion included here will not add significantly to what others have written, although it might suggest new avenues of research.

It is the author's intent to give students and the public (and hopefully, scholars) a solid understanding of the history of the Mongol Empire. The book was written with students in mind and drafts were read by several classes at the University of North Georgia as well as one class taught by Scott C. Levi at The Ohio State University. Despite the varying quality of the early drafts, the students do not appear to have suffered unduly, although the text was alternately hailed as a cure for insomnia and derided as the cause of narcolepsy. I hope the final version has removed these unfortunate aspects. Yet to understand how the Mongol Empire became an Islamic empire and why the transformation occurred, one must start in the beginning, in a region that historically had been quite untouched by Islam.

For
Aidan, Tori and Kira

1

Mongolia before the Mongol Empire

Defining Mongolia is difficult. Although a modern state known as Mongolia exists, it is only part of a historic Mongolia whose borders could be quite fluid. Mongolia as the name of an actual location only came into existence with the rise of the Mongol Empire. Nonetheless, one may consider the Mongolian plateau as historic Mongolia, as the steppe nomads interacted and dominated the plateau for most of known history. It has been the home of numerous empires, some more centralised than others – the Xiongnu (259 BCE–91 CE), the Xianbei (c. 87–181 CE), the Ruruan (c. 400–552 CE), the Gok Turk (552–742 CE), the Uighurs (744–840 CE) and others. Although all of these expanded beyond the Mongolian plateau and ruled impressive empires, none had an impact or shared a legacy like the Mongol Empire. While they extended their control over portions of the sedentary world, most of the empires that originated in Mongolia kept the steppes as their focal point and largely remained there.[1] While their predecessors also controlled sedentary populations, the Mongols, however, controlled extensive sedentary populations that easily dwarfed the nomadic population. Mongolia before the Mongol Empire, however, remains elusive and perhaps chaotic in the minds of scholars, if not in reality. Yet, with the rise of the Mongol Empire, the Mongolian plateau was forever changed, as was the rest of Eurasia.

The plateau has a diverse topography, with the northern and western regions being quite mountainous, while the southern and eastern regions consist of steppes and deserts. The Altai Mountains mark the western borders of the plateau while the Greater Khinggan range demarks the eastern boundaries with Manchuria. To the north, the plateau extends to fringes of Siberia, with Lake Baikal and the Tannu Ola, Sayan, Khamar-Daban, Daur and

---

[1] Thomas Barfield has posited that most empires originating in Mongolia had little desire to conquer China and that the Mongols became the exception. See Thomas J. Barfield, *The Perilous Frontier: Nomadic Empires and China, 221 BC to AD 1757* (Cambridge, MA, 1992).

Onon mountain ranges hemming the plateau. To the south, the Yin Shan and Helan Shan mountains form the boundary. North of these two ranges the plateau is mixed steppe and desert, including the Gobi and Alashan deserts with the Huanghe or Yellow River, so named due to the loess deposits from the Mongolian steppes, located south of the plateau. Mongolia's high elevation allows some mountains in the Altai and Khangai Ranges to have permanent snowcaps above 4,000 metres. Even the steppes extend from 500 to 1,000 metres elevation above sea level.

The climate of Mongolia remains cold and dry. The plateau does not receive enough precipitation to make agriculture sustainable in many areas, with an average of 400 millimetres or 16 inches across the plateau. Indeed, much of the steppe may be considered *gobi* or gravelly with scrubby plant life. Nonetheless, the northern sections receive more precipitation than other areas. The dry climate combines with winds that sweep the plateau from the north and west. As a result, aggressive farming and overgrazing (and mining) can accelerate topsoil erosion. Even today, Inner Mongolia and other parts of China suffer from dust storms that blow loess from the Mongolian plateau.

Although a semi-arid region, historic Mongolia also possessed several lakes and rivers that made pastoral nomadism possible. Lake Baikal, the deepest lake in the world, is also the largest lake in the region although it is located in Russia, outside of modern Mongolia. The western portion of the plateau, particularly in the Great Lakes Basin in north-western Mongolia, holds a number of lakes, with most possessing salt water. The major rivers in the north-east consist of the Onon and Kerulen (Kherlen on modern maps), Khalkha and Hailar Rivers. Some of these join the Amur River, draining into the Pacific. The Selenge, Tula and Orkhon rivers run through north-central Mongolia. The Selenge River originates at Lake Khovsgol, which is the deepest lake in modern Mongolia, while the Orkhon connects to the Selenge. The river basin of the Orkhon has historically been important to a number of confederations.[2] The Tula or Tuul River also played a prominent role in the twelfth century and in the modern era, as Ulaanbaatar, the capital of Mongolia, is situated along it.

The average temperature is 22 degrees Celsius (72 degrees Fahrenheit), but winter comes early with frost appearing at the beginning of September and the possibility of snow in May. Winter temperatures can drop to -34 degrees Celsius (-30 degrees Fahrenheit), but with a winter average of

---

[2] Larry W. Moses, 'A Theoretical Approach to the Process of Inner Asian Confederation', EM 5 (1974), 113–22.

around -12 degrees Celsius (-15 degrees Fahrenheit). While the summer average is 22 degrees Celsius (72 degrees Fahrenheit), the highs can reach into the low 30s Celsius (mid-80s to low 90s Fahrenheit). Although the thirteenth-century climate of Mongolia was wetter than in most eras, it is not surprising that pastoral nomadism rather than intensive agriculture became the dominant form of subsistence as the moist climate allowed the pastures to flourish.³

Climatic Causes for the Mongol Empire?

Prior to the twenty-first century, some scholars hypothesised that the desiccation of the steppes was often responsible for massive nomadic migrations that caused the rise of the Mongols, the Xiongnu, etc. More recent studies based on dendrology and the examination of tree rings show that the era of the Mongol Empire was wetter (probably making the steppes lusher than in most eras), which would then allow for more livestock and perhaps even support more people as well. While intriguing, mono-causal explanations rarely explain anything. Climate may have played a role, but it was not the sole reason for the rise of the Mongol Empire, or any other empire.

Pastoral Nomadism

Contrary to the popular idea that the nomads simply wandered the steppes with their herds and flocks, the life of a pastoral nomad was (and is) quite different. Nomads do not wander. Rather, they migrate between seasonal pastures so as to not overgraze the land. In the steppes of Mongolia the nomads relied on five animals, often referred to as the five snouts, in differing quantities. The importance of the pastoral nomadic economy and lifestyle

---

³ See Gareth Jenkins, 'A Note on Climatic Cycles and The Rise of Chingis Khan', *CAJ* 18 (1974), 217–26; Maria Hvistendahl, 'Roots of Empire', *Science* 337 no. 6,102 (28 September 2012), 1,596–9, doi: *10.1126/science.337.6102.1596* (last accessed 21 August 2013); 'A Horde of Data: The World's Greatest Land Empire Was Probably Encouraged by Climate Change', *The Economist*, 8 December 2012, <http://www.economist.com/news/science-and-technology/21567877-worlds-greatest-land-empire-was-probably-encouraged-climate-change-horde> (last accessed 21 August 2013); Charles Q. Choi, 'Reign Check: Abundant Rainfall May Have Spurred Expansion of Genghis Khan's Empire', *Scientific American*, 21 March 2012, <http://www.scientificamerican.com/article.cfm?id=abundant-rainfall-may-have-spurred-expansion-of-genghis-khans-empire&page=2> (last accessed 21 August 2013).

Figure 1.1 Steppes of Mongolia. Due to the climate of Mongolia, pastoral nomadism has been the dominant form of economy since the ancient period. Nomadism's decline only began in the late twentieth century.

cannot be understated when studying the Mongol Empire. This overview is by no means complete, but should permit the reader to appreciate the role of pastoral nomadism in the Mongol Empire.[4]

Sheep usually made up the largest portion of a family's livestock. Docile and easily controlled, the sheep provided wool from which the nomads created felt cloth. Through the wool being crushed, microscopic barbs on the wool interlock, allowing it to form a solid cloth or felt without the process of transforming it into yarn and then weaving or knitting. From the felt, the nomads constructed their *gers* (commonly referred to as yurts), round tents made with a lattice frame and then draped with layers of felt (depending on the temperature). The *ger*'s size was limited only by the length of the roof beams and amount of felt available. A *ger* could be constructed within an hour by a family. The *ger* was easily stowed in a cart or on the back of camels, thus allowing a sizeable home while retaining mobility. In addition, sheep provided meat and leather.

---

[4] For nomadic medieval Mongolia, see Bat-Ochir Bold, *Mongolian Nomadic Society: A Reconstruction of the 'Medieval' History of Mongolia* (New York, 2001).

The next animal, in terms of quantity, was the goat. As goats could subsist in areas with less pasture, their inclusion aided the nomads in times of drought. In addition, they could be milked and skinned for leather, and their soft undercoat provided cashmere. Goats, however, have sharper hooves than sheep and can damage pastures; hence they are kept in smaller numbers, except in areas where insufficient pasture existed for sheep. Both animals, however, nibble the grass close to the ground, leaving little for other animals. Goats also have a tendency to eat the roots, contributing to desertification of the steppes if not properly managed. Nomads learned how to pasture animals, allowing more efficient use of the same pasture for all of the animals without exhausting the grass.

Oxen and yaks were also kept, but in fewer numbers. Groups that lived in higher elevations typically replaced their oxen with yaks, or a cross-breed of cow and yak known as *khainag* in modern Mongolian. Both were primarily used as draught animals and rarely eaten. Their milk and resulting dairy products, however, were used extensively.

Bactrian (two-humped) camels were highly valued as draught animals. They could carry large loads of up to 400 pounds or pull loads exceeding 900 pounds.[5] While they could be ridden quite comfortably, they were not the ideal form of transportation due to their slower pace. Possessing special adaptations to eyelids and feet, humps for water storage and thick wool, the camel survived quite well in dry climates. Although the nomads used the wool and dairy products of a camel, the animal was rarely slaughtered due to its value as a draught animal as well as its relative scarcity. A female camel's gestation period is considerable – twelve to fourteen months. Camels simply do not breed fast enough to serve as a regular food source.

The final animal is the horse, which permitted pastoral nomadism to exist and was a key to Mongol expansion. The Mongolian horse is small, rarely more than fourteen hands tall (56 inches at the shoulder), similar to the American mustang. By way of comparison, American Quarter Horses tend be fifteen or sixteen hands tall. Like other livestock, the horse was also pasture-fed. Of great importance was the fact that the horses' combination of intelligence and hooves allowed it to dig through the snow, or break ice when it covered the grass, allowing it to feed. Other animals often followed in its wake to graze during winter. While not necessarily the swiftest of animals, it had incredible endurance. In modern Mongolia, as well as medieval, the value of a horse does not lie in how quickly it can run a race, but in the

---

[5] Timothy May, *Cultures and Customs of Mongolia* (Westport, CT, 2009), 35.

Figure 1.2 Bactrian (two-humped) camels were extremely valuable due to their use as draught animals and their low rate of reproduction. Their wool was also useful. In this picture, the camels are still shedding their winter coat.

distance it can travel.[6] To achieve this endurance, the Mongols and other nomads took considerable steps to train and build the animal's stamina as well as ensure its docility.[7] Mares and geldings were preferred for riding for this reason. Stallions were maintained primarily for reproduction as well as to protect the herd from predators.

The nomads rarely used horses as draught animals, riding them with a wooden-framed saddle, covered with leather. The nomads rubbed the saddle with sheep fat to prevent swelling of the wood and the cracking of leather. Stirrups kept the weight of the rider placed in the middle and not on the sides, allowing the rider to stand and turn. The nomads also used horseshoes of iron or wood.[8] The Mongols and other steppe nomads goaded their animals with a whip, rather than with spurs. The whip consisted of a short

[6] May, *Cultures and Customs of Mongolia*, 120–1.
[7] Timothy May, *The Mongol Art of War* (Yardley, PA, 2007), 54–6. Also see *MDBL*, 68–9.
[8] Ruth Meserve, 'An Historical Perspective of Mongol Horse Training, Care and Management: Selected Texts', Ph.D. dissertation, Department of Uralic and Altaic Studies, Indiana University, 1987, 34.

Figure 1.3 Small, but tough, the Mongolian horse was key to the military success of the Mongol Empire.

baton, its thongs rarely exceeding a foot in length. With the mobility of a horse, the nomad could maintain and control his flocks and herds, which might range from a few dozen animals (among the poorest) to hundreds and even thousands of animals.

With these five animals, the nomad survived, albeit not quite self-sufficiently. Trade with sedentary communities, whether directly or with travelling merchants, for goods that the nomads could not make was necessary. This included luxury goods and most metal objects, although local blacksmiths existed. Nonetheless, the five snouts provided most of the basic needs, particularly in terms of food. The diet of the nomads consisted largely of dairy and meat products. Fruit and vegetables as well as grain products tended to be infrequent and procured through trade, foraging and some small-scale farming.

Despite consisting of two basic categories, their diet did have variety. In addition to drinking milk from the various animals, the nomads also enjoyed fresh yogurt and made a variety of cheeses. By exposing it to the wind and sun on top of the roof of the yurt, the nomads cured and preserved the cheese for the long term. They also used cream and butter in a variety of ways. Mare's milk was particularly relished and transformed through occasional stirring and free-floating yeast into *kumiss* or *airagh* – fermented mare's milk. Although it possessed a low alcoholic content (1–3%), distillation increased it exponentially. In its natural form, the slightly fizzy *airagh* was the beverage of choice for the nomads and greatly enjoyed throughout the summer. Unfortunately, supplies dwindled as winter approached and mares stopped lactating.

All animals provided meat, although mutton and goat's meat were staples due to the greater importance of horses, camels and oxen. Nonetheless, the meat was stretched to its fullest use with very little wasted. For the most part, meat was boiled or roasted over a fire, with dried animal dung as fuel. The nomads even ate the marrow from bones. The bones, when boiled, provided a broth for *shulen* or soup, which consisted of bits of meat and perhaps random vegetables and was thickened with millet or other grains. The nomads used sinew in the manufacturing of tools and weapons. Fat, when not eaten, was used to waterproof items and used on the nomad's skin to help prevent chapping from the wind. In addition to meat from the livestock, the nomads supplemented their diet through hunting. Fowl was procured through snares and falconing. While deer or antelopes were hunted, a favourite meal was marmot, a prairie dog-like animal, common throughout the steppes. Fishing was rare and fish not a preferred food among most nomads.

Although a division of labour existed between male and female nomads, their lifestyle was more egalitarian than in sedentary agricultural cultures. For pragmatic reasons, men and women learned to do the other's work simply because if one died or became sick the husband or wife had to take over. The men primarily took the animals out to pasture, hunted and waged war. Women gathered other food when necessary and took care of the camp by cooking and processing food and animal products, although men tended to milk the mares and produce *airagh*.

While a camp could consist of several *gers*, it rarely exceeded a family unit of approximately five people and perhaps a few other relatives, due to pasture constraints. Nonetheless, every nomad considered himself to be part of another group, which for the lack of a better word could be considered a tribe. The tribe itself consisted of a real or fictive ancestor, at least among the upper stratum of society, from which the tribal name originated. The elites then ruled over other affiliated members. Membership of the tribe varied through time and members came and went, both willingly and unwillingly. Nonetheless, as long as the dominant element maintained its hegemony over the sub-groups, the identity of the tribe remained that of the ruling element. This is not to say that the ruling elite had complete dominance. Tribal leaders consulted and listened to the concerns of the sub-group leaders. While leaders did not always heed their advice, failing to do so repeatedly undermined the relationship, thus making the sub-groups more susceptible to rebellion, or else they sought the protection of another tribal confederation, or perhaps even that of a nearby sedentary power. The leader tended to be a quasi-elected position, as the leader needed to demonstrate not only his competence in warfare, but also his capability for fulfilling social obligations towards his followers and subjects. Failure to do so usually meant he would be replaced, forcibly if necessary.[9]

Mongolia in the Late Twelfth Century

Numerous pastoral nomadic tribes dwelt within Mongolia. On occasion, one group dominated much if not all of the northern Mongolian plateau, occasionally extending influence into the southern steppes, which were frequently dominated (directly or indirectly) by a dynasty in China. Sometimes this dominance was military; on other occasions it was through a combination of economic, social, military or political influences. As stated earlier, the dynasty in China could also attempt to extend its influence northward as the Jin Empire (1125–1234) did in the twelfth century. Prior to the Jin Empire, the Liao Empire (960–1125) established a line of forts and garrisons north of the Gobi, the most northern occupation of the steppes by any empire originating outside of Mongolia prior to the Qing (1636–1911). The proto-Mongolian origin of the Khitans, the ruling element of the Liao, perhaps assisted in this effort as they attempted to rule China as a Chinese emperor and the steppes as a nomadic khan. The Liao, as well as the Jin, were exceptional due to their Inner Asian origins, allowing them to function in both the nomadic and sedentary worlds. Most dynasties had less success straddling the divide.

The Liao and Jin dynasties emerged from the Inner Asian world and both did their utmost to control the often-volatile steppe tribes. By the late twelfth century, the Jin were not the only kingdom that kept a wary eye on the steppes of Mongolia. While the Uighur Empire (744–840) was the last group north of the Gobi to pose a significant threat to China in the eighth and ninth centuries, the lurking fear of raids remained and hence was the reason why the Jin Empire, Xi Xia and Qara Khitai all maintained ties to various groups within Mongolia. Located in the modern Ningxia and Gansu provinces of China, Xi Xia varied from being a tributary of the Jin Empire to being a rival. Founded by refugees of the Liao Dynasty escaping Jin domination, Qara Khitai controlled much of the southern portion of modern Kazakhstan, Kyrgyzstan and Xinjiang, as well as Uzbekistan and Tajikistan.

---

[9] For more on the identity of tribes, see Rudi Lindner, 'What Was a Nomadic Tribe?', *Comparative Studies in Society and History* 24/4 (1982), 689–711; David Sneath, *The Headless State: Kinship Society, and Misrepresentation of Nomadic Inner Asia* (New York, 2007).

Owing to their borders, all three kingdoms had an interest in influencing events in the steppes.

In the twelfth century, a number of tribal confederations existed without a single dominant one. The Naiman in the west maintained ties with Qara Khitai. Despite their being a large and powerful group, we do not know what the Naiman called themselves. 'Naiman' is the Mongolian word for eight, and it is believed that eight Turko-Mongolian tribes made up the Naiman confederation, with their ruling elite being Turkic.[10] While a single khan led them, his position was not absolute and he primarily served as a first among equals. The Kereit, who probably also possessed a Turkic ruling stratum, controlled central Mongolia with their pastures based between the Orkhon River and the Tuul or Tula River and its source in the Black Forest.[11] The Kereit had links to the kingdoms of Xi Xia and to Qara Khitai. Deposed Kereit khans typically took refuge with one or other of these kingdoms. In the late twelfth century, the Kereit khan, Toghril, also forged links with the Jin Empire by accepting its suzerainty. Both the Naiman and the Kereit shared a curious feature in that many of them had converted to Christianity in the eleventh century, during which missionaries allegedly converted 200,000 nomads.[12] The particular branch of Christianity was the Church of the East, often derogatively called Nestorian Christianity as it was viewed as a heresy in Western Christendom.

The Merkit occupied the steppes north of Kereit along the Selenge and south of Lake Baikal. There they straddled a divide between the steppe nomads and the semi-nomadic forest tribes of Siberia. The Merkit kept a foot in both worlds as they fished, trapped, hunted and kept herds of reindeer like the Siberian groups, but also were horse nomads like those in the steppes.[13] A Turko-Mongol group, the Merkit posed little threat to the major powers on the steppes such as the Naiman, Kereit and Tatars as the Merkit consisted of three known clans or tribes. Nonetheless, the Merkit posed a menace to weaker groups. Furthermore, their mountainous territory and proximity to the forests of Siberia made it more difficult for steppe nomads to raid them.

In the eastern steppes the Tatars and the Mongols competed for dominance. The Mongols nomadised between the Kerulen and Khalkha Rivers and the Greater Khinggan Mountains. The Tatars posed a serious threat to the Jin and Liao on different occasions and tended to be viewed as the

---

[10] Igor de Rachewiltz, ed and trans., *SHM*, 518; Peter B. Golden, *An Introduction to the History of the Turkic Peoples* (Wiesbaden, 1992), 285.
[11] Golden, *Introduction*, 285.
[12] BH1, 184; Samuel Hugh Moffett, *A History of Christianity in Asia*, vol. 1 (San Francisco, 1992), 400–1.
[13] Golden, *Introduction*, 285.

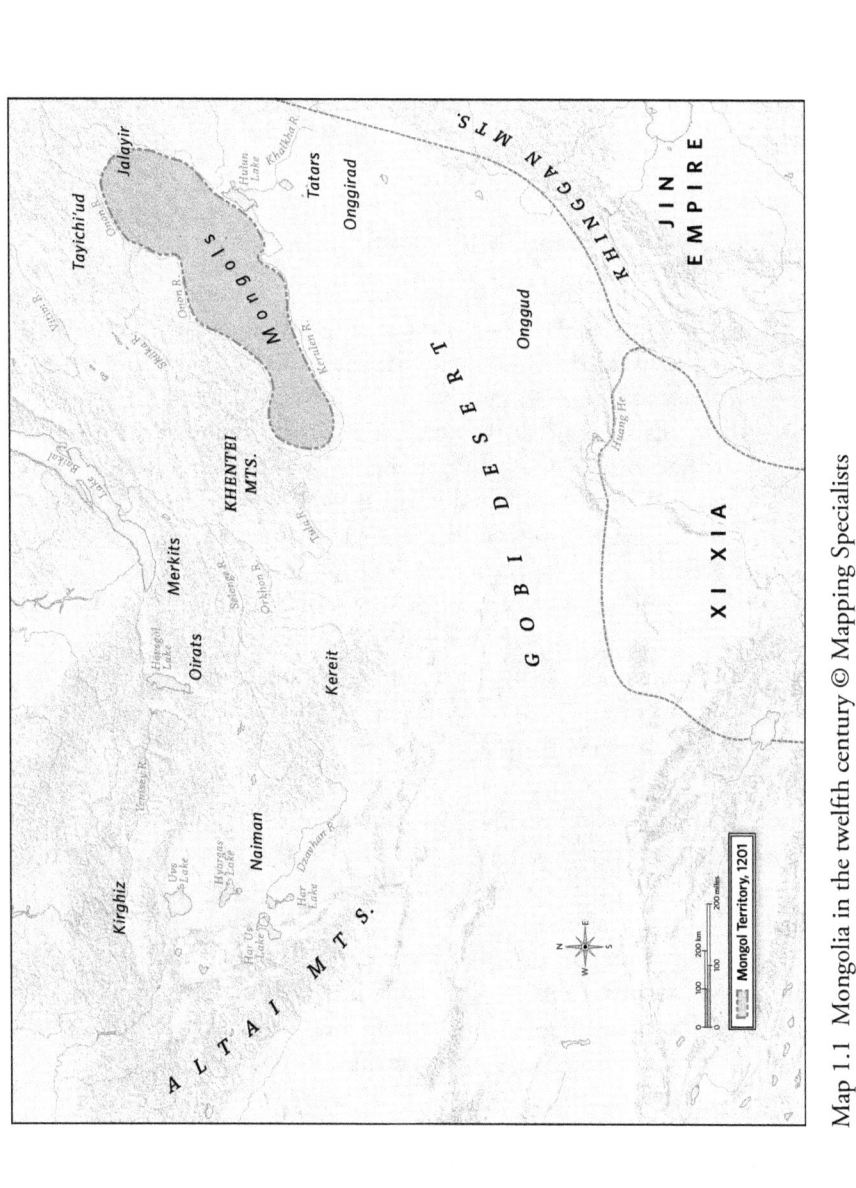

Map 1.1 Mongolia in the twelfth century © Mapping Specialists

most dangerous group, most likely due to their proximity to the Manchurian homelands of the Jurchen. For this this reason, the Jin erected long earthen walls along the eastern foothills of the Greater Khinggan range in order to hamper Tatar attacks. By the late twelfth century, the Tatar threat convinced the Jin Empire to find allies in the northern steppes to break their power. This also happened in the early twelfth century when the Jin sought allies against the rising Mongols.

The Church of the East or Nestorianism

The latter name is derived from its progenitor, Nestorius, Patriarch of Constantinople in 428–31, who believed that Jesus was merely a vessel born of Mary and then filled with the Holy Spirit. Thus, in essence, Mary was not the mother of Jesus, but rather mother of a container or body for the Holy Spirit, thus giving Jesus the dual nature of god and man. Ultimately, at the Third Ecumenical Council of Ephesus in 431, Nestorius' teachings were deemed heretical. Persecuted in the Byzantine Empire, his followers fled into the Sassanid Empire in Persia. There they found refuge and their numbers grew, causing the Zoroastrian clergy to view them as a threat. Nonetheless, a number of bishoprics appeared, including one in Merv in modern Turkmenistan. There the bishop received a request from the Kereit and Naiman for missionaries to teach them about Christianity. By the thirteenth century Nestorian Christianity still existed in the steppes, with several members of the ruling families among the faithful.[14]

Recent arrivals to the steppe, the Mongols moved from the forests of Siberia during the Tang dynasty (618–906). In the early twelfth century, however, they emerged as a powerful confederation under the leadership of Qabul Khan, but after a defeat by the Jin–Tatar alliance in 1164, they fragmented. The Mongols occupied the steppes in the far northern reaches of the Mongolian plateau in the Onon and Kerulen Rivers basin. Like other pastoral nomads, the Mongols consisted of a number of sub-groups with the Borjigin and Tayichi'ud being among the most important.

Shamanism

Although some members of the Naiman and Kereit confederations converted to Christianity, most of the nomads remained shamanic in religious practice.

---

[14] Also see G. W. Houston, 'An Overview of Nestorians in Inner Asia', *CAJ* 24, no. 1 (1980), 60–8.

Shamanism is a primal religion, which lacks a central holy text that provides a defined set of rules or beliefs for the religion. Unlike Christianity or Islam and other religions, shamanism also lacks a transcendental afterlife in which everything is better than in the mundane world. In shamanism, one's status remains the same in the afterlife, with the exception that one is now living in the spirit world. Powerful beings in the mundane world, such as a tribal khan or a shaman, become powerful spirits in the spirit world. A slave or simple herdsman did not see significant change in the spirit world – they had the same status for all eternity. Gods also existed in the shamanic world. The most important deities were Tenggeri, the eternal sky, and Etugen, the earth. Other gods existed, but these two figures received the most attention. A priesthood did not exist, as the gods paid little attention to the lives of the individual. Of greater importance were spirits who interacted with humans on the spiritual plane as well as in the mundane world. Shamans might invoke the gods on occasion, primarily to prevent the displeasure of the gods whose wrath was fearsome. Among the nomads of Mongolia, thunder and lightning in particular were dreadful. With the altitude of the Mongolian plateau and an odd visual perspective in which the very sky seems within reach, one's vulnerability on the open steppe became quite evident.

The shaman was not a priest, but a healer, a mediator and a specialist, who was also different from anyone else in the tribe.[15] The shaman dealt not with gods, but rather with the spirit world that often crossed into the mundane physical world, usually at nexus points, which served as sacred spaces. It was not an occupation that most desired. Indeed, in many instances it was a family occupation passed down from generation to generation. Due to specialised training and knowledge, the hereditary selection of a shaman was preferred; however, this was not always possible. Some shamans entered their vocation through other means, such as a near-death experience from, for instance, being struck by lightning. Others simply had a special affinity for the spirit world – meaning that they could either see spirits or communicate with them. The ability to communicate with spirits did not automatically make one a shaman. The skills were honed; if one did not learn how to control the spirits, they became dangerous, albeit not always intentionally. Nonetheless, they could drive one insane. Thus, the shaman underwent training with other shamans not only in the appropriate use of rites and chanting, but to master entering the spirit world. Most shamans in the medieval era were men, although female shamans did exist.

---

[15] Klaus Hesse, 'On the History of Mongolian Shamanism in Anthropological Perspective', *Anthropos* 82 4/6 (1987), 406.

Sometimes a spirit remained rooted in the physical world and did not enter the spirit world. Usually this was due to their soul being trapped in the physical world. Inner Asian nomads believed that the bone and blood of an individual contained the soul. Thus, there were taboos against the shedding of blood, particularly in executions and with murder – instances where dishonourable or unusual deaths occurred. When the blood seeped into the ground, it potentially trapped the individual's soul, stranding them in the physical world. In these instances, the person became a ghost trapped at that specific locality. Most often, such a ghost became malevolent due to his or her status and potentially dangerous to passing travellers. In order to propitiate the spirit, individuals flicked *airagh*, or fermented mare's milk, to the nearby spirits. With this offering, the shaman placated the ghost. Additionally, a shaman could exorcise the spirit and open a passage for it to the spirit world.[16]

Malevolent spirits also interacted with the physical world, attacking humans and attempting to steal their souls, thus causing illness. In order for an individual to recover, the soul needed to be restored. Only a shaman could provide this service as only the shaman could travel to the spirit world. In order to do so, the shaman wore special clothing which included a ceremonial robe that often included bits of metal and even highly polished metal mirrors. These were spirit placings where the shaman's spirit helpers resided and would come when he called them. They served as his intermediaries between the mundane and spirit world, gathering information and thwarting the actions of hostile spirits. In addition, should the shaman enter the spirit world, his helpers guarded his body and protected it from being possessed by others. The shaman entered the spirit world by entering an ecstatic state or trance through chanting and rhythmic drumming. His drumstick also served as his horse or housed the spirit of his horse. Once the spirit helpers found the evil spirit, if they could not restore the patient's spirit the shaman entered the spirit world. As his spirit left his body, it was a very dangerous situation for the shaman. A spirit journey was not undertaken lightly, as the shaman could be trapped if a spirit possessed his body or his astral form could be slain. On the journey, the headdress served an important function. It usually included a veil of some fashion that obscured the shaman's face, thus making it difficult for spirits to identify him. If hostile spirits recognised the shaman while he

---

[16] For an overview on Mongolian Shamanism see Walther Heissig, *The Religions of Mongolia*, trans. Geoffrey Samuel (Berkeley, 1980), 6–24; John A. Boyle, 'The Thirteenth-Century Mongols' Conception of the After Life: The Evidence of Their Funerary Practices', *MS* 1 (1974), 5–14; Dorji Banzarov, 'The Black Faith, or Shamanism among the Mongols', trans. Jan Nattier and John R. Krueger, *MS* 7 (1981–2), 53–92.

was in the spirit world, his soul could be at risk as they could then attack his body or torment him in other ways.

Beyond Mongolia

Although Christians and even Buddhists existed in the Mongolian steppes, the nearest Muslim population was located in Central Asia and was subject to the Qara Khitai Empire (1131–1213), extending from the Altai Mountains in the east to the Amu Darya River in the west. Founded by Yelu Dashi, a refugee and member of the now toppled Liao Dynasty of northern China, Qara Khitai had a mixed population. The ruling element were the Khitans, a Mongolian people who formed the Liao Dynasty in 907 and then fled westward, first to Mongolia and then to the Ili Valley, where they created their empire in 1125 after the Manchurian Jurchen toppled the Liao.[17] The Khitans were Buddhists, a religion quite alien to the region they settled, although the Uighurs in Uighurstan (roughly the Turfan Depression) were co-religionists. The majority of the population consisted of Turkic pastoral nomads who held shamanic beliefs and Muslim townspeople in the cities of Mawarannahr (Transoxiana or the region between the Amu Darya and Syr Darya rivers) and the Muslim Karakhanids, a Turkic dynasty that had previously ruled much of the region.[18]

Beyond Qara Khitai was Khwarazm, located just south of the Aral Sea and a client state of Qara Khitai after Yelu Dashi defeated the last Great Seljuk sultan, Sanjar (r.1118–53), at the battle of the Qatwan Steppe in 1141. Khwarazm quickly expanded in the absence of Seljuk authority to dominate much of Iran and succeeded in establishing control over modern Afghanistan and much of modern Pakistan with the defeat of the Ghurid Empire (1059–1215) in 1215–16.[19]

Further to the west on the Volga River sat the Volga Bulghar Kingdom, an island of Islam in northern Eurasia.[20] To be sure, Bulghar had contact with the rest of the Islamic world through trade by travelling down the Volga River and through the Caspian Sea as well as travelling in overland caravans, but it was surrounded by infidels. As Bulghar dominated much of

---

[17] For more on Qara Khitai see Michal Biran, *The Empire of the Qara Khitai in Eurasian History* (Cambridge, 2005).
[18] See Peter B. Golden, 'The Karakhanids and Early Islam', *CHIA*, 343–70; Biran, *Empire of the Qara Khitai*, 15–16.
[19] For the Seljuks, see A. C. S. Peacock, *The Great Seljuk Empire* (Edinburgh, 2015); for Khwarazm, see 'Khwarazm', *EI²*, and 'Khwarazm-Shahs', *EI²*.
[20] For more on Volga Bulghar, see Peter B. Golden, 'The Oghur Turks and Volga Bulgharia', *CHEIA*, 234–42.

the fur trade by extracting tribute from Siberian tribes as well as serving as a hub for trade in the region, numerous traders of all religions and ethnicities visited the city. Although the city converted to Islam in the ninth century, Islam had not spread significantly in the region. The nomadic tribes in the region remained largely shamanic, although individuals may have converted to Islam or Orthodox Christianity as the Rus' principalities to the west were the Bulghars' primary rivals in both trade and religion.

North of Mongolia were numerous semi-nomadic tribes dwelling in the Siberian forests known generically as the *Hoy-in Irgen* or Forest People. These tribes formed another fur-trade conduit that reached China and Central Asia through Mongolia and Manchuria. The remoteness of their location granted them independence from other powers such as the Jin. For the most part their involvement in affairs in the steppes was based on their interests. Some of the groups, such as the Merkit, became increasingly involved in the steppe affairs, perhaps showing a transition from semi-nomadic forest dwellers to pastoral nomadism. The Mongols had experienced this same shift centuries previously, a shift that is illustrated metaphorically in the *The Secret History of the Mongols*.[21]

Mongolia's other neighbours were largely Buddhists. Spanning Manchuria and northern China with the Gobi Desert serving as an approximate northern border, the Jin Empire was the major power in the vicinity. Established in 1115, first in Manchuria and then in China with the toppling of the Liao Dynasty in 1125, the Jin Empire was ruled by the Jurchen, a Tungusic people from Manchuria.[22] In addition to ruling Han (ethnic Chinese) and Tungusic populations, the Jurchen ruled the Khitans as most did not flee westward like people of other ethnicities did. The Jin also exerted considerably influence northward into the Mongolian steppes. In the southern steppes, most of the various Turkic and Mongolic tribes submitted to Jin authority and became known as *juyin* and guarded the Jin frontier. In return, the *juyin* received trading privileges as well as protection in return and remained somewhat autonomous, but often found the Jin meddling in their affairs.

North of the Gobi, the Jin followed the custom of previous Chinese emperors and attempted to prevent any particular leader from forming a confederation that could challenge Jin power and interests in the steppe. Therefore, they assisted the rise of one tribe against another but, should one

---

[21] *SHM*, §1.
[22] The Jurchen became known as the Manchus or Manjus in the seventeenth century when their emperors were recognised as the reincarnation of the Manjushiri Boddhisattva. For more on the Jurchen, see Herbert Franke, 'The Forest Peoples of Manchuria: Kitans and Jurchen', *CHEIA*, 412–23.

group become too powerful, the Jin then orchestrated its downfall by backing several other groups. These machinations in the steppes played a pivotal role in the rise of the Mongol Empire.

South-west of Mongolia, and serving as a buffer between the Jin and Qara Khitai empires, rested Xi Xia, a Buddhist kingdom in what are the modern Gansu and Ningxia provinces of China.[23] Comprising a mixed population of Han Chinese, Turkic nomads and Tangut, a Tibetan people who served as the ruling class, Xi Xia was situated along the Silk Road and benefited from trade arriving east from Central Asia and west from China. It also served as entry into the Mongolia steppes and had some ties to various nomadic groups, such as the Kereit.

As the thirteenth century began, it is unlikely that it occurred to anyone that this organisation of states and borders was about to be swept away and irrevocably changed. Of the states mentioned above, none survived the rise of the Mongols. Many medieval states had been invaded and even conquered by steppe nomads previously. While some were destroyed, others continued under 'new ownership', but the Mongols changed the map of Eurasia forever. Furthermore, it is doubtful that anyone would have guessed that large numbers of Mongols would convert to Islam. In the twelfth century, Islam was unknown to the nomads of Mongolia, aside from perhaps a few long-distance traders from Central Asia. Although merchants had long been instrumental in converting new populations to Islam, these Muslims merchants either did not attempt it or had little, if any, success.

---

[23] For more on Xi Xia, see Ruth Dunnell, 'The Hsi Hsia', *CHCAR*, 154–214.

2

The Rise of Chinggis Khan and the Unification of Mongolia

The rise of Chinggis Khan is something of a marvel, as there is no particular reason why Temujin, as he was named, should have become the greatest conqueror in history as well as a lawgiver and the founder of a nation. While one should not consider him a reluctant hero, there are a myriad of possibilities whereby he could have failed, been killed, or simply disappeared in history. Yet, at the same time, if one believes in destiny, it could be said that he was destined for greatness – for if nothing else Temujin learned from his mistakes and from the mistakes of others. He continually improved himself and the situation of his followers while never accepting the status quo. While he could exist quite comfortably within the confines of traditional steppe society, he was something of a revolutionary. His rise to power, however, was tied to four feuds.[1]

The first feud originated before Temujin's birth. The Mongols in the late twelfth century were a broken power, but in the first half of the twelfth century they had emerged as a significant factor in Mongolia, having pushed their way from the forests into the steppes of north-eastern Mongolia. Their success was great enough to attract the attention of the Jin Empire, which then promptly conspired with the Tatars against the Mongols. This was simply part of the Jin Empire's, and indeed most Chinese empires', standard operation procedure of playing one steppe group off against the other to ensure that none became too worrisome. The Jin–Tatar alliance defeated the Mongols, forcing the Mongols to change tactics. Under the leadership of Ambaghai Khan, who was a Tayichi'ud Mongol and marked a shift in leadership to that branch of the Mongols, the Mongols attempted to make peace with the Tatars. Ambaghai arranged a marriage between his daughter and a Tatar chieftain. As part of normal protocol, he travelled lightly armed and with few followers as he escorted his daughter to the Tatar camp. En route,

---

[1] Larry V. Clark, 'The Theme of Revenge in *The Secret History of the Mongols*', in *AAC2*, 33–57. While I agree with Clark's overall thesis, we differ in the details.

the Tatar *juyin* took Ambaghai captive and then sent him to the Jin Empire, where the emperor executed Ambaghai by nailing him to a wooden donkey.² It was not only a horrific death, but a clear insult to the horse nomads of the steppes.

According to *The Secret History of the Mongols*, Ambaghai managed to send a message to his kinsmen before he died, urging them to fight the Jin until their fingers could no longer draw a bowstring.³ The Jin's actions broke the Mongols as a power. Unfortunately, as the Jin learned to their chagrin, it allowed the Tatars to grow unfettered, and decades passed before the Jin found an ally to keep them in check. Nonetheless, the Mongols, led by Qutula Khan, fought thirteen battles with the Tatars. Although they never achieved any major victories, a leader named Yesugei had some success. A member of the aristocratic Borjigid clan, Yesugei was the father of Chinggis Khan.

The Mongols were composed of two major groups (as well as many subgroups), the Durlukin or ordinary Mongols, and the aristocratic Niru'un. The Niru'un clans all belonged to one lineage known as the Kiyad, who were believed to be descended from Alan Goa and her five sons, some of whom had a heavenly father according to Mongolian legend.⁴

According to tradition, a number of Mongol tribes came from the five sons of the Alan Goa. The most important, and highest in terms of hierarchy, came from Buqu Qadagi, Buqatu Salji and Bodonchar – those who had a heavenly father. Some Mongols, however, viewed any tribe descended from the womb of Alan Goa as Niru'un, although others considered those descended from the non-divine sons as Durlukin.⁵ Six generations later, those Niru'un descended from Qabul Khan became known as the Kiyad.⁶

Yesugei's clan, the Borjigid, was descended from Alan Goa's fifth son Bodonchar. For much of the early history of the Mongols, the Borjigid were the dominant Kiyad clan. During the reign of Ambaghai, however, his clan, the Tayichi'ud, assumed the leadership of the Kiyad Mongols. It returned to the Borjigid with the reign of Qutula, however. As for Yesugei, although

---

² *SHM*, §53; RD/Karimi, 59–60; RD/Thackston1, 45; RD/Thackston2, 93. Rashid al-Din indicates that Ambaghai went to the Tatars seeking a wife for himself.
³ *SHM*, §53. It is not known when Ambaghai died or when his reign began. His successor, Qutula, died in 1164. It is likely that the Jin Emperor who executed Ambaghai was either Hailing Wang (1150–61) or the Shizong Emperor (1161–90).
⁴ RD/Thackston2, 56; RD/Thackston1, 79; RD/Karimi, 111; *SHM* §17–22; Christopher Atwood, 'Mongol Tribe', *EMME*, 389–91.
⁵ RD/Thackston2, 81; RD/Thackston1, 117; RD/Karimi, 172.
⁶ RD/Thackston2, 57, 89; RD/Thackston1, 79, 126; RD/Karimi, 112, 190; *SHM* §17–22.

Alan Goa and the Parable of the Arrows

Alan Goa, or Alan the Beautiful, married Dobun Mergen and had two sons with him. While hunting, Dobun Mergen shot a deer and while returning home he encountered a distressed man who exchanged his son for a haunch of the deer. Not long after he returned to his wife and children, Dobun Mergen died. Months later, Alan Goa conceived and gave birth to three more sons, named Buqu Qadagi, Buqatu Salji and Bodonchar. Her two sons grew suspicious and accused their mother of sleeping with a slave. She denied this and explained that a 'Yellow Man' had come through the smoke-hole of their yurt. When he left, he transformed into a yellow dog and exited through the smoke-hole. The implication was clear – heaven favoured her and caused her pregnancy. The three sons were of divine nature.

She further lectured all of her children on the importance of unity. To this end, she gathered five arrows and handed one to each son, ordering them to break the arrows. All five broke their respective arrows with ease. She then bundled five arrows together with a thong and again ordered her sons to break the arrows. Each son attempted and failed to snap the bundled arrows. This, she explained, was the lesson. If they stood alone, they could be broken; if they remained united as brothers, no one could overcome them. After her death, they often forgot this lesson, but the parable reappears throughout Mongolian history.

---

grandson of Qabul Khan and the nephew of Qutula, he was not the khan but a leader of some standing who upheld the prerogatives of the Borjigid Mongols and even defeated the Tatars on a few occasions.

Ho'elun, Temujin's mother, came from the Olqunu'ud, a sub-group of the Onggirad who were Durlukin and lived near the Khalkha River. Yesugei's abduction of Ho'elun gave rise to the second feud. Originally, Ho'elun was the bride of a Merkit, Chiledu. Kidnapping in order to procure a bride was not uncommon and did not always lead to feuds. Indeed, in some regions of Central Eurasia, it existed well into the twentieth century and unfortunately still occurs.[7] Chiledu and Ho'elun were travelling

---

[7] Isolated occurrences still occur in Central Asia. Cynthia Werner, 'Bride Abduction in Post-Soviet Central Asia: Marking a Shift Towards Patriarchy through Local Discourses of Shame and Tradition', *Journal of Royal Anthropological Institute* 15 (2009), 314–31; Cynthia Werner, 'Women, Marriage, and the Nation-State: The Rise of Nonconsensual Bride Kidnapping in Post-Soviet Kazakhstan', in Pauline Jones Luong (ed.), *Transformations of Central Asian States: From Soviet Rule to Independence* (Ithaca, NY, 2004), 59–89.

Figure 2.1 Reconstructed *ger* on a wagon platform. Large *gers* or yurts were often transported fully assembled on wagons. These typically belonged to the elites.

back to Merkit territory in 1160 when Yesugei spotted them. Smitten by Ho'elun's beauty, Yesugei gathered his brothers and warriors and attacked. Faced with certain death, Chiledu and his men fled, leaving Ho'elun to her fate. The event in the *Secret History of the Mongols* reveals Ho'elun's touching farewell to her bridegroom, with her literally giving him the shirt off her back, her blouse, so that he would remember her by her scent. Nonetheless, she became Yesugei's primary wife, the second wife being known as Suchigil-eke.[8]

The event started a feud, as Yesugei violated social conventions. Exogamy was the norm among the nomads, particularly among the elites. For the Mongols, the practice of exogamy made all of the aristocratic Kiyad marry from a Negus clan, the lineage of the Durlukin. Ho'elun's Olqunu'ud clan fell into that category, but as she was already someone else's wife, it violated custom.

---

[8] *SHM* §55–6; Jack Weatherford, *Genghis Khan and the Making of the Modern World* (New York, 2004), 12. The 'eke' attached to Suchigil means 'mother'. She also appears as Sulchigei.

The Wedding Party

While the abduction of women was not uncommon, it carried the risk of retaliation as well, hence the need for some social conventions. These were also aimed at preventing the wedding party from transforming into a war party and attacking an unsuspecting camp. Thus the groom's party came lightly armed and few in numbers. In return, the bride's camp provided hospitality. Hospitality towards travellers was sacrosanct – violating it was taboo. A wedding party was also sacrosanct. If it was not, then all wedding parties travelling back to their distant camps and pastures became fair game and easy targets. Such violations threatened the practice of exogamy. Yesugei's kidnapping of Ho'elun violated the tradition, an offence that would not be forgotten, although the Merkit did not have an opportunity for revenge in Yesugei's lifetime. The lack of immediate retaliation also gives some indication of the Yesugei's prowess and reputation that is not always explicit in the sources.

Despite the unconventional marriage, Yesugei and Ho'elun produced five children. Temujin was their eldest, and was followed by his brothers Qasar, Qachi'un, Temuge, and a sister named Temulun. Temujin's siblings were born in two-year intervals so that by the time Temujin was nine years old his siblings were seven, five, three and one.[9] There is some dispute about the date of Temujin's birth – 1155, 1162, or 1167 have all been posited in the sources, although the Mongolian government has recognised 1162 as the official date, for political reasons although historical data supports it as well.[10] Yesugei's other wife, Suchigil-eke, also gave birth to two sons, Bekhter and Belgutei. Although Suchigil was the second wife, Bekhter was born before Temujin, making Temujin the second-eldest son.

Shortly before Temujin's birth, Yesugei defeated a group of Tatars and took several captives, including a leader named Temujin. In honour of this auspicious event, Yesugei named his first son with Ho'elun Temujin. Legend

---

[9] While this is certainly possible, particularly as breastfeeding would mitigate the chances of pregnancy, the spacing of ages may be symbolic as the number nine has symbolic meaning in Mongolian lore. Larry W. Moses, 'Triplicated Triplets: The Number Nine in the Secret History of the Mongols', *Asian Folklore Studies* 42 (1986), 287–94; Igor de Rachewiltz (ed.), *SHM*, 324–5.

[10] Paul Ratchnevsky, *Genghis Khan: His Life and Legacy*, trans. Thomas Nivison Haining (Cambridge, MA, 1992), 18; Timothy May, *Culture and Customs of Mongolia* (Westport, CT, 2009), 143–4.

also reported he was born clutching a blood clot the size of a knuckle bone – a portent that his son was destined for greatness.[11]

Following Temujin's birth, his life is unknown until he was eight or nine years old. In the interim, the war with the Tatars continued. The significance of the age is that Yesugei began to seek a bride for Temujin, although the actual marriage would not occur until the children reached puberty. One was considered an adult around the age of fifteen. Yet in order to find a suitable bride, among the nobility at least, one started early to secure a suitable arrangement. Negotiations often took considerable time. Marriage among the elite was rarely just a social ritual, but was tied to politics and security as the marriage formed the basis of an alliance. Due to exogamy customs, Temujin's bride had to come from the Durlukin and ideally from a leading family. Although the Durlukin were 'commoners', a hierarchy existed; the key was that Durlukin leaders could not become khans.

Yesugei intended to betroth his son to a girl from the Olqunu'ud, Ho'elun's tribe. This made strategic sense as Ho'elun came to Yesugei through kidnapping; a marriage alliance did not exist between the two. Furthermore, there was a possibility that hostilities existed between them due to the kidnapping. A marriage between Temujin and an Olqunu'ud girl could diminish the hostilities and counter any alliance between the Olqunu'ud and the Merkit against Yesugei. Despite this strategic manoeuvre, fate interceded. While travelling to the Olqunu'ud, Yesugei and Temujin encountered Dei Sechen, a leader among the Onggirad, which included the Olqunu'ud as a sub-group.[12] Militarily weak, Dei Sechen secured his tribe with neutrality in steppe affairs through marriage alliances. The Onggirad were well-known throughout the Mongolian plateau for the beauty of their women.

Offering hospitality to Yesugei, whom Dei Sechen undoubtedly knew by reputation if not personally, Dei Sechen informed the Mongol leader of a recent dream he had experienced. Dei Sechen dreamt of a white falcon that flew towards him, clutching the sun in one claw and the moon in the other. The dream should have been clear to Yesugei. White was an auspicious colour on the steppes and the falcon was the symbol of the Borjigid Mongols.[13] The clutching of the sun and moon indicated that Temujin would rule the universe. Although we have little reason to doubt Dei Sechen, as Sechen means

---

[11] *SHM* §59. The naming of Temujin after a Tatar leader also have been a method of reminding the next generation of the Tatar feud. Clark, 'Theme of Revenge', 36.

[12] Also spelled 'Qonggirad'. The Onggirad had ties with the Jin and Liao before them.

[13] The falcon became the symbol of the Borjigids as their ancestor Bodonchar became known for his falconing skills, which allowed him to survive when his brothers abandoned him. See *SHM* §25 and 26.

'wise', he may also have recognised that Yesugei was an ascending leader on the steppes. Having him as an ally would be beneficial, and so he offered his daughter, Borte, who was only a few months older than Temujin, as a wife to Yesugei's son. Yesugei consented to the arrangement and left Temujin with Dei Sechen.[14]

As the son normally returned home with his father, this was an unusual situation. Perhaps Yesugei preferred to leave Temujin there for safety reasons. As indicated before, on trips such as these the nomads travelled with few men and lightly armed. Considering that Temujin was young and not a warrior yet, perhaps Yesugei felt that he would be safer with Dei Sechen. Regardless, Yesugei could always retrieve Temujin later. Unfortunately, Yesugei had only a short life yet to live.

On the journey home, Yesugei and his supporters halted at a camp for the night. According to custom, the hosts offered Yesugei hospitality and provided shelter, food and drink. Unfortunately, it was a Tatar camp and the Tatars recognised Yesugei. Seeing an excellent opportunity, the Tatars broke protocol and poisoned his food. The poison, however, did not take instantaneous effect, but as he rode home Yesugei became gravely ill. By the time he returned to Ho'elun, Yesugei was on his deathbed. He sent a rider to retrieve Temujin.[15] When Temujin arrived home, his father was dead, thus deepening the feud between the Mongols and Tatars, but it was a feud that would have to wait.

Ho'elun was now left alone with five children, or at least that is what the sources lead us to believe. Of course, Suchigil-eke and her two sons were also present, and perhaps a few others. While Yesugei's death was a result of and affected the Tatar feud, it also triggered the third feud with the Tayichi'ud.[16]

The Tayichi'ud feud originated during the high period of Mongol power when Qabul Khan reigned (c. 1120–40). Qabul Khan and the previous khans were Borjigid Mongols. Qabul Khan, however, named Ambaghai, of the Tayichi'ud lineage, as his successor due his ability, rather than one of his own seven sons. Although the Borjigid Mongols wanted to maintain the line of authority, they complied with Qabul's wishes. Ambaghai's reign ended ignobly as previously mentioned, and the position of khan passed back to the Borjigid with Qutula, one of Qabul's sons, taking the reins of authority. He died in 1164 without an heir while fighting the Jin and Tatars. A

---

[14] *SHM* §63. It should be noted that this dream was probably an apocryphal story used to justify Chinggis Khan's rise to power. Along with the blood clot clutched in his fist at birth, the dream is another portent that Temujin was destined for greatness.
[15] *SHM*, §67–9.
[16] *SHM*, § Clark, 'Theme of Revenge', 38–9.

successor was not selected immediately, which allowed a deep rift between the Tayichi'ut and the Borjigid to grow as the Mongols could not agree upon a khan. Yesugei's death, several years after Qutula died, only magnified the divide.

Although Ambaghai died, his wives still wielded influence, particularly in the rituals of the tribe performed during a *quriltai* or meeting of all of the clans where major decisions, such as the leadership of the tribe, were made. During this *quriltai*, held not long after Yesugei's death, the wives of Ambaghai excluded Ho'elun from the *Qajaru Ineru* ceremony which honoured the ancestors with sacrifices.[17] As the meat and drink sacrificed to the ancestors became part of a feast, Orbei and Soqatai, Ambaghai's widows, denied Ho'elun a role not only in the ceremony, but also partaking in the feast, indicating she was not welcome. This was a grave insult and indicated that with Yesugei's death, her family lacked influence in tribal affairs. With Temujin being perhaps ten and Bekhter a few years older, none of the male descendants of Yesugei had attained his majority.

After the *quriltai* ended, it was clear that a decision regarding the leadership of the Mongols had been made. Once again the Tayichi'ud Mongols were in the ascendant, although it is not certain if anyone was declared khan. As the various clans packed up their belongings and moved off, the majority of Yesugei's followers joined the Tayichi'ud. One of Ho'elun's servants attempted to rally them, but the Tayichi'ud killed him. Ho'elun herself successfully shamed many into remaining by grabbing her husband's *tuq* or standard and riding to the front of their column. Unfortunately, although they could not desert Ho'elun while she looked upon them, they ignominiously abandoned her in the middle of the night. When Ho'elun awoke, she found herself alone with Suchigil and their children.[18]

Left to fend for themselves, they hunted, gathered root crops and berries, and lived a basic life of subsistence. Temujin and his brothers were even forced to fish – something that Mongols rarely did.[19] During this time a rift between Temujin and Bekhter opened. Although Ho'elun was Yesugei's primary wife, Suchigil may have been his first wife, or at least the one who first produced a child. The favoured wife's children were the heirs of the father's legacy. Bekhter, however, being older, may not have wished to concede authority to his half-brother Temujin, who was at least two years younger. Complicating this is the fact that the Mongols practised what is known as levirate marriage, in which the son married his father's wives, excluding

[17] SHM §70–1. Also see Rachewiltz, *Secret History*, 341–435.
[18] SHM §71–5.
[19] SHM §75.

his own mother. Thus, upon attaining his majority, Bekhter could become Temujin's stepfather.[20]

Bekhter did not achieve this, as Temujin murdered him. Whether this was because of family dynamics or was as depicted in the *Secret History*, in which Temujin and Qasar killed him because he repeatedly stole food from them, Bekhter died. Temujin allowed Belgutei, the younger half-brother, to live. Even though Temujin removed his rival, he was not absolved of his actions. Ho'elun realised what her sons had done immediately and castigated them as animals while reminding them of Alan Go'a and the Parable of the Arrows. She also noted that instead of fighting among themselves they should be planning vengeance against the Tayichi'ud.[21] While she may have been shamed and angered by her sons, news of the event spread. The fact that it did spread also makes one wonder just how ostracised Temujin's family really was.

One morning, the Tayichi'ud attacked Temujin's camp; possibly the attack was to punish the murder of Bekhter, a violation of any society's norms, but most likely it was a demonstration of the ascendancy of the Tayichi'ud over the Borjigin. Temujin and his family fled upon hearing the hooves of horses in the distance. Although they hid in a thick forest with Qasar, already an impressive archer, holding off the Tayichi'ud, Temujin still entered captivity. Temujin's life was spared for the time being, perhaps due to his age, to serve as a reminder to Yesugei's former supporters of his family's now-subordinate position. Around his neck he wore a cangue, a wooden device large enough that one could not lie down to sleep and heavy enough to prevent anyone from running far.[22] Cangues could also include holes into which one inserted one's hands, similar to pillories used to punish wrongdoers in colonial America. Another means was to use a cangue large enough for one to have to use one's hands to support the cangue. In short, it was a simple yet effective device.

It is uncertain how long Temujin remained in the Tayichi'ud camp, but while there he found some sympathisers, particularly among Yesugei's former supporters. Temujin quickly learned who was compassionate, as each night he stayed with and was fed by different families so that no single family bore the burden of maintaining the prisoner. In the household of Sorqan Shira of the Suldus, a herdsman, Temujin found the most relief. Sorqan Shira's sons released him from the cangue, allowing him to rest comfortably and treating the sores that the chafing cangue caused.[23]

---

[20] Weatherford, *Genghis Khan and the Making of the Modern World*, 23–5.
[21] SHM, §77–8.
[22] SHM, §81.
[23] *SHM* §82–7; RD/Karimi, 133; RD/Thackston1, 93–4; RD/Thackston2, 66.

Figure 2.2 Cangue, Qing period (nineteenth century). Temujin would have worn something similar as prisoner of the Tayichi'ud. (National History Museum, Ulaanbaatar)

Their treatment of Temujin was fortuitous for Yesugei's heir and his attempt to escape the Tayichi'ud. One night during a festive occasion, Temujin was left in the care of a less capable individual. Using the cangue as a weapon, Temujin rendered him unconscious and fled. He hid in a stream, using the cangue as a float to keep his head up and keeping fairly well hidden in the dark of the night. Although the Tayichi'ud searched for him, Temujin escaped detection. Eventually the Tayichi'ud gave up the search, realising he could not run far with the cangue. Furthermore, it is likely that most of them were inebriated and not in a condition to conduct a diligent search. Ultimately, Temujin took advantage of Sorqan Shira's kindness. The old man and his family burned the cangue in their fire and hid him until a safe escape could be arranged. To ensure that Temujin did nothing further foolhardy and thus endanger his family, Sorqan Shira provided him with a small quantity of food, a horse and a bow with three arrows – sufficient for hunting and perhaps defending himself, but not for revenge against the Tayichi'ud.[24]

[24] *SHM*, §81–7; RD/Karimi, 133–4; RD/Thackston1, 93–4; RD/Thackston2, 66.

Thanks to the kindness of Sorqan Shira, Temujin returned to his family. Strangely, the Tayichi'ud did not attempt to capture him again. It is difficult to understand why. Perhaps they lost track of him in the steppes, or considered him properly humiliated and no longer a concern. In the interim, Temujin began to establish as following.

He gained his first significant supporter while retrieving his family's stolen horses.[25] Temujin pursued them after Belgutei returned from hunting with their remaining horse. Along the way, he encountered Bo'orchu, the son of a very wealthy herdsman. The rustlers had passed by Bo'orchu while he was milking his father's mares. The fact that they did not attempt to steal their livestock provides an indication of Bo'orchu's father's wealth and power, as indicated in his name – Naqu Bayan or Naqu the rich. Bo'orchu not only provided Temujin with a fresh mount, but joined him in his pursuit. The two were successful in their endeavour and Bo'orchu became a fast friend and joined Temujin's family as his first *nokor*, or personal follower.[26]

Shortly afterwards, Temujin attained adulthood and now decided to marry. Accompanied by Belgutei, he retrieved Borte from the Onggirad camp. Interestingly, Dei Sechen and his retinue accompanied them back to Temujin's camp. Dei Sechen apparently decided that security for his daughter was important. The trip gained Temujin not only a wife, but a very valuable black sable cloak, which was a present from Chotan, Borte's mother, to Ho'elun. Temujin immediately invested the present by finding a protector. He travelled to the Kereit *ordo* or camp in the Black Forest near the Orkhon River and reminded Toghril Khan, the Kereit leader, that he was once the *anda* of Temujin's father.[27]

The *anda* relationship was a complicated bond among the nomads of Mongolia. The participants had to be of the same generation and the bond was meant to transcend all other loyalties, including tribe and clan, as well as ethnicity (thus a Mongol and Turk could be *anda*). In a sense, it made blood brothers of the two people and came with many obligations. Men who shared *anda*-hood were to be loyal to each other and protect and defend not only their *anda*, but their family. With Yesugei dead for several years, Toghril no longer had any obligation to Temujin, but Yesugei's son was daring. His presence reminded Toghril that Yesugei's death had not been avenged. Considering that Yesugei had assisted Toghril on several occasions, including restoring him to power after Toghril had been dethroned, Toghril owed much to his *anda*. Indeed, Toghril was in exile until Yesugei came to

---

[25] There is some suggestion the rustlers were Tayichi'ud. See Clark, 'Theme of Revenge', 39.
[26] SHM §90–3, 95.
[27] SHM §94, 96.

Figure 2.3 The Orkhon River Valley was historically significant not only to the Mongols, but to a number of confederations prior to the Mongol Empire.

his aid. Thus, even though Temujin did not have a large following – though it was larger than *The Secret History of the Mongols* hints at – by accepting him as a *nokor* Toghril not only gained another supporter but also gained legitimacy for taking in the son of his former *anda*. The gift of the sable coat demonstrated Temujin's respect for the Kereit khan while also increasing Toghril's wealth.

Although he now basked in the protection of Toghril Khan, the dominant force in central Mongolia, Temujin was not immune from tragedy. One day, riders attacked his camp. Believing the advancing riders to be Tayichi'ud, Temujin and his brothers fled. In their haste, however, Temujin and his brothers forgot Borte. She took shelter in a *ger* mounted on a wagon and driven by an old woman named Qo'aqchin.[28] As the riders approached, Qo'aqchin feigned any knowledge of Temujin, but learned the attackers were not Tayichi'ud but Merkit. Having learned that Temujin now had a wife, the Merkit sought to avenge Yesugei's abduction of Ho'elun. Discovering Borte,

---

[28] SHM §100. Again we have another indication that Temüjin was not as isolated as *The Secret History* wants us to believe. Qo'aqchin was apparently a maid or servant to either Hö'elün or Suchigil.

the Merkit carried her off, along with Suchigil and Qo'aqchin, and did not pursue Temujin.[29]

On his own, Temujin had little chance of rescuing her, but fortunately, he was now a *nokor* of a much more powerful individual. Temujin came to Toghril and informed him of his plight, gaining Toghril's assistance. While retrieving Temujin's wife helped his *nokor*, Toghril also benefited from the anticipated plunder. It took several months to organise the campaign, but he and Temujin marched together and joined Toghril's war chief, Jamuqa, who also happened to be Temujin's *anda* and a Jajirad Mongol. Although they had made their *anda* pact during their childhood, Jamuqa's fortunes had risen while Temujin's life had been unsettling. With their friendship renewed they marched against the Merkit. Under Jamuqa's direction, the attack succeeded, the Merkit were defeated, and a very pregnant Borte was rescued. Suchigil, however, remained with the Merkit of her own volition despite Belgutei's strident efforts to find her. According to *The Secret History of the Mongols*, she did not want to return to her son after having been married to a commoner. The embarrassment was too great.[30]

Afterwards, Temujin remained with Jamuqa, attaching his camp to his *anda*'s. The most obvious reason for this was for protection, although Temujin may have also achieved this by remaining with Toghril. It appears, however, that Toghril encouraged Jamuqa and Temujin to renew their friendship. Furthermore, to make Temujin more useful, Toghril may have wanted Temujin to learn the arts of war from Jamuqa as the death of Yesugei left a large gap in Temujin's education.[31]

Two major events occurred while Temujin stayed with Jamuqa. Besides his education in the arts of war, Borte gave birth to Jochi, Temujin's first son. One etymology for the name is 'Guest' because he was born in Jamuqa's camp. Another version is that he was a guest in Temujin's camp as his parentage was questionable. Borte's rescue was not immediate, and almost a year past before she was re-united with Temujin.[32] Nonetheless, Temujin accepted him as his first son and never questioned it. Unfortunately, the issue was never forgotten, becoming a problem for Jochi as an adult. Islamic sources from the Mongol Empire conceal Jochi's parentage, whereas the *Secret History of the Mongols* does not skirt the topic. In the awkward alternative version, the Merkit abducted Borte, but she is taken to the camp of Toghril,

---

[29] *SHM*, §101–2.
[30] *SHM*, §112.
[31] See Timothy May, 'Jamuqa and the Education of Chinggis Khan', *Acta Mongolica* 6 (2006), 273–86.
[32] *SHM*, §110–11.

who then returns her to Temujin.³³ The difference is that the *Secret History of the Mongols* was accessible only to the Mongol elite; the chronicles written by Muslim authors employed by the Mongols were not restricted. It is unclear whether they altered the story due to their own discretion or whether their patrons offered a different version to protect the prestige of the family, even that of a different Chinggisid line. The second event was that tensions arose between Jamuqa and Temujin. The exact reasons are not clear, but appear to have their roots in Borte's and also Temujin's own charisma.

Borte encouraged Temujin to split from Jamuqa as they moved to new pastures.³⁴ Perhaps she no longer wanted her husband to be Jamuqa's apprentice. Alternatively, perhaps she was jealous that Temujin was spending more time with his *anda* than with her. What is apparent, however, is that Temujin learned not only how to lead by following Jamuqa's example, but also how not to lead. This was demonstrated as several of Jamuqa's followers joined him as well, including many commoners, such as Subedei, who was the cousin of one of Temujin's *nokod* (Jelme) and who became the greatest of all Mongol generals. Some senior Mongol leaders also joined Temujin, including Qorchi, who dreamt of an ox pulling a cart and bellowing that Temujin would rule the Mongols, not Jamuqa.³⁵ Over the following weeks, more and more people left Jamuqa and joined Temujin. While it was not a complete desertion from Jamuqa, small groups steadily trickled into Temujin's camp, including Altan Otchigin, the last son of Qutula Khan, which made him a distant uncle of Temujin's. While the addition of Mongol aristocracy bolstered Temujin's legitimacy among the Borjigid, the most came from Durlukin clans who joined Jamuqa's Jajirad or the Tayichi'ud after the Ho'elun's ostracism.

Altan and other Mongol leaders swore stylised oaths of allegiance to Temujin, and made him khan of the Borjigid Mongols. Toghril also seemed pleased and Jamuqa initially congratulated his *anda*. However, tensions mounted. Temujin and Jamuqa still nomadised in the same vicinity. Before long conflict erupted between their followers over livestock, during the course of which Taichar, Jamuqa's brother, was killed.³⁶ This was somewhat fitting as Taichar initiated the livestock rustling, but Jamuqa viewed it as an act of war. No attempt to resolve the matter diplomatically occurred and the two *anda* fought at Dalan-baljut near the Onon River in 1187. Although their

---

[33] RD/Karimi, 223; RD/Thackston1, 146; RD/Thackston2, 104. Juwayni avoids the topic altogether.
[34] *SHM* §118.
[35] *SHM*, §121.
[36] *SHM*, §129.

forces were approximately the same, Jamuqa soundly defeated Temujin, forcing him to take refuge in the Jin Empire.

Many steppe leaders, including Toghril, took refuge in Qara Khitai, Xi Xia, or the Jin Empire during adverse times. Conversely, rebels and disgraced officials from sedentary realms sometimes fled to the steppe. Such was life along the borderlands. While there is little evidence to confirm that Temujin took refuge with the Jin, besides a lacuna of ten years in Temujin's recorded activities, it is the most likely location due to the proximity of the empire and the Onon River compared to the alternatives.[37] Later events discreetly indicate a more intimate familiarity with the Jin than with Xi Xia or Qara Khitai. Temujin's defeat had a greater impact on the steppe than just a quarrel between two minor chieftains. With Jamuqa's victory, his following increased and upset the balance in Toghril's domains. Toghril's brother Erke-Qara gained Jamuqa's support in an effort to unseat the Kereit khan from his throne. Toghril fled to Qara Khitai while his uncle, Jaqa Gambu, found refuge in the Jin Empire.[38]

Although Temujin remained with the Jin for almost ten years, little is known of his life there. One source indicated he was a slave.[39] Yet, when Temujin returned, he was more powerful than before, which may mean that he was not a slave but rather a servitor of the Jin Empire. Even though Jamuqa defeated him, Temujin gained significantly. After the battle of Dalan-baljut, Jamuqa sought vengeance against many of those who had joined Temujin. Not only did he confiscate livestock, a typical punishment, but he also allegedly boiled seventy people alive and cut off the heads of their leaders before tying them to the tail of his horse and dragging their heads over the ground. This action alone violated any number of taboos and social conventions.[40] Thus, Temujin found a large portion of the Mongols who once supported Jamuqa deserting to him when he returned in 1195. The deserters were not only former followers but new ones as well, such as the Mangqud and the Uru'ud clans who became elite warriors in Temujin's army. Additionally, a former *nokor* of Yesugei joined them, Monglik of the Qongqotad with his sons.[41]

Upon his return to Mongolia in 1195, Temujin gathered his new and former supporters before holding a *quriltai* in 1196 with the Jurkin

---

[37] Ratchnevksy, *Genghis Khan*, 49–50.
[38] Ratchnevsky, *Genghis Khan*, 49–51. Erke-kara may have been Toghril's uncle instead of his younger brother. The sources are unclear and the scholarship conflicting.
[39] *MDBL*, 49; Ratchnevsky, *Genghis Khan*, 50; RD/Thackston2 115; RD/Thackston1, 160–1; RD/Karimi, 243–5. Rashid al-Din has Chinggis Khan defeating Jamuqa.
[40] *SHM*, §129.
[41] *SHM*, §130.

Mongols to renew their relationship and plan a campaign against the Tatars. Undoubtedly, Jin lucre facilitated Temujin's return. This wealth may have influenced many to join Temujin while also providing the Jin with an ally in the steppes. Several had little reason to follow Jamuqa considering how he dealt with those who offended him. As for the Jurkin, they were a branch of the Borjigid Mongols, with the Jurkin being slightly senior to Temujin's line.

As with all diplomatic and social functions, there are certain rules of etiquette that are observed. In the case of the Mongols, individuals received their *airagh* according to social status. If someone received their bowl before another of higher status, it was insulting, and this faux pas occurred at the *quriltai*. It led to the Jurkin beating one of Temujin's men. Then, another fight broke out over a stolen horse, during which Belgutei, Temujin's half-brother, suffered a knife wound. Despite being wounded, Belgutei attempted to ease the tension, but an enraged Temujin, supported by his men, attacked the Jurkin. Fortunately, no weapons were permitted within the vicinity of the *quriltai*, and thus they could only fight with weapons of convenience – branches and paddles used for churning the *kumiss* – as real weapons were kept outside of the drinking area. Temujin's men roundly defeated the Jurkin and resumed the *quriltai*. Nonetheless, the Jurkin did not forget their humiliation, which caused the third feud.[42]

While the *quriltai* ended in a drunken brawl, its intent was not only to consolidate the Borjigid Mongols with Temujin as the khan, but also to plan an attack against the Tatars. It is notable that Toghril also returned to Mongolia and regained control of the Kereit at this time. There is also evidence that Temujin assisted Jaqa Gambu's return to the Kereit as well.[43] Again, Jin support was key. While Temujin and the Borjigid Mongols may have had an axe to grind with the Tatars, the Jin also became wary of the Tatars and sought to break their power as they had grown too powerful since the death of Ambaghai Khan and Qutula Khan. Temujin's presence in the Jin Empire gave the Jin the perfect pawn to assist in breaking Tatar power in eastern Mongolia. The fact that Toghril was out of power and only restored with Jin aid also placed him in the debt of the Jin Emperor. Although the Jin armies could invade the steppes, without support from other nomads there was nothing the Jin could do to prevent the Tatars from retreating and over-extending the Jin lines of supply and communication, rendering them

---

[42] *SHM*, §130–2; RD/Thackston2, 116–18; RD/Thackston, 1998, 163–5; RD/Karimi, 248–52; Clark, 'Theme of Revenge', 40–1.
[43] RD/Karimi, 285; RD/Thackston1, 187; RD/Thackston2, 133.

vulnerable to a counterattack. The combined power of Toghril and Temujin gave the Jin an excellent opportunity to influence events in the steppes.

Although the Jurkin pledged their support for the campaign, they did not appear on the appointed day in 1196. As the campaign depended on timing, Temujin could not wait long and moved out to join Toghril. Caught between the Jin armies and those of Toghril and Temujin, the Tatars were soundly defeated. As a reward, the Jin granted Toghril the title of *wang* or king, which entered Mongolian as Ong: hence Toghril became known as Toghril Ong-Khan. Temujin also received the title of *Ja'ut qori*, a title meaning Commissioner in Charge of Rebel Pacification.[44]

Returning to camp, Temujin discovered that the Jurkin had betrayed him, not only by not fulfilling their pledge, but also by attacking his camp in his absence. Angered, Temujin rode against the Jurkin. He massacred the elite, including Taichu and Sacha Beki who were among those who had sworn oaths when they raised Temujin to the position of khan of the Borjigid. The non-elite Jurkin were then absorbed into Temujin's camp. With the elite destroyed, the Jurkin ceased to exist as a distinct group within the Mongols.

With this victory, Temujin's status increased, and he participated in a number of campaigns with Toghril, which accelerated his rise to power. In 1199, he campaigned with Toghril in western Mongolia against the Naiman. During this campaign, jealousies manifested among other members of Toghril's entourage. Despite their efforts to drive a wedge between Toghril and Temujin, they failed as Temujin rescued Toghril's son Senggum from another Naiman force.[45]

Nonetheless, tensions grew. Temujin remained in Toghril's favour and together they dominated much of eastern and central Mongolia. Several Mongol leaders disliked Temujin as he defied many social conventions, particularly in terms of social hierarchy. Many of his generals and his *nokod* (plural of *nokor*) came from commoners instead of the aristocracy. Furthermore, other tribes became concerned with the rise of the Kereit confederation, which now expanded beyond central Mongolia. In 1201, a *quriltai* of various disaffected groups gathered and elected Jamuqa Gur-Khan (Universal Ruler).

Jamuqa was a natural choice. His Jajirad clan was not large enough to dominate the confederation, thus forcing him to consult others as was

---

[44] SHM, §134; Rachewiltz, *SHM*, 491–3 on the titles. *Ja'ut quri* was a title awarded to *juyin* leaders who assisted the Jin against other nomads. During the time of Ambaghai there was a Tatar chieftain with this title, Mongke *ja'ut quri*.

[45] SHM, §162–4; RD/Thackston2, 127; RD/Thackston1, 178–9; RD/Karimi, 271–2; Ratchnevsky, *Genghis Khan*, 58.

desirable in confederations, which tended to be acephalous.[46] His credentials were considerable as he had formerly served as Toghril's war leader and had defeated Temujin. Forming the confederation were contingents of the Tatars and Naiman. The bulk, however, were Mongols coming from the Tayichi'ud and other Mongol tribes such as the Saliji'ud. The confederation represented the non-Mongol groups who feared the Kereit's growth and then those Mongols who rejected Temujin's increasing power.

Toghril and Temujin met the Gur-Khanid forces at Yedi Qunan in eastern Mongolia, with the Kereit-Borjigid forces emerging victorious. The Gur-Khanid confederation splintered and scattered across Mongolia. Perhaps it could have regrouped, but it proved to be an ephemeral polity as Jamuqa pillaged the camp of some of his former allies as he fled. Most likely, he needed the plunder in order to ensure his own position as khan of the Jajirad.

Toghril and Temujin pursued their enemies to ensure victory. Toghril chased after his former *nokor*, Jamuqa, to the Arghun River where Jamuqa surrendered. Jamuqa being too valuable to kill, Toghril granted him clemency and accepted him as his *nokor* again. Meanwhile, Temujin pursued the Tayichi'ud to the Onon River where he defeated them, despite suffering a life-threatening wound.[47] Although some Tayichi'ud escaped, they ceased to be a threat. Temujin followed a practice that started with the Jurkin and soon became standard procedure by executing the leadership of the clan and then distributing the rest of the Tayichi'ud among his followers to break their collective power. He also accepted members of the Tayichi'ud and their subordinate clans, such as the Suldus, to which Sorqan Shira belonged. Temujin did not forget those who helped him, or those who harmed him. Shortly afterwards, Temujin received also the submission of the Onggirad, who had also been part of the confederation. Although Borte was an Onggirad, any alliance between Temujin and Dei Sechen had long ended, probably with the death of Dei Sechen. In any case, the Onggirad may not have had a choice in joining the Gur-Khanid confederation as it comprised many tribes from eastern Mongolia. With the victory of the Tayichi'ud, Temujin appeared to be the pre-eminent Mongol leader and dominated the Onon-Kerulen basin; even if the more conservative elements did not fully support him, they could not challenge him alone.

Despite all of these successes, none quite compared to the final reward from defeating the Tayichi'ud. Temujin, several days later, accepted the

---

[46] See David Sneath, *The Headless State* (New York, 2007).
[47] *SHM* §145; Timothy May, 'Spitting Blood: Medieval Mongol Medical Practices', in Larissa Tracy and Kelly DeVries (eds), *'His Brest Tobrosten': Wounds and Wound Repair in Medieval Culture* (Leiden, 2015), 175–93.

submission of a common Mongol warrior known now as Jebe. Impressed by his audacity and prowess, Temujin accepted him as a *nokor*.[48]

The Tatars joined the Gur-Khanid confederation due to their weakened status after the 1197 war. With the expansion of the Kereit and Temujin's dominance in the Onon-Kerulen region, the Tatars saw a further diminution of their power. It was only the beginning of the end, however. In 1202, Temujin decided to end the Tatar feud. He launched an attack on the Tatars at Dalan-Nemurges, near the Khalkha River. Prior to the battle, Temujin decreed that no one should plunder until the battle was over and the enemy defeated. Too often, victory turned into defeat as discipline broke down and warriors became preoccupied with looting rather than fighting. His disciplined army crushed the Tatars. In the aftermath, he executed the male Tatar elites, excluding children. His actions have sometimes been called genocidal, but in reality tribes were somewhat amorphous. The identity of a tribe consisted of the leading clan. The rest of the tribe could be polyethnic and even polyglot. Members could leave the tribe and join another through various means.[49] The rest of the Tatars were then absorbed into the Mongols. The fact that the Tatar ethnonym became a synonym for the Mongols as they moved westward indicates that large numbers of Tatars survived Dalan-Nemurges and that the massacre, while dreadful, was not genocide.

Not everyone, however, obeyed Temujin's pillaging order. Senior members of the Borjigid clan defied Temujin. Even worse, the three culprits (Altan, Qucha and Daritai) were among those who had sworn oaths to obey Temujin when they made him khan after leaving Jamuqa. As punishment, Temujin confiscated and redistributed their plunder.[50] Furious, the three departed with their followers and went to Toghril. As Toghril was his suzerain, Temujin could not take any further action against them.

With his victory, Temujin now controlled eastern Mongolia and saw his following increase greatly with the destruction of the Tatars. Yet the battle altered his relationship with Toghril as he achieved victory without Kereit assistance. With the destruction of the Tatars in 1202, three major powers remained in Mongolia. The Naiman dominated the west, while the Kereit held sway in central Mongolia, but now Temujin's Mongols controlled eastern Mongolia.

Temujin's rapid rise caused considerable consternation within the Kereit elite. Some feared that Temujin might become Toghril's heir,

---

[48] *SHM* §147.
[49] See Lindner, 'What Is a Tribe', *passim*; Sneath, *Headless State, passim*.
[50] *SHM*, §153.

indicating that Temujin's Mongols were clearly part of the Kereit confederation.[51] Temujin attempted to further cement their relationship by proposing that his son Jochi marry Cha'ur, the daughter of Toghril. Toghril seemed open to this, but in his old age seemed less decisive. Senggum, his son, found the proposal insulting, most likely because of Jochi's undetermined parentage. Jamuqa also whispered in Toghril's ear against Temujin while Mongol defectors like Altan, Daritai and Qucha denounced Temujin for overturning the rights of the aristocracy, as demonstrated in his confiscation of plunder.[52]

Eventually, Toghril succumbed to these overtures and agreed to turn against his most stalwart supporter. Deciding to eliminate Temujin through conspiracy rather than risk battle, Toghril consented to the marriage in order to lure Temujin into a trap. Two herdsmen, however, learned of the plan and alerted Temujin before he arrived at the Kereit camp. Both sides marshalled their troops and they battled at Qalqajit Sands in 1203. The Kereit defeated the Mongols, shattering Temujin's army. The latter, however, had learned from his defeat by Jamuqa and established a rendezvous point. He and his followers re-formed at Lake Baljuna, with men trickling in over a number of days. According to the *Secret History*, they swore oaths and made a covenant of utmost loyalty to Temujin. Despite the setback, Temujin also received good news in the arrival of the Qorolas tribe, who may have deserted the Kereit and joined Temujin because of Toghril's treachery.[53]

Rested, the Mongols launched a counterattack a few days later. The Kereit paid the price for not ensuring Temujin's death, as he attacked while the Kereit were still celebrating their victory. The Mongols routed the Kereit. Although Toghril, Senggum and Jamuqa escaped with a few followers and fled beyond Temujin's reach, the rest of the Kereit submitted to him. Now a refugee, Toghril fled through Naiman territory and was killed by a Naiman.[54] Senggum took refuge in Xi Xia while Jamuqa found service among the Naiman. Unlike with the Jurkin and Tatars, Temujin did not massacre the Kereit leadership, most of whom he knew from his days in Toghril's service. Despite the marriage proposal of the Jochi and Cha'ur Beki being a *casus belli* between the Mongols and Kereit, Jochi did not marry her after the Kereit's defeat. Cha'ur disappears after the Kereit defeat in 1203. Other marriages, however, did take place. Tolui married Sorqoqtani, the daughter of Jaqa

---

[51] *SHM*, §164.
[52] *SHM*, §165–6.
[53] *SHM*, §182–3, 208. Also see Francis W. Cleaves, 'The Historicity of the Baljuna Covenant', *HJAS* 18, no. 3 (1955), 357–421.
[54] *SHM*, §188.

Gambu, Toghril's brother, as was Begtutmish Fujin who married Jochi. Meanwhile, Temujin married their sister, Ibaqa.[55]

With the defeat of the Kereit, Temujin now controlled central and eastern Mongolia. His meteoric rise attracted the attention of the Naiman. There is no evidence that suggested that Temujin wished to rule all of Mongolia; indeed, while he had a successful encounter with the Naiman in 1199, it also taught him that they were powerful and not to be trifled with. Unfortunately for Temujin, he did not have the opportunity to make the decision. The Naiman viewed Mongol success a result of Toghril's weakness and decided to deal with the Mongols. The Naiman found allies among Jamuqa and other disaffected Mongols as well as the Merkit, but the Onggud, a Turkic tribe in southern Mongolia, delayed in responding and warned Temujin of the Naiman's plans.[56]

Rather than wait for the Naiman to attack, Temujin devised a daring plan to march against the Naiman, across Mongolia in the early spring, when his own horses were weak. It was a risky move, but surprised the Naiman. In 1204, Temujin won perhaps the most important battle of his career at Chakirmaut on the slopes of the Khangai Mountains. Here he displayed a military genius in terms of organisation, discipline, tactics and strategies that completely baffled his enemy, including opponents like Jamuqa who were well-regarded military leaders and familiar with Temujin's style of warfare. The decades of war and experience that Temujin gained, beginning with the campaign against the Merkit, culminated at this moment and revealed a new form of steppe warfare involving not only highly disciplined troops, but also new tactics.[57] Although the Naiman were crushed, some escaped and remained a concern. Temujin, however, was the undisputed master of Mongolia, much to the consternation of his former patron, the Jin Empire. They could do little to halt it, however, due to rebellions in their own territory.

The remainder of 1204 and 1205 consisted of Temujin consolidating his authority, and the capture of Jamuqa. Jamuqa's own men took him captive and turned him over to Temujin. As a reward, he executed them – Temujin clearly disliked disobedience and disloyalty to one's master. To him, disloyalty was the greatest sin. Despite a rivalry spanning decades, Temujin was loath to kill his *anda*. If the *Secret History* is to be believed, Jamuqa convinced him that it would be best to give him an honourable death. Reluctantly, Temujin consented.[58]

---

[55] *SHM*, §186.
[56] *SHM*, §189–90.
[57] SHM, §193–5.
[58] *SHM*, § 200–1.

Yeke Monggol Ulus

Temujin's rule of Mongolia was confirmed in 1206 during a *quriltai*. Here he was given the title of Chinggis Khan, meaning 'firm or fierce ruler'.[59] This was a new title and marked a new era in Mongolian history. As there were still lose ends from the process of unifying Mongolia, which was largely accidental, Chinggis Khan's first priority was to consolidate his rule. Merkit and Naiman refugees were still a potent threat, as was Senggum, who took refuge in Xi Xia. Any of these could serve as a rallying point for the disaffected. Furthermore, the wars wrecked the nomadic economy – battles destroy pasture and inevitably herds and flocks of animals. Furthermore, unity could be ephemeral among the various tribes. Yesterday's enemy was today's friend, but how long before old grudges resurfaced?

To resolve the problem, Temujin conducted a social revolution by reorganising society into a military system based on the *minqan* or unit of one thousand. The members of the Baljuna Covenant and a few others became leaders of the *minqan*, some with more than one *minqan* under their command. The *minqan* was then also organised decimally so that it comprised ten units of one hundred. The latter consisted of ten units of ten. This formation existed not only for the military, but also the households, so that one thousand households formed a *minqan*, which was taxed accordingly. Essentially, a military-industrial complex evolved, with a household *minqan* supporting a military *minqan*.

Chinggis Khan also assigned territory to family members, removed from the centre. He assigned them *minqans* with commanders who advised his sons and brothers. Thus, Chinggis Khan created a system of checks and balances so that his relatives could not conspire against him or seek independence. As the majority of the old tribal leaders, at least those who opposed Chinggis Khan, were killed, the military leaders were his *nokod*, who largely rose through the ranks. Their position and authority rested on Chinggis Khan's favour. The absence of other aristocrats allowed Chinggis Khan to reconstruct the *yasun* hierarchy. His family became the *altan urugh* or Golden Kin or Family, or the imperial family. This became the *chaghan yasun* or white bone. The old aristocracies that were not destroyed became *qara yasun* or black-boned, also known as the *qarachu*. They still wielded authority, but were subordinate to the *altan urugh*. Furthermore, Chinggis Khan attempted to erase old tribal identities. The *minqad* (plural) consisted of those who had

---

[59] Igor de Rachewiltz, 'The Title Činggis Qan/Qayan Re-examined', in W. Heissig and K. Sagaster (eds), *Gedanke und Wirkung. Festschrift zum 90. Gerburtstag von Nikolaus Poppe* (Wiesbaden, 1989), 281–98.

Figure 2.4 Chinggis Khan monument (Tsonjin Boldog). Built in 2008 and standing 40 metres (130 feet) tall on the banks of the Tuul or Tula River, 54 kilometres (33.55 miles) east of Ulaanbaatar, the statue is located where Chinggis Khan found a golden horse whip, according to legend. Made from stainless steel, the statue was designed by D. Erdenebileg, a sculptor. The architect J. Enkhjargal designed the visitor centre and museum that serves as the statue's base.

fought for him. The defeated were then added, but distributed among many units. Thus, the defeated never made up a single coherent body that could rebel. Transfers to another *minqan* were forbidden. In doing this, Chinggis Khan created a single tribe or nation, the *Yeke Monggol Ulus* or Great Mongol State. No longer were they Kereit, Tatars or any other identity, but Mongols. A wonderful plan in theory and even in practice – however, the old identities never truly disappeared. Instead, they transformed and even became the names of some of the *minqad*, essentially names of regiments that morphed into new clan or tribal identities over time.

A key tool for running the empire was also formed at the 1206 *quriltai*. This was the *keshik* or bodyguard, comprising 10,000 men. A smaller one was formed in 1204, but now Chinggis Khan used it to transform his power into a state. It was made up of the sons of the military leaders. It gave Chinggis Khan some leverage to ensure their loyalty, but it also served as a training school for officers and officials. Thus it was much more than a bodyguard, but Chinggis Khan's household staff, and carried out numerous functions pertaining to the empire. As a result, Chinggis Khan became familiar with the abilities of each member of the guard and ensured that they all received similar training in military and administrative leadership.

Yet, his efforts to organise a state were not his only methods of stabilising the *Yeke Monggol Ulus*. Sending the army outside of Mongolia also served as a tool of stability. One can never forget that the *Yeke Monggol Ulus* was forged in the crucible of war. Prior to 1206, the men who made up the *minqad* of Chinggis Khan had been enemies. While peace existed in Mongolia, tensions remained under the surface. Additionally, while many of Chinggis Khan's enemies were dead, several, like Senggum of the Kereit and Guchulug of the Naiman, had escaped. As long as they existed they served as a rallying point for anyone dissatisfied with the Chinggis Khan's rule. Furthermore, although the Jin played a significant factor in Chinggis Khan's rise to power, they had a history of meddling in the affairs of the steppe nomads. Thus, while Chinggis Khan needed to stabilise his rule in Mongolia, one of the mechanisms for doing this was to venture outside of Mongolia.

Figure 2.5 Modern depiction of a Mongol warrior performing the 'Parthian shot'.

An Islamic Empire?

Clearly, at this time the Mongol Empire was not an Islamic Empire or even in extensive contact with *Dar al-Islam*. Indeed, one could question whether the Mongols even knew what Islam was, or whether any Muslims resided within the *Yeke Monggol Ulus*. While converts may not have existed among the tribes of Mongolia prior to or during the rise of Chinggis Khans, Muslims could be found. These few individuals were usually long-distant merchants originating from Central Asia, plying the Silk Road.

While we often envision the Silk Road as a direct route between the Mediterranean Sea and China, it actually consisted of numerous routes and branches that not only traversed the east and west, but also connected the north and south. Furthermore, silk was not the primary commodity; ubiquitous goods that could be sold from market to market to cover the expenses of the merchant were equally important. Luxury goods such as silk, furs and spices were the key to large profits, but pots, iron needles and tools also found markets.

Asan or Hasan the Sartaq, who joined Temujin as Lake Baljuna, was such an individual.[60] Asan originated from Central Asia, hence the Sartaq or Sart identity, which became a Mongolian term for the non-Turkic population of Central Asia.[61] The relevant passage in the *Secret History of the Mongols* indicates that he came from Alaqush Digid Quri of the Onggud. Asan, as he was called by the Mongols, was certainly one of these merchants who ventured from the main routes. The *Secret History of the Mongols* indicates that he was engaged in the fur trade, stating: 'He had a white camel and was driving a thousand wethers among the Ergune River downstream in order to buy pelts of sables and squirrels.'[62] What is notable is that he brought wethers or two-year-old sheep to trade. These he probably purchased from the Onggud after trading with them, most likely in textiles, though other luxury or common goods from Central Asia would also be appropriate.[63] As one does not become wealthy by selling sheep in Mongolia on a normal basis, Asan probably planned to take the sheep to Siberia, to trade sheep for furs with the tribes in Siberia. Another possibility, however, is that he may have been a war profiteer. One must wonder whether he had learned of the war and perhaps Temujin's defeat from Alaqush and sought to sell his stock.

---

[60] *SHM*, §182. Also see Igor de Rachewiltz (ed. and trans.), *The Secret History of the Mongols*, 657–8.
[61] 'Sart', *EI²*.
[62] *SHM*, §182.
[63] Rachewiltz, *The Secret History of the Mongols*, 658.

Certainly there was a risk of being pillaged, but the rewards could outweigh that risk. This also explains his timely appearance at Lake Baljuna.

Regardless of the reason, Hasan soon entered Chinggis Khan's service and would play an important, but unfortunate, role in the future of the Mongol Empire. Nonetheless, Hasan was one of the first Muslims Temujin encountered. If the fur trade was part of Hasan's regular business, he may even have been in Temujin's pastures before, or perhaps at Toghril's camp at the same time as Temujin. One might wonder whether at some point Hasan appraised the sable cloak that was part of Borte's dowry and had been given to Toghril.

Hasan was not the only Muslim Temujin encountered. In addition, there was Jabar or Ja'far Khwaja. Ja'far Khwaja, a *sayyid* or descendant of Muhammad, was with Temujin at Lake Baljuna when Asan arrived. The origins of Ja'far remain nebulous. We know he met Chinggis Khan in the court of Toghril, but not why he was there. Perhaps he accompanied Yelu Ahai and Yelu Tuqa (Khitan brothers), who were Jin envoys.[64] Regardless, Temujin made a positive impression, as Ja'far chose to join Temujin and drank the muddy waters of Lake Baljuna.

Ja'far and Hasan were undoubtedly the first Muslims Temujin encountered and the first to enter the service of the Mongol Empire. The Mongols found little use for their religion, but Hasan's abilities as a merchant (and perhaps as a quartermaster) demonstrated his ability. Ja'far also possessed talents that Temujin appreciated, as he became one of the Baljuntu, or those who took the oath at Lake Baljuna.[65] Additionally, he later played important roles in the expansion of the Mongol Empire in various capacities, particularly in North China.

Were there other Muslims? Merchants did not travel alone, and while Hasan may have hired individuals to assist him at various points, most merchants travelled with at least a small party of trusted partners or employees. Ja'far may also have had friends or family members with him. At this time, however, they had a small impact on the Mongols beyond their immediate occupational abilities.

---

[64] Igor de Rachewiltz, 'Personnel and Personalities in North China in the Early Mongol Period', *JESHO* 9 (1966), 96–7.
[65] Cleaves, 'Historicity of The Baljuna Covenant', *passim*.

3

The Mongols outside Mongolia

Even though Temujin was now the ruler of the Mongolian plateau north of the Gobi Desert, his rule was not undisputed. Several threats existed in 1206. Senggum, Toghril's son, fled to Xi Xia and remained a potent threat. Even though Temujin had amiable relations with many Kereit before their war and his family married relatives of Toghril, the return of Senggum could potentially cleave the Kereit from his new state. Guchulug, a Naiman prince, escaped the debacle at Chakirmaut and was rumoured to be in league with the Merkit leaders who eluded Chinggis Khan's troops. Finally, the Jin Empire still meddled in steppe affairs. Chinggis Khan knew from personal experience and from history that the Jin would not readily accept his dominion over northern Mongolia. A comparable state had not existed in Mongolia since the ninth century with the Uighur Empire, which intervened in the Tang Empire frequently.[1]

While the Jin Empire was certainly a threat, the Jin's strategy of using one group of nomads to weaken another could only be successful if they caused fissures among the Mongols. The easiest way to do this would be to recruit the disaffected or rival leaders such as Guchulug or Senggum, much as they did with Temujin and Toghril against the Tatars. Guchulug and Senggum, however, were a threat even without the Jin. Chinggis Khan's control over Mongolia remained tenuous. Although he had virtually eliminated all other aristocratic lines, the acceptance of the *altan urugh* was not guaranteed and would take time to provide with legitimacy. As evinced by Jamuqa's ill-fated Gur-Khanid confederation, massive tribal confederations were difficult to manage and permanence elusive. Even though Chinggis Khan now held sway from the Altai to the Khalkha River, how long he could do so remained a pertinent question.

Additionally, there were neighbouring groups to the north, known collectively as the *Hoi-yin Irgen* or Forest People, that posed problems. Although

---

[1] See Colin Mackerras, 'The Uighurs', *CHEIA*, 320–42.

the Mongols generally referred to them as a single group, the *Hoi-yin Irgen* were not a confederation but rather a number of independent tribes who lived in Siberia. In most of the steppe wars, they tended to be neutral, but some groups, like the Oirat, had joined Jamuqa's confederation.[2]

The Oirat's fleeting alliance with Jamuqa was not sufficient cause to wage war against them, but, from Chinggis Khan's perspective, the fact that some, like the Oirat, also then aligned with the Naiman could not be overlooked. Nonetheless, there were other reasons to bring the Hoi-yin Irgen to heel. The first reason was the Merkit, who had been at a stage between complete pastoral nomadism and the economy of the *Hoi-yin Irgen*. Although the Merkit had been defeated with the Naiman, many escaped westward. Their traditional homeland was in northern Mongolia and south of Lake Baikal, just south of many of the *Hoi-yin Irgen*. If Chinggis Khan exerted dominance over the region, he then deprived the Merkit of their pastures and eliminated a threat. In addition, the region was economically important. Grain grew in several areas around Lake Baikal and in Siberia; thus he could secure food supplies. Furthermore, by controlling the *Hoi-yin Irgen*, Chinggis Khan then had access to the lucrative fur trade as well as gold deposits along the Yenisei River. Finally, a campaign to subdue the Hoi-yin Irgen also served the purpose of creating a patrimony for his son Jochi. The campaign began in 1207 and quickly overcame most of the *Hoyin-Irgen*. Some, such as the Oirat, submitted without fighting and gained favour. Others, such as the Kirghiz and Kem-Kemjiuts in the Yenisei River basin, submitted only after some resistance.[3]

Meanwhile, Mongol forces also expanded westward. In 1207, a Mongol army, perhaps reinforced by Jochi's army and aided by the Oirat, crossed the Altai Mountains in search of the allied Naiman and the Merkit.[4] The Mongols encountered them at the Irtysh River where they soundly defeated the refugees again in late 1208 or early 1209. Despite their victory, the Mongols were unable to destroy their enemies, although they shattered their army. Guchulug and the Naiman fled south, attempting to take refuge in Uighurstan. The Uighurs, however, drove them away.[5] Guchulug then sought protection among the Qarluqs, a Turkic confederation near Almaliq. The Naiman's propensity for pillaging, however, quickly soured that relationship. Guchulug eventually found shelter with the Gur-Khan of Qara Khitai later in that year.[6]

---

[2] *SHM*, §141.
[3] *SWQZL*, 39–40; RD/Karimi, 308–9; RD/Thackston1, 204; RD/Thackston2, 144–6.
[4] *SWQZL*, 39–40; RD/Karimi, 308–9; RD/Thackston1, 204; RD/Thackston2, 144–6.
[5] RD/Karimi, 308–9; RD/Thackston1, 204; RD/Thackston2, 145.
[6] Juwayni/Qazvini, 46–9; Juvaini/Boyle, 62–4.

Figure 3.1 Sandy steppe land. While they are often viewed as an unending expanse of grasslands, the steppes are actually quite varied in terrain and pasture.

Qara Khitai had long-standing ties with the Naiman, and during the twelfth century had even been their suzerain for a period of time.[7] Since then, however, Qara Khitai had weakened. The Gur-Khan accepted Guchulug as a vassal and even presented his daughter to the Naiman prince as a wife. In Guchulug, the Gur-Khan found a stalwart warrior with a sizeable retinue who could possibly reverse the declining fortunes of Qara Khitai.

Meanwhile, the Merkit continued to seek refuge. As their primary leader, Toqtoa Khan, had died at the Irtysh River, they continued to flee westward under the leadership of Toqtoa's sons, Qutu and Chila'un, skirting Qara Khitai territory. Eventually they halted north of the Aral Sea in the pastures of the Qangli nomads, another Turkic group.[8] The Qangli permitted the Merkit into their territory, suggesting that the wars with Chinggis Khan seriously weakened the Merkit.

In 1208, the victory at the Irtysh was sufficient for Chinggis Khan. He neither forgot nor ignored these refugees, but for the time being Chinggis

---

[7] Michal Biran, *The Empire of Qara Khitai in Eurasian History* (New York, 2005), 46.
[8] *SWQZL*, 40, 49–50; RD/Thackston2, 160.

Khan was directing a number of expeditions, including one that came about while he was pursuing another refugee from Mongolia.

Xi Xia

After the defeat of the Kereit in 1203, Senggum fled to Xi Xia.[9] As a result, Chinggis Khan's gaze focused squarely on this kingdom. Its population was in the tens of millions, much larger than the Mongols', and consisted of nomads and sedentary populations dwelling in fortified cities.

Mongol forces began probing raids into Xi Xia as early as 1205 – after their victory over the Naiman. As they were not certain of Senggum's location, the raids served multiple purposes. First, they gathered intelligence, and secondly, they kept the newly formed army with its multi-tribal formation busy and outside of Mongolia where idleness could reawaken feuds. Theoretically, the raids also weakened a potential enemy. Although the Jin Empire frequently meddled in steppe affairs, Xi Xia's proximity also permitted it to do so. With Senggum's presence, along with a history of close ties with the Kereit, Chinggis Khan could not discount the Tangut's potential involvement in disrupting his empire. Finally, the raids mirrored Chinggis Khan's actions against the Naiman and the Merkit: hunting enemy leaders and eliminating them so that they could not pose a threat. As long as the old aristocracy existed outside of his control, Chinggis Khan's new social order was vulnerable.

The Mongols' efforts at capturing or eliminating Senggum were fruitless. Senggum's own plundering forced the Tangut to evict him from Xi Xia. He fled southward with a few followers, where he was killed in the Tarim basin by Khalaj Turks raiding from modern Afghanistan.[10] Mongol forays continued in 1206 and afterwards, and it is unclear whether Chinggis Khan knew of Senggum's departure. The Tangut attempted to stop the Mongols, but were routinely defeated.[11] Afterwards, the Tangut remained in their fortresses and cities and fought a defensive struggle. This passive policy led to the ruler being deposed and a more aggressive king, Li Anquan, coming to the throne. The shift did little in preventing the Mongol raids and may have actually led to the main invasion in 1209.

Although the Tangut armies also consisted largely of horse archers, the military reforms of Chinggis Khan baffled them as much as they did the Naiman and Merkit at Chakirmaut in 1204. Armies that opposed the Mongols on the battlefield were swept away. Some cities resisted, but

---

[9] Ruth Dunnell, 'The Hsi Hsia', 154–214, in *CHCAR*, 164.
[10] Dunnell, 'His-Hsia, 206–7.
[11] *SWQZL*, 198; RD/Thackston2, 144; RD/Thackston1, 203–4; RD/Karimi, 306–8.

eventually the Mongols stormed or blockaded them. The pivotal point came with the siege of Zhongxing. The Mongols made no headway against the city's stout defences as they lacked more than basic battering rams for siege weapons. As the siege extended into 1210, it appeared that the Mongols might have to abandon it, but then they came up with a novel idea – flooding the city.[12]

With the winter rains, the Huanghe River, which fed the city's irrigation canals, swelled and began to rise. Chinggis Khan ordered his men to redirect the river against the city by building a dyke. The waters soon entered the city and flooded many homes. The damage was great enough to kill many and damage the city's earthen walls. The Tangut attempted negotiations, but the siege continued until the poorly constructed dyke broke and flooded not only the Zhongxing, but also the Mongol camp. Even though the Mongols suffered from their own tactics, their determination to continue the siege convinced the Tangut to make peace.[13]

As a result, in 1210, Li Anquan and Chinggis Khan agreed a treaty. First and foremost, the Tangut submitted to the Mongols and Li Anquan's daughter, Chaqa, became one of Chinggis Khan's wives. Furthermore, the Tangut would provide troops and send tribute to the Mongols as a client state. The tribute consisted of camels, woollen cloth and falcons. Upon receiving the first tribute payment (as many camels as Li Anquan could find) and Chaqa, Chinggis Khan withdrew from Xi Xia.[14]

While the treaty was humiliating and the tribute a burden, the Mongol raids ended and the tribute was certainly less expensive than the damage they had caused. Chinggis Khan gained a steady supply of tribute and demonstrated his military ability. The Mongols did not occupy Xi Xia by leaving a garrison force, nor did they attempt to govern there. Instead, they relied on the peace agreement and for several years it held; Xi Xia became the first sedentary state to survive the Mongol conquests largely intact.

The Jin Empire

Although the Jin had manipulated events in the steppes of Mongolia previously, other events curtailed their ability to intervene. Since 1198, not long after Temujin returned to Mongolia, a rebellion by the *juyin* in southern

---

[12] Ruth Dunnell, *Chinggis Khan* (New York, 2010), 64; Dunnell, 'Hsi-Hsia', 208.
[13] RD/Thackston2, 146; RD/Thackston1, 206; RD/Karimi, 311.
[14] *SHM* §249; H. D. Martin, *Chinggis Khan and His Conquest of North China* (Baltimore, 1950), 119; RD/Karimi, 427; RD/Thackston1, 289–90; Thackston 2012, 146.

Figure 3.2 Camels with saddles. The demand of camels as tribute from Xi Xia is a further indication of their value to the nomads of Mongolia. While primarily draught animals, they could also be ridden.

Mongolia (south of the Gobi) near the Jin Empire's border occupied much of the Jin's attention.[15]

The rebellion dragged on for several years, preventing the Jin from interfering with events north of the Gobi. Furthermore, it also affected trade with the northern nomads as well, leading to a deterioration of economic relations between the Jin and most of the steppe tribes. An added complication was that, although Chinggis Khan controlled the northern Mongolian plateau, his influence filtered southward. Many nomads, including those among the *juyin*, looked to him rather than the Jin for aid and allegiance.[16]

War appeared on the horizon in 1211. By this time, Chinggis Khan was no longer involved in Xi Xia and saw the war as an opportunity to prevent the Jin from meddling in Mongolia once the *juyin* rebellion ended. Furthermore, it also served as an opportunity to avenge Ambaghai Khan. Yet, the invasion

---

[15] Thomas Allsen, 'The Rise of the Mongolian Empire and Mongolian Rule in North China', *CHCAR*, 349; Paul D. Buell, 'The Role of the Sino-Mongolian Frontier Zone in the Rise of Cinggis-Qan', in *SOM*, 66–8.
[16] Buell, 'Role of the Sino-Mongolian Frontier Zone', 66–8.

could not be started without some risk, as Guchulug remained a threat. To this end, Chinggis Khan dispatched the general Toquchar to the west to guard the Mongols' western frontier against Qara Khitai and the Naiman.[17] Chinggis Khan had no interest in a two-front war. As he marshalled his army for the advance against the Jin, Chinggis Khan assigned his youngest brother, Temuge Otchigin as his regent to mind affairs in Mongolia.[18]

The invasion began in 1211 with a three-pronged attack as armies struck western Jin domains and central north China, as well as the Manchurian homeland of the Jurchen. Overall, these were small forays, with the focus being on bringing the *juyin* tribes under Mongol control. This was achieved quickly and without too much effort as several already had established ties with Chinggis Khan. Now, however, they could not easily extricate themselves from him. Mongol raids into the Jin Empire kept the Jin from aiding those *juyin* who might resist Chinggis Khan. Furthermore, the Mongols defeated the Jin in the field and took a significant amount of territory, including Yunnei in the west, where the imperial stud's grazing lands were located.[19] By capturing these territories, the Mongols not only gained more horses, but deprived the Jin cavalry. When the Mongols withdrew in February 1212, they abandoned the territory within the Jin Empire, but Chinggis Khan did achieve several objectives.

The first was control of the *juyin*. Chief among the *juyin* were the Onggud, a Nestorian Turkic tribe. Chinggis Khan married his daughter, Alaqa Beki, to their prince, Buyan-Shiban, and gave Alaqush Digid-Quri, the Onggud ruler, the status of *quda* or in-law.[20] Alaqa's presence was to assure their loyalty and she essentially acted as an ambassador or even viceroy. Many of the Onggud rejected the marriage alliance, however; Alaqush and Buyan-Shiban were killed, and Alaqa escaped with her stepsons Boyaoha and Zhenguo to her father's military camp at Datong. Chinggis Khan swiftly ended the Onggud's rebellion. Alaqa persuaded Chinggis Khan not to massacre the Onggud. She then married her stepson, Zhenguo, and resumed her position as ambassador and viceroy. Alaqa ruled the Onggud peacefully until she died in the 1230s.[21] With control of the *juyin*, Chinggis Khan now controlled the border and access into Mongolia.

---

[17] *SWQZL*, 49–50; RD/Karimi, 320, 427; RD/Thackston1, 213, 290; RD/Thackston2, 151, 197.
[18] RD/Karimi, 412; RD/Thackston2, 212; RD/Thackston1, 281.
[19] *SWQZL*, 42; RD/Karimi, 322; RD/Thackston2, 152; RD/Thackston1, 215; Martin, *Rise of Chingis Khan*, 146.
[20] RD/Karimi, 100; RD/Thackston2, 50; RD/Thackston1, 71.
[21] George Qingzhi Zhao, *Marriage as Political Strategy and Cultural Expression: Mongolian Royal Marriages from World Empire to Yuan Dynasty* (New York, 2008), 150–4.

Onggud Relations

Alaqush Digid-Quri warned Chinggis Khan of the Naiman's plans to attack him in 1204. In gratitude, Chinggis Khan made a marriage alliance with the Onggud. Alaqa Beki was the Chinggis Khan's third daughter with Borte. In total, Borte produced nine children, in the following order: Qojin (daughter); Jochi, Chaghadai, Ogodei (sons); Chechiyegen, Alaqa, Tumelun (daughters); Tolui (son); and Altun (daughter). Alaqa's first husband, Bai Shibu, was also known in the Mongolian sources as Buyan-Shiban. After Bai Shibu's murder, she married her stepson Zhenguo and then Boyaoha after Zhenguo's death. While marrying her stepsons might seem odd to the modern reader, as they were not her sons it was permissible and quite normal in medieval Mongolia. Although Alaqa Beki was the true ruler of the Onggud after Chinggis Khan ended their rebellion, they maintained the pretence that the Onggud royal line still ruled. Chinggis Khan also used his other daughters as viceroys to ensure the loyalty of his vassals through marriage relations. Chechiyegen did so with the Oirat, Altun married the Uighur Idiqut, Tumelun married an Onggirad prince (one of Borte's nephews), and Qojin married Butu of the Ikires, one of Chinggis Khan's early *nokod*.[22]

Even though they did not occupy Jin territory, the Mongols controlled the mountain passes and prevented the Jin from entering Mongolia and, more importantly, from exerting influence in the region. The Mongols may also have withdrawn after they had exhorted tribute from the Jin; even if they did not, the plundering during the campaign ensured that the Mongol troops were happy.[23] Finally, the attack kept the Jin on the defensive and unable to mount an invasion into Mongolia.

The 1211 invasion was only a prelude of things to come. In the autumn of 1212, another invasion came with what appeared to have been long-term objectives. The first was to annex some territory in order to secure Mongolia from potential Jin attacks. This required that the Mongols then administer the territory; however, the cost of doing so was offset by the ability to exert pressure on the Jin from the newly acquired lands.[24] With

---

[22] Anne Broadbridge, 'Marriage, Family and Politics: The Ilkhanid–Oirat Connection', *JRAS* 26, no. 2 (2016), f2, 123.
[23] *SWQZL*, 45; *SHM*, §248.
[24] Martin, *Rise of Chinggis Khan*, 155, Sechen Jagchid, 'Patterns of Trade and Conflict Between China and the Nomadic Peoples of Mongolia', *Essays in Mongolian Studies* (Provo, UT, 1987), 17.

this in mind, the Mongols invaded with two armies, both equipped with a train of camels carrying siege weapons that could be assembled on site. The first army was led by Chinggis Khan and the second by his youngest son, Tolui.[25]

The initial invasion went well, and as the war extended into 1213 the advantage shifted even more to the Mongols as famine swept much of the Jin Empire, accelerated by the war. In addition, an army from Xi Xia invaded the western provinces of the Jin Empire as the Tangut fulfilled their obligations to Chinggis Khan.[26] Another issue was insurrection by Jin subjects. The largest occurred in the eastern regions by Khitans. As early as 1211, the Jin began to settle Jurchen colonists among the Khitans to ensure that they did not join the Mongols. As the Khitans had ruled northern China prior to the Jurchen takeover in 1125, the Jurchen still doubted their loyalty.[27] Perhaps the Jin's caution was merited, but their actions actually provoked rebellion.

Faced with two crises, the recently elevated Jin Emperor Xuanzong (1213–34) offered an olive branch, certain that he could bribe the Mongols into abandoning their campaign. To the court's surprise, the Mongols rejected the peace overtures. It was not clear why they did so, but it may have been that the Mongols had not acquired enough booty to make the invasion profitable. Much of the campaign up to this time had been in regions previously ravaged by the Mongols.

With the rejection of the peace treaty, the Mongols advanced on Zhongdu, the Jin capital.[28] The immensity of the city awed even Chinggis Khan. Rather than attempting to take the city, Chinggis Khan left contingents to blockade it and destroy any relief armies. Attempts to break the blockade by the garrison met with similar results.

Chinggis Khan then divided his own army into three divisions and systematically began to destroy the surrounding regions. Despite bringing siege equipment, the Mongols did not concern themselves with lengthy sieges. Instead, if an attack on a city became protracted, the Mongols simply moved to another location, but they might return. This kept the garrisons wary.

While the Mongol armies wreaked havoc in the provinces near Zhongdu, they also attacked the capital, which then led to more efforts by the Jin to relieve the city. The only results were that the Jin field armies, no longer sheltered by their fortifications, were crushed in battle. The defeats finally

---

[25] SWQZL, 43.
[26] SWQZL, 44.
[27] Martin, *Rise of Chingis Khan*, 150–1.
[28] *SWQZL*, 45.

triggered another effort by the Jin to seek peace in April 1214. They offered regular tribute payments to Chinggis Khan, including horses (which the Jin sorely needed), gold and silk. In addition, the Jin gave Chinggis Khan one of the daughters of the previous emperor as a wife along with a retinue of five hundred followers.[29]

Payments of gold, silk and other luxury goods were not uncommon in relations between the empires of China and the steppes. Several empires found it less expensive to send goods north than deal with raids.[30] The inclusion of horses is an oddity as the nomads usually traded horses for goods. There are two possibilities for the inclusion of horses. The first is that the Mongols perhaps needed more horses due to the loss of mounts during the process of unification. Considering that it was now six years later, this loss of livestock seems less likely, but still a possibility. Considering that the climate was cooler during the thirteenth century, it is also possible that Mongolia experienced a number of *zhuds*, devastating snow and ice storms, which may have also contributed to famine in the Jin Empire. Even in twenty-first century Mongolia, a *zhud* can decimate livestock.[31] Finally, the insistence on horses by Chinggis Khan may also reflect a concerted effort on his part to eliminate the Jin's military capabilities. Without sufficient cavalry, the Jin's military options were limited. Of course, one cannot dismiss the possibility of loss of mounts during the Jin campaign.

The inclusion of a bride in the tribute was not unusual. The Jin exhibited some craftiness by providing the daughter of the previous emperor, as she was viewed as expendable. In addition, this practice of sending a princess to the nomadic leaders was also part of standard operating procedure. Accompanied

---

[29] SWQZL, 45; RD/Karimi, 428; RD/Thackston1, 290; RD/Thackston2, 156; Khwandamir, 12–13.

[30] For a discussion on the *Heqin* treaties during the Han-Xiongnu period see Nicola Di Cosmo, *Ancient China and Its Enemies: The Rise of Nomadic Power in East Asian History* (New York, 2002), 210–17. For a discussion of Sui-Tang and Uighur relations see Jonathan Karam Skaff, *Sui-Tang China and Its Turko-Mongol Neighbors: Culture, Power, and Connections, 580–800* (New York, 2012).

[31] 'Foreign Minister Says Extreme Weather "Draining" Mongolia', *BBC Monitoring Asia Pacific – Political Supplied by BBC Worldwide Monitoring*, 18 January 2010, LexisNexis Academic, Web (last accessed 9 January 2015); 'Red Cross Launches Appeal to Help Mongolian Herders', *BBC Monitoring Asia Pacific – Political Supplied by BBC Worldwide Monitoring*, 18 January 2010, LexisNexis Academic, Web (last accessed 9 January 2015); 'UNICEF Delivers Freeze Aid for Mongolian Children', *BBC Monitoring Asia Pacific – Political Supplied by BBC Worldwide Monitoring*, 2 March 2010, LexisNexis Academic, Web (last accessed 9 January 2015); Miro Cernetig, 'Famine Stalks Mongolian Steppes: A Half Million Nomads on Brink of Starvation', *The Globe and Mail* (Canada), 10 April 2000, LexisNexis Academic, Web (last accessed 9 January 2015).

Zhuds

Zhuds were and still are the bane of Mongolian nomads. '*Zhud*' literally means a disaster caused by famine for livestock. While the most common *zhuds* are due to snow and ice covering the ground so that animals cannot eat the grass, other zhuds also exist due to drought, overgrazing and destruction to the pasture. *Zhuds* happen periodically, and climatic shifts only make them more prolific.

by a large retinue, she was not isolated. The idea was that the princess and her entourage would be a civilising influence on the Mongols and perhaps create a permanent alliance or treaty. Previous dynasties also attempted this, although history shows that results were uneven at best.[32]

Chinggis Khan agreed to the treaty and withdrew his armies, while still maintaining the mountain passes. Peace remained elusive, however. The Jin Emperor, concerned with the ease with which the Mongols had penetrated Jin defences, moved his court to his southern capital, Kaifeng. Furthermore, the provinces of Hebei and Shansi, and the regions north of Zhongdu, were desolate, leaving the capital vulnerable. When the news reached Chinggis Khan, he was livid. In his eyes, the court's relocation was a blatant breach of the treaty and indicated that the Jin were up to something. As a result, the Mongols invaded again in 1214.[33]

The Mongols marched directly onto Zhongdu and laid siege immediately. With the departure of the emperor, the city's morale was low. Unlike in their previous attempts, the Mongols made a concerted effort to capture Zhongdu. Equipped with siege weapons and engineers, many of whom were Jin deserters, the Mongols systematically attacked the city as blockading forces stymied relief efforts.[34] With starvation and panic setting in, the city submitted to the Mongols in 1215. The peace did not allay the fears of the populace, however. According to one chronicler, 60,000 virgins leapt from the walls rather than fall into the hands of the Mongols, although this was probably propaganda, perhaps encouraged by the Mongols.[35]

The fall of Zhongdu carried immense ramifications, not only as a military defeat for the Jin Empire. In addition to the Jin losing their capital, the loss of Zhongdu also undermined the defence of the surrounding areas,

---

[32] Sima Qian, *Records of the Grand Historian: Han Dynasty* II, trans. Burton Watson (New York, 1993), 143; Skaff, *Sui-Tang China and Its Turko-Mongol Neighbors*, 203–20, 238–40.
[33] *SWZQL*, 46; *SHM*, §251; RD/Thackston2, 156–7.
[34] *SWQZL*, 47.
[35] Juzjani/Habibi, 102; Juzjani/Raverty, 964–5.

placing the Mongols squarely in the middle of the empire. Communications between the eastern and western portions were now cut off. Furthermore, this undermined the government's legitimacy, which rested not only on stable rule but the concept that the dynasty had received the Mandate of Heaven, or that Heaven (*tian*) viewed the Jin as the legitimate rulers. While much of the Mandate was simply pretence – legitimacy based on the reality of Jin authority and power – a series of events could convince the population that the dynasty had lost Heaven's favour. This included not only rebellion and natural disasters, but also foreign invasion.[36] Rebellions broke out in many parts of the empire against the Jin, and some of the rebels declared allegiance to Chinggis Khan. The situation worsened for the Jin as well, as the Tangut seized Jin territory in Gansu. The Mongols further prospered, not only from looting Zhongdu, but also by capturing the treasury of the Jin Empire, which had not been removed when Xuanzong had relocated to Kaifeng. Furthermore, they acquired Yelu Chucai (1189–1243), a Khitan and high-ranking minister in the Jin government. His loyalty to the Jin impressed Chinggis Khan, who took the tall Khitan into his service. Yelu Chucai eventually became one of the highest-ranking non-Mongols in the empire, serving as a *bichigchi* or scribe, adviser, court astrologer, and eventually chancellor or chief minister of the Mongol Empire.[37]

Despite the calamity at Zhongdu, Xuanzong, the Jin Emperor, refused to submit. The Mongol armies then divided and struck on multiple fronts, making it near-impossible for the Jin to respond to the Mongol attacks. Chinggis Khan's brother, Qasar, and General Muqali invaded Manchuria. Muqali then split off and invaded the Liaodong peninsula. Here, we have clear signs the Mongols planned on conquering the region and ruling it. A number of Han, Khitan and Jurchen commanders abandoned the Jin Empire and submitted to Muqali. In return, a rudimentary administrative structure was put in place in Liaodong.

As other armies ravaged the western portion of the empire, Chinggis Khan suddenly returned to Mongolia early 1216. Despite his departure, he remained confident in the abilities of his commanders to finish the operation with Muqali in overall command. Although Muqali died in 1223, he executed the war superbly until his death.[38]

---

[36] F. W. Mote, *Imperial China, 900–1800* (Cambridge, MA, 2003), 8–10, 278–9.
[37] For more on Yelu Chucai, see Igor de Rachewiltz, 'Yeh-Lü Ch'u-Ts'ai (1189–1243), Yeh-Lü Chu (1221–1285)', in *ITSOTK*, 136–75.
[38] *YUS*, 44; Igor de Rachewiltz, 'Muqali (1170–1223), Böl (1197–1220), Tas (1212–1239), An-T'ung (1245–1293)', *ITSOTK*, 3–12.

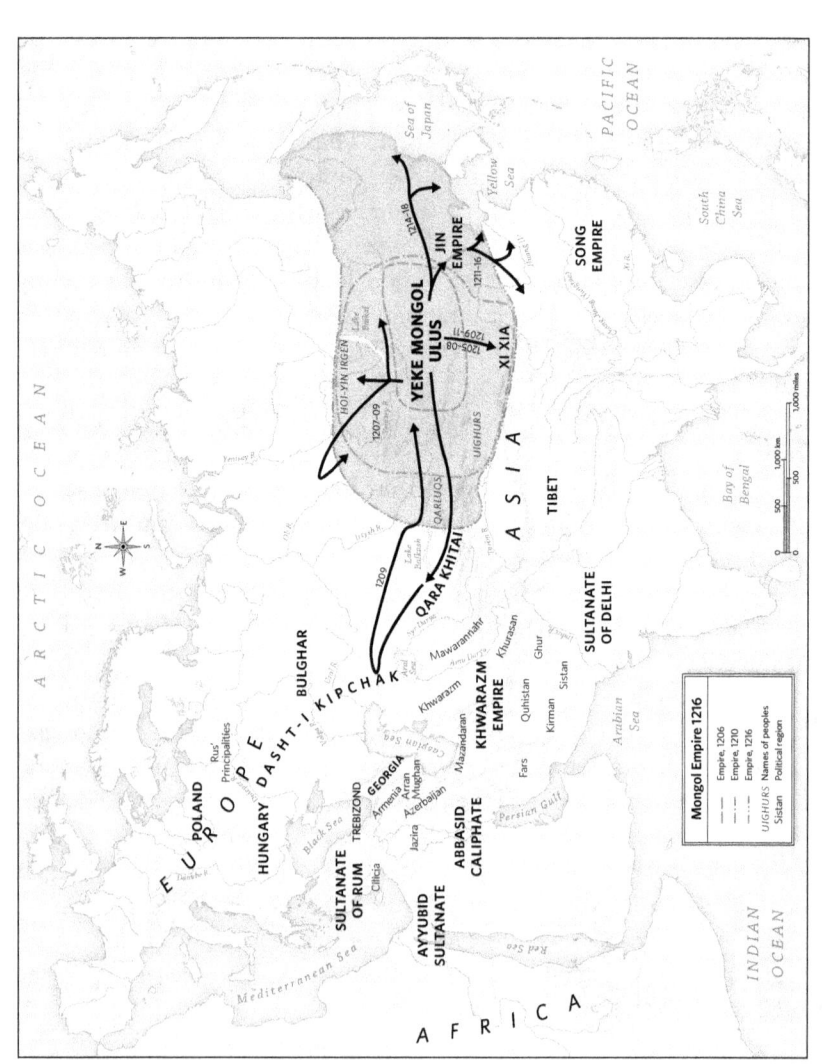

Map 3.1 The Mongol Empire in 1216 © Mapping Specialists

The Hoi-yin Irgen Rebellion

Chinggis Khan's departure was not planned. A rebellion arose in January or February 1216 among the *Hoi-yin Irgen* and was tied directly to the decisions of the *quriltai* of 1206. At that *quriltai* Qorchi, the individual who had prophesied Chinggis Khan's ascendancy over Jamuqa, was rewarded by being appointed the governor of the *Hoi-yin Irgen*. Chinggis Khan had promised him a reward if the prophecy came true, and he remained true to his word. In addition to appointing him governor, he permitted Qorchi to collect beautiful women among his subjects. Qorchi paid little heed to social convention and took whoever he wanted any time he wanted, including women who were already betrothed or even married. This led to a rebellion among the Qori-Tumed, who seized Qorchi.[39]

Quduqa-beki, the leader of the Oirat, attempted to defuse the situation by negotiating with the Qori-Tumed. The rebels, led by Botoqui Tarqun, the wife of the deceased Qori-Tumed chieftain Darduqul-Soqor, also took him captive. Chinggis Khan erupted when he learned the news and wanted to lead the campaign to exterminate them. His advisors calmed him and convinced him to let others handle the situation. Boroqul, a trusted general, led an expedition into the northern forests. While leading his army through the woods, Boroqul was killed by the Qori-Tumed in 1217.[40]

Another general, Dorbei Doqshin, resumed the campaign while Jochi marched with an army against the Kirgiz and other *Hoi-yin Irgen*. This was in part to ensure that they did not join the Qori-Tumed, but also to punish them for not sending troops when Dorbei Doqshin had requested them. Meanwhile, Dorbei Doqshin did not take the primary route into rebel territory. Instead, he and his men cut a new road into the territory. Although it took considerable time and effort, their appearance surprised the Qori-Tumed and crushed the rebellion.[41]

Dorbei's success prevented grave consequences. Although somewhat understandable, the Qori-Tumed's actions were an open act of rebellion during a time when the majority of the Mongol army was in Jin territory. The failure to quell the rebellion risked the cohesion of Mongolia and, at a bare minimum, Mongol control of the *Hoi-yin Irgen*. If the Qori-Tumed had been successful, other tribes could easily have joined. Yet Dorbei's success also demonstrated that the Mongols could fight pitched warfare in thick forests and demonstrated their flexibility in adapting to new terrain and circumstances.

---

[39] SHM, §241.
[40] *SHM*, §240–1; *SWQZL*, 50.
[41] *SHM*, §50; *SWQZL*, 50; RD/Karimi, 429–30; RD/Thackston1, 290–1; RD/Thackston2, 198.

The campaign also revealed many of Chinggis Khan's concerns as a leader. Although the Qori-Tumed's reaction to Qorchi's actions is understandable, they did not seek Chinggis Khan's intervention. Instead, they rebelled and then took an envoy hostage. For the Mongols, envoys were sacrosanct – they had true diplomatic immunity and could not be harmed in any manner. The Qori-Tumed violated this by taking Quduqa-Beki captive. As a result, they had to be punished severely. Killing Boroqul, one of Chinggis Khan's closest associates, only worsened the situation.

As a result, Qorchi was reinstated and permitted to resume his wife-collecting as a punishment to the Qori-Tumed. Chinggis Khan gave the queen and ruler of the Qori-Tumed, Botoqui Tarqun, to Quduqa-Beki as a wife. This removed her from power and placed her under the control of a proven and loyal ally as well as assigning the Qori-Tumed to Quduqa-Beki's supervision.[42] Quduqa-Beki's attempts to resolve the issue greatly enhanced the status of the Oirat leader in the eyes of Chinggis Khan, effectively negating his appearance at the side of the Naiman in 1204.

Western Expansion

Meanwhile, events to the west also came to a head. After the defeat of the Naiman and the Merkit at the Battle of the Irtysh River, they suffered heavy losses, but regrouped at the Chu River. The Mongols never ceased in their pursuit, defeating them again at the Chu River also in 1208. Here, the tenuous Naiman–Merkit alliance fell apart with Guchulug fleeing southward while the Merkit fled west. While Guchulug found refuge in Qara Khitai, the Merkit entered the territory of the Qangli, the eastern branch of the Kipchak confederation that nomadised the steppes between the Caspian and Pontic Steppes, often referred to in Islamic sources as the *Dasht-i Kipchak* or Kipchak Steppes.[43] A Mongol army dealt with the Merkit eventually – at some point between 1209 and 1219, although the dates are uncertain,[44]

Now, far from home, the Mongol general Subedei approached this situation cautiously.[45] They did not attack immediately, but requested that the Qangli hand over the Merkit refugees, as they were rebels. The

---

[42] *SHM*, 241.
[43] *SWQZL*, 38–40; *SHM*, §236; Juwayni/Qazwini, v1, 51–2; Juvaini/Boyle, 69; Thomas T. Allsen, 'Prelude to the Western Campaigns: Mongol Military Operations in the Volga-Ural Region, 1217–1237', *AEMA* III (1983), 8.
[44] For a discussion of the dates see Paul D. Buell, 'Early Mongol Expansion in Western Siberia and Turkestan (1207–1219): A Reconstruction', *CAJ* 36 (1992), 1–32.
[45] *SHM*, §236; *SWQZL*, 40, 49–50; Depending on the date of the event he was either accompanied by Chinggis Khan's son Jochi or by Jebe.

Qangli refused, leading to a Mongol attack. Although the Qangli resisted, the Mongol forces overwhelmed them and destroyed both the Qangli and the Merkit.[46] With their task complete and Guchulug out of reach in Qara Khitai, Subedei began to return to Mongolia. His journey did not go unimpeded, however.

The Mongols were not the only army in the region interested in the Qangli. Muhammad Khwarazmshah, the sultan of the Khwarazmian Empire, which at its peak covered most of modern Iran, Afghanistan, Uzbekistan, Turkmenistan and Tajikistan, was also in the vicinity seeking to punish the Qangli for raids.[47] He came across the battlefield and pursued the Mongols. Subedei had strict orders not to engage in battle with any of the local powers in their pursuit of the Merkit and attempted to extricate his army from a potential battle. Muhammad, however, attacked. Despite having superior numbers, Muhammad quickly found that the Mongols were unlike any other opponent. By nightfall, the battle ended and the armies returned to their camps. Muhammad's troops kept an uneasy watch through the night, but in the morning they found that the Mongols had departed in the night.[48] Muhammad did not pursue. According to Nasawi, who worked for Muhammad Khwarazmshah, the encounter terrified him.[49]

The Mongol presence in the western regions had a larger impact than simply eliminating the Merkit. The far-ranging manoeuvres of Jebe and Subedei along with Jochi's Siberian campaign demonstrated the Mongols' operational abilities. Toquchar's small army stationed west of the Altai Mountains placed a permanent Mongol force in the region.[50] Now the Mongols bordered Qara Khitai, which gave many within that empire something to consider. Although Qara Khitai provided a haven for Guchulug, not all of the subjects within the empire approved, as Guchulug had plundered their territory in the past. Both the Uighurs and the Qarluqs of Almaliq submitted. Their leaders journeyed to Mongolia and offered their submission to Chinggis Khan in 1209 and 1211 respectively.[51]

The transfer of allegiance demonstrated more than just the extension of Mongol power. It also represented the declining power and prestige of Qara

---

[46] SHM, §236; SWQZL, 40, 49–50; Juwayni/Qazwini, v1, 51–2; Juvaini/Boyle, 69.
[47] Juzjani/Habibi, v2, 149; Juzjani/Raverty, 1,096–7. This may have been the reason why the Qangli welcomed the Merkit.
[48] Juwayni/Qazvini, v2, 101–4; Juvaini/Boyle, 370–2; Nasawi, 44–5; Nasawi/Houdas, 18–19.
[49] Nasawi, 44–5; Nasawi/Houdas, 19–20.
[50] SWQZL, 41; 49–50; RD/Karimi, 428; RD/Thackston1, 290; RD/Thackston2, 198.
[51] SHM, §235, 238; Juvaini/Boyle, 45–6; 74–5; Juwayni/Qazvini, v1, 33, 56–8; RD/Karimi, 318; RD/Thackston1, 205–6, 213, 289; RD/Thackston2, 145–6, 197; SWQZL, 40–1.

Khitai. Guchulug and the Naiman were welcomed with open arms by the Gur-Khan of Qara Khitai in an effort to revitalise his military strength.[52] Not only were vassals submitting to Chinggis Khan, but to the south, Muhammad Khwarazmshah had renounced his vassalage and had revolted in 1207. Despite the fact that Guchulug became the son-in-law of the Gur-Khan and had converted from Christianity to Buddhism at his wife's request, he joined Muhammad's rebellion. They agreed to divide the empire, although neither could agree on the specifics of their pact.[53] Once in power, Guchulug proved to be a rapacious ruler, increasing and arbitrarily collecting taxes. His Muslim subjects viewed his actions through a lens of religious persecutions, although there is some question as to whether this was an accurate interpretation of events.[54]

With the ascension of Guchulug in Qara Khitai, the door opened for Chinggis Khan to remove the Naiman threat once and for all. Chinggis Khan dispatched Jebe to resolve the matter in 1218. Jebe's armies only skirmished with the Naiman, as Guchulug refused to chance battle. Upon the Mongol general's arrival, the Naiman prince fled. Locals in Badakhshan killed him and presented his body to Jebe. The Mongols then incorporated Qara Khitai into their empire and Jebe issued an order for religious toleration throughout the poly-religious region.[55]

The Khwarazmian Empire

Now the Mongol Empire's border reached the Syr Darya River, the northern frontier of the Khwarazmian Empire. Seeking to expand trade within his empire, Chinggis Khan sent a caravan to Otrar, a border town along the Syr Darya.[56] Otrar's governor, Inalchuq, saw the enormous wealth of the caravan and could not contain his avarice. Furthermore, he also noticed that the merchants asked many questions, which raised his suspicions. He informed Sultan Muhammad, who then authorised his subordinate to act. Inalchuq

---

[52] Biran, *The Empire of the Qara Khitai*, 77.
[53] Juwayni/Qazvini, v1, 46–8, v2, 83–4; Juvaini/Boyle, 62–4, 351; RD/Karimi, 338; RD/Thackston2, 163. Ostensibly, whoever defeated the Gur-Khan would have preference in the division of spoils. If the Khwarazmshah won, then his territory would extend to Khotan and Kashgar. If Guchulug won (and he did), his territory would extend to Fanakat. Neither had intention of honouring their agreement to the letter.
[54] Juwayni/Qazvini, v1, 49, 53; Juvaini/Boyle, 65–6, 70; RD/Karimi, 338; RD/Thackston2, 163. For the argument against religious persecution see Biran, *Qara Khitai*, 194–6.
[55] Juwayni/Qazvini, v1, 50–1; Juvaini/Boyle, 66–8; *SWQZL*, 50; RD/Thackston2; 163–4.
[56] Juzjani/Habibi, 650–1, Juzjani/Raverty 963–6; Yelu Chucai, 21; Henry Schwarz, 'Otrār', *CAS* (1998), 8.

massacred the caravan in 1218, but one camel tender escaped unnoticed. The governor and the sultan divided the plunder between themselves.⁵⁷

Chinggis Khan became enraged when he learned of the massacre. Bogged down in a war against the Jin and still dealing with the repercussions of the *Hoi-yin Irgen* rebellion, he had no desire to become involved in another war; thus he turned to diplomacy. He sought restitution of the goods – many Chinggisids, including their wives, had invested in the caravan. He also requested that the governor be sent to him. Muhammad refused. Although the earlier encounter with Subedei had unnerved him, Muhammad had expanded his empire by conquering Afghanistan and parts of modern Pakistan. His borders stretched almost to the Tigris River in the west and his cronies called him a Second Alexander. Knowing that Chinggis Khan was at war with the Jin and had meagre forces in Qara Khitai, Muhammad was not concerned. Furthermore, he found Chinggis Khan's letter insulting. Therefore, he killed the Mongol diplomat and burned the beards of the envoy's guards before sending them back to Chinggis Khan.⁵⁸

This insult was more than Chinggis Khan could bear. He left Muqali with a small army in northern China and marched 2,000 miles to invade the Khwarazmian Empire. Along the way, Uighurs and Qarluqs reinforced him.⁵⁹ According to Yelu Chucai, who accompanied Chinggis Khan, the massacre at Otrar 'was the only reason for the western campaign'.⁶⁰ A far cry from attempting to conquer the world.

Although the governor of Otrar expressed concerns about Mongol espionage, it is clear that Khwarazmian spies were also active. Muhammad quickly learned that the Mongols were approaching and met with his advisors to plan for the coming invasion. He settled for dividing his army and defending his cities. While not a popular plan for some of his commanders, including his son Jalal al-Din, it made sense.⁶¹ The Khwarazmian Empire was vast and newly formed. If he did not secure the cities, they might surrender without a fight. Also, the memory of his previous encounter with the Mongols surely haunted him. Muhammad raised new troops, built new fortifications, and then waited for the hammer to fall.⁶²

---

⁵⁷ Juvaini/Boyle, 79–81; Juwayni/Qazvini, v1, 61; Juzjani Raverty, 272; Juzjani/Habibi, 311; RD/Thackston2, 165–6; RD/Karimi, 341; Nesawi/Houdas, 57–9; Nasawi, 83–6; Ibn al-Athir, 361–2; Ibn al-Athir/Richards, 205.
⁵⁸ Juvaini/Boyle, 79–81; Juwayni/Qazvini, v1, 61; Hadid, v3, 71; Nasawi, 87–8; Nesawi/Houdas, 60; Ibn al-Athir, 363–4; Ibn al-Athir/Richards, 206.
⁵⁹ Juwayni/Qazvini, 63; Juvaini/Boyle, 82.
⁶⁰ Yelu Chucai, 21.
⁶¹ Juwayni/Qazvini, v1, 106–8; Juvaini/Boyle, 376–7; Nasawi, 89–90; Nesawi/Houdas, 62; Hadid, v3, 70.
⁶² Nasawi, 89–91; Nesawi/Houdas, 61–3; Ibn al-Athir, 363–5; Ibn al-Athir/Richards, 206–7.

It came swiftly and without mercy. Although Otrar resisted, it fell to the Mongols and the governor suffered an ironic death for his avarice as the Mongols allegedly poured molten silver into his mouth and ears. The Mongols then divided their forces. Jochi marched along the Syr Darya towards Urgench and Khwarazm. Ogodei and Chaghadai took another route in the same direction. Jebe and Subedei took their armies into central and southern Mawarannahr. Chinggis Khan took his army and simply disappeared.[63]

As the Mongols attacked various points south of the Syr Darya along with a few border towns north of the river, Muhammad Khwarazmshah tried to keep track of the multiple Mongol armies. He reeled with shock when he suddenly learned that Chinggis Khan's army had appeared before Bukhara – 300 miles behind enemy lines.[64] The wily Mongol leader led his army through the Kizil Kum desert, thought to be impassable by such a large force. Despite a desperate defence, Bukhara fell.[65]

The attack on Bukhara carried not only shock value. For Chinggis Khan the city held immense importance as it was rumoured that the loot from the caravan massacred at Otrar was stored there. Many of the city's leading citizens underwent interrogation as to its location.[66] The message was clear – one does not steal from Chinggis Khan. Afterwards the population was divided. Talented artisans were sent back to Mongolia while the less skilled marched before the Mongols towards Samarqand. These survivors then filled Samarqand's trenches and moats with debris, manned siege weapons, and served as arrow fodder.[67] Jebe and Subedei also joined the Mongol Khan there.

Despite a large garrison and a contingent of war elephants, Samarqand could not hold against the Mongols.[68] With the fall of two leading cities

---

[63] RD/Karimi, 353, 430–1; RD/Thackston1, 241, 291; RD/Thackston2, 170–3; *SWQZL* 51; Juzjani/Habibi, 367–8, 652–3; Juzjani/Raverty, 273–4, 969–71; Juwayni/Qazvini, 62–75; Juvaini/Boyle, 81–97.
[64] Nasawi, 101–3; Nesawi/Houdas, 75–6.
[65] Juwayni/Qazvini, v1, 82–3; Juvaini/Boyle, 106–7; Juzjani/Habibi, v2, 653; Juzjani/Raverty, 976–8. RD/Karimi, 360–2; RD/Thackston1, 246–7; RD/Thackston2, 173–4; Ibn al-Athir, 365–7; Ibn al-Athir/Richards, 207–9.
[66] Ibn al-Athir, 366–7; Ibn al-Athir/Richards, 208–9.
[67] RD/Karimi, 364; RD/Thackston1, 248–9; RD/Thackston2, 175; Juwayni/Qazvini, v1, 94–7; Juvaini/Boyle, 120–2. Juzjani/Habibi, v2, 665; Juzjani/Raverty, 1,048; Ibn al-Athir/Richards, 209; Al-Athir, 367.
[68] RD/Karimi, 363–4; RD/Thackston1, 248–9; RD/Thackston2, 174–6; BH2, 381; Juwayni/Qazvini, v1, 94; Juvaini/Boyle, 120; Juzjani/Raverty, 274, 979–80; Juzjani/Habibi, v1, 311–12, v2, 107.

of the region, Muhammad retreated across the Amu Darya to Khurasan. Chinggis Khan dispatched Jebe and Subedei after him. With the two generals in pursuit, Muhammad never had an opportunity to rest or rally his forces. He eventually escaped from them, by fleeing to an island in the Caspian Sea, where he died ignobly of dysentery shortly thereafter.[69]

Meanwhile, the destruction of his empire continued. While Chinggis Khan led an army into Afghanistan, Tolui entered Khurasan and destroyed any city that resisted, often returning later to kill survivors who came out of hiding. Those who did submit were to destroy their walls.[70] After the region was devastated, Tolui withdrew north of the Amu Darya. His objective was not to conquer the region, but simply to destroy all strongpoints, leaving it defenceless against future attacks. Writing a generation later, the Persian historian Juwayni, whose father witnessed the Mongol invasion, commented on the destruction: 'With one stroke a world which billowed with fertility was laid desolate, and the regions thereof became a desert, and the greater part of the living dead, and their skin and bones crumbling dust; and the mighty were humbled and immersed in the calamities of perdition.'[71] While Juwayni was prone to hyperbole, his commentary reveals an amount of destruction never seen before in the region.

As for Chinggis Khan, he pursued Jalal al-Din, the most talented son of Muhammad Khwarazmshah. With the death of his father, Jalal al-Din became the de facto leader of the empire. At Parwan, near Kabul, he defeated a Mongol army led by Shigi Qutuqu, but retreated across the Hindu Kush mountains upon the advance of Chinggis Khan. Chinggis Khan treated the defeat as a learning opportunity and conducted what in modern military parlance is known as an After-Action Review (AAR) to determine what went wrong at the battle and also what the commanders did correctly.[72] He then followed Jalal al-Din, finally catching him at the Indus River in 1221. With his flanks crumbling, Jalal al-Din spurred his horse off a cliff and into the river. Other elements of the Khwarazmian army joined him, escaping into India; those that did not were eradicated. Dorbei Doqshin, who suppressed the *Hoi-yin Irgen* rebellion, led the hunt for Jalal al-Din across the Indus.[73]

[69] Juzjani/Raverty, 278–9, 992; Juzjani/Habibi, v1, 313; v2, 108–9; Dhahabi, 208–9, Nasawi, 104–7; Nesawi/Houdas, 79–80; Ibn al-Athir, 370; Ibn al-Athir/Richards, 211.
[70] Juwayni/Qazvini, 126–8, 140; Juvaini/Boyle, 161–4, 178.
[71] Juvaini/Boyle, 152.
[72] Juzjani/Habibi, 372–3, 660; Juzjani/Raverty, 287–9, 1,019–21; Juwayni/Qazvini, v1, 105, v2, 137–8; Juvaini/Boyle, 132, 406–7; Nuwayri, 255. My thanks to Staff Sergeant (ret.) Robert Klemm for the correct terminology.
[73] Juwayni/Qazvini, v2, 140–2; Juvaini/Boyle, 409–11; RD/Karimi, 377; RD Thackston 1998, 257; RD/Thackston2, 183; Juzjani/Habibi, v2, 492–3; Juzjani/Raverty, 534–6.

Although Mongols pursued and laid waste to a few towns, they eventually rejoined the main Mongol forces in reducing other fortresses in Afghanistan. The heat and humidity of India proved to be too much of an obstacle for the Mongols and their horses. Additionally, it weakened their bows, making them less effective.[74]

Then, abruptly, the campaign was over. Chinggis Khan's army regrouped and returned to Mongolia. A force remained in Mawarannahr and Khwarazm, depriving Jalal al-Din of the core of his father's empire. These regions were also the economic centres, which the Mongols turned to their advantage. They abandoned the rest of their conquests, despite the fact that the conquest of the region proved to be a masterpiece of Mongol warfare at all levels.

Return to Xi Xia

It is impossible to determine whether the Mongols would have lingered in the remnants of the Khwarazmian Empire, but they withdrew north of Amu Darya in 1223 after receiving news of a revolt in Xi Xia.[75] The standard story found in the sources is that when Chinggis Khan prepared to march on the Khwarazmian Empire, he ordered the Tangut to provide troops. Already contributing a significant force again the Jin Empire, Asha Gambu, a Tangut general, retorted, 'Since [Chinggis Khan's] forces are incapable of subjugating others, why did he go as far as becoming [khan]?'[76] Thus, the king of Xi Xia heeded his advice and did not send the troops as his client status dictated.

Despite this act of rebellion, Chinggis Khan did not retaliate because the Tangut had previously provided approximately 50,000 men towards the Jin campaign, and Chinggis Khan needed to deal with in the Khwarazmian Empire immediately.[77] Thus, when the Mongols invaded Xi Xia again in 1225, he was dealing with an insult that was seven years old.

It is clear that the Mongols did not forget past grievances. If the Tangut had ignored the request for troops in 1219, ignoring this slight and open act of defiance to his authority contradicts Chinggis Khan's behaviour. With

---

[74] For the effects of humidity on the composite bow see Charles R. Bowlus, 'Tactical and Strategic Weaknesses of Horse-archers on the Eve of the First Crusade', 149–66, *Autour de la Premiere Croisade*, ed. Michel Balard (Paris, 1996), 161.

[75] Juzjani/Habibi, v2, 665–6; Juzjani/Raverty, 1,046–7; Juvaini/Boyle, 139; Juwayni/Qazvini, v1, 110.

[76] *SHM*, §256.

[77] Luc Kwanten, 'The Career of Muqali: A Reassessment', *The Bulletin of Sung and Yüan Studies* 14 (1978), 33–4.

the Hoi-yin Irgen revolt, he dealt with it immediately and even returned to Mongolia rather than remaining in the Jin Empire, which persisted as a powerful opponent. The reality is that Xi Xia's response may not have happened in quite the way the sources depicted it.

While the Tangut may have been exasperated with the constant demand for soldiers, the ruler certainly did not rebel. Indeed, armies from Xi Xia fought against the Jin until 1223, when Muqali died. With the bulk of the Mongol army in Central Asia and far from Xi Xia, they made peace with the Jin. Chinggis Khan quickly learned of it. Again, he attempted to resolve the matter diplomatically, but without success. Although the Tangut engaged in peace talks, these broke down after the Tangut court could not come to terms over which hostages to send to Chinggis Khan. The issue was not so much sending hostages, but who among the Tangut elite should go. Eventually, Chinggis Khan lost patience and declared war. Meanwhile, Chinggis Khan had returned to the Tula River in central Mongolia, after an absence of eight years, before invading Xi Xia in March 1226.[78] The fact that he could return to Mongolia after such a lengthy departure is testament to the foundations of his rule and the governing institutions that he had established in his rise to power.

The Mongols swiftly advanced and captured cities one by one before dividing their forces. While Subedei performed mop-up operations through the region, Chinggis Khan advanced on Zhongxing in 1227. The Tangut made last-ditch efforts for peace, but it was too late.[79] The Tangut almost had a lucky break, however. During the campaign, Chinggis Khan went hunting, during which the sudden appearance of wild asses startled his horse, causing it to rear up and throw the Mongol leader. Unlike those he sustained from a similar fall while hunting wild boar in Central Asia, these injuries were severe.[80] Afterwards, he sickened and grew weaker. The Tangut again sued for peace and his commanders and sons urged Chinggis Khan to grant peace and return to Mongolia, arguing that the Tangut lived in cities and were not going anywhere.[81] Chinggis Khan refused, and ordered that even if he died nothing should be revealed and that the attack should be continued until the Tangut were 'maimed and tamed'.[82]

---

[78] *SWQZL*, 53; RD/Karimi, 385–6; RD/Thackston1, v2, 262; RD/Thackston2, 187.
[79] *SHM*, §265; Yelu Chucai, 24.
[80] For the incident with the boar, see *Xi Youji*, 118. For the wild asses incident see *SHM*, §265.
[81] *SHM*, §265.
[82] *SHM*, §268.

Figure 3.3 Chinggis Khan advising his sons on his deathbed. Fifteenth-century miniature from Marco Polo's *Livre des Merveilles*. (Rue des Archives/ The Granger Collection, New York)

Chinggis died on 18 August 1227. His commanders faithfully carried out his orders, destroying much of the city and the population of Zhongxing. While the population of Xi Xia was not killed in a genocidal spree, the Mongols wiped the kingdom off the map along with the Tangut royalty. It was a necessary step, for as long as the royal family of Xi Xia existed it would continue to view the kingdom as an independent state and not part of the Mongol Empire. It also demonstrated that the Mongols' system of ruling sedentary populations was not an effective form of ruling an empire. Sedentary cultures viewed the land as the kingdom, while the Mongols viewed the people as the empire. The two views did not mesh. As with their first conquest of Xi Xia, the Mongols did not leave an occupying garrison. There was no reason; they destroyed the military might of Xi Xia. Although Xi Xia had been economically important through its tribute, it was now fully incorporated into the Mongol Empire with officials assigned to govern the territory as part of the *ulus* or patrimony of Ogodei.

The Post Chinggis Khan World

Although Chinggis Khan was now dead, he had left a considerable legacy. The most important elements of this included his unification of the Mongolian plateau and the establishment of an effective state. This transformation included a social revolution that altered the fundamental tribal structure of

Figure 3.4 Modern statue of Chinggis Khan, depicting him as the father of Mongolia. Located in the Chinggis Khan pavilion in Sukhbaatar Square, Ulaanbaatar.

the plateau, in which everything was inexorably linked to the *altan urugh*.[83] The key to this state was the political and bureaucratic structure, which promulgated a writing script that the Naiman were already using. Chinggis Khan and his successors developed a keen eye for recognising what was useful among the conquered, such as a writing system, and adapting it to their own use. Even though Chinggis Khan remained illiterate, he decreed that his sons and grandsons would learn to read and write using the new vertical script that remains in use today in Inner Mongolia.

He also built an effective army, incorporating new tactics, strategies and organisation that revolutionised steppe warfare. With this, the *Hoi-yin Irgen* were subdued, along with much of Manchuria and North China. Xi Xia, Qara Khitai, Uighurstan and Mawarannahr were annexed and incorporated into a new steppe empire. Yet now, the *Yeke Monggol Ulus* was without its leader: a man who had not only conquered more territory than anyone else in history, but had also constructed an empire out of a previously declining steppe tribe.

---

[83] See Isenbike Togan, *Flexibility and Limitation in Steppe Formations* (Leiden, 1998), 124–50; David Sneath, *The Headless State* (New York, 2007), 172.

As a result of Chinggis Khan's death, the Mongol Empire faced an immediate crisis. Who would be the next ruler? As the Mongols, like most steppe nomads, did not use primogeniture or ultimogeniture as a succession method, the possibilities for Chinggis Khan's successor were increased. Although the youngest son typically inherited the hearth (the *ger* and personal possessions of his father), inheriting an empire was more complicated than inheriting a few tents and livestock.[84] Furthermore, Chinggis Khan had died far from home; thus, steps had to be taken to ensure that the empire remained cohesive while the Mongol army returned to Mongolia in order that the princes and generals could determine Chinggis Khan's successor.

To this end, Chinggis Khan's youngest son, Tolui, was appointed regent. Why Tolui? For one, he was an able military commander and could lead the army from Xi Xia to Mongolia while maintaining good order. Furthermore, he being the youngest son his father's possessions became his and he became the executor of the estate, although, as Isenbike Togan points out, the title *Otchigin* was never applied to Tolui.[85] Tolui then created, possibly using some previous traditions, practices that regents employed upon the death of the khan.

First, almost all military activity by the Mongols ceased. This did not mean that all fighting ceased, but all offensive actions involving the Mongols ended. Khitans, Han troops and other non-Mongol armies continued to operate in the Jin Empire. Most senior Mongol commanders, however, returned to Mongolia to participate in the *quriltai*. There would also be a period of mourning for all Mongols. The regent oversaw the rites of mourning – propitiating the spirits and escorting the body to burial. The regent also convened the *quriltai* in which the successor would be selected and was also expected to nominate the heir. It is important to remember that while a khan could name a successor, the *quriltai* was not obliged to follow the previous khan's wishes.

There were good reasons why the khan's chosen heir might be bypassed. The most obvious is that the *quriltai* might deem him unworthy or incompetent. New conditions, such as illness or even death, might have changed the situation. In short, all possible contenders were to be considered. Two groups decided the matter. The first was the *altan urugh*. The second group was the *noyad* or military commanders. As many of the leading figures were

---

[84] Isenbike Togan, 'Otchigin's Place in the Transformation from Family to Dynasty', in CEMA, 408–9, 417; Michal Biran, *Qaidu and the Rise of the Independent Mongol State in Central Asia* (London, 1997), 8 and 134; Joseph F. Fletcher, 'Turko-Mongolian Tradition in the Ottoman Empire', *HUS* 3–4 (1979–80), 239.

[85] Togan, 'Otchigin's Place', 409. Togan suggests (pp. 417–19) that Tolui may have been his actual title.

the companions of Chinggis Khan and served in the *keshig* or bodyguard, they were loyal to the wishes and desires of Chinggis Khan.

Prior to Chinggis Khan's death, there were five possible candidates for the throne: his four sons (Jochi, Chaghadai, Ogodei and Tolui) and his youngest brother, Temuge Otchigin.[86] While en route to the Khwarazmian Empire or proceeding against the Tangut, Chinggis Khan chose a successor.[87] The long ride gave him plenty of time to discuss the matter with his sons as well as with his advisors. Jochi, the eldest son, was excluded as an option due to his questionable parentage. It does not appear that Chinggis Khan was concerned about it, but during the discussion Chaghadai exploded at the idea of Jochi being the potential successor, saying 'How can we let ourselves be ruled by this bastard offspring of the Merkit?'[88] Indeed, the two engaged in fisticuffs while in the presence of their father. Ultimately, the issue was moot as Jochi died before Chinggis Khan.

Still, tensions existed between Chinggis Khan and Jochi prior to the latter's death. During the Khwarazmian campaign, Jochi became increasingly distant from his father and appeared more content to stay in his new lands in modern Kazakhstan than to join Chinggis Khan against the Tangut. Chaghadai was also excluded, largely because of his derision towards Jochi. This indicated to Chinggis Khan that Chaghadai could not compromise and was too unforgiving. His stern character was useful, but not for a ruler. Tolui, the youngest son, was perhaps the most logical as he was a brilliant military commander, although there were concerns over his comparative youth. Temuge Otchigin, the youngest brother, was also a contender, but Chinggis Khan preferred his sons over his brother. Finally, there was Ogodei, who, like Tolui, was a drunkard. The fact that his father and other Mongols viewed him as a drunkard was worrisome, as all were known to be a hard-drinking lot. In the end, however, Chinggis Khan named Ogodei as his heir and his brothers swore to obey him.[89]

So why Ogodei? Not only was he a drunkard, he also was a mediocre military commander. Yet, perhaps it was his failings that made him suitable

---

[86] Temuge Otchigin will be the last to use the title Otichigin. Togan, 'Otchigin's Place', 410–12.

[87] *SHM* §254; Juwayni/Qazvini, v1, 142–3; Juvaini/Boyle, 180–2; RD/Karimi, 384–5; RD/Thackston1, 262; RD/Thackston2, 186. This date is not certain. *SHM* §254 gives the impression that this council took place prior to the Mongol march on Khwarazm (1219). Juwayni places the event when Chinggis Khan is on his deathbed during the final Tangut campaign (1227). It is possible that the scenario took place on the march against the Tangut in 1225 as indicated by Rashid al-Din.

[88] *SHM*, §254.

[89] Juwayni/Qazvini, v1, 144; Juvaini/Boyle, 182–3; *SHM*, §255.

for the position. Unlike his stern and serious brothers, he knew clemency. Furthermore, he was likeable and he worked well with others, presumably because he understood the limitations of his own talents. While not gifted in war like Tolui, he learned to trust the advice and judgements of his subordinates. He also knew, unlike Chaghadai, that the ruler could not view all things as black and white, but rather had to see them in many shades of grey. Unlike Jochi, he did not allow perceived slights to define his being. Ogodei recognised his weaknesses and found ways to compensate. It was his ability to find the compromise in difficult situations that gained the trust of Chinggis Khan and was the reason he was named the successor to his father.

Yet in 1227, these decisions were no longer guaranteed. Much had happened, then, as Tolui escorted Chinggis Khan's body back to Mongolia. Tolui may have considered the potential candidates – including himself. He remained a viable candidate. His campaign in Khurasan was brilliant and broke the Khwarazmian Empire. That alone, however, was insufficient for him to gain the throne. In order to do so, he needed support from another branch of the *altan urugh*. Fortunately for Tolui, his wife Sorqoqtani was related to Begtutmish Fujin, the widow of Jochi.[90] As sisters, the two women had close ties that pre-dated their 1203 marriages to the sons of Chinggis Khan. It was clear that the Jochid line of the *altan urugh* would never gain support for the candidacy of the throne, but through the maternal lines they could have strong support if Tolui became khan. Yet, a funny thing happened on the way to the *quriltai*. Chinggis Khan may have died a man, but he entered the spirit world as a powerful demi-god.

In the shamanistic world of the Mongols, the afterlife was very much like the mundane. One's power as a spirit was equivalent to one's position in the here and now. Thus a simple herdsman was still a simple herdsman in the afterlife. Shamanism did not offer a transcendental afterlife. A khan would still be a khan, and thus a powerful spirit. Typically, the Mongols and other nomads propitiate the spirits of their ancestors – asked for protection, to ward off evil, etc. Yet, now Chinggis Khan had entered the spirit world, his ascendancy in the mundane world was unexpected. He not only unified Mongolia, but also rendered all potential enemies impotent. He avenged the massacre at Otrar, the death of Yesugei, the insult to Ambaghai – he was an avatar of vengeance, a god of war, and a creator hero who brought writing and stability to the Mongols. His *sulde*, a part of his soul or genius, took residence in the tuq or standard of the Mongols and offered protection to the ruler and to the Mongols in general.

---

[90] RD/Karimi, 505; RD/Thackston1, 348; RD/Thackston2, 246.

As a result, his words were sacred and became *bileg*, or 'wisdom', and proper behaviour for Mongols (*yosun*); the words, deeds and wisdom of Chinggis Khan became analogous to the *sunna* of the Prophet Muhammad in Islam. Since Chinggis Khan had decreed his son Ogodei his heir, this could not be disputed. In 1229, Ogodei became the second *Qa'an* (*Khaghan*) of the *Yeke Monggol Ulus*.

Islam and the Mongol Empire

By 1227, the *Yeke Monggol Ulus* went from being a state with negligible knowledge of the Islamic world to one that not only interacted with *Dar al-Islam*, or the Islamic world, but also caused it to contract. This was true not only in terms of death and destruction, but also through the mere fact that, in the eyes of the Muslims, *Dar al-Islam* consisted of territories ruled by Muslims. Furthermore, the largest and most powerful Islamic state, the Khwarazmian Empire, was irrevocably shattered, and parts of it ruled by infidels. Afterwards, the Mongols gained more knowledge concerning Islam and the Islamic world, but it was still an imperfect knowledge. At the time of the promulgation of the *Yeke Monggol Ulus*, there were only a handful of Muslims (primarily merchants) within the Mongol realm. These men, however, proved to be quite useful.

A Muslim may have negotiated the 1214 peace treaty with the Jin Empire. According to one source, Jaʿfar Khwaja went to the Jin Emperor Xuanzong (1213–24) as Chinggis Khan's envoy, and asked for his submission. Although the Emperor Xuanzong rejected it, what is significant is that Jaʿfar Khwaja was a Muslim, originally from Yanikant along the Syr Darya River, and in the employ of Chinggis Khan.[91] Jaʿfar's role is not discussed in Juwayni or Rashid al-Din and may be apocryphal, albeit not implausible. Juzjani, however, offers another explanation for Jaʿfar's services. In Juzjani's account, Jaʿfar did not enter the Jin Empire as a diplomat, but as a spy prior to the Mongol invasion. The Jin captured him, although he eventually escaped and provided Chinggis Khan with intelligence regarding the best routes for invading the Jin Empire.[92]

The truth of the matter is likely somewhere between the two accounts. It is unclear from whom either author received his information, Khwandamir writing much later, and Juzjani as a refugee in Delhi. Curiously, the sources from within the Mongol Empire are largely silent about the activities of Jaʿfar

---

[91] *Xi Youji*, 135, fn. 2; Khwandamir, 12. The *Mengda beilu* (p. 64) indicates he was a Uighur, but this seems to be the term the Song Empire used for Central Asians. At this time, most Uighurs were either Nestorian Christians or Buddhists.
[92] Juzjani/Raverty, 954; Juzjani/Habibi, v2, 100.

Khwaja. Still, his role as an emissary or as a spy should not be completely dismissed. Indeed, it is feasible that both events took place. Why Jaʿfar was in Mongolia remains a mystery.

Jaʿfar also commanded troops during the Mongol war against the Jin Empire, but he is best known for his administrative service. Chinggis Khan appointed Jaʿfar Khwaja, already quite old, as a daruqachi or governor of Yanjing (the former Zhongdu) and the surrounding environs in 1214 or 1215. He continued to serve as the chief civil authority in North China during Muqali's vice-royalty there.[93] Ostensibly, he died at the age of 117 or 118.[94] It was during his tenure as *daruqachi* that Jaʿfar Khwaja, a descendant of the prophet Muhammad, may have converted to Daoism. This remains unclear, but it is certain that he held great reverence for the Daoist sage Changchun Zi, whom he met when the latter was summoned to meet with Chinggis Khan. Afterwards, Jaʿfar personally delivered messages to him and eventually implored the sage to build a new temple and presented him with five acres of land for that purpose.[95] It could be argued, however, that Jaʿfar's sponsorship of the temple may simply have been in line with the Mongol practice of religious tolerance and not the result of conversion.

Jaʿfar was not the only Muslim emissary. While the latter may have been a surprising choice to send to the Jin Empire, Muslim emissaries to the Khwarazmian Empire seems an obvious choice. To the modern reader it may seem surprising that Chinggis Khan's envoys for initiating a trade agreement with the Khwarazmian Empire – Mahmud al-Khwarazmi (a.k.a. Mahmud Yalavach), ʿAli Khwaja al-Bukhari and Yusuf Kanka al-Otrari[96] – originated from that empire: nationalism as we know it did not exist yet, although it is also clear that Sultan Muhammad attempted to sway Mahmud by pointing out their ties in location and religion, as well as bribing him with a pearl to spy on Chinggis Khan. Mahmud agreed, although either Chinggis Khan never learned of this or he also continued to serve as a spy for Chinggis Khan.[97] The latter case seems likely, as when the Khwarazmshah pressed him for information about the Mongol ruler's campaign in China, Mahmud allegedly told him the story of the 60,000 virgins leaping to their death at

---

[93] Elizabeth Endicott-West, *Mongolian Rule in China: Local Administration in the Yuan Dynasty* (Cambridge, MA, 1989), 26. Igor de Rachewiltz, 'Personnel and Personalities in North China in the Early Mongol Period', *JESHO* 9 (1966), 122, fn. 2; *MDBL*, 64.

[94] Considering that Chinggis Khan summoned Changchun Zi in order to learn any secrets to immortality, there is some irony here. One must wonder if Ja'far followed the recommendations that Changchun Zi gave to Chinggis Khan to extend his life. *Xi Youji*, 101.

[95] *Xi Youji*, 137.

[96] Nasawi, 84; Nesawi/Houdas, 57.

[97] Nasawi, 84–5; Nesawi/Houdas, 58–9.

Zhongdu and roads lined with hills of bones.[98] Mahmud did not lie about Chinggis Khan's capture of Zhongdu, but he may have embellished it. After the massacre, the Chinggis Khan again sent a Muslim as his diplomat. Ibn Kafraj Bughra, a Turk, was the unfortunate individual whom Muhammad executed.

The role of Muslims in opening trade relations with the Khwarazmian Empire is not surprising. After all, it is very likely that the idea originated among Muslim merchants operating in the *Yeke Monggol Ulus*. Religion had very little to do with it; business and the safety of a secure trade route, however, meant profits for everyone. Yet, due to the avarice and hubris of the Khwarazmshah, the Mongols wiped the most powerful Muslim state off the map. Their fury was unrestrained and the destruction unparalleled in a region that had seen frequent wars. Due to this, the damage inflicted by the infidel armies left a jagged scar on the Muslim psyche in the thirteenth century, and various authors attempted to rationalise the event and explain why God had seemingly abandoned the Believers.

The Islamic world possessed an imperfect view of the Mongol Empire as well, viewing the Mongols both as liberators and as an apocalyptic force of nature. Prior to the Khwarazmian war, the Muslims in Qara Khitai welcomed Jebe as their liberator from the tyrannical oppression and persecution of the infidel Guchulug.[99] While Jebe's edict of religious toleration benefited the Muslims, it did not favour them. Nonetheless, the Mongols appeared more favourable to Islam than Guchulug did.

For the Muslims of the former Khwarazmian Empire, the Mongols were not liberators, but a force of nature and the stuff of nightmares. And the nightmare began swiftly. With the capture of Bukhara, Chinggis Khan allegedly announced: 'O People, know that you have committed great sins, and that the great ones among you have committed these sins. If you ask me what proof I have for these words, I say it is because I am the punishment of God. If you had not committed great sins, God would not have sent a punishment like me upon you.'[100]

The great Arab chronicler Ibn al-Athir also was mortified by the event. Living in Mosul, a region spared by the Mongol onslaught, but a destination for refugees from the east, Ibn al-Athir wrote: 'For several years I continued to avoid mention of this disaster as it horrified me and I was unwilling to recount

---

[98] Juzjani/Habibi, 102; Juzjani/Raverty, 964–5.
[99] Juwayni/Qazvini, v1, 49, 53; Juvaini/Boyle, 65–6, 70; RD/Karimi, 338; RD/Thackston2, 163.
[100] Juvaini/Boyle, 105; Juwayni/Qazvini, v1, 81. RD/Thackston2, 174; RD/Karimi, 499; Khwandamir, 16.

it. I was taking one step towards it and then another back. Who is there who would find it easy to write the obituary of Islam and the Muslims?'[101] In his attempts to rationalise the Mongol invasion and destruction, Ibn al-Athir drew upon apocalyptic descriptions, painting al-Djallal (the Anti-Christ) in a favourable light vis-à-vis the Mongols. Ibn al-Athir wrote, 'As for the Anti-Christ, he will spare those who follow him and destroy those who oppose him, but these did not spare anyone. On the contrary, they slew women, men and children. They split open the bellies of pregnant women and killed the fetuses.'[102]

Juwayni and Ibn al-Athir's examples are but a small sample of the uncomprehending horror that the Muslim world experienced before the Mongol onslaught. Yet shock gave way to attempts to rationalise the Mongol arrival, as will be discussed in Chapter 12.

With the Mongol entry into *Dar al-Islam* there was no indication that the *Yeke Monggol Ulus* would expand it and drift towards becoming an Islamic empire. Indeed, it is clear that they did not understand the religion or the culture. By ruling Muslims and bringing many into their service, whether as soldiers or bureaucrats, they could not avoid Islam or the fact that some might find it attractive. Yet, the expansion of Islam throughout the Mongol Empire and the eventual conversion of much of the empire was not inevitable by any means.

---

[101] Ibn al-Athir/Richards, 202; Ibn al-Athir, 358.
[102] Ibn Al-Athir/Richards, 202; Ibn al-Athir, 359.

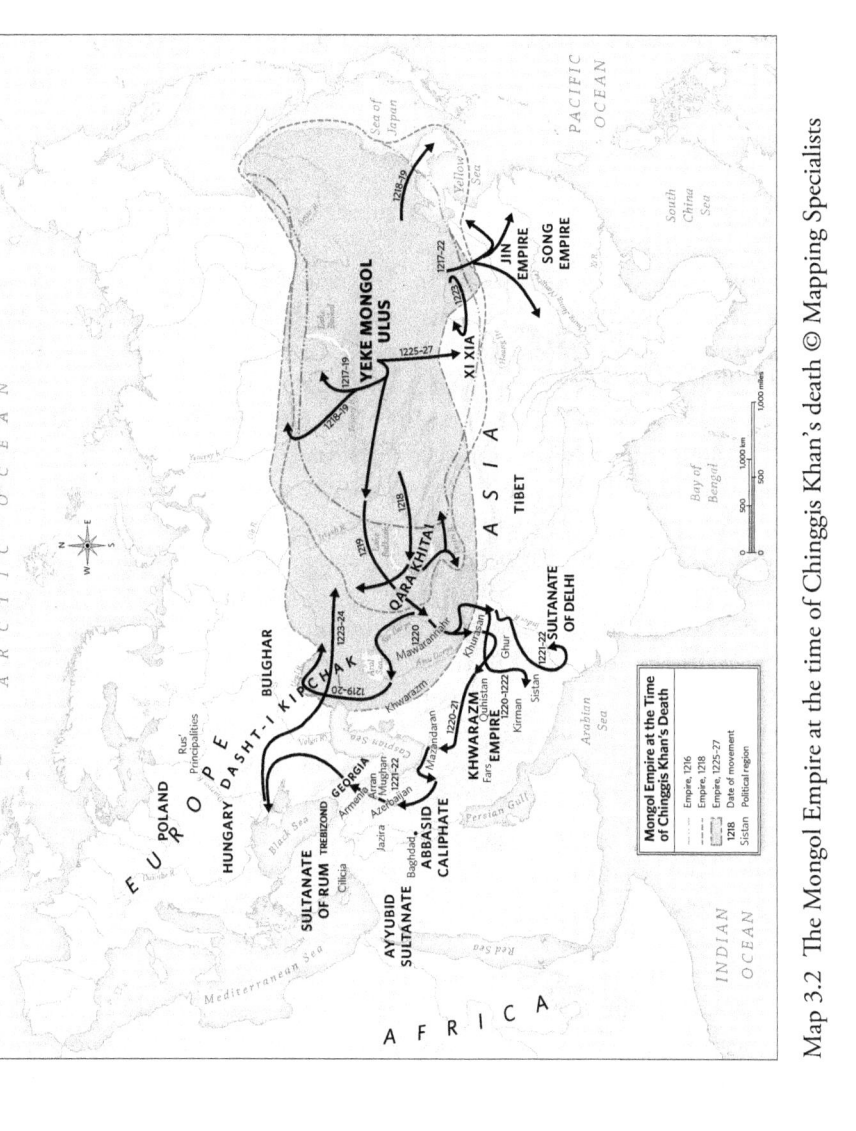

Map 3.2 The Mongol Empire at the time of Chinggis Khan's death © Mapping Specialists

4

The Institutions of the Empire

One of the most under-appreciated moments in the history of the Mongol Empire is the lack of crisis after the death of Chinggis Khan. As suggested in the previous chapter, a succession crisis could have occurred. The conditions were ripe, yet nothing occurred, even though Chinggis Khan had been absent from Mongolia for six years, and then following his departure after a brief visit in 1225. After the *quriltai* of 1206, Chinggis Khan spent twelve and a half years of his final twenty-one years of life outside of his homeland.

Chinggis Khan's initial conquest of Xi Xia lasted from May 1209 to late spring/early summer 1211, or approximately two years. Not long afterwards, he invaded the Jin Empire and campaigned until February 1212, or for nine months. Another invasion occurred in September 1212. While his armies stayed longer, Chinggis Khan withdrew two months later after having been wounded. A third invasion occurred in the autumn of 1213 and lasted until March 1214: approximately six months. His last invasion of the Jin Empire began in September 1214 and lasted until June 1215. He then returned to Mongolia while Muqali took command of the operation. The Mongols departed Mongolia for the Khwarazmian Campaign in the late winter/early spring and reached the Irtysh River by May 1219. Although he learned of the Xi Xia revolt in 1223, Chinggis Khan did not reach Mongolia until 1225; thus the Khwarazmian campaign alone lasted six years, from mobilisation up to his return to Mongolia in 1225. He departed for Xi Xia in November 1225, and died in August 1227, after campaigning for approximately twenty-two months. The frequency of his departures and their duration is startling. Yet, there is very little indication of rebellion or a loss of control. The exception was the rebellion of the *Hoi-yin Irgen*, who were outside of the original *Yeke Monggol Ulus*, in 1217–18 when Chinggis Khan was in the Jin Empire, and then of the Tangut who rebelled in 1223 after Muqali's death. Their rebellion was not solely due to Chinggis Khan's absence, as he had been in Central Asia for almost four years by then.

One must consider also that Ogodei's elevation to *Qa'an* occurred almost three years after the death of Chinggis Khan. In short, regents ruled the homeland for fifteen out of the twenty-three years following the 1206 *quriltai*. Despite the lengthy absences, Mongolia remained stable after effectively undergoing a social revolution in 1206. Although Temuge Otchigin, Chinggis Khan's youngest brother, and Tolui reigned as effective regents, we have little knowledge of their regency. Furthermore, their abilities as regents are not enough to explain the stability of the empire. A sophisticated system of administration, ideology and control was necessary to ensure that the *Yeke Monggol Ulus* was not simply a house of cards precariously built at the 1206 *quriltai*.

Military Administration

So what happened at this *quriltai*? Chinggis Khan assigned ninety-five units of one thousand (*minqan*) to commanders. Most commanders received one *minqan* each, but a few received more, such as Chigu Guregen and Alchi Guregen of the Onggirad, who led three *minqan* each, while Alaqush Digid Quri of the Onggud commanded five *minqad*. This favouritism was a token of their *guregen* or son-in-law and *quda* relationship status. Although the Onggirad had submitted to Chinggis Khan much earlier, Alchi was Borte's brother, and Tumelun's marriage to Chigu by way of a marriage alliance cemented the Onggirad's ties to Chinggis Khan. As for the Onggud, Chinggis Khan's daughter Alaqa Beki married Alaqush's son. Alaqush was considered *guregen* by extension. These *minqad* were Onggud tribal troops.

Chinggis Khan also named Muqali and Bo'orchu as commanders of the left and right wings of the army respectively, commanding a *tumen* or unit of 10,000. This assignment created military districts, with Bo'orchu's extending to the Altai Mountains while Muqali's reached the Qara'un Jidun Mountains. A general named Naya'a commanded the centre with his own *tumen* and thus remained close to Chinggis Khan. Others also received *tumed* (plural of *tumen*). Qorchi received command of the northern frontier (the *Hoi-yin Irgen*) as his administrative district with a *tumen* of troops to ensure order.[1]

Chinggis Khan named his adopted younger brother, Shigi Qutuqu, the *yeke jarquchi* or chief judge. Not only did he have the power to mete out punishment, but he was also in charge of preventing crime, as well as writing down the judicial decisions. In essence, Shigi Qutuqu was placed in charge of enforcing and maintaining the law of the land.[2] The Mongol general Qubilai was placed in charge of military affairs. It appears that this was primarily in terms of organisation, logistics and even training.

---

[1] *SHM*, §203, 205, 206. This was based on a southern orientation.
[2] *SHM*, §204; Paul Ratchnevsky, 'Sigi-Qutuqu, ein Mongolisher Gefolgsmann im 12.–13. Jahrundert', *CAJ* 10, no. 2 (1965), 87–120.

While these commanders rose to power through their performance and ability, they were slowly transformed into a new aristocracy known as the *qarachu* or 'Black-boned'. Black was the colour of the commoners or non-royal, but it also referred to the aristocracy below the *altan urugh* or family of Chinggis Khan. While they earned their positions through a meritocracy, their privileges transformed their military commands into hereditary positions.

Among the most important institutions created at the *quriltai* was the *keshig* or bodyguard, which expanded to 10,000 men. Made up of the sons and companions of Chinggis Khan's commanders, and founded on their ability and appearance, the *keshig* formed a *tumen* comprising 1,000 night guards, 1,000 quiver-bearers and 8,000 day guards. The importance of the *keshig* cannot be overstated as its importance is described in the *The Secret History* in great detail.[3] The account covers recruitment, duties, commanders and functions. The *keshig* served not only as a bodyguard, but also as the household staff for Chinggis Khan. A *minqan* accompanied him in battle at all times while the remainder guarded the camp. In periods of peace, they tended his herds and flocks, cooked his food and poured his drink. By evaluating their abilities in all facets, Chinggis Khan and his successors determined who would be best suited to govern a territory or lead an army. In short, the *keshig* served as bodyguard and military college, as well as school for future governors and administrators of the Mongol Empire.[4]

Through the assignment of military units and territory to govern as military districts, the creation of the judicial branch and the *keshig*, Chinggis Khan laid down the foundation of the Mongol administration. As the empire expanded, so did the administration. The Mongols relied heavily on non-Mongols to administer their empire and its sheer size and scope made it impossible for them not to do so.[5] While it is certainly true that the Mongols recruited large numbers of Khitans, Han, Uighurs and Muslims of various ethnicities into their administration, they remained involved and provided the structure under which the empire functioned.[6] Other than the *keshig*,

---

[3] *SHM*, §224–34.
[4] Timothy May, *The Mongol Art of War* (Barnsley, 2007), 32–6; David Morgan, *The Mongols*, 2nd edn (Malden, MA, 2007), 79–80; Ruth Dunnell, *Chinggis Khan* (New York, 2010), 45.
[5] David Morgan, 'Who Ran the Mongol Empire?', *JRAS* 114, no. 2 (1982) 124–36; Paul D. Buell, 'The Role of the Sino-Mongolian Frontier Zone in the Rise of Cinggis-Qan', in *SOM*, 63–76; Igor de Rachewiltz, 'Personnel and Personalities in North China in the Early Mongol Period', *JESHO* 9 (1966), 88–144.
[6] See David Morgan, 'Mongol or Persian: The Government of Ilkhanid Iran', *HMEIR* 3 (1996), 62–76.

the most important institution within the Mongol Empire was also the most Mongolian – the army.

As an institution, the army was crucial not only for its role in establishing, expanding, and protecting the empire but also for organising it. Within Mongolia, the creation of the units of 1,000 and 10,000 extended beyond just military means. The decimal system, which had been in use in the steppes since the time of the Xiongnu, was a means of organisation that extended into maintaining the military.[7] In order to have the decimal military units, Mongol officials registered the men and their households through a census.[8] Not every man served in a military unit – to take all of the men away threatened economic disaster. Although the women could fulfil many of the roles of the men in a pastoral nomadic economy, the traditional division of labour existed for a reason. If there were not enough people to perform all the duties, the system broke down. A thousand men might form a unit, but 1,000 households supported it. When a military unit was not in the field, the men returned to their families, resumed their normal life and mobilised for war when commanded.

The organisation of the households provided not only manpower, but mounts and provisions for the unit. As the Mongols expanded, other nomads were incorporated into the same system. Other nomads were the most easily inducted. They were given a new hairstyle that inducted them into their new Mongol identity. The haircut was similar to a monk's tonsure, but with a tuft left at the front and then long hair on the sides that was usually braided.[9] The unusual haircut made it difficult for new recruits to desert. They then merged with existing units. Thus, at times, a *minqan* might be slightly larger than a thousand and at times a *tumen* might consist of only a few thousand men. The new nomads then trained with the existing units so that they learned the Mongol art of war. Although the Mongols used many of the same tactics and strategies that had been used by steppe nomads for centuries, significant refinements and changes gave the Mongols a substantial edge.

Troops from sedentary units remained in their own formations and the districts they originated from supplied the recruits with provisions and

---

[7] Hyun Jin Kim, *The Huns* (London, 2016), 15–16; Ch'i-ch'ing Hsiao, *The Military Establishment of the Yuan Dynasty* (Cambridge, MA, 978), 8; Ch'en Yuan, *Western and Central Asians in China under the Mongols: Their Transformation into Chinese*, trans. Ch'ien Hsing-hai and L. Carrington Goodrich (Nettetal, 1989), 73.

[8] Thomas T. Allsen, 'Mongol Census Taking in Rus, 1245–1275', *HUS* 5/1 (1981), 50–1; Grigor of Akanc, 325; YS 98, 73–5.

[9] JPC, 32–3; JPC/Dawson, 6–7; Rubruck/Dawson, 101–2; Rubruck/Jackson, 88; Rubruck, 183–4.

Figure 4.1 The typical nomad's camp consisted of only a few *gers* and not a hundred, due to pasture concerns. Large congregations, such as at a *quriltai*, were infrequent.

equipment. The Mongols did not try to alter their method of war, but allowed them to fight according to their accustomed method. Thus, Khitan heavy cavalrymen served that purpose for the Mongols while the Mongols remained primarily light horse archers. In order to organise them into decimal units, a census of local households also took place, providing the Mongols with an estimate of men and materials, as well as the tax base.

Additional military units also existed, such as the *tamma*. This was a special military unit placed on the frontier of the Mongol military. It protected the frontiers as well as expanding Mongol control either directly through conquest or indirectly through intimidation and influence. The *tamma* were new units, drawing on troops from various *minqad*, such as two from every hundred, etc., to be sent to new locations. These were the the *tammachin*. Their commander (*tammachi*, which also is the singular of *tammachin*) usually came from the *keshig*. There are no examples of a *tamma* unit being disbanded. The *tamma* situated itself in the region with the best pasture, with the *tammachi* serving as the *Qa'an*'s direct representative and as a military

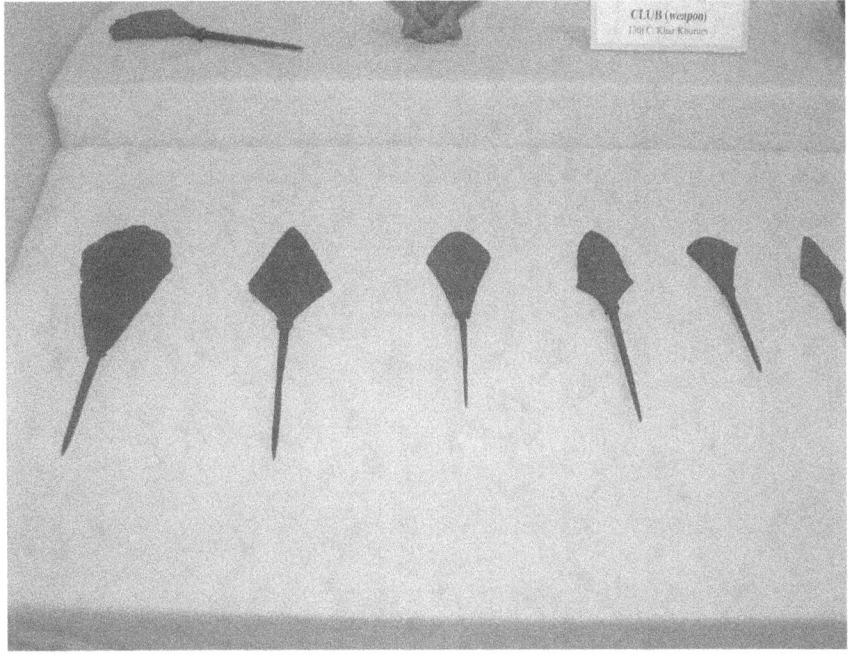

Figure 4.2 Thirteenth-century Mongol arrowheads show the variety of arrows that the Mongol military used. (Mongolian National History Museum, Ulaanbaatar)

governor for the region. *Alginchin* (singular *alginchi*) or scouts rode and communicated between the various units forming the *tamma*, as they often had to be distributed on the basis of available pasture.[10]

While the Mongol military enabled the Mongol Empire to conquer territories quickly, the empire needed an effective civil administration in order to govern and continue to expand. Like the military, the administrative structures of the empire also evolved. Indeed, without the development of an increasing sophisticated civil administration, it is unlikely that the Mongols could have maintained their conquests without the empire collapsing under mismanagement as it ceased to be coterminous with the army. The *tamma* military institution could control newly conquered territories, but it remained a military force. Without the introduction of an effective and efficient civil administration, the majority of the Mongol military would become mired in controlling territory rather than invading new ones. It is the

---

[10] Paul D. Buell, 'Kalmyk Tanggaci People: Thoughts on the Mechanics and Impact of Mongol Expansion', *MS* 6 (1980), 41–59; Jean Aubin, 'L'Ethogenese Des Qaraunas', *Turcica* 1 (1969), 65–95; Donald Ostrowksi, 'The *Tamma* and the Dual-administrative Structure of the Mongol Empire', *BSOAS* 61 (1998), 262–77.

Figure 4.3 The black tuq, made from yak or horse hair, was the war standard of the Mongols. A white one was displayed during peace. These modern Mongolian soldiers, from a special brigade, re-enact scenes from the history of the Mongol Empire, bowing before the standard of Chinggis Khan.

civil administration that allowed the *tammachin* to advance to new frontiers while older conquests became integrated into the Empire. It should be noted that as the *tammachin* remained in a location for years, even decades, often they resented and even resisted relinquishing control of their territories when a civil administration replaced it.[11]

Civil Administration

Just as the *minqan* was the basis for the military, it also served as the basic unit for the organisation of civil society and the fiscal administration of the empire.[12] Despite the importance of the *tammachi* in a particular region, they could only extract tribute and services from the local population. A regular

[11] Timothy May, 'Mongol Conquest Strategy in the Middle East', in *MME*, 15–16, 20–2.
[12] Paul D. Buell, 'Kalmyk Tanggaci People: Thoughts on the Mechanics and Impact of Mongol Expansion', *MS* 6 (1980), 47.

system of taxation was needed. Thus, as a region transitioned into being administered by a civil government, a *daruqachi* accompanied by *bichigchi* or secretaries arrived.¹³ The *daruqachi* position, also known in Turkic as *basqaqs*, *shahna* in Persian and Arabic and *daluhuachi* in Chinese, originated in the Liao Dynasty and also existed in the Qara Khitai Empire. The Mongols adopted its use early on from their Khitan subjects.¹⁴ In a strict form, the *daruqachi* served as the governor of a region or town, but the term was malleable. In some areas, where local authorities remained in place, the *daruqachi* was a Mongol agent or resident. Often, the *daruqachi* was a local official, but reported to the Mongol government rather than to the local potentate. Indeed, most of the Mongols staffed most of their administrative apparatus with non-Mongols not only due to their expertise, but also, of necessity, due to the size of the empire.

After conquests, Chinggis Khan ordered *daruqachin* to be placed in the cities. To supervise and manage all of the *daruqachin*, the Mongols assigned a *yeke* ('great', 'high') *daruqachin*. Mahmud Yalavach and his son Masʿud were among the first *yeke daruqachin*. Chinggis Khan first installed Mahmud as the *yeke daruqachin* over Turkestan. Under Ogodei, Masʿud became the *yeke daruqachi* of Turkestan while Mahmud Yalavach served as the *yeke daruqachin* over much of North China.¹⁵ He assigned this father and son team specifically because they were familiar with the role of the *daruqachi*, presumably from their time as subjects of the Qara Khitai Empire. There has been some conjecture that Mahmud Yalavach was also Mahmud Bey, the vizier of the last Qara Khitan Gur-Khan, Zhilugu (d. 1213), whom Guchulug overthrew in 1211. It is possible that Mahmud became unemployed and fled into Chinggis Khan's territory or back to Khwarazm and became a merchant some time between 1211 and 1213.¹⁶

One of the *yeke daruqachin*'s primary duties, at least in the time of Mongke, was to oversee and carry out the registration of the population in a census. The census was carried out on a fairly regular basis and often the census-takers were protected by a local dynast. This position sometimes merged with another, the *jarquchi*. The *jarquchi* resolved legal disputes, often acting as the judge. This position was somewhat fluid and may have been applied as needed. Nonetheless, we see high-ranking officials in other positions also

---

[13] Buell, 'Kalmyk Tanggaci', 47; May, 'Mongol Conquest Strategy', 20–2. A *yeke jarquci* was a high judge, one who decrees, and one who administers a province.

[14] Paul Buell, 'Sino-Khitan Administration in Mongol Bukhara', *JAH* 13/2 (1979), 266; David Morgan, *The Mongols*, 95.

[15] See Thomas Th. Allsen, 'Maḥmūd Yalavac, Masʿūd Beg, ʿAli Beg, Bujir', *ITSOTK*, 122–30.

[16] SHM, 263. Also see Allsen, 'Mahmud Yalavac, Masʿud Beg', 122.

granted the title of *yeke jarquchi*. Mahmud Yalavach was both *yeke daruqachi* and *yeke jarquchi*.¹⁷ The combination of titles made him and others true viceroys with plenipotentiary powers.

Eventually, an administrator known as the *yeke jarquchi* or *yeke daruqachi* gradually replaced the *tammachi* commander to serve a regional governor. During the conquest phase, administrating conquered territory through the *minqan* units made sense, but as the needs and goals of the Empire evolved, so did the administrative institutions. In the process, a civil administration emerged, separate from the military and concerned with the actual governance of the conquered territories.

While the *minqan* administered the conquered lands, the central administrative institution emerged through the *keshig*, following the frequent process in the pre-modern world by which companions of warlords became heads of administrative offices. Although the *keshig* served as the bodyguard, it also fulfilled royal household and administrative functions. In order to maintain their ties with the khan, the *keshig* member often served a tour of duty, either as an officer or as an administrator away from the court, but returned to the *keshig* upon completion of his duties.¹⁸

The administrative side of the empire underwent substantial changes throughout the history of the empire, transitioning from periods where the military commanders, particularly the *tammachin*, had greater authority and periods where the government functioned more as centralised government. As Thomas Allsen has demonstrated, under Mongke, the fourth *Qa'an*, the administration of the Mongol Empire underwent substantial transformation. Had it continued, the empire would have transformed into a government with an extensive bureaucracy and centralisation of authority comparable to seventeenth-century empires.¹⁹

Mongke's major reforms served to lessen the burden on the sedentary population of the Empire. In this, the Empire sought to organise trade and agriculture to its own benefit. Mongke sought to restore imperial authority over the appanages of the Chinggisids and commanders while reducing the amount of devastation to property and people in war zones in an effort to maintain and preserve the economic prosperity and long-term vitality of the

---

17 Allsen, 'Mahmud Yalavac, Masʿud Beg', 126.
18 Thomas T. Allsen, 'Guard and Government in the Reign of The Grand Qan Mongke, 1251–1259', *HJAS* 46, no. 2 (1986), 517–18, 521; idem, *Mongol Imperialism: The Policies of the Grand Qan Mongke in China, Russia, and the Islamic Lands, 1251–1259* (Berkeley, 1987), 100.
19 Allsen, *Mongol Imperialism*, 80–2, 85. Also see Juwayni/Qazvini, v3, 75–8; Juvaini/Boyle, 598–9.

newly conquered lands.[20] Mongke recognised that the Mongols stood to benefit more in the long term through taxation rather than via short-term gains through plunder and preying on their subjects. Although his reforms originated as a result of the mismanagement of the Empire during the regency of Oghul Qaimish and that of Toregene, as will be discussed, it continued in the same direction as the evolution of the Mongol administration of the previous *Qa'ans*, at least in intent if not practice. This may also be a sign that the Mongol *Qa'ans* changed from being rulers of an empire that centred on controlling people in the traditional steppe sense into rulers of an empire focused on territorial rule.

Taxation

Prior to the establishment of a formal taxation system, the Mongols typically plundered their sedentary subjects.[21] In early Mongol society, tribute was formalised and payment came in the form of goods and service, which demonstrated the subjection of an individual to an overlord, whereas a levy was extraordinary, and used to fulfil a specific need.[22] Eventually, the Mongols set a tithe at approximately 10 per cent of possessions, including men. Additionally, when on campaign, Mongol commanders demanded goods or levied what they needed from subjects, typically those they had recently conquered. This was known as the *alba qubchuri*.[23] The *alba qubchuri* differed in its application for nomads and sedentary populations.

During the reign of Ogodei, the taxation system became regularised, primarily due to the influence of the officials Yelu Chucai and Mahmud Yalavach. In 1235–6, Yelu Chucai and Shigi Qutuqu conducted a census of northern China. Yelu Chucai determined that this was perhaps the best

---

[20] Allsen, *Mongol Imperialism*, 85.
[21] Matters of taxation have been discussed in detail elsewhere. For more detail see Allsen, *Mongol Imperialism*; Ann K. S. Lambton, *Continuity and Change in Medieval Persia: Aspects of Administrative, Economic and Social History, 11th–14th Century* (Albany, 1988); I. P. Petrushevsky, 'The Socio-economic Conditions of Iran under the Il-Khans', in J. A. Boyle, *CHI*, vol. 5 (Cambridge,1968), 483–537; H. F. Schurmann, 'Mongolian Tributary Practices of the Thirteenth Century', *HJAS* 19 (1956), 304–89; Schurmann, *Economic Structure of the Yuan Dynasty* (Cambridge, 1956); John Masson Smith, Jr, 'Mongol and Nomadic Taxation', *HJAS* 30 (1970), 46–85; Smith, 'Mongol Manpower and Persian Population', *JESHO* 18, no. 3 (1975), 271–99.
[22] Schurmann, 'Mongolian Tributary Practices', 311. This formed the basis for the later *alba*. Individuals who owed 'obligations of servitude to a superior were called albatu' (Shurmann, p. 326).
[23] Ibn al-Athir, 380–3, 502. Ibn al-Athir provides numerous examples during the Khwarazmian campaign where Mongol commanders requisitioned cloth, food, mounts and money from cities that submitted to them.

method of demonstrating the importance of the sedentary population to his nomadic overlords.[24] By providing a forecast of tax revenue for Ogodei Khan, the Mongols saw the benefits of taxation rather than plundering. In Central Asia, Mahmud Yalavach adapted the reforms of Yelu Chucai to pre-existing systems in the region. Yalavach's model continued to be used until 1239 or 1240, after which the Mongols transferred Mahmud Yalavach to northern China. Mahmud Yalavach's reforms, while similar to those of Yelu Chucai, differed in certain respects and became the standard for most of the empire. Yalavach's system was based on *qubchur*, a poll tax on adult males paid in cash (perhaps influenced by the *jizya*). Yelu Chucai's version centred on households after the Chinese custom, although he did include a poll tax after 1236, perhaps due to Central Asian influence. In addition, another tax known as *qalan* also was imposed and was often paid in kind rather than in cash.[25]

Just as the empire was divided into military districts and patrimonies (*ulus*) for the Chinggisids, in order to maintain control of the fiscal resources of the empire civil administration divided the empire into fiscal regions. By Guyuk's reign (1246–8), the empire consisted of three revenue districts: Northern China, Turkestan and Khurasan-Mazandaran.[26] While nomads existed in all three regions, the revenue districts primarily consisted of sedentary populations. In the late 1250, the Rus' principalities (conquered in 1238–40) also came under the authority of the fiscal administration as an Onggirad named Kitai was assigned as *daruqachi* over the region in 1257.[27]

By the mid-thirteenth century, taxation was a combination of local taxes (whatever was used in that particular region) and new levies that were applied two or three times a year, often two or three years in advance. Mongke carried out reforms to end this practice. He created a new system of 'Mongol-inspired tribute', to which all adults were subject.[28] In addition, traditional taxes were paid. These included agricultural taxes on sedentary regions (nomads were exempt) and duties on commerce. One important aspect of these reforms was their further concentration of power at the imperial centre, as regional princes were bypassed and a representative of the central government collected taxes. In theory, extraordinary collections did not happen, but that is not to say it did not occur. Mongke's system formed the basis used by the other khanates after the split of the empire.

---

[24] For more on Yelu Chucai see Igor de Rachewiltz, 'Yeh-lu Ch'u-ts'ai, Yeh-lu Chu, Yeh-lu Hsi-ling', *ITSOTK*, 136–72.
[25] Allsen, *Mongol Imperialism*, 147–8; Morgan, *The Mongols*, 101.
[26] Paul D. Buell, 'Cinqai (Ca. 1169–1252)', in *ITSOTK*, 107.
[27] Allsen, *Mongol Imperialism*, 104.
[28] Allsen, *Mongol Imperialism*, 144.

Local Government

Although the Mongols were rather lacking in administrative skill at the time of the establishment of the Mongol Empire into sedentary lands, just as the Mongols sought to control the troop reservoirs of the steppe, they also commandeered the sedentary administrative reservoirs for functions of governance. In governing the conquered territories, the Mongols often used local notables as administrators, particularly at local levels. The Mongols needed people with language skills and knowledge of local customs. In China and Persia, they did not always use local administrative structures, but often promoted others into the administration even though they sometimes had no previous experience. The key to advancement, however, was mastery of the Uighur script used to write Mongolian. They would replace 'local elites, whose status was validated by mastery of indigenous literary and cultural traditions, with those who possessed the inclination and skills outside their own cultural and linguistic milieu'.[29] Over time, other languages also became important such as Persian, Chinese and Turkic, but none replaced Mongolian, although the Mongols did not impose it upon others. Persian, however, did run a close second as it became a *lingua franca* for much of the empire whereas Chinese remained useful only in China.[30]

The Mongols often allowed the native rulers to retain their positions and territories if they submitted without resistance. The Mongols did this for two reasons. The first was that, by giving foreign rulers an opportunity to be part of the empire, the Mongols could avoid unnecessary military actions. Secondly, due to the Mongols' lack of experience in administration they wanted to recruit others with those talents.[31] Furthermore, the Mongols lacked the capability to replace every single local ruler with imperial personnel. Thus, as long as local rulers forwarded taxes, provided troops when required and otherwise behaved, the Mongols had little interest in replacing them. To be sure, the Mongols also did not hesitate to remove local dynasts when the need arose.

At a higher level, the fiscal administrative territories emerged as secretariats, ruled by a civil government. Most of the senior officials of the secretariat

---

[29] Thomas T. Allsen, 'Ever Closer Encounters: The Appropriation of Culture and the Apportionment of Peoples in the Mongol Empire', *Journal of Early Modern History* 1 (1997), 7–8.
[30] David Morgan, 'Persian as a lingua franca in the Mongol Empire', in B. Spooner and W. L. Hanaway (eds), *Literacy in the Persianate World: Writing and the Social Order* (Philadelphia, 2012), 160–70.
[31] Allsen, *Mongol Imperialism*, 63–4.

were Mongols, with a few Uighurs and Khitans during Mongke's time. By Mongke's reign, more Mongols had administrative experience, making it possible for Mongols to govern their empire more directly. Of course, many of the leading figures in the administration were not Mongols, but, as David Morgan indicates, Mongols should never be construed as not having an interest in the operation of their civil government.[32]

Daruqachi, *Basqaq* and *Shahna*

As mentioned earlier, the *daruqachi* was a governor or Mongol agent who handled relations between the empire and a locality. The *daruqachi* was also known as a *basqaq*, *daluhuachi* or *shahna*. Throughout the sources, these three titles are mentioned in several places. Most often the chronicler referred to the terms without further explanation, and modern scholars have struggled to define them. Part of the problem is that each term originates in a different language: *daruqachi* from Mongolian, *basqaq* from a Turkic term, *daluhuachi* from Chinese and *shahna* from Persian derived from Arabic. The second problem is that in some places the terms seem to serve as synonyms while in other sources it is implied that their meanings are not the same. The final problem in understanding these terms is that their meanings evolved and changed over time.

The clearest indication that the terms *basqaq* and *shahna* were synonyms appears in the pre-Mongol era of Turkestan. During the war between Muhammad Khwarazmshah and the Gur-Khan of Qara Khitai, Tort Aba, the governor of Samarqand, is described as a *shahna* in one place and then as *basqaq*.[33] While it is possible that Juwayni, who wrote a history of the Khwarazmshahs, simply utilised terminology in current use in the Mongol Empire, it seems unlikely that the Mongols would have altered the local terminology in order to create a new bureaucratic ranking system.

There is little question that during the period of the *Yeke Monggol Ulus*, the *daruqachi* and the *basqaq* were the same office. The *basqaq* was an official used in Qara Khitai. The office of *daruqachi* was first used between 1206 and 1214 when it first appeared in China.[34] Although Chinggis Khan initiated their use, Ogodei expanded their presence. He instituted *daruqachin* (plural of *daruqachi*) throughout North China. Their primary purpose, as Buell notes, 'seems to have been integration of local administrative systems

---

[32] See David Morgan, 'Mongol or Persian', 62–76.
[33] Juvaini/Boyle, 349 and 351; Juwayni/Qazvini, v2, 81 and 83. On p. 349 *shahna* is used, but on p. 351 Tort Aba is referred to as a *basqaq*.
[34] Paul D. Buell, 'Tribe, Qan, and Ulus in Early Mongol China, Some Prolegomena to Yuan History', Ph.D. dissertation, University of Washington, 1977, 33.

based on these cities, and much was simply taken over unchanged at the time of conquest, with the imperial establishment at large'.³⁵ The presence of the *daruqachin* extended beyond northern China, as seventy-two d*aruqachin* were present in the portion of Korea under Mongol control. A *yeke daruqachi* (high *daruqachi*) may have also existed, although conclusive evidence is not apparent.³⁶ Through the pairing of a *daruqachi* with a local official, a dual administration emerged, local or regional below a Mongol stratum.

According to Carpini, after a conquest the Mongols placed *basqaqs* in countries where they supervised the region and suppressed rebellion.³⁷ In Russia, the institution of *basqaq* began in 1245. The Mongols stationed *basqaqs* in the forest zone, although the khans of the Golden Horde later recalled them. Yet when they were present, the *basqaq* collected or farmed out taxes to whoever would bring in the highest yield and conscripted troops.³⁸

The *daruqachi* were placed in cities and regions of the sedentary world and were accountable to the *Qa'an*. They supervised local governments as well as collecting taxes and sent revenues to the *Qa'an*. They could lead local armies if necessary, but most importantly, through their offices they served as liaisons between local power structures and the imperial government.³⁹

The imposition of the *daruqachin* over the conquered occurred fairly early in the development of the Mongol Empire and perhaps prior to the appearance of the *daruqachin* in North China. Chinggis Khan appointed two Uighurs as *daruqachin* in two small villages in Uighurstan. Curiously, there is no evidence that he assigned *daruqachin* to larger cities in the region.⁴⁰ This is probably due to the lack of change in Uighurstan, as it had been left in the control of the Idiqut, or the ruler of the Uighurs.⁴¹

As mentioned previously, one of the primary duties of the *daruqachi* was to oversee and carry out the registration of the population in a census. The census was carried out on a fairly regular basis, and often the census-takers were protected by a local dynast. Thomas T. Allsen has noted that local

---

³⁵ Buell, *Tribe, Qan, and Ulus*, 87.
³⁶ Buell, *Tribe, Qan, and Ulus*, 90–1.
³⁷ *JPC*, 86; JPC/Dawson, 40.
³⁸ Charles J. Halperin, *Russia and the Golden Horde: The Mongol Impact on Medieval Russian History* (Bloomington, 1985), 33–5.
³⁹ Buell, *Tribe, Qan, and Ulus*, 32–3.
⁴⁰ Thomas T. Allsen, 'The Yuan Dynasty and the Uighurs of Turfan in the 13th Century', in *China Among Equals*, ed. Morris Rossabi (Berkeley, 1983), 251–2. The Uighur cities are not listed in paragraph 263 of the SHM.
⁴¹ Allsen, 'The Yuan Dynasty and the Uighurs of Turfan in the 13th Century', 251–2. This changed with the reign of Ogodei, as under his reign Uighurstan came under the control of Mahmud Yalavach, then Masᶜud Beg, who was headquartered in Beshbaliq.

dynasts as well as the regional khans and princes throughout the empire were to provide support during the census, whether administrative or military.[42] During the invasion of the Khwarazmian Empire, after Jochi conquered the city of Khwarazm he made Chin-Temur, a Qara Khitan, *basqaq* of the region. His position is quite illustrative of the duties and responsibilities of the office. In 1230, several years later after Chin-Temur's appointment, Ogodei issued a *jarligh* or edict that the leaders and *basqaqs* on every side should accompany the levy and render assistance to Chormaqan, the *tammachi* in Iran. Chin-Temur assisted him and also placed at Chormaqan's disposal other commanders representing the Chinggisid princes.[43] In this capacity, Chin-Temur exercised some military command and had authority to quell insurrection.[44]

As with many terms, the meanings of *basqaq*, *daruqaci* and *shahna* changed over the course of time until they no longer held the same definition. Charles Halperin, in discussing the terminology in the Jochid Ulus, noted that by the fourteenth century the *basqaq* had become the equivalent of a nineteenth-century British colonial viceroy, while the *daruqachi* became more similar to a state department desk officer who advised but lacked operational responsibilities. Thus, in his view, although the *basqaq* and *daruqaci* held synonymous meanings at one point, by the fourteenth century, Halperin acknowledges, the two terms were no longer synonymous.[45]

Not all scholars concur with this view, however. Donald Ostrowski views the *basqaq* as a military governor and the *daruqachi* and the *shahna* as civilian governors. A *tammachi*, according to Ostrowski, was the same as a *basqaq*.[46] According to Ostrowski, there is no evidence suggesting anything other than that a *tammachi* could be a *basqaq* in charge of other *basqaqs*.[47]

Istvan Vasary has determined, correctly in this writer's opinion, that the meaning of *daruqachi* changed over time and place but that it always had a common feature: the *daruqachi* was a chief official or a superior of a territorial or administrative unit. Vasary assumes that '[a]s the chief task of civil administration in a feudal nomadic state like the Golden Horde was to assure regular taxation of the subjects, the daruga's [sic] function was surely connected with taxation'.[48] Furthermore, there must have been a state rev-

---

[42] Thomas T. Allsen, 'Mongol Census Taking in Rus', 1245–1275', *HUS* 5/1 (1981), 47–8.
[43] Juwayni/Qazvini, v2, 218; Juvaini/Boyle, 482.
[44] Juvaini/Boyle, 483; Juwayni/Qazvini, v2, 219.
[45] Halperin, *Russia and the Golden Horde: The Mongol Impact on Medieval Russian History*, 39.
[46] Donald Ostrowski, 'The *Tamma* and the Dual-administrative Structure of the Mongol Empire', *BSOAS* 61 (1998), 262 and 275–6.
[47] Ostrowski, '*Tamma*', 264–5.
[48] Istvan Vasary, 'The Golden Horde Term Daruga and Its Survival in Russia', *AOH* 30 (1976), 188.

enue to supervise the collection of taxes. The Soviet scholar Berezin, however, believed that the *daruga* made the census on the subjects while the *basqaq*s did the conquering.[49]

Vasary, as did Claude Cahen, concluded that the terms *basqaq*, *shahna* and *daruqachi* possessed different origins; however, under the Mongols, their meanings became unified and the terms became interchangeable. Furthermore, only 'a certain territorial distribution can be observed'.[50] In China and in the Jochid Ulus both terms were used; over time, however, *basqaq* simply disappeared. *Daruga* (the Russian equivalent of *daruqachi*) was the only term used by the fourteenth century and *daruga* also took on a certain level of status.[51] *Shahna* remained prevalent in the Middle East. The Mongols systematised and universalised local practices, so that while local governance institutions remained intact, the Mongols also applied institutions from one region in other regions.

Patrimonies

While the Mongol imperial government governed military districts through *tammachin* and commanders (*noyan* (sing.)/*noyad* (pl.)) and governed sedentary populations through local dynasts and *daruqachin* while collecting taxes in fiscal districts, there was another layer of administration. While the imperial government attempted to form a cohesive government that could rule an empire, it also had to contend with the Chinggisid princes, who viewed the empire as their own possession.

The root of the problem existed in the inheritance structures of the Turko-Mongolian nomads. Ideally, the youngest son inherited the home pastures while his elder brothers acquired their own.[52] In this way, Chinggis Khan apportioned his own empire among his sons. Jochi was assigned territories to the west. The exact border was 'as far in that direction as the hoof of the Tartar horse has penetrated'.[53] At the 1206 *quriltai*, this meant just beyond

---

[49] I. N Berezin, *Tarchannye jarlyki Tochtamyka, Temur Kuluka i Saadet-Gireja* (Kazan', 1851), 45; Vasary, 'The Golden Horde Term Daruga and Its Survival in Russia', 188.

[50] Istvan Vasary, 'The Origin of the Institution of Basqaqs', *AOH* 32 (1978), 201; Claude Cahen, *Pre-Ottoman Turkey*, trans. J. Jones-Williams (New York, 1968), 41. Cahen concluded that the term *basqaq* was the Persian *shahna* or *shihna*, who were the police chiefs or garrison commanders of the Seljuks. *Basqaq* and *shahna* thus became synonyms during that period.

[51] Vasary, 'The Origin of the Institution of Basqaqs', 201.

[52] Isenbike Togan, 'Otichigin's Place in the Transformation from Family to Dynasty', in Istvan Zimonyi and Osman Karatay (eds), *Central Eurasia in the Middle Ages: Studies in Honour of Peter B. Golden* (Wiesbaden, 2016), 408.

[53] Juwayni/Qazvini, v1, 31; Juvaini/Boyle, 42.

the Altai Mountains. By the 1220s it meant as far as the Black Sea, even if the Mongols did not control it. Tolui received most of Mongolia as his patrimony, while Chaghadai received Mawarannahr and much of Kyrgyzstan and modern Xingjiang. Ogodei's territories overlapped with modern Xinjiang, Mongolia and Kazakhstan. These patrimonies or *uluses* were subordinate to the khan, but in the khan's absence the Chinggisid princes possessed a considerable degree of autonomy, with one prince of a particular branch usually being the highest authority. The Mongols referred to the empire as the *Yeke Monggol Ulus*, meaning it was the people and lands belonging to the Mongols. The patrimonies assigned to Chinggis Khan's sons could rightly be viewed in the same way – as the Jochid Ulus (*Ulus-un Jochi*) (lands and peoples belonging to the family of Jochi), etc. In addition, members of the *altan urugh* and even the khan possessed territories known as *inju*.

Inju originally meant property, meaning the dowry that accompanied a wife, which consisted of material goods, livestock, and even people who accompanied the woman as servants. Most importantly, it was hereditary. Overtime, *inju* property also included land (such as villages and towns) and provided considerable income for the princely class. Additionally, the *Qa'an* himself had what might be termed the *royal inju*, which provided him with wealth outside of the official revenue of the state. He could dispose of his *inju* territories as he saw fit. As such, *inju* could be given as a gift. New conquests automatically became the *inju* of the *Qa'an*, although often the territory could be assigned ahead of time.[54]

Additionally, there was *qubi* territory. *Qubi* literally meant share. As the *altan urugh* often viewed the empire as their property, it was not surprising that the princely families had possessions and interests that were not contiguous with their own appanages. In some cases, a city or region might be *qubi* for all four branches, with an agreement made on the division of revenues. In the conquest of the Jin Empire, much of the territory became *qubi* and was exploited by the princes. The creation of a rational civil government helped mitigate the abuses and converted much of the *qubi* territory into imperial land or *dalay*, meaning that tax revenues went directly to the state coffers and imperial officials governed this territory. *Qubi* territory did not disappear, however. It continued to exist but became more systematic. It also helped ensure that the members of the *altan urugh* did not become too provincial and remained interested in the whole empire. After all, while the Jochids

---

[54] See Kazuhiko Shiraiwa, 'Inju in the Jami' al-Tavarikh of Rashid al-Din', *AOASH* 42 (1988), 371–6; Petrushevsky, 'The Socio-economic Condition', 516, 525–7; A. K. S. Lambton, *Continuity and Change in Medieval Persia*, 118; H. F. Schurmann, 'Mongolian Tributary Practices', 330.

might be content to stay in the Pontic steppes, if they collected revenues from conquests in central China, that part of the empire also necessitated their attention.[55] There were times when *inju* and *qubi* were confiscated, usually due to death without heirs or after rebellion, and converted to *dalay* territories.[56]

It is important to note that the administration of the Mongol Empire often appeared a work in progress. While there is some truth to the statement that some wanted 'to reintroduce Chinese bureaucratic government and rationalize the system of taxation [but] were thwarted by the stiff opposition of the Mongol nobility and the keen competition of the Muslim tax-farmers',[57] this is not the complete picture. As far back as 1206 there were structures in place to help guide the empire, even in the absence of the empire. Although it gradually coalesced into a more rational system, this did not happen at once. Initially, everything was administered as part of a princely patrimony or through *tammachin*.

The creation of an organised civil government took years and expanded over time to the sedentary regions that the Mongols ruled the longest. At the local level, change from the previous administration and that of the Mongols may not have been apparent, as the imperial government was often just a new layer operating above the local. Taxes may have been higher, but in many areas they also decreased as the Mongols eliminated many tolls and tithes on commerce. Yet, change nonetheless occurred that indicated that the empire was marching towards an increasing centralisation of authority. Only the dissolution of the empire in 1260 appears to have halted that progress and opened the door to a return to less systematic governance.

---

[55] Paul D. Buell, 'Saiyid Ajall (1211–1279)', in Rachewiltz et al (eds), *ITSOTK* (Wiesbaden, 1993), 469.

[56] A. K. S. Lambton, *Continuity and Change in Medieval Persia*, 118; A. K. S. Lambton, 'Mongol Fiscal Administration in Persia', *Studia Islamica* 64 (1986), 83–4, fn. 5; Schurmann, 'Mongolian Tributary Practices', 330.

[57] Igor de Rachewiltz, Hok-lam Chan, Hsiao Ch'i-ch'ing and Peter W. Geier (eds), *ITSOTK* (Wiesbaden, 1993), xi.

5

The Reign of Ogodei

The reign of Ogodei began with the *quriltai* of 1229, when he was selected *Qa'an* of the *Yeke Monggol Ulus*. Although Tolui had every right to make the case that he was a more qualified candidate, he remained true to his word and supported his brother's ascent to power.

At the *quriltai*, Ogodei performed a perfunctory refusal of his nomination, saying that his brothers and uncles were far worthier. He noted that Tolui was worthier and that, as the youngest son of Chinggis Khan, it was the *yosun* or custom that he take his father's place and possessions. As the Mongols viewed the conquests as the possession of Chinggis Khan, everything should belong to Tolui. Ogodei also noted that Tolui knew the *yosun* and *yasa* (laws, ordinances) better than he. Naturally, the assembled commanders and princes refused and insisted on his selection as the successor of Chinggis Khan. In the end, the princes all removed their hats and placed their belts on their shoulders, a traditional demonstration of obeisance, and placed him on the throne. It was done quite literally as Chaghadai took his right arm as Tolui grasped the left. Temuge Otchigin, their uncle, then lifted him by the belt and placed him on the throne. Then, the princes came forward one by one and bowed before him and called him *Qa'an*.[1]

As many of the sources were written with the patronage of rulers descended from Tolui, one must also be careful with their account of Tolui. Professor Peter Jackson has amply demonstrated that the Toluid sources took pains to demonstrate Toluid legitimacy, particularly with the dissolution of the empire.[2] Some events, however, may also suggest that the Toluids were never comfortable with Ogodei's ascension. In Juwayni's seemingly innocuous account, Ogodei protests his appointment by saying, 'Ulugh Noyan [Tolui] is the youngest son of the eldest *ordu* [sic] and was ever in attendance on Chingiz-Khan [sic] day and night, morning and evening, and has seen,

---

[1] RD/Thackston2, 222; RD/Thackston1, 312; RD/Karimi, 453; Juvaini/Boyle, 186–7; Juwayni/Qazvini, v1, 146–7; *YUS*, 47.

[2] Peter Jackson, 'The Dissolution of the Mongol Empire', *CAJ* 22 (1978), 186–244.

and heard, and learnt all his *yasas* and customs. Seeing that that all these are alive and here present, how may I succeed to the Khanate?'[3]

As Isenbike Togan has indicated, this particular passage suggests that Tolui had dynastic claims to the throne, even though succession was not based on ultimogeniture.[4] Although Juwayni wrote his history after the sack of Baghdad in 1258, one must wonder where he learned of this statement as Juwayni himself was not present at the 1229 *quriltai*. While it is a bit of a throwaway line demonstrating Ogodei's humbleness and bolstering later Toluid legitimacy, this segment also hints at Tolui's own pretensions.

In addition to raising Ogodei to the throne, Tolui turned over the *keshig* and the central state (*qol-un ulus-i*), demonstrating that not only his regency had ended, but also any claim to the throne.[5] The fact that Tolui once possessed the *keshig* is not an indication that he sought power. As the youngest son of Chinggis Khan and Borte, he inherited the *ordo* or camp of Chinggis Khan, to which the *keshig* belonged and which it protected. It is also a clear indication that Tolui served as regent. The allocation of the 'central *ulus*' is somewhat curious as Ogodei's own *ulus* was located between the Emil and Qobuk Rivers, not in Mongolia. One may conjecture that the *qol-un ulus* was perhaps *dalay* land, meant to support the imperial government as it included the Orkhon River basin and was more centrally located to rule the new empire than the Kerulen-Onan River basin. In effect, Tolui handed Ogodei the 'reins of government'.[6]

Ogodei's own refusal of the throne was not just humility, but part of a court drama to demonstrate that he took the throne only because the rest of the elite wanted him to rule. Yet, by refusing the throne, one was always taking a calculated risk since it might not be offered again, as Raymond of Toulouse learned much to his chagrin during the First Crusade.[7] While Ogodei may have had his private doubts and Tolui may have also desired it, there was little chance that the commanders and companions of Chinggis Khan would have permitted any deviation from Chinggis Khan's succession.

---

[3] Juvaini/Boyle, 186; Juwayni/Qazvini, v1, 146.
[4] Isenbike Togan, 'Otchigin's Place in the Transformation from Family to Dynasty', in *CEMA*, 408. On succession see Michal Biran, *Qaidu and the Rise of the Independent Mongol State in Central Asia* (London, 1997), 8 and 134; Joseph F. Fletcher, 'Turco-Mongolian Tradition in the Ottoman Empire', *HUS* 3/4 (1979–80), 239.
[5] *SHM*, §269.
[6] Thomas T. Allsen, 'The Rise of the Mongolian Empire and Mongolian Rule in North China', in Twitchett and Fairbank (eds), *CHCAR*, 367–8.
[7] Christopher Tyerman, *God's War: A New History of the Crusades* (Cambridge, MA, 2006), 159; Thomas F. Madden, *The Concise History of the Crusades* (Lanham, MD, 2014), 36.

Figure 5.1 Ogodei Khan established the true functioning administration of the Mongol Empire. This statue is located in the Chinggis Khan pavilion in Sukhbaatar Square, Ulaanbaatar.

With his enthronement came the inevitable celebration. Treasure was awarded to the relatives, the commanders and the commoners. Sacrifices of food were made to Chinggis Khan, along with forty beautiful women, all from the families of the military commanders, and prized horses to attend to Chinggis Khan's needs in the afterlife.[8] Then Ogodei's reign truly began.

Although fond of pleasure, Ogodei also took his duties seriously. His first decree verified that all of Chinggis Khan's ordinances remained in effect and without alteration. He pardoned all crimes committed prior to his enthronement, but warned that any new transgressions would be punished.[9] In addition, the Mongols began to plan the next phase of the empire. By this time, the Mongols remained in awe that Chinggis Khan's rise had led not only to the unification of Mongolia, but also to their expansion well beyond their homeland. It was as if *Tenggeri* (Heaven) had decreed the earth to the Mongols. Moreover, the Mongols developed an ideology asserting this claim. While some attribute this to Chinggis Khan, it seems more likely that the idea

[8] RD/Thackston2, 222; RD/Thackston1, 312; RD/Karimi, 445; Juwayni/Qazvini, v1, 149; Juvaini/Boyle, 189.
[9] Juwayni/Qazvini, v1, 149; Juvaini/Boyle, 189–90.

manifested after Chinggis Khan's death. *The Secret History of the Mongols*, at least in some form, also came into being at this time – a record of the life of Chinggis Khan complete with events that demonstrated that Chinggis Khan and his heirs were destined to rule the world.[10]

To that end, the Mongols prepared to live up to *Tenggeri*'s decree. The first priority was to eliminate the Jin. Since the death of Muqali in 1223, the war had entered a stalemate with neither side able to make headway. Ogodei and Tolui would lead the expedition. Subedei was also given permission to venture into the western steppes as far as the Volga River to secure Mongol claims made by Jochi during the Khwarazmian campaign. In 1230, Ogodei also dispatched Chormaqan Noyan, a *qorchi* or quiver bearer from the *keshig*, across the Amu Darya. Part of his army was to deal with Jalal al-Din Khwarazmshah's return from India into Khurasan. Another force, led by Chormaqan's lieutenant Dayir, entered present-day Afghanistan to bring those territories under Mongol control. Although the Mongols had conquered the region during the reign of Chinggis Khan, they did not leave an army of occupation. Finally, troops were also sent into Siberia to secure tribute from tribes beyond the known *Hoi-yin Irgen* territory.[11]

The Jin Campaign

In 1230, the Mongol army returned to the Jin Empire in force. The campaign went well. Tolui continued in his father's footsteps and demonstrated his battlefield acumen. Like his father, however, he could not elude death (1232). Some accounts indicate that he died of alcoholism, while others offer another, more dramatic interpretation in which Ogodei is on his deathbed.[12] Here, Tolui offers himself to the spirits so that they might spare the Great Khan, saying: 'I have sinned more, for I have deprived so many people of life and taken their women and children captive and caused them to weep. If you

---

[10] Thomas T. Allsen, 'A Note on Mongol Imperial Ideology', in *EMLCH*, 1–8; Sh. Bira, 'Mongolian Tenggerism and Modern Globalism: A Restrospective Outlook on Globalisation', *IA* 5 (2003), 107–17; Igor de Rachewiltz, 'Some Remarks on the Ideological Foundations of Chingis Khan's Empire', *PFEH* 7 (1973), 21–36. On the composition of the *SHM*, see Igor de Rachewiltz, 'Introduction', in Igor de Rachewiltz (ed.), *The Secret History of the Mongols*, vol. 1 (Leiden, 2004), xxv–xl; Christopher P. Atwood, 'How the Secret History of the Mongols Was Written', *Mongolica* 49 (2016), 22–53; Christopher P. Atwood, 'Validation by Holiness or Sovereignty: Religious Toleration as Political Theology in the Mongol World Empire of the Thirteenth Century', *IHR* 26/2 (2004), 237–56.

[11] *SHM*, §269–70; Juwayni/Qazvini, v1, 149, 150; Juvaini/Boyle, 190; RD/Thackston2, 222–3; RD/Thackston1, 313; RD/Karimi, 454–5.

[12] Juwayni/Qazvini, v3, 3; Juvaini/Boyle, 549; RD/Thackston2, 224; RD/Thackston1, 316; RD/Karimi, 459; SHM, §272. Juwayni simply says Tolui died by drinking in excess.

are taking the Qa'an away on account of beauty and skill, I am better looking and more skilled. Leave him and take me instead.'[13] Even here the accounts differ and fit their cultural context. Another possibility is that Ogodei had Tolui murdered or consented to the shamans sacrificing his brother, and that Tolui had little choice in the matter.[14] While Ogodei is often depicted as jovial figure, he could be as ruthless as his father.[15]

Despite the untimely death of Tolui, the war continued. Ogodei recalled Subedei from the Volga. Subedei now led the campaign and by 1233 he had reduced the Jin Empire to the environs of Kaifeng.[16] With the Jin threat eliminated and now reduced to a narrow body of land, Subedei returned to the western frontier to prepare for another campaign. At this time, the Song Empire to the south sought an alliance with the Mongols. The Song, who had formed an alliance with the Jin against the Liao Dynasty (907–1125) before them, thought that with the Jin removed, they would then be able to retake lands lost to the Song in the tenth century. The Song's military contribution was largely inconsequential – the Jin routinely defeated them. Nonetheless, the Song provided valuable logistical support, particularly in the form of food supplies for the Mongols. In 1234, Kaifeng fell and even though the Jin Emperor escaped to another small city, his days were numbered and before the end of the year the Jin Empire ceased to exist. The Song, not having learned from their experience with the Jin, then attempted to take territory from the Mongols. Ogodei was furious, and not only did the Song quickly find themselves losing territory in the former Jin Empire, but Mongol incursions into the Song Empire began as well.[17]

With the defeat of the Jin Empire, Ogodei turned his attention to ruling his empire. After Tolui's death, Ogodei did not take an active role in the conquest of the Jin Empire. He lacked the military talent of his brother and his father, but that was not why Chinggis Khan chose him as his successor. In Ogodei, he saw a greater ability to rule than in any of his other sons and Ogodei proved him right. While Chinggis Khan founded the empire, in

---

[13] RD/Thackston2, 224; RD/Thackston1, 316; RD/Karimi, 459; SHM,§272.
[14] Christopher P. Atwood, 'The Sacrificed Brother in the *Secret History of the Mongols*', *MS* 31 (2009), 200–2.
[15] Also see Christopher P. Atwood, 'Pu'a's Boast and Dolqolqu's Death: Historiography of a Hidden Scandal in the Mongol Conquest of the Jin', Conference on Middle Period China, 800–1400, Harvard University, 5–7 June 2014.
[16] Thomas T. Allsen, 'The Rise of the Mongolian Empire', in Herbert Franke and Denis Twitchett (eds), *CHCAR*, 32. See Atwood, 'Pu'a's Boast and Dolqolqu's Death' for more on Dolqolqu.
[17] RD/Karimi, 460–2; RD/Thackston2, 225; RD/Thackston, 1998, 316–18; Allsen, 'Rise of the Mongolian Empire', 372.

many ways Ogodei was the true architect of the empire. Although he followed the examples of his father, he also dealt with new situations.

Ruling the Empire

One of Ogodei's major achievements was the establishment of a capital. It was one thing to rule from a military camp as his father had done while conquering territory; it was quite another to actually rule an empire after the conquest. His tax collectors needed a definite location to which to send tax revenue; subjects needed a place where they could seek redress for grievances; envoys had to be able to find the ruler. The Daoist monk, Changchun zi, was summoned by Chinggis Khan in 1219. As the Mongol ruler invaded the Khwarazmian Empire in the same year, Changchun zi had difficulty finding him, travelling first to Mongol camps in the occupied Jin Empire before proceeding to the Onon-Kerulen basin in northern Mongolia. Temuge Otchigin, Chinggis Khan's brother and regent, then sent the elderly monk in the wake of Chinggis Khan's march to Central Asia. He eventually found the Mongol ruler in modern Afghanistan, in the Hindu Kush Mountains. While it may have been an epic game of hide and seek, clearly this was not the way to conduct personal meetings or diplomacy.

To this end, Ogodei ordered the construction of the city of Qaraqorum in 1235. He chose a site in the Orkhon Valley, which had historic connotations. Previous empires had also used the valley for their own capitals and had even built sizeable towns there, such as the Uighurs' Qarabalghasun.[18] There is some indication that Chinggis Khan planned to use the location as his primary *a'uruq* or base serving as the centre of the *qol-un ulus*.[19] To be certain, Ogodei did not abandon his nomadic life. While the city was built, he nomadised and held court. Using the labour acquired through the conquest of the Jin and the numerous artisans that they imported from the Khwarazmian Empire, the Mongols had the labour and talent necessary to build the city. A number of the Central Asian and Chinese artisans had already been settled in a city known as Chinqai Balghasun, Chinqai City, which also served as a logistical base in western Mongolia. Chinqai was a chamberlain in the empire's bureaucracy, along with Mahmud Yalavach and Yelu Chucai.[20] Chinggis Khan had originally ordered the former caravaneer to build his city with a *tumen* of Chinese prisoners. Originally, it served as

---

[18] Larry W. Moses, 'A Theoretical Approach to the Process of Inner Asian Confederation', *EM* 5 (1974), 113–22.
[19] Igor de Rachewiltz, *SHM*, v2 (Leiden, 2004), 988.
[20] See Paul D. Buell, 'Cinqai', in Igor de Rachewiltz, et al. (eds), *ITSOTK*, 95–100. He was either a Kereit or an Onggud.

Figure 5.2 Qarabalghasun was the capital of the Uighur Empire in the eighth and ninth centuries. Made of earthen walls, much of the citadel remains despite the eroding winds of Mongolia. Orkhon Valley, Mongolia.

state farm but it also evolved into an industrial complex that manufactured goods and weapons for the empire.

Qaraqorum was not a large city. Perhaps no more than 10,000 people populated it.[21] Nonetheless, it was large enough for 900 cartloads a day to be needed to feed the population, most of which consisted of non-Mongols – Han Chinese, Central Asians, Persians, and later even captives from Europe. Even after the completion of the palace, now occupied by the Erdene Zuu monastery, Ogodei and later Mongol khans did not reside in the city. Instead, it served more as 'the office' while they resided in their nomadic camps, moving periodically in the vicinity of the city. When necessary, the khan came to the city to conduct business. The bureaucracy, however, resided largely in the city, which also contained numerous storehouses built specifically to hold the ever-increasing treasury of the Mongol Empire.[22] Furthermore, markets were built to accommodate the growing number of merchants who ventured into Mongolia.[23]

[21] Rubruck/Dawson, 183–4; Rubruck/Jackson, 221; Rubruc, 285.
[22] Rubruck/Dawson, 175; Rubruck/Jackson, 209; Rubruc, 276.
[23] Rubruck/Dawson, 177; Rubruck/Jackson, 211; Rubruc, 278.

Figure 5.3 Erdene Zuu, a Buddhist monastery built in the sixteenth century, sits atop the ruins of Qaraqorum. Kharkhorin, Mongolia.

Although merchants had previous visited Mongolia from abroad, the traffic increased dramatically. This was assisted by Ogodei's generous style of negotiations, in which he often paid double or more for goods regardless of the quality. While the sources clearly show the frustration of his advisors, Ogodei's cavalier attitude towards wealth was not without reason.[24] He realised that in order to make Qaraqorum a desired location for merchants he needed to provide incentives. While the so-called Silk Road was not known by that name until the late nineteenth century, there were well-travelled caravan routes that criss-crossed Eurasia. Ogodei made Qaraqorum a major hub and even had personal shopping assistants ride to meet the merchants as they approached the city so that they could inspect the goods and inform the khan as to what they carried.

With the arrival of the merchants, amenities were necessary. These included religious buildings. Daoist and Buddhist temples sat in view of Muslim mosques and a Christian church.[25] Ogodei continued Chinggis Khan's policy

[24] Juvaini/Boyle, 198, 214–15; Juwayni/Qazvini, v1, 156, 170–1.
[25] Rubruck/Dawson, 184; Rubruck/Jackson, 221; Rubruc, 286.

of religious toleration or indifference, although that never stopped the various faiths from trying to convince the Mongol rulers that one faith was superior to others. As long as the various religious sects included the khan in their prayers and did not cause trouble, anyone could practise their faith without interference. Yet, this policy should not be viewed as one of enlightened philanthropy.[26] There is evidence that the Mongols initially struggled with their own claim to universal rule and religious toleration. This is not to say that they wished everyone to convert to their own form of shamanism or that everyone should worship the *Koke Mongke Tenggeri*, or Blue Eternal Sky. Rather, the Mongols had to adjust to the idea that the *yasa* and *yosun* of Chinggis Khan did not represent a perfect legal system for an entire empire.

Food Preparation

Legal tensions arose not only from major philosophical differences, such as over property, but also ubiquitous events. A major source of contention was the slaughtering of animals. The pastoral nomads of the steppes traditionally placed an animal on its back, made a small slit in the animal's chest and then either squeezed the heart until it stilled or cut an artery so that the animal died somewhat peacefully through internal bleeding. The nomads were careful not to spill any of the blood; they scooped it out and kept it to make blood sausages and other foods. Muslims, however, had a religious mandate of *halal* meat, meaning that an animal's throat was slit with a single stroke and the blood drained while a prayer was uttered. This religio-cultural difference could make meals awkward as Muslims could not eat meat prepared in the Mongol fashion. To be sure, not all Muslims were as particular, but for the devout it was a serious issue that could cause tension when meeting with Mongol officials.

Chaghadai, Ogodei's elder brother, was renowned for his knowledge of the *yasa* and *yosun*. For that reason, he would have made an excellent khan in the eyes of some. Chinggis Khan, however, recognised that Chaghadai was also too stern and too narrow in his interpretation of tradition while lacking Ogodei's liberal perspective on life.[27] In the Islamic sources, Chaghadai is depicted as unwavering in his commitment to the traditions of his father, and assisted his brother by enforcing the *yasa* throughout the realm. It was said that 'a woman with a golden vessel on her head might walk alone without

---

[26] David Morgan, *The Mongols*, 2nd edn (Oxford, 2007), 38–40.
[27] Juwayni/Qazvini, v1, 226–7; Juvaini/Boyle, 271–2; *SHM*, §242.

fear or dread'.²⁸ Security was an obvious benefit for all, but his unstinting enforcement of the *yasa* also had negative consequences. Under his purview, Muslims were forced to eat carrion and other meat slaughtered in non-*halal* fashion.²⁹ Ogodei, however, is depicted as a just ruler, albeit a heathen. In Muslim depictions of the brothers, Ogodei counters Chaghadai's fanatical adherence to the *yasa* and supports religious toleration.³⁰

One must be careful not to read 'religious toleration' in a twenty-first-century connotation (or perhaps twentieth-century connotation, as the current century appears thus far to be less tolerant than the previous one). One should read it with a very literal interpretation. Ogodei tolerated other religions. He being the ruler of an empire comprising a poly-ethnic, poly-religious population, his primary concern was stability. The often-playful banter and contrasting behaviour between Chaghadai and Ogodei has obvious religious tensions in it; however, it should also be viewed as a debate as to how the empire should be ruled. There is no question that the Mongols viewed the empire as their possession, but should everyone be a Mongol? Clearly, that was not possible. Even in war, the Mongols tended to view the enemy more as livestock to be herded than as human beings.³¹ Yet would applying the *yasa* of Chinggis Khan to the subjects create a stable empire, or would it create instability? This is the question that Chaghadai and Ogodei debated, whether or not the chroniclers realised it. While Chaghadai represented the *yasa* as the only legal code, Ogodei viewed it as suitable for the nomads, but recognised that other systems exist. Just as applying the Jin legal system to Central Asia or Islamic law to Manchuria would have caused chaos, one could not apply the *yasa* to sedentary cultures whose lifestyles were as alien to the Mongols as the Mongols' customs were foreign to them. Ogodei being *Qa'an*, his view won, but not without substantial time and effort being expended in convincing Chaghadai and perhaps other conservative members of the ruling elite. Even more remarkable is that Chaghadai showed no interest in reversing course after Ogodei's death. As a result, the Mongols not only maintained their religious toleration, but also allowed existing legal and cultural norms to exist and coexist under the aegis of the *yasa*.³²

---

[28] Juvaini/Boyle, 272, Juwayni/Qazvini, v2, 227.
[29] Juvaini/Boyle, 272; Juwayni/Qazvini, v2, 227.
[30] Johan Elverskog, *Buddhism and Islam on the Silk Road* (Philadelphia, 2010), 237.
[31] Timothy May, 'Livestock and Warfare: Livestock Herding as Warfare in the Mongol Empire', paper presented at the Central Eurasian Studies Society Conference, 3–6 October 2013, The University of Wisconsin-Madison, Madison, Wisconsin.
[32] For more on the *yasa*, see David O. Morgan, 'The "Great *Yasa* of Chinggis Khan" Revisited', in *MTO*, 291–308.

Figure 5.4 The Tortoise of Qaraqorum. A stelae once mounted its back. Its face is discoloured from various offerings, including alcohol and even gummy worms. It is the only intact large object from Qaraqorum. Erdene Zuu is in the background. Kharkhorin, Mongolia.

In addition to building his capital and developing a more comprehensive method of ruling the sedentary populations, Ogodei also invested in the infrastructure of the empire. As discussed previously, the civil administration developed into a rational functioning bureaucracy under the guidance of Yelu Chucai, Mahmud Yalavach and Chinqai. Chinqai, in particular, saw his star rise during the reign of Ogodei and became the prime minister in a sense. As the empire continued to grow, it also became increasingly necessary to ensure that decrees made in Qaraqorum reached the far corners of the empire.

Chinggis Khan began the *jam* (*yam*) system, in which riders switched horses or were replaced at different stations, situated every 20–30 miles apart. In areas not conducive to riding, runners were used. The *jam*, however, did not extend greatly beyond Mongolia at the time of his death.[33] Ogodei extended it, and also developed a system of passports made from wood,

---

[33] See Adam J. Silverstein, *Postal Systems in the Pre-Modern Islamic World* (Cambridge, 2007), 141–64 for a study of the *yam* and discussion of its antecedents.

Figure 5.5 Modern presentation of a *yam* station. The horses were saddled and ready for a messenger to arrive. Note the brand or *tamgha* on the horse in the forefront. This *tamgha* not only helped in the return of the horse, but also noted who contributed to the *yam* system.

iron, silver and gold that indicated the importance of the carrier.[34] The level of passport also dictated what resources the bearer had access to at the *jam* stations – food, horses, lodging, etc. The stations themselves were supported by local nomads or the sedentary population. When the system functioned properly, riders could traverse the empire swiftly. When it failed, not only did the flow of communication slow, but the passports allowed government officials and others to exploit the *yam* stations and burden the local population.

Additionally, Ogodei expanded another infrastructure item, which Chinggis Khan initiated. In Mongolia, Ogodei ordered the digging of wells and the construction of protective walls to ensure that animals did not pollute them. While this benefited the armies as they departed Mongolia, it also promoted commerce as caravans coming to Mongolia now had well-watered routes. He also deployed patrols to ensure that the trade routes remained secure, which also bears the hallmarks of Chaghadai's influence in making policy.[35]

[34] *SHM*, §281.
[35] *SHM*, §281.

The Middle East and the Western Campaign

Although the Jin Empire fell after more than twenty years of war, the Mongols did not rest on their laurels. In the Middle East, the army of Chormaqan Noyan remained active. The reason for the invasion centred primarily on the return of Jalal al-Din Khwarazmshah from India. After his defeat by Chinggis Khan, he fled into India and attempted to re-establish himself along the frontiers of the Sultanate of Delhi (1210–1526), whose ruler, Sultan Iltumish, had no interest in seeing the restoration of a Khwarazmian Empire in any form and supported weaker princes against Jalal al-Din's predations. Eventually, Jalal al-Din went west as the Mongols pressured his holdings in Afghanistan. The Sultanate of Delhi's act of neutrality may also have played a role in why the Mongol armies did not attack the Sultanate of Delhi during Chinggis Khan's lifetime.[36]

Between the death of Chinggis Khan and the arrival of Chormaqan Noyan, Chin-Temur, the *daruqachi* of Urgench in Khwarazm, attempted to deal with Jalal al-Din, but without definite success, in 1227 and 1228.[37] The encounters between his troops and Jalal al-Din ended in draws, although Jalal al-Din also garnered enough prestige to rally more support. Nonetheless, Chin-Temur's efforts convinced Jalal al-Din that remaining in Khurasan and eastern Iran only attracted more attention from the Mongols, so he moved his operations westward and attempted to carve out a new kingdom in western Iran and Transcaucasia.

The arrival of Chormaqan's force drastically changed the situation. After crossing the Amu Darya, one portion of his army under Dayir secured Khurasan and then moved into the regions of Ghur and Ghazna in modern Afghanistan, while he led the rest of the army into northern Iran. From here, he dispatched a special task force commanded by Taimaz with the sole purpose of hunting and destroying Jalal al-Din. After a few sieges, the majority of Iran submitted. The Mongols did not even campaign in southern Iran, as regional leaders pre-emptively sent envoys to submit to the Mongol general. Meanwhile, the Nizari Ismailis (often referred to as the Assassins) in the Albruz Mountains and Quhistan appeared to ally themselves with the Mongols against Jalal al-Din.[38]

---

[36] Peter Jackson, *The Delhi Sultanate: A Political and Military History* (Cambridge, 1999), 33–4, 104.

[37] Nesawi/Houdas, 224–33; Nasawi, 232–8; Ibn al-Athir, 470, 476–7; Ibn al-Athir/Richards, 284, 288–9; Juvaini/Boyle, 436–7; Juwayni/Qazvini, v2, 168–9.

[38] Timothy May, 'A Mongol–Ismaili Alliance? Thoughts on the Mongols and Assassins', *JRAS*, 14/3 (2006), 231–9; Ibn al-Athir, 496; Ibn al-Athir/Richards, 303–4.

Only the city of Isfahan continued to resist, which was not surprising as it also served as Jalal al-Din's de facto capital.[39] He, however, was not present to lead its defence. Furthermore, the Mongols did not immediately lay siege to it. The Mongols isolated and monitored the city while Chormaqan consolidated his control of Iran and directed the pursuit of the Khwarazmshah.[40]

Although Jalal al-Din led the Mongols in an extended pursuit through Transcaucasia, he could not escape. Taimaz caught him by surprise in his camp while the prince made merry, secure in the thought that his scouts found no trace of the Mongols for miles. The Khwarazmian veterans resisted fiercely and even distracted the Mongols long enough for Jalal al-Din to escape. The sultan's escape, however, did not save him, as Jalal al-Din was eventually killed, not by the Mongols but by Kurdish peasants or perhaps others.[41] The Mongols used Isfahan as a beacon to attract the Khwarazmian forces, which the Mongols then ambushed. Many Khwarazmians, however, did not attempt to reach Isfahan, but instead sought greener pastures elsewhere. Many served as mercenaries for a number of regional powers before sacking Jerusalem in 1244 while en route to Egypt. Eventually, however, the Ayyubid rulers of Egypt and Syria destroyed them after the Khwarazmians proved too unruly.

In 1233, Chormaqan's forces then advanced to the Mughan plain in modern Azerbaijan. The lush pastures there made it ideal for him to use as a base for his *tamma*.[42] The following year, he expanded his dominion into the region of Arran, sacking Ganjak in 1235. In 1238, he began the invasion of Armenia and Georgia.[43] The conquest went rapidly. Georgia and Armenia, already militarily weakened by the predations of Jalal al-Din in the late 1220s, did not offer any resistance on the battlefield but sought shelter behind their fortifications. While these mountain fortresses slowed the Mongols, Chormaqan's armies steadily reduced them.[44] Nonetheless, the bravery of many Armenian princes caught the eye of Chormaqan and he often expanded their territory after they submitted to him. To be sure, the princes had to pay tribute and provide troops upon request, but

---

[39] Al-Hadid, vol. 3, 81; J. E. Woods, 'A Note on the Mongol Capture of Isfahan', *JNES* 36 (1977), 49–51.
[40] Nasawi, 213; Nesawi/Houdas, 204; Juzjani/Habibi, 157; Juzjani/Raverty, 1,118–19; Juwayni/Qazvini, v1, 214; Juvaini/Boyle, 479.
[41] Juvaini/Boyle, 250; Juwayni/Qazvini, v1, 205; Nuwayri, 297; May, 'A Mongol–Ismaili Alliance?', 239.
[42] Kiracos, 116.
[43] Vartan, 282; Vardan, 214; Kiracos, 116–17; M. Brosset (trans.), *Histoire de la Georgie: Depuis l'Antiquité Jusqu'au XIXe Siècle* (St Petersburg, 1849), 511.
[44] Kiracos, 119–20, 124–5, 126.

the regional sources attest that the local magnates found Chormaqan to be a just overlord.[45]

Not all of the Georgians agreed. In 1238, the Mongols sacked Tiflis (modern Tbilisi) and then divided into three separate columns to wreak further havoc elsewhere in the region.[46] The Georgian ruler, Queen Rusudan, fled to a stronghold in the western part of Georgia, refusing to submit and appealing to Pope Gregory IX (r. 1227–41) for a Crusade.[47] As the rest of Georgia submitted, the Mongols left her isolated until 1243, when she grudgingly submitted to the Mongols through her intermediaries.

Even as Chormaqan conquered Transcaucasia, his armies were active in the rest of the Middle East. Dayir proved successful in Afghanistan and established Mongol rule there. Meanwhile, Mongol contingents raided the Jazira (northern Iraq) and Iraq al-Arabi (southern Iraq), beginning in 1235.[48] This alarmed the Abbasid Caliphate, now a truncated state whose control was limited to much, but not all, of modern Iraq. When the Abbasid army marched against the Mongols, to the Abbasids' surprise the Mongols always withdrew after brief skirmishes.[49] The Mongols only raided the region. At this time, they did not seek conquest. Their limited actions served as a smokescreen with which to cover their conquest of Transcaucasia as well as a much larger campaign further to the north.

In 1236, another major campaign began. This was the Western Campaign, which had two primary objectives. The first and foremost was to create an adequate realm for the descendants of Jochi. The second goal was to bring the Kipchak Turks of the Caspian Steppe to heel and under Mongol control. The Mongols also targeted the kingdom of Bulghar on the Volga River, as they had previously rejected Mongol terms of submission. Bulghar also attacked Subedei's army when it returned from the Kalka River in the 1220s. In the study of this campaign, much attention is given to the conquest of the Rus' principalities as well as the invasion of Europe, but these actions were ancillary to the Mongols' goals.

The Mongols had a fair understanding of the region. During the Khwarazmian War, the generals Subedei and Jebe led a campaign into the *Dasht-i Kipchak*. Departing from Iran, they devastated Armenia and Georgia, but they also defeated an army of Alans and then a joint force of Rus' and

---

[45] Grigor of Akanc, 299–303, 319; Vardan, 214–15.
[46] Kiracos, 124–5.
[47] Brosset, *Histoire de la Georgie*, 514, 516; Peter Jackson, *The Mongols and the West* (Harlow, UK, 2005), 60.
[48] Ibn al-Athir, 501; Ibn al-Athir/Richards, 307–8; BH1, 402; Al-Dhahabi, 233–2.
[49] BH1, 404; Dhahabi, 235; Hadid, v3, 81.

Kipchaks at the Battle of the Kalka River in 1223. Although Jebe died in the prelude to the battle, Subedei successfully led the army across the Volga to link up with Jochi's armies in 1225.[50]

Subedei began operations along the Volga as early as 1229, halting when he assumed command of the final push against the Jin Empire. Operations resumed in 1233 under the leadership of Berke, one of Jochi's sons.[51] During this time, the Mongols gained the Yayiq or Ural River. These were limited gains, however. Not until the *quriltai* of 1234 did the Mongols decide to permanently occupy the *Dasht-i Kipchak* and other territories.[52]

Only the Kipchak nomads proved to be challenging on the battlefield, and hence the reason why the Mongols sought to bring all of the steppe nomads under their control as ordained by *Tenggeri*. The Mongols prioritised the subduing of other nomads over the reduction of sedentary states due to the nomad's martial prowess. As Tolun Cherbi, a Mongol commander, pointed out about the Tangut, they lived in cities and were not going anywhere. Nomads, on the other hand, could leave and thus pose a recurring threat to the Mongols.[53]

Although the campaign was meant to carve out a realm for the Jochids, it was truly an imperial campaign. Neither Ogodei nor Chaghadai accompanied the campaign, but they both sent sons, such as Qadan and Baidar respectively, and troops to accompany it. Tolui's eldest son, Mongke, also joined the campaign. Estimates put the army at approximately 150,000 men. Batu, the scion of the house of Jochi, led the campaign, but this was more of an honorary position, making him first among the princes. Subedei was the true commander of the army. Ogodei recognised the difficulty presented by the large number of Chinggisid princes in the campaign and granted Subedei the authority to mete out punishment to all but the Chinggisids – those would be sent back to him so Ogodei could deal with them personally if necessary.

As the army crossed the Volga, it divided into two forces. One force attacked the Kipchak nomads led by Mongke, Tolui's eldest son. While many Kipchaks fled westward across the *Dashti-i Kipchak* before the Mongol onslaught, others stood and fought. One such leader was Bachman Khan. He

---

[50] Concerning Jebe's death see Stephen Pow, 'The Last Campaign and Death of Jebe Noyan', *JRAS* 27, no. 1 (2016), 31–51.
[51] Juwayni/Qazvini, v1, 150; Juvaini/Boyle, 190; Juzjani/Habibi, v 2, 717–18; Juzjani, 1,284–5.
[52] Juwayni/Qazvini, v1, 157, 224; Juvaini/Boyle, 190, 269; RD/Karimi, 473, RD/Thackston1, 324; RD/Thackston2, 230–1.
[53] *SHM*, §265.

too, however, was defeated and fled to an island in the estuary of the Volga and Caspian Sea. Unfortunately, the island did not provide shelter against pursuit. When the tide went out, the Mongols were able to advance upon the island and capture and execute the Kipchak khan.[54] Those Kipchaks not killed were then incorporated into the Mongol army.

Nerge Formation

The *nerge* or *jarga* formation stemmed from a technique that the Mongols used in hunting and to train their army. The men formed a line extending over miles. The line eventually became a circle that constricted and drove the animals to the centre. The men were punished if they allowed any animal to escape from the circle, whether it was a tiger or a rabbit. Once the hunting circle contracted to its smallest size, men hunted and demonstrated their bravery before releasing the remaining animals. The Mongols also used the *nerge* in warfare. It could be an encircling tactic or be applied to a campaign strategy where units operated over dozens or even hundreds of miles, forcing the enemy to flee or march to exactly where the Mongols wanted them. As it took place over vast distances, the enemy only realised they were surrounded when it was too late.

Meanwhile, another Mongol army marched north, led by Batu, Orda and Shayban – all sons of Jochi. The Bulghars' defence was stiff, but the Mongols overcame it and brought them and many of the subordinate Siberian and steppe tribes such as the Bashkirs to heel as well. Although Batu and Orda continued westward, there is some indication that Shayban may have continued north in order to gain the formal submission of Siberian tribes, who paid tribute in fur.[55]

In late 1237, the Mongols turned their eyes towards the Rus' principalities. Through their intelligence network, the Mongols already knew of the lack of unity among the Rus' princes. The Rus' did not seem alarmed by the approach of the Mongols, despite their earlier encounter with Subedei in 1223. Furthermore, the Bulghars had approached a few Rus' princes in search of an alliance against the Mongols prior to the 1234 invasion.[56] The

---

[54] Juwayni/Qazvini, v3, 9–10; Juvaini/Boyle, 553; RD/Thackston1, 326; RD/Thackston2, 231–2; RD/Karimi, 476.
[55] Juwayni/Qazvini, v1, 224; Juvaini/Boyle, 269; RD/Thackston2, 230–3; RD/Karimi, 474–6; RD/Thackston1, 325–7; *Novgorod*, 81; Zenkovsky/NC, v2, 307 Thomas T. Allsen, 'The Princes of the Left Hand', *AEMA* 5 (1987), 11.
[56] *Nikon*, v2, 299, 304.

Rus' ignored all warnings and did not seem overly curious about the Mongols either. They may have assumed they were just another group of nomads, like the Kipchaks and the Pechenegs before them. Both were dangerous, but accommodations and relations existed between the steppe zone and the forests of the Rus'. At most, the Rus' seemed to think, these new nomads would be a nuisance, but not a cataclysmic event. The Rus' thought wrong.

The invasion of the Rus' principalities began in the winter of 1237. Unlike other invaders (Napoleon, Nazi Germany), the Mongols did not fear the Russian winter – they welcomed it. The frozen rivers served as highways and not as obstacles. The Mongols descended upon the well-fortified city of Riazan' and encircled it with a palisade, preventing escape and also making good use of the plentiful lumber from the northern forests. Defensive works that had been an asset in disrupting nomadic armies in the past now became a liability as the Mongols brought engineers with them. A relief army attempted to liberate Riazan' from the Mongols, but was defeated quickly. Afterwards, the Mongols stormed and destroyed Riazan', shortly before Christmas.[57]

As with all of their campaigns, the Mongols then split their armies. One marched against the titular ruler of the Rus', Grand Prince Vladimir. Although he attempted to draw the Mongols into a field battle, they deferred engaging with him and shadowed his movements until he entered an area more to their liking along the Sit' River, where the Mongols soundly defeated him in 1238. Meanwhile, the cities of Rostov, Iaroslavl', Torzhok and Suzdal' all succumbed to the Mongols. Armies that met the Mongols on the battlefield encountered not only the usual barrage of arrows, but also assault by catapults deployed as field artillery. Most dramatic, however, was that the Rus' found themselves in a tightening noose. As the Mongols used the *nerge* tactic, which spread out over hundreds of miles, the Rus' had less room to manoeuvre and were often cut off from the cities.[58] Of the major northern Rus' cities, only Novgorod escaped an attack as an early thaw turned the route to it into a muddy swamp.[59] Its ruler, Prince Alexander, however, did not wait for the Mongols to attack him. He promptly came to their camp and submitted to Batu, saving his city from an attack in the future.

With the northern cities subjugated, the Mongols rested in the lush pastures of the Don River steppes before launching an attack on the southern Rus' principalities in the winter of 1238–9. As with the northern campaign,

---

[57] RD/Thackston2, 231–2; RD/Karimi, 476; RD/Thackston, v2, 327; *Novgorod*, 81–2; *Nikon*, v2, 308–9; *IL*, 518–20; *EL*, 104–5; *LPLS*, 437.
[58] *IL*, 518–20; *EL*, 105–6; *LPLS*, 438–40; *Novgorod*, 82–3; *Nikon*, v2, 310–14; RD/Thackston2, 231–2; RD/Karimi, 476; RD/Thackston1, 327.
[59] *EL*, 103; *EL*, 105; *Novgorod*, 83–4.

the Mongols operated on a wide front and the cities fell one by one. Pereiaslavl' fell in March 1239 and Chernigov in October 1239. Afterwards, the Mongols solidified their gains and dealt with nomadic elements in the steppes. Then, in the late autumn of 1240, the Mongols descended upon the religious and cultural capital of the Rus', Kiev.[60] Prince Daniil fled in the face of the Mongol threat. Once the Mongols breached the city walls, many of the citizens fled and took refuge in the great churches of Kiev. The Mongols simply burned them rather than trying to enter. Kiev fell, with columns of smoke reaching towards the heavens, on 6 December 1240.[61] Years later, travellers noted that the roads to Kiev were still lined with the bones of the citizenry.[62] Many other cities submitted swiftly rather than face the Mongols' wrath.

While Batu and Subedei launched the attack on the southern cities, another Mongol army led by Qadan, Berke and Mongke moved into the steppes between the Black Sea and the Caspian Sea. Again the army divided, with Qadan marching against the Circassians while Berke continued the war against the Kipchaks in the region as well as subduing what is now Daghestan and Chechnya.[63] Meanwhile Mongke moved against the Alans, a semi-nomadic, Indo-European group that had been in the region since the first century CE. Although the Alan capital of Magas proved difficult to capture, the region was subdued.[64] Undoubtedly the effort was assisted by Chormaqan's presence in Georgia in 1238–9, thus cutting off possible aid and retreat. The Georgians and Kipchaks had long-standing ties and, while they were not always amiable, they knew each other well enough for an alliance not to be out of the question. As with other regions, leaders who submitted without resistance stayed in power. Berke also established a presence in the region as it became part of his *ordo* or camp.

With the steppes and Rus' cities subdued, the Mongols continued westward and spent much of 1240 resting their horses for the invasion of Europe.

---

[60] *EL*, 108; *Nikon*, v2, 319; Martin Dimnik, 'The Siege of Chernigov in 1235', *Medieval Studies* 41 (1979), 392; Alexander V. Maiorov, 'The Mongol Invasion of South Rus' in 1239–1240s: Controversial and Unresolved Questions', *The Journal of Slavic Military Studies* 29/3 (2016), 481–4.

[61] *IL*, 520, 522–5; *GVC*, 48; *Nikon*, v2, 320–2; Maiorov, 'Mongol Invasion of South Rus'', 484.

[62] JPC, 71–2; JPC/Dawson, 29.

[63] RD/Thackston2, 231–2; RD/Karimi, 476–7; RD/Thackston1, 327; Thomas T. Allsen, 'Mongols and North Caucasia', *AEMA* 7 (1987–91), 17–18, 21; V. Minorsky, 'Caucasia III: The Alan Capital Magas and the Mongol Campaigns', *BSOAS* 16 (1952), 226.

[64] RD/Thackston2, 231–2; RD/Karimi, 477; RD/Thackston1, 327–8; Juwayni/Qazvini, v1, 225; Juvaini/Boyle, 269–70; Allsen, 'Mongols and North Caucasia', 17–18, 20.

Unlike the Rus', the Hungarians, whose realm dominated much of Central Europe, did not sit passively awaiting the Mongols. The Hungarians built new fortifications and improved old ones in the mountain passes of the Carpathians. Hungary also made an alliance with Bulgaria, and King Bela IV welcomed 40,000 Kipchak refugees who had fled from the Mongols. Missionaries based in Hungary had long proselytised (with mixed results) in the Pontic Steppes, so the Hungarians had a fair idea about the Mongols' intentions.[65] Furthermore, Bela IV welcomed the Kipchaks for his own reasons – to bolster his own authority in the face of often recalcitrant vassals. Unfortunately for him, the nomads and Hungarian peasants immediately experienced tensions as the Kipchaks allowed their animals to graze in the cultivated fields. Arguments turned into fights. The Hungarian nobility realised Bela's intent. The Church did not welcome the Kipchaks either. Even though the Kipchak leader Koten had undergone baptism, the Church was rightly sceptical about the Kipchaks' beliefs. In the eyes of the Church, the Kipchaks were still pagans. Tensions reached a head shortly after the Mongol invasion. Many Hungarians believed that the Kipchaks were in league with the Mongols and the nobility hanged Koten.[66] In retaliation, the Kipchaks went on a rampage through Hungary and went southward to escape the Mongols. They left a swath of destruction before dispersing into nomadic bands, or became mercenaries for a number of regional powers.[67]

The refugees did not escape Mongol notice. A Mongol ambassador appeared in Hungary demanding the return of the Kipchaks – explaining that they were the Mongols' slaves and thus their property. Bela refused. Although the ambassador was unharmed, the fact that Bela did not submit and also refused to return the property of the Mongols placed Hungary in state of rebellion against the will of *Tenggeri*. War loomed on the horizon. The Kipchaks fled as the Mongol invasion began in 1241, with the Mongols once again moving on a wide front. Two *tumed* led by Baidar, son of Chaghadai, and Qadan, a son of Ogodei, invaded Poland while Batu and Subedei led the main force against Hungary. Another occupying force remained in the Pontic Steppe to maintain control over the newly conquered regions.

In Poland, Baidar and Qadan made sudden strikes, often dispersing their forces to mask their numbers. With eastern Poland ablaze, the lords of western Poland attempted to assemble an army to face the Mongol threat. Henry of Silesia joined the Teutonic Knights coming from Prussia. King Vaclav

---

[65] Master Roger, 136–55.
[66] Master Roger, 140–1, 172–5.
[67] Master Roger, 174–7; Istvan Vasary, *Cumans and Tatars: Oriental Military in the Pre-Ottoman Balkans, 1185–1365* (New York, 2005), 65.

Figure 5.6 Basilica of St Mary, Krakow, Poland. Krakow was but one of the cities that the Mongols attacked in 1241. A trumpeter still sounds the alarm from the church tower, with his final note dying as the Mongols shot him. While often attributed to the 1241 Mongol attack, it actually occurred during a later raid. (Photo courtesy of T. Christopher Jespersen)

(r. 1230–53) of Bohemia, Henry's brother-in-law, marched with reinforcements. Mongol scouts, however, were aware of their intents and ensured that the battle took place before Vaclav's arrival. The Mongols forced the battle at Liegnitz, attacking the formations of the Poles and Teutonic Knights. After luring the knights into an ambush with a feigned retreat, the Mongols then destroyed the rest of the army. Later, Henry's widow only recognised his body due to him having an extra toe on one foot, as the Mongols took his head and paraded it on a lance before the city of Liegnitz. Not all of the Europeans were killed, however. Many German miners served in the allied army at Liegnitz. Those who survived were sent to work in the mines of the Tien Shan Mountains in modern Kyrgyzstan. William of Rubruck, who, in the 1250s, journeyed to the empire, enquired about their whereabouts as part of his mission.[68]

---

[68] Rubruc, 224–5; Rubruck/Dawson, 135–6; Rubruck/Jackson, 145–6.

After Liegnitz, Baidar and Qadan did not tarry. They realised that Vaclav's army was near; it arrived only a day or two later. They did not engage Vaclav, but drew him away from Hungary. As Vaclav and Bela were related (King Bela III of Hungary was their grandfather), it was possible Vaclav could come to Bela's aid. Their ruse succeeded. Baidar and Qadan eventually split their forces again and rode to Hungary to re-unite with Subedei and Batu.

The major engagement in Hungary occurred at Mohi, along the Sajo River in April 1241. The Mongols broke through several of the fortified passes in the Carpathians and found the Hungarians at Mohi. The two armies were separated by the Sajo River. The river was a sufficient obstacle with few fordable spots. As a result, a pitched battle between the Mongol vanguard and the Hungarians took place at a bridge. The Mongols eventually captured the bridge with a rolling barrage from their siege weapons and drove their opponents off the bridgehead.[69] The Hungarians retreated to their fortified camp or wagon laager – a circle of wagons that provided some protection from the barrages of arrows while preventing sudden charges.

Rather than assault the fortified position, the Mongols pressured the camp, building tension, but then carefully left a gap in their lines. This lured the Hungarians to make a foray to escape. The initial probe soon became a flood as the entire camp rushed for the gap. Mongol units near it fled at the sudden onslaught. Soon thousands of Hungarians fled towards the twin cities of Buda and Pest, narrowly escaping the Mongol trap. The Hungarians then learned that Subedei did not make careless mistakes. The Hungarians went from the frying pan into the fire as the Mongols suddenly attacked from behind. Reasoning that to storm the camp would incur heavy casualties, Batu and Subedei decided to allow the Hungarians to escape. They then attacked the retreating Hungarians after allowing a reasonable amount of time to convince the Hungarians they were truly safe. In full retreat, the Hungarians were less likely to put up an organised resistance. Bela survived, but his army was destroyed.[70]

The residents of Buda and Pest quickly learned that rumour travelled only slightly more quickly than the Mongols. As the destruction of the Hungarian

---

[69] Thomas of Spalato, R106–13, L293–6; Thomas of Split, 262–3; Master Roger, 180–3. Both editions of the *Historia Salonitanorum atque Spalintonorum pontificum* by Archdeacon Thomas contains the Latin text and a translation in Russian (Thomas of Spalato) or English (Thomas of Split). While the English version is on the opposition page, the Thomas of Spalato edition has the Russian translation in a separate section; hence R = Russian pages, L = Latin pages.

[70] Thomas of Spalato, R111–13, L295–6; Thomas of Split, 269; MR, 182–5.

Figure 5.7 This Chinese woodcut depicts Subedei, perhaps the greatest Mongol general, in an almost demonic representation. Undoubtedly, many of his opponents would have agreed with it. (The Granger Collection/New York)

army occurred, rumours reached the cities that the Mongols were a mere hundred miles away – at least three or four days away. The Mongols appeared the next day. The cities were ruthlessly sacked. Bela survived Mohi only to be relentlessly pursued by Qadan, now returned from Poland. Qadan's sole task was to hunt down the Hungarian king. Bela only escaped by fleeing into the Adriatic Sea from Split, now in modern Croatia, leaving Hungary to the pillagers.[71] Bulgaria, Hungary's ally, also suffered. Bulgaria, however, submitted to the Mongols and remained a client state of the Mongols until well into the fourteenth century. Meanwhile Subedei and Batu continued with the conquest of Hungary, pillaging and destroying any opposition.

Europe braced itself for the next onslaught – an invasion of the Holy Roman Empire, at that time ruled by Frederick II (1194–1250). In late 1241, Mongols were spotted near Vienna.[72] It was rumoured that imperial

[71] MR, 214–15; Thomas of Spalato, R117–20, L300–1; Thomas of Split, 288–95; RD/Thackston2, 632–3; RD/Karimi, 483; RD/Thackston1, 332; *Chronica Majora*, v4, 114.
[72] Master Roger, 214–15.

troops captured a few Mongols, including an Englishman who happened to be in their company. Panic began to set in across Europe.⁷³ As early as 1238, the fish market in Yarmouth, England bottomed out as merchants from the Hanseatic League and other ports in the Baltic remained in their ports in case their ships were needed to evacuate the cities.⁷⁴ Pope Gregory IX (r. 1227–41) and Emperor Frederick both made calls for a Crusade against the Mongols, in addition to blaming the other for the disasters that had occurred in Poland and Hungary.⁷⁵ Even in the face of apocalyptic doom, the rivalry between the papacy and the Holy Roman Empire did not abate. Yet for all the worry, the attack never came. Reports soon reached the crowned heads of Europe that the Mongols had disappeared and were no longer in Hungary, as the Mongols withdrew in 1242.⁷⁶

The standard explanation was that news had reached Batu and Subedei that Ogodei had died, and the princes and leading generals needed to return to Mongolia for the *quriltai* to select a new emperor. Others have postulated that the Mongols determined that there was not sufficient pasture in Hungary for them to suitably occupy the region.⁷⁷ Some scholars have suggested that the wars against Hungary and Poland cost the Mongols too many men. The valour of Christendom had been defeated, but the armies of Hungary and Poland inflicted heavy casualties on the infidels. Contemporary chroniclers also touted this idea. Supporters of Frederick wrote that the Mongols fled in fear of his might.⁷⁸ Finally, some scholars suggested that the Mongols departed because they never planned to stay, as they practised a gradual conquest – often devastating an area to make a buffer zone to protect their new conquests among the Rus' and the *Dasht-i Kipchak*.⁷⁹

No matter what the real reason was, the death of Ogodei played a large role in the decision. A *quriltai* had to be convened. Replacing Ogodei was not an easy decision as he had proved to be a very effective khan. The sources, hostile and amiable, all concur on this point. His death in 1241 was a great loss for the empire. Nonetheless, he left behind an effective administration

---

⁷³ Matthew Paris, v1, 317, 357; *Chronica Majora*, v4, 274–6.
⁷⁴ *Chronica Majora*, v3, 488–9.
⁷⁵ *Chronica Majora*, v4, 112, 273; Matthew Paris, v1, 317, 344–5; Peter Jackson, 'The Crusade Against the Mongols (1241)', The *Journal of Ecclesiastical History*, 42/1 (1991), 1–18.
⁷⁶ MR, 218–25.
⁷⁷ Denis Sinor, 'Horse and Pasture in Inner Asian history', *Oriens Extremus* 19 (1972), 171–84.
⁷⁸ Matthew Paris, v1, 357, 489.
⁷⁹ For an overview of the various reasons see Peter Jackson, *The Mongols and the West, 1221–1410*, 71–4; Greg S. Rogers, 'An Examination of Historians' Explanations for the Mongol Withdrawal from East Central Europe', *East European Quarterly* 30 (1996), 3–26.

staffed by capable men. He had also improved communication throughout the empire through an empire-wide installation of the *jam*, a pony-express-style postal system. During the lifetime of Chinggis Khan, this had only existed in Mongolia. Ogodei also established a true capital city, Qaraqorum in the Orkhon Valley of Mongolia, the site of previous capitals for the Gok Turk and Uighurs. Ogodei also gave the Mongols an ideology upon which they could build and rationalise their empire – world conquest as decreed by *Tenggeri*. Yet, Ogodei was not perfect, as evinced by his chronic drunkenness, which may have been the root of his death. More importantly, however, he died without securing his heir and successor, and this indecision took the empire into crisis.

Islam and the Mongol Empire under Ogodei

The reign of Ogodei did not reveal an inevitable transition into the Mongol Empire becoming an Islamic Empire. Although the conquest of larger regions of the Middle East brought more Muslim subjects into the *Yeke Monggol Ulus*, it also brought in numerous Christians through the conquest of Armenia and Georgia, not to mention those living in Iran or Azerbaijan. Furthermore, the conquest of the Jin Empire counterbalanced the additional Muslim population with Daoists, Buddhists and many others. The Western Campaign also did not move the Mongols closer to Islam. Although Bulghar was Muslim in faith, it was an Islamic island in a sea of traditional beliefs. To be sure, Muslim missionaries operated in the *Dasht-i Kipchak*, but Christian missionaries were active as well among the Kipchaks. Additionally, the conquest of the Rus' brought Orthodox Christians, a new element, into the Mongol fold.

Thus in terms of population, Muslims did not become the majority. If anything, the Mongols' religious neutrality only expanded. While mosques existed in Qaraqorum, they existed next to Buddhist temples and Christian churches. More Muslims served in the bureaucracy of the Mongol Empire, but again, they were in the company of members of other religions as well. Nor was the government structure an Islamic one, although some influences may have existed in taxation and offices; the Mongol bureaucracy possessed incredible diversity in structure and influences, as well as flexibility in its operation, based on locality.

Although the Mongols during the *Yeke Monggol Ulus* period were known for their religious toleration or indifference, this is not to say that some religious persecution did not occur. The most notable episodes of religious persecution during the reign of Ogodei involved the curious matter of slaughtering animals by Muslims, as mentioned before. It should be noted that Ogodei was the one who issued the decree prohibiting the *halal* method of slaughter.[80] While the Muslim sources are unstinting in their hostility towards Chaghadai's apparent disdain for Muslims, Ogodei is treated as a 'Just Ruler'.[81] These incidences may indicate a struggle by the Mongols in adapting to ruling sedentary populations, but the question of whether this constituted religious persecution remains.

Muslims were not alone in some forms of religious persecution. During the reign of Chinggis Khan, there was an effort to have the Chinese (and presumably Jurchen and Khitans) cut their hair in the Mongol fashion. Buddhist monks (who shaved their heads completely) and Daoist priests (who did not shave their heads) both complained how this infringed upon their religious practices. Chinggis Khan relented.[82] Likewise, on several occasions Ogodei intervened against Chaghadai's repressive measures against Muslims in addition to relenting on the *halal* prohibition.[83] Additionally, Juwayni's depiction makes it clear that Mongol rulers 'could in fact change their laws as they saw fit'.[84] It is difficult, however, to determine whether Chaghadai's animosity towards Muslims was based on their faith or was simply because they violated the *yasa*. Juwayni and Rashid al-Din's accounts clearly demonstrate that his actions were based on transgressions against the *yasa*, whereas Juzjani is quick to see the spectre of religious persecution in Chaghadai's actions, and views him as a mastermind plotting genocide against Muslims.[85]

In the examples above, the proscription of animal slaughter and the imposition of hairstyles were all abandoned due to the Mongols' practice of religious toleration. Ogodei also appears to have come to terms with the fact that the *yasa* did not function well as a legal code outside of the nomadic world. When examined in isolation, the imposition of nomadic-style animal slaughter and the banning of *halal* do appear to be religious oppression. When placed in the context of the Mongols' imposition of hairstyles, another view comes into focus. When Chinggis Khan created the *Yeke Monggol Ulus*, his social revolution did away with other identities, such as the Merkits,

---

[80] RD/Karimi, 488; RD/Thackston1, 335; RD/Thackston2, 238.
[81] Juwayni/Qazvini, v1, 158–91; Juvaini/Boyle, 201–35; RD/Karimi, 486–503; RD/Thackston, 1998, 334–45; RD/Thackston2, 237–45; Juzjani/Habibi, v2, 151–8; Juzjani/Raverty, 1,106–15; Johan Elverskog, *Buddhism and Islam on the Silk Road* (Philadelphia, 2010), 236–7.
[82] Atwood, 'Validation by Holiness', 244–5; Sh. Bira, 'Mongolian Tenggerism and Modern Globalism: A Restrospective Outlook on Globalisation', *IA* 5 (2003), 107–17; Sh. Bira, 'Mongolian Tenggerism and Modern Globalism', *JRAS* 14/1 (2004), 3–12.
[83] Juzjani/Habibi, v2, 152–7; Juzjani/Raverty, 1,007–15; Juwayni/Qazvini, v1, 161–3; Juvaini; Boyle, 204–6; RD/Karimi, 489; RD/Thackston1, 336; RD/Thackston2, 238.
[84] Elverskog, *Buddhism and Islam*, 237.
[85] Juzjani/Habibi, v2, 1,110–15; Juzjani/Raverty, 154–7.

Naiman, etc., and all became Mongols. We know that the Mongols imposed their hairstyle on nomads conscripted into the military. Perhaps it was initially more widespread, and all who became part of the *Yeke Monggol Ulus* were to have the same hairstyle, thus marking them as Mongol. In a similar fashion, the method of slaughter would also indicate that one was Mongol. Only as the Mongols became more culturally aware did they begin to realise that other identities, such as religious identities, also existed. Their own innate religious tolerance (or disinterest) then permitted them to adjust and limit their attempts to enforce Mongol identity over their subjects. Again, this should not be viewed as a modern form of enlightenment, but rather as a pragmatic assessment of how to rule a diverse population.

Their religious neutrality, however, also permitted religions to spread. Juzjani, who was perhaps the most hostile chronicler, went so far as to call Ogodei 'a great friend' of the Muslims.[86] Juzjani also recorded that mosques were being built in the cities of China and even Tibet. Mosques had existed in some Chinese cities prior to this due to the presence of Muslim merchants, but Juzjani's praise suggests the establishment of new ones. Additionally, he notes that the Mongols relocated Muslim commanders from Iran and Mawarannahr to Turkestan and North China. Juzjani states that Ogodei encouraged the Mongols to allow their daughters to marry Muslims.[87] While Juzjani interprets this as Ogodei's favourable view of Muslims, it also reflected an effort to control both Muslims and the populations of North China and elsewhere. By relocating Muslim commanders to areas in non-Muslim Turkestan and North China, he introduced a new element, who then became beholden to Ogodei for their own protection as outsiders. At the same time, he augmented his military capacity for dealing with an insurrection in North China as well as with outside troops. Nonetheless, Muslims were favourably impressed with Ogodei, and word even reached Juzjani, who had fled to Delhi during the Khwarazmian War, that Ogodei had secretly converted to Islam. Juzjani, however, remained dubious.[88] At the same time, one must also consider that Ogodei's efforts were also an attempt to bring Muslims into *Yeke Monggol Ulus* through the influence of location, and also their daughters, much as Chinggis Khan did by strategically marrying his daughters. The marriage of daughters of Mongol commanders to Muslim (and other) commanders and princes brought their new subjects closer into the Mongol world.

---

[86] Juzjani/Raverty, 1,106; Juzjani/Habibi, v2, 151.
[87] Juzjani/Habibi, v2, 151–2; Juzjani/Raverty, 1,106–7.
[88] Juzjani/Habibi, v2, 157; Juzjani/Raverty, 1115.

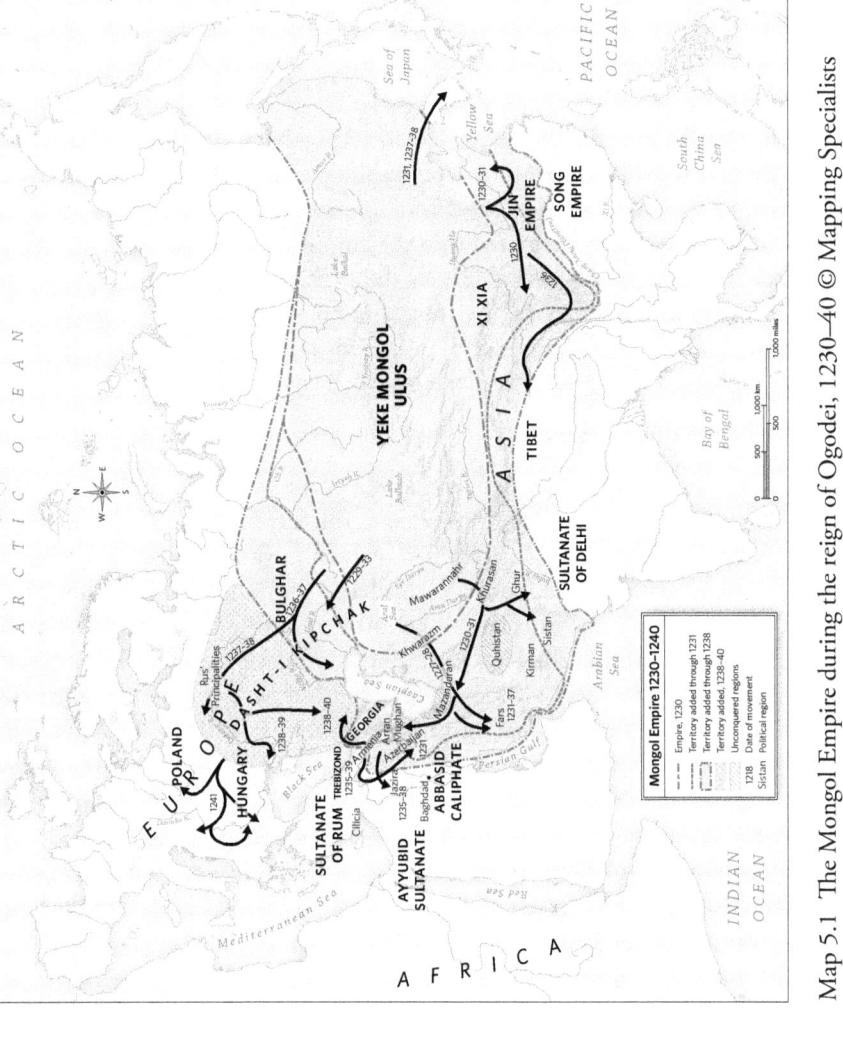

Map 5.1 The Mongol Empire during the reign of Ogodei, 1230–40 © Mapping Specialists

6

The Reign of Guyuk and the Regents

The death of Ogodei in 1241 led to a decade of stability and instability in the Mongol Empire. The stability came from the fact that the Mongol Empire ceased to expand for the most part, which allowed some areas to become better integrated into the empire. On the other hand, political machinations created instability at the very highest levels of the empire and threatened to fracture it. The root of the problem was that Ogodei died without securing his successor and, unlike his father, for all his accomplishments he lacked the *gravitas* to make his word law.

The Regency of Toregene

Upon Ogodei's death, his wife Toregene, a Naiman and former wife of the Merkit prince Qudu, became the regent. Initially she ruled with another wife, Moge Khatun, but Moge died shortly afterwards, allowing Toregene to rule alone with the support of Chaghadai, now the senior Chinggisid prince.[1] As the regent, she declared a period of mourning and was to organise a *quriltai* to determine the new khan and nominate the heir. The military campaigns largely ended, although some fighting still occurred against the Song; it consisted of raids and skirmishes rather than actual campaigns. The only major military action took place in Anatolia, modern Turkey, where Baiju, Chormaqan's (d. 1241) successor in the region, conquered the Seljuk Sultanate of Rum after the battle of Kose Dagh in 1243.[2]

Arranging the *quriltai*, however, was more complicated. With the death of Chaghadai in 1242, Batu became the senior Chinggisid prince on the basis of his primacy in the Jochid Ulus. Although many bore a grudge against him on account of the questionable heritage of his father (Jochi), it excluded him from the throne but not from his position within the empire. Upon learning

---

[1] Juwayni/Qazvini, v1, 196; Juvaini/Boyle, 240; RD/Karimi, 564; RD/Thackston1, 390; RD/Thackston2, 276–7.
[2] Paul Pelliot, *Les Mongols et la Papaute* (Paris, 1923), 51. Baiju replaced Chormaqan after the latter became paralysed and mute, possibly from a stroke.

of Ogodei's death, Batu's army of conquest departed from Hungary and returned to the steppes. The various non-Jochid princes took their contingents and returned to their respective pastures. Batu, however, remained in the *Dasht-i Kipchak* to rule his new patrimony along with the other Jochids. At this time, he also learned the fate of a rival, Guyuk.

Guyuk participated in the Western Campaign, but had been dismissed by Subedei after he and one of Chaghadai's sons, Buri, insulted Batu, either over his parentage or over his ability as a military commander, during a feast following the defeat of the Alans at Magas in 1240.[3] Guyuk departed prior to the invasion of Hungary, probably in the summer of 1241.[4] Although Subedei could not punish the two as they were princes, Ogodei could and he was furious. Ogodei stripped Guyuk of his rank and ordered him to serve in the front lines of the Song war.[5] Before the punishment could be carried out, however, Ogodei died. As Guyuk was one of Ogodei's sons, he was a viable candidate for the throne – something that clearly did not please Batu.

When calls for the *quriltai* came, Batu stalled as he had no interest in seeing his rival come to the throne, even though that was not certain. The fact that Toregene was Guyuk's mother, however, did not assuage his feelings on the matter. Instead, he focused on consolidating his rule and building Sarai, a capital on the Volga. Although he actually nomadised around Sarai and did not live in the city, Batu still needed a capital for the same reasons that Ogodei built Qaraqorum. Between this and a case of gout, Batu stalled for several years and avoided going to Mongolia. Indeed, the *quriltai* did not take place until 1246. Batu's actions, however, were not the only reasons for the postponed *quriltai*.

Toregene used the time to her advantage to secure support for her son Guyuk. At the same time she had an empire to manage. Toregene, by all accounts, was a cunning woman with great ambition. She continued to cultivate relations with various princes, often by sending them valuable gifts. In addition, she made substantial changes to the administration. The changes were necessary for her plan to succeed, so she made no effort to hasten the *quriltai*.[6]

Toregene switched the taxation system developed by Yelu Chucai and Mahmud Yalavach with tax-farming. In tax-farming, the process of tax collection is farmed out to private individuals who petitioned or submitted a

---

[3] *SHM*, §275; Hodong Kim, 'A Reappraisal of Guyug Khan', in Reuven Amitai and Michal Biran (eds), *MTO* (Leiden, 2005), 314–20.
[4] Kim, 'A Reappraisal of Guyug Khan', 316–17.
[5] *SHM*, §277.
[6] See Timothy May, 'Commercial Queens: Mongolian Khatuns and the Silk Road', *JRAS* 26 (2016), 90–5.

bid to tax a territory by agreeing to produce a certain amount of taxes in a given time frame. As the tax collectors were not part of the bureaucracy, they were not paid by the government. Instead, they kept any amount above the agreed-upon tax or a percentage of the revenue produced. The privatisation of taxation created a system that that permitted the tax farmer to exploit the tax base and enrich himself. While this inevitably increased revenues in the short term, the long-term aspects were devastating. Toregene's appointee to oversee the transition in North China, ʿAbd al-Rahman, ensured the system worked to the regent's advantage. Previously, ʿAbd al-Rahman, a Muslim merchant, had not been part of the Mongol civil administration. His entry into Mongol service appears to have been through the suggestion of Fatima, a slave from Meshed who became Toregene's confidante.[7] It is likely that Toregene also knew him from commercial dealings through the *ortoq* arrangement.

Ortoq

The *ortoq* was a relationship between a merchant and an investor, usually from among the Mongol nobility. It is believed that the Mongols adopted the *ortoq* institution from the Uighurs. Most of the merchants involved were either Uighurs or Central Asian Muslims, who dominated much of the Eurasian trade and received funding from a Mongol noble. The *ortoq* conducted business, often in long-distance trade, while the investor received a share of the profit as well as the repayment with interest on the loan. The Mongol noble (very frequently the Mongol *khatuns* or queens and princesses) loaned the *ortoq* merchant money at a very low rate. Benefiting from their ties to the Mongol ruling elite, the *ortoq* merchants sometimes abused the privileges that came from Mongol protection and capital. Their Mongol investors also sometimes made poor decisions and issued large promissory notes when short on funds. Poor decisions on both parts made the empire teeter on the edge of financial disaster on more than one occasion.

Ogodei's efficient administration was dismantled in favour of short-term gains, with key figures removed from their position. Yelu Chucai died shortly after his dismissal from severe depression.[8] It cannot be forgotten that he was the one who demonstrated the value of a rational system of taxation over short-term plundering by forecasting the tax revenue. Others attempted to

---

[7] Juvaini/Boyle, 243; Juwayni/Qazvini, v2, 199.
[8] Igor de Rachewiltz, 'Yeh-lu Ch'u-ts'ai, in *ITSOTK*, 162.

resist Toregene's changes, but quickly found their opinions unwelcomed and their lives threatened. The chancellor, Chinqai, and Mahmud Yalavach fled to the court of Koten, another son of Ogodei. Toregene demanded their return, but Koten refused, telling the messenger: 'Tell my mother, "The kite that takes refuge in a bramble patch from the talons of the hawk is safe from his enemy's might" . . . In the near future a *quriltai* will be held, and I will bring them there with me. In the presence of my relatives and the amirs [commanders] an investigation into their crimes can be undertaken, and they can be punished accordingly.'[9]

Meanwhile, Mas'ud Beg, Mahmud's son, fled to Batu, who was delighted to provide him with a haven. Korguz, the *daruqachi* of Khurasan and Mazandaran, also fled the region and found shelter with Arghun Aqa, an appointee of Toregene. Unlike his assistant, Sharaf al-Din, who was a notorious tax-farmer, Arghun Aqa had a solid reputation as an administrator and mitigated some of the effects of the changes in the administration in Khurasan and Mazandaran. Arghun Aqa, however, was loyal to Toregene and handed Korguz over. He was executed at the insistence of Chaghatayid princes he offended.[10]

Through these changes, Toregene accumulated wealth to finance Guyuk's election.[11] Due to Ogodei's condemnation, as well as a chronic, yet unidentified illness, Guyuk's selection was not guaranteed. At one point he was Ogodei's heir, but the former ruler also considered another possibility, his grandson Shiremun, who was significantly younger than Guyuk. A third contender was Koten, whom Chinggis Khan had recommended as a suitable successor to Ogodei.[12] On paper, Koten was a viable candidate. Not only had he led armies in the final stages of the Jin war, he also began the conquest of Tibet, operating from his appanage in the former territories of Xi Xia. He, parallel with his grandfather's experience with the Daoist sage Changchunzi, met with the Buddhist monk, Sa-skya Pandita (1182–1251). The latter agreed to meet with him in order to halt the invasion of Tibet. Although Koten possessed the military ability and his nomination was supported by the sacred words of Chinggis Khan, his suggestion was made prior to Ogodei's ascent to power. Many things had changed, including Koten developing an unidentified illness.[13]

---

[9] RD/Thackston2, 277; RD/Thackston1, 390; RD/Karimi, 565.
[10] Juvaini/Boyle, 243; Juwayni/Qazvini, 198–9; RD/Thackston2, 277; RD/Thackston1, 390–1; RD/Karimi, 565.
[11] May, 'Commercial Queens', 94–5.
[12] Juwayni/Qazvini, v1, 206; Juvaini/Boyle, 251; *YUS*, 55.
[13] Juwayni/Qazvini, v1, 206; Juvaini/Boyle, 251; RD/Karimi, 564; RD/Thackston1, 390; RD/Thackston2, 278.

Batu never came to the *quriltai* of 1246, but sent representatives, including his brothers Orda and Berke. His absence has been viewed as a boycott, but while his absence was notable, the presence of Orda (Jochi's eldest son) along with that of Berke (Jochi's third son) indicates that the Jochids had not withdrawn from participating in the decisions of the empire. Batu's absence may have been demonstrated his disdain for Guyuk, perhaps even a belief that the *quriltai* could not be held without his presence. If so, he was quite mistaken. Toregene successfully arranged for the *quriltai* and secured the support of the majority of the princes. Although there was much debate about the qualifications of the candidate, Guyuk emerged as the successor due to his experience, seniority and Toregene's efforts. He was elevated to the throne, with Yesu Mongke, son of Chaghadai, and Orda leading him to his seat.[14]

The Reign of Guyuk

Guyuk immediately dealt with a crisis, as Chinggis Khan's youngest brother Temuge Otchigin attempted to seize power when the *quriltai* convened, having grown weary of waiting. The timely appearance of Mengli Oghul, Ogodei's youngest son, with his own retinue en route to the *quriltai* thwarted Temuge.[15] Upon seeing his great-nephew, Temuge Otchigin repented his actions, perhaps realising that no one else considered him a candidate. If he attempted to usurp the throne, he would face the combined might of the offspring of Chinggis Khan. Nonetheless, Temuge Otchigin's actions did not escape notice.

After assuming power, Guyuk ordered an investigation into the affair, which Mongke, the eldest son of Tolui, and Orda carried out.[16] Their participation is noteworthy, as it clear that Guyuk sought the participation of other Chinggisids, thus providing a balanced and collegial perspective. The two princes worked alone in their investigation. They found Temuge guilty of conspiring against the *Qa'an* and executed him.[17] His death marks a signature departure from traditional steppe empires in which the line of succession could be both vertical (father to son) and horizontal (brother to brother). This is not to say that a lateral succession was impossible, but now, it could only occur among those descended from

---

[14] Juwayni/Qazvini, v1, 207; Juvaini/Boyle, 251–2.
[15] Juvaini/Boyle, 244; Juwayni/Qazvini, v1, 199.
[16] Juwayni/Qazvini, v1, 210; Juvaini/Boyle, 255; RD/Thackston2, 279; RD/Thackston1, 393; RD/Karimi, 569.
[17] Juwayni/Qazvini, v1, 210; Juvaini/Boyle, 255; RD/Thackston2, 279; RD/Thackston1, 393; RD/Karimi, 569.

Chinggis Khan. With Temuge's death, the term *Otchigin* also disappeared from use.[18]

Despite the election of Guyuk in 1246, he did not immediately assume the reins of power. Instead, for the next two or three months his mother still wielded power and appears to have relinquished authority only reluctantly. She died shortly thereafter.[19] Almost immediately, Guyuk began reversing her changes to the Mongol administration, with the surviving former ministers resuming their positions. Chinqai resumed his position as chancellor while Yalavach administered the lands of North China, after the rapacious ʿAbd al-Rahman's execution. Arghun Aqa, although an appointee of Toregene, kept his position of authority in Khurasan and as far west as Azerbaijan due to his ability.[20]

It is not exactly clear why Guyuk abandoned his mother's policies so quickly. Perhaps he simply saw the inefficiency of the tax-farming system and its exploitive practices and disagreed with the methods of his mother. Another issue may have involved Toregene's confidant, Fatima, who was accused of witchcraft after Koten died. Before his most recent bout of illness, Koten had sent a dire warning to Guyuk about Fatima, stating that if he died unexpectedly it was due to her. The recently reappointed Chinqai reminded Guyuk of his obligation. After an investigation, Fatima was bastinadoed, tortured and then wrapped in felt and thrown into a river.[21] Guyuk continued to clean house, as it were, with Mongke often serving as judge.

Guyuk then held a *quriltai*. Batu once again claimed illness, but his brothers represented him.[22] Although Batu did not attend, the rest of the empire did, including representatives from all the conquered territories and even beyond. The outsiders included John of Plano Carpini, a Franciscan friar, sent by the Papacy to determine the intentions of the Mongol Empire towards Europe, as well as envoys from Aleppo, who brought tribute to the Mongols, although Aleppo had not formally submitted.[23]

John of Plano Carpini's attendance was particularly fortuitous as Guyuk was fond of Christians, perhaps influenced by his mother and Chinqai, both of whom were members of the Church of the East, as was Qadaq, the

---

[18] Togan Isenbike, 'Otichigin's Place in the Transformation from Family to Dynasty', in *CEMA*, 410–11, 419–20.
[19] Juwayni/Qazvini, v1, 200, 204; Juvaini/Boyle, 244, 248.
[20] Juwayni/Qazvini, v1, 212; Juvaini/Boyle, 257.
[21] RD/Karimi, 566; RD/Thackston1, 391; RD/Thackston2, 277; Juwayni/Qazvini, v1, 200–3; Juvaini/Boyle, 244–7.
[22] Juwayni/Qazvini, v1, 205; Juvaini/Boyle, 249.
[23] JPC, 116–17; JPC/Dawson, 62–3; Juwayni/Qazvini, v1, 205; Juvaini/Boyle, 249–50.

commander who trained Guyuk in the arts of war, serving very much like an *atabeg* in the Turkic tradition.[24] Furthermore, during the *quriltai* Guyuk and other Mongol notables enjoyed listening to the debates of the various religious scholars and others of various faiths who flocked to the Mongol camp in the hope of converting the khan to the One True Religion. No one succeeded. Muslims assumed this was because Guyuk was a Christian, or perhaps even a Buddhist, and favoured these while showing hostility to the Muslims. This may also account for a certain amount of hostility towards Guyuk in the Islamic sources.[25] John of Plano Carpini, who had an audience with the *Qa'an*, noted that he was very intelligent and did not engage in frivolity.[26] Considering that he maintained Mahmud Yalavach and Mas'ud Beg in high positions, one cannot conclude that he discriminated against Muslims. Christian sources tend to paint a more favourable picture. Furthermore, John of Plano Carpini carried back a message from Guyuk to Pope Innocent IV that clearly demonstrated that Guyuk's personal convictions did not interfere with his duties as ruler of the Mongol Empire.[27]

Guyuk also followed Ogodei's example with magnanimous generosity. Like his father, he overpaid for goods from merchants in order to promote commerce. When the storehouses could hold no more, he distributed his largesse to the troops and the people. Often, as his camp moved he distributed cloth and gold to alleviate poverty among the population.[28] He also nullified decrees issued during the interregnum as well as the *jam* passports, which had been given out freely during Toregene's regency, including to many merchants. Abuse of the *jam* system strained the resources and oppressed those nomads and villages that provided support for the *jam* stations. Thus, new passports (*gerege* or *paiza*) were issued and distributed only to officials who demonstrated a clear need.[29]

---

[24] Juwayni/Qazvini, v1, 213–14; Juvaini/Boyle, 259; RD/Thackston, 2012, 279; RD/Thackston1, 394; RD/Karimi, 570.
[25] Juwayni/Qazvini, v1, 213–14; Juvaini/Boyle, 259; RD/Thackston, 2012, 279; RD/Thackston1, 394; RD/Karimi, 570; Juzjani/Habibi, v2, 171–5; Juzjani/Raverty, v1, 157–63. Also see Peter Jackson's commentary on Guyuk's religious views in Jackson, *The Mongols and the West*, 97–9.
[26] JPC/Dawson, 68; JPC, 125.
[27] Guyuk Khan, 'Guyuk Khan's Letter to Pope Innocent IV (1246)', trans. D. A. Maitland Muller, in Christopher Dawson (ed.), *The Mongol Mission* (Toronto, 1980), 85–6.
[28] RD/Thackston2, 280; RD/Thackston1, 394–5; RD/Karimi, 571; Juwayni/Qazvini, v1, 214–16; Juvaini/Boyle, 259–61.
[29] Juwayni/Qazvini, v1, 211; Juvaini/Boyle, 255–6.

Figure 6.1 Gold jewellery at Qaraqorum. The Mongols encouraged merchants to come to Qaraqorum, bringing luxury goods such as this piece as well as ubiquitous items. It is also possible that this piece of jewellery was made in Qaraqorum as a number of skilled artisans dwelled there. (Kharkhorin Museum, Kharkhorin, Mongolia)

Gerege

The *gerege* or *paiza* was a tablet that permitted its bearer to access food, lodging and animals from the *jam* stations throughout the empire. The *gerege* consisted of golden tablets with a tiger head, and gilded silver, silver, and wooden tablets, with each type connoting rank and privilege according to its value. The gilded silver and silver consisted of a rounded rectangle with a hole for a thong to attach it to the bearer's belt or neck. Additionally, the bearer received a *jarliq* or decree which instructed him on the privileges and responsibilities that accompanied the *gerege*.

Guyuk also resumed the Mongol conquests. He dispatched Eljigidei to the Middle East to conquer that region, particularly the Nizari Ismailis, known popularly as the Assassins by their detractors. Since the death of Chormaqan in the region, a low-intensity conflict had brewed with them after they had assassinated a Mongol commander named Chaghadai. It is also notable that the Ismailis sent a representative to the *quriltai*. We do not know whether Guyuk received him. Regardless, Guyuk viewed the Ismailis

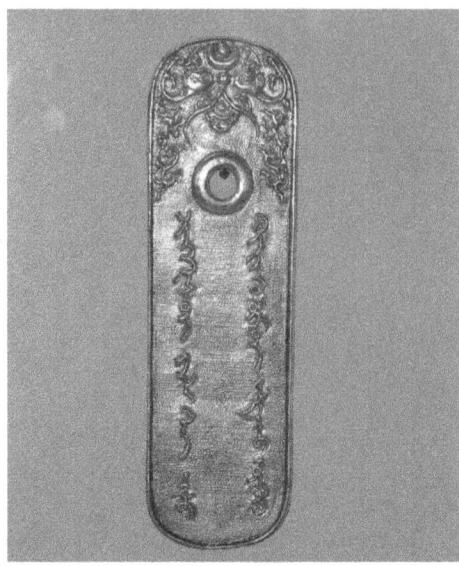

Figure 6.2 A gilded *gerege* or *paiza*. These passports were inscribed with the phrase 'By the power of the Eternal Heaven, [this is] an order of the Khan. Whoever does not respect the bearer will be guilty of offence.' The inscription is on both sides in the vertical script. (National History Museum, Ulaanbaatar)

as insubordinates who needed to be conquered.[30] The venerable Subedei led another army to the Song front.[31] Meanwhile, Guyuk planned to lead a new army to conquer Europe. This is often thought to have been merely a front to strike Batu.[32] Their mutual animosity was well-known, and Sorqoqtani sent Batu a message warning him of Guyuk's intent.[33] While it is often assumed that Guyuk despised Batu for his lineage, there is evidence which suggests that Guyuk's disdain stemmed from Batu's blunderous performance as a military commander.[34] Nothing became of the event, as Guyuk died in 1248 while on the march.

Yet was the campaign really an effort against Batu? There is ample reason to think that Guyuk, while he may have had issues with his cousin, was not

---

[30] Juwayni/Qazvini, v1, 211–13; Juvaini/Boyle, 256–8; RD/Thackston2, 278–9; RD/Thackson 1998, 392, 394; RD/Karimi, 568, 570; Juzjani/Habibi, v2, 159–60; Juzjani/Raverty, 1,150–3.
[31] Juwayni/Qazvini, v1, 212–13; Juvaini/Boyle, 256–8.
[32] Jackson, *Mongols and the West*, 115; J. J. Saunders, *The History of the Mongol Conquest* (Philadelphia, 1971), 99; Morgan, *The Mongols*, 103.
[33] RD/Karimi, 524; RD/Thackston1, 360; RD/Thackston2, 255.
[34] Hodong Kim, 'A Reappraisal of Guyug Khan', in *MTO* (Leiden, 2005), 317–19.

planning to wage war on him. Indeed, letters to Pope Innocent IV, as well as a John of Plano Carpini's account, reveal that the Mongols were indeed planning to return to Europe.[35] If that was part of the ruse, it seems overly elaborate. Yet one must also consider that Orda, Batu's brother, not only literally elevated Guyuk to the throne, but also took part in the investigation of Temuge Otchigin. If there was a dispute between Guyuk and Batu, it did not extend to all of the Jochids. Nonetheless, the arrival of the *Qa'an* with a large army en route to Europe gave Guyuk the opportunity to assert his supremacy over Batu, who would have surely been expected to join the campaign.

Guyuk's death in 1248, however, brought the empire to a standstill. When he passed away, his primary wife, Oghul Qaimish, took control of his *ordo* or camp as was customary. Upon his death, she sent messengers to inform the *altan urugh*.[36] Batu was undoubtedly relieved, but so were others. Guyuk had clearly attempted to restore the centralised authority that Ogodei had created, which removed power from the other Chinggisid princes. Toregene left them to their own devices, which often led to the population being taxed by her administration and then also by the local princes. In addition to re-appointing Ogodei's old officials, Guyuk had assigned them to more clearly demarcated fiscal regions, which placed all fiscal and civil authority in the hands of the central government. Mahmud Yalavach, a Khwarazmian, governed North China, Masʿud Beg governed Central Asia, while Arghun Aqa governed Iran and West Asia.[37] Furthermore, he also appointed individuals to be the heads of the princely *ulus*. Yesu Mongke became the head of the Chaghatayid territories, replacing Qara Hulegu, Chaghadai's grandson and chosen successor. Guyuk believed in seniority and elevated Yesu Mongke to the Chaghatayid throne, which also gained him a firm supporter.[38]

This also adds another dimension to his relationship with Batu. As noted previously, Orda played an active role in Guyuk's coronation. Guyuk clearly viewed Orda differently from his younger brother. Combined with his execution of Temuge Otchigin for his planned, but never executed coup, Guyuk may have considered replacing Batu with Orda. Although Batu never marched with troops against him, his absence from the *quriltai* may have

---

[35] Christopher Dawson (ed.), *The Mongol Mission* (Toronto, 1980), 85–6.
[36] Juwayni/Qazvini, v1, 217; Juvaini/Boyle, 262; RD/Thackston2, 280; RD/Karimi, 571; RD/Thackston1, 395.
[37] Juwayni/Qazvini, v1, 212; Juvaini/Boyle, 257; RD/Thackston2, 279; RD/Karimi, 570; RD/Thackston1, 394.
[38] Juwayni/Qazvini, v1, 210–11; Juvaini/Boyle, 255; RD/Thackston2, 279; RD/Karimi, 569; RD/Thackston1, 393.

been construed as an act of rebellion. Although we may never know Guyuk's intent, Batu certainly had cause to be concerned.[39]

Oghul Qaimish took the body back to the Emil River, where Guyuk's pasture and *ordo* were located.[40] Although the sources reveal very little about Oghul Qaimish, her regency was a pivotal episode in the history of the Mongol Empire. It is directly due to her neglect of the state of affairs of the empire and tradition that a revolution was caused that toppled the house of Ogodei.

The Regency of Oghul Qaimish

When Sorqoqtani received the news of Guyuk's death, she sent clothing, specifically *nasij* or cloth of gold, and a *boqta* or headdress and a message of condolence to the widow. Batu also sent a message of condolence, but as the senior prince also authorised Oghul Qaimish to 'administer the affairs of state together with the ministers and attend to all that was necessary'.[41] Furthermore, Batu declared that all of the other princes and military commanders (*noyad*) should meet with him at Ala Qamaq to choose a new khan.[42]

Here we see a shift of duties. Previously, it had been the regent's duty to call for a *quriltai*. Batu, however, learned from Toregene's regency that the regent could also manipulate the *quriltai*, or that delay bred impatience, as in the case of Temuge Otchigin; thus it was better to schedule it himself with the appointment of a regent. This removed the decision from the regent and shifted power to the senior prince of the realm. The location also was more central for the empire. The exact location of Ala Qamaq is not certain, although it is believed to have been between Lake Issyk-Kul and Ili River.[43] Rashid al-Din, however, indicates that the location was inside the Jochid Ulus.[44] Batu, still ailing from bouts of gout and rheumatism, clearly wanted to be involved, and by determining the location of the *quriltai* not only ensured greater Jochid participation, and thus a sort of home-court advantage, but actually placed the *quriltai* in a more central location for the Chinggisid princes. For the descendants of Chinggis Khan's brothers, situated in eastern Mongolia and Manchuria, the distance removed them even further from the affairs of state.

[39] Kim, 'A Reappraisal of Guyug Khan', 331.
[40] Juwayni/Qazvini, v1, 217; Juvaini/Boyle, 262; RD/Thackston2, 216; RD/Karimi, 445; RD/Thackston1, 305.
[41] Juwayni/Qazvini, v1, 217; Juvaini/Boyle, 262–3; RD/Thackston2, 280; RD/Karimi, 571; RD/Thackston1, 395. Rashid al-Din specifically mentions that Oghul Qaimish should work with Chinqai.
[42] Juwayni/Qazvini, v1, 217; Juvaini/Boyle, 262.
[43] 'Batu', *EI2*; 'Batu', *EI3*.
[44] RD/Thackston2, 284; RD/Karimi, 581; RD/Thackston1, 401.

It is not clear whether Batu entertained notions of securing the throne for himself.⁴⁵ If so, these were quickly dashed as many Ogodeids and Chaghatayids did not attend, partly due to the location. Many were offended by the notion that the event was not held at the *ordo* of Chinggis Khan in the Onon-Kerulen basin.⁴⁶ Nonetheless, they still proceeded with plans to determine a successor. Batu and Sorqoqtani settled on her eldest son, Mongke. Mongke had served in Batu's army of conquest with distinction and was known to him. With a talent for military command and 'a measure of gravity and dignity' that even Ogodei had recognised, Mongke was an ideal candidate.⁴⁷ They further rationalised Mongke's nomination, as he was Tolui's eldest son and Tolui, being Chinggis Khan's youngest son, should have inherited the throne.⁴⁸ By combining concepts of primogeniture and ultimogeniture, the conspirators made a case that could appeal to a wide audience. They also listed reasons why the Ogodeids should be excluded, such as that they did not follow Ogodei's wishes for Shiramun and also executed Chinggis Khan's daughter, Altalun.⁴⁹ Thus, the two families surreptitiously planned a *quriltai* in order to ensure the support of the majority of the Mongol princes, but the fact that so many Ogodeids and Chaghatayid did not attend could not legitimate Mongke's ascension. A second *quriltai* held in the Onon-Kerulen basin was necessary.⁵⁰

Oghul Qaimish, a Merkit, had two sons sired by Guyuk: Khwaja and Naqu. She did not attend the *quriltai*. Her sons attended, but stayed only for two days, leaving a representative named Temur Noyan with instructions to vote along the lines of the other Chinggisids.⁵¹ It is not clear whether they simply assumed that the *quriltai* would come to naught or assumed that, as sons of Guyuk, one or both of them would be nominated. In either situation, their cavalier attitude cost them dear. It appears that only Mongke's name garnered enough support for a vote, particularly in the absence of Naqu and Khwaja.⁵² The regent and her sons were not the only ones who avoided the *quriltai*, as few Chaghatayids and Ogodeids attended. Qara Hulegu, a son of

---

⁴⁵ Juzjani/Habibi, 176, 178–9; Juzjani/Raverty, 1,172, 1,177–81. The fact that this rumour is found in Juzjani, writing outside of the Mongol Empire, also gives one an impression of Batu's magnitude within the empire.
⁴⁶ RD/Karimi, 581; RD/Thackston1, 401; RD/Thackston2, 284.
⁴⁷ RD/Thackston2, 255, 285; RD/Karimi, 524–5, 581–2; RD/Thackston1, 361, 401–2.
⁴⁸ RD/Thackston2, 255, 285; RD/Karimi, 524–5, 582; RD/Thackston1, 361, 402.
⁴⁹ RD/Thackston2, 255; RD/Karimi, 255; RD/Thackston2, 361.
⁵⁰ RD/Karimi, 583–4; RD/Thackston1, 401–2; RD/Thackston2, 285–6.
⁵¹ Juvaini/Boyle, 264; Juwayni/Qazvini, v1, 218; RD/Karimi, 581; RD/Thackston1, 401; RD/Thackston2, 284–5.
⁵² Juvaini/Boyle, 265–6; Juwayni/Qazvini, v1, 220–1; RD/Karimi, 584; RD/Thackston1, 403; RD/Thackston2, 286.

Chaghadai, and Qadan, Ogodei's son, both attended, apparently sensing the shift in the political winds and perhaps also weary of the lack of leadership from Oghul Qaimish, who never seemed interested in convening a *quriltai* of her own. Due to the dearth of Ogodeid leadership, those Chaghatayids and Ogodeids attending abstained from voting, stating that they believed that the *Qa'an* should continue to be an Ogodeid. Yet, the absence of Naqu and Khwaja may have made many doubt their suitability for the throne. Unfortunately for them, the Jochids and Toluids carried the day. Thus, when the time came for the election, Temur Noyan agreed with the other princes and voted for Mongke. The princes also said that in the interim, the sons of Guyuk should be regents and listen to the wisdom of Chinqai until the *quriltai* for the coronation of Mongke could be held.[53]

When Temur Noyan returned, he informed Naqu and Khwaja of Mongke's election. Unfortunately, any pride he took in performing his duties came crashing down as the two princes were furious and reproached Temur Noyan. They then plotted to remove Mongke from contention by setting an ambush along his route from the *quriltai* to the Onon-Kerulen region. Their timing was poor, however, and Mongke passed through the ambush site before Khwaja and Naqu had deployed their men.[54] Still, they conspired for other opportunities.

Although the *quriltai* should have ended Oghul Qaimish's regency, she continued to rule as the Queen-Regent. Although there is little indication that her regency prior to the *quriltai* was ineffective, it is clear that the princes found her abilities lacking, for she spent most of her time with 'qams' or shamans behind closed doors and only rarely attended to matters of the state. Exactly what she did with the shamans is vague. According to Rashid ad-Din, who was biased against shamanism, she carried out the shaman's 'blithering and fables'.[55] According to Juwayni, when she did act as a regent she 'hindered men of goodwill', such as ignoring the efforts and advice of Chinqai in running the government, and mainly dealt with merchants.[56]

At the same time, Khwaja and Naqu held separate courts in opposition to Oghul Qaimish. A rift grew between mother and sons, but the sources do not indicate the source of the disagreement. Thus, three separate courts existed – one for Oghul Qaimish, another for Khwaja, and one for Naqu. Yet, none of them ruled effectively. Indeed, they often contradicted the ministers as

---

[53] Juwayni/Qazvini, 218; Juvaini/Boyle, 264; Rashid/Boyle, 201–3.
[54] Juwayni/Qazvini, 219; Juvaini/Boyle, 264.
[55] Juvaini/Boyle, 265; Juwayni/Qazvini, v1, 219; RD/Thackston2, 280; RD/Thackston1, 395; RD/Karimi, 572.
[56] Juwayni/Qazvini, 220; Juvaini/Boyle, 265.

well as each other.⁵⁷ Rashid al-Din wrote: 'Amir Chinqai sat dumbfounded by the tasks with which he was confronted, and no listened to his advice of counsel.'⁵⁸ Clearly, the creation of three separate courts frustrated his efforts to manage the affairs of the empire. In addition to their misrule, Khwaja and Naqu sent a letter stating that they would not consent to the election of a khan other than one of themselves.

This stalemate led to disorder throughout the empire. Other princes began their own dealings and issued their own orders. No one listened to the ministers of state, or even Sorqoqtani, who was depicted as the paradigm of virtue and role model for all Mongols, as she allegedly never swayed from the *yasa* and *yosun* of Chinggis Khan.⁵⁹

The Coup

At the second *quriltai* in 1251, Sorqoqtani and Batu actively lobbied for Mongke. Although he had been the clear favourite at the first *quriltai*, there was still an opportunity for dissent and debate due to the absence of so many Ogodeids and Chaghatayids at the first *quriltai*. The Jochids and Toluids supported Mongke. Meanwhile, most of the Ogodeids and Chaghatayids postponed making their decision as they felt that the throne should stay in the line of Ogodei. While Batu and Sorqoqtani gathered support for Mongke, they also sent Shilemun Bitikchi to Oghul Qaimish and her sons, with the message:

> Let all the princes come here. We will hold a *quriltai*, elect one who is worthy and whom we consider best, and enthrone him.⁶⁰

Although Naqu went, Khwaja continued to delay. He and his supporters thought that the *quriltai* would surely not start without them. The Jochid prince, Berke, however, had other thoughts. He sent a message to Batu, saying: 'We have been wanting to place [Mongke] Qa'an on the throne for two years. [Ogodei] Qa'an's and Guyuk Khan's sons and Chaghadai's son Yesu [Mongke] have not come.' Batu replied, 'Seat him on the throne! And any creature that disobeys the Yasa will lose his head.'⁶¹

En route to the *quriltai*, Naqu met another embittered contender for the throne, Shiremun, grandson of Ogodei and the most important challenger to Mongke. Guyuk's election, manipulated by the politically savvy

---

⁵⁷ Juwayni/Qazvini, v1, 219; Juvaini/Boyle, 265, RD/Thackston2, 280, RD/Karimi, 572; RD/Thackston, 395.
⁵⁸ RD/Thackston2, 280; RD/Karimi, 572; RD/Thackston, 395.
⁵⁹ RD/Thackston2, 280; RD/Karimi, 572; RD/Thackston, 395.
⁶⁰ RD/Thackston2, 284–5; RD/Thackston1, 401; RD/Karimi, 581.
⁶¹ RD/Thackston2, 286; RD/Thackston1, 403; RD/Karimi, 584.

Toregene, sidelined Shiremun's bid for the throne after the death of Ogodei. As discussed earlier, Toregene effectively painted Shiremun's relative youth as a detrimental quality for a *Qa'an* – a significant triumph considering that Chinggis Khan himself had once commented that Shiremun should be Ogodei's successor. Five years later, Shiremun's youth could no longer be used against him. Nonetheless, Sorqoqtani's deft organisation of a *quriltai* to elect her son ignored any claim to the throne that Shiremun possessed. He recognised that the *quriltai* left no room for any challengers to Mongke and sent word that he would attend. Thus to all appearances it appeared that he had no interest, but sensing the shift in the political winds Shiremun planned his own counter-coup to Toluid supremacy. Finding other like-minded Chinggisids among the Chaghatayids and Ogodeids, including Naqu, he organised a secret army, hiding them in carts that normally hauled the large princely yurts or *gers* of the nobility. Their plan was to arrive late to the *quriltai*, but in all appearances ready to join the large encampment during the festivities celebrating Mongke's election.[62] With Mongke and his supporters revelling in their victory, Shiremun's troops would emerge from their hiding places and take control of the events, through bloodshed if necessary. Unfortunately for Shiremun and Naqu, a stray camel foiled their plot.

With any large nomadic camp, the herds and flocks pastured a distance away from the camp to ensure sufficient pasture. One of Mongke's falconers, named Keshik, noticed that one of the camels had wandered off from the main body of animals. While tracking the lost animal, he encountered Shiremun's camp. Initially, the falconer gave little thought to the large number of wagons as he had seen many other latecomers arrive in the past few weeks.[63] Thus, he continued to search for their stray animal, looking among the animals in the camp – it was quite possible that the stray had entered Shiremun's camp. For the falconer, finding the animal might be tedious, but it was necessary and their claim to the animal easily determined as the animals were branded with the *tamgha* or mark of their owner.

In his search, Keshik came across a broken-down wagon. While assisting in the repair, Keshik found it loaded with weapons and armour. Typically, only the women and children rode in the wagon-bound *ger*. Also, one did not bring the gear of war to a *quriltai*. As a result, Keshik surreptitiously investigated further. The falconer realised that something was amiss and carefully

---

[62] Juwayni/Qazvini, v3, 27–8; Juvaini/Boyle, 567.
[63] Juwayni/Qazvini, v3, 39–40; Juvaini/Boyle, 574–5; RD/Thackston2, 287; RD/Karimi, 587; RD/Thackston1, 405. One must wonder whether Juwayni erred and the name of the falconer was not Keshik, but he was a member of the *keshig*. Thackston believes his name was Kasaga and he appears as Koxiejie in the *Yuan shi*.

extricated himself and his lost camel from the camp to inform Mongke of his discovery.⁶⁴ At first Mongke was incredulous. Only after a long explanation did the falconer convince Mongke. Mongke sent his right-hand man, Menggeser, to investigate with a sizeable force. With little difficulty, Mongke captured Naqu and Shiremun.⁶⁵

Now securely in power, in large part due to the military backing of Batu, Mongke plotted against of those who opposed him. Mongke sent Shilemun Bitikchi (Shilemun the scribe) to Oghul Qaimish and her son Khwaja with messages ordering them to his camp. Khwaja almost executed the messenger, but his wife convinced him not to do so as certainly only ill would befall him if he did. Reluctantly, Khwaja and his followers made their way to the *ordo* of Mongke.⁶⁶ His fate and that of his brother will be discussed in Chapter 7.

Oghul Qaimish's actions were quite different from those of her son. She defiantly countered Mongke's accusations of intrigue with denunciations of rebellion. To Shilemun Bitikchi she gave the following message for him to deliver to Mongke: 'You princes promised and gave [a written oath] that the rule would always remain among [Ogodei] Qa'an's offspring and that you would never rebel against his sons. Now you have broken your word.'⁶⁷

Naturally, Mongke was not pleased. He in turn issued a decree stating:

> The wives of Jochi Qasar, Otchigin, and [Belgutei] Noyan, the brothers of [Chinggis] Khan, have attended the deliberation of the *quriltai*, but Oghul Qaimish has not. If the shamans or Qadaq, Chinqai, or Bala (who were Guyuk Khan's *amir-ordus*) call or proclaim anyone *padishah* or *khatun*, or if anyone becomes a *padishah* or a *khatun* by their word, they shall see what they shall see.⁶⁸

In reality, this was less a decree and more of a challenge to anyone, but specifically to Oghul Qaimish. In Mongke's mind, he was the ruler now. It did not matter that some had not attended the *quriltai*; previous agreements were null and void.⁶⁹

---

⁶⁴ Juwayni/Qazvini, v3, 39–40; Juvaini/Boyle, 574–5; RD/Thackston2, 287–8; RD/Karimi, 587; RD/Thackston1, 405; Juzjani/Habibi, 179; Juzjani/Raverty, 1,182; Rubruck/Jackson, 169; Rubruck/Dawson, 147–8; Rubruc, 241–2.
⁶⁵ Juwayni/Qazvini, v3, 39–42; Juvaini/Boyle, 574–6; RD/Thackston2, 287–8; RD/Karimi, 587; RD/Thackston1, 405.
⁶⁶ Juwayni/Qazvini, v3, 54–5; Juvaini/Boyle, 585–6; RD/Thackston2, 289–90; RD/Karimi, 592; RD/Thackston1, 408.
⁶⁷ RD/Thackston1, 408–9; RD/Karimi, 593; RD/Thackston2, 289–90.
⁶⁸ RD/Thackston1, 409; RD/Karimi, 593; RD/Thackston2, 290.
⁶⁹ See Kim, 324–5 for an extended discussion of the question of legitimacy, both for Mongke and for the legitimacy of Guyuk.

Again, Mongke dispatched envoys to Oghul Qaimish, but this time to escort her. She returned with them, unwillingly and with her hands stitched together with rawhide. Once she was before Mongke, he accused her of treason and sent her to the *ordo* of his mother, Sorqoqtani, along with the mother of Shiremun, Qadaqach, to await trial.[70]

Menggeser Jarquchi (Menggeser the Judge) presided over the trial, during which he ordered that Oghul Qaimish be stripped naked before having her dragged her into court. An interrogation then proceeded. Her only reply, according to Rashid al-Din, was 'How can anyone else look upon a body that only an emperor has seen?'[71] Clearly, this was another jab at Mongke's legitimacy. Found guilty, she was wrapped in felt and then thrown in a river on Ramadan of 650 H., or November/December 1252 CE, a punishment usually reserved for witches.[72]

Whereas Toregene was a political mastermind, Oghul Qaimish is much more difficult to define. In summary, as wife of Guyuk, she became the regent upon his death. She ruled ineffectively, and due to her misconduct others intrigued to establish a new ruler. Furthermore, she never attended any of the *quriltais*, indicating that she did not intend to relinquish power. Unlike Toregene, who actively lobbied for her son Guyuk to ascend to the throne, Oghul Qaimish did not take such action on behalf of her sons.

Was she politically unmotivated? On the contrary, neither she nor her sons attended the *quriltai*, simply because they could not believe that an election could be held without them, nor would they attend one in which they knew they were not going to be considered. Furthermore, her not so subtle jabs at Mongke's legitimacy in holding power are clear indications that she tried to undermine his authority. Finally, Mongke's edict to Oghul Qaimish clearly states that no one shall be declared *khatun* as well as ruler. He legally attempted to prevent her from declaring herself ruler above her position as regent.

Nonetheless, her political manoeuvring was not sufficient cause for the method of execution. Being drowned alive was very unusual even among the Mongols, particularly when one considers other decrees against polluting water.[73] The taboos included bathing, even the hands, in water. The reason is

---

[70] RD/Thackston2, 290; RD/Karimi, 593; RD/Thackston1, 409; Juwayni/Qazvini, v3, 58–9; Juvaini/Boyle, 588.
[71] RD/Thackston1, 409; RD/Karimi, 593; RD/Thackston2, 290.
[72] RD/Karimi, 593; RD/Thackston1, 593; RD'/Thackston 2012, 290.
[73] Mention of these taboos is recorded by a number of observers, but Valentin A. Riasonovsky, *Fundamental Principles of Mongol Law* (Bloomington, 1965), 83–4 remains useful as a compilation of a number of decrees.

fairly simple. Water was the source of life, for not only humans but also their livestock. If the water became polluted, then all would suffer. Then what else could have triggered such a reaction?

Certainly, her personality did not help her case. There is no question that she was an unpleasant person. The Persian historians never wrote anything complimentary about her, but then most of the contemporary sources were written by men from cultures hostile to powerful women. Of the three major women involved in politics after the death of Ogodei – Toregene, Oghul Qaimish and Sorqoqtani – only one fared well in the sources. Sorqoqtani was consistently portrayed as a paradigm of wisdom and virtue. Of course, she was the mother of Mongke, Khubilai, Hulegu and Ariq-Boke, the four major figures in the post-1250 Mongol Empire. In addition, Hulegu was the patron of Juwayni, one of the major Persian chroniclers, and thus it is not surprising that he wrote well of her, while Rashid al-Din wrote from a later period and for his Toluid patrons.

Toregene, on the other hand, although viewed negatively, was always noted for her intelligence. Other authors seem to verify Juwayni's depiction of Oghul Qaimish. It is extremely difficult to find anything complimentary said about Oghul Qaimish. For instance, Mongke openly aired his opinion of her to foreign emissaries. In his description of Oghul Qaimish to William of Rubruck, a Franciscan friar present in Mongolia on behalf of King Louis IX of France, Mongke stated:

> Your envoys arrived at [Guyuk Khan's] residence after his death. [Oghul Qaimish], his wife, sent you *nasic* cloth and a letter. But as for knowing the business of war and the affairs of peace, subduing the wide world and discerning how to act for the best – what could that worthless woman, lower than a bitch, have known of this?[74]

Mongke however, went even further. William wrote, 'Mangu [*sic*] told me with his own lips that [Oghul Qaimish] was the worst of witches and that with her sorcery she had destroyed her whole family.'[75]

Although Mongke was known for his practicality and efficiency, it also clear that he had a reason for carrying a grudge. Still, his accusation is not without merit, as there is other evidence. It has already been mentioned that Oghul Qaimish spent much of her time with *qams* or shamans. This in itself is not highly suspicious, as when we think of modern spirituality and the likes of Rasputin and other sensational figures. Nor is it out of place when

---

[74] Rubruck/Jackson, 249; Rubruck/Dawson, 304; Rubruc, 308.
[75] Rubruck/Jackson, 249; Rubruck/Dawson, 304; Rubruc, 308.

one considers that in the mid-thirteenth century, the Mongols routinely consulted with shamans on a variety of matters. Nonetheless, the phrasing and mention by the sources is odd. Perhaps Juwayni and Rashid al-Din were simply writing a commentary stating that she was not supportive of Islam and/or other religions. Certainly, they wrote in glowing terms when a khan or a *khatun* established a mosque or madrasa, but they also wrote when the Mongols supported other religious establishments or demonstrated toleration for all.[76] Yet rarely did they even mention pagan practices except in a negative manner.[77]

The other and most damning conviction about Oghul Qaimish is her death. First, it was the custom of the Mongols not to shed the blood of royalty. There are numerous examples of people being rolled up in carpets and suffocated or trampled (the most famous being the Abbasid Caliph), or being beaten to death or having their back broken.[78] Oghul Qaimish is the exception to this. The method of execution was the same as that for Fatima, Toregene's confidante, who was a Persian slave from Meshed. Like Fatima, Oghul Qaimish was deemed a witch and executed accordingly. Certainly she was placed in a sack and sewn up, but she was then thrown into a river – not a lake.

The rivers of Mongolia are not particularly deep, and thus not an efficient way of disposing of a body for all time. A lake would be much more practical. Nonetheless, dumping Oghul Qaimish into a river was the method, for a single reason: there is a universal belief that evil cannot cross running water as its purity is a barrier to evil and even removes it.[79]

Islam and the Interregnum

Muslims in the Mongol Empire during the interregnum period and Guyuk's period remained much as they had during the reign of Ogodei. For every depiction of oppression there is equal evidence that the Mongol policy of religious tolerance remained in place. Most claims of religious oppression or discrimination seem to be based more on favouritism towards other religious groups than on true targeted persecution or repression.

---

[76] Juwayni/Qazvini, v1, 11, 159, v3, 8–9; Juvaini/Boyle, 15, 201, 552; RD/Thackston2, 284; RD/Karimi, 581; RD/Thackston1, 401; RD/Thackston2, 291; RD/Karimi, 597; RD/Thackston1, 411.

[77] Juwayni/Qazvini, v1, 28–9, 219; Juvaini/Boyle, 39, 265 RD/Thackston2, 63; RD/Karimi, 128; RD/Thackston1, 90; RD/Thackston2, RD/Karimi, 487–8; RD/Thackston1, 334–5.

[78] Juwayni/Qazvini, v1, 231, v3, 50, 59; Juvaini/Boyle, 275, 583, 588–9; RD/Thackston2, 63; RD/Karimi, 128; RD/Thackston1, 90; RD/Thackston2, 278; RD/Karimi, 567; RD/Thackston1, 391–2.

[79] James G. Frazer, *The Golden Bough*, abridged edn (New York, 1950), 629.

This is evinced most clearly during the reign of Guyuk, during which Muslim authors noted his proclivity towards Christianity, particularly the Church of the East (Nestorianism).[80] This favouritism is borne out by a number of other sources that emphasise Guyuk's affinity, and that if he was not a Christian already his conversion was imminent.[81] As noted earlier, it is clear that whatever his predilection for Christianity, it did not interfere with his Mongol sensibilities towards world domination. Juzjani, however, noted that Guyuk favoured Buddhists, which has support in the Chinese sources.[82] Juzjani relates an episode in which his Buddhist monk advisors (known as *tuin* or *toyin*) plotted to emasculate the Muslims, as massacring them was impractical due to their sizeable population.[83] Why it was thought that castrating the male Muslim population would be easier remains uncertain. A dog foiled the scheme, and made known the will of God as Guyuk placed his *tamgha* or seal on the decree. Juzjani wrote: 'This dog was in [Guyuk's] place of audience, and, like unto a wolf upon a sheep, or fire among wild rue seeds, it seized hold of that impious Tuin, flung him to the ground, and then, with its teeth, tore out that base creature's genitals from the roots; and, by the Heavenly power and Divine help, at once, killed him . . .'[84] This episode is even more curious as dogs are generally viewed as 'unclean' animals by Muslims.

Guyuk and the rest of his court, in a move of testicular fortitude, recognised the will of Heaven and quickly abandoned their plan and destroyed the decree. This plot seems a bit far-fetched and cannot be corroborated by other sources and thus may be consigned to the body of conspiracy theories. The fact that Juzjani recorded it, however, suggests that Muslims worried about persecution, and that Guyuk favoured others as recorded by Juwayni and Rashid al-Din. Juzjani includes another Buddhist-instigated plot to diminish Islam, but it too fails. This one appears to have more grounding in reality as it involves a religious debate. Here the plot device is that Buddhists and Christians prod Guyuk into inviting a distinguished *imam*, Nur al-Din, to prove the superiority of Islam over other religions. If he fails, he will be executed. The *imam* naturally defeats his opponents in debate. During the *imam*'s performance of prayers, some of the Buddhists then interrupt them,

---

[80] Juwayni/Qazvini, v1, 214; Juvaini/Boyle, 259; RD/Thackston2, 281; RD/Karimi, 573–4; RD/Thackston1, 396.
[81] JPC, 43; JPC/Dawson, 68; BH1, 411.
[82] Juzjani/Habibi, v2, 171; Juzjani/Raverty, 1,157; Peter Jackson, 'The Mongols and the Faith of the Conquered', in *MTO*, 270.
[83] Juzjani/Habibi, v2, 171–2; Juzjani/Raverty, 1,157–8.
[84] Juzjani/Habibi, v2, 172; Juzjani/Raverty, 1,159.

sometimes with violence, but the *imam* perseveres. Juzjani recorded that Guyuk died shortly after this event and ties his death directly to the khan's attempt to humiliate the *imam*.[85]

Again, Juzjani delivers a tale that appears exaggerated but nonetheless reveals the anxiety of Muslims. Although Juzjani wrote from the safety of the Sultanate of Delhi, he nonetheless heard much from Muslims who fled there, merchants who did business in the Mongol Empire, and perhaps also from diplomatic contacts. The anxiety among the Muslims of the Mongol Empire was real. This scenario may also have some merit as the Mongols were known to stage religious debates as a form of entertainment and as a method of settling religious strife within the empire, as will be examined in Chapter 7.

At the same time, during this period, one can look to the realm of Batu and find evidence of perceived favouritism towards Muslims. Here we see Batu embracing Muslim merchants, supporting religious experts, and perhaps even converting to Islam, although the latter is reported in only one source.[86] As Professor Jackson has indicated, there is no evidence to support this conversion, although Berke, Batu's brother, was a Muslim.[87] While Batu did not convert to Islam, the fact that Juzjani indicated that he did reveals that, at least in Batu's territories, Muslims experienced less anxiety. Professor Jackson astutely observes, however, that, when dealing with individual Mongol rulers, 'we cannot always be sure to what extent we are dealing with personal conviction or with political favouritism or simply with the wishful thinking of our highly partisan sources'.[88] What Juzjani saw as a preference was probably pragmatism on the part of Batu, and was perhaps encouraged by Muslims, such as Sharaf al-Din (a Khwarazmian), in Batu's service.[89]

What is notable, however, is the continued possible increase in Muslim civil servants, particularly in the areas of taxation. With the switch to tax-farming during the era of Toregene, their expertise was crucial. Most seemed to have been former merchants, perhaps recruited through *ortoq* relationships. On such example was ʿAbd al-Rahman, who ostensibly promised to

---

[85] Juzjani/Habibi, v2, 173–5; Juzjani/Raverty, 1,160–4.
[86] Juzjani/Habibi, v2, 176; Juzjani/Raverty, 1,172–3.
[87] Jackson, 'The Mongols and the Faith of the Conquered', 269. For Berke, also see Rubruc, 209; Rubruck/Jackson, 127; Rubruck/Dawson, 124; Jean Richard, 'La conversion de Berke et les debuts de l'islamisation de la Horde d'Or', *Revue des Etudes Islamique* 35 (1967), 173–84; Istvan Vasary, '"History and Legend" in Berke Khan's Conversion to Islam', in *AAC3*, 320–52; Devin DeWeese, *Islamization and Native Religion in the Golden Horde* (University Park, PA, 1994), 83–6.
[88] Jackson, 'The Mongols and the Faith of the Conquered', 268.
[89] Juwayni/Qazvini, v2, 223, 230; Juvaini/Boyle, 487, 494.

double the revenue from North China.⁹⁰ While ʿAbd al-Rahman was active in the east, his apparent doppelgänger, Sharaf al-Din, drained the coffers of everyone in the west.⁹¹ Their avarice, however, knew no distinction between sect, creed or ethnicity.

Additionally, in the court of Toregene we find Muslim advisors such as the aforementioned Fatima. When Guyuk ascended the throne, so Mahmud Yalavach and Masud Beg returned to their positions. While we (and chroniclers) may be dismissive of the Shia Fatima, from the fact that Toregene, who by all accounts was a very intelligent person, consulted her we may conclude that the regent found her useful beyond her purported sorcery.⁹² Suffice to say, for every high-level individual in the court there were dozens of lower-level Muslim officials just as there were other Christians, Buddhists, Daoists, Confucians, etc. serving the Mongols. Thus while one prince or regent might have favoured one group over the other, it is clear that they maintained officials who had ability and could work towards their goals. It is curious, however, that none of the sources, to my knowledge, mentions any religious persecution or favouritism on the part of Toregene or Oghul-Qaimish.

---

⁹⁰ May, 'Commercial Queens', 91–2.
⁹¹ Juwayni/Qazvini, v2, 244, 274–81; Juvaini/Boyle, 508, 538–44.
⁹² Juwayni/Qazvini, v1, 200–1; Juvaini/Boyle, 244–6.

7

Mongke and the Toluid Revolution

The fractured nature of Oghul Qaimish's regency brought much of the Mongol Empire to a standstill. Sorqoqtani, the widow of Tolui, seized the opportunity. The Toluids and Jochids possessed a tacit alliance through matrilineal ties as well as in response to the tight bonds of the Ogodeids and Chaghatayids. Working behind the scenes, Sorqoqtani secured the support of Batu to have her eldest son, Mongke, make a bid for the throne. Much of Sorqoqtani's behind-the-scenes success was due to her public displays of disinterest in politics after the death of her husband while she also performed the role of the dutiful widow, raising her four sons. She became the model of someone who never veered from the *yasa* and *yosun* of Chinggis Khan, a paragon of virtue. Thus in 1251, Mongke became Qa'an of the Mongol Empire and began the Toluid revolution. While the transition of the position of Qa'an from the house of Ogodei to the house of Tolui was revolutionary in a sense, it was still only a political shift.

While Ogodei and Guyuk cultivated the idea that only an Ogodeid should sit on the throne, it is unclear whether Chinggis Khan said anything that supported this view. The Toluids argued that the failure of Oghul Qaimish to convene a *quriltai* and select a new Qa'an invalidated the Ogodeid mandate of authority – the function and role of the regents was well-defined. The regency was not indefinite. The Toluids were revolutionary as well in the timing. Oghul Qaimish sat as regent for only two years, a brief period compared to the six years of regency held by Toregene. Finally, the outcome of the Toluid Revolution ensured that the Mongol Empire fundamentally and irreversibly changed. Indeed, Mongke and his supporters took steps to ensure that his rule was unchallenged and that it could not slide back into the hands of the Ogodeids, or even the Chaghatayids. Their first step in this process was to deal with other contenders.

Yasa and *Yosun*

The Mongols were governed by the *yasa* and *yosun*. The *yasa* was a legal system based on customary law among the nomads as well as decrees or *jarliqs* made by the *Qa'an*. Generally, when a new ruler came to the throne, he approved the *jarliqs* of his predecessor. It was not a universal law code and primarily applied to the nomads, but it did affect the sedentary population as it could trump other laws. The *yosun* were traditions based on the words and actions of Chinggis Khan. In many ways the *yosun* were analogous to *hadiths* in Islam.

The Toluid Revolution

While awaiting Oghul Qaimish's arrival, Mongke also dealt with the perpetrators of the attempted coup. With Shiremun and Naqu's plot exposed, the two attempted to pass off their arrival as their simply joining the *quriltai* with good intentions and to wish Mongke congratulations. There was little else the conspirators could do since they were surrounded by Menggeser, who wasted little time with formalities. His envoy conveyed the message 'It has been reported to the emperor that you are approaching with evil in your hearts. If this report is false, it will be sufficient proof for you to head to court at once, without stopping to think or hesitate. Otherwise, we are ordered to arrest you and take you there. Which of the two would you prefer?'[1]

Although it appears that Menggeser offered them an opportunity to plead innocence, there was no choice. The first part of the message meant that they were going to be escorted to the court without public humiliation. The second option meant that Menggeser and his troops would crush any resistance. Shiremun, Naqu and other conspirators were escorted by a few horsemen while Menggeser confiscated their men's weapons. Shiremun and company entered the *quriltai*, and performed all of the rituals of obeisance before the *Qa'an*, before participating in the festivities. They were observed carefully for three days without any questioning.

On the fourth day, the investigation began, with Mongke presiding. At the onset Mongke announced that if Shiremun, Naqu or anyone else who had been accused was found innocent, then the accusers would be punished. The princes claimed innocence of any plot and a servitor of Shiremun, the *atabeg* Qata Kurin, testified while being interrogated via bastinado that

---

[1] RD/Thackston2, 288; RD/Thackston, 406; RD/Karimi, 588. While Rashid al-Din surely consulted Juwayni's account, his account of Menggeser's words contains less purple prose. See Juwayni/Qazvini, v3, 45; Juvaini/Boyle, 578.

the Chinggisid princes were not involved. He confessed that he and other commanders had conspired against Mongke. He later committed suicide.[2] Menggeser then took over the investigation, serving as *yeke jarquchi*. The following day Menggeser assembled a number of the *noyad* connected with the accused princes and interrogated them. Many of them included commanders of the highest rank. In the end, seventy-seven *noyad* were executed in a variety of manners.[3]

A massive purge began throughout the empire, its principal targets being the Ogodeids and Chaghatayids and their supporters. A screen of troops intercepted any other latecomers to the *quriltai* and determined their intent.[4] Menggeser Noyan continued as *yeke jarquchi* and investigated all who had been a part of the Ogodeid regime. Menggeser began his efforts by investigating Oghul Qaimish's advisors. Even Chinqai, the chancellor of the empire, and Qadaq, Guyuk's *atabeg*, came under scrutiny due to their close ties to the Ogodeid lineage. Detachments, led by *jarquchin*, were sent throughout the empire with a list of suspects and conducted tribunals. While the actual coup attempt was conducted by a relative handful, Mongke was determined to root out all those who may have sympathised with them. As Thomas Allsen noted, 'A Mongolian prince and his retainers rose together and fell together'.[5] Eljigidei, whom Guyuk assigned as the *tammachi* in Iran, was arrested and sent to Batu.[6] And, perhaps not coincidentally, command of that *tamma* reverted to Baiju, who originated from the Jochid Ulus.

Mongke did not exempt the *altan urugh* from scrutiny. Buri, the grandson of Chaghadai, was also sent to Batu, who executed him.[7] Shiremun was sent to the Song Empire front and then later executed.[8] Yesu Mongke,

---

[2] RD/Thackston2, 288; RD/Thackston1, 407; RD/Karimi, 489; Juwayni/Qazvini, v3, 50; Juvaini/Boyle, 583.

[3] RD/Thackston2, 289; RD/Thackston1, 407; RD/Karimi, 489. The sons of Eljigidei Noyan had their mouths stuffed with stones until they died, Elchitei's head and feet were cut off, and Taunal was trampled. Juvaini/Boyle, 583; Juwayni/Qazvini, v3, 50.

[4] Juwayni/Qazvini, v3, 53–4; Juvaini/Boyle, 585.

[5] Thomas T. Allsen, 'The Rise of the Mongolian Empire and Mongolian Rule in North China', in *CHCAR*, 394.

[6] Juvaini/Boyle, 590; Juwayni/Qazvini, v3, 61–2; RD/Thackston2, 289; RD/Thackston1, 407; RD/Karimi, 489.

[7] RD/Thackston2, 261, 289; RD/Karimi, 536, 591; RD/Thackston1, 369, 408; Juwayni/Qazvini, v3, 59; Juvaini/Boyle, 588; Rubruck/Jackson, 144–5; Rubruck/Dawson, 135; Rubruc, 224. William of Rubruck indicates he was beheaded.

[8] William of Rubruck indicates he was executed. Juwayni and Rashid al-Din mention that he was sent as part of Khubilai's army against the Song Empire. Rubruck/Jackson, 169; Rubruck/Dawson, 147–8; Rubruc, 241–2; Juwayni/Qazvini, v3, 65; RD/Thackston2, 290 591–2; RD/Thackston1, 409; RD/Karimi, 594; *YUS*, 59; Thomas T. Allsen, *Mongol*

the Guyuk's appointed ruler of the Chaghatayid Ulus, was also executed. Juwayni indicates that Yesu Toqa, Qara Hulegu's brother, was sent to Batu along with Buri, but there is no mention as to whether or not Batu executed him along with Buri.[9] Juwayni later indicates that Yesun Toqa went to China.[10] Meanwhile, Rashid al-Din wrote that Mongke ordered Qara Hulegu to execute his uncle, Yesu Mongke, and assume the Chaghatayid throne. Yesu Mongke was viewed as a negative influence on Naqu and Khwaja, and perhaps as the root of their obstinacy.[11] Qara Hulegu died before he was able to carry out the order, so it was carried out by his wife Orghina Khatun.[12] Thus at least two, perhaps three, Chinggisids were executed. It is notable that they were executed on the order of other Chinggisids (Mongke, Batu and Qara Hulegu). Menggeser, the *yeke jarquchi*, was not involved in the sentencing. The *qarachu*, no matter what the circumstances, did not have authority to issue a sentence against the descendants of Chinggis Khan.

Women were not immune from the purge. Toqashi Khatun, wife of Yesu Mongke, grandson of Chaghadai, was kicked to death before her husband's eyes after being tried by Qara Hulegu. The reasons are vague, but she had offended Mongke in some manner.[13] She appears to be the only other queen besides Oghul Qaimish to have been executed. Qara Hulegu's involvement in the execution of his brother's wife is curious and may have been a test of loyalty by Mongke. Others saw their holdings diminish and often were placed under the supervision of Toluids or Jochids.

With few exceptions, those Chaghatayid or Ogodeid princes and their supporters not purged received a military exile, to fight in the sweltering climate of South China. Surprisingly, Oghul Qaimish's sons were not executed. Naqu, who openly bore arms against Mongke, went to the front in China with Khubilai, Mongke's brother.[14] Spared from persecution and war due to the wisdom of his wife, Khwaja was directed to move his camp to the

---

Imperialism: The Policies of the Grand Qan Mongke in China, Russia, and the Islamic Lands, 1251–1259 (Berkeley, 1987), 31.
[9] RD/Thackston2, 290; RD/Karimi, 595; RD/Thackston1, 410; Juwayni/Qazvini, v3, 59; Juvaini, Boyle, 588–9.
[10] Juwayni/Qazvini, v3, 64–5; Juvaini, Boyle, 591–2.
[11] RD/Thackston2, 280, 285–6; RD/Thackston1, 402–3; RD/Karimi, 583.
[12] RD/Thackston2, 263, 266; RD/Thackston1, 372, 376; RD/Karimi, 540, 544.
[13] RD/Thackston2, 289; RD/Karimi, 591; RD/Thackston1, 408; Juwayni/Qazvini, v3, 59; Juvaini, Boyle, 588–9.
[14] Juwayni/Qazvini, v3, 65; RD/Thackston2, 290, 591–2; RD/Thackston1, 409; RD/Karimi, 594.

Figure 7.1 Tile work from Qaraqorum. Although the Mongol Khans rarely resided in Qaraqorum, much of the bureaucracy did. The Mongols ensured that their capital, though small, had the proper appearance of an imperial capital. (Kharkhorin, Mongolia)

Selenge River, near Qaraqorum, the capital, well within the reach and sight of Mongke and outside the Ogodeid Ulus.[15]

The purge then expanded beyond the *altan urugh* and the administration and towards the local dynasts as well as bureaucrats in the far-flung regions of the empire. By custom, with a new ruler all vassal rulers were to come to provide tribute to the new *Qa'an*. This time, a tribunal closely questioned them as well. Those who demonstrated loyalty to the Toluids found their situation improved. Failure to do so did not mean the end of a dynastic line, however. Salindi, the ruler of the Uighurs, was deposed due to his ties to Oghul Qaimish; his brother Ogrunch became the new *idiqut*. He also served as his brother's executioner, possibly as a test of his Toluid loyalty. The ruler of Kirman in southern Iran suffered a similar fate.[16] Officials connected too

---

[15] Juwayni/Qazvini, v3, 65; Juvaini/Boyle, 592; RD/Thackston2, 290; RD/Karimi, 594; RD/Thackston1, 409.

[16] Juwayni/Qazvini, v3, 60; Juvaini/Boyle, 589; RD/Thackston2, 290; RD/Thackston1, 409; RD/Karimi, 593. Also see Allsen, *Mongol Imperialism*, 63–76.

closely to the Chaghatayids and Ogodeids but serving in domains beyond their respective *uluses* were also purged.[17] The Ogodeid patrimony largely disappeared, as did the sons and grandsons of Ogodei. The most notable survivor was Qaidu (1236–1301), a grandson of Ogodei, who was too young to be a threat. He received a patrimony around the city of Qayaliq, south of Lake Balkash. His uncle and Ogodei's youngest son, Melik, who also served in the Western Campaign, received territory along the Irtysh River. The sons of Koten escaped the purge and were confirmed in their territory in the former domains of Xi Xia.[18] A few other Ogodeids survived, but with insignificant holdings or support.

Meanwhile, the Chaghatayid patrimony remained largely intact, but with fewer Chaghatayids. Qara Hulegu, who had succeeded his grandfather Chaghadai in 1242 before being deposed by Guyuk, regained the Chaghatayid throne from Yesu Mongke, as mentioned earlier. Indeed, Guyuk's actions had moved Qara Hulegu in the Toluid camp as soon as Sorqoqtani began her efforts. As Qara Hulegu died en route to the Chaghatayid Ulus, his wife Orghina, Mongke's niece, served as regent for their under-aged son, Mubarak Shah, which had ramifications that were only realised in the next decade.[19]

The Jochids benefited greatly from the Toluid Revolution, but the Toluids were the big winners. While it was unlikely that Guyuk's sons would have attacked Batu, Batu's realm was now secure. The Jochids may even have seen an expansion of their patrimony at the expense of the Ogodeids. And while the Jochids benefited from the change in rulers, they remained very much part of the empire. Any autonomy they had was great only in comparison with the Ogodeid and Chaghatayid realms. Although Berke provided security at the first *quriltai*, the second *quriltai* took place in Mongolia, where the Toluids had dominated since the death of Chinggis Khan. The Toluid revolution occurred through Toluid efforts. The Jochids assisted. That being said, if the Jochids had resisted the Toluids, Sorqoqtani may have found herself removed from politics permanently. Still, Sorqoqtani's careful cultivation of Jochid relations should be commended. Being the sister of Jochi's widow Begtutmish Fujin, and then warning Batu about Guyuk's intentions (real or imagined), only endeared Sorqoqtani to Batu.

---

[17] Allsen, *Mongol Imperialism*, 32–3.
[18] Michal Biran, *Qaidu and the Rise of the Independent Mongol State in Central Asia* (Richmond, UK, 1997), 19–20.
[19] For Orghina see Bruno De Nicola, 'The Queen of the Chaghatayids: Orghina Khatun and the Rule of Central Asia', *JRAS* 26/i–ii (2016), 107–20; Paul D. Buell, 'Some Royal Mongol Ladies: Alaqa-beki, Ergene-Qatun and Others', *WHC* 7/I (February 2010), <http://worldhistoryconnected.press.illinois.edu/7.1/buell.html> (last accessed 11 January 2017).

While force of arms and political scheming placed Mongke on the throne, Mongke realised this was insufficient to legitimate his rule. Although Chinggis Khan had been transformed into a hallowed figure not long after his death, Mongke instituted a true cult of Chinggis Khan in 1252 with official ceremonial worship. Buried next to Chinggis Khan, Tolui was posthumously promoted to *Qa'an* status, despite only having served as regent. He too became the object of official veneration. Mongke also wrapped himself in the mantle of the *yasa* and *yosun* of Chinggis Khan. He did his utmost to live up to that reputation as well.[20] As indicated previously, accusations against Oghul Qaimish included that she had veered from the *yasa* and *yosun*. Two of our major sources for the rise of Mongke, the chronicles of Juwayni and Rashid al-Din, were written by officials who served the Toluid family. Juwayni was a minor official in Hulegu's court, although he later became the governor of Baghdad and his family rose in importance. Rashid al-Din served as the vizier in the Il-Khanid court (the successors of Hulegu). Both stress the importance of the *yasa* and the *yosun*, no matter who ruled, throughout their works. Indeed, Rashid al-Din records one aphorism from Chinggis Khan (perhaps apocryphal) that supports the Toluid Revolution in light of the allegations against Oghul Qaimish:

> Among my offspring, many emperors will come into existence after this. If the grandees and warriors who will serve them do not maintain the *yasaq* [*sic*] strictly, the empire will become shaky and end. They will wish they had [Chinggis] Khan, but they will not have him.[21]

In relation to Sorqoqtani Beki (the Queen Mum, so to speak), her character became irreproachable, while Toregene and Oghul Qaimish were painted in a less favourable light. One source indicated that Sorqoqtani was even preferable to Chinggis Khan's own mother, as instead of remarrying as did Ho'elun (to Monglik, the father of Teb Tenggeri) Sorqoqtani rejected Ogodei's suggestion that she marry Guyuk. She apologised and said:

> 'How can one change the decree of a *yarligh*? Nonetheless, I had thought I would raise my sons to manhood and do my best that they be educated and not part from or detest one another so that, perhaps, something might come of their unity'. When she did not give her consent to be married to Guyuk Khan, no doubt remained as to whether or not she had any inclination to get married. For this reason she had been preferred to [Chinggis] Khan's mother [Ho'elun].[22]

---

[20] Allsen, *Mongol Imperialism*, 34–44.
[21] RD/Thackston2, 201; RD/Thackston1, 294; RD/Karimi, 435.
[22] RD/Thackston2, 274; RD/Thackston1, 387; RD/Karimi, 561.

In this passage she is also invoking the mythical mother of the Mongols, Alan Goa, by alluding to the lesson of unity found in the Parable of the Arrows.[23] Unfortunately, as with all of the Mongol males, the lesson proved elusive.

Mongke was not shy in disparaging Oghul Qaimish publicly. To be sure, Toregene and Oghul Qaimish had their flaws, but Sorqoqtani was not a saint.[24] Nonetheless, she was a remarkable woman. While the latter chronicles cemented Toluid legitimacy for history, the Toluids also attempted to bolster their legitimacy during the purge. Oghul Qaimish accused Mongke and his supporters of violating their solemn vow to Ogodei that the throne would always remain in the line of Ogodei. Mongke countered this by arguing that Oghul Qaimish did not perform her duties and neither did her sons.[25] Thus, it was incumbent upon others to seize the reins of leadership. Two *quriltais* had been convened, which provided opportunity for the heirs of Ogodei to make their intentions and claim to the throne known, but Oghul Qaimish never attended any *quriltais*, nor did her sons express much interest, leaving their affairs to proxies. Whether or not the Toluids or Jochids would have heeded their claims if they had made an effort is a moot point as Mongke emerged victorious. It is difficult to truly know if the interregnum period before Mongke was truly as bad as the pro-Toluid sources and those drawing upon Toluid intelligence (like Rubruck) indicate, as other sources reveal little. Like the Armenian sources, one Muslim source, Juzjani, seem to follow the adage of 'if you can't say something nice . . .' and simply ignores all three women, apparently not wanting to even comment on any the regents or Sorqoqtani – perhaps a silent and disapproving commentary on the role of women in politics in Mongol Eurasia.

The Administration of Mongke

With the purge completed, Mongke then turned his attention to reforming the Mongol Empire's administration. During the previous decade of instability the administration had strayed significantly from Ogodei's reign. Although some of the bureaucracy remained the same, key members such as Chinqai had been purged and needed replacement. Additionally, during the tri-*ordo* administration of Oghul Qaimish, Naqu and Khwaja, conflicting decrees were issued and, in any many cases, Chinggisid princes simply ignored the regents and did as they wished. In essence central authority

---

[23] *SHM*, §19–22.
[24] Timothy May, 'Commercial Queens: Mongolian Khatuns and the Silk Road', *JRAS* Series 3, 26, 1–2 (2016), 105–6.
[25] RD/Thackston2, 290; RD/Thackston1, 409; Karimi, 593.

devolved to local authorities, whether a Chinggisid prince or a regional governor. Corruption and avarice ran rampant.

The Toluid Revolution did not occur spontaneously. Just as Sorqoqtani carefully cultivated alliances and support among the Chinggisid princes, Mongke also had his own household personnel who could step in and ease the transition. Chinqai's replacement was none other than Menggeser, the Jalayir Mongol, who led the tribunals throughout the purge. In addition to his position as *yeke jarquchi*, he served as the de facto chancellor or vizier and handled the day-to-day affairs of the empire and Central Secretariat. Aqa Bulghai, a Kereit and Nestorian Christian, was the second-highest official and became Menggeser's replacement when the latter died in 1253. There is no indication that anyone took over Bulghai's duties as well; thus Bulghai consolidated the two highest positions within the administration after the Qa'an.[26] Like Menggeser, Bulghai emerged from Mongke's personal *keshig*. Although each *Qa'an* possessed a *keshig* of 10,000 men, all the Chinggisid princes had their own bodyguards, which often merged with that of the *Qa'an* when that prince assumed the throne. Undoubtedly, the *keshig* of Guyuk also suffered from the purge as well. Nonetheless, much as it had done during the reign of Chinggis Khan, the *keshig* still remained not only the security service of the khan, but also his personal household staff and the recruiting ground for the *Qa'an*'s generals and administrators.

As with his predecessors', most of Mongke's administration was dominated by Mongols, but the lower-ranking figures were predominantly non-Mongols and consisted of subjects from across the empire. Most of them had served in either Tolui's or Mongke's personal *keshig* prior to their entry into the bureaucracy. Although most of the high-ranking Ogodeid administrative personnel had been purged, lower-ranking officials survived, such as two Muslim *bichigchin*, Amir Imad al-Mulk and Fakhr al-Mulk. Each of the *bichigchin* or scribes had to be fluent in a number of languages as the memorials and decrees were usually written in Mongolian, Uighur Turkic, Persian and Chinese. Additionally, decrees going to specific locations needed to be written in the local language such as Armenian, Tangut or Tibetan for the local dynast.

The Toluid revolution continued in other ways as well. Three fiscal regions came into existence prior to Mongke: North China, Turkestan (Mawarannahr and much of the Tarim region) and Khurasan. Mongke ordered a new census and added the Rus' principalities as a fiscal territory. Although it took place in the Jochid Ulus, both Jochid and imperial agents

---

[26] Allsen, 'The Rise of the Mongolian Empire', 397; Allsen, *Mongol Imperialism*, 96–7.

conducted the census and tax collection, as was done in the other regional secretariats that overlapped with a Chinggisid *ulus*.[27]

As Mongke also purged the administration of many of the appointees of Toregene and Oghul Qaimish, this eliminated many of the *ortoq* merchants and tax-farmers, who had served in a variety of posts. Rather than keeping these regions organised as strictly fiscal regions, controlled by the imperial government, Mongke brought them more directly under centralised rule by transforming them into fully fledged secretariats supervised by the Central Secretariat. Mahmud Yalavach was placed in charge of North China, while his son Masʿud Beg took charge of Turkestan, which included Mawarannahr, Khwarazm, Uighurstan and the Ferghana Valley. Arghun Aqa, who had been part of Oghul Qaimish's administration, retained his position in the Middle East.

Mongke ordered that a census of the empire be conducted. This not only allowed him to return to a more rational tax system with populations paying what they could afford, but he also gained an estimate of the resources of the empire. These three individuals, despite their high rank, survived the purge largely through their ability, but also through the fact that, even though they had served both Ogodei and Guyuk, all three had at some point represented and maintained the interests of the entire *altan urugh*.[28] In short, their integrity remained intact.

Although the Ogodeids and Chaghatayids saw a reduction in their territory, Mongke did not destroy them. He did take steps to ensure that Toluid hegemony could never be challenged. To Khubilai, Mongke allocated the unassigned territories in the former Jin Empire as well as occupied Song land. Although the Mongols occupied much of the Middle East since 1230, it also remained directly tied to the *Qaʾan*. Mongke dispatched his younger brother Hulegu there, although scholars still debate Mongke's intentions.[29] Regardless, both Khubilai and Hulegu received the title of *il-khan* or subordinate khan.[30] Although both enjoyed almost complete autonomy, whether as military commander or viceroy, the title made it clear that they were

---

[27] Allsen, *Mongol Imperialism*, 134–43.
[28] Allsen, 'The Rise of the Mongolian Empire', 398; Thomas T. Allsen, 'Mahmud Yalavac, Mas'ud Beg, ʿAli Beg, Safaliq, Bujir', *ITSOTK* (Wiesbaden, 1993), 126–7.
[29] Michael Hope, *Power, Politics, and Tradition in the Mongol Empire and Ilkhanate of Iran* (Oxford, 2016), 93–4; George Lane, *Early Mongol Rule in Thirteenth-Century Iran* (New York, 2003), 15, Peter Jackson, 'From *Ulus* to Khanate: The Making of the Mongol States', in *MEL*, 28–32.
[30] Reuven Amitai-Preiss, 'Evidence for the early use of the title *Ilkhan* among the Mongols', *JRAS* 1 (1991), 353–61; Reuven Amitai-Preiss, 'An Exchange of Letters in Arabic Between Abaya Ilkhan and Sultan Baybars (AH 667–AD 1268–9)', *CAJ* 38 (1994), 24–6.

subordinate and directly tied to the *Qa'an*. Furthermore, he placed the two most economically important regions of the empire (China and the Middle East) in the hands of the Toluid family. Previously, these regions had been parcelled out throughout the *altan urugh* as *qubi*. Family members extracted some revenue, but no single individual or even family could consolidate their holdings to claim the region even if they wanted to. Mongke altered this.

A major issue was the proliferation of the *ortoq* relationship between the Chinggisids and merchants. The commercial ties were not an issue, but many of these merchants had gained positions within the government through their princely connections while also maintaining their commercial ventures. In effect, the government subsidised commerce yet did not yield any profit. Furthermore, during the regency of Oghul Qaimish, *gerege* or *paizas*, the passports that allowed individuals in government employ to use the *jam* system, proliferated.[31] This was due not only to the tri-*ordo* situation rendered by Oghul Qaimish, Naqu and Khwaja, but also because other Chinggisid princes also issued their own passports for their territories. Even the princes used the *jam* system for their own travel with large entourages, leading to excessive demands on nomadic and sedentary populations for horses, shelter and food and resulting in extreme poverty as well as the abandonment of areas near a *jam* station. In short, the system was breaking under the corruption.

Mongke rectified both situations. He centralised the *jam* system and connected routes set up by individual princes to the imperial system. He also ordered that all of the *gerege* then be turned over to the government and be re-issued.[32] Recipients were registered to ensure that the system was not abused by the Chinggisids, government workers or merchants. The aforementioned Amir Imad al-Mulk and Fakhr al-Mulk were placed in charge of issuing the *gerege* with explicit orders to not issue them to merchants.[33] Restrictions were also put in place to eliminate abuses. Even those carrying the gold *gerege* were limited to fourteen horses and prohibited from requisitioning animals from nomads or villages near the stations. Furthermore, all envoys were to move from one *jam* post to another and not linger unduly, not only to ensure the speed of message delivery but also so as not to burden the populace.

The tax system also received new scrutiny and became standardised due to the Toluid Revolution. Although, as Thomas Allsen indicated, Mongke did not innovate with new institutions, he reformed those that existed.[34] In addition to imposing a unified taxation system, he also ordered that devastated

---

[31] May, 'Commercial Queens', 105–6.
[32] Allsen, *Mongol Imperialism*, 80.
[33] RD/Thackston2, 292; RD/Thackston1, 411; RD/Karimi, 596–7.
[34] Allsen, 'The Rise of the Mongolian Empire', 398.

regions be rehabilitated. This process began prior to Mongke, but it appears to have been haphazard and left to individual initiative as much as policy. Mongke's expansion of central government changed that. To achieve that goal, funds were necessary and thus taxation reform became a priority. One reason was that Oghul Qaimish proved to be even more rapacious than Toregene. Whereas the custom had been to tax nomads at one animal for every hundred, Oghul Qaimish had set the rate at one for every ten, which was unsustainable. Had her administration existed for more than a brief two years, the nomadic economy might have collapsed and sent the base of the empire into poverty.

Mongke restored the *qubchur* tax to one animal for every one hundred of a kind for nomads. If one had fewer than a hundred animals no tax was owed. In sedentary areas reasonable *qubchur* taxes were also restored. Among the sedentary population, the tax system devised by Mahmud Yalavach was expanded beyond Central Asia, with some modification. Whereas individuals paid a tax ranging from one to eleven dinars on the basis of their wealth established at the time of the census in the Muslim regions, in North China the tax operated on a household basis rather than involving just adult males. Another adjustment was that, in China, the tax could be paid in silver as in the rest of the empire, or in goods such as silk. This was also a countermeasure to the policies of Oghul Qaimish. Silver coinage had not been common in North China. Thus, when the tax collectors demanded payment in silver, the population often turned to moneylenders, who were often *ortoq* merchants connected to the administration. Thousands became impoverished by paying the interest on their taxes. During Mongke's reign both silver and silk were permitted as payment. After 1253, paper money issued by the government circulated in North China and became an acceptable form of payment. Similar situations occurred in other regions where silver coinage was uncommon, such as in the Rus' principalities, where furs became an alternative means of payment. Nonetheless, Mongke made a conscious effort to promote the use and circulation of coinage.[35]

Alba, or service, continued to be expected, and the census ensured that the Mongols knew what each location could provide. Although the *qubchur* was standardised, the *qalan* also included agricultural taxes on the sedentary population, implemented according to local custom.[36] In North China it was based on the quantity of land while in Islamic territories the traditional *kharaj* (land tax) served as *qalan*. The *tamgha*, a sales tax of sorts, was also

---

[35] Allsen, *Mongol Imperialism*, 172–3.
[36] Allsen, *Mongol Imperialism*, 153–4.

expanded. Previously it had ranged from 5 to 10 per cent of the value of a merchant's goods. This remained the same, but Mongke also expanded it to other occupations that provided services, such as prostitutes, but also those who produced goods or materials, including not only artisans, but even fishermen![37] Even while some taxes were lowered more were created, with all of them tied to the census registration.

Those granted tax exemptions by Chinggis Khan or by Ogodei maintained that status. This included most religious leaders, among others. Anyone who had gained exemption from Guyuk or the regents resumed paying taxes. Furthermore, Mongke's agents accepted no excuses for not paying taxes. Although Mongke did not tolerate resistance to his new tax policies, he did not seek to recoup previous years' unpaid taxes. Mongke demonstrated a more lenient side, however, by exempting the elderly who no longer could work. In effect, Mongke started his reign with a blank slate for everyone. By and large, with the reign of Mongke the empire saw a reduction in taxes, but the loss of revenue was compensated for by a more efficient administration that eliminated corruption and gathered income from new sources.

The reforms of Mongke were significant and transformed the Mongol Empire by creating a greater level of central authority. According to Rashid al-Din, 'Even during the reigns of ancient kings and sultans of times past, when there was perfect order, had they been alive then they would have followed his example'.[38] Although he surely wrote with hyperbole, Rashid al-Din's statement indicates a greater level of centralisation of authority than in previous eras of the *Yeke Monggol Ulus*.

Religion

Like his predecessors, Mongke followed a policy of religious neutrality. As long as one's religious beliefs did not cause instability within the empire, one could practise whatever faith one desired. As with other rulers, Mongke also found large numbers of various adherents coming to Qaraqorum to convert the *Qa'an*. Despite the vaunted religious toleration of the Mongols, it did not extend to all religions in all manners. Buddhists, Daoists, Christians, Confucians and Muslims all received tax exemptions for their religious sites in return for prayers for the *Qa'an*, whereas Jews, Zoroastrians and

---

[37] David Morgan, *The Mongols* (Cambridge, MA, 1986), 101; Beatrice Manz, 'The Rule of the Infidels: The Mongols and the Islamic World', in David O. Morgan and Anthony Reid (eds), *NCHI*, v3, *The Eastern Islamic World Eleventh to Eighteenth Centuries* (Cambridge, 2010), 142.

[38] RD/Thackston2, 292; RD/Thackston1, 413; RD/Karimi, 599.

Manichaeans did not, largely as they did not have sufficient political clout.[39] As regards religion, he showed favour to none, but appears to have made all feel included and important. During Eid al-Fitr (the feast at the end of Ramadan) in 1252, he distributed alms and listened to the sermon and prayer given by the Qadi Jalal al-Din Mahmud Khujandi. This took place in Qaraqorum, not in a Muslim majority region of the empire.[40]

Mongke took great interest in religions even if he did not subscribe to any. Although numerous missionaries came, they all failed in their proselytisation. Nonetheless, he gave them the opportunity to convince him of the truth of their words so that many went away thinking the *Qa'an* had been swayed. In some instances the Mongols had religious tournaments where the priests and clergy of various faiths debated before the Mongol court. As with many sporting events, it was not uncommon that some of the observers became inebriated during the spectacle. While the contests could be in essence a battle royale, others involved team debates with teams picked by the *Qa'an* or others. For instance, the Franciscan friar William of Rubruck found himself on 'Team Monotheist' with Nestorian Christians and Muslims squaring off against the 'Idolators', which included a variety of Buddhist monks and Daoist priests. According to William of Rubruck, he was the MVP (most valuable priest) of the event, as not only did he debate the key issues of monotheism most eloquently, but the Idolaters could not counter his arguments.[41] Thus, it seemed that Mongke was on the cusp of conversion. William, however, was to be disappointed. Mongke simply explained to the earnest Franciscan, 'But just as God has given the hand several fingers, so has he given mankind several paths.'[42]

These debates also had another purpose, beyond the entertainment and education of the ruler. On occasion, they were also used to settle disputes between groups. In 1258, Mongke's younger brother, Khubilai, presided over a debate between Daoists, Buddhists and Confucians. The primary goal of the meeting was to end violence between Daoists and Buddhists in North China. Disagreement over doctrine had escalated into violence that included not only the destruction of temples, but also Daoists and Buddhists fighting pitched battles in city streets and elsewhere. Mongke specifically selected

---

[39] Christopher P. Atwood, 'Validation by Holiness or Sovereignty: Religious Toleration as Political Theology in the Mongol World Empire of the Thirteenth Century', *IHR* 26/2 (2004), 247.
[40] Juwayni/Qazvini, v3, 79–80; Juvaini/Boyle, 601–2; RD/Thackston2, 292; RD/Thackston1, 413; RD/Karimi, 599.
[41] Rubruck/Jackson, 230–5; Rubruck/Dawson, 190–4; Rubruc, 293–6.
[42] Rubruck/Jackson, 236; Rubruck/Dawson, 195; Rubruc, 298.

Figure 7.2 Rubruck's Tree. The Franciscan friar William of Rubruck described a fountain made in the shape of a silver tree by the Parisian silversmith William Buchier (who was made captive during the 1241 invasion of Hungary). Unlike the original, this modern presentation did not produce *airagh*, rice wine, wine, or mead.

Khubilai to resolve the matter because of his familiarity with both Buddhism and Daoism. In addition, he had some familiarity with Confucians. The latter's presence in the debate seems to have been more of an effort to include the Confucians, many of whom abstained from imperial service, as well as an effort to include a third party to defuse tensions. In the end, the Buddhists won the debate through the oratorical skills of a Tibetan monk known as the Phagspa Lama, who, along with other Buddhist monks, demonstrated that a few Daoist texts were forgeries and not written by Laozi (Lao-Tzu).

Khubilai allowed the Daoists another chance at redemption by demonstrating their supernatural powers. These failed. As a result, Khubilai ordered all copies of the forged texts to be destroyed. Also, any property the Daoists had seized from Buddhists was to be returned. Although this did not resolve all of the issues between the two religions, it did curb the violence. By having brought their dispute before the secular authorities, the Daoists also realised that to continue the strife would only incur the wrath of the Mongol *Qa'an*.

While not happy, they accepted the judgement. For the Mongols, it was also important not to target Daoism as it was an extremely popular religion among their Chinese subjects.[43]

Campaigns

The Toluid Revolution that changed the empire politically and administratively also extended to the military structure of the empire. Although the first year of Mongke's reign consisted of purging the empire of those who opposed him and reforming the government, in the second year he convened another *quriltai* to plan for war. Mongke planned to deal with those powers that remained in a state of rebellion according to the Mongol ideology of *Tenggerism*, or the belief that *Koke Mongke Tenggeri* had bequeathed the earth to Chinggis Khan and his successors. According to this, if one had not submitted to the Mongols, one was a rebel. Mongke had already assigned his brothers Hulegu and Khubilai to govern territory in areas that had not been part of the four *uluses* of the sons of Chinggis Khan. With the *quriltai*, these assignments were transformed into military campaigns. By dispatching Hulegu to the Middle East, Mongke achieved several goals. For the good of the empire, his brother would bring under Mongol authority those who had not yet submitted. At the same time, he would prevent further Chaghatayid expansion southward. There remains some question as to whether all of the territories south of the Amu Darya would become part of an *ulus* Hulegu or whether he simply served as an imperial viceroy or senior military commander.[44] With the tightening of imperial authority over what was now the Turkestan Secretariat and the establishment of Hulegu in the Middle East, the Chaghatayids were not only encircled, but considerably more restricted in their autonomy.

Meanwhile, Khubilai was to campaign against the Song empire. Little headway had been made since the time of Ogodei. Guyuk had sent armies, but due to his short reign the armies made only minimal advances against the Song defences. The primary obstacles for the Mongol advance were the northern defences. Therefore, Mongke ordered Khubilai to open another front. In order to achieve this, Khubilai had to secure the submission of the unconquered kingdom of Dali. Dali was a non-Chinese kingdom, called Qarajang by the Mongols, bordering Tibet, Xi Xia and the Song Empire and

---

[43] Morris Rossabi, *Khubilai Khan: His Life and Times* (Berkeley, 1988), 40–2.
[44] Allsen, *Mongol Imperialism*, 48–9; Peter Jackson, 'Dissolution of the Mongol Empire', *CAJ* 22 (1978), 220–2; Hope, *Power, Politics, and Tradition*, 93; Peter Jackson, 'From *Ulus* to Khanate: The Making of the Mongol States, c. 1220–c. 1290', in *MEL*, 29–30; George Lane, *Early Mongol Rule in Thirteenth-Century Iran* (New York, 2003), 39–40.

included much of Yunnan Province in modern China.⁴⁵ Its conquest would then open a south-west front against the Song. Although Khubilai himself delayed his participation in the war due to gout, he sent his primary general, Uriyangqadai (1199–1271), the son of Subedei, with his army, while he would follow.⁴⁶

During Mongke's coronation, many representatives arrived to offer their tribute and obeisance. While most were princes of conquered states who had retained their throne, there were a few new ones. One such figure was King Hethum, the King of Cilicia or Lesser Armenia. Other parties included local notables from areas around Quhistan and other territories that bordered the domains of the Nizari Ismailis, known more infamously as the Assassins. They lodged complaints about the Assassins, regaling the khan with how no one slept soundly for fear of assassination. The qadi of Qazvin even showed the Khan the chain mail shirt that he wore under his robes. He daringly challenged Mongke's authority, saying that the Mongols were weak as the Assassins held several castles and their religion was contrary to the Muslims, Christians and Mongols. Furthermore, if the Mongols lost power, the Assassins would take their place.⁴⁷ Needless to say, this did not go down well with Mongke. The qadi, however, did not suffer any retribution. Rather, the Nizari Ismailis earned a spot at the top of Hulegu's 'to-do' list as he entered the Middle East.

To assist his brothers in their endeavours, Mongke assigned armies of conquest to them. Mongke ordered that two in every ten would serve in Khubilai's armies and another two in every ten serve under Hulegu's command.⁴⁸ This order referred only to the Mongol population. As a result their armies swelled, and this did not include the armies that Mongke would lead against the Song Empire. Mongke's plan not only augmented the Toluid troops available by drawing on 40 per cent of Mongol nomadic military power, but it also reduced the military capacity of the non-Toluids. While the Jochids were allies, Mongke nonetheless wanted to ensure that the Ogodeid and Chaghatayid military were not idle. Mongke also benefited in that his command was not out of the ordinary. The armies that took part in the Western Campaign and in previous campaigns in China comprised various Chinggisid princes and their retinues. Yet, both of these new armies may have been *tamma* armies. The difference was that *tamma* armies were

---

[45] *YUS*, 60. Ergo, before the Mongol Empire, Yunnan was not part of China.
[46] John E. Herman, 'The Mongol Conquest of Dali: The Failed Second Front', in *WIAH*, 304–5.
[47] Juzjani/Raverty, 1,189.
[48] Juvaini/Boyle, 607; Juwayni/Qazvini, v3, 90.

normally commanded by generals, not princes, and were sent to the frontiers of non-patrimonial lands. Furthermore, *tamma* units did not return to their domains, unlike the princely armies that took part in the Western Campaign or in China, when their service ended.[49]

Mongke could assign 40 per cent of the military to these two campaigns because of the censuses. Although the census was not complete, he had enough information to know the military strength of each *ulus*. At this time, the Mongol military had approximately one million nomads enrolled in the military and untold millions of non-nomadic or *cherik* troops.[50] With this data and manpower, the Mongols no longer concerned themselves with maximising their manpower so as not to over-extend themselves and with withdrawing from much of the conquered land with the tsunami strategy.[51] Instead, now they could use numbers to crush their enemies. Numbers would not be used as sledgehammer or steamroller, but rather allow them to open even more fronts and attack more targets than they had ever done before.

The invasion of Dali began in 1252 and it took three years to pacify, during which time Khubilai arrived. Even though Dali, which also possessed high-quality pastures, was now in Mongol hands and offered an excellent staging base for attacks on the Song Empire, it sufficiently stalled Khubilai's attack on the Song. The delay annoyed Mongke as it prevented his own invasion. Although raiding had been continuous since 1252, the conquest of the Song Empire began in earnest in 1254. Not until 1258, however, did Mongke break through the outer defences with a four-pronged attack. Mongke invaded Sichuan and eastern China while Khubilai invaded central China and headed south. Uriyangqadai, meanwhile, invaded the Song Empire from Dali and moved in a north-eastern direction as another army, led by Prince Taghachar, invaded eastern China and marched north-west.[52]

Terrain and fortifications slowed their advance. The Mongol cavalry was confined to raiding while mountain fortresses often forced the Mongols to use alternative routes. Nonetheless, the Mongol war machine, augmented by thousands of Chinese infantry from the former Jin Empire, advanced inexorably into Song territory. Ultimately, all armies were to converge on various

---

[49] Juvaini/Boyle, 607–8; Juwayni/Qazvini, v3, 90–3; RD/Thackston2, 35; RD/Thackston1, 49; RD/Karimi, 66.
[50] Timothy May, *The Mongol Art of War* (Yardley, PA, 2007), 28.
[51] Timothy May, 'The Mongol Art of War and the Tsunami strategy', in Roman Hautala, et al. (eds), Золотоордынская цивилизация. Научный ежегодник, Выпуск 8 (Казань, 2015), 31–7; Timothy May, 'Mongol Conquest Strategy in the Middle East', in *MME*, 13–37.
[52] *YUS*, 63.

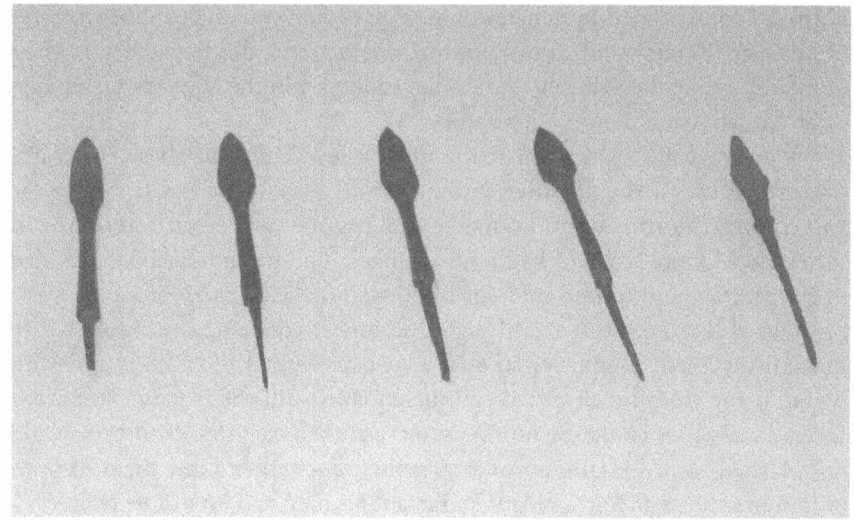

Figure 7.3 The Mongols used a wide variety of arrowheads. These more narrow ones were primarily for piercing armour. (National History Museum, Ulaanbaatar, Mongolia)

locations on the Yangzi River. Unable to cope with the multiple armies, it appeared that the Song Empire was on the verge of collapse as Khubilai began the siege of Ezhou and Mongke attacked Hezhou.

Meanwhile, Hulegu's primary objective was to bring to heel those rulers who had yet to submit to the Mongols in the Middle East. Both the Abbasid Caliph and a few Ayyubid princes had not formally submitted to Mongke, despite having sent tribute in the past.[53] Other rulers had, however, such as King Hethum of Cilicia, a small Armenian state, who did so shortly after the defeats of the Seljuks at Kose Dagh in 1243. Because he submitted, he received an increased realm as well as protection from the Seljuks, also Mongol vassals but who had previously raided his territory.[54] Hethum also convinced Prince Bohemund VI of Antioch and Tripoli (two Crusader states) to submit to the Mongols.

Hulegu's advance has been termed as being leisurely so as to conserve his troops.[55] Although the invasion of Hungary and Khwarazm had been marked by rapid advances, Hulegu did not advance rapidly. For one thing, sizeable

---

[53] JPC, 75–6; JPC/Dawson, 32; *YUS*, 63; BH1, 409.
[54] Matthew Paris, v2, 165; Het'um, 178–9; Hetoum, 36–40; Vardan 1989, 216; Grigor of Akanc, 313–15, 325–7.
[55] See J. M. Smith, Jr, 'Hulegu Moves West: High Living and Heartbreak on the Road to Baghdad', in *BLGK*, 111–34.

Figure 7.4 Mongol archery. Archery was key to Mongol military success. Even today, it remains a popular sport. Here, a Mongolian strings his bow.

Mongol forces were already in the vicinity of the Assassins and operations were under way by the time Hulegu began his march. Logistically, it was impossible to move rapidly as pasture had to be secured to satisfy the needs of the animals as well as additional provisions and water. Indeed, officials had begun this process long before Hulegu moved.[56] This included the movement of Baiju's army from Transcaucasia into Rum. The appearance of a Mongol army in Rum for the long term caused a minor rebellion, but Baiju quashed it at the battle of Aq Saray in 1256. Afterwards, Rum was divided between two Seljuk princes, who continued to see their authority and power diminished due to the Mongol presence.[57]

Ket-Buqa Noyan began his military operation against Nizari fortresses in Quhistan, in central Iran, in 1253/4.[58] The fortresses fell steadily and more frequently as Hulegu approached. Meanwhile, the Mongols demanded

---

[56] Smith, Jr, 'Hulegu Moves West', 113–18.
[57] May, 'Mongol Conquest Strategy', 27–34.
[58] Marshall G. S. Hodgson, *The Order of the Assassins* (New York, 1955), 260; Timothy May, 'A Mongol–Ismaʿili Alliance?: Thoughts on the Mongols and Assassins', *JRAS* 14/3 (2004), 233.

Figure 7.5 The Mongol composite bow, when unstrung, formed an approximate 'C' shape. When it was strung, the tension stored in its arms provided great power to the bow.

that Rukn al-Din Khwurshah, the leader of the Nizaris, come and submit to Hulegu. Khwurshah stalled for time and offered to send relatives, but Hulegu would not accept this alternative. Part of the issue was that hostilities between the Mongols and Assassins reached a point of no return when rumours reached Mongke that the Nizaris had dispatched four hundred Assassins to his enthronement.[59]

As his fortresses fell one by one and the population was slaughtered, Khwurshah submitted to the inevitable. As Ket-Buqa escorted him to Hulegu, the Mongol general also used Khwurshah to secure the surrender of a number of other fortresses. Hulegu admonished the Nizari leader but otherwise treated him well. With Quhistan subdued, the Mongols then turned to the mountain fortresses in northern Iran. Eventually, Khwurshah became less valuable as a negotiating tool, as these citadels refused to submit. Khwurshah was then sent to Mongke.[60]

---

[59] Rubruck/Jackson, 222; Rubruck/Dawson, 184; Rubruc, 287.
[60] RD/Thackston2, 345; RD/Thackston1, 486; RD/Karimi, 697.

The key fortress was Alamut, a formidable fortress perched atop a steep mountain. The Nizaris also made the attack more difficult by removing all rocks within the vicinity; thus the Mongols had to haul rocks for their trebuchets from miles away. They also resorted to cutting down trees and launching wooden missiles. Yet the Mongols had other means of weaponry as well. In Hulegu's company was a *minqan* of Chinese engineers. Some scholars have interpreted this, along with vague statements in one Persian source, as evidence that the Mongols used gunpowder weapons – rockets – to attack Alamut.[61] Thus far the archaeological and textual evidence does not support this hypothesis. Regardless of the weaponry, Alamut did fall, as did the rest of the Nizari strongholds in 1256. A few held out for several more years, but all succumbed to the Mongols. Their libraries were burned, to the delight of one Sunni observer, who viewed them as filled with heretical tracts and treatises.[62] Furthermore, the men were killed and the women and children were sold into slavery. Despite this, the Nizaris were not exterminated and many founded a community in India, beyond Mongol reach, although there was Nizari activity in Iran after 1256 as well.[63] After the fall of Alamut, Khwurshah was executed by his guards.[64]

With the demise of the Nizaris, Hulegu then marched towards Baghdad. Although the Abbasid Caliphate no longer stretched from the Mediterranean to the Syr Darya, it still wielded some authority. The reality, however, was that it was greatly reduced in both influence and power, particularly beginning with the reign of Caliph Mustasim ibn Mustansir. Unlike his father, Caliph Mustansir, who had vigorously attended to the defences of the Caliphate, Mustasim was more interested in pigeon racing and leisure than in affairs of state. These he left in the hands of his vizier Ibn al-Alqami, a Shia Muslim.[65] Ibn al-Alqami was well aware of the truncated power of the Abbasids and the rise of the Mongols and so he opened a line of communication. When Mongol emissaries demanded the Caliph's submission, the Caliph gave them dire warnings of what would happen, unaware that his vizier had begun negotiations with the Mongols. Even when his generals intercepted messages Mustasim ignored the warnings.[66]

---

[61] See Juvaini/Boyle, 630–1; Juwayni/Qazvini, v3, 128; Stephen G. Haw, 'Cathayan Arrows and Meteors: The Origins of Chinese Rocketry', *Journal of Chinese Military History* 2 (2013), 35–6, Smith, Jr, 'Hulegu Moves West', 126–8.
[62] Juvaini/Boyle, 725; Juwayni/Qazvini, v3, 278.
[63] Nadia Eboo Jamal, *Surviving the Mongols: Nizari Quhistani and the Continuity of Ismaili Tradition in Persia* (London, 2002), *passim*.
[64] Juwayni/Qazvini, v3, 277; Juvaini/Boyle, 724.
[65] BH1, 409.
[66] Dhahabi, 260, 265; Juzjani/Habibi, v2, 701; Juzjani/Raverty, 1.229–35; RD/Thackston1, 490–1; RD/Thackston2, 347; RD/Karimi, 703–5.

Thus, even before Hulegu's armies arrived from the east and were joined by Baiju's army along with Georgians, Armenians and Muslim vassals, Baghdad's fate was sealed. The Abbasid army rode out in an effort to prevent the Mongols from laying siege, but the Mongols broke a dyke and flooded the Abbasid camp. People who fled the city southward by boat found their path blocked by Mongol detachments that shot their ships with arrows and catapults. While some dared the gauntlet, others turned back upstream. Mongol siege engines bombarded the city while Ibn al-Alqami and others continued to negotiate. When the Caliph finally surrendered on 10 February 1258, the Mongols pillaged the city for thirty-four days. The Caliph was not even sent to Mongke. Instead, after revealing his hidden wealth and being chastised by Hulegu, he was executed by being rolled into a carpet and trampled to death, although rumours of a more ironic death persisted.[67] Ibn al-Alqami, however, was left as the vizier of the city with a *daruqachi* named ʿAli Bahadar and two Mongol *noyad*, Elgai and Qara Buqa, to restore order and repair the damage to Baghdad.[68]

Afterwards, other regional and local powers in northern Syria, Iraq and Anatolia formally showed obeisance to Hulegu, with the curious exception of al-Nasir Yusuf, the Ayyubid ruler of Aleppo and Damascus. A sizeable army, including many units of Armenians, Georgians, and even some troops from the Principality of Antioch, approached Aleppo. The Mongols wasted no time and directed their siege engines against the Bab al-Iraq gate. Within five days, the city fell. The citadel held out for a short time under the command of Muazzam Turanshah, but even this formidable structure could not last against the Mongols.[69] The Syriac monk Bar Hebraeus wrote: 'And there took place in Aleppo a slaughter like unto that of Baghdad only more terrible.'[70]

As the Mongols attacked Aleppo, al-Nasir Yusuf deliberated over a plan of action. Some of his commanders, including a Mamluk named Baybars, urged him to attack the Mongols while they laid siege to the city. Aleppo, however, fell before al-Nasir reached a decision. As the Mongols approached Damascus, al-Nasir fled southward, intending to reach Egypt. The Mongols

---

[67] Dhahabi, 266–7; Grigor of Akanc, 333–5; Juzjani/Habibi, v2, 708; Juzjani/Raverty, 1,252–3. Grigor of Akanc wrote that, before the execution, Hulegu berated the Caliph for hoarding his wealth rather than having spent it on the defence of Baghdad. Marco Polo made this rumour famous in the Western world. MP1, 30–1; MP/Cliff, 23–4; MP/Latham, 52–3; MP/Marsden, 27–8; MP/YC, 63–4; Hetoum, 40.
[68] RD/Karîmî, 714; RD/Thackston1, 499; RD/Thackston2, 354.
[69] RD/Thackston2, 356–8; RD/Thackston1, 502–3; RD/Karimi, 719–23; Nuwayri, 386; Maqrizi, v1, 422–3; Maqrizi/Quatremere, vol. 1, 90; Abu Shamah, 203; Grigor of Akanc, 349.
[70] BH1, 436.

captured him at Nablus after a brief skirmish. Ket-Buqa put al-Nasir to good use and secured the submission of a few other fortresses including Ajlun in northern Jordan before sending him to Hulegu. When the Mongols came to Damascus, the city leaders opened the gates and offered their submission. While some pillaging occurred, primarily by the Georgians and Armenians, the city suffered relatively little damage.[71] Afterwards, the majority of the Mongol army returned north while Ket-Buqa mopped up the remaining centres of resistance in Syria. On the basis of his operations, he most likely used the Biqa' Valley in Lebanon as his base of operations. It provided adequate pastures and placed him in a central position where he could control the most independent-minded population. Another Mongol force took up position at Gaza. The Mongols were firmly in control. A few skirmishes with crusaders in the Kingdom of Jerusalem demonstrated that the occupation force was not to be trifled with. Yet Mongol control of Syria proved ephemeral. They secured their position in Syria by the end of April and lost it on 3 September 1260 at the Battle of ʿAyn Jalut.

Egypt became the destination for refugees in Syria, including al-Nasir Yusuf's general Baybars, who abandoned al-Nasir in disgust. Baybars' return to Egypt was risky as he had fled from it during a coup. Yet with the Mongol threat looming on the horizon, the new sultan, Qutuz, welcomed him. Just a decade earlier, the Mamluks had seized control of Egypt from the Ayyubids. The Seventh Crusade of King Louis IX had thrown Egypt into turmoil as its ruler had died in the middle of the invasion. Although the Mamluks, slave soldiers, halted the invasion and took King Louis IX and the majority of his army captive, the heir to the throne did not reward them or appreciate the Mamluks to their own satisfaction. As a result, the Egyptian Mamluks committed regicide. They placed an Ayyubid child on the throne as a puppet. Instability continued for the next decade, with factions competing for power. Baybars found himself on the losing side and fled Egypt with many others. The Mongol threat, however, opened the door for reconciliation.[72]

---

[71] Thomas Agni of Lentini, 'Thomas Agni of Lentini, Papal Legate and Bishop of Bethlehem, to All Kings, Priests, Prelates and Nobles (1 March, 1260). Acre', in *LOE*, 154–55; Hulegu, 'Hulegu, Mongol Il-Khan of Persia, to Louis IX, King of France (1262). Maragha', in *LOE*, 158; Grigor, 349; Nuwayri, 389–90; Maqrizi, 423–4; Maqrizi/Quatremere, v1, 94; BH1, 436; RD/Thackston1, 503; RD/Thackston2, 357; RD/Karimi, 720.

[72] R. S. Humphreys, From Saladin to the Mongols: The Ayyubids of Damascus 1, 192–260 (Albany, 1977), 345–8; A. A. Khowaiter, Baibars the First: His Endeavours and Achievements (London, 1978), 18–20; Peter Thorau, *The Lion of Egypt: Sultan Baybars I and the Near East in the Thirteenth Century* (London, 1992), 65–6; Reuven Amitai-Preiss, *Mongols and Mamluks*, 35–6.

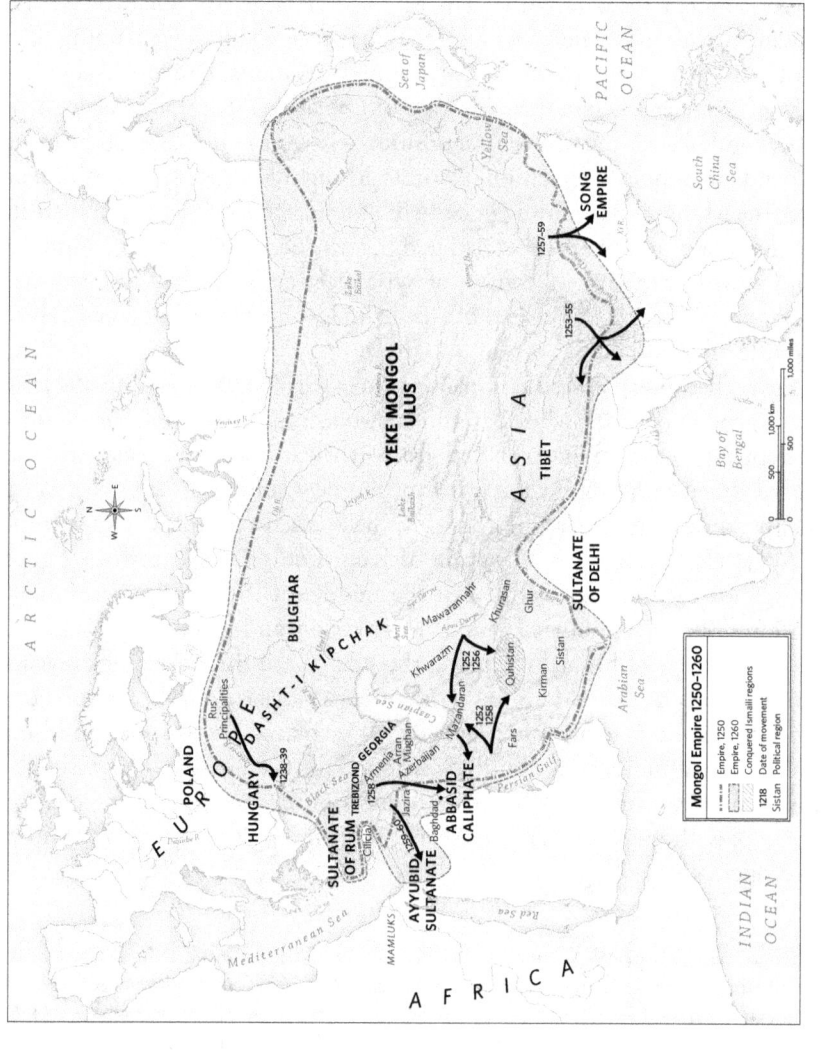

Map 7.1 The Mongol Empire during the reign of Mongke, 1250–60 © Mapping Specialists

When Mongol emissaries reached Cairo to demand the submission of the Mamluks, Qutuz, who had removed the Ayyubid child king from the throne in the face of the Mongols, executed the emissaries.[73] In his war council, Qutuz told his commanders they could flee across North Africa, submit like slaves, or resist. Encouraged by Baybars, he did not plan to wait for the Mongols to arrive, but to invade their territory and do so before they could mobilise.[74]

His plan was sound, as there were probably no more than 12,000 Mongols in Syria and Palestine. While their forces could be augmented by others, the loyalty of the Syrian *amirs* was dubious. The boldness of Baybars and Qutuz paid dividends. They quickly overran the Mongol force at Gaza and then secured the neutrality of the Kingdom of Jerusalem (which consisted of strongholds on the coast, but not actually Jerusalem). As Ket-Buqa marched southward, he encountered the Mamluks at ʿAyn Jalut in the Jezreel Valley in modern Israel. In an evenly matched battle, the Mamluks emerged victorious, killing Ket-Buqa.[75]

With Syria liberated, the Mamluks then began to plan for their possible retribution, which never occurred in the expected fashion. Yet, despite that possibility, with the immediate threat removed, old tensions between the Mamluk leaders resurfaced and Baybars killed Qutuz to claim the throne. Fortunately for Baybars, vengeance did not come immediately.[76] News reached Hulegu that proved to be of higher priority than Ket-Buqa's defeat at ʿAyn Jalut.

Even as the empire reached its greatest territorial heights in China and the Middle East, it suddenly came to a halt. Although the Mamluks defeated the Mongols, the conquests would have halted anyway, at least briefly. Mongke died in southern China in 1259 at the siege of Chongqing. Reports vary as to whether it was from illness or from wounds sustained in the siege.[77]

---

[73] RD/Karimi, 722; RD/Thackston1, 504–5; RD/Thackston2, 358; Maqrizi, 427–8; Maqrizi/Quatremere, v1, 101–2; Amitai-Preiss, Mongols and Mamluks, 36. Depending on the source, the execution was crucifixion, being cut in half, or beheading.

[74] RD/Karimi, 722; RD/Thackston1, 504–5; RD/Thackston2, 358. Also see Amitai-Preiss, *Mongols and Mamluks*, 35–7.

[75] For the analysis of the battle see Reuven Amitai-Preiss, 'ʿAyn Jalut Revisited', *Tarih* 2 (1992), 119–50; Amitai-Preiss, *Mongols and Mamluks*, 39–45; Peter Thorau, 'The Battle of ʿAyn Jalut: A Re-examination', in *Crusade and Settlement*, ed. P. W. Edbury (Cardiff, 1985), 236–41; John Masson Smith, Jr, 'ʿAyn Jalut: Mamluk Success or Mongol Failure?', *HJAS* 44 (1984), 307–45; J. J. Saunders, 'The Mongol Defeat at Ain Jalut and the Restoration of the Greek Empire', in *Muslims and Mongols: Essays on Medieval Asia* (Christchurch, 1977).

[76] Amitai-Preiss, *Mongols and Mamluks*, 45–8.

[77] RD/Thackston2, 294–5; RD/Thackston1, 415–16; RD/Karimi, 603; *YUS*, 67–8. Also see S. A. Shkoliar, *Kitaiskaia doognestrel'naia artilleriia* (Moscow, 1980), 251–2.

Race to the Throne

Ariq-Boke b. Tolui, Sorqoqtani's fourth son, received the news and immediately began to carry out his duties as regent. Unlike prior khans, Mongke had left the duties of regent to his brother rather than to a wife. It is not clear why. Perhaps he decided to follow the example of Chinggis Khan and his father Tolui. Perhaps he viewed the experiences of the 1240s as having been a direct result of female regents. He named Ariq-Boke as his regent prior to his invasion of the Song Empire. As a result, Ariq-Boke remained in Mongolia and did not take part of the Song campaign.

Mongke's son Asutai escorted his father's body back to Mongolia, where it was buried next to Chinggis Khan and Tolui.[78] Ariq-Boke then began to convene a *quriltai*. What happened next is a matter of dispute. According to the official accounts, Ariq-Boke did not wait for the return of all of the princes, including his brothers Hulegu and Khubilai, although he sent messengers to inform them. Although Khubilai received the news in a reasonable time frame, he did not immediately return. Instead, he insisted on finishing the campaign, saying, 'We have arrived here with soldiers like ants and locusts. Why should we turn back without having done anything just because of rumors?'[79]

Khubilai not only ignored the message but continued the invasion by crossing the Yangzi River with his army, no small feat in any era.[80] As he waged war for two months in the south attempting to capture the city of Ezhou, he received word from his wife Chabi that Ariq-Boke was acting suspiciously. She assumed he was seizing the throne.[81] Rashid al-Din's account suggests that Ariq-Boke plotted to have Khubilai arrested en route to the *quriltai*.[82] Ariq-Boke did indeed proceed with the *quriltai* in the absence of Hulegu and Khubilai Khan. Representatives from the Ogodeids, Chaghatayids and Jochids, along with the Asutai and Urungtash, Mongke's sons, and one of his wives all supported the nomination of Ariq-Boke, and he was elected.[83]

Ariq-Boke's election, however, convinced Khubilai to end his assault on the Song Empire. As a number of princes were in his army along with high-ranking commanders, he could also claim wide support for the throne. Khubilai then convened his own *quriltai* with those princes and generals who accompanied him, although he acknowledged that Hulegu and the Jochids

---

[78] RD/Karimi, 603; RD/Thackston1, 416; RD/Thackston2, 295.
[79] RD/Thackston1, 425; RD/Karimi, 617; RD/Thackston2, 300.
[80] Rossabi, *Khubilai Khan*, 49. See *Yuan Shi* 61.
[81] RD/Karimi, 617–18; RD/Thackston1, 425–6; RD/Thackston2, 301–2.
[82] RD/Karimi, 618–19; RD/Thackston1, 618–19; RD/Thackston2, 301–2.
[83] Rossabi, *Khubilai Khan*, 50–1.

were too distant to be involved. This hastily convened *quriltai* then raised Khubilai to the throne.[84] Curiously, none of the sons of Mongke was considered by either faction. And perhaps as a result, civil war loomed on the horizon.

The war between Ariq-Boke and Khubilai is often depicted as an ideological one. The fact that Ariq-Boke and Khubilai could both hold *quriltais* and be elected also reveals much about their opposing views and what has become the typical view of the civil war factions. Ariq-Boke was very much the emblem of the conservative or traditional faction among the Mongols. He preferred that the empire continue to be exploited for the benefit of the nomads and that they should rule from the steppes and not become assimilated into the sedentary population. Khubilai, on the other hand, represented progressive elements among the Mongol elites who believed that, in order to rule and maintain the empire better, they needed to be more integrated with the sedentary population. Khubilai was not concerned about assimilation as he believed steps could be taken to prevent it. Nonetheless, he did not believe the Mongols could maintain their rule by being apart from the majority of the empire's population.[85] The Mongol princes aligned more or less according to their belief, although some chose sides because of other issues. This was the case with the Jochid Khanate's ruler, Berke. Batu died in 1256, and then his son Sartaq and his successor both died in rapid succession, which led to the ascension of Berke, Batu's brother, to the throne. Berke had other reasons to side with Ariq-Boke as well, since Hulegu occupied territory that Berke viewed as being part of the Jochid patrimony. There are hints, however, that he played both sides.[86] Hulegu may have sided with Khubilai not because he shared the same view as him but rather because he wanted assistance against Berke, and he did not give allegiance to Khubilai until 1262.[87] His son Jumghur, who remained in Mongolia when Hulegu first moved west, had actually fought alongside Ariq-Boke before joining Hulegu.[88] While some areas were not directly involved in the war, no area was immune from the war's effects. In truth, the war had less to do with ideology and more with the two brothers' rivalry for power.

[84] RD/Karimi, 620; RD/Thackston1, 427–8; RD/Thackston2, 302.
[85] Rossabi, *Khubilai Khan*, 53–6.
[86] Peter Jackson, *The Dissolution of the Mongol Empire*, CAJ 22 (1978), 208–27. Also see RD/Karimi, 623; RD/Thackston1, 429; RD/Thackston2, 304.
[87] Jackson, 'Dissolution of the Mongol Empire', 234; RD/Karimi, 623; RD/Thackston1, 429; RD/Thackston2, 304.
[88] RD/Karimi, 621, 680; RD/Thackston1, 428, 472; RD/Thackston2, 303, 335. Rashid al-Din suggests that he was forced to fight beside Ariq Boke and departed as soon as the opportunity arose. This is not completely convincing.

Having a large army already assembled, Khubilai marched north towards Mongolia, leaving but a few token forces to engage in holding actions against the Song. Despite possessing Qaraqorum and Mongolia, Ariq-Boke was at a decisive disadvantage. Qaraqorum was only sustainable because it received 900 cartloads of provisions per day. Once Khubilai cut this off, Qaraqorum was crippled. The city fell in 1262.[89]

Ariq-Boke continued his war in the steppes and attempted to procure provisions from Central Asia. He placed his own Chaghatayid supporter, Alghu, on the throne there, but this backfired as he proved to be independent-minded and sided with Khubilai not long afterwards.[90] Ariq-Boke found himself increasingly isolated and Alghu's desertion crippled him. The Jochids, although nominal supporters of Ariq-Boke, were involved in their own war with Hulegu and did not send support to Mongolia. As a result, Ariq-Boke surrendered in 1264.[91] Khubilai considered executing him, but Hulegu, Alghu and Berke all prevaricated on this sentence. Neither Hulegu nor Berke would set aside their own war to come to Mongolia to pass sentence. Alghu pointed out that he had taken the throne in the Chaghatayid Ulus without consulting Khubilai or Hulegu, insinuating that if Ariq-Boke was executed, then so should he be. Nonetheless, a purge of Ariq-Boke's supporters took place among the *noyad*.[92] Ariq-Boke died in 1265 from illness, leaving Khubilai the sole claimant to the throne.[93] As neither Hulegu, Alghu nor Berke attended a formal *quriltai*, and the other major princes never formally conferred their approval on Khubilai's enthronement nor made formal obeisance, an aura of illegitimacy haunted Khubilai despite assertions that he had always been the legitimate claimant to the throne.[94] Hulegu, the Chaghatayids and even the Jochids gave him recognition to some extent, but none went to him to make formal submission.

In truth, Khubilai was the usurper. Rossabi indicates that Khubilai painted himself as the rightful emperor on the basis of Chinese precepts so as to cultivate support there.[95] The myth that Ariq-Boke challenged Khubilai's right appears to be largely influenced by Marco Polo, Khubilai's greatest unofficial propagandist, as well as Rashid al-Din, who gained much

---

[89] RD/Karimi, 622; RD/Thackston1, 428–9; RD/Thackston2, 303–4.
[90] RD/Karimi, 622–8; RD/Thackston1, 428–32; RD/Thackston2, 303–5.
[91] RD/Karimi, 628–9; RD/Thackston1, 432–3; RD/Thackston2, 306; Peter Jackson, *The Mongols and the Islamic World* (New Haven, 2017), 149.
[92] RD/Karimi, 631; RD/Thackston, 434–43; RD/Thackston2, 307–8.
[93] RD/Karimi, 632; RD/Thackston1, 435; RD/Thackston2, 308.
[94] Rossabi, *Khubilai Khan*, 62.
[95] Rossabi, *Khubilai Khan*, 55–6.

of his information on Khubilai's realm from Bolod, a high-ranking official in Khubilai's administration.[96] Due to Bolod's influence, Rashid al-Din's account must be viewed with skepticism, perhaps not in terms of the course of events, but in interpretation. Despite Rashid al-Din's protestations otherwise, Hulegu seems only to have declared for Khubilai after Ariq-Boke lost Qaraqorum and perhaps after Alghu turned on him. At one point Rashid al-Din writes that Ariq-Boke, having fled to the Kemkemjiut territory in Siberia after losing Qaraqorum, tried to trick Khubilai into an ambush by offering a peace overture:

> We younger brothers have committed a crime and done wrong out of ignorance. You are my elder brother. The rule is yours. Wherever you say, I will come, and I will not disobey my elder brother's command. Let me fatten my flocks and horses and then come to you. [Berke], Hulagu, and Alghu are also coming, and I am expecting their arrival.[97]

Here Rashid al-Din overplays his hand. First, he is suggesting a primogeniture succession, which had never been Mongol custom, although certainly some (Guyuk) preferred it. Secondly, he indicates that Berke, Hulegu and Alghu would join Ariq-Boke. In doing so, Rashid al-Din inadvertently suggests that they supported him. Otherwise, why would they join him prior to meeting Khubilai? As indicated above, both Alghu and Hulegu joined Khubilai, but only after Khubilai gained the upper hand. Berke never committed himself. In truth, Ariq-Boke appears to have been the preferred successor from the beginning.[98] Khubilai's efforts to gain glory against the Song were an attempt to surpass Ariq-Boke's credentials by defeating a foe that not even Mongke had defeated.[99]

Although he was now the ruler of the eastern regions, resistance to his rule continued. With the defeat of Ariq-Boke, many of his supporters moved westward to Zhungaria (Lake Balkhash and the Ili River Basin). Here they coalesced around the scion of the House of Ogodei, Qaidu. Augmented by these, Qaidu became a force undaunted by Khubilai's title or resources. While Qaidu could not topple Khubilai, over the decades it became clear that Khubilai could not remove Qaidu from power. As a result, their struggle had a tremendous impact on the empire.

Both Qaidu and Khubilai vied for influence over the Chaghatayid

---

[96] MP/Cliff, 87; MP/Lathem, 113; MP/Marsden, 97; MP1, 122; MP/YC, 332–3; Thomas T. Allsen, *Culture and Conquest in Mongol Eurasia* (Cambridge, 2001), 72–83.
[97] RD/Thackston2, 303–4; RD/Karimi, 622–3; RD/Thackston1, 429.
[98] Kiracos, 184; BH1, 489.
[99] Rossabi, *Khubilai Khan*, 49.

Khanate. As it was the centre of the empire, it dominated communication lines between Khubilai and Hulegu. Therefore, it was crucial that Qaidu should control it. It also sat in the middle of the overland trade routes. The Jochids were also interested in it because of trade, as well as the possibility of opening a second front against Hulegu. Many Chaghatayids also opposed Khubilai, as they often had to concede to Qaidu because of his immediate proximity. Khubilai had his own stable of Chaghatayid supporters, but in his own territories, and he could only insert 'his man' given the right circumstances.

Even with the defeat of Ariq-Boke, the capital could no longer exist at Qaraqorum. Khubilai's victory exposed the city's vulnerability and with Qaidu just across the Altai Mountains, it remained susceptible to attack. Furthermore, Qaraqorum was too far north to serve as an administrative centre if Khubilai wished to finish conquering the Song Empire, which he did. During the reign of Ogodei, Qaraqorum served its purpose, being roughly equidistant from the Ili River, Xi Xia, Siberia, Manchuria and the Jin Empire, but with the shift in empire and the logistical difficulties in maintaining the city, it no longer served a purpose. Although the city

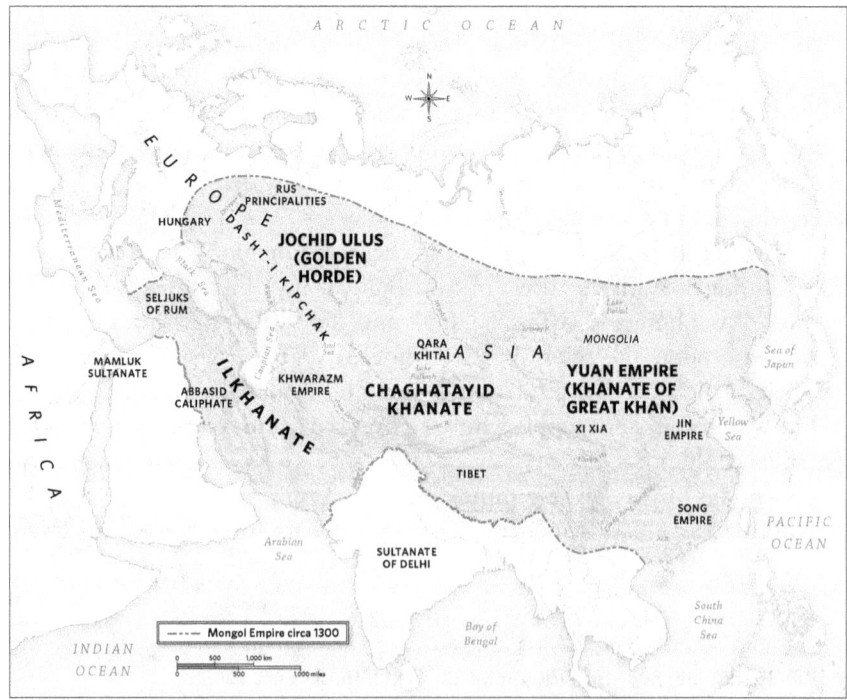

Map 7.2 The Mongol Empire in c.1300 © Mapping Specialists

continued to receive supplies, its population of 30,000 people gradually diminished.

Khubilai built a new city that is now incorporated by Beijing, named Daidu. The location was chosen wisely. It remained close enough to the steppes for Khubilai still to exert control over Mongolia, which remained sensitive to Ariq-Boke's defeat. At the same time, its location permitted Khubilai to rule from northern China and have firm control over his sedentary subjects. Daidu was also safely removed from the reach of Qaidu. At the same time, because of the shift of capitals, Mongolia receded in importance. With the removal of the capital, Mongolia once again became peripheral to trade and served primarily as a troop reservoir. Hopes of unity for the entire empire now collapsed.

Muslims in the Reign of Mongke

Despite writing from the safety of the Sultanate of Delhi, the Persian chronicler Juzjani was well-informed about activities within the Mongol Empire. Yet it is also apparent he did not receive all the details of events, as his account has omissions. Nonetheless, Juzjani includes some events not recorded elsewhere and the historian must determine whether these occurred and were omitted in other sources, or whether Juzjani understood events in a particular way that suited his own dogmatic outlook.

One occasion that demonstrates Juzjani's peculiar historical approach is Mongke's ascent to the throne. On the one hand Juzjani describes the discovery of Shiremun and Naqu's plot, but lays the entire scheme at the feet of the Chaghatayids.[100] He also states that Mongke became the first Muslim ruler of the Mongol Empire.[101] According to Juzjani, Mongke's conversion came through the intercession of Berke, who said:

> The empire of the infidels hath departed, and the dominion of every pagan monarch who ascends the throne of sovereignty will not endure. If ye desire that the rule of [Mongke] continue, and be prolonged, let him pronounce the confession of faith, in order that his name may be inscribed in the register of Islamis [sic], and then let him ascend the throne.[102]

Although Berke's role in Mongke's alleged conversion is not surprising, as he both was a Muslim and attended the *quriltai*, Mongke may have been surprised, as there is no other indication of his conversion. Indeed, William

---

[100] Juzjani/Habibi, v2, 179; Juzjani/Raverty, 1,182.
[101] Juzjani/Habibi, v2, 179; Juzjani/Raverty, 1,181–2.
[102] Juzjani/Raverty, 1,182; Juzjani/Habibi, v2, 179.

of Rubruck became quite aware that Mongke had no interest in converting to any religion, as mentioned earlier.[103] As indicated in Chapter 6, Juzjani viewed the Jochid Ulus as being quite favourable to Muslims, not only due to Berke's influence, but also due to Batu's own alleged conversion. William of Rubruck, however, noted that Batu was not completely comfortable with Berke's choice of religion.[104] Despite Juzjani's allegations (and perhaps wishes), neither Batu nor Mongke converted to Islam.

The other curious aspect of this is that Juzjani omitted the role of the Ogodeids in the coup against Mongke, even though Shiremun and Naqu were the primary conspirators. One must remember that Juzjani alleged that Ogodei was a friend to Muslims and may have even converted to Islam.[105] Thus the Ogodeids, while not perfect in the eyes of Juzjani, were not quite infidels. The Chaghatayids, however, were the descendants of the arch-foe of Islam, Chaghadai – at least from Juzjani's perspective.[106] Thus, if Mongke converted to Islam, it would be natural for the Chaghatayids to oppose him, while the involvement of the Ogodeids is politely ignored as a good Muslim should not rebel against a just ruler.

Juzjani was not alone in viewing opposition to Mongke through an Islamic lens. He does not, however, place the Chaghatayids at the forefront of the plot. As noted earlier, the Ogodeids were primary participants, but Juwayni indicates that when Shiremun and his co-conspirators gathered 'it was rumored that they were hatching some plot against the Moslems [*sic*]'.[107] Perhaps this was just a cover to hide their ill intentions towards Mongke, but it seems more of an effort to portray Mongke as a just ruler and one who protected Muslims. Other than this almost-passing remark, there is no indication that Shiremun or the other Ogodeids had a particular animosity towards Muslims. Indeed, Khwaja's very name suggests a certain affinity towards Islam, although I have not found any evidence that he was a Muslim. His one known son (Tugma) did not have a Muslim name, either.[108]

We also have a curious episode at Mongke's enthronement beyond Juzjani's claims of Mongke's conversion. Juwayni writes:

> He therefore made a yasa that on that lucky day no man should tread the path of strife and contention; people should not engage in acts of hostility and enmity towards one another but should enjoy themselves and make

---

[103] Rubruc, 298; Rubruck/Jackson, 236–7; Rubruck/Dawson, 195.
[104] Rubruc, 209–10; Rubruck/Jackson, 127; Rubruck/Dawson, 124.
[105] Juzjani/Habibi, v2, 151–2, 157; Juzjani/Raverty, 1,106–7, 1,115.
[106] Juzjani/Habibi, v2, 154; Juzjani/Raverty, 1,110.
[107] Juvaini/Boyle, 566; Juwayni/Qazvini, v3, 28.
[108] RD/Karimi, 445; RD/Thackston1, 305; RD/Thackston2, 216.

merry. And since the human species was receiving its due of life in all manner of enjoyment and self-indulgence, so too all the other animals should not go without their share, and therefore those domesticated animals used for riding or as beasts of burden should not be subjected to the discomfort of loads, chains, hobbles, shackles, and straps, while as for those which are slaughtered for their flesh in accordance with the just Sharia͑at, their blood should remain unshed in the asylum of security, so that for one day, like the doves in a sanctuary, they might pass their time in ease and tranquility.[109]

Eventually they feasted and the animals were then slaughtered in *halal* fashion due to Berke's presence.[110] This violated the *yasa* of Chinggis Khan, as the Mongols normally slaughtered animals in another fashion, according to which, if it was strictly enforced, all of the participants (including Mongke) should have been executed.[111]

So what is happening here? As noted earlier, there were strong cultural aversions among the Mongols to *halal* slaughter. While Ogodei tolerated Muslims performing it in private, there is no indication that it became acceptable for Mongols. Thus with this account we must conclude that *halal* did indeed become acceptable for all Mongols, or alternatively something else is occurring in this passage.

Only Juzjani mentions Mongke's conversion. If he had converted, surely Juwayni, Wiliam of Rubruck and others would have known and recorded it. Thus we may conclude that Mongke never converted. But did they violate the *yasa* and slaughter animals in *halal* fashion simply to accommodate Berke? Although Rashid al-Din mentions that all animals were slaughtered in this fashion, Juwayni is less specific. So perhaps only some were. Yet there is more to be read into this. While Juwayni and Rashid al-Din both mention that animals were slaughtered in *halal* fashion, Rashid al-Din records that 'the blood of those that could lawfully be eaten should not be spilled'.[112] This statement is subtly different from Juwayni's account, which specifically refers to the *shari͑a*. The Mongol method of slaughter, however, does not actually spill blood. It remains within the animal's body.

On the surface, both Rashid al-Din and Juwayni depict the Mongols as abiding by the *shari͑a* on dietary measures. Yet, it seems unlikely that an entire *quriltai*'s worth of Mongols suddenly shifted their method of slaughtering

---

[109] Juvaini/Boyle, 569; Juwayni/Qazvini, v3, 31–2.
[110] Juwayni/Qazvini, v3, 38; Juvaini/Boyle, 573; RD/Karimi, 586; RD/Thackston1, 404–5; RD/Thackston2, 286–7.
[111] David Ayalon, 'The Great Yasa of Chingiz Khan. A Reexamination (Part A)', *Studia Islamica*, 33 (1971), 119.
[112] RD/Thackston1, 404; RD/Karimi, 586; RD/Thackston2, 286.

animals, particularly when '300 horses or oxen and 3000 sheep' were served.¹¹³ While the numbers might have symbolic meaning, this still indicates that the Mongols slaughtered a large number of animals for the feast.¹¹⁴ Furthermore, a key aspect of the official propaganda concerning the Toluids was that they followed the *yasa* and *yosun* and no one could find fault in them. It seems a flight of fancy to suggest that this was a key point in the Toluids maintaining their legitimacy, but that they then suddenly reversed course at the very *quriltai* that raised the first Toluid ruler to the throne. Such an action could have undermined Mongke's support.

Thus, while Mongke was not a Muslim, he was subtly depicted as either being one or as being favourable towards Muslims. Unquestionably, there were many Muslims in the employ of the Mongols at various levels, particularly at the regional level in regions with Muslim populations.¹¹⁵ Furthermore, Sunni Muslim writers were swift to praise Mongke for his efforts to dispense justice against those who plotted against Muslims, such as the Idiqut of the Uighurs, and also for dealing with those deemed heretics, such as the Nizari Ismailis.¹¹⁶

As both *Ithna' Ashari* Shias and Sunnis found the Nizaris distasteful, the Mongol actions were greeted with applause. However, Hulegu's campaign against Baghdad only confirmed the worst aspects of the Mongols. Juwayni curiously ends his history with the destruction of the Nizaris, even though he became the governor of Baghdad. Juzjani places most of the blame for the Abbasid fall on Ibn al-Alqami, the vizier. Undoubtedly, much of his ire was because of Ibn al-Alqami's Shia identity.¹¹⁷

What is curious is that Ibn al-Alqami was not executed despite betraying his sovereign, although Juzjani recorded that he was, and that he did so with good reason.¹¹⁸ Typically, the Mongols executed traitors, and since they betrayed one master, what would prevent them from doing it again?¹¹⁹ However, one must keep in mind that the Mongols had recently deposed the titular head of the Sunni world. By keeping Ibn al-Alqami, they maintained a high-ranking individual who knew the conditions of the region. Furthermore,

---

¹¹³ Juvaini/Boyle, 573; Juwayni/Qazvini, v3, 38.
¹¹⁴ See Larry Moses, 'Triplicated Triplets: The Number Nine in the *Secret History* of the Mongols', *Asian Folklore Studies* 45, no. 2 (1986), 287–94.
¹¹⁵ Allsen, *Mongol Imperialism*, 107, 110.
¹¹⁶ RD/Karimi, 593; RD/Thackston1, 409; RD/Thackston2, 290; Juzjani/Habibi, v2, 180–5; Juzjani/Raverty, 1,187–97; Juwayni/Qazvini, v3, 60–1, 275–8; Juvaini/Boyle, 589, 723–5.
¹¹⁷ Juzjani/Habibi, v2, 1901; Juzjani/Raverty, 1,229.
¹¹⁸ Juzjani/Habibi, v2, 199–200; Juzjani/Raverty, 1,260–1.
¹¹⁹ SHM, §188, 200.

this may have served as a signal to Shia Muslims that there was a new order that did not give preference to a particular sect. It also must have served as a very visible reminder that Sunni Muslims were no longer at the top of the hierarchy. Shias did thrive under the Mongols. While Baghdad suffered, the Shia towns of Hilla, Kufa and Najaf submitted as Hulegu entered Iraq.[120] The fact that the major Shia centres submitted without resistance certainly won them favour in the eyes of the Mongols.

Sunni decline was even more apparent, as Christian troops from Armenia, Georgia, Cilicia and the Principality of Antioch supported Hulegu not only at Baghdad but also in Syria. Their involvement not only demoralised the Muslim population, but enhanced the apocalyptic, lachrymose foreboding that infected the Islamic world with the Mongol conquests. While the conquests were traumatic, the recently conquered also had to adjust to Mongol rule. The destruction of Baghdad and the execution of the Caliph dealt a deep psychological blow to the Muslim psyche, particularly those who had previously been outside of Mongol domains. Even though the Abbasid Caliph's power had waned, the concept still carried weight, as did the very real and durable grandeur of Baghdad. The Mongols swept it away. While the Mongols allowed Muslims to continue their religious practices, the fading lustre of Islamic civilisation reminded Muslims (whether Sunni or Shia) that they were just another group of devotees of one of the several religions within the empire.

The newly acquired subjects of the *Yeke Monggol Ulus* now experienced changes that Mongke's other Muslims subjects faced. While many Muslims had been taxed since the Mongols had first come into their regions, other Muslim groups found themselves further integrated into the Mongol Empire during the reign of Mongke. The *Hui Hui*, or ethnic Chinese (Han) Muslims, were registered through a census for the first time in 1252, which allowed the Mongols to collect the *qubchur*.[121] For Muslims, this was akin to paying the *jizya* or poll-tax that non-Muslims normally paid to their Muslim ruler.[122] The Mongols, however, abolished the *jizya* as part of their policy towards religion. While the Christians and Jews of the Middle East also paid *qubchur*, the Muslim population now experienced a new reality in which they now understood they were no longer in control.

While the Mongols maintained a policy of religious toleration, occasional outbursts of persecution did occur, particularly in the wake of

---

[120] Peter Jackson, *The Mongols and the Islamic World* (New Haven, 2017), 167, 321–2.
[121] Allsen, *Mongol Imperialism*, 127.
[122] Allsen, *Mongol Imperialism*, 167–8.

conquest.[123] These, however, need to be viewed carefully as it is not clear whether the destruction and persecution were religiously motivated (perhaps among Christian troops), or whether they represented the braggadocio of the Christian writers revelling in the destruction of the Caliphate whereas the Mongols seemed well-disposed towards Christians. For instance, the Armenian author Grigor recorded that the Hulegu collected pigs as tribute from the Armenians and then sent 2,000 pigs to every Arab city. Not only were the swine to be well-treated, but upon slaughter, anyone who did not eat pork would be decapitated.[124] As this is not reported elsewhere, it is unlikely to have happened. Not even Juwayni or Rashid al-Din could have ignored such an action.

At the same time, not everything was doom and gloom. Juwayni saw many optimistic signs for *Dar al-Islam* while attempting to come to terms with the impact of the Mongol conquests on the Muslim world. One must remember that even though Juwayni worked for the Mongols, he still had misgivings towards them. Thus, his work can be read as his personal struggle and coming to terms with living and working within the Mongol Empire.[125]

While Mongke and Batu did not convert, Juwayni noted that other Mongols embraced Islam during the reign of Mongke.[126] One may forgive Juzjani's exuberance and wishful thinking concerning Mongke's conversion. King Hethum of Cilicia believed that he had converted Mongke to Christianity.[127] Furthermore, while most of the Mongols remained infidels and adhered to the *yasa* and *yosun* of Chinggis Khan, Juwayni noted, 'There are many of these ordinances that are in conformity with the Shariᶜat.'[128] Additionally, under Mongol rule, the economy was flourishing, 'so it has come to pass that the present world is the paradise of that people'.[129] While this certainly applied to the Mongols as well as many merchants, Juwayni, like many modern commentators, also reckoned that if the economy was strong life was not all bad, even under infidel rule.[130]

---

[123] Hetoum, 42.
[124] Grigor of Akanc, 343.
[125] Also see Judith Kolbas, 'Historical Epic as Mongol Propaganda? Juwayni Motifs and Motives', in *MME*, 155–71.
[126] Juwayni/Qazvini, v1, 11; Juvaini/Boyle, 16.
[127] Hetoum, 39.
[128] Juwayni/Qazvini, v1, 18; Juvaini/Boyle, 25.
[129] Juwayni/Qazvini, v1, 15; Juvaini/Boyle, 22.
[130] Kolbas, 'Historical Epic', 164–6.

8

The Yuan Empire

In 1264, Khubilai decisively ended the war with Ariq-Boke and became the ruler of the eastern portion of the Mongol Empire. Although his claim to the leadership of the entire empire remained disputed, there was little anyone could do to prevent him from claiming the title as war wracked the rest of the empire. With Ariq-Boke's death in 1265, Khubilai consolidated his authority in northern China and Mongolia and then planned to legitimise his rule in a traditional way – by conquering an enemy. Rather than turning his attention to asserting his authority over the rest of the *Yeke Monggol Ulus* and risk civil war, he rested his eyes on the Song Empire. The Mongols had just begun to make headway against the Song when Mongke died, but his death had led to an abandonment of the campaign, permitting the Song to regroup. Khubilai sought to complete the conquest, which would be the hallmark of his career. Yet, one could argue that the conquest of the Song proved detrimental to the dynasty he founded.

Conquest of the Song Empire

Although the Song armies, with over a million men under arms and a large navy, were inferior to those of the Mongols, it was not because of lack of effort. Technologically, the Song Empire was the most advanced state on the planet. It also learned from many of its mistakes and possessed tremendous resources that allowed it to continue to prosecute the war without the state collapsing, even after numerous defeats. Even as the Mongols advanced, the war became more difficult as the Mongols lost their mobility due to mountainous terrain and well-situated mountain fortresses. Once the Mongols exited the mountains, they then encountered cities with populations in the hundreds of thousands, or rural areas with rice paddies, which impeded cavalry warfare. The Song also planted trees as obstacles to break up cavalry formations.[1]

---

[1] Huang K'uan-chung, 'Mountain Fortress Defence: The Experience of the Southern Sung and Korea in Resisting the Mongol Invasion', in Hans Van de Ven (ed.), *Warfare in Chinese*

As the war continued, the Mongols incorporated increasing numbers of Han infantry from northern China as well as Song deserters, allowing them to conduct more sieges, but also hold territory while their cavalry raided. Additionally, the wide rivers and coastline dictated naval warfare. Without a navy, the Mongols could not completely isolate key cities or deliver troops to where they were needed in a timely manner.

While geography slowed the Mongol advance, internal rot doomed the Song, as feuds at court undermined imperial objectives and local elites placed local and regional interests ahead of imperial priorities. Those who commanded in the field were often disconnected from strategic planning at the imperial level. As orders were issued without explanation of the strategic and operational plan, Song generals could not see the larger context and often chose to ignore commands. In general, the military was excluded from the court because of Confucian prejudices against military careers. While some of the prejudices were superficial, other concerns were well-founded. Prior to the Song Dynasty, successful generals sometimes became sources of upheaval in previous dynasties such as the Tang Dynasty (618–907). The Song consciously wanted to avoid that issue. Furthermore, fiscal and agrarian reforms intended to raise additional funds for the war alienated all groups within the Song Empire. In many cases, provinces bordering the Mongols remitted fewer taxes to the central government as the funds were needed for local defence. Efforts to find more revenue often led to an increase in the bureaucracy that then outstripped the tax income. Corruption led to troops not being paid, who then deserted and became bandits. Many units transitioned back and forth from banditry and serving in the Song army. Hyperinflation also ran rampant in some regions as the government exhausted its gold, silver and silk reserves.[2]

Many of the issues stemmed from the leadership of the Song. Emperor Lizong (r. 1224–64) appreciated loyalty and even accepted criticism, but was blind to the shortcomings of his ministers, such as their personal and often petty rivalries that hamstrung the government.[3] By the rise of Khubilai Khan, the Song had faced the Mongols in intermittent warfare for approximately thirty years, yet the Song frequently reacted to events rather than anticipating war. Lizong lacked vision in a crisis. Often he was found in the company of his concubines rather than with his ministers. He allowed his eunuchs,

---

History (Leiden, 2000), 222, 226–7; James Waterson, *Defending Heaven: China's Mongol Wars, 1209–1370* (London, 2013), 91.

[2] Richard L. Davis, 'The Reign of Li-Tsung', *CHCSD*, 908–12.

[3] Richard L. Davis, 'The Reign of Tu-Tsing (1264–1274) and his Successors to 1279', *CHCSD*, 913; Waterson, *Defending Heaven*, 85–6.

Zhongwen Qingwu

The Song Empire emerged in the aftermath of the Tang Empire. Recognising that the rise of warlords destabilised the Tang, the Song followed a policy known as *Zhongwen Qingwu*. This policy emphasised the civil administration while de-emphasising the importance of the military. This was further enhanced with a promotion of Neo-Confucian values and the use of an examination system for government officials. This contributed to the devaluation of martial skills. The policy was successful in bringing internal stability to the Song, but it also left them very vulnerable to outside forces, such as the rise of the Khitan Liao Empire, the Jurchen Jin Empire, and then the rise of the Mongols.

such as Dong Songchen, to run the affairs of court, which then insulated the emperor from the affairs of the provinces. Provincial officials contributed to the internal rot by hiding defeats out of pride.

Despite these issues, Khubilai's conquest did not come easily. Fortunately, for the Song, a few able ministers and generals existed. Ding Dachuan, an inept official in Sichuan, was replaced by Jia Sidao (1213–75), who gained prominence through family connections. Jia Sidao's father had served with distinction as a military commander and his sister was a former consort of the emperor. Jia Sidao had the right connections, but also extensive military and civil experience.[4] His success in previous positions also bred arrogance. Emperor Lizong's blindness to the flaws of his favourites truly manifested with Jia Sidao.

Jia Sidao took over Sichuan and led armies against Khubilai during Mongke's invasion. He had the good fortune to be at Ezhou when Khubilai withdrew to deal with Mongke's death and the civil war with Ariq-Boke. While Jia Sidao's appearance was coincidental, Khubilai's withdrawal made Jia Sidao a war hero. He attempted to revive the economy by buying land from the wealthy landowners in an attempt to secure grain supplies. In many instances it was outright seizure of land and compensation given in paper money, which became worthless due to hyperinflation, alienating many of the landowners. Furthermore, the fiscal efforts were undermined by the extravagance of the court, which did not adopt any form of austerity.[5] Jia Sidao's authority only grew when Lizong's crippled nephew, Duzong, succeeded Lizong after the emperor died in 1264.

---

[4] Richard L. Davis, 'The Reign of Li-tsung (1224–1264)', in *CHCSD*, 890–1.
[5] Davis, 'The Reign of Li-tsung', 893–4; Waterson, *Defending Heaven*, 89.

Because of his unchecked power, Jia Sidao undermined every successful action through hubris. Rather than work towards an armistice or even a peace treaty in order to plan for the next Mongol invasion, Jia Sidao ensured that war continued by imprisoning Mongol envoys.[6] It seems unlikely that Khubilai would have ignored the Song Empire or that a permanent peace was possible, but his actions necessitated an immediate reaction from the Mongols. Although Jia Sidao strengthened the defences of Sichuan, particularly at the pivotal city of Xiangyang, he and his cronies, who also included generals, downplayed the Mongol threat, falsified reports and denounced rivals. In one such instance Liu Zheng, a Song general, deserted to the Mongols with his army rather than suffer the continual abuse of Jia Sidao. Jia Sidao also played the court like a lute in times of distress. In one power play, he resigned, causing the court to beg him to return; the court then dismissed his political rivals. We must keep in mind that he was a hero and his own propaganda only made his 'victories' more grandiose. Even without a 24-hour news cycle, it was still possible to spin and create unnecessary and exaggerated hype for someone. When Jia Sidao returned, he possessed more power than before.

Meanwhile, the Mongols were not idle. To overcome the Song navy, they followed the advice of the renegade Song general, Liu Zheng, who convinced them that the Song could never be defeated until their navy had been neutralised.[7] He persuaded them to focus on a single point rather than employ their traditional pincer strategies. His logic was sound. Although the Mongols stretched the Song defences, the Song had the resources to slow them. By focusing on one location at this juncture, the Song would be unlikely to move all of their armies for fear of the pincer strategy, but they would move more men to hold the line at Xiangyang, thus providing the Mongols with an opportunity to destroy more armies at the location of their choosing. Furthermore, by breaking key fortifications, the Mongols exposed the interior of the Song Empire. Thus, a fleet became a top priority.

While the Song and Mongols fought only a few battles between 1264 and 1268, the Mongols committed to the conquest of the Song Empire in 1268. The Mongols developed their own fleet, manned by Han and Koreans. Their major attack focused on Xiangyang and its neighbour Fancheng on the

---

[6] Davis, 'Reign of Tu-Tsung', *CHCSD*, 926.
[7] Morris Rossabi, 'The Reign of Khubilai Khan', *CHCAR*, 431; Waterson, *Defending Heaven*, 93–4.

Han River. Although Liu Zheng advised the Mongols on the battle, Aju, Subedei's grandson, executed the plan.⁸

With the aid of the Mongol navy, the Mongols blocked the Song from supplying and reinforcing the cities via the Han River. The key to victory, however, was the arrival of Muslim engineers from the west sent by the Il-Khan Abaqa to assist his uncle against the Song. These Muslim engineers, Talib, Abu Bakr, Ibrahim and Muhammad, built seven counter-weight trebuchets, which previously had not been known in China.⁹ These were capable of hurling stones weighing hundreds of pounds, and the cities of Xiangyang and Fancheng surrendered in 1273. Marco Polo credited his father, his uncle and himself with the construction and design of the trebuchets, but he arrived in China a few years after the fall of Xiangyang and Fancheng.¹⁰

The Muslim engineers were not Abaqa's only gifts for Khubilai. A military officer named Bayan accompanied the engineers. He became Khubilai's greatest general.¹¹ Bayan originally accompanied Hulegu to the Middle East, but returned east as Hulegu's envoy to Khubilai Khan. Although his record with Hulegu was insignificant, he immediately impressed the Mongol ruler, who acquired him for his own service and promoted him to the position of *chingsang* (*chingxiang*), or junior grand counsellor. Bayan also married the niece of Chabi, Khubilai's primary wife. In 1274, Khubilai assigned to Bayan an army of 100,000 men and tasked him with the final destruction of the Song Empire. Accompanied by Aju Noyan and 10,000 ships, the Mongols advanced down the Han River. They bypassed fortresses and sought out the riverine navy and field armies of the Song, destroying a major fleet (10,000 ships) on 12 January 1275. On 19 March 1275, Bayan and Aju defeated Jia Sidao at the battle of Dingjia Island, where Jia Sidao led an army considerably larger than Bayan's (approximately 130,000), and over 1,000 boats. With the string of losses, the Empress Xie dismissed Jia Sidao, who was later murdered.

Under Bayan's leadership, the Mongol armies moved faster and more efficiently. Bayan adeptly deployed combined arms corps of Mongol cavalry and Chinese infantry. The sight of his red banner caused towns to surrender. In the summer of 1275, Khubilai convened a *quriltai* in Shangdu to plan the final campaign against the Song, and prevent his armies from remaining in the humid climate of South China during the summer. Aju led one

---

⁸ RD/Thackston2, 291; RD/Thackston1, 415; RD/Karimi, 602.
⁹ RD/Thackston2, 318; RD/Thackston1, 450; RD/Karimi, 651.
¹⁰ MP1, 224–5. The texts on Marco Polo vary; in some instances, Marco gives credit to his father and uncle, but he was not involved. See MP/Cliff, 190–1; MP/Lathem, 207–8; MP/Marsden, 189; MP/Yule, v2, 158–9.
¹¹ RD/Thackston2, 310; RD/Thackston1, 438–9; RD/Karimi, 637.

Figure 8.1 Portrait of Khubilai Khan on silk, National Palace Museum, Taipei. (The Granger Collection/New York)

army against Yangzhou while Bayan led the main army against the city of Changzhou and the Song capital of Lin'an (modern Hangzhou).[12] Although Changzhou resisted the Mongols and suffered a massacre, Lin'an entered negotiations. The Empresses Dowager Xie submitted on behalf of the child emperor and handed over the imperial seal. She opened gates to Lin'an to the Mongols on 28 March 1276; the Mongols spared the city. The Song had little choice. Bayan's army was but one of three Mongol corps descending upon the city. Bayan then escorted the Song royal family to Khubilai Khan with much fanfare. Most of the empire surrendered afterwards, but one faction continued to resist by propping up child emperors.

In 1279, the Mongols, led by a Tangut named Li Heng and Zhang Hongfang, a former Song commander, manoeuvred the Song into one last battle at Yaishan, near modern Macau. Yaishan was an island and the Song fleet found itself bottled up by the Mongols as the Mongols employed the *nerge* via land and sea. The Song, commanded by Zhang Shijie (Zhang Hongfang's nephew), made this their last stand and commanders lashed their ships together to ensure that no one abandoned the cause. This, however, also eliminated all mobility for the Song. The Mongols rode the tide in from the

[12] RD/Thackston2, 310–11; RD/Thackston1, 438–9; RD/Karimi, 636–8.

sea to begin their attack, while other Mongol forces rode the tide out from the mainland to reinforce. The additional momentum increased their mobility and added force to the Mongol naval attack. The Battle of Yaishan went poorly for the Song, causing one courtier, Lu Xiufu (1238–79), to grab the last emperor, a seven-year-old child named Zhao Bing (1271–9), and leap into the water, preferring to drown instead of allowing the child to fall into Mongol hands. Thousands of Song loyalists followed suit.[13] While some Song loyalists continued to resist, the Song Empire had fallen.

Khubilai as Ruler

With the conquest of the Song Empire, Khubilai Khan now ruled an empire stretching from the forests north of Lake Baikal to the South China Sea, ruling more territory than any emperor of China before him. In many ways, he was the ideal Mongol khan to rule over China as he had a clear interest in eastern religions and cultures before his reign, as evinced by his role in the Daoist–Buddhist religious debates. During his own reign, he favoured Buddhists throughout his entire career. Nonetheless, he demonstrated support for Daoists when necessary for political reasons. Daoists, however, also suffered from periodic government-supported persecution. Muslims and Christians also found Khubilai sympathetic, and numerous Muslims from beyond his territory found employment. Despite Marco Polo's claims that Khubilai Khan requested from the Pope a hundred priests to teach and preach Christianity, it is doubtful whether he sought to convert to Christianity.[14] He did, however, desire individuals who could debate the merits of their faith against other religions. Aside from Polo's tales, much of Khubilai's early religious policy simply followed what was in place under Mongke and other khans. Buddhists, Daoists, Christians and Muslims all received official sanctions to practise their religion and often found Mongol patronage.[15]

Although he recognised that his empire was much greater than China, with the addition of the millions of Song inhabitants, Khubilai altered his style of government considerably from Mongke's. While he continued the vision of imperial rule that had existed since the time of Chinggis Khan, with the *Qa'an* being a true steppe ruler and the empire being the personal property of the *altan urugh*, other changes were necessary. The imperial institutions of governance continued, but Khubilai did not apply the *minqan*

---

[13] Davis, 'The Reign of Tu-Tsung', 956–7; David C. Wright, 'Navies in the Mongol Yuan Conquest of Southern Song China, 1274–1279', *MS* 29 (2007), 208–11. The mass suicide is disputed.
[14] MP1, 13–14; MP/Cliff, 6–7; MP/Lathem, 33–6; MP/Marsden, 7–10; MP/YC, v1, 13–14.
[15] Rossabi, 'The Reign of Khubilai Khan', 457–62; Rossabi, *Khubilai Khan*, 141–7.

system to the former Song Empire. *Daruqachin* were used, but existing Song practices continued with a parallel Mongolian government operating behind the local officials to supervise the Chinese, not dissimilar from what occurred in the Ilkhanate and other areas prior to Khubilai, but now carried out on a scale not seen before.

Khubilai's administration divided the Chinese territories into twelve provinces. Although he banned the Confucian civil service system, Khubilai ruled the Chinese provinces as a Confucian emperor. He became familiar with the works of Confucius through his tutors and Confucian advisors, although he never learned to read Chinese. Khubilai realised that implementing a Confucian-style civil service would make his government dependent on Chinese personnel.[16] Additionally, he wanted to retain the ability to appoint his officials, which the civil service system restricted.[17] A key point in shaping his opinion on this was the revolt of Li Tan in the Shandong peninsula. Li Tan submitted to Mongke and fought against the Song in Mongol service. In 1262, however, he rebelled, taking advantage of Khubilai Khan's war with Ariq-Boke. The rebellion was crushed, but afterwards, Khubilai Khan does not appear to have completely trusted his Chinese officials. Although the Mongol military aristocracy remained with their *minqad*, after the Li Tan incident Khubilai made it difficult for Chinese elites to maintain private armies. Nonetheless, he realised the need to appeal to the majority of his subjects. He declared a new dynasty in 1271, the *Da Yuan* or Great Yuan, and declared that the Song had lost the mandate of heaven. The dynastic name was chosen from one of the five classics of Confucius, the *Yijing* or *I Ching* (Book of Changes). In essence, the *Da Yuan* was a new convention to express the *Yeke Monggol Ulus*, but in Chinese terms.[18] In order to maintain the Mandate of Heaven, Khubilai performed the proper ceremonies and rites that a typical Chinese emperor was expected to perform. As regards the sacrificial rites to Confucius, a proxy often performed them in his place, although he did have two hundred Mongols familiarised with the rites.[19] He also dressed in imperial regalia as befitting a proper Chinese emperor and was carried on a sedan rather than on horseback in public. It is, however, not certain whether he maintained a Chinese diet.

Khubilai ensured that the Confucian scholar elite would not dominate his government by recruiting non-Han Chinese. Still, he also took measures to gain Confucian support, which was an important key to legitimating

---

[16] Rossabi, 'The Reign of Khubilai Khan', *CHCAR*, 418; Rossabi, *Khubilai Khan*, 131–41.
[17] Rossabi, 'The Reign of Khubilai Khan', 427.
[18] Hodong Kim, 'Was "Da Yuan" a Chinese Dynasty?', *JSYS* 45 (2015), 300–1.
[19] Rossabi, 'The Reign of Khubilai Khan', 458.

his rule among the Chinese population.[20] As he built his capital of Daidu, designed by the Muslim architect Yeheitie'er, in 1267, he included in it the construction of an imperial ancestral temple, as a Chinese emperor would do.[21] He also gave his eldest living son Jingim (Dorji, Khubilai's first son, died young from illness) a Confucian education, foreseeing that his heirs would need to understand the consciousness and culture of their Chinese subjects. The name 'Jingim' was the Mongol version of Zhenjin (True Gold). Jingim, was not, however, to be a Confucian scholar. Instead, he also received instruction in and exposure to Buddhism and Daoism. Jingim gradually assumed more responsibilities, and named the heir-apparent in 1273, perhaps an effort by Khubilai to sidestep the Mongol custom of deciding the ruler through a *quriltai*. Having participated in one civil war and having witnessed the Toluid Revolution, Khubilai had good cause to find a smoother path for the succession.

Although to the Chinese his outward appearance was that of a proper Chinese emperor, Khubilai still viewed himself as a Mongol khan. His primary wife, Chabi, served as a key and noticeable advisor in the court, unlike with most Chinese emperors. He also carried out Mongol-style hunts in a large hunting park that he established in Shangdu, his summer capital, kept an area of steppe grass on the palatial grounds to remind him of his origins, drank *airagh*, and often slept in a *ger* rather than in the sumptuous quarters of his palaces at Daidu and Shangdu.[22] Unlike previous Mongol khans, he did not nomadise, although moving to Shangdu during the summer months may have served as his equivalent of a migration. Nomadising would have identified him more as a nomad and thus a foreign ruler of a Chinese population, which in turn would only have made ruling China more difficult. His failure to nomadise, except between his capitals of Daidu and Shangdu, alienated some of the more traditional Mongol princes and commanders. On the other hand, the lack of formal Chinese imperial protocol in Khubilai's court in Daidu made the Chinese uncomfortable.[23]

Although Khubilai attempted to appear as a Confucian emperor, his system of government was firmly tied to that of the Mongol Empire, but

---

[20] MP1, 162; MP/Cliff, 106; MP/Lathem, 133; MP/Marsden, 132; MP/YC, vol. 1, 418; Rossabi, *Khubilai Khan*, 119, 125–6, 141, 154.

[21] Ch'en Yuan, *Western and Central Asian in China Under the Mongols*, 2nd edn, trans. Ch'ien Hsing-hai and L. C. Goodrich (Nettetal, 1989), 219–20; Rossabi, *Khubilai Khan*, 131.

[22] MP1, 107–8; MP/Cliff, 82–3; MP/Lathem, 108–9; MP/Marsden, 90–1; MP/YC, v1, 298–302.

[23] MP1, 158; MP/Marsden, 128; MP/YC, v1, 410–11; Rossabi, 'The Reign of Khubilai Khan, 454–7.

modified for his needs. Khubilai's version of the Central Secretariat took elements of the Mongol version (itself influenced by Jin and Khitan models) and tied it to a Chinese style of central government. The Central Secretariat consisted of the *Qa'an* and six ministers who led the ministries of war, justice, public works, rites, revenues and the bureaucracy. Although the Mongol secretariat had ministries for the military, justice, revenue and bureaucracy, the addition of rites and public works was clearly Chinese. Initially, several of the key ministers were Chinese who had advised Khubilai since his youth, but these were gradually replaced as they died with non-Chinese personnel. Most were Mongols, but a few non-Mongols demonstrated Khubilai's increased use of non-Chinese personnel. A mirror of this secretariat existed at the provincial and local levels as well. The key ministry, however, was the *Shumi Yuan* or Ministry of War, headed by Prince Jingim, who also served the director of the Central Secretariat. Although the *Shumi Yuan* was technically part of the civilian government, it often acted independently and was crucial to controlling the army and as well as the nomads in Mongolia. It remained the most Mongolian of all the parts of the government.

Outside of these ministries, the *keshig* remained important. Every member of the *keshig*, even the lowest-ranking, held a position not only as a bodyguard, but also in the bureaucracy on the civilian side.[24] Some served as *daruqachin* in the provinces and thus served as the personal representatives of the *Qa'an*. The *Qa'an* controlled the government through the Censorate (*Yushi tai*), which provided intelligence about happenings not only within the empire, but also within the government. Part of its mission was to prevent corruption, which it did by spying on government officials.[25] Originally, the Censorate was led by a Confucian, Zhang Dehui (1197–1274), but he resigned after a dispute with Khubilai over how the law applied to the *Qa'an* (Khubilai said it didn't) and was replaced by a Mongol aristocrat (Oz-Temur).

Although the *keshig* provided many officials, it could not provide all of them. A major problem that Khubilai faced was staffing the government. He had no trust in staffing it, or desire to staff it, with former Song officials. Even so, many refused to work with what they considered an alien and barbarian regime, and instead retired to lives of scholarly and artistic pursuit. As a result, Khubilai recruited foreign personnel heavily. Marco Polo is probably the best-known example, although his actual position was not quite as grandiose

---

[24] Ch'i-ch'ing Hsiao, *The Military Establishment of the Yuan Dynasty* (Cambridge, MA, 1978), 39–40.

[25] Rossabi, 'The Reign of Khubilai Khan', 427; MP1, 165–6; MP/Cliff, 126–7; MP/Lathem, 149–50; MP/Marsden, 136; MP/YC, v1, 430–1.

as he related to European audiences.²⁶ Khubilai also constructed a hierarchy through which he sought to control the vast population. At the top were the Mongols, which included other nomads. Secondly, a source from which he recruited many government officials was the *Semuren*, also known as the round-eyed or coloured-eyed people.²⁷ These included all westerners, that is, those dwelling west of China, and included not only Venetians like Polo, but also Persians, Central Asians, Arabs, Rus' and Alans, as well as Uighurs, who were among the most important source of personnel for the empire. After the *Semuren* came the *Hanren*, comprising northern Han, Jurchens, Khitans, Tanguts and Koreans. The fourth category consisted of *Nanren* or southern Chinese and other ethnic populations in the south. The hierarchy was fluid, however, as considerations of ability, religion, occupation, and how one came to be a subject of the Mongol Empire enabled individuals to transcend their categories. It was, nonetheless, quite effective in keeping power in the hands of the Mongols.²⁸

Governor Polo?

The exact occupation of Marco Polo in the Yuan Empire is problematic. Although he was the son of Venetian merchants and his writings maintain a keen eye on merchandise and commerce, this can also be attributed to his audience. One issue is that the various texts of Marco Polo are all different. Some indicate that he was the governor of the city of a province, or perhaps the city of Yangzhou. Other texts are silent on his exact position. It is possible that he served in the *keshig*, which would have placed him in a position to have direct knowledge of Khubilai Khan, but also in a position to travel as widely as he did throughout the empire.

The ethnic hierarchy served as a mechanism for controlling the population, but was also a legal necessity. The *yasa* still applied to the nomads. In northern China, Khubilai allowed those *Hanren* to use their own legal system, largely based on the Jin legal system, which had been practised during the *Yeke Monggol Ulus*. In 1262, however, he authorised a new law code

---

[26] MP/Marsden, 187; MP/Latham, 206; MP/YC, v2, 154; MP 2012, 222; MP/Cliff, 188.
[27] See Michael C. Brose, *Subjects and Masters: Uyghurs in the Mongol Empire* (Bellingham, WA, 2007). Although Brose's work focuses on the Uighur *Semuren*, it also provides a good overview of the *Semuren* in general.
[28] Brose, *Subject and Masters*, 39–41, 49; Elizabeth Endicott-West, 'The Yuan Government and Society', in *CHCAR*, 608–25.

Figure 8.2 Statue of Marco Polo. Located in Ulaanbaatar, Marco Polo is dressed as a Mongol warrior. Although he may have exaggerated his position in the Mongol Empire, there is little question that he visited the court of Khubilai Khan.

which took effect in 1271. While it was based on Chinese law from previous dynasties, the *yasa* still influenced it. Nonetheless, as regards the recently conquered *Nanren*, Khubilai did not completely replace their law code, but maintained it, with the new legal code gradually replacing Song practice as Mongol control solidified. As for the *Semuren*, their own various customs were respected; thus Muslims could uphold the *shariʿa* in Hangzhou or in Daidu while Armenians could follow their own customs. The hierarchy also demonstrated which legal system had greater priority in settling disputes. Still, inter-group disputes were decided by a conference comprising representatives from the various groups involved. Generally speaking, however, Mongol prerogatives had the advantage.[29]

Despite the Mongols' reputation for cruelty, the new Yuan law code of 1271 contained only 135 capital crimes, half of those the Song legal code held

---

[29] Paul Heng-chao Ch'en, *Chinese Legal Tradition under the Mongols: The Code of 1291 as Reconstructed* (Princeton, 1979), 82–5.

and also fewer than in the Ming code.[30] Nonetheless, the Yuan implemented the traditional punishments used by previous dynasties. These punishments (*wuxing*) included death, exile, prison, beating with a heavy stick and beating with a light stick. There were other revisions. In pre-Yuan punishments, the most common forms of execution were strangulation and decapitation. The Mongols maintained decapitation, but replaced strangulation with slow slicing (*ling chi*), a most un-Mongol punishment. *Ling chi* consisted of eight cuts to the face, hands, feet, chest, stomach and head so that the offender died slowly and painfully. Slow slicing was 'employed against offenders guilty of the most serious crimes, such as treason'.[31] Despite it being a gruesome method of death, the death penalty appears not to have been a common form of punishment. Between 1261 and 1306 executions ranged in number from three (1302) to 278 (1283).[32] By way of comparison, in the USA, executions between 1977 and 2014 ranged from a low of zero (1978, 1980) to 98 (2000). The average number of executions per year was 59.63 in the Yuan, as against 36.89 in the USA.[33] Life-exile varied from one being sent a set distance from one's home to one serving on farms, at *jam* stations, or in the military. Indeed, military service became an acceptable substitute in many situations and had the advantage of being part of Mongol tradition as well.[34] Yet, some sentences were never carried out as Khubilai and his successors granted amnesty, particularly if requested to do so by Buddhist monks. It happened frequently enough that Chinese advisors criticised the Yuan rulers for their leniency.[35] Regardless of this, the 1270 legal code became the basis for the empire and remained the foundation for subsequent legal codes. Indeed, it appears that later codes were alterations of the 1270 code rather than being a new and unique legal code.

The twelve provinces Khubilai created were ruled by a *jarquchi* with *daruqachin*, who were usually Mongols or *Semuren*, in cities and regional secretariats that mirrored the imperial Central Secretariat.[36] The provincial reorganisation was quite different from in previous dynasties and continued to be used during the Ming dynasty and, with some alteration, during the Qing

---

[30] Heng-chao Ch'en, *Chinese Legal Tradition*, 43; Rossabi, 'The Reign of Khubilai Khan', 453.
[31] Paul Heng-chao Ch'en, *Chinese Legal Tradition*, 42–3.
[32] Heng-chao Ch'en, *Chinese Legal Tradition*, 44–5.
[33] See 'Death Penalty Information Center', <http://www.deathpenaltyinfo.org/executions-year> (last accessed 10 March 2015).
[34] Heng-chao Che'en, *Chinese Legal Tradition*, 47.
[35] Heng-chao Che'en, *Chinese Legal Tradition*, 46.
[36] MP1, 165–6; MP/Cliff, 127; MP/Lathem, 150; MP/Marsden, 137; MP/YC, v1, 430–1; RD/Karimi, 644–6; RD/Thackston1, 444–6; RD/Thackston2, 314–16.

Figure 8.3 Statue of Khubilai Khan as lawgiver. Located in the Chinggis Khan pavilion in Sukhbaatar Square, Ulaanbaatar.

period. Part of the reorganisation at the provincial level was possible because, for the first time in three hundred years, China was unified and provided the territorial borders for later dynasties. As a means of tying the new lands together, the *jam* was extended, runners being used in areas not suitable for horses. In addition, the Grand Canal was built. Extending approximately 1,000 miles, the canal linked the south with the north, thus allowing food supplies to come to the northern provinces without using the coast, which was often plagued by pirates. Although canals had been in use prior to the Yuan, the Grand Canal exceeded anything before it.[37]

Other reforms were connected to the organisation of society to ensure that the southern Chinese or *Nanren* could not rebel, a reasonable concern as many never accepted Mongol rule. Military reforms included relieving the Chinese population of weaponry, which included many farming instruments. Finally, no horses could be sold to *Nanren*, continuing a policy begun by Ogodei.

---

[37] RD/Karimi, 640; RD/Thackston1, 441; RD/Thackston2, 312; MP1, 228; MP/Cliff, 193; MP/Lathem, 210; MP/Marsden, 190; MP/YC, v2, 174–5.

While it is often thought that the Mongols strove to resist assimilation into the Chinese population, many of Khubilai's efforts appear to have ensured that the subject population could not become Mongols. Khubilai attempted to segregate the Chinese and Mongols as much as possible. He decreed that the Chinese could not learn Mongolian; nor could they dress like Mongols, particularly with the *deel*, the traditional coat/robe which all Mongols wore and which was fastened on the right-hand side. Additionally, Khubilai ensured that his offspring, even though they were perhaps steeped in Chinese education and culture, remained Mongol. Although he had a large harem of women, all of his concubines were Mongolian.[38]

Khubilai's Foreign Ventures

Khubilai's somewhat schizophrenic identity of being a Chinese emperor while not wanting to be assimilated into Chinese culture continued with foreign policy. Here we see the Mongol ideology of conquering the world fusing with the Chinese identity of the Middle Kingdom (*Zhongguo*), or centre of the world. In the ideal of the Middle Kingdom, China was surrounded by lesser dependencies, which paid China tribute due to its superior culture and civilisation. Beyond the lesser dependencies were barbarian people and beyond that demonic territories. To be properly considered as ruling over the Middle Kingdom, however, Khubilai needed to restore the tribute system by which the lesser dependencies came and paid tribute to the Middle Kingdom. This had fallen into disrepair during the late Song era and was then completely abandoned with the Mongol conquest. Thus, the era from the 1270s to Khubilai's death in 1294 saw an effort to restore the tribute system.[39]

The old tribute system consisted of many kingdoms. Originally, the tribes of Mongolia were included as barbarians, as were the Tibetans. Both areas, however, were part of the Yuan Empire and thus excluded from that category. Korea was also part of it, and paid tribute as a subject of the Yuan. Indeed, Korean became among the most loyal (and often overburdened) vassals of the Mongols. To gain autonomy, Korean kings often married Mongolian princesses, who then served as the eyes of the *Qa'an* in Korea. Other regions remained outside of Mongol control. These included Japan, Pagan (modern Myanmar), kingdoms in Vietnam, and even Indonesia. For Khubilai, the combined mission of a Sino-Mongolian government was clear; these regions had to be brought under his dominion.

---

[38] Rossabi, *Khubilai Khan*, 174.
[39] Michael C. Brose, 'Realism and Idealism in the "*yuanshi*": Chapters on Foreign Relations', *Asia Major*, 3rd series, 19 (2006), 327–47.

Khubilai began to his quest to extend his control before completing his conquest of the Song. Initially, these efforts were tied to his strategy of defeating the Song. Japanese pirates were a problem, but of greater importance was commerce between Japan and the Song Empire. While the Mongols could prohibit Koryo (modern Korea) from trading with Japan (although smuggling occurred), they had no control over Japan. By bringing Japan under Mongolian control, Khubilai could strike at the Song economy and Song ability to fund the war. Japan, however, was quite aware of Mongolian activities, and the Kamakura Shogunate (1192–1333) was more than a little apprehensive about Mongolian intentions. The Japanese were certain that the Mongols wanted to conquer Japan so that the samurai could bolster the Mongol armies.[40]

Khubilai sent envoys for the first time in 1268, demanding not only that the Japanese refuse Song ships at Hakata Bay (the primary port), but also that they submit to Mongol authority and pay tribute.[41] The Bakufu (samurai military government) was uncertain how to deal with Khubilai's emissaries. On the one hand, it did not desire a war with the Mongols, but on the other it was annoyed by the envoys' haughty message. Thus, the envoys were sent to the emperor in Kyoto. The Emperor Kameyama (r. 1260–74) ignored the envoys for several days, as well as ignoring the letter, before sending them back without a response. Nonetheless, the Japanese did not ignore Khubilai's intentions and prepared their defences.[42] Since an official response was not given, Khubilai sent another envoy as per protocol, but also ordered 1,000 Korean ships to be built. As these were being constructed, the second envoy returned empty-handed while a third envoy never met with the emperor. Officials at Hakata Bay immediately sent him back.

The invasion began in 1274 after the Mongols had captured the Song city of Xiangyang. With this strategic city's fall, the rest of the Song Empire was now vulnerable to annihilation, including annihilation of its economic ties to Japan. Thus began the Bun'ei War, named after an era in Japanese chronology. Khubilai's army consisted largely of captive Song troops. The army that sailed from Pusan, Korea numbered roughly 23,000 and included

---

[40] Rossabi, *Khubilai Khan*, 99–100; Togen Eian, 'A Letter Concerning the Mongol Threat', trans. Thomas D. Conlan, in Thomas D. Conlan, *In Little Need of Divine Intervention* (Ithaca, 1994), 201.

[41] Rossabi, *Khubilai Khan*, 99–100.

[42] Hojo Tokimune and Hojo Masamura, 'A Mobilization Order Issued by Kamakura', trans. Thomas D. Conlan, in Thomas D. Conlan, *In Little Need*, 202; Otomo Yoriyasu, 'Organizing Defenses', trans. Thomas D. Conlan, in Thomas D. Conlan, *In Little Need*, 203–4.

Mongols, Koreans and Chinese, transported by 6,700 sailors. They overran the islands of Tsushima and Iki before advancing upon Hakata Bay. There the Mongols found 6,000 samurai opposing their landing, but Mongol archery and trebuchet-launched explosives forced them back. During the fighting, however, one of the Mongol generals was wounded.[43]

With his injury, the invasion stalled. As the Mongols decided on their next step, their army retreated to its ships, rather than wait on the exposed coast. While they fended off some attacks by Japanese ships, disaster struck when a storm destroyed hundreds of ships, scattering the fleet. As a result, the Mongols abandoned the attack and returned to Korea. The Mongols viewed the incident as a minor event. Most of the ships lost were poorly-made and -maintained ships captured from the Song, while the Korean-built ships survived. Furthermore, the Mongols believed that their attack had made its point – Japan was not immune from the Mongols, and thus submission was preferable. Furthermore, Hakata Bay, the major port for trade with the Song, had been wrecked.[44]

Nonetheless, Khubilai Khan continued his attempts to gain Japanese submission, but without success. The final diplomatic effort came in 1275 when the Bakufu decapitated the envoys and sent back their heads. Khubilai delayed further attacks and focused on finishing off the Song, but after the Battle of Yaishan (1279) he ordered the construction of a new fleet.

The Japanese remained steadfast. While they savoured the divine intervention (as they interpreted the storm as representing), they remained pragmatic and prepared for invasion. Hakata remained the most likely landing area, so they improved defences, with walls extending for twelve miles, and only fifty yards from the beach, preventing the Mongols from establishing a beachhead.[45]

Using Song resources and manpower, Khubilai built a larger navy and ordered King Chongyol of Koryo to prepare 1,000 ships and 20,000 men, augmented by roughly 30,000 Mongol troops. While the fleet sailed from Korea in 1281, another fleet of 3,500 ships left southern China with approximately 100,000 Chinese troops. A planned rendezvous at the island of Iki did not occur. The Chinese ships were of lesser quality, with many hastily repaired or built to meet Khubilai's quota. The Korean fleet also left its port early.

While the Korean fleet captured Tsushima and Iki before the Chinese fleet appeared, the commanders grew impatient and moved against Hakata

---

[43] He was ethnically a Korean, Yu Puk-Hyong.
[44] James P. Delgado, *Khubilai Khan's Lost Fleet* (Berkeley, 2008), 97; Randall J. Sasaki, *The Origins of the Lost Fleet of the Mongol Empire* (College Station, TX, 2015), 26–7.
[45] Conlan, *In Little Need*, 34–41.

without waiting for the Chinese fleet.[46] The Mongols landed, but found that the Japanese walls prevented them from establishing a camp. They then retreated to ships and bombarded the wall. With the Mongols confined to their ships, the Japanese attacked in small boat-raiding parties and launched flaming boats against the Mongol armada at night.

Meanwhile, the Chinese fleet bypassed Hakata and sailed to Imari Bay, thirty miles south-west of Hakata. Imari fell quickly and then the army marched over land to Hakata. Japanese forces intercepted it and fought a two-week battle in the hills and countryside near Imari Bay. At the same time, the Chinese fleet at Imari found itself under attack from the same tactics as had the fleet at Hakata. To counter this, and so that ships could not be singled out and culled from the fleet, the Chinese ships formed a floating fortress by lashing themselves together, the better to fend off small boat raids. This, however, made the fleet more susceptible to fire ships. While losses were inevitable, the Chinese considered there was plenty of water to counter any fires. As a result, a stalemate occurred, at both Hakata and Imari, that lasted two months. The situation altered when a typhoon hit in August. The Chinese floating fortress was destroyed because the ships were lashed together, which led to them crashing into each other. Some accounts put the death toll close to 100,000, with 4,000 ships destroyed.[47] The Korean fleet remained largely intact, as it was able to ride the waves. It retreated to Korea, however, upon receiving news of the Chinese fleet's destruction. Those troops who remained on the island were captured, with many executed or enslaved.

Khubilai Khan wanted a third invasion, but his advisors convinced him otherwise. Even though the Korean fleet returned intact, repairing, building new ships and supplying was beyond the ability of the Korean economy. The burden to supply the last fleet had stretched the economy and logistical abilities of Koryo to its limits. Khubilai's advisors also pointed out that the expense was too great, particularly when the threat of Qaidu remained, and although the Song were defeated the south was not completely pacified. Even if tax revenues were increased, it would not satisfy the need for another invasion and would probably cause more unrest. One method was to get more revenue from overseas trade. Ignoring this advice, Khubilai Khan ordered a new fleet and new army for Japan, including many soldiers conscripted from prisoners. Fortunately, the invasion was called off in 1286 due to the unrest caused by the heavy tax burden, as forecast by Khubilai's advisors.[48] Other

---

[46] Delgado, *Khubilai Khan's Lost Fleet*, 101–8.
[47] MP1, 259–61, 264–6; MP/Cliff, 228–32; MP/Lathem, 243–7; MP/Marsden, 219–22; MP/YC, v2, 253–60; Delgado, *Khubilai Khan's Lost Fleet*, 108.
[48] Rossabi, *Khubilai Khan*, 212.

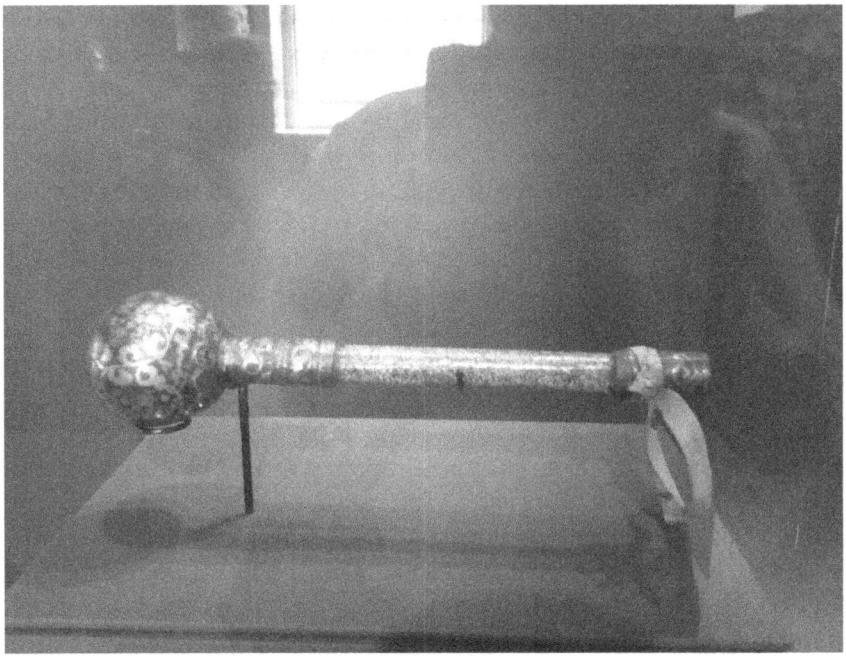

Figure 8.4 Yuan mace. Maces were carried not only as weapons but as symbols of authority. The intricate design of this mace indicates that it was primarily an instrument of authority. (Tower of London, London)

factors may have played a role in the decision as well, such as the fear of failure. Also, one cannot dismiss the death of Khubilai's wife, Chabi, in 1281 as an influence. She was not only his beloved wife but also a trusted counsellor. After her death, Khubilai withdrew somewhat from imperial affairs and delegated many duties.[49]

The failure with Japan did not prevent other invasions, however. In 1279, the Mongols invaded Pagan or Burma (modern Myanmar). The invasion came after the ruler of Pagan, King Narathihapate (r. 1256–87), refused to submit to the Mongols and pay tribute. The Muslim general Nasir al-Din, the son of Sayyid Ajall, led 10,000 Mongol cavalry into Pagan, using the lush pastures of Yunnan as his base of operations.[50] Here he encountered the enemy, which greatly outnumbered his own army as well as possessing large numbers of elephants. Not even the Mongol bow could completely penetrate the thick hides and leather armour of the elephants. Furthermore, their

---

[49] Rossabi, *Khubilai Khan*, 224–5.
[50] MP1, 20–7; MP/Cliff, 165–8; MP/Lathem, 184–7; MP/Marsden, 170–3; MP/YC, v2, 101–4.

scent made the Mongol horses restless and difficult to control. Nasir al-Din adapted his tactics and dismounted, taking positions behind the trees of the jungle. Even though the arrows did not deliver killing blows to the elephants, they could still wound and annoy them. By focusing on the elephants, Nasir al-Din broke the elephant attack and sent them into the ranks of the enemy. King Narathihapate agreed to pay tribute to the Mongols. Nasir al-Din withdrew his troops, returning the following year to enforce Pagan's submission.[51] Furthermore, over 100,000 households along the border were registered, effectively placing the frontier under direct Mongol control.

In 1282, Khubilai Khan cast his gaze over the region now known as Vietnam, which consisted of two kingdoms in the thirteenth century: Champa in the south and Annam or Dai Viet (1050–1400) in the north.[52] Annam had submitted to Uriyangqadai in 1258, after he invaded in 1257 from Dali, seeking to open a southern front against the Song. After a short war, King Tran Thanh Tong agreed to pay tribute. Uriyangqadai withdrew, finding that the climate and tropical diseases greatly curtailed his military strategy.[53] Now, the Mongols sought to pursue survivors from the battle of Yaishan who fled to Annam and Champa, as well as expand their realm.[54] Furthermore, Khubilai was annoyed that both King Tran Thanh Tong of Annam and King Jaya Indravarman VI of Champa sent tribute but refused to come to his court and submit.[55]

To eliminate further escape by Song loyalists, Champa was made the initial target of invasion. By conquering it, Khubilai would gain the maritime trade in Southeast Asia, and place Annam in a vice between Champa and the Mongol army in Yunnan, or Qarajang as the Mongols termed it. The invasion of Champa began in 1281 when an army led by Sogetu disembarked from a fleet of a hundred ships, a small one compared to those used in the efforts against Japan. The Mongols quickly seized the capital and major cities, but the leaders fled into the mountains. Again, the Mongols fought armies equipped with elephants, but continued their success against the terrifying animals.

With Champa under Mongol control, although still not completely conquered, Khubilai planned his conquest of Annam. Using the pretext that

---

[51] Rossabi, *Khubilai Khan*, 214–15.
[52] Annam was the Chinese term for Dai Viet or northern Vietnam. Dai Viet was the proper name of the kingdom that existed.
[53] Paul D. Buell, 'Indochina, Vietnamese Nationalism, and the Mongols', in *EMLCH*, 22.
[54] See Hok-Lam Chan, 'Chinese Refugees in Annam and Champa at the End of the Sung Dynasty', *JSAH* 7/2 (1966), 1–10.
[55] Buell, 'Indochina, Vietnamese Nationalism and the Mongols', 24–5.

his armies needed reinforcements to subdue Champa, Khubilai proposed to Annam to allow the Mongols to march through their territory from Yunnan to Champa. After the inevitable refusal, the Mongols invaded while Sogetu marched north. The Vietnamese realised the futility of facing the Mongols in a pitched battle and carried out a scorched-earth policy, while Prince Tran Hung Dao carried out guerrilla warfare. His strategies reappeared in the twentieth century as the Vietnamese studied and used his plans in wars against the Japanese, French and Americans.[56]

As with the later invasions of Vietnam, the Mongol army was bogged down in the field. Its cavalry was less useful in the jungles, not only because of the terrain, but also because the climate affected the health of both men and horses. Furthermore, much as modern invaders of Vietnam learned, while the Mongols could control the cities domination of the countryside remained elusive.[57] The Mongols withdrew, but both Champa and Dai Viet agreed to continue to pay tribute, realising that it was a small price to pay compared to the damage from repeated invasions.[58] Thus, while militarily the Mongols failed to conquer, they still achieved the dual goals of world domination and restoring the tribute system.

Although the Mongols did not invade Japan in 1286, they continued their naval operations and goals of overseas conquest. Previously, a number of kingdoms in what is present-day Indonesia had sent tribute to the Mongols. The Mongols' activities in Champa, as well as their substitution for the Song dynasty, ensured that these kingdoms were aware of their power. By 1286, however, Kertanagara unified most of Java and ceased sending tribute.[59] The Mongols sent envoys to diplomatically settle the issue and gain the submission of Kertanagara. In addition to restoring the tribute, Khubilai also desired a new wife, learning of the beauty of the Princess of Tumapel in Java. Kertanagara, however, sliced off the noses of the Mongol envoys and returned them to Khubilai.[60] A Mongol fleet set sail in 1292.

Upon landing, the Mongols learned that Kertanagara was dead and there was rebellion against his son-in-law, Raden Vijaya. Raden Vijaya quickly came to terms. In return for Mongol support, Khubilai would receive the

---

[56] Buell, 'Indochina, Vietnamese Nationalism and the Mongols', 26–9.
[57] Buell, 'Indochina, Vietnamese Nationalism and the Mongols', 26–7.
[58] MP1, 269; MP/Cliff, 234–5; MP/Lathem, 249–51; MP/Marsden, 224–5; MP/YC, v2, 266–8.
[59] MP1, 274; MP/Cliff, 235–6; MP/Lathem, 251–2; MP/Marsden, 225–6; MP/YC, v2, 272–4.
[60] Delgado, *Khubilai Khan's Lost Fleet*, 165.

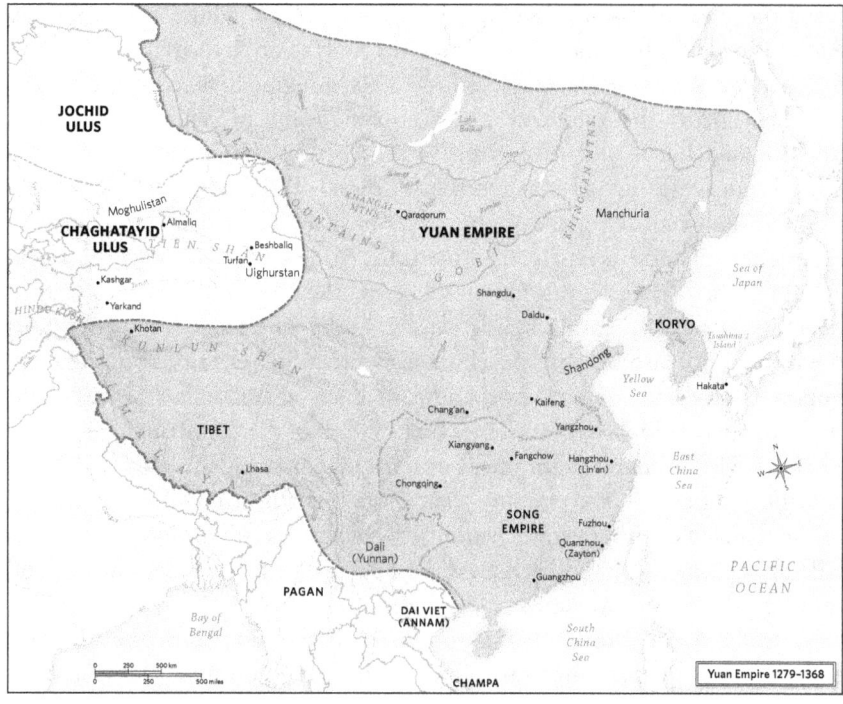

Map 8.1 The Yuan Empire, 1279–1368 © Mapping Specialists

princess and tribute while Raden Vijaya ruled Java as Khubilai's *jarquchi*. Although the conquest went smoothly, Raden Vijaya betrayed the Mongols, evicting them from Java without the princess.[61] With another foreign venture ending in failure, Khubilai was furious. The shiploads of plunder that the retreating Mongols carried may have assuaged his feelings somewhat. More importantly, his advisors persuaded the Great Khan that despite the plunder, the campaigns were not worth the expense, particularly when other matters needed his attention.

Internal Matters

The greatest threat that remained to the Yuan Empire was Qaidu (r. 1265–1301), Khubilai's cousin who dominated the remaining Ogodeid and Chaghatayid territories. Their conflict consisted largely of sporadic fighting along the border and occasional larger invasions into Mongolia

---

[61] See David Bade, *Of Palm Wine, Women and War: The Mongolian Naval Expedition to Java in the 13th Century* (Singapore, 2013); Odoric, 446–7; Odoric/Yule, 106–8.

and Xinjiang. Mongolia became a backwater province of Khubilai's empire due to the moving of the capital from Qaraqorum to Daidu and Shangdu, but it remained an important reservoir of troops and horses. Symbolically, Qaraqorum also held great importance – how could Khubilai call himself the *Qa'an* of the Mongol Empire without holding Mongolia? Thus, with Qaidu's forays and the fact that many in the steppes sympathised with Qaidu, he remained a constant threat and risked rebellion within Khubilai's domains.

Indeed, Nayan, a descendant of Chinggis Khan's half-brother Belgutei, and a Nestorian Christian, rebelled in Manchuria and eastern Mongolia against Khubilai while Qaidu invaded from the west in 1287.[62] Nayan's supporters were drawn largely from the nobility descended from Chinggis Khan's brothers, who had supported Khubilai Khan, but who now felt disenfranchised and ignored. Nayan's rebellion was short-lived as Khubilai learned of it before Nayan could co-ordinate effectively with Qaidu. Khubilai personally led the army that quelled it.[63]

Khubilai, however, could not defeat Qaidu, although Bayan prevented Qaidu from making significant gains in Yuan territory. When Yuan forces invaded Qaidu's territory, Khubilai lost his economic and logistical advantage. Furthermore, he also risked the desertion of many Mongols who did not savour a civil war or who viewed Qaidu as being more Mongol – Khubilai's policies often appeared Sinocentric to many Mongols. Thus, Qaidu remained a rallying point for anyone dissatisfied with Khubilai, and the dispute remained unsettled when Khubilai died in 1294 after a reign of approximately thirty years.

Rebellion and the threat from Qaidu were not the only issue in the latter years of Khubilai's reign. The death of Khubilai's beloved wife Chabi's death in 1281 affected him deeply. Although Khubilai had other wives and even remarried, Chabi's presence as a counsellor was missed. She had been a steadying influence on Khubilai.[64] Through her guidance, the Yuan Empire shifted

---

[62] Louis Hambis (trans.), 'Le Chapitre du Yuan Che CVII', *TP* 38 (1945), 40, 62, 151. Rashid al-Din indicates that Nayan is a descendant of Temuge Otchigin. RD/Karimi, 208; RD/Thackston1, 138; RD/Thackston2, 99.

[63] MP1, 122–7; MP/Cliff, 88–93; MP/Lathem, 114–19; MP/Marsden, 97–102; MP/YC, v1, 332–44.

[64] Francis W. Cleaves (trans.), 'The Biography of the Empress Cabi in the Yuan Shih', *HUS* 3, pt. 1(1979–1980) 145–8; George Qingzhi Zhao, *Marriage as Political Strategy and Cultural Expression: Mongolian Royal Marriages from World Empire to Yuan Dynasty* (New York, 2008), 241; RD/Karimi, 612; RD/Thackston1, 422; RD/Thackston2, 298; Rossabi, *Khubilai Khan*, 206. Rashid al-Din indicates 1284 as Chabi's death while the *Yuan Shi* lists 1277.

Figure 8.5 A *gerege* with Phagspa inscription. With Khubilai's institution of the Phagspa script, it began to appear on all forms of government communication, including this *gerege* or *paiza*. The message reads: 'By the power of the Eternal Heaven, [this is] an order of the Khan. Whoever does not respect the bearer will be guilty of offence.' (Kharkhorin Museum, Kharkhorin, Mongolia)

into a more Buddhist orbit.[65] Although Khubilai continued the practice of religious tolerance, he favoured Buddhism, particularly Tibetan Buddhism. To this end, he made a monk, Phagspa, the state preceptor and head of all monks in 1261, as well as his personal chaplain. When Phagspa went to Tibet, he assisted in enforcing Mongol rule there. He returned to Khubilai in 1267 and designed a script, known as the square script or Phagspa script, that was meant to unify the empire – a script for all languages. Although functional, it never completely replaced any script, including Mongolian. Indeed, Phagspa script largely disappeared after the end of the Yuan. Although Phagspa retired as imperial preceptor in 1274, his influence was great. He initiated the priest–patron relation in the Mongol Empire. In private, Khubilai showed Phagspa

---

[65] Paul D. Buell, 'Some Royal Mongol Ladies: Alaqa-beki, Ergene-Qatun and Others', *WHC*, <http://worldhistoryconnected.press.illinois.edu/7.1/buell.html> (last accessed 11 April 2017).

great respect, but in public, it was clear that the *Qa'an* was the unquestioned authority.[66]

In his later years, Khubilai's tolerance for other religions wavered. Muslims found themselves at odds with the court on the basis of their practices such as the *halal* method of animal slaughter versus the Mongol method. The difference made it awkward for Muslim dignitaries, emissaries and officials to eat at Khubilai's court, which the *Qa'an* viewed as an insult.[67] Khubilai's ire led to the issuing of a rescript banning Muslims and Jews from slaughtering animals in their traditional manner. Additionally, it ordered them to take wives in the same manner (levirate) as the Mongols, leading many Muslims to exit from the Yuan Empire.[68]

While discrimination occurred, when desultory results occurred, such as Muslim merchants exiting from the empire or unrest among the Chinese population, the court mitigated some of the excesses. As with the situation of the Daoists, who experienced discrimination due to the court's predilection for Buddhism, some of the discrimination towards Muslims may have also been reactionary and part of a growing rivalry in the bureaucracy or broader discontent among the Chinese population. Although Khubilai Khan introduced many non-Chinese into the bureaucracy, Muslims constituted a significant number and thus represented a direct threat to Confucian dominance of government.

While Muslims had long served the Mongol government, Khubilai's amalgam of Confucian and Mongol practices created tensions as his administration appeared Chinese. The tension between Muslims and the Confucians intensified when a Central Asian Muslim, a favourite of Chabi's named Ahmad Fanakati, became a key minister of state. He had served in various capacities in Khubilai's appanage since 1247 and rose to become one of the most powerful figures in the empire outside of the *altan urugh*. In addition to overseeing the government monopolies on salt, medicinal herbs and iron production, he proved to be a talented finance minister.[69] His success nurtured even greater ambitions as he sought to maintain Khubilai's favour, which earned him jealousy and hatred from a number of individuals.

---

[66] Sh. Bira, 'Qubilai Qa'an and 'Phags-pa bLa-ma', in *MEL*, 240–9.
[67] RD/Karimi, 654; RD/Thackston1, 451; RD/Thackston2, 319; 'Yuan tien-chang: Chin Hui-hui mo-sha yang tso su-na', trans. Francis W. Cleaves, *JTS* 16 (1992), 72–3; Johan Elverskog, *Buddhism and Islam on the Silk Road* (Philadelphia, 2010), 227–41.
[68] RD/Karimi, 654; RD/Thackston1, 451; RD/Thackston2, 319; 'Yuan tien-chang', 72–3; MP1, 163; MP/Cliff, 108; MP/Lathem, 135; MP/Marsden, 134; MP/Yule, v1, 420.
[69] RD/Karimi, 650–3; RD/Thackston1, 449–51; RD/Thackston2, 318–19; MP1, 160–3; MP/Cliff, 104–8; MP/Lathem, 131–5; MP/Marsden, 130–4; MP/YC, v1, 415–20; also see Herbert Franke, 'Ahmad (?–1282)', in *ITSOTK*, 538–57.

While Khubilai favoured Ahmad as he increased revenues, Prince Jingim did not conceal his distaste for him.[70] Ahmad's rivals eventually assassinated him in 1282. After an investigation revealed Ahmad's embezzlement, he was posthumously accused of cronyism and nepotism. The tribunal flayed his sons, and when Khubilai Khan learned the depths of his corruption, he had Ahmad's body exhumed, hanged and then cast into the street for dogs to devour.[71] To be sure, some criticism of Ahmad's tenure is fair, but as the Chinese sources are hostile towards Ahmad it is difficult to ascertain whether he was a bad minister or simply envied. His boundless ambition certainly made many enemies at all levels of the government ranging from the low-level officials who assassinated him to Prince Jingim. According to Marco Polo, Khubilai Khan's discovery of the extent of Ahmad's crimes led him to issue the decree banning *halal* slaughter and other aspects specifically tied to Islam.[72]

Although Marco Polo's account emphasises that he was present for the event, one should not assume that Ahmad was killed due to his religion.[73] Ahmad, however, employed many non-Muslims as well as Muslims. Most of these shared Ahmad's vision, and his avarice.[74] It is uncertain whether Ahmad's religious identity played a role in the intrigues against him, but it certainly affected events afterwards.

Khubilai's decree may have been a knee-jerk reaction and perhaps penance for himself, as Ahmad's actions took the *Qa'an* by surprise. In addition to his embezzlement, Rashid al-Din indicates that Ahmad had accumulated forty wives and 400 concubines, along with the fortune needed to support them.[75] Marco Polo supports Rashid al-Din's account not in numbers, but by revealing the method by which Ahmad acquired his women:

> Moreover, there was no beautiful woman whom he might desire, but he got hold of her, if she was unmarried, forcing her to be his wife, if otherwise, compelling her to consent to his desires. Whenever he knew of any one who had a pretty daughter, certain ruffians of his would go to the father and say: 'What say you? Here is this pretty daughter of yours; give her in marriage to the Bailo Achmath [*sic*] (for they called him 'the Bailo,' or, as we should say, 'the Viceregent'), and we will arrange for his giving you such

---

[70] RD/Karimi, 650–3; RD/Thackston1, 449–51; RD/Thackston2, 318–19, Franke, 'Ahmad', 549.
[71] MP1, 163; MP/Cliff, 108; MP/Lathem, 134; MP/Marsden, 133; MP/YC, v1, 420.
[72] MP1, 163; MP/Cliff, 108; MP/Lathem, 134–5; MP/Marsden, 133–4; MP/YC, v1, 420.
[73] MP1, 163; MP/Cliff, 108; MP/Lathem, 134–5; MP/Marsden, 133–4; MP/YC, v1, 420.
[74] Franke, 'Ahmad', 249.
[75] RD/Karimi, 653; RD/Thackston1, 451; RD/Thackston2, 319.

a government or such an office for three years.' And so the man should surrender his daughter.[76]

It is not surprising that one of Ahmad's assassins was also a victim, with his mother, wife and daughter falling into Ahmad's clutches. The fact that low-ranking officials carried out the assassination indicates that Ahmad's intrigues affected more than his court rivals. Indeed, Marco Polo insinuates that Ahmad's acquisition of women also provoked thoughts of rebellion in the minds of the Chinese. [77] If Rashid al-Din's account is accurate, we can also conclude that Ahmad was not the most devout Muslim, as forty wives clearly exceeds the four that most jurists found acceptable in Islamic law. That being said, Khubilai's reaction was most likely a corrective measure against a growing resentment towards Ahmad and those he employed. While Ahmad employed many individuals of varying ethnicities and religion, Marco Polo observed that Muslims and Christians served as officials over the Chinese.[78] With Ahmad's fall from grace and life itself, other Muslim officials surely came under scrutiny. For Khubilai, retaliation against a group was necessary to mollify the majority of the empire's population. Nonetheless, Ahmad's excesses also demonstrated the extent of Khubilai's withdrawal from the management of the empire.

A protégé of Ahmad's named Lu Shirong succeeded him. Initially in the tea administration, Lu Shirong somehow survived the purge of Ahmad's appointees, most likely because he was in the provinces. To prevent future abuses, Ahmad's former position was divided into two positions (Office of the Left and Office of the Right), with Lu Shirong surviving as the Chancellor of the Left while the Mongol Antung, a great-grandson of Muqali, served as the Chancellor of the Right.[79] Antung had been among those who had opposed Ahmad, and he became a formidable opponent to Lu Shirong as well. Lu Shirong's duties, however, still entailed fiscal responsibilities. These he embraced, and found new ways to increase state income from the salt monopolies as well as from liquor, copper and silver. He used the confiscated copper and silver to further back and expand the use of paper currency in the Yuan Empire.[80] He also recruited merchants into tax positions, possibly as tax-farmers. It was not long before complaints of exploitation surfaced among

---

[76] MP1, 161. Also see MP/Cliff, 105; MP/Lathem, 130–1; MP/Marsden, 131–2; MP/YC, v1, 416–17.
[77] MP1, 161; MP/Cliff, 105–6; MP/Lathem, 131–2; MP/Marsden, 132–3; MP/YC, v1, 417–18.
[78] MP1, 162; MP/Cliff, 106; MP/Lathem, 133; MP/Marsden, 132; MP/YC, v1, 418.
[79] Igor de Rachewiltz, 'Muqali', in *ITSOTK*, 9–11.
[80] Rossabi, *Khubilai Khan*, 190–1.

the populace. Political rivals also emerged. While these rivalries became quite heated and even led to executions on both sides, Lu Shirong appeared safe due to his efficiency in raising revenues, at least until Prince Jingim became involved. Emboldened by Prince Jingim's animosity towards Lu, his enemies charged Lu Shirong with profiteering. Khubilai executed him in May 1285.[81]

A Buddhist from Tibet named Sangha became Chancellor of the Left in 1287. Previously, he had replaced the Phagspa lama as head of the Buddhist monks and crushed a rebellion in Tibet in 1280.[82] His duties as Commissioner of Buddhist Affairs gave him influence in the court, but his political acumen and interest in fiscal affairs made him a prime candidate to replace Ahmad as the chief official of the empire. Soon his influence permeated virtually all the Yuan ministries. Rashid al-Din referred to him as Khubilai's vizier.[83]

As minister of finance and state affairs, Sangha attempted to correct the economy and strengthen the silver and silk reserves that backed the paper money of the empire. Realising the importance of Muslim merchants and the *ortoq* institution to the empire, he convinced Khubilai to end his persecution of Muslims.[84] The exodus of Muslims drained the empire of talent and the economy experienced a notable decline as Muslim merchants avoided the empire. It is curious that other merchants (like the Polos) were unable to fill the gap. Like the talented Ahmad, Sangha's ability created enemies. Antung, the Chancellor of the Right, opposed Sangha's actions, but Khubilai favoured the Tibetan over the Antung, who then resigned in 1289.[85]

Although Sangha rooted out inefficiencies and corruption, he was not immune to bribes. Although many Chinese officials disliked him, his downfall came when he angered Mongol and Turkic officials, who denounced him before Khubilai. A Persian Muslim rival, Mubarakshah, added the final straw by demonstrating that Sangha had embezzled jewels. With Sangha's execution in 1291, his supporters who rode his coat-tails to power were also dismissed.[86]

The 'Three Villainous Ministers', as they are referred to in the Chinese histories, Ahmad, Lu Shirong and Sangha, were, however, symptoms of a larger problem. Although Khubilai found talented individuals for his staff, his withdrawal from active participation permitted their abilities to develop

---

[81] Rossabi, *Khubilai Khan*, 191–2.
[82] Herbert Franke, 'Sangha (?–1291)', *ITSOTK*, 558–9.
[83] RD/Karimi, 654; RD/Thackston1, 451; RD/Thackston2, 319; Franke, 'Sangha', 559–64.
[84] RD/Karimi, 654–5; RD/Thackston1, 451–2; RD/Thackston2, 319–20.
[85] Igor de Rachewiltz, 'Muqali', 11.
[86] RD/Karimi, 655–6; RD/Thackston1, 452–3; RD/Thackston2, 320–1; Franke, 'Sangha', 575–82.

into hubris due to lack of oversight. Furthermore, his longevity became problematic. One minister suggested he abdicate in favour of Jingim, which led to Khubilai fearing that a conspiracy was brewing. Jingim's death in 1285 averted potential conflict.

Jingim's death left the Yuan Empire in a curious situation. In many ways, Khubilai's longevity fuelled the demise of the empire. He outlived his designated successor, Jingim (1243–85), and most of his other sons, so that his grandson Temur Oljeitu (r. 1295–1307) came to the throne. While Temur proved to be a very capable ruler and even defeated Qaidu on a few occasions, much of his reign dealt with correcting issues that occurred during the last decade of Khubilai's life. After Chabi's death, Khubilai's inattention to imperial responsibilities appears to have been due to a combination of heavy drinking and depression. While the ministers of state were capable of managing the empire, those who abused their power caused unnecessary upheaval within the government.

The Middle Period

Temur Oljeitu's accession was not without challenge. His elder brother Kammala (1263–1302) also vied with him for the throne. As Khubilai's efforts to ensure smooth succession failed due to the death of Jingim in 1285, it was not guaranteed that Temur Oljeitu, Jingim's son, would be elected khan. He benefited, however, from the support of many members of the Secretariat, as well as from the support of the general Bayan and from the tireless efforts of his mother, Kokojin.[87] In a *quriltai* in April 1294, Temur became *Qa'an*.

Temur Oljeitu continued many of his father's policies and held the line against Qaidu. With Qaidu's death in 1301, the war with the Ogodeids lost its momentum as fractures between the Chaghatayids and the Ogodeids manifested themselves. Unlike his father, Temur Oljeitu did not see the need to expand the empire and even cancelled plans to invade Annam and Japan, viewing them as an unnecessary expense, particularly when Annam continued to send tribute. His only foreign campaigns were punitive actions against Pagan in 1300–1 and then northern Thailand in 1301–3, which ended with desultory results.[88]

---

[87] RD/Karimi, 671; RD/Thackston1, 463–4; RD/Thackston2, 328–9.
[88] *Yuan che*: 'Notice sur les expeditions en Birmanie faites sous la dynastie des Yuan', in Edouard Huber, "Etudes indochines: V-La Fin de la dynastie de Pagan", *BEFEO* 9 (1909), 676–9; *Hman-nan Yazawin* (la Chronique royale birmane), Edouard Huber (ed. and trans.), 'Etudes indochines: V-La Fin de la dynastie de Pagan', *BEFEO* 9 (1909), 659–61; Hsiao Ch'i-ch'ing, 'Mid-Yuan Politics', in *CHCAR*, 501.

Figure 8.6 Copper mirror from Qaraqorum. Although Khubilai Khan moved the capital to Daidu, Qaraqorum remained symbolically important. This mirror reveals a pastoral scene. (Kharkhorin Museum, Kharkhorin, Mongolia)

Instead, he focused on the return of the *Pax Mongolica* in 1304.[89] With the end of the war against the Ogodeids and Chaghatayids, overland trade resumed and the four Mongol khanates co-operated with each other for the most part. Realising the limitations of Yuan power during the Qaidu war, Temur Oljeitu worked diligently to promote peace with his cousins throughout the Mongol world. In return, they recognised him as *Qa'an* of the Mongol Empire, although in reality his authority was limited to the Yuan territories.[90] With the stability, Temur Oljeitu could then turn to internal matters.

With Khubilai's diminished role in affairs of state in the waning years of his reign, this focus was crucial. Temur Oljeitu sought reconciliation with his relatives in Mongolia proper and Manchuria. Although numerous Mongols lived in China (and throughout the Yuan Empire), significant numbers remained in the steppes. Temur sent lavish gifts, even though it caused financial strain. Other policies promoting stability continued, such as cancelling tax debts caused by ruinous fiscal policies in the last years of Khubilai's life. Temur's government also endeavoured to eradicate corruption. In 1303,

---

[89] For the *Pax Mongolica*, see Hodong Kim, 'The Unity of the Mongol Empire and Continental Exchanges Over Eurasia', *Journal of Central Eurasian Studies* 1 (2009), 15–42.

[90] Oljeitu, 'Lettre d'Olejeitu à Phillippe le Bel, datée de 1305', in Antoine Mostaert and Francis Woodman Cleaves (eds and trans.), *Les Lettres de 1289 et 1305 des ilkhan Aryun et Oljeitu à Philippe le Bel* (Cambridge, MA, 1962), 55–7.

18,373 officials were convicted; however, punishment was lenient and many regained their posts.[91] While Temur Oljeitu promoted stability, it was short-term as lavish gifts to members of the *altan urugh* and governmental corruption meant that costs outstripped income, and began to deplete the monetary reserves of the empire.

This problem was not insurmountable, however. Unfortunately, court intrigues ensured that instability at the highest level occurred after Temur Oljeitu died. After Temur's primary wife Shirindari died in 1299, he made Buluqan empress. A woman of great ability and ambition, Buluqan played an influential rule in the instability that followed Temur Oljeitu's death, which is unfortunate as even hostile sources indicate that most of her policies and actions were just.[92] During Temur Oljeitu's lifetime, Buluqan accumulated power and wealth, often confiscating the property of those charged with corruption. In some cases, she was the one who framed the accused.[93] Using her wealth and influence, Buluqan secured support for her son, Deshou, as the heir apparent and removed all rivals, all of them cousins, from the court, placing them in distant regions.[94] Deshou, however, died in 1306, and when Temur Oljeitu died in 1307 he left no heir.

With all potential successors spread throughout the empire, the race for the throne became literally that. He who could gain the support of influential members of the Central Secretariat and military had the best chance of success. Factions emerged during Buluqan Khatun's regency. Buluqan sought to place Ananda (d.1307), Jingim's Muslim nephew, on the throne. It has been suggested that his Muslim affiliation damaged his support. Another faction supported Qaishan, the son of Temur Oljeitu's elder brother Darmabala (1264–93). Other factions also existed, and bloodshed occurred as Qaishan's younger brother Ayurbarwada stormed the palace in Daidu and arrested Prince Ananda and Buluqan.[95] Although Ayurbarwada seized the capital and considered himself a contender, Qaishan emerged victorious due to his superior military support and seniority. Rather than more bloodshed occurring, their mother Targi (d. 1322) mediated a resolution, leaving Qaishan as *Qa'an* (r. 1307–11) and Ayurbarwada as the heir apparent.

Qaishan differed from Khubilai and Temur Oljeitu on a number of policies.[96] Much of this was due to his education. Although he received some

---

[91] Hsiao Ch'i-ch'ing, 'Mid-Yuan Politics', in *CHCAR*, 499.
[92] Ch'i-ch'ing, 'Mid-Yuan Politics', 504.
[93] Ch'i-ch'ing, 'Mid-Yuan Politics', 504.
[94] RD/Karimi, 670; RD/Thackston1, 463; RD/Thackston2, 328.
[95] Ch'i-ch'ing, 'Mid-Yuan Politics', 506.
[96] Ch'i-ch'ing, 'Mid-Yuan Politics', 508.

Confucian influence, he spent much of his time commanding Yuan armies in the steppes. He ruled as a steppe khan, relying on personal retainers rather than the Secretariat to ensure compliance with his whims.[97] Unfortunately, his empire was too vast and diverse to be ruled as such; thus he was largely ineffective. Unlike Ogodei and Khubilai, he failed to realise the need for different styles of governance. Financial difficulties inherited from Temur Oljeitu increased as he expanded the Secretariat with his supporters and built new Buddhist temples and palaces, including ones for his retainers. His expenses soon outstripped new taxes.

His death in 1311 permitted his brother Ayurbarwada (r. 1311–20) to peacefully transition to the throne. Despite his peaceful ascent to the throne, bloodshed followed as he purged the government of many of Qaishan's ministers and reversed Qaishan's policies.[98] Unlike his brother, he embraced his Confucian education (and perhaps filial piety influenced his agreement to Qaishan and Targi's proposal).

Unlike most, if not all, Yuan emperors, Ayurbarwada could read and write Chinese. During his reign, he trimmed the bureaucracy to manageable levels and in 1313 reinstituted the civil service exams based on neo-Confucian interpretations of the classic texts. Although the status of Confucian scholar-officials increased, Mongols and *Semuren* still dominated the government in terms of power. While the exams prevented appointments based on personal connections, Mongols and *Semuren* received preference in the tests. Furthermore, Ayurbarwada attempted to codify the regulations and laws implemented since Khubilai Khan's death, a process which was not completed until 1323 (two years after his death). He found it difficult to curtail the privileges of the elites, particularly those granted by Qaishan. In these situations, he picked his battles rather than risk rebellion. Like Khubilai, he sought to find a balance between the reality of the Chinese population who needed an emperor and the necessity that he maintain Mongol prerogatives as a steppe *Qa'an*. While Ayurbarwada managed to control some excesses, his death at age 35 limited his impact. As one scholar noted, although his reign 'added more Chinese features to the Yuan state, it failed to curb the vested interests of the Mongolian and the *se-mu* elites and hence did not fundamentally affect the "constitution" of the Mongolian-Yuan state'.[99]

Ayurbarwada's eighteen-year-old son, Shidebala (r. 1230–1323), took power in April 1320 without opposition. Assassination ended his reign in

---

[97] Ch'i-ch'ing, 'Mid-Yuan Politics', 507–8.
[98] Ch'i-Ch'ing, 'Mid-Yuan Politics', 514–15.
[99] Ch'i-Ch'ing, 'Mid-Yuan Politics', 526–7.

1323. Tensions between Ayurbarwada's and Shidebala's pro-Chinese sympathies and the more conservative Mongol elite led to his death. In the end, his bodyguard assisted in his disposal and raised Yesun Temur (r.1323–8) to the throne at a *quriltai* along the Kerulen River, the homeland of Chinggis Khan.

Yesun Temur, a nephew of Prince Jingim, legitimated his reign by arresting the assassins and attempted to support his predecessor's policies. At thirty-one years of age, he was not a pawn. Unlike Ayurbarwada, he had been raised in the steppes of Mongolia and was decidedly not pro-Chinese. Whereas Ayurbarwada was a devout Buddhist and discriminated against non-Buddhists, particularly Muslims, Yesun Temur returned to the more neutral religious tolerance of the early Mongol Empire. Several Muslims found positions in his administration and Confucians once again found themselves on the outside looking in, although not all were removed from their posts. Nonetheless, Yesun Temur recognised the need to portray himself as a Chinese emperor and provided patronage to Confucian scholars outside of the bureaucracy. Despite his support of both Muslims and Confucians, he showered his patronage upon Buddhists, particularly those who followed the various Tibetan sects.[100]

Yesun Temur died at Shangdu in August 1328. His death, while natural, ushered in a new round of violence. His nine-year-old son, Aragibala (r. 1328), vanished during the conflict as court factions attempted to place Qaishan's sons on the throne. Two of his sons, Qoshila and his half-brother Tuq Temur, both claimed the throne after his death. Qoshila (r. 1328–9) assumed the throne through the efforts of a Kipchak commander named El Temur, who had served Qaishan and was a veteran of the wars against Nayan and Qaidu. Furthermore, El Temur controlled the *keshig*. The coup found widespread support. Many of the Confucians found themselves supporting the conservative Mongols due to Yesun Temur's support for Christians and Muslims.[101]

Many of Yesun Temur's ministers, especially Muslims, were purged as El Temur seized Daidu. Capturing Shangdu proved more difficult as the coup was discovered. Those loyal to Yesun Temur eventually submitted, although resistance continued in the provinces. While Qoshila became *Qa'an*, his reign only lasted six months as neither El Temur nor Qoshila's half-brother Tuq Temur were ready to concede power. Tuq Temur (r. 1328, 1329–32) seized the throne by fratricide.[102] Tuq Temur's reign lasted only three years, in which he was decidedly pro-Chinese and Confucian. A few *Semuren*, but

---

[100] Ch'i-Ch'ing, 'Mid-Yuan Politics', 537–41.
[101] Ch'i-Ch'ing, 'Mid-Yuan Politics', 542–3.
[102] Ch'i-Ch'ing, 'Mid-Yuan Politics', 545.

not a single Muslim, served in the administration. Tuq Temur, however, was a puppet king as El Temur and Bayan the Merkit (a subordinate of El Temur and not Khubilai's general) wielded the real power. They spent much of their time quelling rebellions, however. Whereas rebellions were rare prior to Yesun Temur's reign, with increasing coups and civil wars, no matter how brief, insurrection became more frequent. Most were not in support of a losing faction, but simply tired of exploitation. El Temur and Bayan faced another challenge when Tuq Temur died without an heir in September 1332.

In agreement with the Empress Dowager Budashiri, El Temur raised a six-year-old Irinchinbal (r. 1332) to the throne, hoping that the youth would not only be easy to control, but would also limit a war between possible contenders. His reign, however, ended after 53 days when he died from illness. His death allowed his elder brother Toghon Temur, exiled in Korea at the time, to take the throne.

End of the Yuan Empire

Toghon Temur (1332–70) inherited a disaster. In many ways, the empire should have been at its peak as the Mongols certainly had sufficient time to stabilise it. While Toghon Temur ultimately 'lost' China, it was not entirely his fault. With brief reigns and constant overturnings of policies, long-term stability proved elusive after Temur Oljeitu's reign.

Mongol control declined most obviously in southern China, which wore Mongol rule uneasily and with great reluctance. Banditry and rebellion increased. Mongolia also began to slip from Yuan control as the dissonance between the Yuan and those in the steppe increased to the point where the nomads no longer viewed the Yuan as true Mongols but essentially as Chinese. The Yuan were caught in a perspective of being Chinese to the Mongols but Mongols in the eyes of the Chinese. This untenable situation came to a head during the reign of Toghon Temur. Additionally, corruption was rampant among various members of the bureaucracy as well as among the imperial family. Although the old Confucian civil service had been reinstated, it did not result in an efficient administration as nepotism and cronyism dominated the ranks.

Despite a thirty-year reign, Toghon Temur could not stop the impetus of collapse. Attempts were made to overcome ethnic friction through loyalty to institutions and the dynasty. The examination system assisted the process, but it only touched those in the government, not the majority of the subjects. Toghon's youth further hampered his reign. He came to the throne at the age of thirteen and under the domination of El Temur and the chancellor, Bayan the Merkit, who became rivals. In 1335, Bayan instigated a coup that ended the influence of El Temur's clique.

Bayan attempted to restore the government and policies to what they had been in the time of Khubilai Khan, but it is uncertain what that meant – Khubilai's own policies had varied considerably during his thirty-year reign.[103] Regardless, Bayan sought to stabilise and improve the status of the empire. Unfortunately, reversing fifty years of change is virtually impossible in any era. Nonetheless, he attempted to reinforce the four-division ethnic hierarchy. This, however, had become greatly blurred, with many Chinese not only assuming Mongolian names but also learning Mongolian and enmeshing themselves into the Mongolian hierarchy. Similar things happened with other groups. Many *Semuren* were culturally Chinese.[104] Bayan's efforts to reverse this caused resentment. His fiscal measures, many sensible, added to the opposition, particularly in light of his own acquisition of property and wealth. In 1340, Bayan's own nephew, Toghto Temur, led a coup that unseated Bayan, who died in exile.[105]

The coup was led primarily by a younger generation of Mongols who had lived in China and saw the ethnic distinctions in a different light. As leader of this faction, Toghto Temur became the Chancellor of the Right in 1340.[106] He ceased the purges and removed the ethnic restrictions while also reinstating the civil service examinations and Confucian ceremonies. Additionally, he made a significant reversal by allowing Chinese to own horses.[107] He also attempted to improve and expand the canal system.

Having participated in the coup, Toghon Temur also began to take an active part in the government. Unfortunately, even as he took the reins of power, a series of natural disasters wreaked havoc within the empire. Efforts to improve the Grand Canal came late as it had fallen into disrepair, along with many dykes and dams along the Huanghe River. The resultant flooding led to famine and refugees.[108] Repairing the damage required massive numbers of men and the only way to achieve those numbers was through corvée labour, which caused resentment. Part of the effort included shifting the course of the Huanghe River, which was successfully completed in 1351.[109] The state of the Grand Canal added to the famine, as food supplied from the south could not reach the north.

---

[103] John Dardess, 'Shun-Ti and the End of Yuan Rule in China', in Herbert Franke and Denis Twitchett (eds), *CHCAR*, 568.
[104] Brose, *Subjects and Masters*, 260–70.
[105] YS 135, 14–16.
[106] YS 135, 14–16.
[107] YS 135, 17–18.
[108] YS 135, 19.
[109] YS 135, 22.

Civil wars prior to Toghon Temur's reign had increased the independence of many generals and governors. The destruction of the war also fed into the rebellion and banditry. A millenarian movement emerged among a Buddhist sect known as the White Lotus, which, in turn, influenced the rise of a rebel movement known as the Red Turbans, so named for the red bands that tied their hair back. The rebellion had been in existence since the 1330s in southern China and sought to restore the Song dynasty. Although the Mongols crushed numerous uprisings, the movement remained alive and grew as Mongol authority diminished. The fact that the Red Turbans were not a single organisation aided the movement as there was not a single source of leadership and it remained somewhat amorphous.[110] Thus a single defeat had little impact on the Red Turbans. Eventually the Red Turbans successfully drove the Mongols out of China. One of their leaders, Zhu Yuanzhang (r. 1368–98), emerged as the dominant figure in post-Mongol China and established the Ming Dynasty (1368–1644).

The Yuan Dynasty did not disappear, however. It continued to function until 1388 before internecine fighting definitively ended any chance of a cohesive state. Two Yuan emperors or khans ruled after Toghon Temur, Ayushiridara (1370–8) and Toghus Temur (1378–88). Until then, the Mongols planned to reconquer China, which often placed former vassals, such as Korea, in tenuous diplomatic situations. While the Ming proved to be xenophobic, the Yuan Empire left an indelible mark on China as well as Tibet and Korea in terms of culture, history and politics. While the Yuan Dynasty ended, the Northern Yuan began in Mongolia in 1388.

Islam and the Yuan Empire

The Yuan Empire could never be viewed as an Islamic empire. Despite Marco Polo's claims that Khubilai was on the verge of converting to Christianity, his account indicates that the Mongols dwelling in China favoured Buddhism just as those in the Ilkhanate favoured Islam.[111] Yet, one may wonder what would have happened if the circumstances had been different. On the surface, it seems unlikely, but a brief exercise in counterfactual history can be useful.[112]

While Khubilai was not a candidate for conversion, his grandson Ananda did convert to Islam. Raised in a Muslim household, Ananda likely converted

---

[110] YS 135, 23.
[111] MP1, 8, 98; MP/Cliff, 7, 75; MP/Lathem, 36, 101; MP/Marsden, 7–8, 81; MP/YC, v1, 13–14, 260.
[112] Jeremy Black, *Other Pasts, Different Presents, Alternative Futures* (Bloomington, IN, 2015), 2–19.

early in life despite his Buddhist name. He ruled the former Tangut region and, according to Rashid al-Din, most of the 150,000 troops under his command also converted to Islam through his efforts; thus he had considerable military backing. Rashid al-Din also notes that while Buddhists and others existed in Ananda's territories, most of the urban population was now Muslim – a considerable change from the time of Chinggis Khan. Marco Polo, however, indicates that although Muslims and Nestorian Christians dwelt in those regions, Buddhists remained the majority.[113] One must also not forget that after Temur Oljeitu's death, Buluqan Khatun sought to raise Ananda to the throne. Ayurbarwada foiled their plans when he stormed the palace. Ananda and Buluqan were arrested and Ananda then died in 1307, possibly by execution.

Yet what if Ananda had secured the throne? With the Yuan *altan urugh* tending towards Buddhism, Ananda's faith would have been a concern, but not necessarily a non-starter. After all, Berke's Muslim faith did not cause a crisis within the Jochid Ulus. With his own sizeable army and other Muslim forces, such as in Yunnan and in the western regions, Ananda had the military strength, which he failed to mobilise during Buluqan's efforts to crown him. Furthermore, we cannot assume that his faith would have mattered tremendously to the rank and file. We have no knowledge of the prevailing religiosity of the Yuan army. Opening the treasury coffers might have been sufficient to win their loyalty.

Additionally, we cannot forget that Muslims had always played an important role within the empire. This ranged from commerce to government officials, as well as culture brokers. Early in his reign, Khubilai Khan seems to have shown Muslims great respect. In 1289, at the instigation of Sangha, Khubilai even established the National College for the Study of Muslim Script, where students could learn Arabic and Persian.[114]

While emphasis is given to Khubilai Khan's attempts to placate the Confucians by participating in their religious rites, he did the same with other religions. Marco Polo observed that Khubilai Khan attended feasts in honour of Easter and Christmas for Christians as well as feasts for Muslims, Jews and Buddhists.[115] Certainly, these sovereign duties contributed to his later obesity, but his actions demonstrated that early in his reign at least Khubilai adhered to the Mongol idea of religious tolerance and that he had learned

---

[113] RD/Karimi, 673; RD/Thackston1, 465; RD/Thackston2, 329; MP1, 72–81; MP/Cliff, 58–66; MP/Lathem, 85–92; MP/Marsden, 64–72; MP/YC, v1, 203–24.
[114] Rossabi, *Khubilai Khan*, 194.
[115] MP/Cliff, 93; MP/Lathem, 119; MP/Marsden, 103. The Yule–Cordier translation does not include this passage.

from the example of his mother, Sorqoqtani.[116] For the Muslims, this meant that Khubilai perhaps attended the *Eid al-Fitr* at the end of Ramadan and the *Eid al-Adha*, celebrated in conjunction with the *Hajj* on the tenth day of the month of *Dhu al-Hijjah*, even by Muslims who did not participate in the *Hajj*. In the latter, and most certainly in the former, the Muslims sacrificed sheep and then consumed them as part of the feast. Considering that they slaughtered the sheep in *halal* fashion, one must consider Khubilai Khan's seemingly peripatetic views on *halal* methods of slaughter. Additionally, Muslims constituted a large number of the *Semuren*, who formed the second tier of Khubilai's social hierarchy.[117]

Judging from the number of Muslim functionaries in the government and from the fact that Khubilai Khan participated in Muslim holidays, it is clear that Khubilai did not have an inherent bias towards Islam. While the Chancellor Ahmad is perhaps the most famous and notorious Muslim associated with Khubilai, many others also served. The most important included Sayyid Ajall and his sons. Sayyid Ajall, the governor of Yunnan, brought numerous Muslims into the region although he did not attempt or encourage conversion of the native population. His administration, however, included some overt efforts at sinicisation with the introduction of Confucian temples and ceremonies.[118] When Khubilai became ruler of the eastern territories of the Mongol Empire, Sayyid Ajall became one of his chief ministers, or, as Rashid al-Din indicates, vizier.[119] His son Nasir al-Din then assumed the role of governor of Qarajang or Yunnan. Nasir al-Din also served with distinction in Annam and Pagan.

The Ahmad Fanakati affair appears to have unleashed a wave of persecution and oppression towards Muslims, including the edict that forbade Muslims from slaughtering animals in *halal* fashion. Instead, they had to use the Mongol method of slitting the belly of the animal. Furthermore, Khubilai Khan commanded them 'to take their wives according to the law of the Tartars', that is to say, the adoption of Levirate marriage.[120]

Johan Elverskog noted:

> With how much zeal the Yuan authorities followed this decree is debated. At first, however, it seems as if it was enforced with draconian glee. Seeking to practice their religion many Muslims therefore left the territory of the

---

[116] Rossabi, *Khubilai Khan*, 13.
[117] Rossabi, *Khubilai Khan*, 117.
[118] Rossabi, *Khubilai Khan*, 202–3.
[119] RD/Karimi, 659–60; RD/Thackston1, 455–6; RD/Thackston2, 317.
[120] MP1, 163; MP/Cliff, 108; MP/Lathem, 134–5; MP/Marsden, 133–4; MP/YC, v1, 420.

Yuan dynasty. In so doing they also took with them their businesses, and this hit the Mongol economy hard. When this unintended side effect became apparent to the Yuan court they subsequently revoked the anti-halal decree in hope that Muslims would not only stay, but also possibly return. But the damage had been done and in many ways this decree set the tone for the remainder of the dynasty.[121]

Although Sangha convinced Khubilai Khan to rescind the edict in 1287, it did have a deleterious impact on the empire, although Elverskog's assessment may be overstated.[122] The role of Muslims in commerce cannot be understated, and they, like Nestorian Christians, were active in various occupations throughout China. When considering the role of Muslim merchants, one must not limit oneself to the caravaneers who traversed Eurasia along the various silk roads; the maritime routes must be also be considered, as trade networks connected Muslim merchant families in the Middle East with relatives in India and China. Friar Odoric estimated that 40,000 Muslims dwelled in Kinsai or modern Hangzhou, which he deemed the greatest city in the world; Marco Polo was also suitably impressed.[123] The ports of Guangzhou and Zayton were also a marvel to Marco Polo, Friar Odoric and Ibn Battuta.[124] Muslim merchants were everywhere. Thus, when Muslims began exiting from the Yuan Empire or simply did not enter the realm to conduct business, an economic boycott took place. The repercussions remained, whether it was intentional or not, although Ibn Battuta noted that some Chinese entrepreneurs took steps to encourage Muslim merchants to transact business in their cities.[125] In the period of Toghon Temur, Muslim butchers were active not just in the hinterland, but in Daidu.[126] Thus, while the edict may have had a grievous effect on Muslims and the Yuan economy, by the fourteenth century there is scant evidence that it still affected the Yuan Empire, although this is not say that prejudice did not exist.

Khubilai's divergence from supporting Muslims may have stemmed not only from the rivalries within his own court, but also from the fact that Muslim Turks on his border with Qaidu tended to support the latter. As

---

[121] Elverskog, *Buddhism and Islam*, 229–30.
[122] Rossabi, *Khubilai Khan*, 194.
[123] MP1, 231–45; MP/Cliff, 197–206; MP/Lathem, 213–31; MP/Marsden, 193–200; 207–8, MP/YC, v2, 185–216; Odoric, 463–7; Odoric/Yule, 127–8.
[124] IB1, 488–90; IB2, 264–8; MP1, 250; MP/Cliff, 192–3, 219; MP/Lathem, 235, 237–9, 348–9; MP/Marsden, 181–2, 185, 212–14; MP/YC, v2, 234–7; Odoric, 458–61; Odoric/Yule, 121–4.
[125] IB1, 489; IB2, 263–4.
[126] IB1, 497; IB2, 268.

a large number of the merchants in the empire, and many of the Muslim officials, were former merchants, Khubilai may have also sought to mollify Confucian elements who possessed a traditional animosity towards merchants.[127] Not all Muslims in the Yuan were merchants, however. In addition to soldiers and engineers, there were also scientists, such as Jamal al-Din, an astronomer. He came from the Ilkhanate at Khubilai's invitation in 1267. Not only did he work with other scientists, including Buddhists and Confucians, but he also created a new and more accurate calendar.[128] Other Muslim scholars took part in academic endeavours with their Chinese peers as well. This included geography and medicine.[129] Yeheitie'er, who supervised the building of Daidu, was a Muslim. Additionally, foreign Muslims brought their own cultural influences which subtly influenced change in China and beyond. Some of the most significant areas were also the most ubiquitous, such as cuisine.[130]

Furthermore, the sizeable Muslim community in the environs of Daidu and perhaps beyond found representation to Khubilai not only among the numerous high-ranking officials, but also through their *Shaykh al-Islam*, a religious official who often served as an intermediary between the Muslims and Khubilai. Ibn Battuta commented on the position of *Shaykh al-Islam* as well, demonstrating that it also existed in the latter Yuan period. The situation, at least on the surface, appears analogous to the role of the Nestorian Catholicus in the Ilkhanate and later the Greek Orthodox Patriarch to the Ottoman Sultan in the *millet* system.[131] Indeed, one may wonder whether the *millet* system found its inspiration in the Mongol Empire.

Still, functionaries such as the *Shaykh al-Islam* could not halt all oppression. While antipathy and rivalry existed between Muslims, Confucians and Buddhists, Christian bureaucrats did not turn the other cheek either. According to Rashid al-Din, Aixue, a Nestorian Christian, accused the Maulana Burhan al-Din Bukhari of an unspecified crime. Aixue also encouraged slaves to inform and spread lies about their Muslim masters.[132]

---

[127] Rossabi, *Khubilai Khan*, 122, 199–201.
[128] Rossabi, *Khubilai Khan*, 125–7; Thomas T. Allsen, *Culture and Conquest in Mongol Eurasia* (Cambridge, 2001), 161–75.
[129] Allsen, *Culture and Conquest*, 154–6; Eugene N. Anderson, *Food and Environment in Early and Medieval China* (Philadelphia, 2014), 202–10. Paul D. Buell and Eugene N. Anderson, *A Soup for the Qan* (London, 2000), *passim*.
[130] Allsen, *Culture and Conquest*, 131–3, 138–40; Buell and Anderson, *Soup for the Qan*, *passim*; Anderson, *Food and Environment*, 203–10.
[131] IB1, 191–2; IB2, 265–7; Rossabi, *Khubilai Khan*, 142; Marshall G. S. Hodgson, *The Venture of Islam*, vol. 3 (Chicago, 1977), 125–6; RS, *passim*.
[132] RD/Karimi, 654; RD/Thackston1, 452; RD/Thackston2, 320.

The actions of Ahmad had a great impact on all Muslims within Khubilai's domains, as indicated above, even in the most distant outposts of the empire, such as in Yunnan. Sayyid Ajall, the trusted counsellor and governor of Yunnan, died a natural death and served without any accusations of corruption.[133] Nasir al-Din, however, suffered a different fate and was executed over accusations of embezzlement in 1292.[134] Nasir al-Din's brothers, however, continued to serve with distinction, demonstrating that Ahmad's character did not impugn all Muslim officials.

In the case of Ananda, evidence of antipathy towards Muslims appears after the death of Khubilai as well. Ananda's life remains an enigma, but Rashid al-Din notes that his faith and his rejection of Buddhism concerned Temur Oljeitu early in his reign. While defending his faith, Ananda refers to the Ilkhan Ghazan's conversion to Islam as a defence for his own beliefs, indicating that, if Ilkhan was a Muslim, the religion must not be a work of evil. While this is certainly panegyric flattery on Rashid al-Din's part, it was effective. Kokejin, Temur Oljeitu's wife, counselled her husband not to antagonise Ananda as he had a large army and much of the population in Ananda's appanage were Muslims. Furthermore, Ananda's territory was close to enemy (Qaidu's) territory. Finally, she also makes the statement that the soldiers and population were 'opposed to this state of affairs'.[135]

This statement referred to both Temur Oljeitu's statements towards Ananda and the hostile atmosphere towards Muslims. Although Sangha convinced Khubilai Khan to revoke his *jarliq*, this did not end animosity towards Muslims, as indicated by Temur Oljeitu's relationship with Ananda. Convinced by the Kokejin's wisdom, Temur Oljeitu ceased his hostilities towards Ananda and, by all appearances, towards other Muslims.[136] While aversion to Islam may still have existed in Temur Oljeitu's heart and within the Yuan Empire, it no longer affected policy. The same can be said of the later Yuan period. Muslims were still active in the court of the *Qa'an* during Friar Odoric's time in the Yuan Empire (c. 1324–30).[137]

Returning to the counterfactual question of whether or not the Yuan Empire could have become an Islamic empire, the answer is yes. Supposing Ananda became the ruler, he did not need the rest of the empire to Islamicise. Nor did he even need to have the majority of the subjects become Muslims.

---

[133] RD/Karimi, 659–60; RD/Thackston1, 455–6; RD/Thackston2, 317.
[134] Rossabi, *Khubilai Khan*, 203.
[135] RD/Karimi, 674, RD/Thackston1, 466; RD/Thackston2, 330.
[136] RD/Karimi, 674–5; RD/Thackston1, 466–7; RD/Thackston2, 330.
[137] Odoric, 474; Odoric/Yule 139–40.

One only needs to look at the Sultanate of Delhi (1210–1526) as an example.[138] So what made an Islamic empire? Certainly, having a Muslim ruler was necessary, but more was needed, as no one considers Berke's reign over the Jochid Ulus to constitute the rise of an Islamic state. While Islamic states shared common governing institutions, most were universal among all civilisations, with only slight modifications. The active promotion of Islam was necessary, however. Ananda demonstrated this in his own domains. Undoubtedly, he would have continued to encourage it as emperor. Additionally, others were active in propagating Islam, including officials in the employ of Temur Oljeitu.[139] All Muslim rulers, at least hypothetically, enjoined good and forbade evil, which also fits with any ruling system that desired a just ruler.[140] The employment of the *shariʿa* would be a factor, of course. Replacing the Yuan law code and the *yasa* would be a major challenge. As will be demonstrated in the following chapters, *shariʿa* never completely replaced the *yasa* in any Mongol state. Rather, what evolved was a syncretic legal system that was able to cope with the hybrid nature of the Mongol world and the Islamic world. The polyglot and polyethnic nature of the Yuan Empire would have made the implanting of an Islamic empire difficult, but not impossible. Indeed, one only needs to look at the Ottoman Empire and its balance of sacred law (*shariʿa*) and the secular (*kanun*).[141] A syncretic approach to governing most likely would have taken place, just as the Mongols adopted in the Confucian world. While some Confucians rituals, such as sacrifices honouring Confucius, would not have meshed with Islam, it is apparent that many Muslims did not see any conflict between their religion and other Confucian tenets. Several Central Asian Muslims found a place among Confucian scholars, bureaucrats and poets even without Ananda's influence, although some of these families lost their Muslim identity over time.[142] The most difficult aspect would have been continuing with a Muslim ruler, particularly considering not only the Buddhist proclivities of the *altan urugh* in the Yuan Empire, but also the fissiparous nature of Mongol succession.

---

[138] See Peter Jackson, *The Delhi Sultanate* (Cambridge, 1999).
[139] RD/Karimi, 675; RD/Thackston1, 466; RD/Thackston2, 330.
[140] Qur'ān 3:110.
[141] Colin Imber, *The Ottoman Empire* (London, 2002), 216–51.
[142] See Ch'en Yuan, *Western and Central Asians*, 57–62, 150–64.

9

The Ilkhanate

Most of the population of the Ilkhanate were Iranians, but it also included large numbers of Turks, Arabs, Kurds, Armenians, Georgians and others. Muslims were the majority, but sizeable contingents of Nestorian and Monophysite Christians existed as well, particularly in the western portion of the empire. Additionally, Buddhists, Jews and Zoroastrians practised their faiths. With thriving trade cities and mixed populations of pastoralists and agriculturalists, the empire was diverse. The imposition of Mongol rule did not radically change the style of government, as the ruling elite had been Turkic military elites since the eleventh century and Mongol rule had been established in much of the region since the 1230s. Nonetheless, the Ilkhanate faced many challenges as it entered the Middle East as a religiously neutral empire based on Mongol ideology instead of one rooted in Islam. For non-Muslim groups it permitted new freedoms, while for Muslims it was bewildering and often frightening as they experienced a complete paradigm shift as other religious groups now found equal standing under infidel rule. Yet, in a few decades the empire transformed into a true Islamic Empire, although aspects of Mongol political ideology and culture never disappeared.

The name of the state itself is interesting, as it is the only section of former *Yeke MonggolUlus* that regularly acknowledged a subordinate status to another Mongol ruler. As explained previously, Mongke made Hulegu his viceroy in the region with the title of *il-khan*, although it was not used in diplomatic correspondence until after Mongke's death.[1] It is curious that Hulegu continued to use the title as the *Yeke Monggol Ulus* drifted into civil war and dissolution, as it was not immediately clear who was *Qa'an*. Much of his reign (1260–5) was complicated by incessant war with the Jochid Ulus as well as the creation of a functioning state. One might wonder whether Hulegu would have contended for the throne had it not been for the war with

---

[1] Reuven Amitai, 'Evidence for the Early Use of the Title Ilkhan Among the Mongols', *JRAS* 1 (1991), 360–1.

the Jochids. It was not until his successor and son, Abaqa, that the Ilkhanids Mongols were truly Il-Khans, in both title and function. Nonetheless, Hulegu used the title during his reign even though Chaghatayid rulers who submitted to Khubilai did not.

In addition to the Mongol government and military, the other major institutions were the religious elite of all sects. With the largest population, the Muslim religious elite posed the greatest challenge. The largest group was the *ulema*, the learned men of religion and law, who were connected to legal schools of thought or *madhhabs*. The *madhhabs* advocated a particular interpretation of the *shari^ca* or Islamic law (Hanifi, Shafa^ci, Maliki and Hanbali). In some cities, these schools had rivalries with each other, which the Mongols exploited. Finally, there were the Sufi *tariqats* or brotherhoods. While the *ulema*, *madhhabs* and *tariqats* were outside of the Mongol government, they exerted an impressive amount of influence over the majority of the population. Proper manipulation and use of these groups made ruling easier just as ineffective handling of them made policy implementation difficult. A complicating factor was that none of these groups was organised at an imperial level and they could only dictate affairs at the local level. For the Mongols this was both a benefit and a headache. Finally, the Mongols left many local rulers in place. Their obedience and compliance with Mongol rule were expected. Compliance, however, did not rule out internal issues and even feuds between local rulers and the aforementioned groups.

Other religious groups also wielded influence. In the western portion of the empire, a sizeable Christian population existed embracing several interpretations of Christianity, including the Church of the East (Nestorians), Greek Orthodox Christianity, and a variety of Monophysite views such as those of the Armenian, Georgian and Jacobite churches. In some regions, such as Georgia, Armenia and Cilicia, and Trebizond, Christian majorities existed. For these, their rulers primarily represented their interests to the Ilkhanid court. In mixed regions, Christian interests found representation through their primary religious leaders, such as the Catholicus of the Church of the East, in what may have been a forerunner of the *millet* system of the Ottomans. Jewish populations also existed, but found themselves on the outside. They were not necessarily oppressed, but without ties to a significant military or political power they lacked influence. Only when Jewish individuals entered the administration did the Jewish community's circumstances change.[2] Buddhism, on the other hand, grew due its popularity among the

---

[2] Christopher P. Atwood, 'Validation by Holiness or Sovereignty: Religious Toleration as Political Theology in the Mongol World Empire of the Thirteenth Century', *IHR* 26/2 (2004), 255.

Mongols. Although Buddhism had a long history in the regions comprising modern Afghanistan and eastern Iran, it had almost disappeared with the spread of Islam, but with the arrival of the Mongols temples were now found in western Iran and Iranian Buddhism experienced a spiritual renewal.

The Reign of Hulegu

Hulegu immediately faced challenges as he began ruling his new empire. Encouraged by the defeat at ʿAyn Jalut, Mosul rebelled in 1261. Sultan Badr al-Din Lu'lu', who had submitted to Hulegu and sent troops against Baghdad, died in 1259. His son and successor, Malik Salih, initiated contact with the Mamluk Sultan Baybars. Tarkan Khatun, Malik Shah's wife and daughter of the old Mongol enemy Jalal al-Din Khwarazmshah, informed Hulegu of her husband's correspondence. Although the Mongols dispatched troops, Mosul's resisted, trusting in aid from Syria. The Mongols, however, intercepted the messenger pigeon and defeated Baybars' troops near Sinjar. The Mongols then donned their armour and wore their hair long like Kurds (rather than in braids) so that the Mosulis thought the Mongols were the expected reinforcements. When the garrison of Mosul sallied forth to attack the besieging Mongols, they discovered the ruse too late.[3]

The city resisted for another six months, but Malik Salih finally surrendered in the summer of 1262. The Mongols showed clemency and sent him to Hulegu, but most of the city was massacred with the usual exception of skilled artisans. After the Mongols departed, refugees who had escaped the slaughter gradually returned to the city. Malik Salih's reprieve, however, was short-lived. According to Rashid al-Din, Hulegu ordered that Malik Salih be 'covered with sheep fat, trussed with felt and rope, and left in the summer sun. After a week, the fat got maggoty, and they started devouring the poor man. He died of that torture within a month.'[4] Hulegu also ensured that Mosul would not rebel again by having Malik Salih's three-year-old son cut in half and left hanging on the bank of the Tigris as a warning to all.[5]

With internal issues settled, Hulegu pondered whether the old Mongol system should continue or whether it was time to change it to fit the unique composition of the territory he ruled. Although he retained many of the institutions and methods of the Mongol Empire, Hulegu (r. 1260–5) bolstered his bureaucracy with many officials native to the Middle East and appointed Sahib Shams al-Din Muhammad Juwayni as his vizier. To be sure, Hulegu's focus remained on the nomads and the hereditary military elites. Two of his

---

[3] RD/Thackston2, 362; RD/Thackston1, 509–10; RD/Karimi, 729–30.
[4] RD/Thackston2, 362; RD/Thackston1, 510–11; RD/Karimi, 731.
[5] RD/Thackston2, 362; RD/Thackston1, 510–11; RD/Karimi, 731.

sons received substantial appanages to govern with Abaqa in Khurasan and Mazandaran, while Yoshmut went to Arran and Azerbaijan.[6] It is notable that he entrusted these regions to his sons, rather than his generals, as the territories also bordered the frontiers of the Chaghatayids and Jochids respectively. Other commanders and elites (Mongols and Turks who arrived with them) also received territories to govern, serving as a stratum of authority above the local notables.

Despite the dissolution of the empire and subsequent civil wars, the Mongols still clung to the idea that *Koke Mongke Tenggeri* bequeathed the earth to the Chinggisids to rule.[7] Therefore, they still needed to expand. Opportunities for expansion, however, became more limited with the end of the *Yeke Monggol Ulus*, largely due to wars with other Mongols. The Ilkhanate itself was bordered by the Jochid and Chaghatayid Uluses, the Mamluk Sultanate and the Sultanate of Delhi. In addition, the Kingdom of Jerusalem was close at hand, as was eastern Arabia. Furthermore, with the dissolution, parts of what is now Afghanistan became quasi-independent. Opportunities were there, but achieving them proved more challenging. At any given time, the Ilkhanate was at war with the Jochid Ulus and the Mamluks, who became allies. The border with the Chaghatayids remained tenuous and ill-defined, leading to many skirmishes and wars. Expansion into India was possible, but the Sultanate of Delhi placed greater emphasis on their defences against the Mongols, limiting most incursions to plundering expeditions. During Hulegu's reign, circumstances prevented him from invading the Sultanate, although his efforts to secure modern Afghanistan had an indirect impact on the Sultanate via refugees.[8] Furthermore, the wars that yielded little plunder were a drain on the economy, which suffered enough problems.

The region comprising the Ilkhanate suffered greatly from the Mongol conquests. Although the chroniclers' claims of apocalyptic destruction in Khurasan and other areas must be ignored, one should not dismiss the notion that the destruction and death reached a level that astounded contemporaries.[9] The Mongols rebuilt many cities not only during the era of the *Yeke Monggol Ulus* but also during the Ilkhanid period. Nonetheless, some locations never fully recovered. Baghdad transformed from a major international city to a less significant regional commercial hub, although it remained a centre of learning. At the same time, peasant flight was a constant concern.

---

[6] RD/Thackston2, 364; RD/Thackston, 513; RD/Karimi, 734.
[7] Reuven Amitai, *Holy War and Rapprochement* (Turnhout, 2013), 38–61.
[8] Peter Jackson, *The Delhi Sultanate* (Cambridge, 1999), 115–16.
[9] Juzjani/Habibi, v2, 120–8; Juzjani/Raverty, 1,026–51; Juwayni/Qazvini, v1, 118–19; Juvaini/Boyle, 152; Ibn Athir, 390–3, 398; Ibn Athir/Richards, 225–7, 230.

Unfortunately, when wars yielded little plunder, some Mongols raided the peasants as the army was a non-salaried institution. Being nomads they could subsist, but without the goods and wealth provided by plundering the enemy or the local population, the average nomad's life was poor. Compounding the issue were the wars with the Chaghatayids and Jochids. The borders became war zones and led to peasants and nomads eschewing the frontiers, unless they were directly tied to the military. In many areas, this led to the breakdown of the *qanat* or *karez* system of irrigation. Furthermore, the wars also interrupted international caravan trade. At times, the wars with the Chaghatayids completely disrupted overland routes to the Yuan Empire in the east. As a result, the Wakhan Corridor in modern Afghanistan was often the only land link between the Yuan Empire and the Ilkhanate.[10]

Qanat or *Karez*

The *qanat* or *karez* irrigation system brought water from the highlands to the lowlands through a series of underground canals and reservoirs. By keeping the water underground, less was lost to evaporation and this made arid regions bloom. It was, however, labour-intensive to maintain, and without a population to maintain it the *karez* system broke down and arable areas returned to scrub or desert. The system had been widely used since the ancient period, and some areas of Central Asia, Iran and Afghanistan still use it today. Access points followed the underground portion and permitted repairs to the underground channels. Additionally, the water cooled these spots, providing relief to workers during the summer.

Such was the Ilkhanate at the time of Hulegu and the situation that his successors faced. Greater challenges confronted Hulegu as he transitioned from conqueror to ruler in a very short amount of time in an age of uncertainty. War with the Jochids began almost immediately, giving Hulegu little time to create a government other than by cobbling together existing systems from the *Yeke Monggol Ulus* and incorporating the recently submitted local elites. Prior to his arrival, many of the regions in southern Iran were largely autonomous, without much oversight from the Mongols. Hulegu continued this practice and maintained a symbiotic relationship with a few states, such as the Salghurids in Shiraz and the Qutlugh Khanids in Kirman, as well as the

---

[10] MP1, 62–4; MP/Cliff, 52–3; MP/Lathem, 79–80; MP/Marsden, 56–7; MP/YC, v1, 170–2.

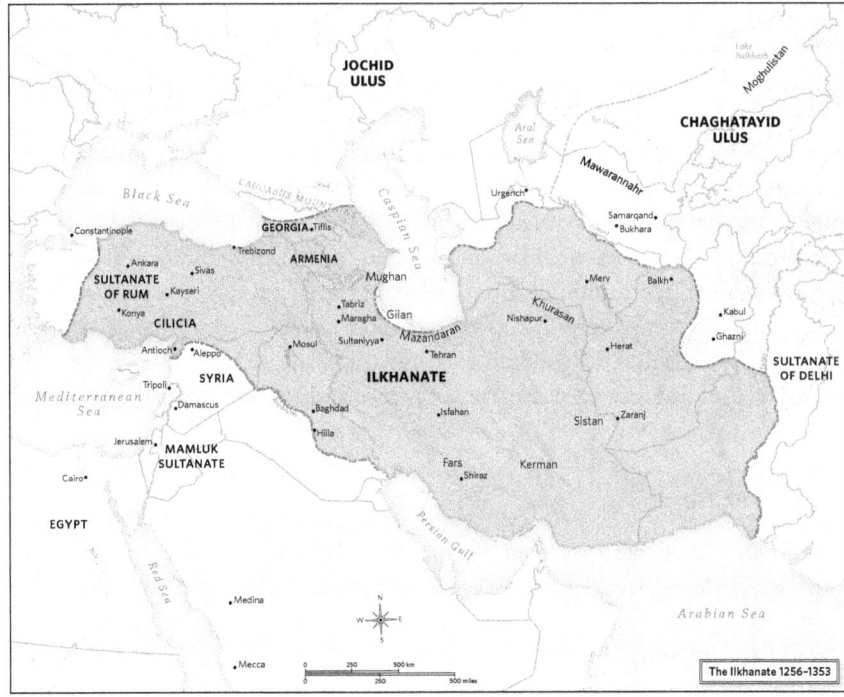

Map 9.1 The Ilkhanate, 1256–1353 © Mapping Specialists

Kartids in Herat.[11] Hulegu also continued the Mongol practice of favouring minorities as a way of hedging their bets against assimilation; thus Buddhists and Christians of all varieties found their situations improved and quite favourable.

The presence of Hulegu's wife, Dokuz Khatun, a Nestorian Christian, lent greater emphasis to this for Christians, and she encouraged the building of churches throughout the Ilkhanate.[12] Dokuz Khatun, a former wife of Tolui, was also a trusted counsellor; indeed, Mongke advised his brother to consult her on all matters.[13] The presence of a Christian queen, however, is not to say that the Muslims were oppressed. Certainly, Muslims did not enjoy the privileged position in society that they once did. Hulegu's continuation of religious tolerance allowed for religious practice of all varieties and prevented anyone from prohibiting others from practising theirs. Nonetheless, the

---

[11] George Lane, *Early Mongol Rule in Thirteenth-Century Iran* (New York, 2003), 96.
[12] BH2, 444; Grigor of Akanc, 341, 343, 351; Hetoum, 40–4; Kiracos, Kirakos, §60, RD/Karimi, 678; RD/Thackston1, 472; RD/Thackston2, 334; Vardan, 217.
[13] RD/Karimi, 687; RD/Thackston1, 479; RD/Thackston2, 340.

extension of favour to other religious groups in the Middle East assisted in extending Ilkhanid control by breaking the monopoly of power held by Muslims. At the same time, the Ilkhanid government employed numerous Muslims in various capacities within the government, as their priority was men of talent regardless of ethnicity or religion, as evinced by the presence of Hulegu's Muslim vizier, Shams al-Din, and his brother ᶜAla al-Din Ata Malik Juwayni as governor of Baghdad.[14]

The war with the Jochid Ulus was a territorial war. The siege of Mosul was extended by it, as Hulegu withdrew many troops to reinforce the Jochid frontier. The Jochids claimed the regions of Arran and Azerbaijan. This territory, in their minds, fell into the category of having been trod by the hooves of Mongol horses, which was the original designation given by Chinggis Khan for the limits of Jochi's appanage.[15] Mongke had apparently confirmed this early in his reign as Batu also acquired rights over the cities of Maragha and Tabriz.[16] Other issues intensified the situation, including the execution of three Jochid princes, Balaghai, Tutar and Quli, who had been part of the army that accompanied Hulegu. Balaghai and Tutar had been convicted of sorcery, and Berke, the Jochid ruler, agreed with the findings.[17] Their men, however, then attempted to flee back to Jochid territory. Some went north through Derbend, while others fled to another Jochid commander named Neguder stationed in modern Afghanistan as part of the *tamma* established by Dayir during Ogodei's reign. Jochid sympathies in Afghanistan eroded Ilkhanid control of the Indian frontier. Still others fled into Mamluk territory and were welcomed by the Mamluks in alliance with the Jochids. Berke may have also nursed a grudge against Hulegu as the latter supported Batu's widow, Boraqchin, and the claim of her infant grandson (Ulagchi) to the Jochid throne over Berke.[18] Regardless, war began in 1262 as Berke Khan attempted to claim Azerbaijan. Much of the warfare was inconclusive with the Ilkhanids winning some battles and losing others. The frontier rarely moved.

In spite of the wars and of the creation of a state, Hulegu initiated the cultural life of the Ilkhanid state. This evolved into an astonishing period

---

[14] See Lane, *Early Mongol Rule in Thirteenth-Century Iran*, 177–212; Esther Ravalde, 'Shams al-Din Juwayni, Vizier and Patron: Mediation between Ruler and Ruled in the Ilkhanate', in *MME*, 55–78.
[15] Juvaini/Boyle 42; Juwayny/Qazvini, v1, 31; Peter Jackson, 'The Dissolution of the Mongol Empire', *CAJ* 22 (1978), 209.
[16] Jackson, 'Dissolution of the Mongol Empire', 209.
[17] J. A. Boyle, 'Dynastic and Political History of the Il-Khans', in J. A. Boyle (ed.), *CHI*, v5, 353.
[18] Jackson, 'Dissolution of the Mongol Empire', 223–4.

of creativity in Islamic arts and sciences due to Hulegu and his successors' patronage of the arts; their support only increased with time. Near Maragha, his capital, Hulegu constructed an observatory for the Shia scholar Nasir al-Din Tusi. Although its primary importance was in enabling Nasir al-Din Tusi to stargaze and create accurate horoscopes for the royal family, Nasir al-Din Tusi also practised astronomy. As a result, the Shia polymath determined the Copernican discoveries almost two hundred years before Copernicus concluded that we live in a heliocentric solar system. He is said to have also invented trigonometry.[19] Numerous other scholars and intellectuals also found Hulegu a generous patron and continued their research and work while receiving salaries. Religion or research topic did not matter. The Syriac monk Bar Hebraeus found patronage not only for his church, but also for writing a chronicle of the era. His work remains an important source for the Mongol period of the Middle East.

Judging from Rashid al-Din's caustic but ironic comments, Hulegu invested vast amounts of lucre in his scholars, but not necessarily on results, particularly among the alchemists. According to Rashid al-Din, 'In transmutation they had no luck, but they were miracles of cheating and fraud, squandering and wasting the stores of the workshops of lordly power'.[20] Although Hulegu initially established his capital in Maragha in north-western Iran, his successors gravitated towards Tabriz. Tabriz's transformation into the capital of the Ilkhanid state also made it into a centre of international trade and industry, not to mention the cultural centre of the Ilkhanid world.[21] As with Qaraqorum during the *Yeke Monggol Ulus* period, the Ilkhans tended to nomadise around their capital rather than dwelling within it.

The Ilkhans were not the only patrons of culture. Their wives also sponsored building projects and the arts. Famed for supporting the construction of religious buildings, Dokuz Khatun, a niece of Toghril Ong Khan, was often described in Armenian, Georgian and other Christian sources as an almost saintly figure in her charitable acts. Yet, despite her faith, she did not limit her good works to her own denomination or faith. Muslims and Buddhists also found ample support from Dokuz Khatun, and she appears to have enjoyed great favour among the entire population.[22]

---

[19] Lane, *Early Mongol Rule*, 213–25.
[20] RD/Thackston2, 364; RD/Karimi, 1,048–9; RD/Thackston1, 513.
[21] For more, see Roxanne Prazniak, 'Tabriz on the Silk Roads: Thirteenth-Century Eurasian Cultural Connections', *Asian Review of World Histories* 1: 2 (2013), 169–88.
[22] RD/Karimi, 678; RD/Thackston2, 334; RD/Thackston1, 472; BH1, 435; Kirakos of Gandzakets'i, *Kirakos Gandzakets'i's History of the Armenians*, trans. Robert Bedrosian (New York, 1986), 327.

Abaqa

Hulegu died in February 1265, after months of battling an illness. His Buddhist doctors and other physicians could not cure the disease.[23] Dokuz Khatun died in June of that year. Although the founder of the new state had died, his policies continued with his son Abaqa (r. 1265–82). The *quriltai* for Abaqa's enthronement appears to have been little more than a formality, although his brother Yoshmut briefly challenged it.[24] Like his father, Abaqa became immersed in the wars with the Jochids, the Chaghatayids and the Mamluks, failing to devote proper attention to issues of governance despite a lengthy reign. This is not to say that the government was in a state of crisis, but rather that the state remained subservient to military needs and was largely a ramshackle assemblage of methods without well-developed institutions. Abaqa kept his father's vizier, Shams al-Din Juwayni, which eased the transition of the new Ilkhan. Additionally, Abaqa enjoyed the support of the *noyad*. He also formally acknowledged Khubilai Khan as the *Qa'an* of the Empire.[25]

The wars increased in severity during Abaqa's reign, and in many ways became institutionalised, which enhanced the power of the *noyad* at the expense of the *divan* or bureaucracy.[26] The Mamluk war also became more aggressive. Sultan Baybars did not attack the Ilkhanate directly, but eliminated and reduced Ilkhanid clients, such as the Principality of Antioch and the Kingdom of Cilicia, which the Mamluk Sultanate bordered. He even invaded Anatolia, timing his invasions for when the Ilkhanid army was engaged with Jochid or Chaghatayid forces. The reasons for the wars became less important than simply the idea that they needed to be fought. Efforts at peace were rare because of the increasing institutionalisation of the wars. Of course, this affected the limited efforts to shore up the bureaucracy of the Ilkhanate, as the wars continued to drain fiscal resources as well as devastating the frontier zones.[27]

War with the Jochids halted temporarily with the death of Berke Khan in 1265/6. Abaqa did not push into Jochid territory, having enough problems on his hands. Instead, he erected a wall defended by a deep ditch along the

---

[23] RD/Thackston2, 365; RD/Thackston1, 514; RD/Karimi, 736.
[24] Michael Hope, 'The Transmission of Authority through the Quriltais of the Early Mongol Empire and the Ilkhanate of Iran (1227–1335)', *MS* 35 (2012), 98.
[25] RD/Karimi, 742–3; RD/Karimi 1999, 517; RD/Thackston2, 367–8.
[26] Michael Hope, *Power, Politics, and Tradition in the Mongol Empire and the Ilkhanate of Iran* (Oxford, 2016), 111.
[27] Hope, *Power, Politics, and Tradition*, 117. For the Mamluk–Ilkhanid wars, see Reuven Amitai-Preiss, *Mongols and Mamluks: The Mamluk–Ilkhanid War, 1260–1281* (Cambridge, 1995).

Kur River.²⁸ This respite also allowed him to attend to matters on his northeastern frontier with the Chaghatayids, who also sought to claim Ilkhanid territory. As his father had dealt with Jochids within his own army, Abaqa dealt with Chaghatayids who had accompanied Hulegu's army. The Chaghatayid Khan, Baraq, attempted to persuade them to join him. Most, if not all, did, but few reached Chaghatayid territory.²⁹ A Chaghatayid invasion, however, met with defeat near Herat in modern Afghanistan on 22 July 1270. Unlike with Berke's death, when Baraq died (9 August 1270) Abaqa crossed the Amu Darya into Chaghatayid territory and sacked Bukhara.³⁰ Threats from Central Asia were minimal thereafter.

Abaqa also made considerable diplomatic efforts. He sent emissaries to Europe, who met with various rulers as well as the pope to discuss potential alliances against the Mamluks. Abaqa even promised that once Syria was conquered he would turn Jerusalem over to the Europeans.³¹ Yet, Abaqa's diplomacy was not restricted to a western focus. Abaqa established formal relations with the Yuan Empire by formally acknowledging the primacy of Khubilai Khan as *Qa'an*. Their lines of communication extended over the land routes (when possible) and via sea routes. By formally establishing relations with Khubilai Khan, the Ilkhanate and the Yuan Empire exchanged not only material goods and technology but also personnel, as discussed in the previous chapter.

Abaqa's life was largely consumed by the wars and by rebellions by the Qaraunas and Negudaris, groups that had links to the Jochids and Chaghatayids.³² He proved to be a strong and capable leader in a time of war, defending the empire on a number of fronts. He died on 1 April 1282 at Hamadan after a night of heavy drinking. While Abaqa upheld what Michael Hope has termed Collegial Rule, in which the *noyad* had considerable influence on the affairs of the state, Abaqa possessed a dynamic personality. Although the *noyad* wielded great power, Abaqa could keep them in check.

---

[28] RD/Karimi, 745; RD/Thackston2, 519; RD/Thackston2, 368.
[29] RD/Karimi, 750; RD/Thackston2, 522–3; RD/Thackston2, 371.
[30] For the Battle of Herat see Michal Biran, 'The Battle of Herat (1270): A Case of Inter-Mongol Warfare', in *WIAH*, 175–220.
[31] RS, 182–3.
[32] Jean Aubin, 'L'ethnogenese des Qaraunas', *Turcica* 1 (1969), 65–95; Timothy May, 'Ил-хаант улс ба Афганистан', pp. 299–325, trans. D. Tod and D. Bayarsaikhan, in Dashdondog Bayarsaikhan and Christopher P. Atwood (eds), ИЛ-ХААДЫН СУДЛАЛ ШИНЭ ХАНДЛАГА ӨГҮҮЛЛИЙН ЭМХЭТГЭЛ (Ulaanbaatar, 2016); Hirotoshi Shimo, 'The Qaraunas in the Historical Materials of the Ilkhanate', *The Memoirs of the Toyo Bunko* 33 (1977), 131–81.

While the *noyad*'s influence grew, Abaqa took a *laissez-faire* approach to his civil government. As long as he had funds for the various wars, he allowed Shams al-Din Juwayni, his *Sahib Divan* or prime minister, to act autonomously. During this time a bureaucrat named Majd al-Mulk Yazdi gained Abaqa's favour. Majd al-Mulk gradually accumulated evidence against the *Sahib Divan* and accused him of embezzlement as well as of conspiring with the Mamluks. While the latter charge was probably based on circumstantial evidence, the embezzlement was easier to prove. To his credit, Abaqa did not accept the evidence immediately, but investigated the matter privately. Ultimately, Shams al-Din remained as *Sahib Divan*, but Majd al-Mulk Yazdi now gained control over the income of the Ilkhan's property, thus depriving Shams al-Din of access to it. He also made Majd-al Mulk Shams al-Din's equal in status.[33] With Shams al-Din humbled, Majd al-Mulk turned his ire against Ata Malik Juwayni. Although the charges appear trumped up, the Juwaynis had accumulated enough enemies over the previous twenty years for Majd al-Mulk's efforts to gain support.

In addition to accusing him of embezzlement, Majd al-Mulk insinuated that Ata Malik Juwayni planned to turn Baghdad over to the Mamluks. Juwayni was imprisoned.[34] Furthermore, since Mu'in al-Din Sulayman, also known by his title of Parvane, the *daruqachi* of Rum had conspired with the Mamluk Sultan Baybars, culminating in not only a Mamluk invasion, but also a Mongol defeat at Abulustayn in 1277, Abaqa had reason to be suspicious of his non-Mongol civil servants.[35] He appears to have never fully trusted his Muslim officials again.[36] Majd al-Mulk may have risen in power, but he simply became a check to Shams al-Din's authority.

The most powerful *noyad*, often referred to as the *qarachu*, sought to protect their own interests and a weak civil government aided them. With Abaqa's death, the *noyad* sought a ruler who protected and upheld the *yasa* as well as their own prerogatives.[37] Unlike the *quriltai* that had selected the *Qa'an* during the height of the *Yeke Monggol Ulus*, the division of the empire into smaller states meant that fewer members of the *altan urugh* participated in the *quriltai*. Indeed, the only Chinggisids considered for the throne were the descendants of Hulegu; even other Toluids were excluded. Furthermore,

---

[33] RD/Karimi, 766; RD/Thackston2, 543; RD/Thackston2, 384–6; Khwandamir, 62–3.
[34] RD/Karimi, 777; RD/Thackston2, 544; RD/Thackston2, 384–5; Khwandamir, 64.
[35] RD/Karimi, 775; RD/Thackston2, 542–3; RD/Thackston2, 385; Hope, *Power, Politics, and Tradition*, 120–1.
[36] Amitai-Preiss, *Mamluks and Mongols*, 168–78; Hetoum, 46; Grigor of Akanc, 367.
[37] Hope, 'The Transmission of Authority through the Quriltais', 108.

fewer Chinggisids not only limited the number of potential candidates for the throne, but also restricted their influence.

The *quriltai* focused on two candidates, Teguder, the seventh son of Hulegu and his wife Qutui Khatun, and Abaqa's son Mongke-Temur, whose mother Oljei Khatun also wielded considerable influence in the Ilkhanate.[38] Mongke-Temur, however, also died, on 26 April 1282 near Mosul, possibly en route to the *quriltai*, which sunk Oljei Khatuns' faction.[39] This allowed the *noyad* to wield greater influence in the selection and approval process, leading to the selection of Teguder (r. 1282–4).

The Middle Period

Teguder, a Muslim convert, is largely viewed as an ineffective ruler, not without reason, and as perhaps having been overly influenced by his Muslim viziers and his wives. It is not known when he converted, only than he converted from Nestorian Christianity to Islam in his youth, taking the name Ahmad.[40] Internal plots and attempted coups complicated his reign, but it is not clear if these arose from dissatisfaction with his abilities as ruler or were simply sour grapes on the part of the *quriltai*.

Internally, the rivalry within the civil government continued between Majd al-Mulk and Shams al-Din. Majd al-Mulk informed Arghun, Abaqa's other son, that Shams al-Din had poisoned Abaqa.[41] Shams al-Din, however, turned the tables and convinced Teguder that Majd al-Mulk conspired with Arghun to overthrow him. Evidence may also have been planted that associated Majd al-Mulk with sorcery. Investigators found a piece of lion skin covered in illegible writing in yellow and red ink. The court shamans and Buddhist monks agreed that it was a talisman of some sort. Thus we have one Muslim faction seeking to eliminate a Muslim rival by using devices that would convince shamans and Buddhists of a suspect's ill intent. While Majd al-Mulk denied any wrongdoing, he failed to convinced the *jarqu* or tribunal. Although Shams al-Din sought to oust him from power and perhaps imprison him, his brother, the historian Ata Malik Juwayni and others with grievances against Majd al-Mulk demanded his execution. According to Rashid al-Din, 'Ahmad's decree was issued for him to be turned over to his adversaries to be put to death . . . and he was turned

---

[38] Bruno de Nicola, *Women in Mongol Iran: The Khatuns, 1206–1335* (Edinburgh, 2017), 95.
[39] RD/Karimi, 778; RD/Thackston2, 545; RD/Thackston2, 95; De Nicola, *Women in Mongol Iran*, 95.
[40] Reuven Amitai, 'The Conversion of Teguder Ilkhan to Islam', *JSAI* 25 (2001), 17–20.
[41] RD/Karimi, 785–6; RD/Thackston2, 548–9; RD/Thackston2, 389–90.

over at night to a crowd that tore him limb from limb'.⁴² This occurred on 14 August 1282.

The fact that Majd al-Mulk sought Arghun's support and that Shams al-Din accused his rival of conspiring with Prince Arghun hints at a greater challenge for Teguder. Arghun was briefly considered for the throne. Many of the Persian sources suggest that Teguder gained the throne illegitimately and that Arghun was forced to consent to his election or risk his life. Yet, as Michael Hope has demonstrated, most of the *noyad* supported Ahmad – not only the regular military commanders, but *qarachu* as well. His mother, Qutui, played a crucial role in rallying support for Teguder, as did two of his wives, Toquz and Armani.⁴³

Nonetheless, Arghun felt aggrieved and eventually found support. He began his resistance to Teguder by replacing officials in certain cities with his own men. Teguder then countered and restored his own men, often beating or torturing Arghun's representatives. When it appeared that Arghun was gathering troops while wintering near Baghdad, Teguder stationed his army within striking distance. Arghun, probably from frustration, then arrested one of Teguder's *daruqachin*, placed him in a *dushakha* (a type of cangue), mounted him on a donkey, and sent him to Ahmad. The blatant and humiliating interference with Teguder's rule could only be viewed as rebellion.⁴⁴

One member of the *qarachu*, Hindu Noyan, attempted to resolve the crisis, telling Arghun not to march against Teguder, insisting that Arghun had support in Khurasan, but that it would fail him if he actually took action against the Ilkhan. Arghun refused to listen. Hindu Noyan, apparently frustrated with the headstrong prince, joined the Ilkhan.⁴⁵ This, however, did not avert war. Unbeknown to Teguder, despite their early support many of the *noyad* became disgruntled.

It was thought by some scholars that Teguder's conversion to Islam would also reduce tensions with the Mamluk Sultanate, something many commanders did not desire. Indeed, the coup against Teguder was long thought to have occurred because the generals disliked his conversion and his goal of transforming the Ilkhanate into an Islamic state. His correspondence with the Mamluks, however, suggests that religion did not alter Mongol political ideology. While one might have suspected that he would seek peace with his co-religionists, Ahmad Teguder maintained the Mongols' right to rule the world and believed that because he was a Muslim the Mamluks should now submit

---

⁴² RD/Karimi, 786–7; RD/Thackston2, 549–50; RD/Thackston2, 390.
⁴³ Hope, *Power, Politics, and Tradition*, 126–8.
⁴⁴ RD/Karimi, 789–91; RD/Thackston2, 551–2; RD/Thackston2, 391.
⁴⁵ RD/Karimi, 790; RD/Thackston2, 552; RD/Thackston2, 391.

to him.⁴⁶ Not surprisingly, the Mamluks disagreed. Little came of his efforts as his generals deposed him, largely for incompetence and a haughty attitude. He failed to reward key supporters and belittled them publicly.⁴⁷ There were also concerns about his morality. Although many senior commanders also disapproved of his conversion and his pressure on others to convert, it was minor compared to other reasons as religion did not prevent them from supporting him initially.⁴⁸ One may also wonder if their disapproval came from the fact that Teguder never led them on a campaign against Mamluks, despite the tough talk in his letter to Sultan Qalawun. It is clear that despite their failed attempts, the Ilkhanid military viewed it as their duty to invade and conquer Syria. Teguder had no inclination for a campaign.

Teguder's actions increasingly drove his former supporters into the arms of Arghun. While Arghun embraced the anti-Islamic sympathies of many *qarachu*, he had to be careful as many of the younger Mongols commanders had embraced Islam.⁴⁹ Arghun, however, still had insufficient support. Oddly enough, his moment came in defeat. As Ahmad advanced on Arghun, driving him from Rayy, Nawruz, a *qarachu*, advised Arghun to retreat across the Amu Darya. Instead, he surrendered. Teguder did not execute him, perhaps not willing to shed the blood of his nephew, rejecting the advice of his *noyad*, but he did execute some of Arghun's supporters. A number of *noyad*, frustrated with Teguder's lack of resolve, liberated Arghun in Teguder's absence. With the new shift in loyalties, Arghun seized Teguder's camp. With this, the loyalty of the entire Ilkhanate shifted and soon Teguder was captured, judged and executed.⁵⁰

Hulegu's grandson Arghun (r. 1284–91) was selected as the next Ilkhan. A *jarliq* from Khubilai Khan legitimised his position as well.⁵¹ His selection was not surprising considering his role in the deposal of Teguder. Although he had the support of the *noyad*, Arghun also recognised the weakness of the military-dominated state. While he did not agree with Teguder's desire to create an Islamic state, Arghun recognised the need to create a stronger civil administration that effectively not only supported the prerogatives of the Mongols, but also attended to the needs of the population so that the empire could thrive.

---

⁴⁶ Reuven Amitai, 'The Conversion of Teguder, 30–34; A. Allouche, 'Teguder's Ultimatum to Qalawun', *IJMES* 22 (1990), 437–46.
⁴⁷ RD/Karimi, 793–5; RD/Thackston2, 554–5; RD/Thackston2, 393–4.
⁴⁸ Amitai, 'The Conversion of Teguder', 38–43.
⁴⁹ Amitai, 'The Conversion of Teguder', 38–43.
⁵⁰ RD/Karimi, 796–800; RD/Thackston2, 556–9; RD/Thackston2, 394–6.
⁵¹ RD/Karimi, 812; RD/Thackston2, 566; RD/Thackston2, 401.

This idea, however, only came about after Arghun was firmly in power. Initially, Arghun ruled with the consent of the leading *noyad*, Buqu, who liberated him from captivity. Shams al-Din Juwayni also saw his fortunes fall. He was executed in 1284. Despite the numerous accusations against him, outsiders viewed him as quite capable and efficient.[52] Buqu Noyan assumed the position of *Sahib Diwan* (prime minister) as well as *amir al'umara* (Commander in Chief), thus giving him control over the civil government as well as the military.[53] While Buqu wielded an amazing level of power, the other *qarachu* became governors of provinces and in many ways served as *atabegs* for Arghun's relatives, who were also assigned appanages, Arghun's brother Gaikhatu to Rum and Arghun's son Ghazan to Khurasan and Mazandaran.

Buqu's power was not unlimited. His *qarachu* rivals prevented him from intruding on their own prerogatives. Additionally, the *altan urugh* gradually asserted their own power. Buqu's demise occurred because his arrogance alienated the other *qarachu* as well as the bureaucracy. When Buqu became implicated in a plot against him, Arghun could no longer ignore it. The Ilkhan ordered Buqu's execution on 16 January 1289.[54]

Buqu's replacement was a Jewish physician, Saʿd al-Daula, who proved to be quite competent as *Sahib Diwan*.[55] The rise of a Jew in a Muslim dominated bureaucracy did not go unchallenged by others who coveted the position. After Arghun executed Malik Jalal al-Din, the primary complainant, Saʿd al-Daula's faced no more open opposition.[56] While Saʿd al-Daula could not directly challenge the *noyad*, he did restore the independence of the civil bureaucracy.

Although Buqu no longer was a threat, Nawruz Noyan raised the standard of rebellion in Khurasan in 1289. The son of Arghun Aqa, Nawruz dominated much of Khurasan, even with the presence of Arghun's son, Ghazan. Some princes even joined Nawruz.

In addition to the internal intrigues, Arghun's reign also faced external challenges. A Jochid army invaded in March 1289, but the Ilkhan personally led his army to victory. Arghun never mounted an invasion of Syria, possibly because of the number of rebellions. Nonetheless, his rise to the throne did cause great concern to the Mamluks, possibly because they thought he

---

[52] BH1, 473; RD/Karimi, 821; RD/Thackston2, 573; RD/Thackston2, 406.
[53] RD/Karimi, 814–15; RD/Thackston2, 568; RD/Thackston2, 403.
[54] RD/Karimi, 817–18; RD/Thackston2, 570; RD/Thackston2, 404–5; Khwandamir, 72–3.
[55] J. A. Boyle, 'Dynastic and Political History of the Il-Khans', *CHI*, v5, 369–70.
[56] RD/Karimi, 819–20; RD/Thackston2, 571–2; RD/Thackston2, 405.

would fulfil his father's ambitions.⁵⁷ Although the Mongols did not invade, the Mamluks raided the Ilkhanid frontiers.⁵⁸ Arghun engaged the Mamluk Sultanate in diplomacy and perhaps psychological warfare.⁵⁹ The success of the latter is debatable, but Arghun realised that despite imperial pretensions, he could not successfully fight a two-front war against the Jochids and the Mamluks. To this end, he not only received European ambassadors but also sent the Nestorian monk Rabban Sawma as an envoy to Europe in order to secure an alliance.⁶⁰ Rabban Sawma left a detailed account of his travels. Perhaps because of their concern about an Ilkhanid–Latin alliance, the Mamluks attacked Acre, the last major Crusader stronghold in Palestine, upon Arghun's death.⁶¹ By then, the Mamluks had given the defenders of Acre no chance of rescue.

Arghun's reign was not noted for military expeditions, unlike Abaqa's. He did, however, restore the civil government to respect and authority at least equal to, if not greater than, the *noyad*'s.⁶² His reforms, however, proved somewhat ephemeral as Arghun died on 10 March 1291, presumably from mercury- and sulfur-based medicines prescribed by his Buddhist doctors in an attempt to gain longevity, although some suspected a Jewish doctor's malpractice.⁶³ With his death, the *qarachu* took their revenge. Saʿd al-Daula was killed and his supporters (Jews and Muslims) found their possessions pillaged.⁶⁴

Nonetheless, during his reign there was at least one significant change. Prior to Arghun, Anatolia had been largely viewed as a frontier region governed by a combination of *tammachin* and local rulers, which was a curious situation as much of the silver coinage of the realm was minted with Anatolian silver (known for its purity).⁶⁵ Anatolia also experienced much disorder, ranging from rebellions to Mamluk invasions. Under Arghun,

---

⁵⁷ BH1, 472.
⁵⁸ BH1, 483.
⁵⁹ Reuven Amitai, 'An Exchange of Letters in Arabic between Abaγa Ilkhan and Sultan Baybars (A. H. 667/A. D. 1268–69)', *CAJ* 38 (1994), 11–33.
⁶⁰ BH1, 492; RS, *passim*. Also see Denise Aigle, *The Mongol Empire between Myth and Reality* (Leiden, 2014), 184–8; Reuven Amitai, *Holy War and Rapprochement*, 52–3; Reuven Amitai, 'Edward of England and Abagha Ilkhan: A Reexamination of a Failed Attempt at Mongol–Frankish Cooperation', in M. Gervers and J. M. Powell (eds), *Tolerance and Intolerance: Social Conflict in the Age of the Crusades* (Syracuse, NY, 2001), 75–82.
⁶¹ BH1, 492–3.
⁶² BH1, 490; Khwandamir 73.
⁶³ RD/Karimi, 823; RD/Thackston 1999, 574; RD/Thackston2, 407; BH1, 490.
⁶⁴ RD/Karimi, 824–5; RD/Thackston 1999, 575; RD/Thackston2, 408; BH1, 490–1.
⁶⁵ See Judith Kolbas, Timothy May and Vlastimil Novak, *Anatolian Early 14th Century Coin Hoard* (Prague, 2011).

Anatolia experienced proper incorporation into the Ilkhanid state. The exact method whereby this was achieved remains murky, but it may be presumed that it was assisted by the fact that a Chinggisid prince, Arghun's brother Gaikhatu, resided in the region and brought some stability with his presence as his commands could trump those of local rulers as well as the *tammachin*.

Anatolia's importance increased as the patrimony of Prince Gaikhatu. Gaikhatu's access to the silver mines may also have assisted him in gaining the throne. His ascent was not without issue, however. His cousin, Baidu, was the initial claimant to the throne. A brief internecine struggle occurred as not all parties recognised Baidu's claim. Rashid al-Din portrays Baidu as being manipulated by commanders who saw him as being more malleable than other Chinggisid princes. Baidu's bid for the throne ended, though, in 1291 when the majority of his supporters decamped and joined Gaikhatu's party in Anatolia.[66] Gaikhatu ascended the throne on 23 July 1291.

Once in power and having dealt with Baidu's supporters, Gaikhatu returned to Anatolia. It is not clear what he did there. Although he appointed Shiktur Noyan as his deputy (*jarquchi*) in Iran, nothing is explicitly said about Anatolia.[67] Afterwards he went to Tabriz but apparently did not stay their long, wintering in Arran at Qara Chali along the Kura River. There is some indication that Gaikhatu ruled from Anatolia, as late in 1291 there was a rumour that rebellious Turkmen nomads had killed Gaikhatu in battle. The rumour proved false, and it appears to have been instigated to frame Prince Anbarchi, a Chinggisid, as a rebel.[68] Gaikhatu reaffirmed his position by summering at the Ala Tagh pastures where the *noyad* and the *altan urugh* came before him and not only visibly offered their loyalty but submitted written pledges as well.[69]

During Gaikhatu's absence from Anatolia, the Mamluks proceeded to invade and lay siege to Qalat al-Rum on the Euphrates River. Gaikhatu sent two armies by different routes to Anatolia to deal with the situation. In 1292, Qalat al-Rum fell before reinforcements arrived. The Mamluks withdrew without further incident.[70] Despite this episode, Gaikhatu's reign did not face external threats as the Jochids initiated a détente in 1294.[71] Numerous rebellions, however, occurred. Not only did these include a rebellion in Yazd

---

[66] RD/Thackston2, 408; RD/Thackston2, 576; RD/Karimi, 826.
[67] RD/Thackston2, 411–12; RD/Thackston2, 581; RD/Karimi, 832.
[68] RD/Thackston2, 411–12; RD/Thackston2, 582; RD/Karimi, 832.
[69] RD/Thackston2, 412; RD/Thackston2, 582; RD/Karimi, 833.
[70] RD/Karimi, 833–4; RD/Thackston2, 582–3; RD/Thackston2, 412.
[71] Boyle, 'History of the Ilkhans', 374.

and Luristan by native leaders, but also many *qarachu* acted with virtual autonomy in the eastern portions of the empire.[72]

Although Gaikhatu was an active military leader, he was best known for his efforts at modifying the economy. From the personnel who arrived from Khubilai Khan's realm, Gaikhatu learned how Khubilai Khan made paper money or *chao* the currency of his empire. Gaikhatu attempted this as well, recognising that the paper money would be more difficult to counterfeit or clip. In the modern era the use of paper money is ubiquitous; in the thirteenth century, however, its use was limited to Mongol China. Its implementation in Iran did not go too well. No one appreciated or completely understood how it functioned. Nor did they like Gaikhatu's efforts to monopolise all silver coinage. Part of the issue was that Gaikhatu had exhausted the treasury through his own generosity and spending. His *Sahib Divan*, Sadr al-Din Ahmad Zanjani, who had complete fiscal authority and could ignore the *noyad*, also contributed to the crisis by failing to curb Gaikhatu's expenses. As they introduced the *chao*, the *bazaaris*, the merchants in the bazaars of Tabriz, boycotted the change, causing commerce to come to a halt. Riots and rebellions erupted throughout the empire. They did not amount to much as they were not organised or unified, and thus easily quelled. However, because of the reaction in Tabriz, the only location where the government issued *chao*, it was abandoned within a fortnight. While the riots did not threaten to overthrow the empire, they did disrupt it. Compounded with Gaikhatu's generosity and his *Sahib Divan*'s own fiscal policies, which left the treasury drained, the introduction of paper money was disastrous, albeit not quite as it has often been portrayed.[73] The message was clear: the world was not ready for paper money outside of China.

Counterfeiting and Coin Clipping

Paper money was a newer technology and thus difficult to counterfeit, unlike coins, which could be debased through counterfeiting. Typically, this was achieved by using less precious metals and then coating with them with silver. Coins were also clipped, meaning the edges were shaved or clipped, thus causing them to have less silver and less value even though they appeared to be the same size to the naked eye. It was a simple yet effective method for cheating the system.

---

[72] Hope, *Power, Politics, and Tradition*, 148–51.
[73] BH1, 496–7; RD/Karimi, 835–6; RD/Thackston2, 584; RD/Thackston2, 413–14; Khwandamir, 76–7; Judith Kolbas, *The Mongols in Iran* (London, 2006), 290–1.

After the failed effort to make *chao* the currency of the Ilkhanate, many commanders reconsidered their loyalty to Gaikhatu. His fiscal reforms also began to impinge on revenues the *qarachu* derived from their personal appanages as well as offices that had become hereditary.[74] Some of the *noyad* also accused Gaikhatu of debauchery.[75] Baidu, still nursing a grudge against Gaikhatu, found many supporters in 1295.[76] Gaikhatu did not act decisively on the matter. Indeed, there is some indication that he considered abdicating and retiring to Anatolia. His advisors convinced him otherwise, but Baidu's rebellion was short, swift and successful. On 24 March 1295, Gaikhatu and his chief supporters were executed.[77]

Baidu's reign was brief and he barely had time to secure the throne. In Khurasan, Arghun's son, Ghazan, emerged as a challenger. A rebellion in the east by the Mongol general Nawruz prevented Ghazan from pursuing the throne when Arghun died. Although Ghazan was not pleased with Gaikhatu, he did not challenge him as Gaikhatu had been elevated to the throne through a *quriltai*. With Gaikhatu's death, Ghazan no longer felt restrained, and gaining the throne through regicide did not legitimate Baidu as the ruler. While serving in Khurasan, Ghazan developed a considerable following among generals and administrators. When he advanced to make his claim to the throne, he learned that several *noyad* preferred Baidu. These, along with some other princes, held an impromptu *quriltai* (to which Ghazan was not invited) and formally elected Baidu to the throne. Baidu, however, seemed reluctant and appears to have served out of obligation rather than desire.[78] Ghazan's army, however, won an initial encounter which led to a flurry of diplomatic exchanges. For a brief moment, it appeared as if peace would prevail with the Ilkhanate being divided between Baidu and Ghazan.[79] In the end, most of Baidu's army deserted to Ghazan, ostensibly because of the latter's conversion to Islam.[80] With the reinforcements, he had no difficulties in evicting Baidu from the throne in 1295. Baidu was captured and executed in 1295.

Did his conversion play a role? It cannot be ruled out, but there are plenty of signs that Baidu's reluctance to be the ruler inhibited his leadership at this time of crisis. As a result, many of the *noyad* and state officials,

---

[74] Hope, 'The Transmission of Authority through the Quriltais', 108.
[75] BH1, 494; Khwandamir, 75.
[76] BH1, 494–500; RD/Karimi, 835–6; RD/Thackston2, 583–5; RD/Thackston2, 414–15.
[77] RD/Thackston2, 415; RD/Thackston1, 586; RD/Karimi, 837–8; RS, 208.
[78] RD/Thackston2, 433; RD/Thackston, 613–14; RD/Karimi, 884–5; RS, 208.
[79] RD/Thackston2, 435–5; RD/Thackston1, 614–16; RD/Karimi, 885–90.
[80] RD/Thackston2, 437–8; RD/Thackston1, 619–20; RD/Karimi, 900–3.

including those who opposed Ghazan, abandoned Baidu. Ghazan Khan's reign (1295–1304) became a transformative one for the Ilkhanate, and during it Ghazan was viewed as either a reformer or a destroyer.

An Islamic Empire?

Ghazan proved to be one of those rare individuals in history who was both a good military leader and a good administrator, a combination the Ilkhanate sorely needed. Ghazan realised that the system was broken, yet Ghazan was even more revolutionary than most people realised at the time, perhaps even his supporters. He transformed the Ilkhanate into an Islamic empire. While the sources paint him as a Sunni with a predilection towards Sufism, Ghazan was also sympathetic towards Shia Islam, particularly in terms of the importance of the family of Ali.[81]

Naturally, this transformation angered many among the nobility and raised worries among many populations within the empire, yet in some ways it was unsurprising. Teguder's conversion was not an aberration, and by Ghazan's era it was increasingly common. Ghazan, despite receiving much of his education at the hands of a Buddhist monk, converted to Islam under the tutelage of a Sufi and the former rebel general Nawruz. Ghazan's conversion before the battle with Baidu was dramatic, but he was probably leaning towards Islam prior to the battle. According to the Islamic sources, Nawruz convinced him and the army to convert after storms frustrated Ghazans battle plans and he then learnt that Baidu heavily outnumbered him. Ghazan and his newly Muslim army observed Ramadan before advancing against Baidu. Ghazan crushed his enemy and won a victory with the assistance of God.[82] It is all a little too neat and tidy, but it did make excellent propaganda and certainly legitimated his cause.

When Rashid al-Din indicates that the army, inspired by Ghazan's conversion, converted, he obscures a deeper change within the empire. Many Mongols had already converted to Islam long before Ghazan.[83] Ghazan's own conversion was more in line with the majority of the Ilkhanid. At the time of their battle, Baidu was a Muslim, although he seems to have been rather lacking in belief as he also claimed to be a Christian, depending on the audience.[84]

---

[81] RD/Thackston2, 472; RD/Thackston1, 676–7; RD/Karimi, 984–5; Hope, *Power, Politics, and Tradition*, 176; Charles Melville, 'Padshah-i Islam: The Conversion of Sultan Mahmud Ghazan Khan', *Pembroke Papers* 1 (1990), 160.

[82] RD/Karimi, 903–4, 912–15; RD/Thackston2, 621, 625–6; RD/Thackston2, 438–9. For alternative accounts see Melville, 'Padshah-i Islam', 159–77.

[83] BH1, 505.

[84] BH1, 505; RS, 206; Melville, 'Padshah-i Islam', 166.

Figure 9.1 A Mongol prince studying the Qur'ān. Illuminated manuscript page from *Jamia'at al-Tawarikh* (Universal History), by Rashid al-Din (1247–1318). Iran, Tabriz, c.1330 CE. Inv.: Diez A, fol. 70, p. 8, no. 1. Photo Ellwardt, Oriental Division. Staatsbibliothek zu Berlin. Art Resource, NY.

Ghazan also began his reign as many new converts do – with ardour to prove his new identity. Once in power, the long-standing practice of religious toleration came to an end almost immediately as Ghazan issued an edict 'that all the *bakhshis*' [Buddhists'] temples and houses of worship, as well as Christian churches and Jewish synagogues were to be destroyed in Tabriz, Baghdad, and other Islamic places, and for that victory most of the people of Islam rendered thanks since God had not seen fit to grant this wish to past generations'.[85] It is safe to say that not all were destroyed, particularly in regions where the population was almost entirely of a particular religion, such as in Georgia and Armenia. Indeed, the *jarliq* indicated that the destruction should only take place in Muslim majority regions. Thus, in Tabriz and

---

[85] RD/Thackston2, 439, 471; RD/Thackston2, 471; RD/Thackston2, 676; RD/Karimi, 983–4.

Baghdad, despite its cosmopolitan population, and other areas, clear religious repression began. Yet this was short-lived.

By 1296, Ghazan realised that, as a ruler, he could not persecute populations simply because of their religion. Charles Melville demonstrates that Nawruz initiated the campaign of destruction and Christian sources reveal that Ghazan had some difficulty in curbing Nawruz's prejudiced tendencies. Nawruz even razed churches in Armenian territories. A mob tortured the Nestorian Catholicus in an attempt to convert him to Islam.[86]

Ghazan restored the privileges that the Georgians and Armenians held, including the right to build churches, and developed an amiable relationship with the Church of the East (Nestorians). He also cracked down on religious pogroms and revoked the *jizya*.[87] Periodic pogroms, however, did flare up, as in 1296–7, but they do not appear to have been state-sponsored as Ghazan punished the perpetrators.[88] For Buddhism, however, it was too late. He did not restore the Buddhist shrine dedicated to his father or allow other Buddhist temples to be rebuilt. Those temples converted into mosques were not restored. The other religions clearly fit the idea of the *'Ahl al-kitab* or People of the Book. Despite also having scriptures, Buddhism was difficult to portray as a monotheistic religion.[89] Furthermore, although Ghazan had a Buddhist childhood, the dire economic situation of the Ilkhanate made it unlikely that Ghazan had any interest in spending funds on repairing damage, even if those funds came from the plunder of Buddhist temples.[90] Buddhism survived Ghazan, but its foundations were undermined during his reign; as a result, Buddhism in Iran largely disappeared in the fourteenth century after making a resurgence under early Ilkhanid rule.

Ghazan's faith did not deter him from fighting other Muslims. The Mamluks, protectors of the Holy Cities of Mecca, Medina and Jerusalem, faced invasion in 1299. Ghazan still adhered to Mongol imperialism, but may have sought retaliation for Mamluk support for rebels in Rum. Furthermore, civil war in the Jochid Ulus gave Ghazan a window for fighting a one-front war.[91] Ghazan not only defeated the Mamluks near Homs at Wadi al-Khaznadar but also captured Damascus, although the Mongols

---

[86] Melville, 'Padshah-i Islam', 170; BH1, 506–8; RS, 210–19.
[87] RS, 221.
[88] RS, 226–30.
[89] RD/Thackston2, 471; Richard Foltz, *Spirituality in the Land of the Noble* (London, 2004), 73; Richard Foltz, *Religions of Iran from Prehistory to the Present* (London, 2013), 103–4.
[90] Johan Elverskog, *Buddhism and Islam on the Silk Road* (Philadelphia, 2010), 41; Kolbas, *Mongols in Iran*, 311–13.
[91] Reuven Amitai, 'Whither the Ilkhanid Army? Ghazan's First Campaign into Syria (1299–1300), in *WIAH*, 221–2.

withdrew to the Ilkhanate in February 1300 as inadequate pasture prevented the long-term Mongol occupation.[92] Two subsequent invasions followed. While the second invasion in 1300 ended prematurely due to severe weather, the invasion of 1303 ended with an Ilkhanid defeat at Marj al-Suffar.

Ghazan also implemented a series of reforms throughout the empire. Among the most important was reviving agriculture.[93] The key component was protecting the peasants from the army's depredations. If the peasants were safe, then the irrigation systems could be rebuilt and restore arable lands. Thus, the most important change for agriculture actually involved changes in the military.

In order to alter the attitude of the military towards the peasants, Ghazan needed to find a method of tying their relationship together. Aided by his remarkable *Sahib Divan* Rashid al-Din, he turned to an Islamic method of administration and assigned *timars*, or land grants. As a result, the Mongol warriors now received income from the revenues produced by villages and farms. Although some scholars have concluded that the Ilkhanid army became a medium-heavy cavalry force supported by fiefs, this did not happen. Instead, the military remained nomadic light horse archers.[94] The difference was that they now received a salary or stipend from their *timar*. While pillaging villages yielded short-term plunder, by not plundering the villages the nomads now had regular access to income.

Since the army now received stipends, they needed to be paid in a useful currency. Ghazan minted new coins, which were symbolic in many ways. The new coins were significant as they marked a return to silver and away from paper backed by silver. They also allowed him to mint coins in his name. Finally, he was able to demonstrate his commitment to Islam through the coins, as he replaced Mongolian inscriptions with *La ilah illa Allah, Muhammad rasul Allah* (There is no God but God, and Muhammad is the Messenger of God). Furthermore, his coins also indicated he was the *Pad-i Shah-i Islam* or Emperor of Islam.[95]

The new coins led to other reforms in the economic system such as unifying the system of weights and measures in the market-places. With

---

[92] Amitai, 'Whither the Mongol Army?', 258–60.
[93] RD/Thackston2, 499, 527–31.
[94] A. P. Martinez, 'Some Notes on the Il-Xanid Army', *AEMA* 6 (1986), 129–242. For the refutation, see Reuven Amitai, 'Turko-Mongolian Nomads and the Iqta' System in the Islamic Middle East (CA. 1000–1400)', in Anatoly M. Khazanov and Andre Wink (eds), *Nomads in the Sedentary World* (London, 2001), 152–71. Also see Reuven Amitai, 'Continuity and Change in the Mongol Army of the Ilkhanate', in *MME*, 38–52.
[95] Kolbas, *Mongols in Iran*, 295, 300, 322–33.

his relatively lengthy reign, Ghazan helped revived the caravan trade, which coincided with a true *Pax Mongolica* among the khanates. Finally, with the new coinage and unified system of weights and measures, Ghazan could standardise the tax system and form a more rational and institutionalised government.[96]

In all of these endeavours, Ghazan was assisted by one of the most remarkable individuals of the age, Rashid al-Din. A former Jewish doctor, Rashid al-Din converted to Islam and became the grand vizier of the Ilkhanate. He promoted the reforms of Ghazan although there remain many questions as to just how extensive they were. Rashid al-Din was also the author of the *Jamia't al-tawarikh* or *Compendium of Chronicles*, our main source on Ghazan. Ghazan's successor Oljeitu commissioned Rashid al-Din to write a history of the known world, one of the first efforts at a world history, although the focus of the book was on the Mongol Empire. He also included many regions outside of the Mongol Empire and demonstrated an incredible talent in research and organisation. While it is true that he wrote the book with a stable of assistants, the overall production of the book was his, particularly as he gained access to Mongolian sources, including the *Shengwu Qinzheng lu*, a Mongolian chronicle concerning the life and campaigns of Chinggis Khan. Copies that exist today are written in Chinese, but with a clear Mongolian idiom.[97] Rashid al-Din also copied large sections for the *Jamia't al-tawarikh*. Additionally, he interviewed many Mongols from the court, including the ambassador from the Great Khan in East Asia, Bolod Chingsang.[98] Bolod was of particular use not only due to his age and deep knowledge of Mongol customs, but also from his time as a highly placed official in the Yuan Empire. While Rashid al-Din's work remains as one of the most important sources available, upon reading the sections on Ghazan one comes away with the idea that prior to Ghazan's reign the Ilkhanate was in a state of anarchy. It is worth noting that Rashid al-Din may have done this intentionally to demonstrate that, once Ghazan converted to Islam, the age of *jahiliyya* or ignorance (and anarchy) ended and just rule began.

Rashid al-Din also built a separate quarter in the city of Tabriz known as the Rabi' al-Rashidi (Rashid's Quarter). Here he housed not only his scholars, but also scientists and artists. Art production facilities saw Chinese, Persians, Armenians and even a few Italians working together and transforming art in new ways that affected Chinese arts and later influenced the

---

[96] RD/Thackston2, 506–7.
[97] *EMME*, 499; David Morgan, *The Mongols* (Oxford, 2007), 11.
[98] Thomas T. Allsen, *Culture and Conquest in Mongol Eurasia* (New York, 2001), 59–82.

Renaissance.⁹⁹ Rashid al-Din did not limit his efforts to history and art. He wrote extensively on agriculture as well as on religion.¹⁰⁰ He did all of this while also managing the day-to-day operations of the empire; this in itself was no small feat.

Rashid al-Din continued his position as vizier after Ghazan Khan died from illness in 1304. Ghazan's brother Oljeitu became the next Il-khan. Oljeitu (1304–16) made a monumental shift by building a new capital, Sultaniyya, located in Zanjan province in north-west Iran approximately two hundred miles south-east of Tabriz. Not only did the 1305 construction of Sultaniyya provide a physical demonstration of Oljeitu's power, but the region provided excellent opportunities for hunting and other recreation. Oljeitu's impressive mausoleum is the city's signature architectural piece. Sultaniyya became a centre for artists and scholars due Oljeitu's support of the arts.

Like his brother, Oljeitu also experimented with religions and eventually converted to Islam. His journey, however, was significantly different. He was baptised as a Christian as a child and named Nicholas, his godfather being Pope Nicholas IV.¹⁰¹ He later converted to Buddhism, and adopted or used the Mongolian Buddhist name of Oljeitu. He converted to Sunni Islam as an adult and adopted the name of Muhammad Khudabanda (servant of God). His conversion came more from the influence of his wives than his brother's example. Disgusted with the incessant quarrels between members of the Hanafiyyah and Shafaiyya *madhhabs* over what he considered insignificant points of religion, which often led to riots, Oljeitu abandoned Sunni Islam. He briefly reverted back to Buddhism, but found this politically unsustainable, which also demonstrated just how far the Ilkhanate state had come since the rise of Ghazan. After visiting the shrine of Ali in Najaf, Iraq, Oljeitu converted to Shi'ism in 1309.¹⁰² He did not attempt a mass conversion, but his new faith did cause some blowback among the *ulema*, who made a pun on his name with a slight change in the script, so that *Khudabanda* became *Kharbanda* (donkey servant or donkey herder, a clear insult to a Mongol).

---

⁹⁹ Timothy May, *The Mongol Conquests in World History* (London, 2012), 241–7.
¹⁰⁰ Allsen, *Culture and Conquest*, 116–22; Dorothea Krawulsky, *The Mongol Ilkhans and Their Vizier Rashid al-Din* (Frankfurt, 2011), 123–7; Ann K. S. Lambton, 'The *Athar wa ahya*' of Rashid al-Din Fadl Allah Hamadani and His Contribution as an Agronomist, Arboriculturist and Horticulturalist', in *MEL*, 126–54.
¹⁰¹ 'Oldjeytu', *EI*².
¹⁰² IB1, 157; IB2, 71; also see Judith Pfeiffer, 'Conversion Versions: Sultan Oljeytu's Conversion to Shi'ism (709/1309) in Muslim Narrative Sources', *MS* 22 (1999), 35–68.

What's in a Name?

For decades, many assumed that Oljeitu's sobriquet Kharbanda was simply part of Mongolian tradition, in which the child is named after the first thing that catches the mother's eye or as something that confuses spiteful spirits who might harm the child. According to J. A. Boyle, 'Partly, at least, for euphemistic reasons the name was afterwards changed to Khuda-Banda ("Slave of God")'.[103] I suspect this is not quite accurate. Why would a Mongolian mother name her child Khar-banda or donkey-herder? The fact that '*khar*' means donkey is not an issue. After all, one of Chinggis Khan's wives was Qulan, which refers to the wild asses of Mongolia and was certainly not a reflection of her appearance or personality. The issue is, why would a Mongolian mother name her child with Persian terminology? None of Orug Khatun's other sons had a Persian or Muslim name until he converted. Qulanchi, the Mongolian equivalent of Khar-banda, would be understandable, but then it is not mentioned in the sources, and considering that the Persian chroniclers did not translate Mongolian names into their Persian equivalent, it is not likely that Oljeitu's sobriquet would be the sole exception. Thus, I maintain that Khar-banda arose as an insult by the *ulema*.

Oljeitu's reign was peaceful in the larger scheme of things. Oljeitu's armies, led by Amir Choban brought the region of Gilan under Mongol control.[104] The mountainous area by the Caspian Sea had eluded Mongol control since the era of Chormaqan. He also swiftly dealt with the Kartid dynasty in Herat, which rebelled and had long sheltered and supported Negudari raiders in modern Afghanistan. During Ghazan's reign, Oljeitu skirmished with Negudaris to discourage their depredations in Khurasan. He now decided to deal with them decisively, including those who abetted them.[105] As Oljeitu annexed Negudari territory, it provoked an invasion by the Chaghatayid Khanate in 1313 as the Negudari and Qarauna had entered Chaghatayid service. The invasion mounted to little, however, and the Chaghatayids soon withdrew. Peace continued with the Jochids, and while espionage and political intrigues continued along the Mamluk border, all was relatively peaceful, although Oljeitu did attack one fortress. This did not, however, appear to

---

[103] IB1, 173; IB2, 77; J. A. Boyle, 'Dynastic and Political History of the Il-Khans', in *CHI*, v5, 398; IB2, 77.
[104] See Charles Melville, 'The Ilkhan Oljeitu's Conquest of Gilan (1307): Rumor and Reality', in *MEL*, 73–125.
[105] Khwandamir, 83, 210–13.

Figure 9.2 Fourteenth-century Mongol chain mail. Although the Mongols tended to favour lamellar armour, chainmail was not uncommon. (National History Museum, Ulaanbaatar, Mongolia)

affect trade between the Ilkhanate and the Mamluk Sultanate.[106] So good was the situation that, in 1305, Oljeitu wrote to King Phillip IV (the Fair) of France (r. 1285–1314) and informed him that the Mongol Empire was once again united as the Jochids, Chaghatayids, Ilkhanids and Yuan had all resolved their differences and recognised Temur Oljeitu, Khubilai's son, as the *Qa'an*. He also suggested this might be an appropriate time to deal with their common enemies (i.e. the Mamluks).[107] The *Pax Mongolica*, however, did not last and the Mamluks avoided an invasion. In 1316, Oljeitu died from a stomach ailment with excessive diarrhoea, most likely caused by excessive drinking.

---

[106] Khwandamir, 109; Amitai, *Mongols and Mamluks*, 211.
[107] Oljeitu, 'Lettre d'Olejeitu à Phillippe le Bel, datée de 1305', in Antoine Mostaert and Francis Woodman Cleaves (eds and trans.), *Les Lettres de 1289 et 1305 des ilkhan Aryun et Oljeitu à Philippe le Bel* (Cambridge, MA, 1962), 55–7.

The Golden Age and End of the Ilkhanate

With Oljeitu's death, Abu Saʿid (1316–35) came to the throne at the age of twelve. The real power, however, rested with Amir Choban, the leading Ilkhanid military commander, but it was the perfect time for some to settle scores. A major change in the Ilkhanate occurred in July 1318, with the execution of Rashid al-Din after decades of loyal service. Accused of poisoning Oljeitu, Rashid al-Din denied it, but admitted prescribing a laxative to purge Oljeitu of his ailment. This only hastened the Mongol ruler's dehydration and demise.[108] Although he had served Ghazan and Oljeitu, Rashid al-Din was not immune from intrigue, particularly from rivals within the bureaucracy. Indeed, the fact that his trial and execution took place indicates that his rivals meticulously built a case to challenge the powerful vizier. Rashid al-Din possessed numerous enemies – political foes envied his power and wealth, rival scholars were jealous of his patronage and success, and then there were those who questioned his faith. Although Rashid al-Din had converted to Islam by the age of twenty-one (1268), his detractors never forgot his Jewish heritage. It was not an easy task to convince the court to remove him due to his performance as vizier and his character, but in the end they did.[109]

Almost immediately afterwards, Abu Saʿid faced a rebellion in the east and an invasion by the Jochids in Transcaucasia. The rebellion was crushed quickly, but the Jochids proved to be more difficult. Abu Said (age 14–15) marched against Uzbek Khan and met defeat as many Ilkhanid commanders fled. Fortunately, Choban arrived with reinforcements and defeated Uzbek Khan in a second battle. Choban then chastised the fleeing commanders. These commanders later rebelled and marched on Tabriz to place Abu Saʿid's uncle, Irenjin, on the throne. Abu Saʿid and Choban defeated them in 1319.[110]

Abu Saʿid and Choban continued to function well together and even achieved a peace treaty in 1322 with the Mamluks, ending their conflict that had begun in 1260. Even with peace, however, some tension remained. Abu Saʿid, as a powerful Muslim ruler, exerted influence in the region and even proposed going on the Hajj and sending to the officials in Mecca the *kiswa* or black cloth that covered the Kaaba, much to the Mamluks'

---

[108] Krawulsky, *The Mongol Ilkhans and Their Vizier Rashid al-Din*, 133–4.
[109] Krawalusky, *The Mongol Ilkhans and Their Vizier Rashid al-Din*, 122.
[110] Khwandamir, 114–15; also see Charles Melville, 'Abu Saʿid and the Revolt of the Amirs in 1319', in Denise Aigle (ed.), *L'Iran Face à La Domination Mongole* (Tehran, 1997), 89–120.

chagrin.¹¹¹ Yet these were diplomatic issues and the peace held for the rest of Abu Saʿid's reign.

Perhaps because no external threats existed, internal intrigue increased. Choban was not only the power behind the throne: he was also Abu Saʿid's brother-in-law as he had married Abu Saʿid's sister Sati Beg.¹¹² We must also consider that tensions between the two men occurred because Abu Saʿid was no longer a twelve-year-old boy. By the time of the Mamluk peace treaty he was in his early twenties and most likely anxious to rule on his own and not in the shadow of Choban. Furthermore, Abu Saʿid disliked Choban's son (not Sati Beg's) Dimashq Khwaja. When Choban ignored complaints presented to him concerning Dimashq's behaviour at court, it annoyed the Ilkhan, who then encouraged Dimashq's assassination. The final break came as a result of Abu Saʿid's infatuation with Choban's daughter (not Sati Beg's), Baghdad Khatun, who was married to Shaykh Hasan of the Jalayirs. Choban would not support a divorce, which deepened the rift. Open rebellion occurred, but Choban was killed in Herat when the Kartid dynasty refused to support the rebellion, having only recently regained the favour of the Ilkhans.¹¹³ Afterwards, Baghdad Khatun became Abu Saʿid's wife.

Abu Saʿid continued to deal with intrigue, but overall the Ilkhanate prospered under his competent rule. In many ways, his reign represented the golden age of the Ilkhanate. Yet, it proved to be ephemeral due to a Golden Horde invasion. Abu Saʿid promptly rode to meet the invasion but died en route. There were rumours that Baghdad Khatun poisoned him and even encouraged Uzbek Khan to invade. Her alleged betrayal came after she fell out of favour, either due to her conspiring with her former husband or because she became jealous when Abu Saʿid favoured a younger wife named Dilshad Khatun, who also happened to be Choban's granddaughter.¹¹⁴

Abu Saʿid lacked a male heir and no other Huleguids proved to be strong enough in the Ilkhanate to be viable contenders. The day after Abu Saʿid's death, the *noyad* selected Arpa Khan, a descendant of Ariq-Boke, to be the new Ilkhan. He rose to the occasion and drove back the Jochids and also executed Baghdad Khatun.¹¹⁵ Yet, his Toluid legitimacy was inadequate

---

[111] Anne Broadbridge, *Kingship and Ideology in the Islamic and Mongol Worlds* (Cambridge, 2008), 103–14; Charles Melville, '"The Year of the Elephant": Mamluk–Mongol Rivalry in the Hejaz in the Reign of Abu Saʿid (1317–1335)', *Studia Iranica* 21 (1992), 197–214.
[112] Khwandamir, 115.
[113] IB1, 174; IB2, 78; Khwandamir, 116–18; Hope, *Power, Politics, and Tradition*, 192–3.
[114] IB1, 174; IB2, 78; Khwandamir, 120, 122, 124; IB2, 78.
[115] IB1, 174; IB2, 78; Khwandamir, 123–4; De Nicola, *Women in Mongol Iran*, 102.

to secure the throne. He further legitimated his rule by marrying Sati Beg, Abu Saʿid's sister.[116] Still, rebellions from other *amirs* arose. As he attempted to quell them, the rebel commanders captured and executed Arpa Khan on 15 May 1336. A strong Ilkhan did not emerge. During this period, Sati Beg Khatun ruled albeit as a puppet.[117] While military commanders vied to find a Chinggisid to raise to the throne, they also fought to ensure that their candidate would be the ruler. Between 1335 and 1344, eight Chinggisids sat on the throne, 'ruling' from various locales.[118] Eventually, the *qarachu* dispensed with the charade and began to rule in their own name. Thus the Ilkhanate disintegrated into a small powers dominated by Ilkhanid military commanders, including the sons of Choban, and local dynasties all vying for power.

The Islamic Ilkhanate

Unlike with the Yuan Empire, there is no reason to employ counterfactuals to determine whether the Ilkhanate was an Islamic empire. It was by virtue of having Muslims rulers who also viewed the state as part of *Dar al-Islam*. Of course, it did not begin as such. With the elimination of the Abbasid Caliphate, Muslims had a very good reason to view it as infidel rule even as Muslim troops fought alongside the Mongols at Baghdad. Nonetheless, the foundations for an Islamic state were laid early in the Ilkhanate's history. Beatrice Manz contends that the very destruction of the Abbasid Caliphate assisted Mongol conversion to Islam, stating: 'A ruler could now become Muslim without placing himself beneath a higher power.'[119] While conversion did not happen overnight, the door was now open.

Almost immediately, the Ilkhans used an Islamic-style bureaucracy, albeit one subordinate to the military. While an Islamic administration came into place early in the Ilkhanate, it is clear that Muslims were to the Mongols simply just another group of subjects without any exceptional rights or privileges.[120] During Arghun's reign, more Jews found positions within the bureaucracy, largely due to the influence of Saʿd al-Daula. The Muslims took issue with this as they had previously dominated the civil government. Some Muslim sources, such as Khwandamir who wrote much later, viewed Arghun as a sworn opponent of Islam although there is little to support this. Indeed,

---

[116] De Nicola, *Women in Mongol Iran*, 103.
[117] De Nicola, *Women in Mongol Iran*, 103.
[118] Hope, *Power, Politics, and Tradition*, 196.
[119] Beatrice F. Manz, 'The Empire of Tamerlane as an Adaptation of the Mongol Empire', *JRAS* 26/i–ii, 282.
[120] BH1, 490.

while he may have disestablished Teguder Ahmad's efforts to establish Islam as a state religion, there is no indication he purposefully persecuted Muslims for their faith.[121] The bureaucracy remained predominantly Muslim, even if the upper echelons were not.

While Teguder reigned as the first Muslim ruler of the Ilkhanate, Ghazan rightfully deserves credit for transforming the empire into an Islamic state. Unlike his overzealous commander, Nawruz, Ghazan recognised the rights of non-Muslims. Muslim rulers traditionally protected non-Muslims and in returned they paid the poll-tax known as the *jizya*. Ghazan briefly permitted the *jizya* before rescinding it.

While other factors also played a role, Islam influenced the ending of the Mamluk–Ilkhanid war. Ghazan's campaigns against the Mamluks demonstrated that even if they defeated the Mamluks, the Mongols still could not occupy Syria, at least not without dramatically altering their military and thus their nomadic identity.[122] With the exception of some skirmishing, Ghazan's invasions were the Ilkhanate's last major military operations. Although Reuven Amitai downplays the role of Islam in ending the war, as Muslims have fought Muslims almost since the beginning of the religion, there is a perceptible shift in attitude after Ghazan's death.[123] While it is conceivable that the Ilkhanids wearied of the perpetual war, the fact that the Ilkhanate was an Islamic Empire also opened other avenues to extend influence if conquest was not possible. As Muslims, the Ilkhanids could now negotiate as equals, particularly as Abu Saʿid restored the Ilkhanid to Sunnism after Oljeitu's flirtation with Shi'ism, making peace politically acceptable to the Mamluk Sultan.[124]

Abu Saʿid reign did not immediately end the war. While military action ceased, the Ilkhanid–Mamluk rivalry did not end. It just shifted, as Abu Saʿid asserted his credentials as a Muslim ruler. As a result, the Mamluks discovered they had competition for the hearts and minds of the Muslim world. While Ghazan asserted his authority, his invasions did not win over the Mamluk population (or people elsewhere). It is doubtful if the Syrian population viewed the Ilkhanid Mongols with anything but hostility due to the looming shadow of war over sixty years, but Muslims removed from the omnipresent threat did not experience the immediacy of invasion. The most

---

[121] Reuven Amitai, 'Sufis and Shamans: Some Remarks on the Islamization of the Mongols in the Ilkhanate', *JESHO* 42/1 (1999), 32.
[122] Reuven Amitai, 'The Resolution of the Mongol–Mamluk war', in *MTO*, 374.
[123] Amitai, 'Resolution of the Mongol–Mamluk War', 377.
[124] Amitai, 'Resolution of the Mongol–Mamluk War', 378–84; Broadbridge, *Kingship and Ideology*, 101.

crucial front in this diplomatic war was the Hejaz, the home of Medina and Mecca. Here Abu Saʿid encroached on the duties of the Mamluk Sultan (and protector of the Holy Cities), by sending curtains for the Kaʿaba along with other items with pilgrims from Iraq in 1319. This forced Sultan al-Nasir Muhammad (third reign, 1310–41) to also go on pilgrimage, 'with the object of asserting his role as protector of pilgrims and paramount patron in the Hijaz'.[125] This was all the more important as Abu Saʿid managed to have the *khutba* or Friday sermon read in his name in 1318, challenging Sultan al-Nasir Muhammad's hegemony over the Hijaz.[126] Additionally, Choban went to Mecca and funded the restoration of a well in Mecca and a *madrasa* in Medina, which then caused Sultan al-Nasir Muhammad to also perform similar good works in 1327–8.[127]

Although Sultan al-Nasir reasserted his primacy in the Hejaz, Abu Sa'id continued to meddle. Ibn Battuta noted Abu Saʿid's magnanimous donation of alms to the Holy Cities.[128] Abu Saʿid also once sent an elephant with the Iraqi pilgrimage to carry the *mahmal*. Charles Melville wrote:

> The elephant was taken through the stations of the pilgrimage but perished outside of Medina on the way home. The foreboding provoked by the elephant appeared to be justified by the rioting that took place in Mecca, and its presence probably heightened tensions in the city. The inhabitants called 730 the 'Year of the Elephant', thus recalling the attack on Mecca in the year of Muhammad's birth, though the threat on that occasion came from the Yemen. The upkeep of the elephant is said have cost 30,000 dirhems by the time it died, and no-one understood Abu Saʿid's motives in sending the beast. However, in the context of the rivalry for prestige in the Hejaz, it was clearly an ostentatious gesture designed to create an impression of the majesty and splendor of the Mongol ruler, building upon the position achieved by his earlier munificence.[129]

These actions compelled Sultan al-Nasir Muhammad to respond and assert his authority in the Hejaz. Actions included patronage and political murders, as well as replacing officials as needed to maintain his status (and the Mamluks' in general) as the Protector of the Holy Cities. As for Abu Saʿid, while he failed to control the Hejaz, it did allow him an

---

[125] Broadbridge, *Kingship and Ideology*, 102–3; Charles Melville, 'The Year of the Elephant', 202–4.
[126] Melville, 'Year of the Elephant', 201.
[127] Melville, 'Year of the Elephant', 206.
[128] Melville, 'Year of the Elephant', 207.
[129] Melville, 'Year of the Elephant', 208.

opportunity to demonstrate his piety. The pilgrims could not fail to notice the Ilkhanid display of wealth and generosity, of which they informed others in their homelands, thus providing publicity and propaganda for the Ilkhan.

Abu Saʿid also forced the Mamluks to demonstrate their piety in other ways as well. After a series of storms in 1320, he became convinced that it was a punishment from God. As a result he campaigned against vice. His actions included dumping wine and cracking down on other illicit activities. In another example of 'Keeping up with the Joneses' or Chinggisids, Sultan al-Nasir Muhammad followed suit so as not to be outdone.[130]

Abu Saʿid's actions assisted in removing the lingering taint of the infidel from the Ilkhanids. The conversion of the Ilkhanate did not take place overnight. Sufis played a key, but perhaps overstated, role in the conversion of the Ilkhans, the *noyad* and, undoubtedly, the rank and file.[131] The Mongol *khatuns* became patrons of Sufi orders as well as more mainstream imams and members of the *ulema*, funding *khanaqahs*, mosques and *madrasas* just as the Ilkhans did. The relative independence and power of Mongol women also caused some awkward moments for the *ulema*, as the Mongol women normally were unveiled in public.[132] As Bruno De Nicola noted, it is difficult to determine how the *khatuns* converted to Islam, but it appears that Mongol women converted at a more or less glacial rate, as did the men. Rather than dramatic conversions, it happened over time. Surely, the presence of Sufis and imams in the *ordos* of the *khatuns* contributed to the elite's conversion, but our understanding of how the ordinary Mongols converted remains unknown.[133]

Despite the transformation of the Ilkhanate, not all Muslims (within and without the Ilkhanate) accepted the conversion of the Ilkhans at face value. Besides the obvious lack of trust that manifested with the decades-long war, the *ulema* in the Mamluk Sultanate looked askance at the Ilkhanid Mongols due to their affiliation with Sufis and Shia Muslims, as well as their loose use of the *shariʿa* alongside their adherence to the *yasa*.[134] The latter point continued to be a sticking point for the *ulema* well into the later fourteenth century. For the most part, though, the successor states of the Ilkhanate were viewed as Islamic polities. It must be remembered that while an Ilkhan no longer ruled,

---

[130] Broadbridge, *Kingship and Ideology*, 104.
[131] Reuven Amitai, 'Sufis and Shamans', 27–9; Devin DeWeese, 'Islamisation, 120–34.
[132] De Nicola, *Women in Mongol Iran*, 194–8.
[133] De Nicola, *Women in Mongol Iran*, 205–7.
[134] See Denise Aigle, *The Mongol Empire between Myth and Reality: Studies in Anthropological History* (Leiden, 2014), 134–56, 283–304.

the majority of the new rulers came from the Ilkhanid *qarachu* families, such as the Jalayirids and Chobanids.[135]

While Abu Saʿid ruled as a Sunni, both Sufism and Shi'ism made considerable gains during Ilkhanid rule. Ghazan's dalliance and Oljeitu's conversion to Shia Islam were not coincidental. Hulegu's destruction of the Abbasid Caliphate created a leadership vacuum in the Islamic world. The psychological trauma of the destruction opened the door to a shift from societal emphasis to a focus on individual morality and spiritual needs, which Sufism could provide.[136] Shias also benefited as the death of the Caliph 'removed one of the pillars on which the constitutional theory of Sunnism had been built'.[137] Thus, Sunni claims to primacy were now in question. Furthermore, as the idea of a Caliph did not mesh with Mongol claims to domination, there was interest in other ideas of legitimacy. Undoubtedly, this also led to a number of post-Ilkhanid states, including the Jalayirids and Chobanids, having Shi'a leanings, culminating in the Safavids.

---

[135] Patrick Wing, *The Jalayirids* (Edinburgh, 2016); H. R. Roemer, 'The Jalayirids, Muzaffarids and Sarbadars', in Peter Jackson (ed.), *CHI*, v6, 1–41.
[136] Moojan Momen, *An Introduction to Shiʿi Islam* (New Haven, 1985), 90.
[137] Momen, *Shi'i Islam*, 91.

10

The Ogodeid and Chaghatayid Uluses

The political situations of the Chaghatayid Ulus and the Ogodeid Ulus were chaotic after the death of Mongke. As the dissolution of the empire came only a decade after the Toluid Revolution in the early 1250s, neither *ulus* had recovered. Quite simply, there were fewer Chaghatayids or Ogodeids in existence. The Ogodeids also experienced a loss of territory. Ogodei's *ulus* originally included the Emil and Qobuq river valleys, a region also referred to as the Zhungar Basin or Zhungaria, located between the Altai and Tien Shan Mountains. The Ogodeid Ulus may have reached the Orkhon River in Mongolia during the reign of Ogodei and Guyuk, but after the Toluid Revolution Mongke allocated the territory between the Altai Mountains and the Orkhon to the *ulus* of the centre, or to that of the *Qa'ans*. Chaghadai's appanage stretched from the frontiers of Uighurstan in the east bordered by the southern slopes of the Tien Shan and the northern Kunlun Mountains to the Amu Darya, and to roughly the Talas River and Lake Balkhash in the north.[1] Central Asia also became the focal point for resistance against Khubilai after 1262, which led to it being drawn into the war as the Ogodeid prince Qaidu and Khubilai competed for influence over the region. Finally, Chaghatayid princes pursued their own prerogatives through civil wars, as well as fighting the Ilkhanate and the Jochid Ulus. As a result, there was very little effort in developing a coherent state in the wake of imperial collapse.

In both territories, the population consisted of a mix of nomads and caravan towns benefiting from the Silk Road trade. Ruling the region presented challenges, as although most of the region had been part of the ephemeral Qara Khitai Empire, the territory lacked a coherent identity such as in Iran or China. The eastern regions had, at various points, been dominated by steppe powers (Xiongnu, Turks) and Chinese states (Han, Tang), and even Tibetans. The western regions had been ruled by pagan Turks and Muslim states, such

---

[1] Peter Jackson, 'From Ulus to Khanate: The Making of the Mongol States c. 1220–1290', in *MEL*, 23–4.

as the Abbasids, Samanids, Karakhanids, Seljuks and Khwarazmians. The benefit was that no pre-existing ideologies or forms of government challenged that of the Mongols, unlike in the Yuan or Ilkhanid territories. The Mongols in Central Asia did not gravitate to the cities, perhaps because the nomadic population was still quite large in the region; thus the court remained largely in the steppes. Furthermore, the cities did not hold the vast urban populations that those in China did. While the sedentary population was sizeable, it was not nearly as populous as in the Middle East or East Asia.

Almaliq initially served as the Chaghatayid capital, but the Chaghatayid *ordo* continued to nomadise. Thus, Almaliq primarily served as a geographic point for those who sought access to the court, whether merchants, scholars or missionaries.[2] Certain cities remained important, such as Samarqand and Bukhara, but none of the Central Asian cities served as a true capital in the way Tabriz, Daidu or Qaraqorum did, although Almaliq remained prestigious well into the fourteenth century. Furthermore, the Chaghatayids remained true to their nomadic roots, viewing the cities as a source of wealth to be exploited through taxation or, for some, plunder. The sedentary areas remained peripheral to their interests for most of the khanate's existence.

The location of the Chaghatayid territories, however, kept them relevant not only for the civil wars, but for communications and trade. Merchants from the west still needed to pass through it to reach China and other destinations, as did missionaries, adventurers and envoys from other khanates, and vice versa. While the Ogodeids and Chaghatayids eschewed city life, they recognised the need for cities and even built new ones to facilitate trade, such as Qaidu and Du'a's construction of Andijan.[3] As such, the Chaghatayid Ulus remained the communications hub of the Mongol Empire and disruptions inevitably affected the rest of the empire.

Post Dissolution

Immediately after the rise of Mongke, Qara Hulegu gained the Chaghatayid throne with Mongke's support, replacing Yesu Mongke, Guyuk's appointee. Qara Hulegu, however, died in 1252, leaving his wife Orghina, an Oirat and daughter of Chinggis Khan's daughter Chechiyegen, as regent for their young son Mubarak Shah.[4] After Mongke's death, Orghina appears to have

---

[2] Michal Biran, 'Rulers and City Life in Mongol Central Asia (1220–1370), in David Durand-Guedy (ed.), *Turko-Mongol Rulers, Cities and City Life* (Leiden, 2013), 261–2, 270.
[3] Biran, 'Rulers and City Life', 268.
[4] RD/Thackston2, 40, 263; RD/Thackston1, 55–6, 371; RD/Karimi, 77; 539. Her name also commonly appears as Orghana, Orqina and Ergene.

supported Ariq-Boke's candidacy for the throne.[5] Once war erupted between the Ariq-Boke and Khubilai, however, she then attempted to remain neutral in the conflict, preferring to wait for a winner rather than risk the war in her own territory. Described as beautiful, wise and a discerning ruler, she held the khanate together, but the stability was short-lived through no fault of her own as the civil war entered into Chaghatayid territory.[6] In the early stages she was able to toe the line of neutrality. Although she ruled the Chaghatayids, her sister married Ariq-Boke and one of their daughters married Orghina's nephew.[7] Additionally, her sister Qutui Khatun and step-sister Guyuk Khatun were wives of Hulegu in the neighbouring Ilkhanate.[8] As a result, she had little desire to see conflict and even less to be involved. The location of the Chaghatayid Khanate, however, prevented that neutrality from enduring.

In need of another front, as well as food and material for the war, Ariq-Boke sought to dominate the Chaghatayid Khanate. In the absence of a khan, Ariq-Boke nominated a grandson of Chaghadai named Alghu for Qara Hulegu's throne. With Alghu on the throne, Ariq-Boke could procure resources of the *ulus* as well as prevent Khubilai's contact with the rest of the *Yeke Monggol Ulus*. Unfortunately for Ariq-Boke, Alghu proved to be unreliable.

With Ariq-Boke's support, Alghu gained control of the Chaghatayid Khanate and removed Orghina from power, but as soon as Ariq-Boke's attention returned to dealing with Khubilai, Alghu sought independence. He expanded his realm by conquering Jochid possessions in Khwarazm.[9] Nonplussed, Ariq-Boke not only expended considerable effort in supporting Alghu, but now Alghu attacked the Jochids, who were Ariq-Boke's allies. Additionally, Mas'ud Beg, who Ariq-Boke needed administratively, complained about Alghu's rule while Orghina took refuge at Ariq-Boke's court. She stayed there until 1263, complaining that her regency had been shunted aside, violating tradition.[10] When Ariq-Boke sent envoys to deal with the matter in 1262, as he still needed supplies from the region, Alghu killed Ariq-Boke's envoys. He also established friendly relations with Khubilai, perhaps

---

[5] RD/Thackston2, 303; RD/Thackston1, 428; RD/Karimi, 620.
[6] For more on Orghina, see Bruno De Nicola, *Women in Mongol Iran* (Edinburgh, 2017), 76–82; Bruno De Nicola, 'The Queen of the Chaghatayids: Orghina Khatun and the Rule of Central Asia', JRAS 26, 1–2 (2016), 107–20; Paul D. Buell, 'Some Royal Ladies: Alaqa-beki, Ergene-Qatun and Others', *WHC* 7, no. 1 (2010), <http://worldhistoryconnected.press.illinois.edu/7.1/buell.html> (last accessed 6 June 2017).
[7] RD/Thackston2, 40; RD/Thackston, 1998, 56; RD/Karimi, 77–8.
[8] RD/Thackston2, 40; RD/Thackston, 1998, 56; RD/Karimi, 77–8.
[9] RD/Karimi, 625; RD/Thackston1, 430–1; RD/Thackston2, 304–5.
[10] RD/Karimi, 625; RD/Thackston1, 431; RD/Thackston2, 304–5.

because Ariq-Boke sought to restore Orghina to her throne.¹¹ Having been forced from Qaraqorum, Ariq-Boke then attacked Alghu and moved into the Almaliq region. His victories were short-lived as famine, perhaps the result of *zhuds* in the winter, stalked the steppes. Between this and other omens, Ariq-Boke withdrew. Alghu attacked his rearguard. With Ariq-Boke's withdrawal, Alghu reconciled with Orghina and Masʿud Beg.¹² The latter two had little choice since Ariq-Boke was unable to remove Alghu from power. Alghu may have had no choice either, and the reconciliation suggests that Orghina had considerable support among the Chaghatayids, not easily dismissed.¹³

With the threat of war subsiding, Orghina married Alghu in 1264 with the condition that Mubarak Shah would be his successor. In terms of him shoring up his support, the arrangement suited Alghu. In doing so, he foiled any possibility of Ariq-Boke overthrowing him, but also found a position that kept Khubilai from invading as well, as Khubilai had been amenable to Orghina's regency despite an unsuccessful attempt to place his own Chaghatayid candidate on the throne.¹⁴ Alghu also benefited from the wisdom of Masʿud Beg, who had served in the Mongol bureaucracy for decades. Masʿud Beg became his financial administrator and began to stabilise the fiscal affairs of the empire, particularly with regard to the caravan cities. Alghu's betrayal of Ariq-Boke was also the key to Khubilai's victory as it deprived Ariq-Boke of troops, provisions and strategic depth.

Peace was fleeting, though. Not only did Alghu attack Jochid possessions, but he also crept towards the remaining Ogodeid territories in an effort to bring all of the former fiscal district of Turkestan under his control.¹⁵ Alghu may have been influenced by Masʿud Beg, who headed the branch secretariat of Turkestan before the dissolution of the empire. With Masʿud Beg's governance, the Chaghatayids' coffers overflowed even with some revenue going to Khubilai, providing Alghu with the funds to consider expansion. The Jochids did not immediately take action due to their war with Hulegu, but the Ogodeids were a different manner.

They were led by Qaidu (1235–1301), a grandson of Ogodei and Toregene. Qaidu had been among those Ogodeids who escaped the purged. At the time of the Toluid Revolution, Qaidu was too young (approximately fifteen) to be any threat. Thus, he remained in his pastures around Qayaliq,

---

¹¹ RD/Karimi, 625; RD/Thackston1, 431; RD/Thackston2, 305.
¹² RD/Karimi, 625–7; RD/Thackston1, 431–32; RD/Thackston2, 305–6.
¹³ Buell, 'Some Royal Ladies'.
¹⁴ Morris Rossabi, *Khubilai Khan* (Berkeley, 2009), 58; De Nicola, 'The Queen of the Chaghatayids', 119.
¹⁵ Khwandamir, 46; Paul D. Buell, 'Some Royal Mongol Ladies'.

between the Emil and Ili rivers.[16] Initially, Qaidu remained neutral in the war between Ariq-Boke and Khubilai. He may have sympathised with Ariq-Boke in terms of being true to the nomadic heritage. Even if he did support Ariq-Boke, Khubilai does not appear to have begrudged him.[17] Many Ogodeid and Chaghatayid princes switched sides as they often lacked the resources to resist the more powerful Toluid rivals. Qaidu's feud with Khubilai, however, arose because of Khubilai's support of Alghu's expansion into Qaidu's appanage.[18]

With Ariq-Boke's defeat in 1264, there was no one to check Alghu's ambition, so Qaidu formed an alliance with Berke. Berke, occupied with the Ilkhanid war, provided what aid he could with a promise that he would support Qaidu's claim to any territory or people taken from Alghu. Jochid support was imperative. With the Toluid Revolution, not only had the Ogodeid territories been reduced, but many of the princes purged and their troops redistributed through the empire. It is not clear whether the *ulus* or appanage structure had been retained, with a khan presiding over the other princes, as it had been with the Chaghatayids. As Michal Biran indicates, the Ogodeids 'had no representation in the regional administrations or in the *tamma* forces that were sent under Mongke to conquer West Asia'.[19] The Ogodeids were no longer a major military power.

After Ariq-Boke's defeat, Khubilai expected all of the princes to come to his court and show due respect at a *quriltai*. Most did not because of the distance, but it was largely symbolic, as was Khubilai's division of the empire. The Jochids were confirmed in their territories (although one may question whether they cared about Khubilai's opinion) and Hulegu was confirmed as the lord of everything from the Amu Darya to Egypt (the Jochids did not recognise this). Furthermore, Khubilai effectively dissolved the Ogodeid Ulus, as all territory from the Amu Darya to the Altai Mountains now fell under the rule of Alghu, while everything east of the Altai was Khubilai's.[20] All of this left Qaidu at a severe disadvantage as he lacked the troops and resources to withstand any challenge alone, particularly as Alghu began to assert his authority in his new territories.

With Berke's reinforcements, Qaidu successfully defeated Alghu in one battle, but lost the next. Indeed, it appeared that Qaidu was on the ropes, but a series of timely deaths intervened and reversed Qaidu's fortunes. Alghu died

---

[16] Michal Biran, *Qaidu and the Rise of the Independent Mongol State in Central Asia* (Richmond, UK, 1997), 20.
[17] Biran, *Qaidu*, 21.
[18] Biran, *Qaidu*, 23.
[19] Biran, *Qaidu*, 16.
[20] RD/Karimi, 622; RD/Thackston1, 429; RD/Thackston2, 304.

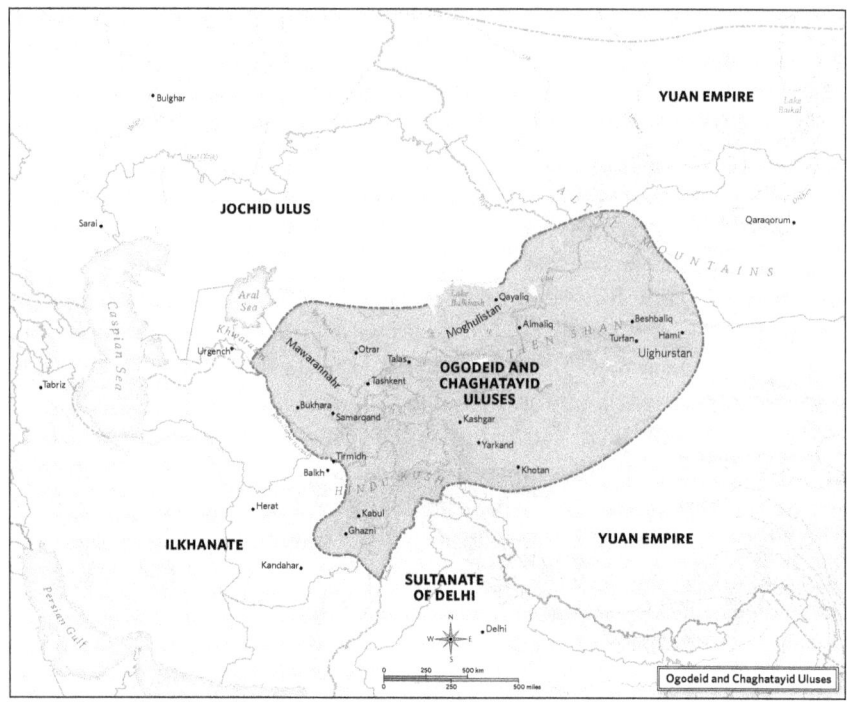

Map 10.1 The Ogodeid and Chaghatayid Uluses © Mapping Specialists

in 1265/6. Qaidu also benefited, indirectly, from the deaths of Hulegu in 1265 and Berke in 1266. With Khubilai busy consolidating his territory and renewing the war on the Song, Qaidu now had the opportunity to reverse his fortunes while the major powers were preoccupied.

The Era of Qaidu

Taking advantage of Alghu's death, Qaidu expanded westward to the Talas River and perhaps to the Syr Darya, reclaiming Ogodeid pastures. Qaidu captured Almaliq, where Alghu had been buried. From there he pushed towards Uighurstan in the Yuan Empire; while never formally Ogodeid territory, portions had been ruled by sons of Ogodei.[21] This attracted Khubilai's gaze and he dispatched an army against Qaidu, forcing him to abandon most of his eastern conquests by 1268. With Khubilai's aggressive defence of his borders, Qaidu opted for strategic depth and made the Talas region

---

[21] Thomas T. Allsen, 'The Yuan Dynasty and the Uighurs', in Morris Rossabi (ed.), *China Among Equals* (Berkeley, 1983), 249–50.

his headquarters, although Talas itself did not become his capital. Indeed, Qaidu did not have a capital city.[22] Qaidu's activities found support among many of the former supporters of Ariq-Boke who took refuge with him and augmented his forces. While Khubilai checked his advances into Uighurstan, he could not dislodge Qaidu from power. This began a decades-long border war, but Qaidu also intervened elsewhere, taking advantage of the problems that arose from the deaths of Alghu, Hulegu and Berke.

With Alghu's death, issues arose in the Chaghatayid Ulus. Orghina married Alghu on the condition that Mubarak Shah became his successor. With Alghu's death, and in agreement with the *noyad* and viziers, Mubarak Shah ascended the throne as the Chaghatayid khan in 1266. While this arrangement had been fine with the Chaghatayids, affairs within the Chaghatayid state needed approval from beyond their borders. Alghu and Orghina both recognised Khubilai as the *Qa'an*, and thus his endorsement carried great weight. Khubilai's disapproval may have simply been the *Qa'an* exerting his authority, as Orghina placed Mubarak Shah on the throne without consulting Khubilai. The issue became moot with the arrival of Baraq, a great-grandson of Chaghadai.[23]

Baraq grew up in Khubilai's camp after the Toluid Revolution and was viewed as loyal. Despite the support for Orghina that existed in the *ulus*, Baraq successfully gained the trust of Mubarak Shah's *noyad* and took him captive.[24] It is not clear as to why they backed Baraq, although Rashid al-Din insinuates that one of Mubarak Shah's *noyad* suggested the coup.[25] As with Ariq-Boke's efforts to control the Chaghatayid Khanate, Khubilai's plan backfired as well.

Baraq proved to be quite independent and raided towns such as Khotan on the Yuan western frontier.[26] Baraq, however, soon also found himself under pressure from Qaidu's expansion towards the Syr Darya. With Qaidu's presence, Baraq settled into peace with Khubilai, who granted him a patent of investiture in 1268.[27]

Despite repeated efforts, Qaidu rejected all of Khubilai's overtures for recognition. Spurned, Khubilai promised Baraq all of Qaidu's territory. He

---

[22] Biran, 'Rulers and City Life', 266–7.
[23] RD/Thackston2, 261; RD/Thackston1, 370; RD/Karimi, 536–7.
[24] Khwandamir, 47; RD/Thackston2, 261; RD/Thackston1, 370; RD/Karimi, 536–7. The dates in Khwandamir are slightly off by two years. I follow the chronology established by the meticulous study of Michal Biran for the events in the Ogodeid and Chaghatayid Uluses.
[25] RD/Thackston2, 261, 267; RD/Thackston1, 370, 377; RD/Karimi, 536–7, 546.
[26] Khwandamir, 47.
[27] Biran, *Qaidu*, 25.

defeated Qaidu initially, but in 1267 Qaidu, with Jochid reinforcements sent by Berke's successor, Mongke-Temur, inflicted a devastating defeat on Baraq at Khojand. Baraq retreated to Mawarannahr to regroup and in the process undid much of Masʿud Beg's wise governance by plundering Samarqand and Bukhara to fund a new army.[28]

Before conflict arose anew between Qaidu and Baraq, the Chinggisids attempted to resolve their conflict peacefully and in the name of unity. Qaidu's envoy to Baraq was an old friend of the latter named Qipchaq.[29] Masʿud Beg and other advisors urged Baraq to accept the invitation. As a result, the two agreed to discuss matters before subjecting the region to further destruction as it had suffered immensely in terms not only of lives and livestock, but also of the looting of towns from Alghu and Ariq-Boke's war. Continuing warfare would only send the region's economy and population into a downward spiral.

The actual meeting took place in 1267 on the Qatwan Steppe south of Samarqand or in 1269 at the Talas River.[30] At the peace conference, which included Jochid representation, Qaidu received the Ili Basin and Zhungaria, which included much of the Chaghatayid territory north of the Syr Darya River. Meanwhile Baraq received Mawarannahr. Two-thirds of Mawarannahr would be Chaghatayid, while the remaining third would be divided by Mongke-Temur and Qaidu. The revenues from the nomads and the workshops of the two principal cities of the region, Samarqand and Bukhara, were divided between the Jochids, Qaidu and Baraq. The Jochids had previously collected revenues from Samarqand and Bukhara as *qubi*, but lost them during Alghu's reign. Masʿud Beg would supervise the distribution of funds. They also divided the pastures in those vicinities, thus allowing Qaidu to maintain troops in the region. Furthermore, to prevent the plundering, Qaidu and Baraq agreed that neither princes nor troops were permitted into Samarqand or Bukhara. Finally, Qaidu and Baraq became *anda* and exchanged gifts.

Although it appeared that Baraq received the significantly lesser end of the deal, Qaidu and the Jochids agreed to support Baraq in expanding south of the Amu Darya, at the expense of the Ilkhans. Baraq had little alternative against Qaidu with Jochid support, which included 50,000 troops. It was doubtful that Khubilai would lend sufficient aid to Baraq to offset Qaidu's advantage. As part of the final agreement, the Jochids, Chaghatayids and

---

[28] Biran, *Qaidu*, 25.
[29] RD/Thackston2, 261; RD/Thackston1, 370; RD/Karimi, 536–7; Khwandamir, 47.
[30] The confusion occurs because the sources vary, with Rashid al-Din indicating 1267 and Wassaf 1269. See Biran, *Qaidu* 26.

Ogodeids allegedly sent a letter chastising Khubilai for his sinicisation of the Mongol Empire.[31] Needless to say, the letter (if real) did not endear any of them to Khubilai. Furthermore, it is doubtful if any of the three desired Khubilai to return the empire to 'the good old days'. With Khubilai ensconced in Daidu and not in Qaraqorum, he could not effectively control Central Asia: it was just too remote. Michal Biran noted: 'Indeed, the very fact of gathering and deciding to allocate territories and cities without asking the Qa'an's opinion was also a breach of the customary usage of the Mongol empire.'[32] Furthermore, the fact that Khubilai was not even invited to the *quriltai* speaks volumes for Qaidu, Baraq and Mongke-Temur's disdain for his authority. They were concerned with expanding and ruling their own territories, not the overall welfare of the former *Yeke Monggol Ulus*.

The main outcome of the Peace of Qatwan was that Qaidu's new state took shape. Even with the peace, and perhaps because of it, Baraq did not trust Qaidu's intentions, but nonetheless took advantage of his support and began his war with the Ilkhanate. Despite some initial successes, Baraq met defeat at the battle of Herat, where he encountered the Ilkhan Abaqa in 1270.[33] Abaqa's victory was complete, with Baraq fleeing across the Amu Darya in complete disorder as Qaidu's forces deserted him. Baraq, rightfully, suspected foul play on Qaidu's part and planned vengeance, but died in 1271 before he could act.[34] It is questionable whether he would have succeeded, as most of his commanders and Masʿud Beg joined Qaidu upon Baraq's death rather than seek service with another Chaghatayid candidate.[35] With this, Mawarannahr came under Qaidu's sway.

With the defeat and death of Baraq and Mawarannahr under his control, Qaidu now held a *quriltai* in which he was crowned Khan in September 1271, one month after Baraq's death. He did not claim to be the *Qa'an*. Qaidu may have eschewed the title to avoid difficulties with the Jochids; friction between Mongke-Temur and Qaidu already existed. Mongke-Temur, at one point, may have proposed a joint action by Khubilai and himself against Qaidu. As Qaidu and Mongke-Temur continued relations it is difficult to say how accurate this was, but it is clear that Mongke-Temur was wary of his neighbour and perhaps annoyed that Qaidu no longer appreciated Jochid

---

[31] Biran, *Qaidu*, 27 and p. 144, n. 80. Biran makes it clear that the date of this letter (mentioned in only one Chinese source) is highly uncertain.
[32] Biran, *Qaidu*, 28.
[33] See Michal Biran, 'The Battle of Herat (1270): A Case of Inter-Mongol Warfare', in *WIAH*, 175–220.
[34] Khwandamir, 48.
[35] Khwandamir, 49.

support. Qaidu certainly did not view himself as subordinate in any way to anyone.[36]

Most of the Chaghatayids acquiesced to Qaidu, as Qaidu did not claim to be their khan, but had the right to appoint one as Guyuk once did. His candidate was Negubei b. Sarban, who became the Chaghatayid khan in 1271.[37] Some Chaghatayids, however, resisted, actively or passively. These included the sons of Alghu (from wives other than Orghina) and Baraq. Negubei joined the rebellion in 1272. It is not clear whether Negubei joined the Alghu/Baraq faction or acted independently. Regardless, his rebellion was short-lived as he died in 1274. The sons of Alghu and Baraq failed in their revolt as well. Qaidu split them by naming Du'a, Baraq's second son, Chaghatayid Khan in 1282. Du'a's acceptance of Qaidu's suzerainty finally ended the conflict in Mawarannahr. With the loss of their allies, Alghu's heirs took refuge in Khubilai's domains.[38]

Tensions existed with the Ilkhanids as Qaidu remained a threat to their borders. An Ilkhanid army invaded Mawarannahr in 1273, sacking Bukhara as a preemptive measure.[39] Abaqa, the Ilkhan ruler, did not seek to occupy the region, but the invasion was a clear warning to both Qaidu and the Chaghatayids not to incur his wrath. Abaqa appears to have achieved his intended results, as Qaidu professed friendship with Abaqa and sought his assistance to ensure Chaghatayid rebels did not find refuge in Ilkhanid lands.[40] Most of Qaidu's attention, however, went on consolidating his hold over the Chaghatayid realm and attacking Khubilai.

Qaidu's attacks had an unintended impact on Khubilai's state. Even though Mongolia gradually became a backwater, the region of modern Xinjiang garnered more of Khubilai's attention and resources even as he fought the Song Empire. To defend the region from Qaidu, he not only increased the number of troops, but also developed infrastructure to support the war effort. This included a new census to determine existing resources, establishment of new *jam* stations, and the stationing of artisans in Khotan and Kashgar, whose purpose was not only to equip the army but also to help revive the economy after Qaidu's raids.[41] In effect, Qaidu's attacks forced Khubilai to strengthen his position in the region. Khubilai also sent emissaries to Qaidu, attempting to cow Qaidu into submission with logical and

---

[36] Biran, *Qaidu*, 30.
[37] RD/Karimi, 548; RD/Thackston1, 378; RD/Thackston2, 268; Khwandamir, 49.
[38] Biran, *Qaidu*, 33; RD/Karimi, 548; RD/Thackston1, 379; RD/Thackston2, 268.
[39] RD/Karimi, 766–7; RD/Thackston1, 636–7; RD/Thackston2, 380–1.
[40] Biran, *Qaidu*, 35.
[41] Biran, *Qaidu*, 38.

pragmatic discussions of comparative resources. While Qaidu was willing to engage in such conversations, there is no indication that he considered submission.

Despite the Yuan build-up on the frontier, Khubilai's generals and sons who commanded the army found little success. While many sources paint Qaidu as a rebel and usurper, a closer examination reveals that he was a competent ruler. Furthermore, the fact that he reigned for such a long time indicates that he had a strong base of support. The nomadic Mongols viewed him as a true Mongol, not only for challenging the sinicised Khubilai, but also in his observance of the *yasa* of Chinggis Khan and for remaining true to his heritage. Although disgruntled Chaghatayid princes fled to Khubilai, many Mongol princes and commanders departed Khubilai's service and joined Qaidu. Although the frontier with the Yuan empire was somewhat fluid, the borders of Qaidu's state were ironically the same as those Khubilai had assigned Alghu, although Du'a successfully incorporated much of non-Khurasan Afghanistan by gaining the support of the *tamma* that Dayir had established during the reign of Ogodei.[42] This then pushed Qaidu's borders virtually to the Indus River. Furthermore, he was able to retake Almaliq. Beshbaliq in Uighurstan remained out of reach as Khubilai made a conscious effort in 1281 (after the fall of the Song) to prevent Qaidu's expansion. Khubilai linked more frontier postal stations with Daidu to stay apprised of the situation. This did not prevent Qaidu from finding success. Du'a's siege of Qara Qocho in Uighurstan only ended after the Uighur ruler lowered his daughter from the walls as a peace offering to Du'a.[43] The following year in 1286, Du'a and Qaidu attacked Beshbaliq and successfully captured it.

Qaidu's success demonstrated that even though Khubilai invested heavily in the region in both manpower and infrastructure (governmental and physical), it did not guarantee control. The massive financial expenditure amounted to little success as Qaidu's border now reached Qara Qocho and his influence extended into Beshbaliq, Kashgar and Khotan by 1290. Rebellions in Manchuria and Tibet, and his own withdrawal from affairs prevented Khubilai from dealing with Qaidu in more than a reactionary manner.

Meanwhile, Qaidu continued to nibble away at the frontier, including incursions into Mongolia. His approach on Qaraqorum roused Khubilai, who had successfully crushed Nayan's rebellion in Manchuria in 1287, to lead an army to Mongolia. Qaidu abandoned Qaraqorum and retreated

---

[42] RD/Thackston2, 262; RD/Thackston1, 371; RD/Karimi, 538–9.
[43] Biran, *Qaidu*, 43.

Figure 10.1 The steppes and hills near Qaraqorum in Mongolia. Although Khubilai moved his capital to Daidu, Qaraqorum remained symbolically important to the Yuan.

in 1289. Fearful of losing Mongolia, Khubilai stationed the great general Bayan in Qaraqorum to direct the defence of Mongolia from 1290 to 1293.[44] Bayan's replacement, Tuq Tuqa, successfully regained the Yenisei region from Qaidu. Khubilai appeared willing to accept losses in the contested areas around Uighurstan to secure Mongolia, which was essential to his own legitimacy as *Qa'an*.

Even after Khubilai's death, Qaidu maintained pressure on the *Qa'an*'s empire. Only Qaidu's death in 1301 ended the war. Before he died, however, Qaidu found Temur Oljeitu to be a more stalwart opponent, as he gave his western frontiers proper attention and priority over foreign conquests, maintaining the seven sizeable garrisons Khubilai established along this frontier stretching from the Upper Yenisei to the Tarim Basin.[45] At one point in 1298 there was even a proposal by Bayan, the Khan of the Blue Horde (the Jochid territory of Orda), that Yuan, Jochid and Ilkhanid armies should attack

---

[44] Biran, *Qaidu*, 91; Rossabi, *Khubilai Khan*, 224.
[45] RD/Karimi, 646–8, 671–3; RD/Thackston1, 446–7, 464–5; RD/Thackston2, 316–17; 329; Biran, *Qaidu*, 49–50.

Qaidu's realm, a significant change from the Peace of Qatwan.[46] Temur Oljeitu, however, declined, satisfied with defending his borders and more interested in consolidating his authority over the Yuan Empire. Other events changed his attitude. Qaidu and Du'a apparently learned of the proposal, but perhaps not of Temur Oljeitu's response. In 1298, Du'a attacked the Yuan border. He also seized Korguz, the *Qa'an's* brother-in-law, and withdrew after a series of successful raids.[47] Although Yuan troops pursued, they failed to liberate Korguz.

The Yuan responded with an invasion. It began in 1300 with a series of battles that permitted the Yuan forces to penetrate the Altai region. The major encounter took place in the autumn of 1301 near Mount Teijiangu on the southern edge of the Altai Mountains. Qaishan, the future *Qa'an*, commanded the Yuan army and defeated Qaidu, who regrouped with Du'a reinforcements. Qaidu and Du'a met the pursuing Yuan army at Qara Qada, located on the banks of the Irtysh River.[48] In a two-day battle, Qaidu emerged victorious. Qaishan retreated to Qaraqorum, burning the steppe behind the Yuan army to prevent pursuit. It is not clear whether Qaishan's tactic prevented Qaidu from following or whether it was because Qaidu suffered too many losses. In the end, it did not matter as Qaidu died not long afterwards.

Post-Qaidu Central Asia

Qaidu's eldest son (by a concubine), Chapar, assumed the mantle of leadership and continued his father's policies, but he lacked his father's ability. Qaidu intended his youngest son, Orus, to succeed him. Du'a, however, supported Chapar.[49] Chapar's selection immediately caused an outcry and factionalism among the Ogodeids. Qutulun, Qaidu's daughter who led armies and was a wrestling champion, withdrew from politics with Chapar's selection.[50] Although the Ogodeids did not fight a civil war over Chapar's selection, Du'a successfully divided them. The Ogodeids attempted to challenge Du'a as he gradually increased his authority, but failed. Du'a also initiated peace overtures with Temur Oljeitu, leading to him and Chapar acknowledging Temur Oljeitu as *Qa'an*. Temur Oljeitu reciprocated and confirmed them as the khans of the Chaghatayids and Ogodeids respectively. By 1303, Du'a reigned independently as the Chaghatayid Khan. This may have been

---

[46] RD/Karimi, 678; RD/Thackston1, 468–9; RD/Thackston2, 332; Biran, *Qaidu*, 50.
[47] RD/Karimi, 675–6; RD/Thackston1, 467; RD/Thackston2, 331.
[48] Biran, *Qaidu*, 52–3.
[49] RD/Thackston2, 218; RD/Thackston1, 307; RD/Karimi, 448; Biran, *Qaidu*, 69.
[50] RD/Thackston2, 219–20; RD/Thackston1, 309–10; RD/Karimi, 450; MP/YC, 463–4; MP2012, 333; Biran, *Qaidu*, 70.

his plan from the beginning. *Pax Mongolica* existed throughout the Mongol Empire by 1305. As with the Yuan and the Ilkhanate, Du'a recognised the need to revive the caravan trade.

Although peace existed, it proved imperfect in Central Asia. Skirmishes occurred between the Chaghatayids and Ogodeids in 1305. Some Ogodeids plundered Samarqand and Bukhara, apparently because they could, rather than for any strategic reason. Du'a even convinced Qaishan, still commanding the Yuan frontier, to attack Ogodeid forces led by Qaidu's son Orus. After this, the Yuan fully supported the Chaghatayids, even sending reinforcements led by the sons of Alghu. By 1307, the war ended with Chapar completely defeated.[51] The Ogodeids' resistance was not unreasonable as they opposed peace with the Yuan simply as devotees of Qaidu's war with Khubilai as well as Du'a's machinations. The other Mongol rulers viewed Chapar and Du'a as equals. Furthermore, as part of the *Pax Mongolica*, Chapar had been forced to relinquish some Chaghatayid territory.[52]

To end any military challenge, most of the Ogodeid army was transferred to the Yuan and Chapar was put out to pasture, literally. Du'a gave him pastures in the steppes and stripped his authority. Du'a made Yangichar b. Qaidu the new Ogodeid khan, but merely as a pawn without support. Du'a further divided the Ogodeid Ulus into smaller appanages and limited Yangichar's authority over his kin. Du'a also purged the house of Qaidu, including the princess Qutulun.[53] It now appeared that the house of Ogodei was truly removed from power, but with Du'a's death in 1307 and then the death of his son and successor Konchek (r. 1307–8) the circumstances changed. As the Chagahtayids contended over the throne, the Ogodeids found new opportunity.

The next Chaghatayid to claim the throne was Naliqo'a (r. 1308/9), a grandson of Buri. Kebek, the youngest son of Du'a, challenged him not only because he felt that Du'a's line should reign; he also found support among others who opposed Naliqo'a's Muslim faith and Islamic policies.[54] Kebek defeated Naliqo'a in late 1308 or early 1309. He had little time to savour his victory, as a coalition of Ogodeid princes, including Yangichar, Orus and Chapar, attacked him at Almaliq. Although the Ogodeids found initial success, Chaghatayid reinforcements gave Kebek victory. It became clear that although each family might fight among themselves, they both viewed their own line as the dominant one in Central Asia.

---

[51] Biran, 'The Ogodeid and Chaghadaid Realms', *CHIA*, 54.
[52] Biran, 'The Ogodeid and Chaghadaid Realms', *CHIA*, 54–5.
[53] Biran, *Qaidu*, 76.
[54] Biran, *Qaidu*, 77; Biran, 'Ogodeid and Chaghadaid', 55.

Kebek also received aid from Qaishan, the new *Qa'an* of the Yuan Empire. Due to his time on the Central Asia frontier, Qaishan was sensitive to the civil war and how it might impact on his own borders. He supported Kebek and also gave him permission to kill certain Ogodeid princes. Chapar, however, surrendered to Qaishan in 1310 and then went to the Yuan court at Qaishan's invitation, effectively ending the Ogodeid Ulus.[55] While some Ogodeid territory around the Altai Mountains became Yuan, most shifted to the Chaghatayids. Qaishan bestowed Ogodeid revenues to Chapar in the Yuan Empire, which had been frozen since the war with Qaidu. Additionally, Qaishan awarded Chapar rank and territory in Yuan territories. His successors continued in this capacity until 1328, when one supported the losing faction in the Yuan struggles for the throne.[56] Although Orus also found refuge among the Yuan, some Ogodeids remained in Central Asia, but after 1309 none obtained real political power.

Curiously, Kebek did not take the throne. His brother Esen-Boqa (r. 1309/10–1319/20) became the khan. Kebek then became the governor of Mawarannahr. Although major wars, such as those that erupted after the death of Mongke, did not flare up, border clashes did occur. The border between the Chaghatayids and Ilkhanids remained contested, particularly in present-day Afghanistan, and in the former Ogodeid territories split between the Chaghadaids and the Yuan. Esen-Boqa feared an alliance between the Ilkhanids and the Yuan.[57]

Esen-Boqa's death led to the enthronement of Kebek (r. 1320–7) at Almaliq in 1320. In Khurasan that year, Kebek also defeated and killed Yasa'ur, who had defected to the Ilkhanids during Esen-Boqa's reign. Additionally, the Chaghatayids eventually held the lion's share of Afghanistan as the Qaraunas shifted their loyalties to Kebek, allowing him to launch raids against the Sultanate of Delhi. Their goals appear to have been less in conquest and more focused on plunder. Kebek, however, launched an invasion of the Ilkhanate in conjunction with Uzbek Khan in 1322, although the Ilkhanids were victorious. His brother, Tarmashirin, raided the Sultanate of Delhi as well.[58]

Known as a just ruler, Kebek advanced the economy and administration of his realm by introducing a monetised economy. The silver coins became known as *kebeks*, or in Russian *kopeika*.[59] Additionally, Kebek formally

---

[55] Biran, 'Ogodeid and Chaghadaid', 56.
[56] Biran, *Qaidu*, 78.
[57] Khwandamir, 50; Biran, 'Ogodeid and Chaghadaid', 56.
[58] Khwandamir, 51.
[59] Khwandamir, 51; Biran, 'The Ogodeid and Chaghadaid', 57.

submitted to the Yuan in an effort to reopen borders to trade, but only after dealing with those Chaghatayids who preferred raiding the Yuan border as a show of good faith. He also built a western capital in Qarshi, a sensible move as Almaliq was vulnerable to Ogodeid rebels as well as the Yuan and Jochids.[60] The location in Mawarannahr also demonstrated Kebek's affinity with that region. Kebek decimalised the khanate, assigning *tumens* to princes and the *qarachu* with appanages to support them.[61] As Turkestan had been a fiscal district that underwent a census during the *Yeke Monggol Ulus* period, this may have been a reorganisation meant to quell the *noyad*'s urge to pillage and reduce tensions with neighbours. By controlling the *noyads*' wealth, Kebek could assert more control over his them, thus subtly centralising his authority.

Kebek's death in 1327 led to another lateral succession with his brother Eljigidei (r.1327–30) coming to the throne. He continued cordial relations with the Yuan and the only major external operations consisted of raiding the Delhi Sultanate from Afghanistan.[62] Unlike his brother, Eljigidei preferred the open steppe and returned the government to Almaliq. Administratively, his reign marked a demonstrable shift from Kebek's capable reign, as the khanate remained stagnant as its nomadic rulers did little more than extract tribute from the sedentary population and raid India. Eljigidei's brief reign, however, tended to favour Buddhists and Christians over Muslims, showing that Islam had yet to become a dominant element among the Mongols of Central Asia.

The reign (1330–1) of Kebek's successor, Dore Temur, was too brief for it to make any substantial impact, but the rise of Tarmashirin (r. 1331–4) marked a distinct shift. The brother of Kebek, Eljigidei and Dore Temur, Tarmashirin converted from Buddhism to Islam. Although he was not the first Muslim Chaghatayid (see Mubarak Shah and Naliqo'a), his conversion altered Chaghatayid policies. His conversion did not mean an immediate change, but he preferred Muslim regions and actively encouraged proselytisation. Although Muslims existed north of the Syr Darya, Tarmashirin, like Kebek, preferred to dwell in Mawarannahr, which became the political centre of the empire as well.

The Muslims of the Sultanate of Delhi in India did not find any relief from Mongol raids due to Tarmashirin's new religion; indeed, during Kebek's reign, Tarmashirin frequently raided Delhi as the governor of Ghazna. Nonetheless, he gradually curbed the rapacious Qaraunas. Tarmashirin,

---

[60] Biran, 'Rulers and City Life', 271.
[61] Biran, 'The Ogodeids and Chaghadaid', 57
[62] Khwandamir, 51.

however, maintained favourable relations with the other Mongol states. Residing in Mawarannahr also made Tarmashirin highly aware of the importance of agriculture and commerce to the region. The cities of Mawarannahr flourished during his reign.[63]

While those outside the Chaghatayid Khanate might have questioned Tarmashirin's religiosity, the Chaghatayid Mongols did not, and for many, it and his political shift to Mawarannahr became a major point of contention. Those Mongols in the Ili River Basin, who still held shamanistic and even Buddhists beliefs, viewed the conversion as a betrayal, as was his move to, and perceived favouritism towards, the sedentary regions of the empire. It was clear that the two factors, like Khubilai's own changes, called into question his Mongol identity. Could one be a Muslim (or subscribe to any other religion) and be sedentary and still be a Mongol? For the majority of the Chaghatayids, one could not. In the eastern (and largely non-Muslim) regions, antipathy built as Tarmashirin remained in Mawarannahr. His distance also allowed the non-Muslim Chaghatayids (both Chinggisid and *qarachu*) to believe he had abandoned the *yasa* in favour of *shariʿa*. A rebellion led by Tarmashirin's nephew, Buzan b. Dore Temur, led to Tarmashirin's overthrow in 1334.[64]

Despite Tarmashirin's removal, his actions laid the foundation for a deeper split within the khanate. While Buzan's coup clearly demonstrated that the Chaghatayid Khanate was not a Muslim state, the fact that Tarmashirin rose to power to 'enjoin good and forbid evil' also demonstrated that there was a segment open to the idea. Of greater concern was the unravelling of authority within the Chaghatayid state. While Buzan claimed the Khanate, other pretenders appeared, including Ogodeids and even a Toluid. In 1335, the Buddhist Changshi (r. 1335–7), Du'a's grandson, took the throne. He returned the capital to its traditional location at Almaliq. Although he was a devout Buddhist, Christians also found favour during his reign, although it is alleged he "had [Buddhist] images painted in painted in all the mosques in the ulus".[65] His reign ended when his brother Yesun-Temur (r. 1337–39/40) murdered him. Despite an unsavoury reputation, Yesun-Temur proved to be an able ruler, minting coins and asserting his authority, not only in the eastern regions but also in Mawarannahr.[66]

An outbreak of the Black Plague in the Issyk Kul region cut his reign short and contributed to instability of Central Asia (and the Mongol Empire).

---

[63] IB1, 293–4; IB2, 143.
[64] Michal Biran, 'The Chaghadaids and Islam: The Conversion of Tarmashirin Khan', *JAOS* 122/4 (2002), 742–52.
[65] Biran, 'Ogodeid and Chaghadaid', 59.
[66] Biran, 'Ogodeid and Chaghadaid', 59.

Into this arose ʿAli Sultan (r.1340–?), an Ogodeid. Unlike Tarmashirin, he was a fanatical Muslim who persecuted the Christians of Almaliq (his treatment of Buddhists is unmentioned).[67] While his faith played a role, his usurpation played a greater role in his overthrow as all of his successors were Muslims.

The rapid succession of rulers attracted the eye of Uzbek Khan, the Jochid ruler, who invaded in 1340–1. Only his death ended the campaign in 1342. The invasion, however, did not unite the Chaghatayids. Instead, rivals competed for the throne, Muhammad b. Bolod (r. 1340–1) ruling from Almaliq, followed by the sons of Yasa'ur Qazan (r. 1341–6) from Almaliq and his brother Khalil Sultan (r. 1341–5) in Bukhara ruling over Mawarannahr.

What is certain is that the eastern and western portions of the Chaghatayid state drifted apart. The eastern portion became increasingly known as Moghulistan. It was not quite Mongolia, but in the eyes of those who dwelt in Mawarannahr, Moghulistan was truly the place of the Mongols, by which they meant nomads. Furthermore, it marked a religious border that predated the Mongol era. Moghulistan remained pagan with a sizeable Buddhist population. Christians (even Catholics) existed along with Muslims, but the majority were shamanistic or Buddhist. While the sedentary population might have viewed them as nomads in a pejorative sense, the Mongols viewed the ascription as a compliment and remained true to their ways. They viewed themselves as stalwarts and protectors of the heritage of the Mongol Empire. Those who remained in Mawarannahr converted to Islam over time. Although the cities remained Sunni, the nomads adopted Islam from Yasaviyya, Kubraviyya, and later Naqshbandiyya Sufis, although the latter tended to be urban-based. Indeed, Islam helped bring the nomads closer to the sedentary population.[68] While the nomads existed in Mawarannahr, the commercial cities carried greater importance because of the lucrative wealth of the overland caravan routes. This was the realm ruled by Khalil Sultan b. Yasa'ur.[69]

Again demonstrating that conversion and acceptance was a slow process, roughly fifteen years after the death of Tarmashirin, Islam became the primary religion of the entire khanate. The Chaghatayid Khan, Tughluq Temur (r. 1347–63), converted to Islam under the tutelage of the relatively minor Sufi Kataki *tariqa*.[70] Allegedly, a large number of nomads followed suit, finally transforming Moghulistan into a Muslim majority.

---

[67] Biran, 'Ogodeid and Chaghadaid', 59.
[68] Biran, 'Rulers and City Life', 274.
[69] Biran, 'Ogodeid and Chaghadaid', 59.
[70] Dughlat/Thackston, 4–7.

Mawarannahr remained tied to the Chaghatayid Khanate, but almost as a colony that the Chaghatayids exploited. In some ways, this was not radically different from the situation in the thirteenth century, yet there was a difference. While a Chaghatayid prince sat on the throne in Mawarannahr, the Chaghatayids in Moghulistan carried more importance and intervened in affairs of Mawarannahr when necessary. This occurred in the mid-fourteenth century. In 1347, Qazghan, a Turkic commander, deposed Qazan Khan, the Chaghatayid ruler of Mawarannahr.[71] Qazghan then ruled Mawarannahr as his own kingdom. During this period those in the western regions (Mawarannahr) viewed themselves as the true Chaghatayid Ulus and referred to themselves as Chaghatayids while they referred to those in the eastern portion (Moghulistan) as Moghuls when feeling kind, but the dismissive term *chetes* found equal usage. The Moghuls, naturally, viewed themselves as the true Chaghatayids, referring to their more sedentary neighbours as Qaraunas, meaning they were no longer true Mongols.[72] Eventually, Qazghan ceased his tribute payments and increasingly acted without regard to the Chaghatayids in Moghulistan.

As a result, Tughluq Temur Khan, the Chaghatayid ruler, invaded. His invasion crushed Qazghan and brought Mawarannahr to heel. Tughluq Temur did not remain in the region for long, leaving his son, Ilyas, to govern it.[73] The removal of Qazghan also opened the door for other personalities in the region to find opportunity. Qazghan had deftly kept a lid on the various leaders of the region; one such figure was Timur, who eventually took over the entire region in 1370. He is better known as Tamerlane.

An Islamic Empire in Central Asia

The Chaghatayid Khanate was the last to Islamise, but as Devin DeWeese has indicated, 'there is as much justification, if not more, for recognising the Chaghatay *ulus* as the *most* Muslim of the Mongol successor states'.[74] After all, it was in Bukhara, a centre of Islamic education, that Chinggis Khan announced from the pulpit that he was the punishment of God. Unlike with the Ilkhans, the Chaghatayids also seemed confident in their belief, never trying to convince a larger audience (such as the Mamluk Sultanate). Nonetheless, in hindsight the conversion of the Ilkhans was not surprising considering that the majority of the population of their territories were

---

[71] Khwandamir, 51.
[72] Beatrice F. Manz, 'The Empire of Tamerlane as an Adaptation of the Mongol Empire', *JRAS* 26/i–ii (2016), 286.
[73] Khwandamir, 52; Dughlat/Thackston, 7–8.
[74] Devin DeWeese, 'Islamization in the Mongol Empire', CHIA, 128.

Muslims. Although Islam entered Central Asia in the eighth century with the Arab conquests of Mawarannahr, only with the conversion of the Chaghatayids did the eastern steppes embrace Islam.

The Chaghatayid Khanate consisted of Mawarannahr with a clear Muslim majority and other regions beyond the Syr Darya possessing a more diverse population. In addition to Muslims, the region had a sizeable number of Buddhists, largely due to the appearance of the Qara Khitai Empire and the Uighurs, although Buddhism entered Central Asia much earlier. Additionally, Nestorians who had been actively proselytising since the tenth century remained. Finally, Manichaeans and Zoroastrians still existed, albeit in negligible numbers.[75]

While Qara Khitai (1124–1218) had dominated much of the region prior to the Mongols, the Khwarazmian Empire (1156–1221) was a Muslim state, as were the Karakhanids (840–1212) and the Samanids (819–999), with the latter emerging from the frontiers of the Abbasid Caliphate (750–1258).

As many of the imperial administration, including the Yalavach family, had been part of the Khwarazmian government prior to the Mongol arrival, they were well-grounded in the principles of Islamic government. Additionally, Islam spread among the newcomers in ways similar to those of its earliest successes – through Sufis, whose syncretic views made the transition easier, as they did not force the Mongols and Turks to abandon their own culture to adopt a foreign one. Additionally, merchants (who were often affiliated with Sufis as well) worked closely with the Mongols not only in commercial transactions but by serving in the administration. Conversion took place over years, typically happening in the second and third generation of exposure to Islam.[76] Although the Chaghatayids (both elites and non-elites) remained largely nomadic, increased contact with the urban centres of Mawarannahr and in the steppes such as Almaliq and Qayaliq exposed them to Muslim communities, leading them to convert in the same way in which the Oghuz and Qarluq Turks converted in the tenth and eleventh centuries.[77]

That the Chaghatayid state divided into two halves is not surprising in hindsight. Although it is uncertain whether they referred to the western (Mawarannahr) as the white and the eastern (Moghulistan) as the blue horde (*aq* (T.) or *chaghan* (Mon.) *ordo* and *koke ordo*, respectively), this type of division was common among both the Xiongnu and the Gok Turks. Regionally, the Karakhanids, whose state corresponded roughly with that

---

[75] Peter B. Golden, 'The Karakhanids and Early Islam', *CHEIA*, 344.
[76] Bruno De Nicola, *Women in Mongol Iran* (Edinburgh, 2017), 205–8.
[77] Golden, 'Karakhanids and Early Islam', 353; DeWeese, 'Islamization in the Mongol Empire', 129.

of the Chaghatayids, also divided into western and eastern halves, with the Ferghana Valley and Semirech'e being the approximate border between Mawarannahr and Moghulistan.[78]

Mubarak Shah was the first Muslim Chaghatayid, and it is not unreasonable to suppose that his faith may have been one reason why the Chaghatayid *noyad* gravitated to other princes such as Alghu and Baraq. Only slightly more than a decade had passed since the death of Chaghadai, with his well-known devotion to *yasa* and *yosun* and his antipathy towards Muslims. This is not to say that religion and tradition were the only factors; both Alghu and Baraq possessed military skills superior to those of the youthful Mubarak Shah.

Despite this, Islam had some influence even among the non-believers, as Baraq allegedly converted upon his deathbed.[79] While Islam surely found converts after Baraq among the Mongols, it wasn't until the 1330s that it truly became a political factor. DeWeese suggests that during this period some used Islam as a method of gaining support in a rather contentious political environment.[80] Indeed, as only a Chinggisid descended from Chaghadai was deemed legitimate, the heirs of Chaghadai had to find novel ways to legitimise their candidacy and rule. Certainly, personal charisma, wealth and military abilities mattered, but more was needed to ensure success. At the same time, the sincerity of their belief should not be dismissed out of hand. The fate of a fraud or hypocrite was precarious.

Kebek probably moved the capital to Mawarannahr for security against external threats, but Tarmashirin's residence in Mawarannahr may have reflected his Muslim sensibilities – it was more Islamic than Moghulistan. Kebek's religiosity remains uncertain – it does not appear that he was a Muslim, but his reign demonstrated the traditional religious tolerance of the Mongols. For Tarmashirin, Mawarannahr not only gave him a strong economic base but also a population sympathetic to his pro-Muslim policies. Even his throne advertised his faith. According to Ibn Battuta, it resembled a *minbar*.[81] Furthermore, it was also closer to Afghanistan, where he served as governor prior to becoming khan. From there it was likely that he could also call upon the *noyad* that still served there.

Nonetheless, Tarmashirin's disposal demonstrated the limits of that support. While Rashid al-Din recorded examples of top-down conversions in the Ilkhanate and the Yuan Empire, in which the leader converted and then facilitated the conversion of the masses, this did not occur in the Chaghatayid

---

[78] Golden, 'Karakhanids and Early Islam', 364.
[79] DeWeese, 'Islamization in the Mongol Empire', 130.
[80] DeWeese, 'Islamization in the Mongol Empire', 130.
[81] IB1, 286–7; IB2, 142.

Khanate.[82] Al-'Umari indicated that while Tarmashirin advocated and promoted Islam, most of the Chaghatayid nomads had already converted.[83] Khwandamir meanwhile indicates that most of the Chaghatayid Ulus became Muslim during Kebek's reign.[84] While it is certain that events did not occur in quite the way Rashid al-Din depicted, it is also certain that the rank and file of the Chaghatayid army did not contain sufficient numbers of Muslims to force the *noyad* to acquiesce to Tarmashirin's conversion efforts.[85] The later conversion narrative of Tughluq Temur also indicates this, which leads one to consider whether perhaps the Chaghatayids in Mawarannahr were largely Muslims by Tarmashirin's reign, but that Muslims in Moghulistan practised *taqiyya* to avoid persecution.[86]

After Tarmashirin, some of the rulers were hostile to Islam. It is difficult to ascertain the veracity of this as most of the authors discussing it were Muslims writing from a later period, who may have viewed the pre-Islamic Chaghatayid world as a period of *jahiliyya*. What is notable is that, a decade later, there was sufficient mass present to support Muslim rulers, leading to the enthronement of Tughluq Temur, so that a Muslim who actively propagated Islam came to the throne once again. Although his conversion story reads in a hagiographic manner, complete with a miracle-producing holy man, it should be read with caution.[87] While the history of Tughluq Temur is scant, the conversion story is meant to demonstrate the Khan's emergence from *jahiliyya*.[88]

Yet, apparently even in Tughluq Temur's time, much of Moghulistan remained committed to other religions, as Dughlat mentions that most of the Moghuls (the Chaghatayid nomads dwelling in Moghulistan) converted to Islam during the time of Muhammad Khan, the Chaghatayid ruler of Moghulistan and grandson of Tuhgluq Temur.[89] Furthermore, if Muhammad Khan learned that a person was not a Muslim, 'he would have a horseshoe nail driven into the man's head. He made many such efforts.'[90] Besides keeping blacksmiths employed, Muhammad Khan ignored Qur'ānic injunctions against forcible conversions and had a selective memory with regard to the

---

[82] See the previous discussion of Ghazan and Ananda.
[83] Umari, 38–41.
[84] Khwandamir, 51.
[85] DeWeese, 'Islamization in the Mongol Empire', 131.
[86] Dughlat/Thackston, 6.
[87] DeWeese, *Islamization and Native Religion*, 160–6.
[88] Dughlat/Thackston, 6–11.
[89] Dughlat/Thackston 21.
[90] Dughlat/Thackston, 21.

'verse of the sword'.⁹¹ While the horseshoe threat might be (hopefully) simple hyperbole, the actions of religious zealots in the twenty-first century force us to consider that it was still in the realm of possibility.

Now we must return, even if reluctantly, to the question of whether the Chaghatayid state could be considered an Islamic empire. Considering the basic criteria, one must conclude that no, it was not. It is true that the administrative apparatus was strongly based (if not wholly) on previous Islamic empires with modifications that always occur as one empire replaces another. It is also true that the Khanate was an empire ruling over a multi-ethnic, multi-lingual and multi-religious population and thus not homogeneous.

The sticking point, however, was the ruler. While Muslim rulers appeared, their brief reigns and opposition to their rule demonstrate a clear instability and an inability to implement Islamic rule (however one might define that). Only Tughluq Temur's reign might be considered to constitute an Islamic empire, due not only to his position as a strong Muslim potentate but also to his reign's length. Yet, as the Chaghatayid state fragmented after his death, can one conclude that it was an empire? Its fragmentation, with Mawarannahr becoming the stronghold of a true Islamic Empire under Amir Timur, demonstrates that Tughluq Temur's rule lacked strong institutions for an empire's continuation even though heirs existed. He was not the only one at fault, but as he was the last in the room, so to speak, he does bear the lion's share of responsibility. Thus, while the Chaghatayid Khanate cannot be considered an Islamic empire, the post-Tughluq Temur Chaghatayids should be considered Muslim rulers, albeit of a truncated and ill-defined state.

---

⁹¹ Qurʾān 2:256 and 9:5 respectively.

11

The Jochid Ulus or Golden Horde

Popularly called The Golden Horde, the domains of the heirs of Jochi were not known by that name. The term 'Golden Horde' does not enter the sources until the sixteenth century, when Russian chroniclers referred to the domains as *Zolotaia Orda*, the Golden Camp or Palace.[1] During the Mongol era, they were known as the Kipchak Ulus or Khanate or the Jochid Ulus or Khanate. The Kipchak Khanate appellation came later and was a substitution for the *Dasht-i Kipchak*, or the Kipchak Steppes. As Kipchaks constituted the largest portion of the population and much of the territory, particularly the political centre, was in the *Dasht-i Kipchak*, the name made sense from a certain perspective. The *ulus* stretched from Bulgaria to the Ob and Irtysh Rivers in Siberia. To the south, the Caucasus Mountains and the southern shores of the Aral Sea marked its boundary. To the north, the Rus' principalities were a part of it, and we are unsure just how far north the khanate held sway. Even when they did not rule Siberian tribes directly, the tribes were tied to the khanate via the fur trade dominated by Novgorod and Bulghar.[2] In addition to its immense size, the Jochid Khanate existed the longest, with its end coming in the early sixteenth century. Even then, successor states to the Jochid Khanate lasted well into the eighteenth century and a case could be made for the nineteenth century as well.

Scholars believe that the *ulus* consisted of relatively few Mongols as Chinggis Khan apportioned to Jochi only 9,000 men.[3] The bulk of the Jochid population and military came from the Kipchak and Qangli Turks who lived

---

[1] Istvan Vasary, 'The Jochid Realm: The Western Steppe and Eastern Europe', in *CHIA* (New York, 2009), 68. For the symbolism of the name see Timothy May, 'Color Symbolism in the Turko-Mongolian World', in Sungshin Kim (ed.), *The Use of Color in History, Politics, and Art* (Dahlonega, GA, 2015), 51–78.

[2] IB1, 262–3; IB2, 127; MP1, 345–6; MP/Cliff, 324–5; MP/Lathem, 330–1; MP/Marsden, 286–7; MP/YC, v2, 480–1, 484; Janet Martin, 'The Land of Darkness and the Golden Horde: The Fur Trade Under the Mongols XIII–XIVth Centuries', *CMRS* 19, no. 4 (1978), 401–21.

[3] See SHM, §242. At five persons per household, this could be 45,000 Mongols.

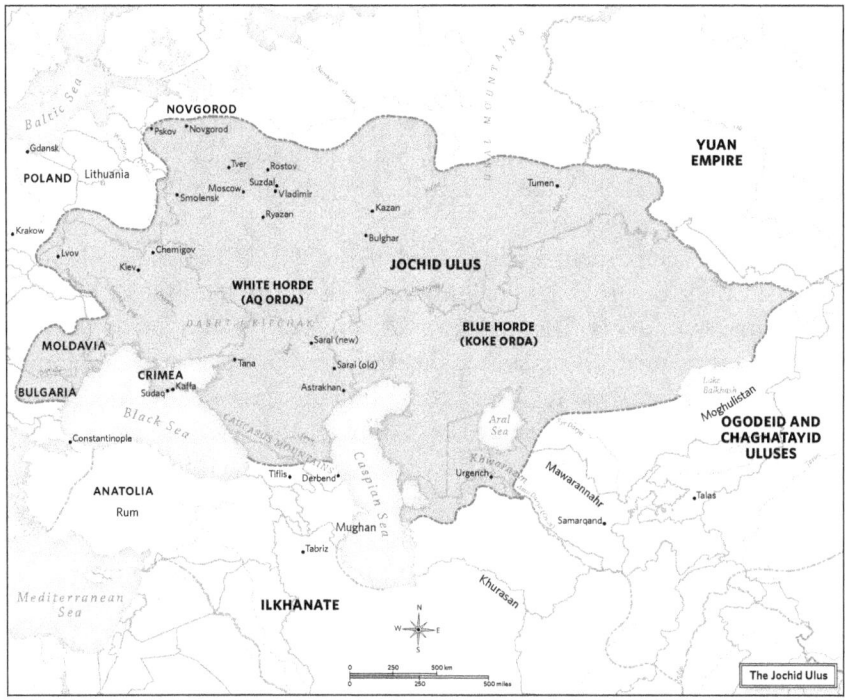

Map 11.1 The Jochid Ulus © Mapping Specialists

in *Dasht-i Kipchak*. As a result, Turkicisation occurred rapidly, including the increased use of Turkic in the Jochid. The latter did not occur overnight, but there is some indication that the Jochids assimilated sooner than the other states, although Mongolian elements lingered in the successors to the Jochid Ulus.[4]

Organisation of the Jochid Ulus

Although the Jochids ruled from the steppes, they remained involved in trade, following models established by Ogodei to promote and encourage merchants to travel to their capital (Sarai) on the Volga River. Much of the trade was consumption in which the khans purchased goods and then distributed it

---

[4] Д.Н. Маслюженко, 'Тюрко-монгольские традиции в «государстве кочевых узбеков» хана Абу-л-Хайра', *Золотоордынское Обозрение* 2/3 (2014), 121–38; Дариуш Колодзейчик, Попытки восстановления монгольской традиции в Крымском ханстве начала XVII века: байса, Тат ве Тавгач', *Золотоордынское Обозрение* 4/3 (2015), 91–101; Istvan Vasary, 'Mongolian Impact on the Terminology of the Documents of the Golden Horde', *AOH* 48 (1995), 479–85.

to their supporters, but archaeological evidence is increasingly demonstrating that the trade was much more complex than previously thought.[5] Persian and Chinese goods appeared in the Russian cities and amber and Siberian furs were sold in the Middle East. Furthermore, the Jochid Khanate also exported wheat and other crops from the Black Sea region. Kipchaks constituted the dominant commodity in the slave trade, sold to the Mamluk Sultanate to form the core of its military.

The state and economy were focused on the Volga River basin. Although east–west trade occurred, the majority travelled north–south using the great river systems of Eurasia. This, in itself, was not new. The location of Sarai followed historical predecessors such as the Khazars, who established their capital of Itil on the Volga, near the river's outlet into the Caspian Sea. The location was strategic as it not only benefited from the trade that travelled the Volga and Caspian routes, particularly from a revitalised Bulghar, but it was sufficiently close to the Black Sea and thriving ports on the Crimean peninsula such as Sudak and Kaffa.[6] The lush steppes in the region also permitted the khans to maintain a pastoral lifestyle without sacrificing their nomadic identity.

Divided between the many sons of Jochi, the Jochids still followed a traditional bifurcation between left (east) and right (west) wings, with a southern orientation and with the Ural River serving as the dividing line. These halves were known as the Blue (*koke* or *koko*) and White (*aq* or *chaghaan*) *ordas* or Hordes respectively, following a colour identification that had existed since the Xiongnu period (c. 209 BCE–91 CE).[7]

Orda, the eldest son, ruled the Blue or eastern wing of the *ulus* while his brother Batu ruled the White or western. Their brother Shayban ruled a region in the northern section as well, although this may have been considered part of either the White or Blue Hordes. The other brothers had territories assigned in these larger polities. While all of Jochis's sons had territories, Batu served as the ruler, perhaps as *primus inter pares*, of the entire Jochid *ulus*. In addition to other Jochids ruling their own patrimonies, the Jochid khan was assisted in maintaining the khanate by the *qarachu*, later known as the *qarachi beys*, who were the leaders of the *minqans* originally assigned to Jochi.[8] They

---

[5] See A. Fedorov-Davydov, *The Silk Road and the Cities of the Golden Horde*, ed. Jeanine Davis Kimball, trans. Alexander Naymark (Berkeley, 2001).
[6] Martin, 'Land of Darkness', 409–12.
[7] See May, 'Color Symbolism'.
[8] Uli Schamiloglu, 'The Qaraci Beys of the Later Golden Horde: Notes on the Organization of the Mongol World Empire', *AEMA* 4 (1984), 286–7; Christopher P. Atwood, 'Titles, Appanages, Marriages, and Officials: A Comparison of Political Forms in the Zungar and Thirteenth-Century Mongol Empires', in David Sneath (ed.), *Imperial Statecraft: Political*

remained influential advisors and military commanders throughout the existence of the khanate and its successors. Although the khan could rule without them, this was not easily done. Without their co-operation, the khan's authority diminished when he was absent.

Colour Confusion

The identities of the territories have been a source of consternation for historians as to which half was Blue or White. Much of the confusion stems from seemingly indifferent usage in some of the later Persian sources, which often referred to the left (eastern) portion as the Aq or White Ordo. This misled modern historians, leading them to refer to the east as the White Horde and the west as the Blue. Adding to the confusion is the fact that many scholars adopted the practice of referring to the western portion, which had more interaction with Russian principalities, as the Golden Horde on the basis of later Russian sources and continued to refer to the eastern portion as the White.

It is difficult to determine the government structure beyond the presence of the *qarachu* and the *basqaq/daruqachi*.[9] The court structure took an Islamic cast, but when remains uncertain. Curiously, it lacked a *Sahib Divan*, unlike the Ilkhanate. While viziers existed, none rivalled the *qarachu*.[10] Most importantly, the Jochid government was similar to other Mongol states; while they may have adopted other institutions, the overarching structure remained firmly rooted in Mongol practice. Furthermore, as what we know of the Jochid government comes from outside sources, we only know how it was perceived and not how it was actually structured. Thus, just as Rashid al-Din described Ahmad Fanakati as Khubilai's vizier, it does not mean that Khubilai's government adopted Islamic governmental institutions.[11] One must remember that Marco Polo described the same individual as a *bailo*, a term familiar to his European audience.[12]

Forms and Techniques of Governance in Inner Asia, 6th–20th Centuries (Bellingham, WA, 2006), 207–42; May, 'Color Symbolism', 64.

[9] JPC, 86–7; JPC/Dawson, 40; Istvan Vasary, 'The Tatar Factor in the Formation of Muscovy's Political Culture', in Reuven Amitai and Michal Biran (eds), *Nomads as Agents of Cultural Change* (Honolulu, 2015), 255–7; Vasary, 'The Origin of the Institution of Basqaqs', *AOH* 32 (1978), 201–6; Vasary, 'The Golden Horde Term Daruga and Its Survival in Russia', *AOH* 30 (1976), 187–97.

[10] Umari, 67; Schamiloglu, 'Qarachi Beys', 288–90.

[11] RD/Karimi, 650; RD/Thackston1, 449; RD/Thackston 2012, 318.

[12] MP 2012, 161; MP/Cliff, 105; MP/Lathem, 132; MP/Marsden, 130–1; MP/YC, v1, 417.

In short, we must be careful when applying non-Mongol/Turkic terminology to describe any Mongol state as it only describes the viewer's comprehension of institutions, not necessarily that of the Mongols.

Islam had been present in the territory of the Jochid Khanate since the ninth century, as had Orthodox Christianity. While Christianity was largely confined to the Rus' principalities (although Catholic missionaries from Hungary did attempt to convert the Kipchaks) and the shores of the Black Sea, Islam found a home in Bulghar on the upper Volga river. It had not noticeably spread from Bulghar prior to the Mongol conquests; the Mongols' arrival, however, changed the status quo. The Jochid Khanate's first true ruler, Batu, was not a Muslim, but Muslim influences increased in the court of his brother Berke during Batu's lifetime. Indeed, Batu even considered moving Berke's *ordo* from its location near the Caucasus to remove from him from proximity to Muslim merchants.[13]

Berke's conversion to Islam is somewhat confusing. Sources indicate that either he was raised as a Muslim, by his wet nurse, or that he converted as a young adult through the influence of a Sufi.[14] In truth, both stories may have an element of truth to them. In either case, Berke's conversion did not lead to the conversion of the khanate. It did lead, however, to changes in how he ruled, such as prohibiting the consumption of pork.[15] The vast majority of the population, however, remained unaffected and Berke did not seem inclined to encourage its conversion although he welcomed Muslim scholars and theologians to his court. While he may not have been a zealous proselytiser (and this is perhaps why he did not face a rebellion), Berke did not interfere with conversions either, as members of his family and retinue converted, including his wife Chichek Khatun and brother Berkecher.[16]

Conversion occurred, however, with some unintended consequences. The focus of the state from its inception had been in the south and east for economic and political reasons, but with the gradual conversion of the Kipchak population the state became polarised, with the south and the steppe regions becoming Muslim while the northern forested areas were oriented towards a Christian and sedentary identity. To be sure, the urban areas in Crimea and Sarai were blended, but outside of the more cosmopolitan areas the differentiation was noticeable.

Much of what we know about the Jochid Khanate comes from Russian sources, which naturally centred on the khanate's interactions with the Rus'

---

[13] Rubruc, 212; Rubruck/Jackson, 127; Rubruck/Dawson, 124.
[14] Istvan Vasary, '"History and Legend" in Berke Khan's Conversion to Islam', in *AAC3*, 230–52.
[15] Rubruc, 212; Rubruck/Jackson, 127; Rubruck/Dawson, 124.
[16] Kirakos, §69; Vasary, 'History and Legend', 250–1.

principalities. The other major sources come from the Mamluk Sultanate due to their alliance with the Jochids against the Ilkhanate. Ilkhanid and Yuan sources fill in some gaps, but much of the Jochid history remains elusive.

In the Russian sources, the vast majority of Rus'–Mongol interactions involved the collection of taxes and tribute, and related activities which included the establishment of a census. The Jochid Khanate carried out the census at regular intervals, even as often as every five years, in order to establish baselines for tax collection as well as to determine how many soldiers the Rus' could provide. As part of the census, officials organised the population into decimal units of households, an activity that caused great resentment among the Rus' and sometimes riots. These vitriolic activities eventually painted the Mongol rule over the Rus' as the Tatar (as the Mongols became known in Russia) or Mongol Yoke, which then was later used by Russian nationalist historians to explain every misery known to Russia, particularly why Russia was backward compared to Western Europe.[17]

In reality, the Mongols considered the Rus' to be backwards as well and peripheral to their main interests. From 1241 to 1290, the focus of the state was not only on the southern portions of the khanate as it solidified, but also beyond its borders. With the death of Mongke and the subsequent dissolution of the empire, war between the Jochids and the Ilkhanate became the primary activity of the Jochid state. Berke's alliance with the Mamluks occurred not only because he sought to establish ties with the Muslim state, but also for strategic reasons – to open another front against Hulegu. Jochid ties with the Mamluks are much more complex than previously thought, and there is evidence that Berke did not see the relationship as one of equals, but rather that the Mamluks submitted to him.[18]

The Early Post-dissolution Period

Berke being the first ruler of the Jochid Ulus in the post-dissolution era, his actions set the tone for the Jochid Khanate. Not long after receiving the news of Mongke's death, Berke attacked Hulegu. Although some sources link Berke's war against Hulegu to religion with Hulegu's execution of the Abbasid Caliph, a close examination of the sources reveals that the reasons for the war had more to do with territory than religion.[19] According to the Persian chronicler Juwayni, Chinggis Khan bequeathed to Jochi and his descendants

---

[17] See Charles J. Halperin, *The Tatar Yoke* (Bloomington, IN, 2009).
[18] Anne Broadbridge, *Kingship and Ideology in the Islamic and Mongol Worlds* (New York, 2008), 58.
[19] Peter Jackson, 'Dissolution of the Mongol Empire', *CAJ* 22 (1978), 208–12.

the earth as far west as the Mongol horses had trod.[20] This included territory in Iran and Azerbaijan, particularly the lush Mughan plain. While some have indicated that Hulegu's territory was not meant to be this region, it is likely that Mongke planned to curtail Berke's power.[21] Although Mongke and Batu may have reached an accommodation so that Batu was practically autonomous, apparently this did not extend to Berke (r. 1257–66) who came to the throne after Sartaq b. Batu (1256–7) and then Ulagchi (r. 1257), both of whom died under mysterious circumstances. At the very least, Mongke realised that approximately half of the empire theoretically belonged to his cousins, thus greatly reducing the authority of the *Qa'an*.

Hulegu fended off Berke's invasion and then invaded the Jochid domain. Even with an alliance with the Mamluks, Berke was unable to decisively defeat Hulegu. The war became bogged down, with the major front being the Caucasus Mountains and neither side gaining an advantage. As with the Ilkhanids, the war became institutionalised despite the stalemate.

The alliance with the Mamluks altered the war, in that one Mongol faction sided with non-Mongols against another Mongol faction. Initially, Mamluk interests with the Jochid were economic – to ensure a flow of slaves from the steppes to renew the Mamluk ranks. Once Sultan Baybars realised Berke was a Muslim with a shared animosity towards the Ilkhanate, a military alliance was only natural. In 1262, Baybars played up their shared faith and emphasised his own role as a Defender of the Faith against the infidels. He reminded Berke that even the Prophet Muhammad fought his own infidel relatives and that Berke should become a *mujihad* as well. Additionally, he suggested that Hulegu abandon the ways of the Mongols and adopt the Christian faith of his wife, Doquz Khatun.[22] Hulegu had not – he remained Buddhist or shamanist, despite the efforts of Doquz.[23] Considering the course of events between the Jochids and Ilkhanids, it is doubtful whether Berke needed encouragement for war.[24]

Nonetheless, the Baybars' initiative bore fruit, as the Jochids posed a serious threat to the Ilkhanids. Additionally, it also provided Berke with alternative means of justifying his actions against the Ilkhanate. For a Muslim audience, he could play the Islam card regarding *jihad* and the murder of the Caliph. For the traditional Mongol audience, Berke could argue that Hulegu

---

[20] Juvaini/Boyle, 42; Juwayni/Qazvini, v1, 31.
[21] George Lane, *Early Mongol Rule in Thirteenth-Century Iran* (London, 2003), 39–40.
[22] Anne Broadbridge, *Kingship and Ideology*, 50–1, Reuven Amitai-Preiss, *Mongols and Mamluks* (Cambridge, 1995), 81.
[23] Kirakos, §65.
[24] Amitai-Preiss, *Mongols and Mamluks*, 86.

had contravened the *yasa*, not only by seizing Jochid pastures, but also by executing Jochid commanders.

In addition to opening a second front, this gave the Jochids another route via which to escape the Ilkhans. As Hulegu's army was composed of troops from most of the *altan urugh*, once war started Berke authorised Jochid troops to depart to the Mamluk Sultanate. While they arrived as infidel refugees, these warriors converted and became known as the *wafidiyya*.[25] While the term meant refugee, it also became a term for foreign troops in the Mamluk army. It is unclear if any returned to the Jochid Ulus.

The war continued after Hulegu's death in 1265, with Berke invading to take advantage of the instability after Hulegu's death. Hulegu's sons Yoshmut and Abaqa (the Ilkhan) defeated the Jochid armies.[26] Berke died as he began to engage Abaqa near Tiflis (modern Tbilisi).

With Berke's death, Mongke-Temur (r. 1267–80) came to the throne. He continued the war, although as a non-Muslim he did not view the war as a *jihad*. As Professor Broadbridge has noted, his ties with the Mamluks were purely economic.[27] Like Berke, Mongke-Temur encouraged trade throughout his realm as Sarai and other towns became thriving commercial centres, benefiting from Italian merchants (including the Polo family) as well as the trade with the Mamluk Sultanate. Commercial activity led to the establishment of separate districts for foreign merchant, including those coming from the Italian maritime cities such as Venice and Genoa as well as merchants from the Mamluk Sultanate. Armenian and Persian merchants from the Ilkhanate also established successful businesses within Sarai during respites in the war, such as during Mongke-Temur's peace agreement with Abaqa in 1268–9.

The Russian sources view Mongke-Temur more favourably than Berke. The *Nikonian Chronicle* indicates that the 'violence of the Tatars over Russia lessened' after the death of Berke.[28] This may have been not only because Mongke-Temur was not a Muslim (the Orthodox sources were usually hostile to Muslim rulers), but also because of the temporary cessation of hostilities against the Ilkhanate. While the Mongols raided Europe, pillaging required fewer men and material resources than the campaigns against the Ilkhanate. Rus' princes such as Prince Gleb Vasil'kovich of Rostov accompanied Mongke-Temur in the Ilkhanid wars.[29] Taxation may have been eased

---

[25] Reuven Amitai, *Mongols and Mamluks*, 71–2; Broadbridge, *Kingship and Ideology*, 52.
[26] RD/Karimi, 526, 744–5; RD/Thackston1, 362; RD/Thackston2, 518–19; RD/Thackston2, 256, 368.
[27] Broadbridge, *Kingship and Ideology*, 59.
[28] *Nikon*, v3, 41.
[29] *Nikon*, v3, 59.

with the detente. While the Jochid administration may have been voracious, nonetheless the Mongols did more than simply extract resources from the Rus'. Mongol troops assisted the Rus' against the Teutonic Knights, the Sword Brethren and the Lithuanians.[30]

Sarai

Sarai was built in the vicinity of the lower Volga River to serve as Batu's administrative capital even while he remained nomadic. The city was located along the Akhtuba River, running parallel to the Volga River. Situated to overlook the river, Sarai was approximately 62 miles (100 kilometres) north of Astrakhan, the centre of a successor state to the Golden Horde. As an urban centre, it was relatively small and extended for 2–2.5 square miles, but it served the purposes of the Golden Horde. The khans preferred to nomadise around the city during the winter before moving to pastures deeper in the steppes during the summer.

Archaeology reveals that the city was diverse in its buildings, ranging from simple houses to palaces with tiled floors and walls. As with Qaraqorum, evidence suggests that yurts were erected in the city by the nomad elite. Many of these were in the gardens of the wealthy homes. By the early fourteenth century, however, Sarai had grown to a respectable size with thirteen mosques, paved streets, and separate quarters consisting of markets and neighbourhoods for the four major ethnic groups: Mongols, Alans, Kipchaks and Russians. An abundance of caravanserais, madrasas and palaces testifies to the wealth and culture of the Sarai, demonstrating that it was more than an administrative centre. While Islam became the dominant religion, Sarai also boasted an Orthodox metropolitan.

Mongke-Temur exerted influence into Eastern Europe as Jochid armies raided Poland and Hungary, particularly during the detente with the Ilkhanate.[31] Mongke-Temur attempted to exert soft influence over Hungary as well, but without great success. In Bulgaria, the Jochids were more successful. Bulgaria submitted to the Mongols during the Western Campaign. During Berke's reign, the Jochids reminded the Bulgarian king of his duties

---

[30] *Nikon*, v3, 45, 54, 63. Also see William Urban, *The Teutonic Knights* (London, 2003) for more on the Teutonic Knights and Sword Brethern; for Lithuania see S. C. Rowell, *Lithuania Ascending: A Pagan Empire Within East-Central Europe, 1295–1345* (Cambridge, 1994).

[31] Peter Jackson, *The Mongols and the West* (Harlow, UK), 198–9.

by having a Mongol army use it as a bypass to reach the Byzantine Empire in the war against the Ilkhanids.[32] This demonstration, which was more a show of force to the Byzantines than to the Bulgarians, convinced the Bulgarians that despite the turmoil in the Mongol Empire, it was in Bulgaria's best interest to remain loyal to the Jochids. The Mongols also meddled in Bulgarian succession matters as well.[33] Not all subjects were as loyal, however. In 1278, Mongke-Temur quelled a revolt by the As or Alans.[34]

Despite the lengthy reigns of Berke and Mongke-Temur, the Jochids faced the same problem that the Mongol Empire faced throughout its history – the problem of succession. Any Chinggisid could make a claim for the throne. Certainly, some princes had stronger claims than others, but there was no shortage of potential claimants. This then created opportunities for some individuals to gain additional power by supporting princes, particularly those who were not as strong-willed or as experienced. Through this systemic flaw, kingmakers emerged. For the Jochid Khanate, the most influential man for the last quarter of the thirteenth century was not the khan, but the general and kingmaker Noghai (d. 1299).

The Ascendancy of Noghai

Noghai was a minor Jochid prince, probably born to a concubine and thus eliminating any claim to the throne.[35] Excluded from power, he became a well-regarded *tumen* commander in the 1260s. He led the invasion of the Ilkhanid realm in 1262 and 1266 as well as the campaign through Bulgaria into the Byzantine Empire. He became Berke's right-hand man. By the time of Berke's death, Noghai was practically autonomous in the lands between the Don and Danube Rivers.[36] His strategic position also made him the primary Jochid representative in affairs in Hungary and the Balkans, which is probably why the Byzantine Emperor Michael VIII Palaiologos (r. 1259–82) married his illegitimate daughter Euphrosyne to Noghai in 1272.[37] This proved fruitful, as Noghai later helped Michal VIII quell a rebellion in Thessaly. Noghai also converted to Islam and in 1270 urged the alliance between the Mamluks and the Jochids to a *jihad* against the Ilkhanids.[38] Professor Broadbridge has suggested that Noghai courted Sultan Baybars by insinuating that he was a

---

[32] Istvan Vasary, *Cumans and Tatars* (Cambridge, 2005), 72–9.
[33] Vasary, *Cumans and Tatars*, 80–5.
[34] Agusti Alemany, *Sources on the Alans: A Critical Companion* (Leiden, 2000), 384.
[35] Vasary, *Cumans and Tatars*, 71.
[36] Vasary, *Cumans and Tatars*, 72.
[37] Vasary, *Cumans and Tatars*, 79.
[38] Amitai-Preiss, *Mongols and Mamluks*, 89.

favourable (Muslim) alternative to Mongke-Temur.[39] Baybars, wisely, had no desire to become involved in Jochid politics.

Noghai remained a valued advisor and general during the reign of Mongke-Temur, but Noghai's independence increased when a weaker ruler came to the throne, as evinced by coins bearing Noghai's name from 1286 and perhaps earlier. Tode-Mongke (r. 1280–7) succeeded his brother, Mongke-Temur, but lacked his resolve. As with his predecessors, the wars against the Ilkhanids continued, but without major successes. Noghai's experience, however, prevented the Ilkhan Abaqa from making gains at the Jochids' expense. Without a strong khan, Noghai also found new opportunities to strengthen his position via Bulgaria. For all intents and purposes, Noghai was the kingmaker in Bulgaria as well as the Jochid Ulus.[40]

Although military victory eluded Tode-Mongke on the Ilkhanid front, he is best known for continuing the growth of Islam within the Jochid Khanate. Scholars and religious leaders from the Mamluk Sultanate and from other parts of the Middle East continued to arrive at his court; Tode-Mongke, however, preferred the company of Sufis.[41] The number of Muslims increased, but widespread conversion did not occur. Instead, conversion remained a personal event. Nonetheless, the Mongol and Turkic population slowly, but steadily, shifted to Islam. Tode-Mongke turned to the Mamluk Sultanate as well, viewing it as an inspiring model. This contact benefited also Sultan Qalawun (r. 1279–90), whose own political legitimacy was shaky.[42]

Tode-Mongke's reign also marked a changing identity for the Jochid Khanate, not only in terms of religiosity, but linguistically. While Mongolian was still used in the court, Turkic increased in usage, including replacing Mongolian on coins although Mongolian influenced the Turkic parlance of the Jochids.[43] Furthermore, Persian and Turkic (Kipchak and Uighur) served as *linguae francae* for the Jochid Ulus, just as they served during the *Yeke Monggol Ulus*.[44] It should be remembered that by Tode-Mongke's reign a full

---

[39] Broadbridge, *Kingship and Ideology*, 60.
[40] Vasary, *Cumans and Tatars*, 86–7, 90.
[41] Istvan Vasary, 'The Jochid Realm', in *CHIA*, 77.
[42] Broadbridge, *Kingship and Ideology*, 61–3.
[43] See Istvan Vasary, 'Mongolian Impact on the Terminology of the Documents of the Golden Horde', *AOH* 48 (1994), 479–85.
[44] See David Morgan, 'Persian as a *lingua franca* in the Mongol Empire', in B. Spooner and W. L. Hanaway (eds), *Literacy in the Persianate World: Writing and the Social Order* (Philadelphia, 2012), 160–70; Peter B. Golden, 'The World of the *Rasulid Hexaglot*', in *KDRH*, 7–8; Istvan Vasary, 'Oriental Languages of the *Codex Cumanicus*', in F. Schmider and P. Schreiner (eds), *Il codice cumanico e il suo mondo* (Rome, 2005), 104–24.

generation had passed since the dissolution of the empire. Large numbers of Mongols no longer arrived from the east to refresh the Mongolian identity.

Tode-Mongke, however, failed as a ruler and lacked the ability to make difficult decisions, which led him to abdicate after a brief civil war, while the Rus' princes who had fallen from favour with the Jochid court took refuge with Noghai.[45] The fact that Noghai forced Tode-Mongke to abdicate indicates the Noghai was, at least initially, looking for more than a puppet. As Noghai rose to power during the reigns of two very strong rulers in Berke and Mongke-Temur, he may have sought a similar ruler before settling into his new *modus operandi*.

Noghai replaced Tode-Mongke with Tole Buqa (r. 1287–91). During this period, Noghai's appanage was independent, with the Jochid khan having no authority over his actions. Indeed, even subjects within the empire viewed the situation with confusion. Many Russian princes believed that Noghai was the ruler. They may have simply recognised the reality of the situation. The fact that Bulgaria dealt exclusively with Noghai only added to the reality.[46] Furthermore, Noghai brought Serbia into the Mongol orbit, solidifying his image in Europe as the true ruler of the Golden Horde. In 1290, Tole Buqa finally asserted himself and attempted to organise against Noghai, but Tole Buqa did not hide his intentions well enough and civil war erupted. Noghai deployed Toqta, the son of Mongke-Temur, against Tole Buqa.[47] Noghai was not so brazen as to execute a Chinggisid prince. Instead, Toqta did it and claimed the throne in 1291.

Reassertion of the Crown

Toqta (r. 1291–1312) came to the throne at a young age and served as the dutiful puppet that Noghai hoped for, allowing Noghai to continue his own agenda. Toqta proved to be much like his father – strong-willed and quite capable. As he grew older, he steadily increased his independence and carefully acquired supporters to challenge Noghai. He married a Byzantine princess named Maria, complicating matters for Noghai.[48] In 1297, Toqta initiated war against Noghai. For two years, Noghai and Toqta fought for control of Noghai's appanage in the vicinity of the Don and Dnieper Rivers. The conflict affected not only the nomads, but even sedentary subjects. The violence from Toqta's war with Noghai and the Rus' feuds may have

---

[45] *Nikon*, v3, 68–73.
[46] *Nikon*, v3, 72–4; Charles J. Halperin, *The Tatar Yoke* (Bloomington, 2009), 85; Vasary, *Cumans and Tatars*, 86–7.
[47] *Nikon*, v3, 80; RD/Karimi, 528; RD/Thackston1, 363; RD/Thackston2, 257.
[48] Donald Ostrowski, *Muscovy and the Mongols* (Cambridge, 2002), 138.

prompted Maxim, the Metropolitan of Kiev, to move to Vladimir in Suzdal, an unprecedented move.[49] Despite initial success, Noghai's situation became so dire that he appealed to the Ilkhan Ghazan. Ghazan, however, had no desire to intervene. With Toqta's victory, Noghai and his sons were removed from the scene and Toqta asserted his authority as the paramount ruler of the Jochid Khanate in late 1299–1300.[50] In the aftermath, many of Noghai's supporters fled to the Balkans, the Byzantine Empire, and even into Anatolia, where their arrival may have changed the course of events.[51] Toqta, meanwhile, turned his attention to foreign merchants.

In 1266, Berke permitted Genoese merchants to trade with the empire in the Black Sea ports. The Genoese established a consulate in Kaffa in 1281.[52] For forty years, they had almost unrestricted trading rights in the city and exerted an enormous amount of influence in the region, largely with Noghai's co-operation. During his war with Toqta, however, Noghai demonstrated to the Italians and other merchants in the region his wrath after his son Aqtaji was murdered by Genoese merchants in 1298.[53] Despite his rampage, the Italians did not abandon their trade settlements in Crimea.

Toqta altered the arrangement with Genoa in 1307. He ordered the arrest of Genoese merchants in Sarai and stripped them of their goods. Then in 1308, he sacked Kaffa and drove the Genoese out. Later, he pragmatically permitted the Genoese to rebuild the city and resume trading. The Kaffa commerce was too important, but Toqta made it clear to all foreigners who was the true khan and that, within the Jochid realm, all were subject to him.[54]

Toqta's actions reflect the complex situation of trade in the post-dissolution empire. The Genoese were allies of the Ilkhans, but they also

---

[49] *Nikon*, v3, 85–6; Donald Ostrowski, *Muscovy and the Mongols* (Cambridge, 2002), 18; also see Donald Ostrowski, 'Why Did the Metropolitan Move from Kiev to Vladimir in the Thirteenth Century?', *California Slavic Studies* 16 (1993), 83–101.

[50] MP1, 350–2; MP/Cliff, 335–41; MP/Lathem, 339–43; MP/Marsden, 293–5; MP/YC, v2, 498–9; *Nikon*, v3, 82, 87; RD/Karimi, 529–32; RD/Thackston1, 363–6; RD/Thackston2, 257–9.

[51] Vasary, *Cumans and Tatars*, 107–13, 122–31; Scott Jessee and Anatoly Isaenko, 'The Military Effectiveness of Alan Mercenaries in Byzantium, 1301–1306', *Journal of Medieval Military History* XI (2013), 107–32; C. J. Heywood, 'Filling in the Black Hole: The Emergence of the Bithynian Atamanates', in K. Cicek, et al. (eds), *The Great Ottoman-Turkish Civilisation*, vol. 1 (Istanbul, 2000), 107–15; Alemany, 252.

[52] Virgil Ciociltan, *The Mongols and the Black Sea Trade in the Thirteenth and Fourteenth Centuries* (Leiden, 2012), 93–102; Jackson, *Mongols and the West*, 304.

[53] Ciociltan, *Mongols and the Black Sea Trade*, 161–2; RD/Karimi, 530; RD/Thackston1, 365; RD/Thackston2, 258.

[54] Ciociltan, *Mongols and the Black Sea Trade*, 164–5.

aided Toqta against Noghai.⁵⁵ Although the Venetians began to trade further inland from Tana, the Genoese navy had the capability to stifle the Venetian trade and prevent the Jochids from creating a navy. The final event leading to Toqta's attack on Kaffa was the arrogance of the Genoese. When the Mongols first ventured into Crimea, Kaffa's fortifications held them at bay; thus the Genoese were relatively secure. Yet, security bred arrogance as the Genoese participated in the lucrative commerce in Kipchak slaves for the Mamluks. Since the time of Berke, the Jochids permitted this; the Genoese, however, brazenly took Mongol children as slaves as well – some captured, but some purchased from their parents. Incensed, Toqta decided not only to terminate the Genoese arrogance, but also to end the Mongol slave trade within his realm. Although Kaffa held out for eight months, it finally fell.⁵⁶

Toqta's long reign stabilised the empire. During Noghai's era, the Rus' princes enacted private and often destructive feuds, although between 1273 and 1299 the Mongols conducted punitive raids. In 1299, Toqta sent an envoy to help settle affairs. With Noghai removed, Toqta continued to arbitrate issues between the Rus' princes. Although the Rus' princes continued their internecine wars, they also turned to the Jochid khan to mediate and lobby support. At times Toqta intervened forcibly.⁵⁷ The empire also benefited from the return of the *Pax Mongolica* between all of the khanates, which initiated new diplomatic contact as well as trade. The fact that Noghai's rise to power and a concurrent decline in the khan's power occurred during the civil wars may have convinced Toqta that the war with the Ilkhanids was unproductive. Like peace in any age, this peace was ephemeral. With the death of Ghazan Khan, the Ilkhanid ruler, in 1304, Toqta once again considered invading the Ilkhanate and attempted to persuade the Mamluks to open a second front. His overtures were unsuccessful, although he briefly cut off the flow of slaves to Egypt in 1307 in a display of economic coercion.⁵⁸ The stability achieved in second half of his reign, however, laid the foundation for what might be considered the Golden Age of the Golden Horde, the reign of Ozbeg Khan (r. 1312–42), Toqta's nephew.

The Jochid Blues

Noghai's activities did more than destabilise the authority of the khan in Sarai. It also created fractures in the Jochid Ulus. Since the time of Batu, the Jochid Ulus had maintained unity among all of the sons of Jochi. Each

---

⁵⁵ Ciociltan, *Mongols and Black Sea Trade*, 160.
⁵⁶ Ciociltan, *Mongols and the Black Sea Trade*, 163–8.
⁵⁷ *Nikon*, v3, 90–2, 95–6.
⁵⁸ Ciociltan, *Mongols and the Black Sea Trade*, 170–1.

Figure 11.1 White jade *tamgha* or seal. With the *Pax Mongolica*, trade flourished across the Mongol states. The seal is believed to that of Prince Tukel-Buka, son of Toqta. He ruled Nogai's ulus after Toqta defeated Noghai.

Figure 11.2 Tukel's Phagspa seal. While it is uncertain how extensively Phagspa was used in Jochid territories, this seal was most likely sent as a gift by a Yuan emperor and also was a sly attempt to demonstrate his suzerainty over the Jochids.

received their own patrimony with the bulk of the Jochid realm divided into the White and Blue *uluses*. Although Orda was senior to Batu, Orda deferred to him and the khan of the White Horde remained the de facto leader of the Jochids after Batu's death – authority rested in Sarai. The Blue Horde, including Orda's son Quli, took part in Hulegu's conquest of Baghdad. When war erupted between the Jochids and Ilkhanate, Orda's troops stranded in Iran fled to Afghanistan. His son Quli died in the attempt.[59]

Although it is uncertain when Orda died, his son Qurumshi and Qarachar b. Udur b. Jochi attended Ariq-Boke's *quriltai* as representatives of the *Ulus Orda*. Qarachar even led armies on Ariq-Boke's behalf against Khubilai.[60] At some point, perhaps in the 1260s, Orda's fourth son, Qongqiran, succeeded him and he appears to have died in the early 1270s.[61] Qongqiran died without sons, so Orda's throne passed to Qonichi (r. 1275?–1300), the son of Orda's eldest son, Sartaghtai.[62] It is with Qonichi that the Blue Horde becomes noticeable in the sources. Both Marco Polo and Rashid al-Din noted that Qonichi ruled independently and answered to no one.[63] Initially, however, it appears that he continued to defer to the ruler of the White Horde, at least until Noghai's authority became too apparent, making it difficult for the Blue Horde to maintain a pretence of subordination. Despite the Jochid–Ilkhanid war, Sartaghtai had amiable relations with the Ilkhan Arghun and Ghazan, confirming the Blue Horde's independence during Qonichi's reign.[64]

Qonichi pursued his own agenda particularly with regard to Qaidu, his Ogodeid neighbour. Initially, Qonichi supplied him with both men and material aid, as well as a haven for deserters from Khubilai Khan's armies. Nonetheless, as Qaidu's power grew Qonichi became wary and shifted towards neutrality. He and Tode-Mongke eventually came to an agreement with Khubilai to contain Qaidu. In 1283/4 Tode-Mongke returned Nomuqan, Khubilai's fourth son, whose army had rebelled.[65] Qonichi also made a separate peace with Arghun Ilkhan and then even requested an alliance with Khubilai and Arghun against Qaidu.[66]

---

[59] RD/Karimi, 510, 526; RD/Thackston1, 350, 362; RD/Thackston2, 248, 256.
[60] RD/Karimi, 620, RD/Thackston1, 427; RD/Thackston2, 302.
[61] RD/Karimi, 511; RD/Thackston1, 351; RD/Thackston2, 249.
[62] RD/Karimi, 507; RD/Thackston 1, 349; RD/Thackston2, 246.
[63] MP1, 344–5; MP/Cliff, 323; MP/Lathem, 329; MP/YC, v2, 479; RD/Karimi, 507; RD/Thackston1, 348–9; RD/Thackston2, 247.
[64] RD/Karimi, 507; RD/Thackston 1, 349; RD/Thackston2, 246.
[65] RD/Karimi, 633–6; RD/Thackston1, 436–8; RD/Thackston2, 309–10; Thomas T. Allsen, 'The Princes of the Left Hand', *AEMA*, 5 (1985), 21.
[66] RD/Karimi, 507; RD/Thackston1, 349; RD/Thackston2, 247.

The alliance did not occur until after Qonichi's death, undoubtedly abetted by his obesity.⁶⁷ Bayan Khan (1300–12), his eldest son, gained the throne after a civil war with his brother Mumkqiya. The conflict touched all parts of the Mongol Empire. Toqta Khan, the ruler of the White Horde, aided Bayan in defeating Mumkqiya. Soon, however, Bayan faced another challenge from his cousin Kupalak, supported by Qaidu and Du'a, to fracture the Blue Horde's alliance with the Yuan and Ilkhanate.

With Toqta distracted by his conflict with Noghai, Kupalak defeated Bayan. While Toqta Khan could not aid him directly, he appealed to other Jochids to legitimise him. Bayan also took advantage of Qonichi's diplomacy to co-ordinate efforts against Qaidu, which would also weaken Kupalak.⁶⁸ The Yuan victory over Qaidu at Qayaliq in 1301 led to Qaidu's death and the fracturing of the Ogodeid–Chaghatayid union. With incursions on multiple fronts, Chapar and Du'a agreed to the *Pax Mongolica* in 1304 and abandoned Kupalak, whom Bayan then defeated in 1304.

Unfortunately, with the death of Qaidu and the *Pax Mongolica* both the Chinese and Persian sources lost interest in the affairs of the Blue Horde. With the fragmentation of the Ogodeid and Chaghatayids, the Blue Horde acquired Otrar, Jand and other towns along the Syr Darya river. It is also apparent that the Blue Horde resumed its subordinate role in the Jochid Ulus. Most likely this was the price Bayan paid for Toqta's support against Kupalak. With Toqta's defeat of Noghai, neither Bayan nor Sasi Buqa (r. 1312–1320/21), Bayan's son and successor, could ignore the White Horde any longer. Toqta's successor and son, Ozbeg Khan, ensured that it continued.

The Golden Age

Several important events occurred during Ozbeg's reign (r. 1312–42), including more issues with Italian merchants but also the rise of Muscovy, yet the single most important event during Ozbeg's reign was his conversion to Islam. As with the conversion of many Mongols, Sufism played a role. According to the conversion narratives, which reflect myth as much as reality, Ozbeg converted when the Sufi known as Baba Tukles demonstrated his superior spiritual powers in magical combat against shamans. The shamans and Baba Tukles both underwent trials by fire, in which they stood in fire. While the shamans endured the heat for a while, Baba Tukles asked if they would put more wood on the fire as he was chilled. This and other events

---

[67] RD/Karimi, 507; RD/Thackston1, 349; RD/Thackston2, 247.
[68] RD/Karimi, 508–9, 678; RD/Thackston1, 349–50, 468–9; RD/Thackston2, 248, 332. Rashid al-Din refers to Bayan as Nayan.

convinced Ozbeg that Islam was superior to his native beliefs.⁶⁹ While the Baba Tukles story is appealing, the truth is rather less sensational. The official histories make no mention of Baba Tukles. It is alleged that Ozbeg converted to gain the support of an influential *noyan*, Qutlugh Temur, which allowed him to gain the throne.⁷⁰

Ozbeg's conversion followed the slow trend whereby the common Mongols gradually converted to Islam. The fact that a khan converted influenced further conversions, but rarely did they make the religion the state religion. Most of the claims of such, as with Ghazan, appear to be panegyrical interpretations by court historians demonstrating the piety of the ruler.⁷¹ Rather than a top-down conversion, in which the ruler converted and then the masses followed, conversion of the Mongols, it appears, involved a steady conversion of the commoners, and then the ruler gradually converting.

Ozbeg's conversion did not go unchallenged. His predecessor, Toqta, promoted Buddhism, much to the consternation of the Mamluks. Many of the nobility resented Ozbeg's adoption of Islam, concerned that he adopt *shariᶜa* and abandon the *yasa* of Chinggis Khan, a situation mirrored in both the Ilkhanate and the Chaghatayid Khanate. Their fears were sufficient for them to attempt a coup, but, as with Ghazan, Ozbeg held the loyalty of the rank-and-file soldiers, so the coup failed. Ozbeg did not institute a dramatic shift to the *shariᶜa* and use of the *yasa* continued, but increasingly Islamic law (Hanifi interpretation) was used in situations that the *yasa* did not cover. The fact that Hanifi interpretation permitted the consumption of *kumiss* certainly played a role.⁷²

As with most new converts, Ozbeg went through a zealous phase, although some of his actions may have been motivated by revenge against those who opposed him. Those who challenged him on the basis of his conversion were defeated and executed. The Buddhist clergy then also felt his wrath. The Christian population experienced momentary discomfort when Christians were ejected from the port of Soldaia in Crimea and perhaps elsewhere, with churches converted into mosques. Ozbeg relented and permitted the clergy to retain their tax exemptions while providing services for Catholic missionaries.⁷³ Ozbeg's sister, Konchek, married a Christian, Prince Yuri of

---

[69] Devin DeWeese, *Islamization and Native Religion in the Golden Horde* (Philadelphia, 1994), 90–125.
[70] Umari, 298; *Nikon*, v3, 97.
[71] DeWeese, *Islamization and Native Religion*, 95.
[72] IB1, 250–1; DeWeese, *Islamization and Native Religion*, 132, 206.
[73] M. Bil and A. C. Moule, 'De duabus epistolis Fratrum Minorum Tartariae Aquilonaris an. 1323', *Archivum franciscanum historicum* 16 (1923), 89–112; DeWeese, *Islamization and Native Religion*, 96–7.

Moscow, and was baptised into the Christian faith.[74] When Ibn Battuta visited the cities of Crimea and Sarai, he noted numerous Christian subjects as well as Christian, Muslim and even Jewish merchants from Andalusia.[75] Thus, while Ozbeg was a Muslim, many of his actions showed the flexibility one might expect from a Mongol prince, yet at the same time his actions were consistent with those of a Muslim ruler.

Ozbeg's new faith did not prevent him from warring against other Muslims. The war with the Ilkhanids was renewed when Ozbeg invaded the Ilkhanate in 1318, effectively ending the *Pax Mongolica*. While he sought to recover lost Jochid territory in Azerbaijan, it once again became a stalemate.

Mongols and Muscovy

The Russian principalities had recovered from the destruction of Batu's campaign and greatly benefited from commerce encouraged by the Mongol Empire. Furthermore, most of the Russian principalities adopted Mongol military methods in organisation and in equipping their soldiers, making them more capable of participating in the Jochids' wars. This, however, also made them more confident and resistant to Mongol demands. Due to the Russians' hatred of the Mongol *basqaqs* who collected taxes, riots often occurred whenever they appeared. As the Russians princes were responsible for protecting the *basqaq*, the riots placed the Russian princes in a tight spot. Failure to protect the *basqaq* often resulted in the arrival of a Mongol army and ensuing destruction. No city was too removed to avoid retribution. To control the Russian principalities and prevent any unification, the Jochid khans manipulated the princes by shifting favouritism.[76]

Prior to the reign of Ozbeg, the Mongols shifted the tax responsibilities to the Russian princes, permitting one to collect the taxes. In return, the prince kept a share of the collection, but a *daruga* (*daruqachi*) supervised him. This indirect approach was not necessarily due to revolts, but rather due to the administrative breakdown during the frequent civil wars within the Jochid Ulus.[77]

Gaining the *jarliq* to collect taxes was transformational for a prince. Moscow benefited the most. This began with the marriage of Konchek, Ozbeg's sister, to Prince Yuri of Moscow (r. 1303–25). With the prestige derived from the alliance, Yuri challenged Prince Mikhail of Tver's primacy among Russian princes. The alliance, however, did not work as well as Yuri

---

[74] *Nikon*, v. 3, 102–3.
[75] IB1, 251; IB2, 123.
[76] Charles J. Halperin, *Russia and the Golden Horde* (Bloomington, 1987), 53.
[77] Halperin, *Russia and the Golden Horde*, 37–41.

intended. Tver' had been a leading city prior to the Mongol invasion and still had strength, as Dmitri of Tver' defeated Yuri's army, capturing Konchek. She died in Tverian captivity in 1317.[78]

Perhaps, as retribution, Ozbeg Khan granted Yuri the *jarliq* to collect taxes in 1319. If a Russian principality was reluctant to pay its taxes, the Muscovite prince could call upon Mongol assistance to persuade them. Despite the unfortunate death of Konchek, Ozbeg's policy made Moscow the 'bad guy', alleviating tensions for the Mongols. Other princes could appeal to the khan against Moscow's transgressions, and he could intervene. Indeed, Yuri was to be placed on trial for embezzling tax collections, but Dmitri, Mikhail of Tver's son, murdered him in Sarai in 1325 before the trial occurred. Dmitri was later executed.[79] The policy of keeping the Russian princes divided worked well as long as the khan was in a position to intervene and ensure that none became a threat.

Moscow was unintentionally aided by the destruction of Tver'. In 1327, Ozbeg's relative, Shevkal, sought to rule Tver' directly and convert the citizens to Islam. A rebellion ensued. In addition to the Mongols who accompanied Shevkal, merchants from Sarai also died in the fighting. Ozbeg, accompanied by Prince Ivan I (r. 1328–40) of Moscow and other Rus' princes, sacked the city, leaving Moscow as the most powerful principality among the Rus'.[80]

A Plague on their House

Ozbeg Khan's long reign finally ended in 1342 and his son Tinibeg came to the throne. His brief reign began well enough, but his career ended abruptly with his sudden death in 1342, with him perhaps being murdered by his brother, Janibeg.[81] Janibeg's career peaked with the capture of Tabriz and the pastures of Azerbaijan in 1357. Jochid claims now were recognised, although Janibeg rationalised the conquest, at least to the Mamluks, in terms of Islamic kingship as members of the *ulema* fled from Azerbaijan to Sarai in the post-Ilkhanid chaos. According to Janibeg, he came to restore order.[82] The lustre of the victory was quickly tarnished as the Ilkhanate had collapsed in in 1335 with Abu Said's death; thus Janibeg defeated minor kingdoms and not the long-time rival of the Jochids.

Prior to this, however, Janibeg had numerous issues. One of the most important involved Italian merchants, both Venetians and Genoese. In 1343,

---

[78] *Nikon*, v3, 103.
[79] *Nikon*, v3, 117.
[80] *Nikon*, v3, 124–5.
[81] *Nikon*, v3, 150.
[82] Broadbridge, *Kingship and Ideology*, 161.

large-scale brawls erupted between the Christians and Muslims in Tana, which now housed both Venetians and Genoese. Janibeg quickly retaliated and the Venetians fled to Kaffa. Although rivals, the Genoese gave shelter to the Venetians even though the Mongols approached for a siege. The Genoese had improved Kaffa's fortifications since the Toqta's attack.

A Mongol siege was worrying, but the Genoese were not overly concerned, as they could abandon the city via the Black Sea, and they had destroyed a fledgling Jochid navy in 1345.[83] Although the Mongols had destroyed the city before, they permitted its restoration and resolved other matters diplomatically. Furthermore, the Mongols valued the Italians too much for complete destruction. It was in the best interests of all to resolve the matter peacefully. Nonetheless, the Mongols engaged in aggressive negotiations through siege warfare. The fact that the siege continued for two years gives some indication that the Mongols were not necessarily seeking to destroy the city. Meanwhile, the Genoese awaited favourable terms, such as the expansion of their trading privileges, but the siege took an unexpected turn when the Mongols began launching corpses into the city.[84]

There have been many terrifying epidemics throughout history – smallpox, Spanish Flu after the First World War, AIDS in the 1980s, and even Bieber fever. The most feared, however, has been the Bubonic Plague that ran rampant across Eurasia in the mid-fourteenth century, with cameo appearances thereafter. It affected all of the Mongol khanates, not to mention the rest of Eurasia. It undermined Mongol rule, regardless of location, on a number of levels. As the nomadic population was the basis of Mongol rule and the Mongols' military, the loss of life depleted their militaries. Although the total number of deaths among sedentary populations was much greater, the nomads had less ability to recover, whether among the Yuan, Chaghatayids or the Jochids. Furthermore, these deaths also disrupted their economies by wreaking havoc on trade routes. The siege of Kaffa was but one example.[85]

It is unclear whether the account of Mongols launching corpses into Kaffa is accurate. It is bizarre enough to be fiction, yet a pragmatic enough action to be accurate. If true, the Mongols loaded their trebuchets with bodies infected with the plague in order to get rid of them in the most efficient manner, after realising that those who washed the dead Muslim Mongols died as well as those who simply moved the shamanistic Mongols to the open steppes. The effect terrified the Genoese, who then fled Kaffa, taking the plague with them

---

[83] Ciociltan, *Mongols and the Black Sea Trade*, 210.
[84] Historia de Morbo, 17.
[85] Uli Schamiloglu, 'Preliminary Remarks on the Role of the Disease in the History of the Golden Horde', *CAS* 12 (1993), 447–57.

as they left the Black Sea and bringing it to the Mamluk Sultanate and, most famously, to Europe. Due to the effects of the plague and his inability to control the sea, Janibeg also had to give up his assault.[86]

Bubonic Plague

Caused by the bacterium *Yersinia pestis*, the Bubonic Plague spread throughout Eurasia, travelling on the trade routes made secure by the Mongol Empire. Scholars estimate that the death toll ranged from one third to one half of the total population of Europe, Asia and North Africa between 1346 and 1353. In some areas, it was even higher. The primary transmitter of the disease is thought to have been fleas inhabiting rats, marmots and other animals, which then bit humans and regurgitated the bacteria into the bloodstream. The bacteria infected the lymph nodes and formed buboes in the neck, groin and armpit regions. While the origins of the plague remain disputed, it is certain that Kaffa was one of the major nexus points, although it is unclear whether the Mongols launched infected bodies into the city. While the death toll was staggering in all areas, the impact of the plague dramatically changed the world, with a collapse of trade routes, social systems and even empires throughout Afro-Eurasia.

With the Italian issue was temporarily resolved through the intervention of the plague, other merchants, including other Italians, attempted to fill the vacuum left by the Genoese and Venetians as Janibeg embargoed the two cities. The embargo failed as the combined fleets of Venice and Genoa blockaded the Black Sea coasts until Janibeg restored their trading privileges in 1347, including the rebuilding of Tana.[87] Both Kaffa and Tana recovered from the Mongols and the plague and resumed their commercial importance within the empire.

Islam continued to flourish during the reign of Janibeg. Like Berke and Ozbeg, Janibeg favoured the Hanafi *madhhab*, although the *yasa* continued beside *shariʿa* among the nomads. Janibeg was less religiously tolerant than his father. While the Russians and Italians could practise their own religion, he did not welcome this.[88] The state promulgated Islam. The religious tensions made the divide between the steppes and the Russian forests even greater.

---

[86] Ciociltan, *Mongols and the Black Sea Trade*, 213; *Nikon*, v3, 157.
[87] Ciociltan, *Mongols and the Black Sea Trade*, 213–14.
[88] *Nikon*, v3, 153–4.

Janibeg's reign, although fraught with crises, continued as an era of strength and relative stability for the Jochid Khanate. It proved ephemeral, however. Although Janibeg captured Tabriz, he died while returning to Sarai in 1357. His son, Berdibeg, who remained in Tabriz as its governor, hastened back to Sarai to take the throne. Almost immediately, Tabriz and Azerbaijan were lost to the Jochids as the Jalayirids and Chobanids, successors to the Ilkhanids, fought to control them.[89] Berdibeg had little time to consider retaking the region as rivals assassinated him in 1359, plunging the Jochid Khanate into anarchy.

The War of Five Contenders

With Berdibeg's death, internecine feuds left the Jochid Khanate leaderless and drifting. Kulpa killed his brother Berdibeg in 1359, but then their brother Nawruz killed Kulpa in 1360. Nawruz ruled as the last Batuid khan until 1361, when he died. In the east, Berdibeg's death permitted the Blue Horde to end its subservient position, although, as in the west, a series of coups and counter-coups occurred before stability came in 1366.

The new Blue Khan, Mubarak Khwaja Khan (1366–8), minted his own coins in the city of Sighnaq, revealing his independence from Sarai. Most notably, Mubarak Khwaja Khan and his immediate predecessors were not of Orda's line but descended from Toqa-Temur, Jochi's thirteenth son. Meanwhile in the west, Qidyr, a descendant of neither Berke nor Batu but Shayban, ascended the throne and marked the rise of the eastern Jochids. Intrigue and assassination accompanied a list of rulers after Qidyr. Orda Malik (1361), Temur Khwaja (1361), Murid (1361–4), Aziz (1363–5), Bolat (1365, 1367,1369), Asan (1368–9), and Mehmet (1370–7) all ruled briefly and without significance, except perhaps in demonstrating that Muslim names became increasing popular among the Jochid khans, further marking the deeply rooted Islamic identity of the Jochid Khanate. Nonetheless, one may wonder whether much of the turbulence throughout the Jochid Khanate resulted not only from the intrigues of kingmakers and politics in general, but also from a struggle over which line of Jochids had true legitimacy.[90]

Mehmet's death in 1370, however, triggered a larger affair that affected much of Eurasia: the War of Five Contenders.[91] The war lasted over thirty years and could be considered a series of wars rather than a single affair. Yet,

---

[89] See Patrick Wing, *The Jalayirids: Dynastic State Formation in the Mongol Middle East* (Edinburgh, 2016).
[90] *Nikon*, v3, 186–9.
[91] I believe my late mentor at Indiana University, Larry W. Moses, coined this term.

it is proper to consider it a single war, as two participants were involved in most of the struggle and ultimately all of those involved possessed the same goal – to control the Jochid Khanate.

The first participant was not a Chinggisid, but a member of the *qarachu*. Mamai, a commander and kingmaker, became the real power behind the throne after Berdibeg's death and played the role of kingmaker in the fashion of Noghai. He could not claim the throne as he lacked Chinggisid ancestry, but he was not above selecting and disposing of rulers in order to strengthen his own authority. Mamai was recognised as the ruler, but not with the title of khan. A Chinggisid sat on the throne, but was khan in title only. The arrangement was understood not only in the steppe, but also among the Rus'.[92] Mamai found a willing partner among the Rus' in Mikhail II of Tver' (r. 1368–99), whom he made Grand Prince of Vladimir.[93]

With the death of Mehmet in 1370, Mamai ceased this pretence and began to rule the western portion of the Jochid realm outright.[94] His seizure of the throne had an unintended effect – Moscow stopped paying tribute. Mamai first attempted to persuade Prince Dmitri of Moscow to pay, but to no avail. Dmitri refused, contending that Mamai was not a true khan (a Chinggisid) and thus an illegitimate usurper. It should be noted that this hyperbole probably entered the sources later in order to justify Dmitri's later actions.[95] Nonetheless, it is clear that Dmitri had paid tribute to Mamai, but not the tribute that Moscow had paid during Janibeg's reign. Furthermore, Dmitri and Mamai had, at one point, agreed to a lesser sum. Possibly, Mamai did this in order to gain Dmitri's compliance when Mamai ruled with a puppet khan.[96]

Mamai responded by sending a punitive force, which Dmitri defeated in 1373. Mamai retaliated and defeated Muscovite forces in 1376. Dmitri remained unbowed and the war escalated. In 1378, Dmitri defeated Mamai's army (commanded by Begich Noyan) on the Vozha River, but not decisively. Seeking to eliminate the Muscovites once and for all, Mamai met Dmitri's army on the field of Kulikovo in 1380. The battle of Kulikovo had wide-ranging implications with Dmitri's victory over Mamai. Mamai's prestige plummeted. Although Mamai did not die in the battle, his defeat led to a cascading array of problems.

---

[92] *Nikon*, v3, 261.
[93] Halperin, *Russia and the Golden Horde*, 55; *Nikon*, v3, 211.
[94] *Nikon*, v3, 267.
[95] Charles J. Halperin, *The Golden Horde*, 98–9; Donald Ostrowski, *Muscovy and the Mongols* (Cambridge, 2002), 156.
[96] *Nikon*, v3, 272.

The Genoese and Venetians in the Crimea ceased to pay. Furthermore, Mamai's defeat ended his credibility for most of the Aq Orda. Muscovy, however, enjoyed a rise in prestige in some circles, although a number of rival princes remained wary of Dmitri's intentions as well as those of the defeated (but not destroyed) Mamai. The Russian sources depict an epic victory, which threw off the oppression of the Mongol Yoke and liberated Russia. Unfortunately for Dmitri that was not quite true, although Moscow did enjoy a brief period of independence from tribute. In truth, Dmitri benefited little as his army was later mauled by Mamai's Lithuanian allies, who arrived late to the battle.[97] Furthermore, events to the east dictated a different outcome from the liberation of Russia.

The second contender for control of Jochid realm was Urus Khan (r. 1368–78), the ruler of the Koke Orda. He began to consolidate power, not only in the eastern portions of the Jochid realm. Urus sought to take advantage of the disorder in the west, even before Mamai's defeat. He did have, however, an obstacle to overcome in the form of a third contender, Toqtamysh, another Toqa-Temurid. After Urus Khan defeated Toqtamysh in their struggle over the Blue Horde, Toqtamysh fled south and sought refuge in Mawarannahr, which now was under the control of the Amir Timur, also known as Timur-i Leng or Tamerlane.[98]

Timur's involvement in Jochid affairs demonstrates how the post-dissolution khanates cannot be studied in isolation. Just as the Jochid Ulus reeled from conflict, so did the Chaghatayid domains. Qazghan, the *qarachu* ruling Mawarannahr, died in 1358. The Chaghatayids restored dominion thereafter, with Tughluq Temur's son, Ilyas, serving as viceroy in Mawarannahr. Chaghatayid rule ended in 1365, with Ilyas driven out by Amir Husayn, a grandson of Qazghan, and his ally, Timur, who had started his career in the Ilyas' service.[99] With the withdrawal of the Chaghatayids, Timur and Husayn fought, no longer bound by a common threat. In 1370, Timur emerged victorious. Although lame on one side of his body (the result of a raid in his youth), Timur was the consummate strategist, both on the battlefield and in the palace.[100] He achieved the independence of Mawarannahr from the Chaghatayids, but did not attempt to claim the throne for himself. Instead, he ruled with a series of Chinggisid princes on the throne while he wielded real power, as did Noghai and Mamai. With Timur now in power, Toqtamysh became his protégé. With Timur's support, Toqtamysh defeated

---

[97] Ostrowski, *Muscovy and the Mongols*, 157.
[98] Khwandamir, 238.
[99] Khwandamir, 225.
[100] Khwandamir, 226.

Urus in 1378, with Toqtamysh becoming the khan.[101] Toqtamysh also had the good fortune that a number of *qarachu* families supported him.[102] While Toqtamysh (r. 1378–98) consolidated his hold over the Blue Horde, Mamai was defeated at Kulikovo.

The confrontation between Mamai and Toqtamysh occurred in 1380 at the second battle of the Kalka River.[103] Here Toqtamysh acted independently of Timur and defeated Mamai. With his second major victory, Toqtamysh rapidly became one of the most capable generals of the age. Mamai again escaped destruction, seeking refuge in Crimea with the Genoese while he licked his wounds. Mamai found no succour in Kaffa. Bereft of support, he was robbed and murdered in 1382.[104]

With Mamai defeated, Toqtamysh then dealt with the former vassals of the Jochid Khanate. Initially, the Russians resisted, but with the destruction of several towns and fortresses most of the Russian cities quickly submitted. Toqtamysh sacked Moscow in Dmitri Donskoi's absence. Toqtamysh was a firm believer in the prerogatives of the *altan urugh* and submission was expected. He razed Moscow and restored Mongol sovereignty over the Jochid domains.[105]

In addition to internal disorder, Toqtamysh had to deal with interlopers from outside the empire. The primary threat, besides Timur, were the Lithuanians. Lithuania began as a small power that primarily resisted the expansion of the Teutonic Knight state in Prussia and the Baltic. A marriage alliance with Poland, which also became alarmed at the expansion of the Teutonic Knights, not only increased the strength of Lithuania, but also brought it into the Catholic fold in 1386.[106]

When not at war with the Teutonic Knights, Poland-Lithuania expanded to the south and east, at the expense of the Jochid Khanate. Prior to the tumultuous era after Janibeg, the khan made numerous punitive raids, often accompanied by Rus' princes, against the Lithuanians in retaliation. Still, in periods of weak khans, some of the western Russian cities submitted to Poland-Lithuania; others submitted when Jochids, such as Ozbeg Khan, focused on their wars with the Ilkhanids. With the turmoil following Berdibeg's death, Lithuania expanded into much of modern Belarus and Ukraine. In

---

[101] Khwandamir, 238.
[102] I. M. Mirgaleev, 'Succession to the Throne in the Golden Horde', *GHR* 5, no. 2 (2017), 348.
[103] *Nikon*, v3, 302–3.
[104] *Nikon*, v3, 303.
[105] *Nikon*, v4, 2–12.
[106] *Nikon*, v4, 22; also see S. C. Rowell, *Lithuania Ascending* (Cambridge, 1994).

1362, Algirdas (r. 1345–77), Grand Duke of Lithuania, defeated Murad Khan (r. 1362–4) and acquired Chernigov, Kiev and other western cities. Lithuania's support for Mamai may have been in exchange for territorial concessions. Toqtamysh, however, reversed this trend. In 1382, Toqtamysh soundly defeated Lithuania at Poltava and reclaimed lost Jochid territory.

With the Jochid Khanate now restored and a Chinggisid established on the throne in Sarai, what would Toqtamysh do next? The only task that remained was to reclaim Jochid territory to the south, renewing a struggle that began in 1260. For Toqtamysh, the task was made more difficult as Timur had expanded into Azerbaijan. Additionally, Khwarazm broke away from Jochid dominance during Mamai's tenure as ruler. Timur brought Khwarazm into his sphere of control in 1372–3, formally annexing it in 1379.[107] While Toqtamysh was one of the great military leaders of the era, Timur was the greatest and became the fourth contender for Jochid dominion. Thus, in 1387 began a war with both men attempting to restore the Mongol Empire, but with different approaches.[108] Timur claimed he was restoring Ilkhanid rights.[109] Indeed, the territories he ruled in the Middle East were Ilkhanid. While his armies ventured beyond those borders, he did not establish rule in Syria or western Anatolia.

Toqtamysh, as a Chinggisid and a Jochid, had legitimate claims to Azerbaijan as well as some territories in Mawarannahr. He probably also chafed at the non-Chinggisid Timur's success. Although not a Chinggisid, Timur claimed kinship to Chinggis Khan through the mythical sons of Alan Go'a, the mother of the Mongols.[110] Finally, in addition to the Chinggisids whom Timur kept on the throne, he married a Chinggisid princess and thus claimed the title of *guregen* or son-in-law (of Chinggis Khan). Thus, restoring the empire was a natural process for his position. Yet, Timur's non-Chinggisid lineage was an issue for Toqtamysh, particularly when Timur conquered Azerbaijan from the Jalayirids, one of the successors to the Ilkhanids, in 1385–6. Toqtamysh saw this as a usurpation of Jochid prerogatives, triggering war.[111]

Timur defeated Toqtamysh when he invaded Azerbaijan in 1387, but no reconciliation occurred between mentor and his former protégé. While

---

[107] Khwandamir, 235–6, 239.
[108] For differing views see David O. Morgan, 'The Empire of Tamerlane: An Unsuccessful Re-run of the Mongol Empire?', in J. R. Maddicott and D. M. Palliser (eds), *The Medieval State: Essays Presented to James Campbell* (London, 2000), 233–41; Beatrice F. Manz, 'The Empire of Tamerlane as an Adaptation of the Mongol Empire', *JRAS* 26 (2016), 281–92.
[109] Manz, 'Empire of Tamerlane', 286.
[110] *SHM*, §46; Khwandamir, 221.
[111] Khwandamir, 243.

Timur was still in western Iran in 1387, Toqtamysh invaded Mawarannahr along with the *qarachu* Qamar al-Din leading Chaghatayid forces.[112] Upon receiving the news Timur hurried back, but Toqtamysh abandoned Mawarannahr before he arrived. Toqtamysh invaded again the following year. Timur defeated the Jochids and razed Khwarazm, which had aided the Jochids. Timur, determined to end the issue, crossed the Syr Darya River in pursuit but found that the Jochid army had dispersed across the steppes, making it impossible to follow.

Although Mawarannahr was secure for the moment, it remained vulnerable, as was Azerbaijan. Timur resolved to end Toqtamysh's threat and invaded the Koke Orda in January 1391. This was a precarious strategy as his horses were not in peak condition and he ran the risk that snow and winter storms would eliminate pasture. The Jochid army proved elusive and it took four months before Timur's scouts found signs of Toqtamysh. Timur finally caught up with the Jochid khan at Kunduzcha, near modern Orenburg, in early June 1391 and defeated him in one of the largest battles of the age.[113] Toqtamysh escaped and fled. Nonetheless, his defeat permitted Timur to place another, and hopefully less bellicose, Jochid on the throne in the form of Temur Qutlugh (r. 1391–3). Upon his return, he allowed Khwarazm to be rebuilt.[114]

Timur was well aware that he could not annex the Jochid Khanate, just as he could not annex Moghulistan from the Chaghatayids. Due to his non-Chinggisid lineage, the Chinggisid princes there would never accept his suzerainty.[115] It was one thing to rule over the sedentary regions of Mawarannahr and the former Ilkhanate, both of which had grown accustomed to non-Chinggisids as well as Chinggisid puppets, but the nomads of the steppes maintained their proud Chinggisid heritage and considered it the sole indicator of supreme political authority. Thus, as he did with the Chaghatayids of Moghulistan, Timur demonstrated his military supremacy and hoped that it would be sufficient to keep them in line. Furthermore, Timur used large numbers of Chaghatayid nomads in his army and the promise of plunder aided him in maintaining their loyalty to him as a general if not as their king. His record of fulfilling those promises only bolstered his credentials.

Though defeated, Toqtamysh remained resilient. He quickly assembled new support and overthrew Temur Qutlugh in 1393. Toqtamysh realised that

---

[112] Khwandamir, 244–5.
[113] Khwandamir, 247–50.
[114] Khwandamir, 245; *Nikon*, v4, 47.
[115] Manz, 'The Empire of Tamerlane', 286–8; Manz, *The Rise and Rule of Tamerlane* (Cambridge, 1989), 13–14.

Timur could not be defeated easily. He formed an alliance with the Mamluks and Ottomans. For the Mamluks, Timur's conquest of Iraq brought him to the borders of their domains in Syria. Furthermore, the Mamluks knew the dire threat of Timur from the Jalayirid and Qara Qoyunlu refugees who had sought Mamluk protection after Timur conquered Baghdad and northern Iraq. Meanwhile, Timur's presence in Azerbaijan and eastern Anatolia threatened Ottoman control of the Turkic beyliks in Anatolia.[116] As the threat of Timur loomed large, all aligned with Toqtamysh.

The alliance, however, was not fully functional as the Mamluks and Ottomans were wary of each other. Furthermore, they lacked the means of bringing their power against Timur due to his wily genius. In 1395, he marched west and showed every intention of invading Mamluk domains, but then suddenly dashed north to invade the Kipchak steppe through Derbend in the Caucasus Mountains. Toqtamysh rode south from Sarai to meet him at the Terek River. Timur once again defeated Toqtamysh in April 1395. With the Jochid army defeated and dispersed, Timur now roamed freely through the western Jochid domains. He pursued Toqtamysh north. Although the latter fled and escaped Timur once again, Timur raided the Russian principalities extensively. He then sacked Tana and Sarai.[117] As a result, Timur destroyed not only Sarai the city, but also the archives and chancelleries of the Jochid Khanate, leaving us largely dependent on outside sources for our understanding of the Golden Horde. While historians may lament this historic loss (and we do!), the sack of Sarai sounded the death knell for the Jochid Khanate. With the destruction of Sarai as well as Tana, Timur destroyed the commerce of the region. It never fully recovered. Afterwards, merchants avoided trade via the overland route through Jochid territory and ventured through the more secure regions of Timur's empire. In effect, Timur rerouted the Silk Road through his domains while destroying Toqtamysh's power base and his legitimacy as khan. Timur also left insurance to prevent Toqtamysh from challenging him again, while also inadvertently creating the fifth contender, Edigu, a descendant of Noghai.[118] Edigu did not rule, but he became the muscle that supported Timur's Jochid proxy khan, the newly restored Timur Qutlugh.

After Timur departed, Toqtamysh attempted to resume power, emerging from his refuge in Lithuania, where descendants of his forces still dwell today. In Timur's absence, Toqtamysh engaged in warfare with Temur Qutlugh Khan and Edigu. Although Timur's destruction of the trading cities also

---

[116] Wing, *Jalayirids*, 147–75.
[117] Khwandamir, 256; *Nikon*, v4, 94–100.
[118] Vasary, 'The Jochid Realm', 84; Ciociltan, *Mongols and the Black Sea Trade*, 113–14.

weakened Timur Qutlugh's position, Edigu's military prowess and Timur's subsidies overcame Toqtamysh and his Lithuanian allies in 1399. Timur Qutlugh remained the Jochid khan until 1400 when his cousin Shadibeg (r.1400–7) succeeded him, still under the tutelage of Edigu.[119] Toqtamysh, who had fled to Siberia, found Timur's pardon; the latter hedged his bets that Toqtamysh might be a useful pawn against Edigu. Toqtamysh, however, died in battle against Shadibeg near the city of Tumen (modern Tiumen) in 1406.[120]

Although Timur's career continued for another decade after the Battle of the Terek River, his military career largely ceased to involve the Jochid Khanate. His influence, however, lingered even after he died at Otrar in 1405, preparing to invade Ming China. Although Shadibeg was the khan, Edigu, Timur's protégé, was the true power in the western part of the khanate and the fifth contender for the Jochid dominions. After Temur Qutlugh died in 1400, Edigu, like his ancestor Noghai, was able to exert more influence over Shadibeg and his successor, Pulad (1407–12). In addition to maintaining order in the steppes, Edigu ensured that the Russian principalities remained vassals and that the Lithuanians were kept at bay.[121] Although Toqtamysh's son Kadir Berdi killed Edigu in 1419, Edigu's legend grew among the nomads and he became an important folk hero to later generations.[122]

The Jochid Khanate continued, but never recovered from Timur's depredations. It slowly dissolved into other khanates, such as Crimea, Kazan (northern Volga), Astrakhan (southern Volga), the Noghai Orda (between the Black and Caspian Seas), Sibir (centred near Tobolsk) and the Shaybanids (much of Kazakhstan), the Kasimov (a vassal of Muscovy), and the Great Khanate, which was the titular seat of the Jochid khan. In reality, the subsections acted increasingly independently, with Muscovy becoming more of an equal, until it too became independent with the defeat of Ahmad Khan of the Great Horde in 1480 at the 'Battle' of the Ugra River. Very little fighting occurred, but a great deal of posturing did.[123] The fact that Ahmad Khan was unable to defeat or gain Prince Ivan III's submission sealed Ahmad's doom. Noghai nomads killed Ahmad Khan afterwards and the Jochid Khanate disappeared, although its successors lasted well into the eighteenth century before succumbing to their former subjects to the north. While the Jochid

---

[119] *Nikon*, v4, 130.
[120] 'Toktamish', *EI²*.
[121] *Nikon*, v4, 116–19.
[122] 'Toktamish', *EI²*.
[123] Halperin, *Russia and the Golden Horde*, 70–2; *Nikon*, v5, 211–15.

Ulus disappeared, its successors still linked themselves to its legacy, even when subservient to other powers, such as Muscovy.[124]

Islam and the Jochid State

The Jochid transition to an Islamic empire was curious and gradual. A sizeable Christian population existed, particularly of the Orthodox variety, but it was largely confined to the Rus' cities and Greeks in the cities of the Black Sea. Additionally, Christians existed in the steppes among the Kipchak and Alans. Armenian and Georgians were also present in some of the cities, often as merchants, but perhaps there were some missionaries as well.[125] Even Catholic missionaries were active, as noted previously. Curiously, unlike with the Ilkhanids, there is little evidence that Nestorians influenced the state. Nonetheless, in the early Jochid state some members of the elite were Christians.[126]

Yet, while this Christian population existed, Islam had firm roots as well. Bulghar had been a Muslim island along the Volga River for centuries and, if William of Rubruck is to be believed, isolation had not diminished Bulghar's ardour.[127] Khwarazm proper (the territory just south of the Aral Sea) was also a Muslim centre and was regaining its commercial importance after being destroyed by Chinggis Khan's armies. While Berke became the first Muslim ruler, Sartaq had been the first Christian khan (allegedly). Yet, many khans who followed them often did not subscribe to either religion. Indeed, if they preferred a world religion it tended to be Buddhism; even then, their proclivities fit with the traditional mode of Inner Asian religious tolerance as Buddhism seems to have only entered the Jochid territories because of the Mongol arrival.

The Islamisation of the Jochid Ulus began with Berke, as he began to fuse the legitimacy of Chinggisid lineage with the role of a Muslim sultan by adopting ideas of Islamic kingship, although not to the extent of Ghazan in the Ilkhanate.[128] His alliance with the Mamluks was rooted in their shared faith as well as strategic interests. In this, the Mamluks were the senior partner

---

[124] Uli Schamiloglu, 'The *Umdet Ul-Ahbar* and the Turkic Narrative Sources for the Golden Horde and the Later Golden Horde', in Hasan B. Paksoy (ed.), *Central Asian Monuments* (Istanbul, 1992) 85–90.

[125] Alemany, 147–9, 153–4, 159, 239, 256, 258; Bridia, 78–9; Benedict, 137; Benedict/Dawson, 80; Rubruc, 191–2, 209; Rubruck/Dawson, 110, 124; Rubruck/Jackson, 102, 126; IB1, 247; IB2, 120.

[126] Uli Schamiloglu, 'The Islamic High Culture of the Golden Horde', in Andras J. E. Bodrogligeti (ed.), *The Golden Cycle* (Sahibqiran, 2002), 201–2.

[127] Rubruc, 212; Rubruck/Dawson, 126; Rubruck/Jackson, 131.

[128] Broadbridge, *Kingship and Ideology*, 10, 27.

in terms of religion and, as Anne Broadbridge has demonstrated, 'role models in the system of thought and belief that was Islam, which helped the khans think about their sovereignty in new ways and justify their oppositions to other Chingizids [sic]'.[129] That being said, considering the Jochids' interests in Azerbaijan and the view of Hulegu as an usurper, one might wonder if the Jochids also played the Islam card simply to maintain ties with the Mamluks, as the alliance continued even when infidels sat on the Jochid throne. Additionally, Berke cemented ties with the Mamluk Sultanate by emphasising that his war with Hulegu was based on liberating *Dar al-Islam*.[130] From Berke's point of view, their shared religion also made it easier for Baybars to submit to Mongol rule.[131] While it is doubtful whether Baybars intended to submit, he at least could adopt some ironic consolidation with King Louis IX of France, who had made the same mistake in the past. Thus, while Berke may have viewed Baybars as a subject, Baybars viewed their relationship as an alliance.

Despite the rhetoric of *jihad*, Islam had little to do with Jochid–Ilkhanid hostilities. While individuals may have viewed the war as a *jihad*, it was quite impossible for non-Muslims to view it in the same way. They may, however, have viewed it as holy war in the sense that the Huleguids contravened the *yasa*, but really it was a war over territory. As Professor Amitai has demonstrated, 'no common strategy was ever developed against the Mongols of Iran. In addition, we have attempted to show that the Jochid–Ilkhanid conflict developed without Mamluk interference.'[132] While Jochid–Mamluk relations came to naught militarily, they did have an impact economically and religiously. If nothing else, Berke was no longer isolated religiously.

While conversion to Islam remained a personal event, albeit one with increasing popularity, Tode-Mongke began the shift to an Islamic empire. He requested banners (including Caliphal) and an Islamic name from Sultan Qalawun. Tode-Mongke also informed the Mamluk Sultan that he planned to implement the *shariʿa* in the Jochid realm, although this appears to have been unfulfilled.[133] Tode-Mongke clearly viewed the Mamluk Sultanate as the model Muslim state and sought its approval for his own transformation into an Islamic ruler. In essence, he was proving that he, and not the Ilkhan Teguder, was the true Muslim ruler among the Mongols. Additionally, he

---

[129] Broadbridge, *Kingship and Ideology*, 51.
[130] Broadbridge, *Kingship and Ideology*, 53–4.
[131] Broadbridge, *Kingship and Ideology*, 58; Anne F. Broadbridge, 'Mamluk Legitimacy and the Mongols: The Reigns of Baybars and Qalawun', *Mamluk Studies Review* 5 (2001), 101.
[132] Amitai, Preiss, *Mongols and Mamluks*, 90–1.
[133] Broadbridge, *Kingship and Ideology*, 62.

adopted the title *padshah-i Islam* (Emperor of Islam), although one suspects that Sultan Qalawun would have disapproved.[134]

Whereas Tole Buqa was a Muslim, Toqta's religious inclinations appear to have been more traditional, with no one being wholly certain of them. It was said by some that he was baptised and died a Christian; meanwhile Muslim sources indicated that he was an idolator (meaning Buddhist, usually), although he showed affinity with Muslims.[135] What is significant, however, is that Toqta felt no compulsion to convert, even though the Muslim Noghai handed him the throne. Clearly, while Islam was growing in religious and cultural significance among the Jochids, it had not become politically necessary.

By the reign of Ozbeg Khan, Islam appears to have been the dominant religion among the nomads. With the exception of a period of time after Ozbeg's conversion, his adoption of Islam did not end Mongol religious tolerance, although Buddhists were targeted, perhaps because they were not deemed 'People of the Book'.[136] Nonetheless, Islam took firm root, as noted by Ibn Battuta, who visited the Jochid realms during Ozbeg's reign.[137] Yet, with the number of mosques, madrasas and khanqahs in Sarai and New Sarai, it is clear that momentum and support for Islam appeared much earlier and were not an overnight occurrence. This suggests that the Mongol elite (*altan urugh* and *qarachu*) provided patronage for building. Additionally, noble women continued to endow religious buildings, much as they had done since the *Yeke Monggol Ulus* period.[138]

As with the Ilkhanate, the entrance of Islam into the lives of the Mongols did not necessarily change fundamental aspects of their lives. For instance, *airagh* remained very much part of their lives, even by the reign of Ozbeg Khan.[139] Women still enjoyed greater equality and freedom of movement.[140] For instance, Ozbeg's wife Bayalun Khatun, a daughter of the Byzantine Emperor Andronikos III Palaiologos (r. 1328–41), returned to Constantinople to give birth. While she was accompanied by a suitable retinue, there is no evidence that a male relative accompanied her. The fact that Ibn Battuta had a number of audiences with her also demonstrates her liberty, which he noticed. This is even more notable since not only was Bayalun

---

[134] Broadbridge, *Kingship and Ideology*, 62.
[135] Jackson, *Mongols and the West*, 272–3.
[136] Schamiloglu, 'Islamic High Culture', 203.
[137] IB1, 247–66; IB2, 119–30.
[138] IB1, 280; IB2, 139.
[139] IB1, 250; IB2, 120.
[140] IB1, 253–7; IB2, 123–6.

not a Mongol, but she was not a Christian either, at least while within the Jochid Ulus. Thus, while Bayalun converted to Islam, she embraced Mongol norms, rather than Muslim practices. Bayalun displayed a savvy that allowed her transition from one role to another – a Muslim to her husband and a dutiful Christian to her father.[141] She also played a key role in Ozbeg's rise to power after the death of her previous husband, Toqta.[142] The marriage of Ozbeg to Bayalun also demonstrates the facility of the Mongols in adapting Islam to their own cultural norms – one might even suggest it was a fusion of *yasa* and *shariᶜa*.

As Islam does not permit levirate marriage, as was customary among the Mongols, as a Muslim Ozbeg should not have married Bayalun, one of his father's wives. As she was not Ozbeg's birth mother, their marriage *per* Mongol custom was acceptable. In order to permit it, a *faqih* or Muslim jurist had to find a loophole. This *faqih* legitimised the marriage as Bayalun's previous husband (Toqta) had been a *kafir* or infidel. Thus, in his eyes she was never truly married in the eyes of God.[143]

Another curious aspect of Jochid Islam was the use of mamluks.[144] Although the mamluk institution had been in use since the eighth century, most mamluks came from the nomadic people. While the Seljuks had used mamluks, the court had become more sedentary and wished for a more reliable element than the tribal component of their armies. While the Jochid khans possessed mamluks in addition to normal household slaves, their numbers are unclear, as was their ethnicity. Still, the adoption of the mamluk institution demonstrates not only a significant shift from nomadic norms, but also a conscious adoption of Islamic institutions.

The other transformation was the end of Mamluk religious superiority. While the Jochids viewed their political legitimacy as greater due to their Chinggisid lineage, the Mamluks, via their control of Mecca and Medina as well as via having the Caliph reside in Cairo, were clearly the senior members in religion, no matter how shaky the Mamluk sultans may have viewed their own religious credentials as being.[145] Ozbeg Khan, however, altered this. When Muhammad al-Nasir sought a Chinggisid bride, negotiations almost collapsed before Tulunbay Khatun became his wife. Additionally, Shaykh Nuᶜman (a Sufi favourite of Ozbeg's) accompanied Tulunbay Khatun in 1320. Ozbeg also demanded an enormous dowry, suggesting that the

---

[141] IB1, 266–70; IB2, 128–30.
[142] DeWeese, *Islamization and Native Religion*, 118.
[143] DeWeese, *Islamization and Native Religion*, 118–19.
[144] IB1, 251; IB2, 123.
[145] Mona Hassan, *Longing for the Lost Caliphate* (Princeton, 2016), 71–83.

marriage (the first Chinggisid *khatun* married to a Mamluk sultan) was not a continuation of the Jochid–Mamluk alliance, but rather the securing of a vassal.[146] The latter may have been necessary, as Muhammad al-Nasir had amiable relations with the Ilkhan Abu Saʿid. Although Professor Broadbridge asserts that Ozbeg continued to acknowledge Sultan Muhammad's senior position in terms of religion, his frustrations with Sultan Muhammad with regard to military alliances, Muhammad's insult towards Shaykh Nuʿman, who was not permitted to build a *khanqah* in Jerusalem, and Muhammad's own treatment of Tulunbay (including a divorce), diminished the Mamluk Sultan's standing as an ideal Muslim ruler.[147] At the same time, it may also have raised Ozbeg's own standing.

Missionary activity by Sufis existed during the era of Ozbeg Khan. As Berke was converted (or at least taught) by a Sufi, it seems likely that Sufis had been active in the Jochid Ulus previously as well.[148] It is difficult to believe that if the Mongols permitted Catholic missionaries from outside their empire they would prevent native missionaries. Yet, one must not attribute the conversion of the Jochids solely to Sufi activity, as monocausal explanations rarely hold water. As time went by, not only were missionaries active, but the Jochid Ulus had sufficient educational institutions to produce their own clergy and members of the *ulema*. These came not only from older bastions of Islam like Khwarazm and Urgench, but also from Sarai and New Sarai.[149] Sufis, the prestige of Islamic culture, the influence of Muslim merchants and the desire to find other means of political legitimisation beyond the Chinggisid lineage all played a role in the transformation of the Jochid Ulus into an Islamic empire. And while scholars may quibble over the definition of an Islamic empire, they should never forget that the Rus' subjects within the Jochid Ulus certainly viewed the Jochids after Ozbeg as Muslims.

---

[146] Broadbridge, *Kingship and Ideology*, 134.
[147] Broadbridge, *Kingship and Ideology*, 133–7.
[148] Schamiloglu, 'Islamic High Culture', 205.
[149] Schamilolgu, 'Islamic High Culture', 206.

12

Anxiety and Accommodation

Islam's relationship with the Mongol was rarely simple or well-defined, and was frequently marked by anxiety and accommodation, even after many Mongols converted to Islam. During the Khwarazmian War, after capturing Bukhara Chinggis Khan made one of the most memorable and frightening speeches in history. He ascended the *minbar* at the Friday Mosque in 1221 and said, 'O People, know that you have committed great sins, and that the great ones among you have committed these sins. If you ask me what proof I have for these words, I say it is because I am the punishment of God. If you had not committed great sins, God would not have sent a punishment like me upon you.'[1]

A powerful and dramatic speech made by a terrifying figure at the pulpit. When reading this passage in Juwayni, one must question whether or not Chinggis Khan actually uttered these words. For someone with limited contact with Islam, Juwayni's explanation fits quite patently into Islamic thought, particularly regarding the legitimisation of authority and a fatalistic explanation of why bad things happen. Yet did Chinggis Khan actually say this? Or was it a simply a method by which medieval Muslims rationalised the violence that upturned *Dar al-Islam*? Certainly, other writers wrote in similar vein, recognising that the Mongols threatened the Islamic world as a menace like no other. Other motifs were soon attached to the Mongol invasion, transforming the destruction from an expanding empire into an apocalyptic nightmare; nor was Juwayni alone in his penitential response to the Mongol invasion.[2]

Muslims were not the only group that viewed the Mongols as divine

---

[1] Juvaini/Boyle, 105; Juwayni/Qazvini, v1, 81; RD/Thackston1, 247; RD/Karimi, 361; RD/Thackston2, 174; Khwandamir, 16.
[2] Devin DeWeese, '"Stuck in the Throat of Chingiz Khan": Envisioning the Mongol Conquests in Some Sufi Accounts from the 14th to 17th Centuries', in Judith Pfeiffer and Sholeh A. Quinn (eds), *History and Historiography of Post-Mongol Central Asia and the Middle East* (Wiesbaden, 2006), 25–6.

Figure 12.1 Persian miniature depicting Chinggis Khan lecturing the grandees of Bukhara from the *minbar* of the Friday Mosque. (The Granger Collection/New York)

punishment. Christians of all sects also interpreted the Mongols' actions in this manner. The best-known expression of this is the desultory lamentation found in the Rus' chronicles after the Battle of Kalka River in 1223:

> In such a way did God bring confusion upon us, and an endless number of people perished. This evil event came to pass on the day of Jeremiah the prophet, the 31st day of May. As for the Tatars, they turned back from the Dnieper, and we know neither from whence they came nor whither they have now gone. Only God knows that, because he brought them upon us for our sins.[3]

---

[3] Serge A. Zenkovsky, *Medieval Russia's Epics, Chronicles, and Tales* (New York, 1974), 196; *EL*, 100–1; *Nikon*, v1, 290.

And even if the Rus' did not know who the Mongols were, they created an explanation that fits an apocalyptic ideology.[4] The Monophysite Armenians wrote of the Mongols in a similar vein, transforming Chinggis Khan into a Christian king and instrument of God. According to Grigor of Akanc, an angel appeared before Chinggis Khan and presented him with the *yasa*, the laws of the Mongols, as well as the title of *Qa'an*, and ordered him to rule over many lands. Furthermore, Grigor wrote: 'Thus this wild <and bestial> folk not only once brought the cup, but also the dregs of bitterness upon us, because of our many and varied sins, which continually roused the anger of the Creator our God at our deeds. Wherefore the Lord roused them in his anger as a lesson to us, because we had not kept his commandments.'[5]

Western Christendom, remote from the nomadic world, found the Mongols alien as they had no agriculture, and ate unclean food such as raw meat, *kumiss*, etc. Peter Jackson summarises Western Christendom's response best:

> However, the advent of a race from the east which was much more powerful and destructive than other steppe peoples naturally touched the apocalyptic sensitivities of medieval Christians, and in their attempts to make sense of the cataclysm, they turned to the historical and geographical material found in Scripture and Classical writings, as mentioned above. The dimension of this response should not be exaggerated. Gog and Magog did not necessarily carry any apocalyptic associations, although the same cannot be said for the Ishmaelites. Neither the letters of Popes Gregory IX and Innocent IV nor those of the Emperor Frederick II deploy any apocalyptic terminology; and indeed many annalists dismiss the Mongol invasion in one brief sentence or, in keeping with their habitually parochial outlook, neglect to mention it at all. It is surprising that Albert of Stade, whose annals had earlier included references to Pseudo-Methodius, makes no connection whatever between the latter and the Mongols. The restraint of the chronicler of St. Pantaleon at Cologne is especially marked. He has heard about the origins, religion and diet of this barbarian race, he says, much that is incredible and utterly inhuman; but since it is not yet known for certain he will refrain from inserting it here . . .[6]

Thus, while some writers in Christendom considered the Mongols the *flagellum dei*, an idea that lingered since Attila's invasions, this was by no

---

[4] Peter Jackson, 'Medieval Christendom's Encounter with the Alien', in *TIWBME*, 41.
[5] Grigor of Akanc, 290–1. Also see Zaroui Pogossian, 'Armenians, Mongols and the End of Times: An Overview of 13th Century Sources', in *CDMP*, 169–98.
[6] Jackson, 'Medieval Christendom's Encounter', 37.

means universal. Indeed, for some (both Jewish and Christian) writers, the Mongols were the Lost Tribes of Israel, despite their ignorance of Hebrew and Mosaic Law.[7] Rational explanations, however, were not needed as the invasion fits a penitential explanation quite nicely, as well as providing an explanation for Christian guilt regarding treatment of Europe's Jewish population. Christendom responded curiously. Rather than the Christians atoning for their sins and seeking forgiveness, pogroms against German Jews resumed, with the culprits justifying their actions on the grounds that the Jews were in league with the Mongols and planned to avenge themselves against Christian persecution.[8] Of course, the idea that Jews were shipping weapons to the Mongols is ludicrous in hindsight, considering the Mongols' weapon-manufacturing capabilities.[9] Furthermore, the annalists overlook the irony of the German reaction to the possibility that the Jews sought vengeance for earlier persecution and that pogroms only encouraged an alliance with the Ten Lost Tribes or whomever the new mysterious invaders were.

This concept of revenge did not escape the European Jews, either. Hebrew sources indicate that the invasions caused a stir among the Jews as 1240 marked the year 5000 in the Judaic calendar – a year ripe with millenarian expectations.[10] Jackson also noted that the *Relatio de Davide rege* referred to 'King Israel' as the father of the eponymous King David. As this work circulated in 1221, it may have promoted some messianic beliefs and perhaps influenced a prophecy in 1241 that predicted 'inter alia the Jews' deliverance from captivity. Even as late as 1250–60, at the time of the Mongol advance under Hülegü towards Palestine, there were still Jewish writers who thought the Mongols were the Lost Tribes.'[11]

Needless to say, not all Jews believed that the Mongols were coming to save them or were the Ten Lost Tribes.[12] The same lack of consensus existed

---

[7] Sophia Menache, 'Tartars, Jews, Saracens and the "Jewish–Mongol Plot" of 1241', in *TIWBME*, 263.

[8] Menache, 'Tartars, Jews, Saracens', p. 263; Jackson, 'Medieval Christendom's Encounter', 38. As Menache comments, ideas of vengeance for the pogroms that took place during the First Crusade still existed in the European Jewry of the mid-thirteenth century.

[9] Timothy May, *The Mongol Art of War* (London, 2007), 63–5.

[10] Menache, 'Tartars, Jews, Saracens', 262; Jackson, 'Medieval Christendom's Encounter', 38.

[11] Jackson, 'Medieval Christendom's Encounter', 38. Also see Menache, *passim*. As Menache indicates, the stories of King David became fact in the minds of many Christians and, with slight alteration, for many Jews as well, particularly with King David being recognised as an ancestor of the Messiah in Jewish tradition, giving the Mongols the status of 'God's emissaries'.

[12] Menache, 'Tartars, Jews, Saracens', 264.

in the Islamic world. Indeed, even within the penitential explanation of the Mongol invasions not everyone was in agreement on exact details.

The matter of sin is a curious one, as not everyone was agreed as to whether it was a collective sin or just certain individuals whose sins caused the invasion regardless of location. In the more selective case, the Mongols could be viewed as avenging angels. Many Sufis initially viewed the Mongols in this manner. Kubraviyya Sufis saw the Mongol invasions of Khwarazm and Central Asia as a result of ninety years of misrule by non-Muslims and the persecution of Sufis by the Muslim Khwarazmshah. The execution of Majd al-Din Ahmad ibn 'Umar Baghdadi by Sultan Muhammad II in 1219, according to the Sufis, was the true cause of the invasions.[13] It was expected that through the invasions the other meaningless forms of Islam would disappear and the insincere believers and hypocrites such as Muhammad Khwarazmshah would be eradicated as infidels.[14] Mawlawiyya Sufis viewed the Mongols in a similar manner as well, telling potential oppressors that the Mongols would punish them. This idea continued well past the initial Mongol invasion. In one anecdote from Aflaki's *Manaqib al-ʿarifin*, the Seljuk administrator Sulayman Muʿin al-Din Pervane (d.1277) asked the great Sufi Rumi when Mongol rule would come to an end. Rumi replied:

> When the great Master [Baha' al-Din, Rumi's father] – God be pleased with him – became sore at heart because of the [Khwarazmshah's] disagreeable behavior which had taken a bad form, and being very annoyed, departed from Balkh, he invoked God in accordance with His name the Avenger to take revenge on those innovators on the road of the *shariʿat*, for *God is All-powerful, the Avenger*. When God Most High had brought forth the enormous Mongol army from the east, they destroyed the capital city Balkh, as well as Khorasan.
>
> He then recited a hadith where God tells Muhammad that, 'I possess an army which I have given an abode towards the east, and I have called them the Turks. I created them with (both) My wrath and My anger, and I will inflict them upon which ever of My bondsmen and bondswomen neglects my command, and I will take revenge on the latter by means of them'.[15]

---

[13] Leonard Lewisohn, 'Overview: Iranian Islam and Persianate Sufism', *The Legacy of Medieval Persian Sufism*, ed. Leonard Lewisohn (London; New York, 1992), 30.
[14] Leonard Lewisohn, *Beyond Faith and Infidelity: The Sufi Poetry and Teachings of Mahmud Shabistari* (Richmond, 1995), 57–8.
[15] John Dechant, 'Depictions of the Islamization of the Mongols in the *Manaqab al-ʿarifin* and the Foundation of the Malawi Community', *Mawlana Rumi Review* 2 (2011), 158–9.

Rumi also explained that the Mongols would eventually fall, but only when they neglected God's command – primarily that they would show disdain for Rumi's offspring (Sufis, Mawlawiyya Sufis specifically). Hagiographers such as Aflaki pointed to this prophecy regarding why the Ilkhanid state would end – persecution of the Mawlawiyya order.[16] Yet at the same time, Aflaki wrote the *Manaqib al-ᶜarifin* from the perspective that the Mongols would convert to Islam over time.[17] Thus their prophesied 'disdain' for the Sufis was due not to their pagan identity but to the hubris of the secular sultans and the Caliphs who frowned upon Sufism, ultimately reflecting back upon Muḥammad Khwarazmshah's actions towards Sufis.

It is apparent, though, that some Sufis had qualms about the Mongol invasions. Although these Sufis still claimed a connection to the Mongols' arrival, their interaction was defensive. Rather than the Mongols being brought as a punishment, it was because of the Khwarazmshah's actions that the Sufis could no longer restrain the Mongols with their spiritual power, as his persecutions of Sufism hampered their activities. Other circumstances existed as well. Often, the circumstance was not due to the failing power of the Sufis, but because custom and propriety forced the Sufis to conform to the dictates of society rather than focusing on what was truly important.

In a story involving Najm al-Din Kubra, the founder of the Kubrawiyya Sufi order, a group of people entered his house with the saint Shaykh Maslahat Khujandi. Najm al-Din was sitting on the floor with one foot extended out towards Turkestan. He was urged to stand up in the august presence of Khujandi. Najm al-Din commented that he had been holding a dog off by keeping his foot in its mouth, but if he must stand because of decorum, he will, though it would release the dog. A few months later Chinggis Khan invaded.[18]

From the perspective of the later Sufis, such as Rumi, the destruction wrought by the Mongols was offset by the role played by the Sufis in converting the Mongols to Islam. According to Devin DeWeese, some Sufis were credited 'precisely [with] the destructive impact of the Mongol conquest upon the institutional structures of the Muslim world'.[19] Indeed, in another story concerning Najm al-Din Kubra, he foresaw the Mongol invasion, which was due to Majd al-Din's execution, and sent his disciples out of the region. He remained behind and died as a martyr fighting the Mongols, but before his death the Mongols, impressed by his piety, gave him an opportunity to

---

[16] Dechant, 'Depictions', 158.
[17] Dechant, 'Depictions', 142.
[18] DeWeese, 'Stuck in the Throat', 50–1. On this symbolic story, see also below, pp. 15–16.
[19] DeWeese, 'Stuck in the Throat', 24.

leave. Kubra rejected it, and said: 'I will attain the blessing of holy war and martyrdom from you, and you will obtain the blessing of Islam from us.'[20] This is usually accepted as a prophecy of the Mongols' conversion to Islam. Thus, by punishment of both the temporal and the religious authorities for their treatment of the Sufis, everything else that the Mongols did was justified, for that damage was fleeting compared to the long-term achievements of Sufism. In some Sufi accounts, the Mongols not only invade to punish those who have oppressed Sufis, but are also led by Sufis and could not be defeated because they were under the protection of Sufis.[21]

DeWeese notes that this motif was extended further and that mere mortal Sufis were not those leading the Mongols, but the *Khizr*, who is 'the immortal prophet of the unseen world'.[22] The use of the *Khizr* as well as other unseen people (*rijal al-ghayb*) in conjunction with the infidel Mongols to kill and punish the wicked Muslims, who are, as DeWeese indicates, still considered as belonging to the Muslim community, is part of a larger penitential explanation of the Mongol invasions.[23] Furthermore, the style in which many of these accounts were written in the late thirteenth and the fourteenth centuries was deliberately crafted to legitimate not only the conquests, but the role and importance of Sufis. Often they included passages in Arabic placed in a Persian text, a style not dissimilar to Juwayni's, which by virtue of the language 'lends an air of divine authority and quasi-Qur'ānic sanction to the legitimacy of the Mongols' destructive impact'.[24]

Other chroniclers had difficulty accepting the calamity, and that God had sent a punishment such as the Mongols, but gradually rationalised it through Qur'ān 13:11: 'When God wills evil to a people, there is no averting it and they have no protector other than Him.'[25] Even so, Ibn al-Athir appears to have had great difficulty justifying the Mongol irruption. Shortly before citing the Qur'ān, he refers to the Tatars (the Mongols) and then writes, 'God damn them.'[26] Thus, he is tacitly damning the instrument of God. His difficulty in rationalising the conquests continues, as he states that he has delayed writing because the events have horrified him too much, and that he had no desire to write the obituary of Islam and wished he had never

---

[20] DeWeese, 'Stuck in the Throat', 42–3.
[21] DeWeese, 'Stuck in the Throat', 32, 34.
[22] DeWeese, 'Stuck in the Throat', 36–7.
[23] DeWeese, 'Stuck in the Throat', 41.
[24] DeWeese, 'Stuck in the Throat', 41.
[25] Ibn al-Athir, 361; Ibn al-Athir/Richards, 204.
[26] Ibn al-Athir, 360; Ibn al-Athir/Richards, 204.

been born.[27] His melodramatics continued with him stating that nothing like this calamity had occurred before in history, and it was unlikely that anything such as this would appear again until the end of the world. Ibn al-Athir's distress is so great that he gives the Anti-Christ (*al-Dajjal*) a more favourable review, stating that 'even the Antichrist spares those who follow him and destroys those who oppose him, but these did not spare anyone'.[28] This statement is magnified, as it directly contradicts a *hadith* in which the Prophet Muḥammad states, 'No tribulation on earth since the creation of Adam will be worse than the tribulation of the Dajjal.'[29] Ibn al-Athir's account is not mere hyperbole. Ibn Kathir (1301–73), while not writing explicitly about the Mongols, wrote extensively on apocalyptic topics, possibly, but not conclusively, influenced by Ibn al-Athir and others who experienced the Mongol conquests. Furthermore, Ibn Kathir being a former student of Ibn Taymiyya and a resident of Damascus in the Mamluk Sultanate, the ardent foes of the Ilkhanid Mongols, it is doubtful whether he ever viewed the Mongols in a positive light.

Nonetheless, his writings shed light on a larger Muslim perspective of apocalyptic events. In Ibn Kathir's work, it is easy to see how the Mongols could be connected to Yaʾjuj (Gog) and Maʾjuj (Magog). While never directly tying the Mongols to Gog and Magog, he includes hadiths foreshadowing their appearance. In one hadith from the Bukhari's Kitab al-Fitan, 'Zaynab bint Jahsh said, "The Prophet got up from his sleep; his face was flushed and he said, 'There is no god but Allah. Woe to the Arabs, for a great evil which is nearly approaching them. Today a gap has been made in the wall of Gog and Magog.' Someone asked, 'Shall we be destroyed even though there are righteous people among us?' The Prophet said, 'Yes, if evil increases.'"'[30] Yet at the same time, Ibn Kathir records a hadith that can tie the Mongols to Dajjal: 'The Prophet said, "The Dajjal will emerge in a land in the east called Khurasan. His followers will be people with faces like hammered shields."'[31] While this *hadith* could easily fit the Turks, during the era of the Mongol irruption into the *Dar al-Islam* (Abode of Islam) one does not need to stretch one's imagination to see the connection with the Mongols. Furthermore, the wall of Yaʾjuj and Maʾjuj also fits nicely into

---

[27] Ibn al-Athir, 358; Ibn al-Athir/Richards, 202.
[28] Ibn al-Athir, 358–9; Ibn al-Athir/Richards, 202.
[29] Ibn al-Kathir, *The Signs Before the Day of Judgment*, 2nd edn, trans. Huda Khattab (London, 1992), 56. Ibn Kathir attributes this *hadith* to Abu Umama al-Bahili.
[30] Ibn Kathir, *The Signs*, 25.
[31] Ibn Kathir, *The Signs*, 66.

the ultimate cause of the Mongol invasions – the actions of Muhammad II Khwarazmshah.

The Khwarazmshah of course offended Chinggis Khan by massacring his caravan, but in the eyes of many this is not what triggered the invasion. While the apocalyptic Sufi stories indicate his execution of a Sufi, other stories hint at his other grave sin. If one recalls the tale of Najm al-Din Kubra, in order to behave according to accepted decorum he had to stand to meet a visiting saint, removing his foot from the maw of a dog.[32] Najm al-Din's efforts at staving off the dog carry additional meaning in connection with the wall of Ya'juj and Ma'juj. In the popular mind, this wall did not exist as a true physical manifestation, but rather as the empire of Qara Khitai. While this imagery may have been the result of hindsight, several compared the Qara Khitans to the wall of Dhu al-Qarnayn, which protected *Dar al-Islam* from Ya'juj and Ma'juj.[33] Although the Qara Khitans were Buddhists and thus infidels, the overall impression of their rule was that they were just and held at bay the pagan hordes of the steppe who otherwise would have overrun the Islamic world. Thus, when Muhammad Khwarazmshah, in conspiracy with Guchulug, overthrew Qara Khitai, they toppled the Wall of Dhu al-Qarnayn. Indeed, Guchulug's rapacious behaviour verified this opinion. His presence also opened the door for the Mongols to enter the region, thus setting the stage for the Otrar massacre.

As a result, apocryphal stories arose in connection to this, such as the tale of Najm al-Din Kubra and the dog. Another popular tale was that Tekish Khwarazmshah (r. 1172–1200), Muhammad II's father, warned his sons never to war with the Khitans as they were a wall that protected them.[34] Juwayni also cites that Qara Khitai was like the wall of Dhu al-Qarnayn.[35] The theme resurfaced when the Mongols invaded Transcaucasia in 1231 in pursuit of Muhammad II's son, Jalal al-Din (r. 1220–31), the last Khwarazmshah. Jalal al-Din attempted to forge an alliance with the Ayyubids and the Saljuqs of Rum and compared himself to the Wall of Alexander. Unfortunately for Jalal al-Din, his eloquence failed to rally an alliance, as his previous behaviour made the Ayybids and Seljuks view him as a larger danger than the Mongols.[36]

It is clear that Ibn al-Athir was overwhelmed by the events, and he

---

[32] DeWeese, 'Stuck in the Throat', 50–1. See above, fn. 25 for more details.
[33] See Michal Biran, '"Like a Mighty Wall:" The Armies of the Qara Khitai (1124–1218)', *JSAI* 25 (2001), 44–91.
[34] Jackson, 'Medieval Christendom's Encounter', 42–3.
[35] Juwayni/Qazvini, 80; Juvaini/Boyle, 347.
[36] Juwayni/Qazvini, 83; Juvaini/Boyle, 452.

ascribed them to the will of God, but reluctantly and only because he could find no other explanation. His account of the sack of Bukhara differs from that of Juwayni. While the details of the military actions are similar, Ibn al-Athir does not mention any speech by Chinggis Khan in which he claims to be the Scourge of God or any other representative of God. In Ibn al-Athir's account, Chinggis Khan's only announcements concern people showing their wealth, or to take part in the actions against the Bukharan citadel or risk the consequences. Indeed, Chinggis Khan's wrath against Bukhara is due to his belief that Muhammad Khwarazmshah stored the loot from the Otrar caravan there.[37]

Juzjani, who fled to Delhi during the invasion, also tied the Mongols to a sign of the end of the world and stated that their coming into *Dar al-Islam* triggered the beginning of the end.[38] He does not, however, appear to subscribe to the concept that the Mongols were the punishment of God, particularly since he cannot mention a Mongol's name without also damning him to hell. Indeed, Juzjani's description of Chinggis Khan's rise to power begins 'When the father of the Chingiz Khan went to hell . . . [*bidozakh raft*]'.[39] The rest of the work follows in the same vein. Chinggis Khan is often referred to as 'The Accursed'. Nonetheless, Juzjani accepted that the success of Chinggis Khan was due to the will of Heaven and attributed it to destiny, although he was not happy about it.[40]

The Mongols were not the first invasion viewed as divine punishment. The ʿAbbasid Revolution was viewed in this way on account of the sins of the Umayyad Dynasty (661–750).[41] In addition, Napoleon's invasion of Egypt almost five hundred years after the Mongols received a similar treatment, as Bonaparte painted himself as a just ruler, unlike the Mamluks.[42] Nonetheless, the Mongol invasion was of a different sort. While the ʿAbbasids (750–1258) toppled the Umayyads, they were at least Muslims. While Napoleon was not a Muslim, he was at least not a pagan. The savagery of the Mongols, along with the fact that they were a new entity altogether, added to the consternation. Furthermore, the Qurʾān is replete with warnings that a punishment

---

[37] Ibn al-Athir, 365-7; Ibn al-Athir/Richards, 207–9.
[38] Juzjani/Ḥabibi, v2, 97–8; Juzjani/Raverty, 935. In relation to the wall of Dhu al-Qarnayn, Juzjani refers to the reign of the Ghurid Sultan Ghazi Muḥammad Sam.
[39] Juzjani/Ḥabibi, v2, 99; Juzjani/Raverty, 937.
[40] Juzjani/Ḥabibi, v2, 90; Juzjani/Raverty, 869.
[41] Moshe Sharon, *Black Banners from the East, vol. 2, Revolt: The Social and Military Aspects of the 'Abbasid Revolution* (Jerusalem, 1990), 187–8, 199–200.
[42] Al-Jabarti, *Napoleon in Egypt: Al-Jabarti's Chronicle of the French Occupation, 1798*, trans. Shmuel Moreh (Princeton, 1993), 24, 29–33, 101–2, 113–14.

would be sent to those who forgot God or ignored his Prophet.[43] Qur'ān 7:2–5, in particular, fits the Mongols' *modus operandi*:

> Follow what has been sent down to you from your Lord, and follow no friends other than He; little do you remember. How many a city We have destroyed! Our might came upon it at night, or while they took their ease in the noontide, and they but cried, when Our might came upon them, 'We were evildoers'.[44]

Thus we have this curious conflict for Juzjani, similar to that of Ibn al-Athir – how does one rationalise the Mongol invasion and the resulting destruction of much of the Islamic world by a clearly pagan army when one also accepts that Islam is the true faith and that God is compassionate and merciful, even when the Qur'ān is quite explicit about sending a punishment? From the writings of all of the authors, it is clear that such a rationalisation did not come easily and without considerable thought. At some point Juzjani, like Ibn al-Athir, came to terms with the tragedy and realised that God moves in mysterious ways.

As stated above, Juzjani initially did not accept the Mongols at the punishment of God. In his introduction to the section on the Mongol irruption, their role as God's instrument is not mentioned. Yet, there is a slight change of heart once he discusses the Otrar incident. Here he accepts that the Khwarazmians acted in a perfidious, and thus sinful, manner. Like others, he rationalises the subsequent events by intermixing Qur'ānic verses with his prose. Juzjani wrote: 'and as Almighty God had so willed that this treachery should be the means of the ruin of the empire of Islam, it became evident that "the command of God is an inevitable decree", and the instruments of the predetermined will of fate became available – From Thy wrath preserve us, O God!'[45] Indeed, his seemingly reluctant acceptance of the Mongols as the Scourge of God or Punishment of God aligns with Qur'ān 17:60, 'No city is there, but We shall destroy it before the Day of Resurrection, or We shall chastise it with a terrible chastisement; this is in the Book inscribed', as well as

---

[43] Qur'ān 32:14. 'So now taste, for that you forgot the encounter of this your day! We indeed have forgotten you. Taste the chastisement of eternity for that you were doing.' Also see Qur'ān 73: 15–18. 'Surely we have sent unto you a Messenger as a witness over you, even as We sent to Pharoah a Messenger, but Pharoah rebelled against the Messenger, so We seized him remorselessly. If therefore you believe, how will you guard against a day that shall make children grey-headed? Whereby heaven shall be split, and its promise shall be performed. Surely this is a Reminder; so let him who will take unto his Lord a way.' The translation used in this chapter is A. J. Arberry (trans.), *The Koran Interpreted* (London, 1955).
[44] Qur'ān 7:2–5.
[45] Juzjani/Habibi, v2, 104; Juzjani/Raverty, 967.

with Qur'ān 18:58–59: 'But thy Lord is the All-forgiving, full of mercy. If He should take them to task for that they have earned, He would hasten for them the chastisement; but they have a tryst, from which they will find no escape. And those cities, We destroyed them when they did evil, and appointed for their destruction a tryst.'[46]

In essence, he has accepted the idea that God's decree pre-determined events, perhaps as a lesson concerning treachery – a harsh lesson, one might argue. Nonetheless, the concept of predetermination is a convenient salve to apply to a world turned upside down. At the same time, Juzjani does not view the course of history as being purely deterministic, nor, should we say, pre-deterministic. Indeed, he allows for the hand of God to work in mysterious ways, as he records a scenario where Chinggis Khan had a dream about wrapping a turban. When the dream was interpreted, it was revealed that the turban represented the Muslim lands that would come under his control, and it was because of this dream that he decided to conquer *Dar al-Islam*.[47]

Thus it appears that Juzjani coyly rejects the idea that the Mongol invasion was God's will, without directly saying it, and even as his own writing aligns with verses from the Qur'ān. Unlike most authors, Juzjani merely mentions the destruction of Bukhara in a few scant lines, with virtually no detail, and quickly moves on to other events. For Juzjani, the Mongols were dreadful and damned to hell upon their death, but he does not necessarily view them as the scourge of God, except where he must fit this trope in according to the writing style of the era.

Of these authors, only those who worked for the Mongols record Chinggis Khan's speech. And among these, Rashid al-Din reused much of Juwayni in his own work. This raises suspicion about the motives of Juwayni. Yet, at the same time Juwayni had access to Mongols who may have been there. So, is it possible that Chinggis Khan provided a message similar to the one which Juwayni indicated that he preached from his pulpit on that fateful day in Bukhara? Not those exact words spoken in purple prose by his interpreter for his learned audience, or even by Juwayni, whose own eloquence is reflected throughout his work, but perhaps something similar to what might be found in *The Secret History of the Mongols*. Pragmatic and direct. My thought would be something along the lines of 'Your rulers committed crimes against me – because of that I have come to punish them'. This seems in line with Chinggis Khan's policy that, if a city surrendered, it would be spared. He informed the citizenry of Bukhara that this fight was between him and the Khwarazmshah.

[46] Qur'ān 17:58; Qur'ān 18:58–9.
[47] Juzjani/Habibi, v2, 101–2; Juzjani/Raverty, 974–5.

If they wronged him, then they should expect retaliation; if they remained out of the feud, they would be spared.

Furthermore, this interpretation fits with the Mongols' *modus operandi*. The Mongols were known to punish those who transgressed them. There are numerous reasons for the invasion of the Jin Empire, but one of the most important was vengeance – for when the Altan Khan (the Jin Emperor) tortured and killed the Mongol Khan Ambaghai by impaling him on a wooden donkey.[48] Although Ambaqai's death occurred before Temüjin's birth, it still weighed in the back of the Mongol mind as a wrong that needed righting, although the Mongols did pillage part of the Jin Empire not long after the event.[49] The Mongols also invaded the Jin Empire again in 1215 when the Jin Emperor Zhenyu, reign name Xuanzong (1213–17), moved his capital from Zhongdu to Kaifeng, which Chinggis Khan viewed as a violation of a treaty. Finally, the ruler of Xi Xia, Xiangzong (r. 1206–11), submitted to the Mongols in 1209. He remained a client and provided tribute to the Mongols as well as troops for the war against the Jin. Nonetheless, Xi Xia rebelled after the death of the Mongol general Muqali in 1223. Again, because of a treaty violation, Chinggis Khan ended his war in the Khwarazmian Empire. In all instances, we see one party wrong the Mongols and then Chinggis Khan seeking justice. The punishment was typically harsh due to the violation of an agreement or established custom.

In many ways the question of the Bukhara speech is one of the chicken and the egg. Did Islamic thought influence the Mongols' conception of divine rule? I have argued elsewhere that Chinggis Khan had no intention of conquering the world and that his empire was often one of happenstance.[50] Indeed, the fact that Chinggis Khan sought to resolve the Otrar incident through diplomacy and compensation and even maintain ties suggests that he did not seek to conquer the world. As Thomas Allsen has indicated, 'it was at bottom a pocket book issue'.[51] Other scholars have also noted that, at least in the case of Khwarazm, the Mongols had no desire to take over the world.[52] Rather, it

---

[48] *SHM*, §53. The mention of the wooden ass comes from Rashid al-Din. See RD/Karimi, 194 and RD/Thackston1, 129.

[49] RD/Karimi, 194; RD/Thackston1, 129.

[50] See Timothy May, 'The Mechanics of Conquest and Governance: The Rise and Expansion of the Mongol Empire, 1185–1265', Ph.D. thesis, University of Wisconsin-Madison, 2004; Timothy May, 'Grand Strategy in the Mongol Empire', *Acta Historica Mongolici* 16 (2017), 78–105.

[51] Thomas T. Allsen, 'Mongolian Princes and Their Merchant Partners, 1200–1260', *Asia Major* 2 (1989), 92.

[52] David Morgan, *The Mongols*, 69; Luc Kwanten, 'The Career of Muqali: A Reassessment', *The Bulletin of Sung and Yuan Studies* 14 (1978), 33.

was during Ogodei's reign that the Mongols took stock of the situation and saw what they had accomplished under Chinggis Khan and then rationalised their empire as representing the will of heaven: conferred on Chinggis Khan and subsequently bequeathed to his successors and the message was universal in its character.

Under this ideology, the Mongols customarily sent orders of submission to neighbouring countries prior to initiating hostilities, as they claimed to have the right, if not the duty, to extend their sway over the entire world. All peoples outside their frontiers were considered members of the Mongols' 'World Empire-in-the-making', and all, after appropriate and formal notification, were required to acknowledge Mongolian suzerainty without hesitation or question. As the Mongol expansion was decreed by Heaven, anyone who refused to submit therefore was in rebellion against Heaven and merited punishment.[53] In this sense, the Mongols were the Scourge of God.

The Mongols always justified their conquests in letters demonstrating that, as Shagdaryn Bira indicated, the campaigns were 'were ideologically and politically motivated actions similar to those which, in different aspects, happened until recently rather often in world history'.[54] In addition to the well-known letters from Güyük (r. 1246–8) to Pope Innocent IV, correspondence between Hulegu (d. 1265) and King Louis IX (r. 1226–70) in 1262 demonstrates that the Mongols still held this view over time and space.[55] Academician Bira also viewed the Mongol campaigns as being ones in which those who resisted were rebels. He wrote:

> In the opinion of the imperial Mongols, whoever did not accommodate themselves to the Divine order (the order of Tenggeri) were rebels (*bulqa irgen*), not only against the khan but also against Tenggeri. Therefore, Mongols had a divine right, as well as an obligation, to punish people who were against them and to unite them under the rule of their khans. In this way, as correctly pointed out by Antti Ruotsala, the Mongols legitimated

---

[53] Thomas T. Allsen, 'Guard and Government in the Reign of The Grand Qan Möngke, 1251–1259', *HJAS* 46.2 (December 1986), 495–6.

[54] Shagdaryn Bira, 'Mongolian Tenggerism and Modern Globalism. A Retrospective Outlook on Globalisation', *JRAS* 14.1 (April 2004), 7.

[55] Guyuk, 'Guyuk Khan's Letter to Pope Innocent IV (1246)', English version based on the trans. by D. A. Maitland Muller (see p. xxxix), in Christopher Dawson (ed.), *Mission to Asia* (Toronto, 1980), 85; the facsimiles of the original letter are available at <http://www.asnad.org/en/document/249/> (last accessed 16 December 2015); Hulegu, 'Hulegu, Mongol Il-Khan of Persia, to Louis IX, King of France (1262). Maragha', in *LOE* (Burlington, VT, 2010), 157.

their expansion on sacred grounds, just as the Western Christians did for their crusades and the Muslims for their jihad.⁵⁶

So, did the Mongols truly believe that they were the instruments of Heaven? Without question. Not only did they tell other rulers that Tenggeri sanctified their rule and use their conquests as evidence, but they themselves also subscribed to the idea. The usual justification of this is the prophecy of the shaman Teb Tenggeri found in *The Secret History of the Mongols*.⁵⁷ While the *Secret History* was classified material meant for the ruling elite, it was clear that the Chinggisid princes learned their history and indeed were indoctrinated in the ideals of Mongol supremacy not only through empirical evidence of conquests, wealth and territory, but also through the power of prophecy. Writing from Maragha in 1262 to King Louis IX, Hulegu revealed to Louis IX the prophecy of Teb Tenggeri, in which Tenggeri instructed the shaman to inform Chinggis Khan:

> I alone am the Almighty God on high and I have set thee over the nations and over the kingdoms to be king of all the world, to root out and to pull down and to destroy and to throw down, to build and to plant. I tell you to announce my command to all the nations, tongues and tribes of the east, the south, the north and the west, to promulgate it in all the regions of the whole world where emperors, kings, and sovereigns rule, where lordships operate, where horses can go, ships sail, envoys reach, letters be heard, so that they who have ears can hear, those who hear can understand and those who understand can believe. Those who do not believe will later learn what punishment will be meted on those who did not believe my commands.⁵⁸

In the same letter, Hulegu indicates that Baghdad fell for the same reason, even though the Caliph claimed his descent from Muḥammad, and that God had created the world for the Muslims. Despite the claims of divine legitimisation, through force of arms the Mongols proved which side Heaven truly supported.⁵⁹ This belief continued even after the dissolution of the Mongol Empire, as evinced by the Il-Khanid–Mamluk wars.⁶⁰

Use of the Teb Tenggeri prophecy to legitimise the Mongol conquests, however, is a bit disingenuous. Teb Tenggeri's prophecy reads '*tende Teb*

---

⁵⁶ Bira, 'Mongolian Tenggerism', 7.
⁵⁷ *SHM*, §244.
⁵⁸ Hulegu, 156–7.
⁵⁹ Hulegu, 157–8.
⁶⁰ Reuven Amitai-Preiss, 'Mongol Imperial Ideology and the Ilkhanid War against the Mamluks', in *MEL*, 63–9.

Tenggeri Chinggis Khaghan-a ugulerun mongke tenggeri-yin jarliq qan ja'arit ugulemu niken-te Temüjin ulus barituqai', which translates as 'Then Teb Tenggeri said to Chinggis Khan, the decree of the eternal Heaven (*tenggeri*) concerning the ruler, one will be that Temüjin will seize the nation (*ulus*)'.[61] *Ulus* was used to refer to the Mongol state at all times. People who were not part of the Mongol power (such as the *Hoy-in Irgen* or Forest People) were typically called *irgen*. Once the Mongols conquered a group, particularly nomads, and incorporated them into the Mongol *ulus* they were considered part of it and no longer *irgen*.[62] Furthermore, the title of *Chinggis Khaghan* is a posthumous promotion for Chinggis Khan. During his lifetime his title was simply Chinggis Khan; thus this line was at least slightly redacted after Chinggis Khan's death. We see that in later periods Teb Tenggeri's prophecy is expanded to suit the new reality of the Mongol world, one in which other world views needed to fit into a framework that was ruled by the *Yeke Monggol Ulus*. Furthermore, the revised and expanded prophecy (or Prophecy 2.0) was supported by undeniable empirical evidence as the Mongols had indeed conquered virtually everything. Defeats or setbacks, such as with the Mamluks at ʿAyn Jalut, were seen as mere impediments that would be overcome by the will of Heaven.[63]

Thus, the idea of the Mongols as the 'Scourge of God' served not only to later justify and explain Mongol success for the Mongols, but also served as a psychological crutch for the Muslims of the Khwarazmian Empire. Only a decade before, Sultan Muhammad II appeared as a second Alexander with a massive army. Even though the decisions that led to the Otrar incident make one question Muḥammad's ability to lead, this is hindsight. At the time he ruled a vast empire with no significant challenges to his rule. The distant Mongol threat was not credible at the time. Furthermore, they did not seem much different from the type of threat posed by Guchulug – a danger, but not durable. Indeed, prior to the arrival of the Mongols in Qara Khitai, it was questionable as to just how long Guchulug could maintain power as the Qarluqs and the Uighurs had already revolted and sought protection under Chinggis Khan. Others near the Khwarazmian borders may have considered a similar plan with Sultan Muhammad.

In conclusion, it is unlikely that Chinggis Khan's sermon in the mosque ever took place, or at least not the speech that Juwayni ascribes to him. It is possible that he said something, but according to Ibn al-Athir, Chinggis

---

[61] *SHM*, §244.
[62] Lhamsuren Munkh-Erdene, 'Where Did the Mongol Empire Come From? Medieval Mongol Ideas of People, State and Empire', *IA* 13 (2011), 213–15.
[63] Hulegu, 159.

Khan on entering Bukhara claimed: 'I want from you the bullion that Khwarazm Shah sold you, for it is mine; it was taken from my followers and you have it.'[64] The Punishment of God is certainly more dramatic, but does not appear to fit with Chinggis Khan's own actions and behaviour. Nonetheless, the speech does, however, fit with later Mongol rhetoric and reflects an effort by not only Juwayni to revise the events of Chinggis Khan's life to fit with the now expanded prophecy of Teb Tenggeri, that the Mongols (and certainly not the meek) had inherited the earth. At the same time, Juwayni works within an Islamic framework in which the Mongols had to serve some function in God's plan. Juwayni also demonstrates how Ogodei was truly a just ruler, although a pagan, and that Muslims were much better off being ruled by the Mongols rather than by unjust tyrants such as Muhammad Khwarazmshah. Yet, even for those who might question the idea that pagans who pillaged and plundered the faithful were the instruments of God, the idea gained credence over time, as demonstrated by Aflaki in his *Manaqib al-ᶜarifin*, which states that the pagans did not need to be aware of God's plans, He set them in motion.[65] Furthermore, even as Juwayni tacitly accepts that the Mongols are just rulers compared to Muhammad Khwarazmshah, he ties the concept of promoting good and forbidding evil to the Mongols through Chinggis Khan as the Punishment of God. The concept of promoting good and forbidding evil was tied to what a just ruler did. Indeed, the punishment of wrongdoing was symbolised in the role of the Caliph as evinced by an Umayyad coin where the Caliph ᶜAbd al-Malik's hand rests on his sword hilt, ready to behead a transgressor. His image promises threat rather than protection.[66] Indeed, Juwayni incorporates the concept of the just ruler enjoining good and forbidding evil throughout his work, particularly with Ogodei Khan.

Juwayni is not alone in demonstrating the Mongol leaders as enjoining good. The Chisti shaykh Nizam al-Din Awliya told an apocryphal story that can be dated from 15 November 1308 about a Chisti Sufi, Khwaja ᶜAli, who was captured by the Mongols during their invasion of the Khwarazmian Empire. Khwaja ᶜAli happened to be brought before Chinggis Khan for judgement while another Chisti Sufi was present. This Sufi recognised

---

[64] Ibn al-Athir, 366; Ibn al-Athir/Richard, 208.
[65] Dechant, 'Depictions', 149–51.
[66] My thanks to Istvan Kristo-Nagy for mentioning this coin, which I later inspected at the British Museum. To my knowledge, he is the only one who has interpreted the coin's image in this manner. Judging from the baleful glare and the posture of the figure, I believe it is clear that the coin represents the Caliph as the dispenser of punishment with his hand resting on his sword hilt.

Khwaja ʿAli and informed Chinggis Khan that Khwaja ʿAli's father was a saint (*mardi-yi buzurg*) and very charitable to the poor. He also urged Chinggis Khan to release him. The Mongol Khan then asked his Chisti advisor whether or not he gave food to his own people or strangers. The Sufi responded that he gave food to strangers, and added, 'Everyone gives food to his own people, but this man's father gave food to strangers.'[67] Chinggis Khan was pleased and affirmed 'It was a good person indeed who gave food to the people of God' and then released him and gave him a new cloak while asking Khwaja ʿAli for his forgiveness. According to DeWeese, Shaykh Nizam al-Din concluded that this story demonstrated that providing food to the poor and strangers 'is praised in all doctrines'.[68] It is also a clear demonstration of Chinggis Khan enjoining good as well as showing his respect for Sufis.

His peers, of course, would disagree with Juwayni's assessment of the Mongols as just rulers as well as perhaps being chosen instruments of God, as they wrote safely out of reach from the Mongols. This idea was further complicated by the fact that even if the Mongols were not the Scourge of God, they could be associated with Gog and Magog. The connection to Gog and Magog was clear, as it was assumed that they were a race descended from Noah's son Yafith (Japeth), the father of the Turks in Islamic lore.[69] This interpretation also fit into Christian interpretations of the Mongol invasions as well. Christians and Muslims alike credited Alexander the Great (Dhu al-Qarnayn) with sealing Gog and Magog behind a wall that would last until the end of days. For Muslims, this was even revealed in the Qur'ān in detail.[70] Then, the wall will finally collapse due to their eternal efforts to escape, and when it collapses, they would then spread across the earth, slaying and destroying all before them and uprooting plants.[71] This motif of rampant destruction, with the touch of uprooting plants, which should be construed as perhaps turning farmland into pasture, certainly seemed to describe the Mongols to all those experienced the Mongol invasions. Indeed, Matthew Paris recorded their invasions along these lines:

> Roving through the Saracen territories, they razed cities to the ground, burnt woods, pulled down castles, tore up the vine trees, destroyed gardens, and massacred the citizens and husbandmen; if by chance they did spare

---

[67] DeWeese, 'Stuck in the Throat', 28–9.
[68] DeWeese, 'Stuck in the Throat', 29.
[69] Ibn Kathir, *The Signs*, 77–8.
[70] Qur'ān 18: 84–100.
[71] Ibn Kathir, *The Signs*, 77–8.

any who begged their lives, they compelled them, as slaves of the lowest condition, to fight in front of them against their own kindred.[72]

A survivor of Bukhara described the Mongol actions along similar lines.[73] Nonetheless, through the intercession of ʿIsa (Jesus), the hordes of Gog and Magog would finally be defeated, including, in one account, their meeting a particularly grisly fate through a worm that will burrow into their necks.[74] Curiously, among some in Europe, this story took a strange twist with Alexander the Great sealing the Ten Lost Tribes of Israel behind the wall rather than Gog and Magog – hence the reason for the Ten Lost Tribes wanting vengeance, although why they specifically wanted vengeance against Christians when a pagan Macedonian committed the act is another question.[75] Still, some Latin writers found ways to reconcile the Ten Lost Tribes with Gog and Magog by determining that the offspring of Gog and Magog were actually Jewish. This was based on Mongol writing. The Europeans deduced that the Uighur script was Hebrew and the Mongols were taught it by Pharisees and Sadducees – an attempt to explain Uighur Buddhist monks and other functionaries who entered Mongol service.[76]

Yet the tendency of Muslim authors to tie the Mongols to Gog and Magog is not without problems, as it is clear in both the Qurʾān and in commentaries and a *hadith* that Gog and Magog would only appear after the appearance and defeat of al-Dajjal, who was prophesied to appear only after the fall of Constantinople.[77] So why did so many disregard this chronology? Another *hadith* recorded by Ibn Kathir may have contributed to it the idea that the Mongols were connected to al-Dajjal, even though it confirms that al-Dajjal would only appear after the capture of Constantinople. The *hadith* in question originates from Fatima bint Qays:

> The Dajjal will be permitted to appear at the end of time, after the Muslims have conquered a Roman city called Constantinople. He will first appear in Isfahan, in an area known as the Jewish quarter (al-Yahudiyyah). He will be followed by seventy thousand Jews from that area, all of them armed. Seventy thousand Tatars and many people from Khurasan will also follow him. At first he will appear as a tyrannical king, then he will claim to be a

---

[72] Matthew Paris, v1, 312.
[73] Juwayni/Qazvini, 83; Juvaini/Boyle, 107. This survivor, when asked what happened, replied, 'They came, they sapped, they burnt, they slew, they plundered and they departed.'
[74] Ibn Kathir, *The Signs*, 77.
[75] Menache, 'Tartars, Jews, Saracens', 260.
[76] Jackson, 'Medieval Christendom's Encounter', 39–40.
[77] Ibn Kathir, *The Signs*, 36.

prophet, then a lord. Only the most ignorant of men will follow him; the righteous and those guided by Allah will reject him. He will start to conquer the world country by country, fortress by fortress, region by region, town by town; no place will remain unscathed except Makkah and Madinah. The length of his stay on earth will be forty days: one day like a year, one day like a month, one day like a week, and the rest of the days like normal days, i.e. his stay will be approximately one year and two and a half months. Allah will grant him many miracles, through which whoever He wills will be led astray, and the faith of the believers will be strengthened.[78]

The inclusion of the Tatars (as the Islamic authors referred to the Mongols) leads one to question whether the *hadith* truly came from the era of the Prophet. Other *hadiths* from the era include mention of the Turks; 'Tatar', however, was used to refer to Mongols. The term 'Tatar' was first recorded in the Orkhon Inscription from the eighth century in Mongolia. Although Chinese sources begin to refer to Tatars by 842, the earliest known mentions in Islamic sources are in the *Hudud al-ᶜalam*, written in the late tenth century, and Mahmud al-Kashghari's *Diwan al-lughat al-turk* written in the late eleventh century.[79] Considering that contact with the Turks occurred earlier in the Transoxiana, it is possible that Muslims knew of the Tatars prior to the tenth century, but unlikely. Furthermore, it is quite evident that the *hadith* had changed by the time Ibn Kathir encountered it. Thus, even though Constantinople was not conquered in Ibn Kathir's era, the rest of the account could apply to the Mongols, particularly with the mention of the Tatars and the statement that many people from Khurasan would join them although the Mongols did not capture Isfahan until 1237. Furthermore, in the thirteenth and even in the fourteenth century, there was anxiety that the Mongols would attack Mecca and Medina. This *hadith* and others, however, indicate that al-Dajjal would never enter Mecca, and by the time of Ibn Kathir's writings the Mongol threat to the Holy Cities was non-existent. The Ilkhanid kingmaker, Choban, had participated in the Hajj and even restored a well and built his tomb there.[80] Finally, in times of anxiety, it is not uncommon to select the parts of prophecy and scriptures that fit the situation and ignore the larger context that otherwise casts doubt on efforts to understand a divine plan.

One likely reason is that, regardless of whether one adhered to the Sufi interpretation, penitential explanations, or the ideas of the *ulema*, there were

---

[78] Ibn Kathir, *The Signs*, 77.
[79] 'Tatar', in *EI*².
[80] Anne Broadbridge, *Kingship and Ideology in the Islamic and Mongol Worlds* (Cambridge, 2008), 115–16, 125. For the other *hadiths* see Ibn Kathir, *The Signs*, 68–9.

simply so many prophecies and stories about the Mongols connecting them in both word and deed to an apocalyptic vision that even the most resistant writers could not ignore them. Regardless of whether the Mongols were the Scourge of God, the hordes of Gog and Magog or the agents of al-Dajjal, what mattered to most was that they were a force of unparalleled destruction and they came from the east, which fitted with a *hadith* related by Ibn ᶜUmar, who said: 'I heard Allah's Messenger on the pulpit saying, "Verily, afflictions (will start) from here", pointing towards the east, "whence the side of the head of Satan comes out"'.[81]

It is significant that Juwayni's account of Chinggis Khan's speech in Bukhara became the standard interpretation of events over Ibn al-Athir's and consequently appears in the Rashid al-Din and Khwandamir accounts.[82] While it was not a salve for the conscience, Muslim writers wrestled with the concept of the overwhelming destruction of the *Dar al-Islam* by infidels, and thus tacitly accepted the violence perpetrated by the Mongols as the will of God. Even if they did not fully like the idea, no other explanation provided a satisfactory cause.

---

[81] The *ḥadith* came from Bukhari, *Kitab al-Fitan*, <http://sunnah.com/bukhari/61/21> (last accessed 6 January 2016). Sahih al-Bukhari 3511.

[82] Juwayni/Boyle, 105; Juwayni/Qazwini, 81; RD/Thackston1, 247; RD/Karimi, 361; Khwandamir, 16.

13

Conclusion: End of the Chinggisids and the Rise of the Qarachu

Most books concerning the Mongol Empire end with a chapter discussing its long-term impact. For decades, and perhaps even centuries, historians viewed the Mongols as simply a destructive phenomenon that left neither a Parthenon nor a philosophy. In the more recent era, this view has reversed. Indeed, some writers now even view the Mongol Empire from an almost Pollyanna-ish perspective in their zeal to reverse the trend.[1] Most historians, however, view it with the measured balance one should expect from professional historians – a breed not generally known for their excitable nature. As a result, a re-evaluation of the Mongol Empire has taken place, along with lengthy commentary regarding its legacy and impact.[2] To this end, instead of the obligatory legacy chapter, I would prefer to consider not only why the Mongol Empire fractured after the death of Mongke, but why it continued to do so. It is hoped that the reader will also see that, even after the dissolution of the empire, similar tensions and trends affected its successors, regardless of time and space. This should be viewed as a contemplative chapter and not definitive, and, more importantly, something for the reader to consider after having read this book.

In the post-dissolution empire, five states emerged from a single hyperpower: the Yuan Empire, the Jochid Khanate, the Ilkhanate, the Ogodeid Khanate and the Chaghatayid Khanate. Peter Jackson makes a case for the Negudaris/Qaraunas, but I am not convinced – although one should never

---

[1] Jack Weatherford, Genghis Khan and the Making of the Modern World (New York, 2004).
[2] Denise Aigle, *The Mongol Empire between Myth and Reality* (Leiden, 2014) Thomas T. Allsen, *Culture and Conquest in Mongol Eurasia* (New York, 2001); Michal Biran, *Chinggis Khan* (London, 2007); Michal Biran, 'The Mongol Empire and the Inter-Civilizational Exchange', in *CHW*, v5, 534–58; William Fitzhugh, Morris Rossabi and William Honeychurch (eds), *Genghis Khan and the Mongol Empire* (Washington, DC, 2009); Linda Komaroff, *BLGK*; Linda Komaroff and Stefano Carboni (eds), *LGK: The Legacy of Genghis Khan* (New York, 2003); Timothy May, *The Mongol Conquests in World History* (London, 2012); David Morgan. *The Mongols*, 2nd edition (Malden, MA, 2007). These are but a few.

discount a Qarauna.³ Of course, the Ogodeid Khanate disappeared shortly after 1300, swallowed up by the Chaghatayids, leaving four superpowers. Three of the four eventually adopted Islam as the state religion, while Buddhism became the state religion of the Yuan Empire. The Yuan Empire also became more sedentary-centric in its outlook, at least on the surface. While it adopted many aspects of Chinese civilisation, the elite still viewed themselves as Mongols. The same could be said about the Ilkhanate. Despite its Islamisation and adoption of many attributes of Islamic governments and Persian kingship, the elite remained Mongol in many respects. It is typical to note that the Mongols of the Jochid Khanate did not adopt Russian culture or convert to Orthodox Christianity. This, however, is not surprising. The Rus' lands were never their core territories. Indeed, they were peripheral, as the leadership and governing institutions remained in the steppes. The greater emphasis on the Rus' principalities in scholarship on the Golden Horde is largely due to the fact that we have Rus' sources but very few from the Jochids. The Jochids fused Mongol and Turkic elements with Islamic institutions to rule over their empire. Besides the Rus', other sedentary elements existed, particularly in Sarai and other commercial cities. There is a very good reason why the most of the successors of the Golden Horde tended to centre on towns (Crimea, Kazan, Astrakhan and Sibir). Meanwhile, the Chaghatayid territory is often referred to as the khanate that retained its nomadic heritage the longest and was most resistant to assimilation.

The Chaghatayid Mongols did not assimilate into the local population, unless one considers the existing nomadic population. Their particular region was perhaps the most diverse, as it consisted of Turks of various sorts (Oghuz, Kipchaks, Uighurs) along with Iranian elements, particularly in Mawarannahr. Additionally, the religious climate included Muslims, Buddhists, Nestorian Christians, some Manichaeans, and of course shamanists. A single entity that could truly dominate the Mongol element did not exist, as even the Turkic population was diverse in language and religion. The fact that the eastern portion became known as Moghulistan suggests that nomads underwent a process of Mongolisation, not unlike the Golden Horde's Turkicisation. It should be kept in mind that the Turkic language known as Chaghatay that arose in Central Asia in the fifteenth and sixteenth centuries referred to the language of the Timurids and not that of the Chaghatayids of Moghulistan.

The question of whether or not one khanate became sedentary assumes that the Mongols functioned as a single entity. Certainly, the rulers gradually did out of necessity, but there is no reason to consider that the bulk of the

---

³ Peter Jackson, *The Mongols and the Islamic World* (New Haven, 2017), 183.

Mongols did so, particularly when one views these regions through history. While the focus of the Yuan Empire generally rests on China, one should not forget that China made up only part of the empire. Furthermore, historic China was not equivalent to the modern PRC. Although the government was situated in northern China and what is now Inner Mongolia, large numbers of Mongols remained in the Mongolian homeland. This population receives scant attention in the study of the Yuan Empire, but there is nothing to suggest that they significantly altered their way of life or nomadic perspective. As for the Jochid territories, more attention is given to the so-called Golden or White Horde, situated in the western half of the khanate. Our understanding of the Jochids remains incomplete. While the population certainly Turkicised and underwent conversion to Islam, there is insufficient evidence to suggest that the Mongols there did not retain a nomadic identity. Certainly, the court may have altered their identity and urban populations existed, but large numbers of nomads remained in the region even as the Jochid Khanate fragmented. As for the Ilkhanate, similar circumstances existed. Despite the existence of a large Persian-speaking population, the successors to the Ilkhanate had Mongol identities and the Uighur script continued to be used, although Turkic appears to have slowly replaced Mongolian. Persian, however, became the dominant court language.

The continued nomadic heritage of the Turko-Mongol world manifested most clearly in succession matters. Succession issues plagued the Mongol Empire from the beginning. Neither primogeniture nor ultimogeniture became the method of succession. Lateral succession, in which a brother or an uncle became the successor, also remained a possibility. While Guyuk's execution of Temuge Otchigin seemed to eliminate that possibility, a peaceful lateral succession occurred on several occasions throughout the post-dissolution Mongol world, as has been noted in the Yuan Empire with Ayurbarwada succeeding Qaishan. Gaikhatu succeeded Arghun in the Ilkhanate and Oljeitu succeeded Ghazan.[4] This occurred in the Jochid Khanate as well, as Tode-Mongke followed his brother Mongke-Temur. One should also not forget that Khubilai and Ariq-Boke both vied for power after Mongke's death; regardless of who won, a lateral succession would occur. With no clear method of succession, new avenues to power opened for those who supported the winning contender.

With all of the post-dissolution Mongol states this succession issue was tied to the rising power of the *qarachu* or non-Chinggisid Mongol elites.

---

[4] The latter may have occurred because all of Ghazan's sons died before he did. My thanks to Peter Jackson for pointing this out.

Chinggis Khan is often credited with instituting a meritocracy within the empire. This was certainly true, and it helped fuel the rapid rise and success of the *Yeke Monggol Ulus*. Yet, by the time of the dissolution of the Mongol Empire, this meritocracy no longer existed. To many of those that Chinggis Khan elevated, he also awarded hereditary privileges, thus preventing their heirs' status from relying on merit alone.[5] Certainly, men of talent and ability could find opportunities and rise through the administration and military ranks. The empire was too large for this not to happen, before and after the dissolution. Nonetheless, those who arose to the highest ranks during the period of the *Yeke Monggol Ulus* became an aristocracy as entrenched and invested in their positions as any other aristocracy. The *qarachu*, as with any elite, jealously guarded its privileges.

As was demonstrated during the Toluid Revolution, the status of particular *qarachu* and other officials rose and fell with the status of the Chinggisids they supported. This did not change during the post-dissolution period. What changed, however, was the number of Chinggisids. The Toluid Revolution purged several Chaghatayids and most of the Ogodeids. Although Qaidu was the most recognisable Ogodeid in the post-dissolution period, he was not alone. The Toluid Revolution, however, was successful in removing the legitimacy of the Ogodeid line. Qaidu's success owed more to his own ability than his grandfather's name or the intent of Chinggis Khan when he named Ogodei as his successor. The rapid disappearance of Ogodeids in positions of real power and authority in the aftermath of Qaidu's demonstrates this more than anything else.

As for the Chaghatayids, the purge during the Toluid Revolution certainly affected them, but as some Chaghatayids supported Mongke, not all was dire. Furthermore, most of the Chaghatayids who found themselves out of favour were not executed, but sent to the Song front. That Khubilai possessed Chaghatayid proxies indicates that he had a stable to choose from. As Khubilai supported Chaghatayid claims, he also served as a source of legitimacy for their house. With the death of Qaidu, no other Ogodeid had the credentials or the resources to assert himself over other Chinggisids.[6]

This left the house of Tolui and Jochi with the most Chinggisids. The Toluids, however, were quickly divided between the rise of the Yuan Empire and the Ilkhanate. While the Ilkhanate was initially subservient to the Yuan Empire, it functioned independently. Furthermore, only those Chinggisids

---

[5] *SHM*, §204–24.
[6] Timur-i Leng did use Ogodeid puppet khans, however. Beatrice Forbes Manz, 'Tamerlane and the Symbolism of Sovereignty', *Iranian Studies* 21 (1988), 112–13 sees this choice as a conscious bid to reassert the universalist empire of the thirteenth century.

descended from Hulegu could rule the Ilkhanids. Within the subset of Huleguids, those descended from his son Abaqa frequently ruled, and connection to Hulegu through Abaqa's line may have been the 'main criterion to legitimise a new ruler in the eyes of many of the Ilkhanid elite'.[7]

In the east, Ariq-Boke's defeat combined with Khubilai's longevity guaranteed that only Khubilai's lineage would rule the Yuan Empire. Khubilai's longevity cannot be understated. If he had died within the first decade or so of Mongke, or even his victory over Ariq-Boke, it may have opened the door for the sons of Mongke to claim the throne. Khubilai's plan for a Chinese-style heir apparent was new and not yet developed into an accepted institution. Furthermore, while the Ariq-Bokeids had been discredited with Ariq-Boke's defeat, Mongke's sons still had a legitimacy that those unhappy with the direction that Khubilai took could have rallied to. Khubilai's longevity, however, not only meant that he outlasted his own heir apparent, but it also permitted the circumstances for Khubilai's own dynasty to coalesce into a distinct and unassailable (at least within the Yuan Empire) identity.

The Jochids benefited from Jochi's proclivity for procreation. With thirteen sons, the Jochid Ulus was never short of Chinggisids (or perhaps just Jochids, as Chaghatay may have said with a sniff of disdain). A Batuid dynasty dominated, albeit with an interruption due to the untimely deaths of Sartaq and Ulaghchi. While it remains uncertain whether Berke had a hand in orchestrating those deaths, he failed to produce a dynasty due to a lack of sons. Additionally, the Jochid Khanate was divided into a traditional Left and Right Wing model (Blue and White Ordos). Orda, the elder brother, deferred to Batu, but it is not exactly clear why. Nonetheless, he was present at both Guyuk's and Mongke's coronations and demonstrated great ability as the Jochid representative. The fact that the Blue Horde remained the junior partner into the mid-fourteenth century indicates that its members understood its position. Only when the White Horde fell into a period of anarchy did the Blue Horde assert its independence. The fact that Toqtamysh Khan, a Toqta-Temurid, not only re-united the Blue and White Hordes but also primarily ruled from west of the Volga indicates the greater prestige of the White Horde. The fact that he achieved this unification also demonstrates the continued legitimacy of the Jochid identity within the Jochid Khanate. It also should be kept in mind that the sons of Shayban later stepped in the forefront of leadership in the eastern regions in the fifteenth century.

While kingmakers emerged from among the *qarachu* and often wielded great power, they lacked the ability to assert their authority over the entire

---

[7] Bruno De Nicola, *Women in Mongol Iran* (Edinburgh, 2017), 102–3.

ulus. There is no indication that Noghai attempted to meddle in affairs east of the Volga, nor did Mamai. Edigu proved to be a bit different, but he also benefited from a trend that existed throughout much of the former *Yeke Monggol Ulus* – the rise of the *qarachu*.

With the dissolution of the *Yeke Monggol Ulus*, the new Mongol states found themselves in the curious situation of having fewer Chinggisids. Although the *qarachu* participated in the *quriltais* that had selected new rulers since the rise of Chinggis Khan, the *altan urugh* was the deciding factor. While the *qarachu* influenced the decisions of the Chinggisids, just as the *khatuns* did, ultimately the opinion of the *altan urugh* mattered the most. Although the voice of the Chinggisids still mattered in the post-dissolution period, the *qarachu* increased in importance as they now filled a space at the *quriltai* previously occupied by other Chinggisids. They shaped the course of events in all of the post-dissolution states.

Actions of the *qarachu* factored in to the end of the Ilkhanate. After Abaqa, the *qarachu* wavered between a strong khan and a weak ruler. The ideal ruler would lead them to glory and uphold the prerogatives of the Mongol elite, both Chinggisid and *qarachu*, without also creating a strong centralised state that threatened the autonomy of the *qarachu*. On the other hand, a weak khan could easily be controlled in terms of protecting the interests of the *qarachu*; they were less effective in protecting the Ilkhanate. Powerful qarachu such as Nawruz and Choban played dramatic roles in the rise of new Ilkhans while also assisting them in wielding power. At the same time, their accumulation of power incited jealousy among other *qarachu* and stretched the patience of the ruler, leading to their downfall. As long as a leading *qarachu* maintained the support of the lesser *qarachu*, or at least the majority, he could rival the ruler and demonstrate why the ruler needed him. Conversely, the dominant *qarachu* needed the ruler's support in order to weather the plots of other qarachu who sought to supplant him. Abu Said's death without an heir exposed not only the tensions of the *qarachu* but also the scarcity of Chinggisids. While young puppets could be found, their legitimacy was questionable at best and insufficient to rally support from the rank and file or the lesser *qarachu*. While regicide was a serious crime, it was no longer something that carried an immediate threat of retaliation. As the *qarachu* began ruling independently, they still legitimised their rule through ties to the Ilkhanate.[8]

The rise of the *qarachu* was not restricted to the Ilkhanate. The Jochids experienced their share of kingmakers in Noghai and others. Noghai's

---

[8] Beatrice F. Manz, 'The Empire of Tamerlane as an adaptation of the Mongol Empire', *JRAS* 26/i–ii, 286.

questionable ancestry may have helped blur the line of distinction between being *qarachu* or Chinggisid. Mamai's ascent to power worked only as long as he maintained a khan. His abandonment of that led to difficulties with Moscow and opened himself up to challenges from the Blue Horde (Toqtamysh). Unlike in the Ilkhanid state, a plethora of Chinggisids remained to challenge the *qarachu*. Even Edigu needed a Chinggisid cover. When he lost power, the sons of Toqtamysh gained their revenge. Nonetheless, a powerful *qarachu* could still shape the course of events in the Jochid Khanate, as demonstrated by the continuation of the Noghai Horde; this confederation of tribes that recognised and supported Edigu did not disappear. It remained an independent entity in the steppes. More than once, they were the weight that tipped the scales in favour of one power or another. While the Noghai Horde may have been the ultimate manifestation of the *qarachu* power in the Jochid state, the *qarachu* continued to influence the successors to the Golden Horde.

Considering that the *qarachu* were first analysed in connection with the Crimean Khanate, one of the many successors to the Jochids, one can determine that once again the scarcity of Chinggisids magnified the importance of the *qarachu*.[9] With the fracturing of the Golden Horde into the Crimean Khanate, the Noghai Horde, the Astrakhanate, the Kazan Khanate, the Sibir Khanate and then the Ozbeg and Kazakh Khanates, one can truly see the manifestation of the qarachu beginning in the fifteenth century. As the Golden Horde fractured, the number of Chinggisids again diminished. While the overall number of Chinggisids may have remained the same or even increased, they were now divided among a seemingly increasing number of polities. The Chinggisid principle still mattered, but it was diluted as the number of *qarachu* also increased. While the Crimean Khan was truly the khan, the khan's control over the *qarachu* varied with each leader.

Gradually, these states ceased to exist in the same mould of the Chinggisid Khanate, in which the khan's authority was absolute. True, all of the *Qa'ans*, from Chinggis Khan to Mongke, and many of the post-dissolution khans, relied on the advice, opinions and wisdom of others, whether Chinggisid or *qarachu*, but the ruler's word still carried great weight. Instead, the successors to the Golden Horde became more akin to a confederation, in which the khan had to balance the various interests of each sub-unit. As the balkanisation of the *Yeke Monggol Ulus* and successor states continued, new opportunities existed. The khan had to be cautious with his authority as a disgruntled

---

[9] See Uli Schamiloglu, 'The Qaraci Beys of the Later Golden Horde: Notes on the Organization of the Mongol World Empire', *AEMA* 4 (1984), 283–97.

qarachu could desert and take his service (and his troops) to another khan. In essence, the *qarachu*'s behaviour devolved from the loyal *noyan* that Chinggis Khan created and cherished to that of the *nokor* that existed in Mongolia prior to Chinggis Khan's social revolution that accompanied the rise of the Mongol Empire.[10]

The Chaghatayids were similar to the Jochids in terms of their experience with the *qarachu* conundrum. The division of the Chaghatayid territory into Mawarannahr and Moghulistan almost mirrored the East–West division of the Jochids. There the difference ends, however. The true power of the Chaghatayids rested in the eastern portion of the empire, but it did not preclude *qarachu* acting as kingmakers, as Qamar al-Din placed Tughluq Temur on the throne. Meanwhile, in the western portion, a number of *qarachu* emerged and culminated in the appearance of the Amir Timur. He solidified his position by not only marrying a Chinggisid princess, thus gaining the title of *guregen*, but also by maintaining a Chinggisid prince on the throne. Unlike Mamai (and perhaps learning from that example), he never used the title of khan. No one was fooled by this ruse, however. But Timur's success stemmed from his military genius. His empire was over the lands of the *qarachu* successors in Mawarannahr and the ruins of the Ilkhanid state, where the ideal of a *qarachu* ruler was not alien. The Chinggisid principle still had value, but it was not mandatory. Timur only attempted to control events and diminish threats to his power in the regions where Chinggisids were dominant. He learned from his experience with Toqtamysh that if he placed a Chinggisid on the throne, he needed a powerful *qarachu* proxy to minimise the threat of Chinggisid legitimacy to his own plans. At the same time, the presence of the Chinggisid could counter the proxy's ambition. Furthermore, Timur's longevity also ensured his own dynasty's legitimacy by developing his charisma and achievements to underpin the rule of his family as a dynasty free of Chinggisid ties.[11]

Timur also affected Moghulistan. His invasions to keep the Chaghatayids in check undermined their legitimacy just as his victories over Toqtamysh did. Although he died in 1405, preparing to invade the Ming Empire and restore Chinggisid rule there, one cannot but wonder whether he would have also firmly brought the Chaghatayids under his control. Indeed, Timur benefited, as Qamar al-Din, a Dughlat *qarachu*, assassinated Tughlaq Temur's successor Ilyas in 1365 along with several other Chinggisids and then assumed power

---

[10] Timothy May, 'Nokhod to Noyad: Chinggis Khan's Social Revolution', *Mongolica* 19 (2006), 296–308.
[11] See Beatrice Forbes Manz, *The Rise and Rule of Tamerlane* (New York, 1991); Manz, 'Empire of Tamerlane', 290–1.

with a Chaghatayid puppet, before proclaiming himself khan.[12] It was in this vacuum that Timur came to power. Qamar al-Din's actions may have been retaliation for Tughluq Temur's efforts to reduce Dughlat power and influence. Tughluq Temur sought to centralise authority, and the *qarachu* reacted violently after he died.[13] Many of Qamar al-Din's *qarachu* rivals eventually joined Timur. Hodong Kim has suggested that without Qamar al-Din's actions, Timur's success might have been much slower.[14] Indeed, one might wonder whether he would have risen to power, recalling Tughluq Temur's retribution against Qazghan.

The Yuan Empire, on the surface, seemed the most immune to the rise of the *qarachu*. While Temur Oljeitu proved to be a worthy successor, the great *noyan* Bayan secured Temur Oljeitu's ascent to power. Chinggisid authority was not seriously challenged for the existence of the Yuan Empire, as other factors than just *qarachu* influenced the decisions as to who sat on the throne. Qarachu figures such as El Temur and Bayan the Merkit emerged during periods of weak rulers or rapid series of successions. They benefited from young and docile rulers, but there is no indication that any of the Yuan *qarachu* considered an independent route until the end. In the waning years of the Yuan Empire, certain generals did become *de facto* rulers in their respective regions, but they still clung to the legitimacy of the Yuan Emperor.

Two factors inoculated the Yuan Empire from the rise of the *qarachu*. As with all matters involving real estate, location was one. The Yuan Empire was based in China. The ruling elite, both Chinggisid and *qarachu*, were outsiders. No matter how sinicised they might become, they were still outsiders, particularly in the former Song Empire. The concept of the Mandate of Heaven legitimated the Chinggisid Principle in the Chinese mind to some extent, but the undercurrent of the Yuan being an alien regime never vanished as the Mongols attempted to maintain their identity and privileges. No matter whether they were progressives who recognised the need to understand and use Chinese culture to their advantage or conservatives who only sought to maintain the Mongol identity, in the eyes of the Chinese the Mongols were still Mongols whether progressive or conservative. A *qarachu* could have seized power, but success was unlikely as it would have opened the door for other non-Chinggisids beyond the *qarachu*.

It was not until after the Yuan emperor Toghon Temur abandoned the Chinese territories and the establishment of the Northern Yuan state

---

[12] Dughlat/Thackston, 12–13; Hodong Kim, 'The Early History of the Moghul Nomads: The Legacy of the Chaghatai Khanate', in *MEL*, 299–300.
[13] Kim, 'Early History of the Moghul Nomads', 304,
[14] Kim, 'Early History of the Moghul Nomads', 299.

Figure 13.1 *Tamgha* or seal in Phagspa script. Even though Qaraqorum became isolated, the Phagspa script was still used for official business, as shown on this seal. (Kharkhorin Museum, Mongolia)

that the *qarachu* truly emerged. The highest-ranking non-Chinggisids were known as *taishis*, meaning grand preceptors or regents. Due to their status, the *taishis* also attained *quda* or marriage alliance status with the imperial family. With an elevated status and close connections with the *altan urugh*, the *taishis* would use their positions to secure power and rule in the name of the emperor.

Driven from their stronghold in China, Toghon Temur's successors were now in the territories of other Chinggisids. The Ariq-Bokeids found support from the Oirat *qarachu*. The Oirat gradually emerged as an influential tribe in the *Yeke Monggol Ulus*. Not only did they grow in number, but they remained an important tribe through their practice of maintaining a *quda* status that had begun during the time of Chinggis Khan. Meanwhile, the Asud *qarachu*, Arugtai, supported Ogodeid princes. The Asud were Alans who served in the *keshig* and as other military troops. Over time, they Mongolised and became a discrete tribe within the Mongolian tribal structure.

While the power struggle could be interpreted as a war between competing Chinggisid families, in reality it was between the *qarachu*. One Ogodeid Northern Yuan ruler, Bunyashir (r. 1408–12), was actually procured from

Samarqand so that Argutai had a suitable Chinggisid to claim the throne. Eventually the Oirat gained the upper hand, and their leader Esen actually became the first non-Chinggisid khan of the Northern Yuan in 1452.[15] His actions, however, caused a backlash, as an anti-Oirat faction fought him until his death in 1454. Oirat influenced diminished, but true Chinggisid supremacy was not restored until the rise of Batu-Mongke Dayan Khan (r. 1480–1517). This was achieved only with the meticulous planning of the regent and widow of the previous khan, Mandukhai, who married the seven-year-old boy despite the great age difference (she was 33 years old). Indeed, Mandukhai was the driving force for the Chinggisid restoration as she defeated the Oirat *qarachu* Ismayil Taishi in battle in 1483. Mandukhai also abolished the *taishi* system, which had permitted the Oirat to gain power.[16]

Religion was another factor. In the Yuan Empire, the Mongols developed an affinity with different sects of Tibetan Buddhism. Due to the multifarious nature of religion within the Yuan Empire, a single sect did not achieve dominance throughout the empire. While certain lamas were not opposed to being involved in political affairs, the diversity of religion and religious matters with the Yuan Empire prevented it from becoming an ideology that could ever challenge the Chinggisid principle. Later, however, Buddhism became a key method of legitimating rulers in the absence of Chinggisid identity.[17] Esen used this, although it did not unify the Mongols in quite the way he had intended. Later Oirat leaders employed it with great success as well.

The Islamicisation of the Mongols in the west contributed to the rise of *qarachu* in unforeseen ways. While the conversion of the khans in the Ilkhanate, Jochid Ulus and the Chaghatayid Ulus initially met resistance from the *qarachu*, the Islamicisation benefited the *qarachu* in ways in which it did not benefit the Mongols. In the Ilkhanate, the resistance of the *qarachu* to the conversion of the khan can be seen as a reaction of the first generation of the post-dissolution world. These were men who were raised and previously fought for the *Yeke Monggol Ulus*, which did not subscribe to a single religion or favour one above the other. While they may have practised one religion or

---

[15] For the further use of the title Khan by the Oirat see Junko Miyawaki, 'The Legitimacy of Khanship among the Oyirad (Kalmyk) Tribes in Relation to the Chinggisid Principle', in *MEL*, 319–31.

[16] For more on these events see L. Jamsran, 'The Crisis of the Forty and the Four', in David Sneath and Christopher Kaplonski (eds), *The History of Mongolia, vol. 2, Yuan and Late Medieval Period* (Leiden, 2010), 497–507; Gongor, 'The Twelve Tumen of the Aglag Khuree Khalkha Mongols', in David Sneath and Christopher Kaplonski (eds), *The History of* Mongolia, vol. 2, Yuan *and Late Medieval Period* (Leiden, 2010), 508–21.

[17] Johan Elverskog, *Buddhism and Islam on the Silk Road* (Philadelphia, 2010), 206.

another, they also abided by the *yasa* and *yosun* of Chinggis Khan. While not a god, he was the model of proper Mongol behaviour and still the guiding light of the empire. The conversion of the khans only found support with sufficient members of the army converted, enough to embrace the religion of their khan and offset the resistance of the *qarachu*. Certainly, members of the *qarachu* also converted, but as a corporate entity, but as beneficiaries of the empire they tended to be conservative and they maintained the primary Mongol identity longer.

The Ilkhanate made the transition earlier than the other khanates for obvious reasons. More Muslims made up the Ilkhanid population than in the other khanates. While this may, at least initially, have caused a revanchist reaction among some Mongols, the fact that many Muslim Turkic nomads were in the Middle East prior to the Mongols eased the transition and perhaps accelerated it among the rank and file. Syncretic forms of Sufism also contributed to conversions, as it did not require a dramatic lifestyle change, particularly in terms of diet.[18]

By the second generation within the Middle East, conversions among the elites were commonplace but not overwhelming. Although Ghazan was not raised a Muslim, his conversion is unsurprising as he was a third-generation Mongol within the Middle East. Islam was no longer foreign, but part of the Ilkhanid landscape.

Additionally, Islam provided a new ideology. The old ideology found in Tenggerism no longer possessed the same allure. The key issue was that, after 1279, there were no more significant conquests. The wars between the Jochids and the Ilkhanate prevented both states from carrying new campaigns of conquest. For the Ilkhans, Syria proved tempting, but even Ghazan's conquest was ephemeral and only possible when no other distractions existed. For the Jochids, western expansion into Europe was possible and raids into Eastern Europe demonstrated that they had the capability. It seemed, however, that as long as Azerbaijan remained in Ilkhanid hands, the Jochids lacked the interest. Meanwhile, the Chaghatayids were surrounded and had no avenue for future conquests until the fourteenth century, except at the expense of other Mongols. Yet, in the fourteenth century, their only avenue was to India, where they faced a militarised Sultanate of Delhi. Much like the Mamluk Sultanate in Syria and Egypt, much of the legitimacy of the Sultanate of Delhi and its *raison d'être* was its defence against the Mongols. Combined with the insalubrious climate of India, the Sultanate of Delhi

---

[18] Timothy May, 'Converting the Khan: Christian Missionaries and the Mongol Empire', WHC 12, no. 2 (2015), <http://worldhistoryconnected.press.illinois.edu/12.2/forum_may.html> (last accessed 16 December 2017).

halted the expansion of the Chaghatayid Khanate, although it remained an attractive location for pillaging and plundering.

With most of their military effort expended in internecine warfare, the façade of Tenggerism was less awe-inspiring. While Berke's faith had little to do with the war with the Ilkhanids, the rhetoric of *jihad* used by a Muslim ruler was useful.[19] It could be used to justify the continued war against the Ilkhanids for Muslim rulers.

Once the khan converted and the religion was also the dominant form among the commoners, the *qarachu* risked alienation on the account of their faith. The converted *qarachu* not only found favour with the ruler, but also undoubtedly had stronger support among the faithful troops. One of the most common rationales for resisting a khan's conversion was the fear of abandoning the *yasa* in favour of the *shariʿa*. Oddly enough, the *shariʿa* could also serve as a counterweight to the authority of the khan, particularly if a member of the *qarachu* was more devout. The *yasa* and *yosun* stemmed from Chinggis Khan and then from his successors. It justified the rule of the Chinggisids. The *shariʿa* offered another avenue.[20] Ghazan and Oljeitu, in particular, may have realised this in their dalliances with Shi'ism and its emphasis on the ʿAlid family. Michael Hope has argued that their interest in Shi'ism was based more on the devotion and support of that family line. Ghazan, at least, clearly saw the need to bolster Chinggisid authority in the face of the increasing power of the *qarachu*. The majority of the Mongols, however, converted through Sufism or favoured Sunni Islam. While the family of Ali was still respected, it did not monopolise devotion.[21]

For *qarachu* such as the Amir Timur, Islam offered an avenue to power as a defender of Islam and a legal system that could justify their actions. Timur was savvy enough to understand when to emphasis his Muslim identity and when to emphasise his status as *guregen*. Timur was one of the few who convincingly balanced on the 'twin pillars of Mongol legacy and Islam'.[22]

Sufi saints and *sayyids* also served as a counter to Chinggisid authority. While it was unlikely that either could directly challenge a Chinggisid, they nonetheless served as an alternative source of authority and influence. These differed from local dynasts whose authority and charisma were dependent

---

[19] Elverskog, 186.
[20] Denise Aigle, *The Mongol Empire between Myth and Reality: Studies in Anthropological History* (Leiden, 2014), 134–56.
[21] Michael Hope, *Power, Politics, and Tradition in the Mongol Empire and the Ilkhanate of Iran* (Oxford, 2016), 174–8.
[22] Elverskog, 202.

on location. For instance, the ruler of Mosul may have found some respect among the Kartids in Herat, but he was unlikely to receive the same amount of respect as a *sayyid* or Sufi *pir* from another part of the empire, or even from another khanate.

The authority of Sufis and *sayyids* lucidly manifests in the later years of the Chaghatayid Khanate. When Tughluq Temur converted, Islam served as a centralising policy.[23] As has been discussed, his successor Ilyas was assassinated and power came into the hands of the kingmaker Dughlat's *qarachu* family. In the mid-fifteenth century the Dughlats lost their own position to Naqshbandi Sufis, who became a dynamic force in Central Asia in the fourteenth century. Unlike some Sufi *tariqas*, the Naqshbandis involved themselves in politics and were not above marrying into important families. Furthermore, they emphasised the importance of *shariʿa*. In the fifteenth century, they were able also to rally the Chaghatayids in a *jihad* against the Timurids, who favoured the Yasaviyya *tariqa*, another and more syncretic Sufi sect.[24] Gradually, two factions arose among the Naqshbandis in Moghulistan, known as the Ishaqiyya or Black Mountain (*Qara taghliq*) Sufis and the Afaqiyya or White Mountain (*Aq taghliq*) in the sixteenth century. While a Chaghatayid Khan still existed, real power rested in their hands, at least until another *qarachu* branch, the Zhungars, a new Oirat confederation, broke their power.

Similarly, another *qarachu* broke the power of the khans in the former Jochid Khanate. It has been well established that Muscovy was a successor state with deep roots in the Mongol Empire. Muscovy must be viewed as a successor state as the Chinggisid lineage remained important there well into the seventeenth century. It only diminished with the reforms of Peter the Great.[25] In this context one can view Ivan IV as a *qarachu*, although the Noghai Tatars attributed to him 'white status', and thus a Chinggisid lineage, although Ivan never claimed it.[26] While Ivan viewed his conquest of Kazan in 1552 and Astrakhan 1556 in terms of holy war, these were also wars to assert dominance in the steppe. Ivan had backed a Chinggisid faction in Kazan, but

[23] Kim, 'The Early History of the Moghul Nomads', 301–2.
[24] Elverskog, 202.
[25] Charles J. Halperin, *Russia and the Golden Horde* (Bloomington, 1987), 101. Also see Donald Ostrowski, *Muscovy and the Mongols: Cross-Cultural Influences on the Steppe Frontier, 1304–1589* (Cambridge, 2002); Charles J. Halperin, 'Ivan IV and Chinggis Khan', in Charles J. Halperin, *Russia and the Mongols: Slavs and the Steppe in Medieval and Early Modern Russia* (Bucharest, 2007), 277–97.
[26] Charles J. Halperin, 'Ivan IV and Chinggis Khan', in Charles J. Halperin, *Russia and the Mongols: Slavs and the Steppe in Medieval and Early Modern Russia* (Bucharest, 2007), 277–97.

Figure 13.2 Chinggis Khan pavilion. Although the influence of Chinggis Khan diminished during the socialist period (1921–90), the construction of the pavilion in Ulaanbaatar is a clear indication of his importance to Mongolian history.

went to war when his candidate was overthrown. In 1554, he also placed his own Chinggisid candidate on the throne in Astrakhan. When his candidate proved to be too independent-minded and sought Crimean aid, Ivan conquered Astrakhan and annexed it in 1556. Thus Ivan was not opposed to playing the role of kingmaker when necessary, and played the role much as any of the Jochid kingmaker *qarachu* did. When Ivan abdicated, he placed a Chinggisid, Symeon Bekbulatovich, the Kasym Khan, on the throne, who ruled (at least in theory) for a year (1575–6).[27] It is difficult to understand Ivan IV's motives from a twenty-first-century perspective, especially as his contemporaries confessed ignorance as well.

The dissolution and continued fracturing of the Mongol Empire may be attributed to one failed lesson. Despite the efforts of Alan Goa, the mythical ancestress of the Mongols, and Mother Hoelun, the Mongols failed to heed the Parable of the Arrows. As long as they remained united like a bundle of

---

[27] Ostrowski, *Muscovy and the Mongols*, 188; also see Donald Ostrowksi, 'Simeon Bekbulatovich's Remarkable Career as Tatar Khan, Grand Prince of Rus', and Monastic Elder', *Russian History* 39/3 (2013), 269–99.

arrows, nothing could break their empire. Yet, the dissolution of the empire left five single arrows. They snapped one by one. Their splinters could not reconstitute a single arrow over time. In his *Jamiat al-Tawarikh*, Rashid al-Din recorded an aphorism of Chinggis Khan's. It proved prophetic: 'Among my offspring, many emperors will come into existence after this. If the grandees and warriors who serve them do not maintain the *yasaq* strictly, the empire will become shaky and end. They will wish they had [Chinggis] Khan, but they will not have him.'[28]

---

[28] RD/Thackston2, 201.

Appendices

Appendix I
Regnal Dates of the Mongol Khans and Rulers of the Yuan Empire, Ilkhanate, Chaghatayid Khanate and Golden Horde[1]

Rulers and Regents of the *Yeke Monggol Ulus* (Mongol Empire), 1206–1259

Name	Reign
Chinggis Khan (Temujin)	1206–1227
Tolui (regent)	1227–1229
Ogodei Khan	1229–1241
Toregene (regent)	1241–1246
Guyuk Khan	1246–1248
Oghul Qaimish (regent)	1248–1251
Mongke Khan	1251–1259
Ariq-Boke Khan	1260–1264 (contested)
Khubilai Khan	1260–1294 (contested)

The Yuan Empire

Name	Reign
Khubilai Khan	1260–1294
Temur Oljeitu	1294–1307
Qaishan	1307–1311
Ayurbarwada	1311–1320
Shidebala	1320–1323
Yesun Temur	1323–1328

---

[1] Dates are based on those provided by C. E. Bosworth, *The New Islamic Dynasties: A Chronological and Genealogical Manual* (Edinburgh, 2004); Christopher P. Atwood, *Encyclopedia of Mongolia and the Mongol Empire* (New York, 2004); Gizat Tabuldin, *Vsemirnaya Genealogiya Chingizidov* (Kokshetau, Kazakhstan, 2012).

Name	Reign
Aragibala	1328 (contested)
Qoshila	1328–1329
Tuq-Temur	1328, 1329–1332
Irinchinbal	1332
Toghon Temur	1332–1370
Ayushiridara	1370–1378
Toghus-Temus	1378–1388

Successors become the Northern Yuan Dynasty.

The Ilkhanate

Name	Reign
Hulegu	1260–1265
Abaqa	1265–1282
Ahmad Teguder	1282–1284
Arghun	1284–1291
Baidu	1291 (contested)
Gaikhatu	1291–1295
Baidu	1295
Ghazan	1295–1304
Oljeitu	1304–1316
Abu Said	1316–1335

Ilkhanate disintegrates as rival *qarachu* elevate their own Chinggisids.

The Jochid Ulus

Name	Reign
Jochi	d. 1225
Batu	1225–1255
Sartaq	1256–1257
Ulaghachi	1257
Berke	1257–1266
Mongke-Temur	1267–1280
Tode Mongke	1280–1287
Tole Buqa	1287–1291
Toqtoa	1291–1312
Ozbeg	1313–1341

Name	Reign
Tinibeg	1341–1342
Janibeg	1342–1357
Berdibeg	1357–1359
Qulpa	1359
Nawruz	1360
Khidyr	1361
Abdullah	1361–1365?
Temur Khwaja	1361
Murid	1362–1364
Aziz	1364–1367
Bolat-Temur	1365, 1367, 1369
Mamai (king maker)	1370–1380
Toqtamysh (ruled Blue Horde first)	1380–1398
Edigu's period of domination begins	1398
Temur Qutlugh	1391–1393, 1398–1400
Shadibeg	1400–1407
Pulad (Bolod)	1407–1410
Temur Khan b. Temur Qutlugh	1410–1412
Jalal al-Din b. Toqtamysh	1412
Karim Berdi b. Toqtamysh	1412–1414
Kebek b. Toqtamysh	1414–1417
Yeremferden b. Toqtamysh	1417–1419
Edigu's period of domination ends	1419
Ulugh Muhammad	1419–1427 (contested)
Dawlat Berdi	1420–1427 (contested)
Baraq	1422–1427 (contested
Ulugh Muhammad	1427–1433 (second reign uncontested)
Sayyid Ahmad I	1433–1435
Kuchuk Muhammad	1435–1465
Ahmad	1465–1481
Shaykh Ahmad b. Ahmad	1481–1499 (co-ruler)
Sayyid Ahmad II b. Ahmad	1481–1499 (co-ruler)
Murtada b. Ahmad	1481–1499 (co-ruler)
Shaykh Ahmad	1499–1502 (sole ruler)

Golden Horde disintegrates with defeat of Shaykh Ahmad in 1502. His death in 1505 truly ends the Jochid Ulus as a single empire.

The Chaghatay Khanate

Name	Reign
Chaghadai	d. 1242
Qara Hulegu	1242–1246
Yesu Mongke	1246–1251
Orghina (regent)	1251–1260
Alghu	1260–1266
Mubarak Shah	1266
Baraq	1266–1271
Negubei	1271–1272
Buqa Temur	1272
Domination of Qaidu	1272–1301
Dua	1281–1307
Konchek	1307–1308
Naliq'oa	1308–1309
Esen Buqa	1309–1318
Kebek	1318–1327
Eljigidei	1327–1330
Dore Temur	1330–1331
Tarmashirin	1331–1334
Buzan	1334–1335
Changshi	1335–1338
Yesun Temur	1338–1340
Ali Sultan (Ogodeid)	1340
Ali Khalil Sultan	1341–1343
Muhammad b. Bolod	1342–1343
Qazan	1343–1346/47
Danishmend	1347–1348 (western portion)
Buyan Quli	1348–1358 (western portion)
Temur Shah	1359–1360 (western portion)
Tughluq Temur	1347–1363

Mawarannahr comes under the control of Amir Timur (Tamerlane, Timur-i Leng). Qamar al-Din dominates Moghulistan.

Appendix II
Genealogical Charts

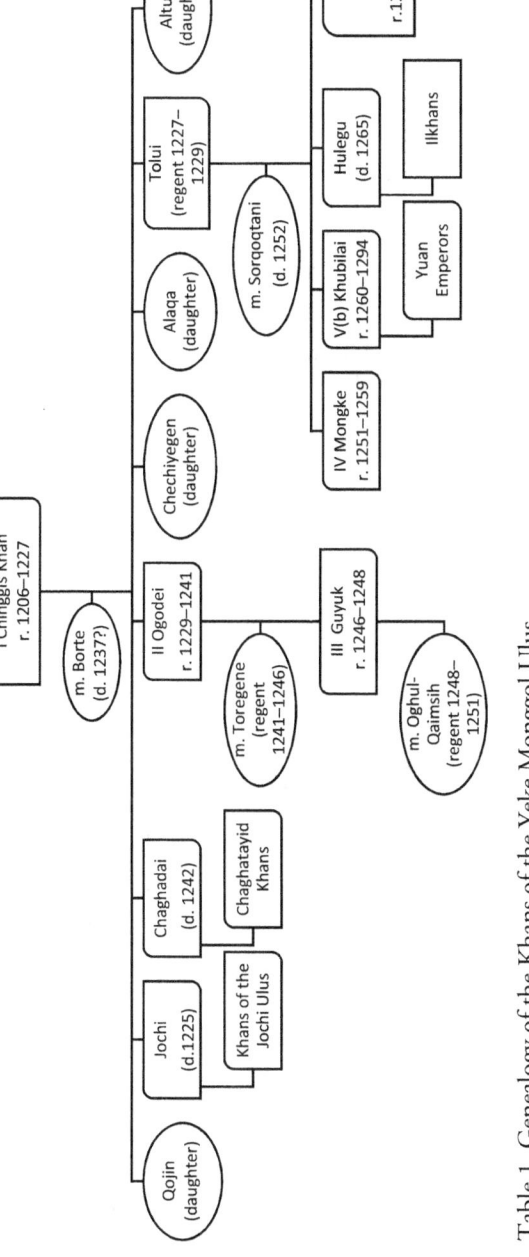

Table 1 Genealogy of the Khans of the Yeke Monggol Ulus

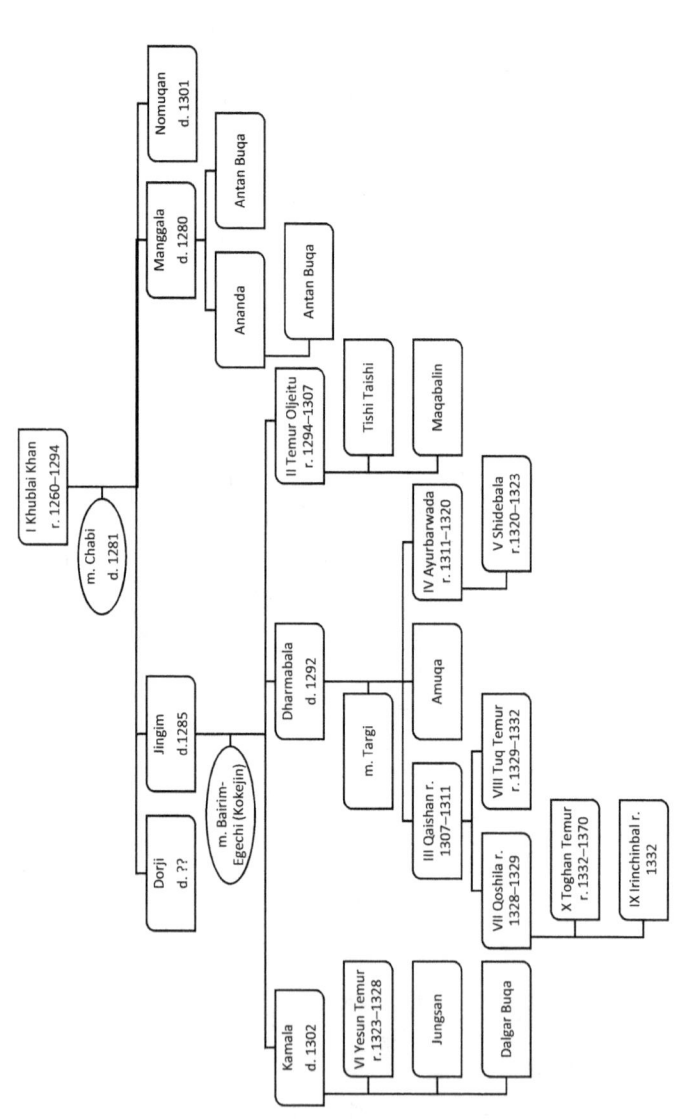

Table 2 Genealogy of the Yuan Emperors (with partial listing of Khubilai Khan's sons)

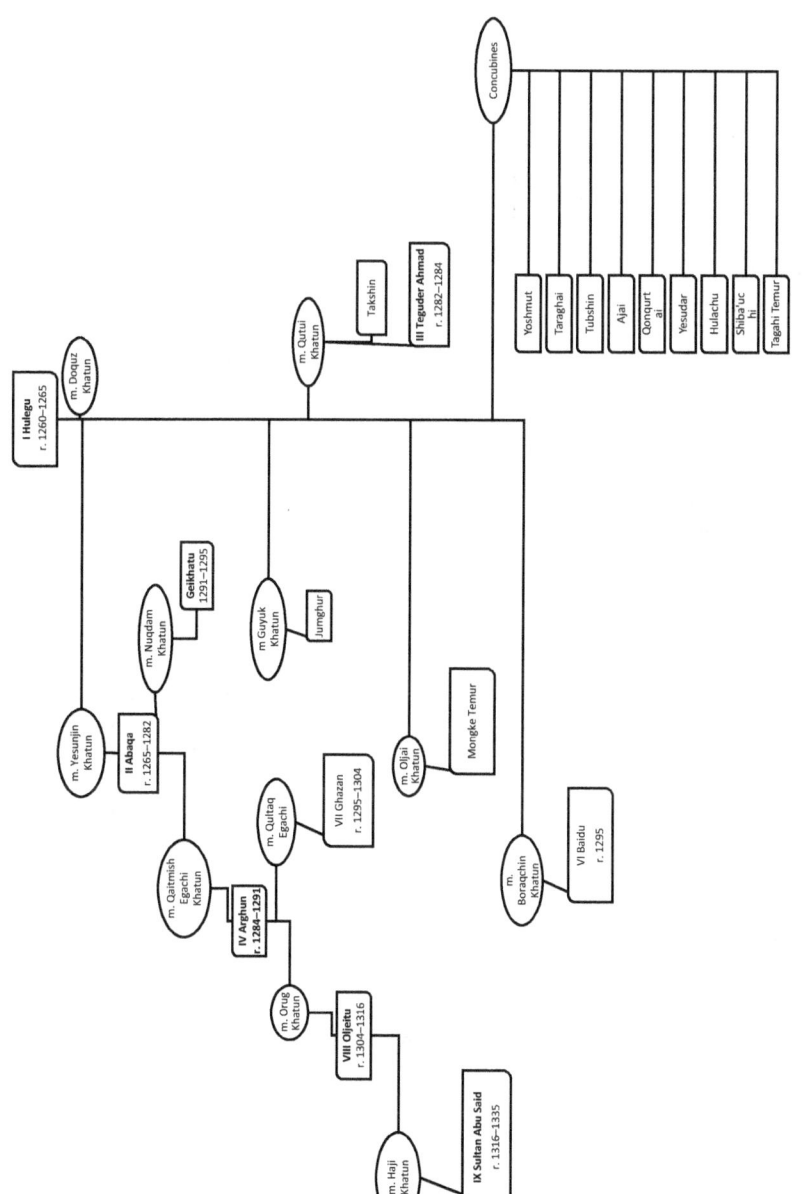

Table 3 Genealogy of the Ilkhans

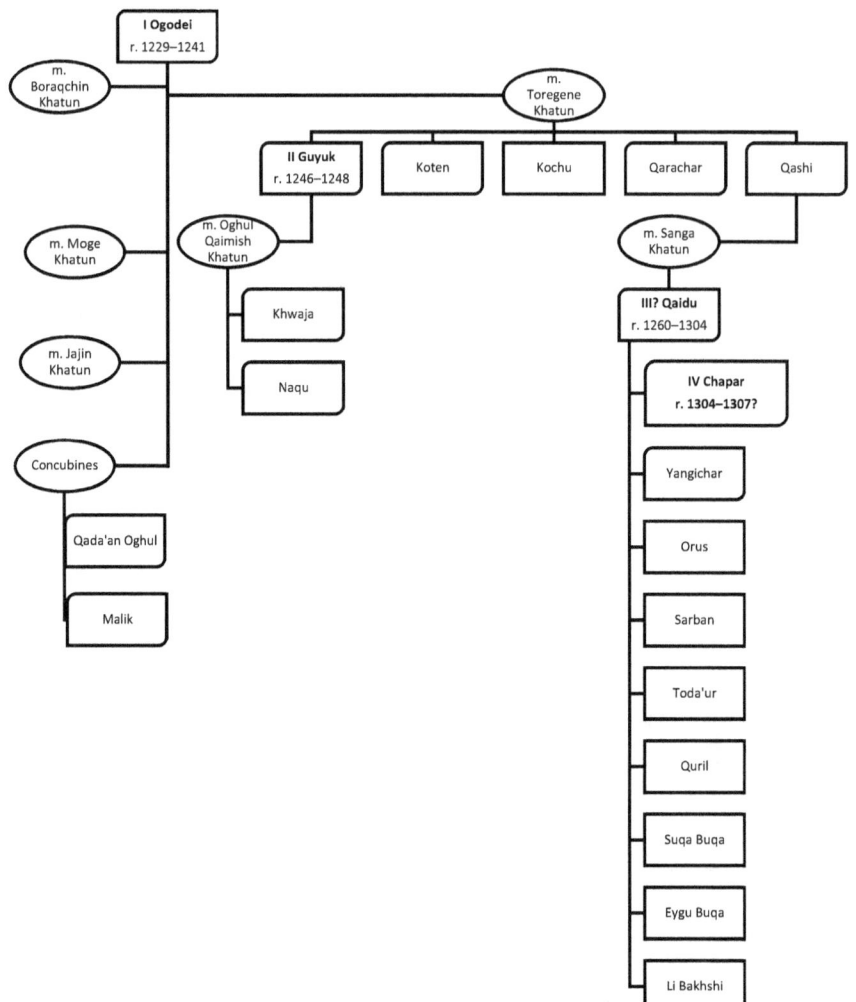

Table 4 Genealogy of the Ogodeids

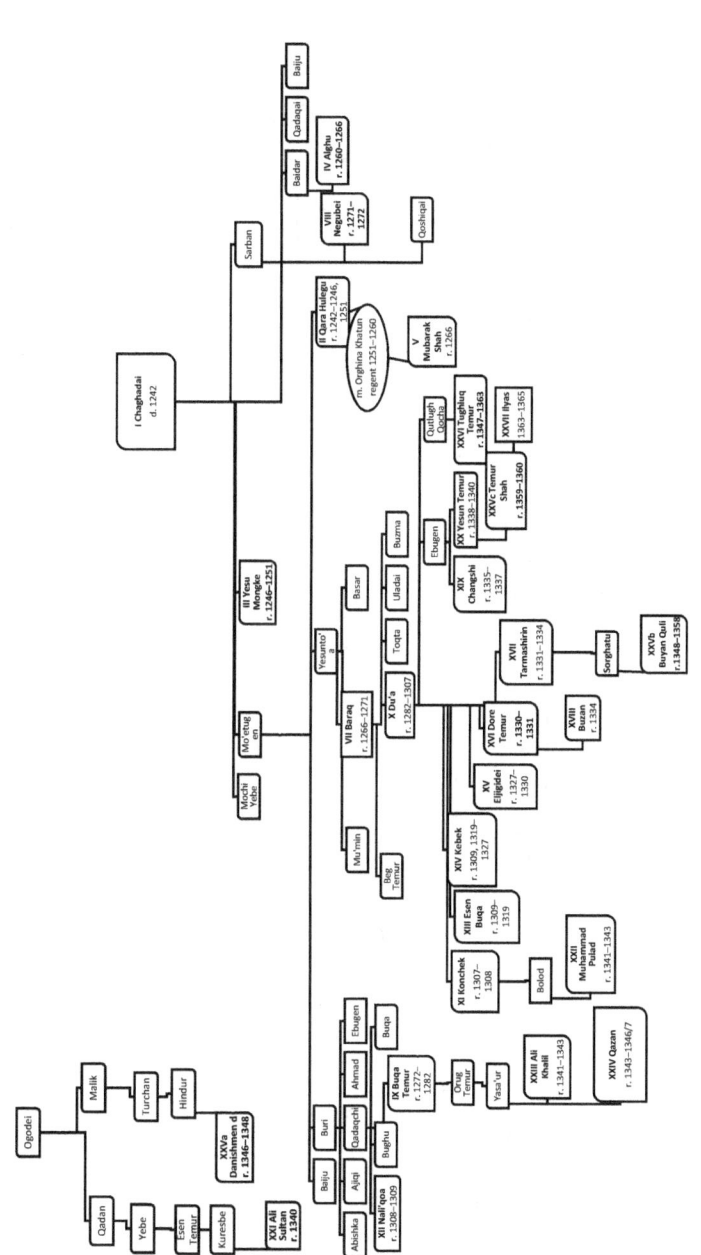

Table 5 Genealogy of the Chaghatayids (mothers excluded as they are omitted for a number of children, *khatun* or otherwise)

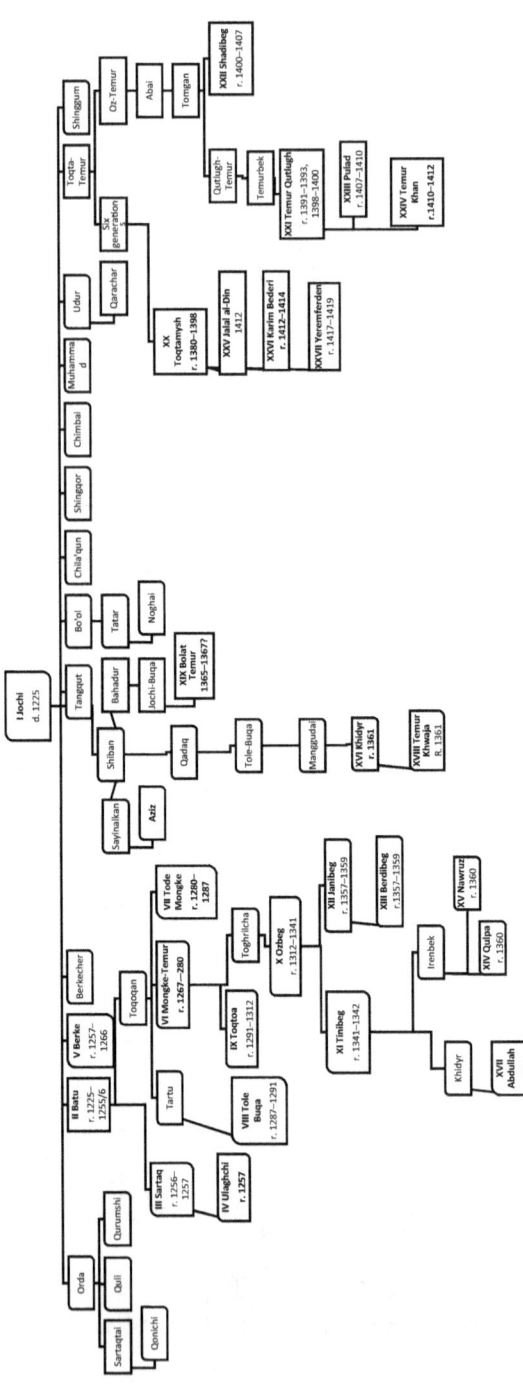

Table 6 Genealogy of the Jochids (after Toqtamysh's sons, the genealogy becomes quite confused)

Appendix III
Chronological Outline

Date	East Asia
1115	Jurchen tribes unify and form the Jin state.
1125	Jin Empire conquers the Liao Empire.
1160	Yesugei takes Borte as a wife.
1162	Temujin (Chinggis Khan) is born.
1164	Mongol confederation defeated by Jin–Tatar alliance; death of the Mongol Khan, Qutula.
1187	Jamuqa defeats Temujin at Dalan-baljut. Temujin takes refuge in Jin Empire.
1195	Temujin returns to Mongolia.
1196–1197	Temujin and Toghril ally with Jin Empire against the Tatars.
1198	*Juyin* rebel against the Jin Empire.
1199	Temujin and Toghril campaign against the Naiman.
1201	Jamuqa forms Gurkhanid confederation against Temujin and Toghril.
1202	Mongols defeat Tatars at Battle of Dalan-Nemurges.
1203	Temujin defeats Toghril and the Kereit at the Battle of Qalqajit Sands.
1204	Mongols defeat the Naiman at Chakirmaut and unify Mongolia.
1205	Mongols begin to raid Xi Xia.
1206	Temujin becomes Chinggis Khan at *quriltai*.
1207	Jochi gains submission of the Hoyin-Irgen.
1209	Mongols invade Xi Xia.
1210	Xi Xia submits to the Mongols.
1211	Chinggis Khan invades the Jin Empire.
1212	Mongols withdraw from the Jin Empire and invade again in autumn.
1214	Jin send tribute to Chinggis Khan; Jin Emperor moves to Kaifeng and war renews.
1215	Zhongdu falls.

1216	Hoi-yin Irgen rebel.
1218	Hoi-yin Irgen subdued.
1223	Muqali dies; Xi Xia rebels.
1225	Chinggis Khan invades Xi Xia again.
1227	Chinggis Khan dies; Xi Xia destroyed.
1229	Ogodei becomes new *Qa'an* (*Khaghan*) of the *Yeke Monggol Ulus*.
1230	Mongols invade Jin Empire again.
1234	Jin Empire is destroyed.
1235–1236	Qaraqorum is built; Mongols conduct census of North China.
1240	Ogodei dies; Toregene becomes regent.
1246	Guyuk becomes ruler of the Mongol Empire.
1248	Guyuk dies. Oghul Qaimish becomes regent.
1250	Toluid Revolution; Mongke becomes ruler of the Mongol Empire.
1252	Formal ceremonial worship of Chinggis Khan begins; Dali submits to Mongols.
1256	Major invasion of Song Empire begins.
1258	Annam submits to Mongols.
1259	Mongke Khan dies.
1260	Dissolution of the Empire; Ariq-Boke and Khubilai hold separate *quriltais* and become khan. Civil war begins.
1261	Phaspa Lama becomes state preceptor and head of all monks.
1262	Khubilai captures Qaraqorum; Li Tan revolts in Shandong peninsula.
1264	Ariq-Boke surrenders.
1265	Ariq-Boke dies.
1267	Daidu constructed; Phagspa Lama develops new universal writing script for the Yuan Empire.
1268	Envoys demand Japan's surrender.
1271	Khubilai new legal code takes effect.
1273	Mongol armies seize the cities of Xiangyang and Fangcheng in the Song Empire; Prince Jingim named Khubilai's heir-apparent.
1274	Khubilai sends Bayan with an army of 100,000 against the Song Empire; first Mongol invasion of Japan; Phagspa Lama retires as imperial preceptor.
1275	Song Chancellor Jia Sidao is defeated at Dingjia Island.
1276	Song capital of Lin'an submits to Bayan.
1279	Mongols win naval victory at Yaishan; end of Song Empire; Mongols invade Pagan (Burma).

1281	Second Mongol invasion of Japan; Chabi Khatun dies; Mongols invade Champa (southern Vietnam).
1285	Prince Jimgim dies.
1286	Third Mongol invasion of Japan is cancelled; Mongols invade Java.
1287	Prince Nayan rebels in Manchuria; Qaidu invades Mongolia.
1294	Khubilai Khan dies.
1295	Temur Oljeitu becomes Emperor of the Yuan Empire.
1300–1303	Temur Oljeitu sends punitive raids into Burma and Thailand.
1304	Peace throughout the Mongol Empire – *Pax Mongolica*.
1307	Temur Oljeitu dies.
1307	Qaishan becomes Khan.
1311	Ayurbarwada takes throne and reverses Qaishan's policies in favour of Sino-centric ideas.
1313	Ayurbarwada reinstituted Confucian civil service exams.
1320	Shidebala succeeds his father.
1323	Shidebalas is assassinated due to pro-Chinese policies; Yesun Temur becomes Khan.
1328	Aragibala is enthroned, replaced by Qoshila.
1329	Tugh Temur takes throne through fratricide with assistance from El Temur.
1330s	Red Turban rebellions begin in South China.
1332	Toghon Temur takes throne in Yuan Empire.
1340s	Black Plague is present.
1368	Yuan driven out of China; establishment of the Ming Dynasty.
1370	Toghon Temur dies in Mongolia.
1388	Yuan Dynasty ends; Northern Yuan Dynasty begins.
1400s	Period of civil wars in Mongolia.

Date	Central Asia
1131	Qara Khitai established.
1141	Yelu Dashi of Qara Khitai defeats the Seljuk Sultan Sanjar at the battle of Qatwan Steppes.
1208	Mongols defeat Naiman and Merkit at the Battle of Irtysh River.
1209	Uighurs submit to Chinggis Khan.
1216	Muhammad II Khwarazmshah defeats the Ghurid Empire in Afghanistan.
1218	Guchulug killed; Qara Khitai submits to Jebe; Mongol-sponsored caravan massacred at Otrar.

1219	Chinggis Khan marches on the Khwarazmian Empire.
1221	Mawarannahr conquered by the Mongols; Jalal al-Din defeated at the Indus River.
1230	Dayir moves *tamma* into Ghur and Ghazna.
1242	Chaghadai dies.
1250–1252	Purge of Ogodeids and Chaghatayids opposed to Mongke.
1252	Orghina becomes regent of Chaghatayid Ulus.
1260	Dissolution of the Empire.
1262	Chaghatayid prince, Alghu, occupies Central Asia for Ariq-Boke.
1263	Alghu rebels against Ariq-Boke.
1264	Alghu allies with Khubilai Khan and marries Orghina Khatun; census of the Chaghatayid Ulus.
1266	Alghu dies; Mubarak Shah becomes Chaghatayid Khan; Baraq becomes Khan.
1267	Qaidu and Baraq Khan war. Peace of Qatwan is negotiated.
1268	Khubilai forces Qaidu to withdraw from Yuan territory.
1270	Battle of Herat. Baraq is defeated by the Ilkhan Abaqa. Baraq dies.
1271	Qaidu is crowned as Khan; Chaghatayid Khanate is subordinate to Qaidu.
1273	Ilkhan Abaqa sacks Bukhara.
1282	Baraq's son Du'a becomes Chaghatayid Khan.
1300	Yuan forces invade Qaidu's territory.
1301	Yuan armies defeat Qaidu; Qaidu later dies.
1303	Du'a takes control of Ogodeid and Chaghatayid Khanates.
1304	Peace throughout the Mongol Empire – *Pax Mongolica*.
1307	Du'a dies.
1308	Konchek takes throne, defeating Nali'qoa.
1333	Tarmashirin Khan overthrown.
1340s	Black Plague strikes.
1347	Qazghan usurps power in Mawarannahr; Tughluq Temur becomes Khan in Moghulistan.
1358	Chaghatayid rule restored in Mawarannahr.
1365	Direct Chaghatayid rule in Mawarannahr ends.
1370	Timur (Tamerlane) assumes power in Mawarannahr.
1370s and '80s	Timur conquers former Ilkhanid domains.
1387	Toqtamysh begins war with Timur (Tamerlane).

Date	Middle East
1220s	Mongols pillage Khurasan and northern Iran; Fifth Crusade in progress.
1230	Chormaqan invades.
1234	Chormaqan's *tamma* move to the Mughan Steppe.
1238	Chormaqan invades Armenia and Georgia.
1240	Chormaqan dies; Baiju assumes command.
1243	Baiju defeats Seljuks at Kose Dagh.
1244	Khwarazmians sack Jerusalem.
1256	Ket-Buqa invades Quhistan; Baiju ends Seljuk rebellion at Aq Saray; destruction of the Ismaili Assassins by Hulegu.
1258	Siege of Baghdad and fall of the Abbasid Caliphate.
1260	Mongol conquest of Damascus, defeated by Mamluks at ʿAyn Jalut; dissolution of the Empire.
1261–1262	Mosul rebels against Mongols.
1262	War with Golden Horde begins.
1265	The first Ilkhan, Hulegu, dies.
1266	Abaqa becomes Ilkhan.
1268	Rashid al-Din converts to Islam.
1282	Ilkhan Abaqa dies; Teguder becomes Ilkhan.
1284	Teguder is assassinated.
1284	Abaqa's son Arghun becomes il-Khan.
1291	Baidu and Gaikhatu compete for throne; Gaikhatu becomes il-khan.
1291	Mamluks end the Crusader states.
1292	Mamluks invade Anatolia.
1295	Gaikhatu overthrown; Baidu become il-Khan; Ghazan overthrows Baidu.
1304	Peace throughout the Mongol Empire – *Pax Mongolica*; Ghazan dies; Oljeitu becomes il-khan.
1305	Oljeitu starts construction of new capital of Sultaniyya.
1310	Oljeitu converts to Shia Islam.
1316	Oljeitu dies, Abu Sa'id becomes the ruler and Amir Choban serves as regent.
1318	Rashid al-Din executed on suspicion of poisoning Oljeitu.
1319	Attempted coup against Abu Sa'id thwarted by Choban.
1322	Peace Treaty with Mamluk Sultanate is achieved.
1335	Abu Sa'id dies; Ilkhanate ends in succession squabbles.
1340s	Plague stalks the Middle East.
1357	Janibeg of the Golden Horde conquers Tabriz.

1387	Toqtamysh begins war with Timur (Tamerlane); invades Azerbaijan.
1391	Timur invades Golden Horde; Battle of Kunduzcha.
1402	Timur defeats Ottomans at Ankara.

Date	Western Steppes and Europe
1223	Battle of Kalka River.
1236	Mongols attack Bulghar and Kipchaks.
1237	Mongols attack Rus' principalities.
1239	Conquest of the Rus' completed.
1241	Mongols invade Poland and Hungary.
1245	Mongols send *basqaqs* to Rus' principalities.
1250	Rus' territories become a fiscal region.
1254–1259	Census of Rus' territories.
1256	Batu dies.
1260	Dissolution of the Empire.
1262	War with Ilkhanate begins.
1266	Genoese permitted to trade at Kaffa; Berke Khan dies.
1267	Mongke-Temur comes to throne.
1280	Mongke-Temur dies; Tode-Mongke comes to throne and Noghai becomes kingmaker.
1287	Noghai replaces Tode-Mongke with Tele Buqa.
1290	Tole Buqa rebels against Noghai and is executed; Toqta becomes Jochid Khan.
1297	Toqta rebels against Noghai.
1299	Noghai dies; Toqta rules unopposed.
1304	Peace throughout the Mongol Empire – *Pax Mongolica*.
1308	Toqta's armies sack Kaffa.
1312	Toqta dies; Ozbeg takes throne.
1319	Yuri of Moscow gains *jarliq* to collect taxes in Rus' cities.
1340	Ozbeg Khan dies.
1340s	The Black Plague strikes.
1341	Tinibeg Khan takes throne; dies from plague.
1342	Janibeg becomes Khan of the Golden Horde.
1343	Janibeg attacks Tana after sectarian riots; attacks Kaffa; Kaffa becomes an epicentre of Black Plague.
1347	Genoese and Venetians blockade Golden Horde ports; trading privileges restored.
1357	Janibeg conquers Tabriz.

1359	Berdibeg Khan assassinated; Golden Horde descends into civil war.
1360s	Blue Horde becomes independent.
1370s	Ascension of the *qarachu* Mamai in the west.
1378	Toqtamysh takes control of Blue Horde with assistance from Tamerlane.
1380	Mamai defeated by Dmitri Donskoi at Kulikovo; Toqtamysh defeats Mamai at Kalka River.
1382	Toqtamysh defeats Lithuanians at Poltava.
1387	Toqtamysh begins war with Timur (Tamerlane); invades Azerbaijan.
1391	Timur invades Golden Horde; Battle of Kunduzcha.
1393	Toqtamysh overthrows Temur Qutlugh, Timur's Golden Horde proxy.
1395	Timur invades Golden Horde; Battle of Terek River and sack of Sarai.
1400s	Edigu's period of dominance.
1406	Toqtamysh dies.
1480	Ahmad Khan defeated at the Battle of Ugra River.
1502	Ahmad Khan defeated by Crimean Tatars.
1505	Golden Horde truly ends.

Glossary

A. = Arabic
C. = Chinese
K. = Khitan
M. = Mongolian
P. = Persian
T. = Turkic

Airagh (M.)	Fermented mare's milk.
Alba qubchiri (M.)	Tribute or levy usually taken in form of service or in kind (livestock).
Alginchi (M.)	A scout.
Altan Urugh (M).	The Golden Kin or Family; referred to not only Chinggis Khan's family and descendants, but those of his brothers as well.
Amir (A.)	A military commander or prince.
Anda (M.)	A sworn brother or blood brother.
Arban (M.)	A unit of ten in the Mongol military.
Atabeg (T.)	A guardian to prince.
Baljuna Covenant	A possibly legendary event where a number of commanders pledged their loyalty to Temujin after initially being defeated by the Kereit.
Basqaq (T.)	A local governor or representative of the khan.
Beg (T.)	A tribal chieftain.
Boqta (M.)	Tall headdress worn by Mongol women that could be lavishly decorated.
Chao (C.)	Paper money.
Chingsang (M.)	Mongolian form of the Chinese *chingxiang* or junior grand counsellor.
Dalay (M.)	State-controlled land directly controlled by the imperial government and separate from *inju* or *qubi* designated territory.

Daruqachi (M.)	A local governor or representative of the khan. Daruga becomes the Russian form.
Dasht-i Kipchak (P.)	The steppes in Eurasia which include the Pontic and Caspian steppes and which were populated primarily by Kipchak Turks.
Diwan (A. and P.)	A governmental ministry or department.
Etugen (M.)	The earth goddess in native Mongolian religious belief.
Faqih (A.)	Muslim jurist.
Ger (M.)	The round felt tent used by the steppe nomads.
Gerege (M.)	A passport or tablet that allowed one to access the *jam*.
Gobi (M.)	A gravelly desert with scrubby plant life.
Gur-Khan	A term that meant Universal Ruler. Primarily used by the rulers of Qara Khitai, but also used by Jamuqa in his short-lived confederation.
Guregen (M.)	A son-in-law, someone who married a Chinggisid princess.
Hadith (A.)	The sayings and actions of the Prophet Muhammad, seen as a model of proper behaviour, action and thought.
Hanren (C.)	Northern Chinese people. Term used in the four-tier hierarchy of the Yuan Empire. Included Han, Jurchen, Khitans, Tangut and Koreans.
Hoi-yin Irgen (M.)	Literally, the People of the Forests. A collective term for the various tribes of the Siberian forests north of Mongolia (and perhaps beyond), who were not pastoral nomads.
Inju (M.)	Property of the Khan.
Iqta (A.)	A land grant.
Jaghun (M.)	A unit of one hundred in the Mongol military.
Jam (M.)	The Mongolian government's postal system. Also known as *yam* (T.).
Jarliq (M.)	Decree, order.
Jarqu (M.)	Tribunal or an investigation.
Jarquchi (M.)	A judge or governor of a large region.
Ja'ut quri (M.)	Title given to foreign commanders by the Jin Empire with a meaning that roughly corresponds to 'Commissioner in Charge of Rebel Pacification'.
Juyin (K.)	Nomadic tribes and other groups that served as guards on the Jin's borders with the steppes. In

	return for service they received trading privileges and protection.
Keshig (M.)	The bodyguard of the Mongol khan.
Khaghan (M. and T.)	Turkic and Mongolian term for Emperor.
Khan (M. and T.)	Turkic and Mongolian term for king.
Kharaj (A.)	Land tax.
Khatun (M.)	Queen or princess.
Khutba (A.)	Sermon given during Friday service at a mosque. Mention of the ruler's name assists in legitimising the ruler. Omission also implies illegitimacy.
Kiswa (A.)	The black cloth that adorns the Kaaba.
Kumiss (T.)	Turkic term for fermented mare's milk.
Madhhab (A.)	School of Islamic jurisprudence, usually for one of the four major Sunni schools of interpretation: Hanifi, Hanbali, Maliki and Shafa'i.
Madrasa (A.)	Islamic educational institution.
Mamluk (A.)	Generically a slave, but usually refers to a military slave.
Mengguren (C.)	The Mongol people; term used in a hierarchy system in the Yuan Empire.
Minbar (A.)	Pulpit in a mosque.
Minqan (M.)	A unit of one thousand in the Mongol military.
Nanren (C.)	The South Chinese people. Term used in the four-tier hierarchy of the Yuan Empire. Referred to population of the former Song Empire, including non-ethnic Chinese.
Nasij (A.)	A gold brocade cloth cherished by the Mongols.
Nerge (M.)	A hunting and battlefield technique in which the Mongols formed a gradually contracting ring, forcing those inside into the centre.
Nokor (M.)	A companion or bondsman to a more powerful figure. The plural is *nokod*.
Noyan (M.)	Mongolian term for a military commander. Plural is *noyad*.
Ordo (M)	Mongolian word for someone's camp. Also spelled *orda* and *ordu* (T.). It also became the term for 'palace' and is the basis of the English word 'horde'.
Paiza (C.)	A passport or tablet that allowed one to access the *jam*.
Qarachu (M.)	The Mongol aristocracy – non-Chinggisids. Also referred to as Qarachi.

Qubchur (M.)	A poll-tax on adult males.
Qubi (M.)	A share of property or *inju*. A city might be divided among members of the *altan urugh*, with each receiving a *qubi*.
Quda (M.)	A marriage alliance.
Quriltai (M. and T.)	A congress or meeting of nomadic leaders. Held to select new rulers and to make major decisions such as planning for war.
Sayyid (A.)	A descendant of the Prophet Muhammad.
Semuren (C.)	Term used for the 'round eye' people or westerns (west of China). Used in the four-tier hierarchy of the Yuan Empire.
Shahna (P.)	A local governor or representative of the khan.
Shari'a (A.)	Islamic law. Literally, 'path'.
Shulen (M.)	Mongolian term for soup.
Shumi Yuan (C.)	Ministry of War.
Sulde (M.)	The soul or genius or a particular person or group.
Sunna (A.)	The way or path of the Prophet Muhammad.
Taishi (C.)	Grand Preceptor or regent.
Tamgha (M.)	Literally, stamp or seal. Also a Value Added Tax or tariff paid on goods.
Tamma (M.)	Mongol military unit stationed on the frontier.
Tammachi (M.)	A member or commander of a *tamma*.
Tariqat (A.)	The order or brotherhood of a particular branch of Sufism.
Tenggeri (M. and T.)	Mongolian term that referred to Heaven or gods in general. Usually, Tenggeri referred to Koke Mongke Tenggeri, the Blue Eternal Sky – the primary deity in Mongolian religious belief.
Tumen (M.)	A unit of 10,000 in the Mongol military.
Ulus (M.)	Mongolian term that referred to a patrimony or even a nation. Typically only used to refer to the Mongols. *Irgen* was used to refer to non-Mongols.
Wafidiyya (A.)	Refugees. Used as a general term for Mongols who deserted to the Mamluk Sultanate, including as a military force.
Wang (C.)	King, prince.
Yasa (M.)	The law code or system of Chinggis Khan. It primarily applied to the nomads.
Yasun (M.)	Bone or family line. There were two types: White (*chaghan*) and Black (*qara*). White meant

	royalty (the Chinggisids or *altan urugh*) while Black referred to the aristocracy. Qara could also refer to commoners.
Yeke Jarquchi (M.)	High judge or governor.
Yosun (M.)	The customs and traditions of the Mongolian nomads. It primarily guided proper behaviour.
Yurt (T.)	Turkic term that has entered common usage for the round felt tents used by the steppe nomads.
Zhongwen Qingwu (C.)	Chinese policy that emphasised the civil administration while de-emphasising the importance of the military.
Zhud (M.)	A devastating snow and ice storm that may not only freeze the livestock of nomads, but also cover the grass to the extent that animals are unable to eat.

Bibliography

Primary Sources

Abu Shamah, Shihab al-Din ᶜAbd al-Rahman ibn Isma'il al-Shafi, *Tarajim rijal, al-qarnayn al-sadis wa'l-sabi al-ma'ruf bi-dhayl al-rawdatayn*, ed. Muhammad Kawthari (Cairo, 1947).

Arghun, 'Lettre d'Arɣun à Philippe le Bel, datée de 1289', pp. 17–18, in Antoine Mostaert and Francis Woodman Cleaves (eds and trans.), *Les Lettres de 1289 et 1305 des ilkhan Arɣun et Oljeitu à Philippe le Bel* (Cambridge, MA, 1962).

Bar Hebraeus, *The Chronography of Bar Hebraeus*, trans. E. A. W. Budge (London, 1932).

Bar Hebraeus, *The Chronography of Gregory Abu'l Faraj*, trans. E. A. W. Budge (Piscataway, NJ, 2003).

Baybars al Mansuri, *Mukhtar al-Akbar: ta'rikh al-dawlah al-ayyubiyah dawlat al-mamalik al-bahriyah haata sanat 702 h*, ed. ᶜAbd al-Hamid Salih (Cairo, 1993).

Benedictus Polonus, 'Relatio Fr. Benedicti Poloni', in P. Anastasius Van Den Wyngaert (ed.), *Sinica Franciscana: Itinera et Relationes Fratrum Minorum Saeculi XIII et XIV* (Florence, 1929), 131–43.

Benedict the Pole, 'The Narrative of Brother Benedict the Pole', trans. Christopher Dawson, in Christopher Dawson, *Mission to Asia* (Toronto, 1980), 77–84.

Blake, R. P. and Frye, R. N. (ed. and trans.), 'The History of the Nation of the Archers by Grigor of Akanc', *HJAS* 12 (1949), 269–399.

Bretschneider, E. (ed.), *Medieval Researches from Eastern Asiatic Sources*, 2 vols (New York, 1967).

Bridia, C. de, *The Tatar Relation*, trans. George D. Painter, pp. 54–101, in R. A. Skelton, Thomas E. Marston and George D. Painter (eds), *The Vinland Map and the Tatar Relation* (New Haven, 1965).

Chan, Hok-lam (trans.), *The Fall of the Jurchen Chin: Wang E's Memoir on the Ts'ai-Chou Under the Mongol Siege (1233–1234)* (Stuttgart, 1993).

Chih-Ch'ang, Li. *The Travels of the Alchemist: The journey of the Taoist Ch'ang Ch'un form China to the Hindukush at the summons of Chingiz Khan*, trans. Arthur Waley (Westport, CT, 1976).

Clavijo, Gonzalez de, *Embassy to Tamerlane 1403–1406*, trans. Guy Le Strange (London, 1928).

Cleaves, Francis W. (ed. and trans.), *The Secret History of the Mongols* (Cambridge, MA, 1982).

Cleaves, Francis W. (trans.), 'The Biography of the Empress Cabi in the Yuan Shih', *HUS* 3/4, pt. 1 (1979–80), 138–50.
Conlan, Thomas D. (trans.), *In Little Need of Divine Intervention: Takezaki Suengaga's Scrolls of the Mongol Invasions of Japan* (Ithaca, 1994).
Currie, Richard Paul (trans.), 'An Annotated Translation of the Biography of Togto Temur from the Yuan Shih', MA thesis, Department of Uralic and Altaic Studies, Indiana University, 1984.
Dawson, Christopher, ed. *Mission to Asia* (Toronto, 1980).
Demchigdorzh, Ch (trans.), *Yuan Ulsyn Sudar*, B. Sumiyabaatar and J. Serjee (eds) (Ulaanbaatar, 2002).
Dulaurier, M. Éd (ed. and trans), 'Les Mongols d'après les historiens arméniens: Extrait de l'histoire universelle de Vartan; *Journal Asiatique* 13 (1860), 273–315.
Dulaurier, M. Ed (ed. and trans.), 'Les mongols d'après les historiens armeniens: fragments traduits sur les textes originaux', *Journal Asiatique* 11 (1858), 192–255, 426–73, 481–508; 16 (1860), 273–322.
Al-Dhahabi, *Kitab Duwal al-Islam* (Les Dynasties de L'Islam), trans. Arlette Negre (Damascus, 1979).
Dughlat, Mirza Haydar, *Tarikh-i-Rashidi: A History of the Khans of Moghulistan* (Books 1 and 2), trans. Wheeler M. Thackston (London, 2012).
Ermonlinskaia Letopis, ed. A. E. Tsepkov (Riazan', 2000).
Grigor of Akner, 'The History of the Nation of the Archers by Grigor of Akancʻ', R. P. Blake and R. N. Frye (eds and trans.), *HJAS* 12 (1949), 269–399.
Golden, Peter B. (ed.), *The King's Dictionary The Rasulid Hexaglot*, trans. Tibor Halasi-Kun, Peter B. Golden, Louis Ligeti and Edmund Schutz (Leiden, 2000).
Guyuk, 'Guyuk Khan's letter to Pope Innocent IV (1246)', English version based on the trans. by D. A. Maitland Muller (see p. xxxix), in Christopher Dawson (ed.), *Mission to Asia* (Toronto, 1980), 85.
al-Hadid, ʿAbd al-Hamid ibn Hibat Allah Ibn Abi. *Sharh Nahj al Balaghah* (Beirut, 1963).
Hambis, Louis (trans.), 'Le Chapitre CVII du Yuan Che', *TP* 38 (1945), 1–181.
Hayton, 'La Flor des Estoires de la Terre D'Orient', *RHC: documents armeniens*, Vol. 2. Paris, 1896–1906.
Hetoum, *A Lytell Cronycle*, trans. Richard Pynson, ed. Glenn Burger (Toronto, 1988).
Het'um, 'The Journey of Het'um I, King of Little Armenia to the Court of the Great Khan Möngke', trans. John Andrew Boyle, *CAJ* 9 (1964), 175–89.
Hman-nan Yazawin (la Chronique royale birmane), Edouard Huber (ed. and trans.), 'Etudes indochines: V-La Fin de la dynastie de Pagan', *BEFEO* 9 (1909), 635–62.
Hojo Tokimune and Hojo Masamura, 'A Mobilization Order Issued by Kamakura', trans. Thomas D. Conlan, in Thomas D. Conlan, *In Little Need of Divine Intervention* (Ithaca, 1994), 202.
Hu Szu-Hui, 'Yin-Shan Cheng-Yao', in Paul D. Buell and Eugene N. Anderson (eds and trans.), *A Soup for the Qan: Chinese Dietary Medicine of the Mongol Era as seen in Hu Szu-Hui's* Yin-Shan Cheng-Yao (London, 2000).
Hulegu, 'Hulegu, Mongol Il-Khan of Persia, to Louis IX, King of France (1262). Maragha', in *LOE* (Burlington, VT, 2010), 156–60.
Ibn al-Athir, *Al Kamil fi al-Tarikh*, Vol. XII (Beirut, 1979).

Ibn al-Athir, *The Chronicle of Ibn al-Athir for the Crusading Period from al-Kamil fi'l-ta'rikh*, Pt 3, trans. D. S. Richards (Burlington, VT, 2008).
Ibn Battuta, *The Travels of Ibn Battuta*, trans. H. A. R. Gibb (Cambridge, 1962).
Ibn Battutah, *The Travels of Ibn Battutah*, trans. H. A. R. Gibb, ed. Tim Mackintosh-Smith (London, 2002).
Ibn Battuta, *Rihala Ibn Battuta* (Beirut, 1995).
Ibn al-Kathir, *The Signs Before the Day of Judgment*, 2nd edn, trans. Huda Khattab (London, 1992).
Ipat'evskaia Letopis', ed. A. I. Tsepkov (Ryazan', 2001).
Al-Jabarti, *Napoleon in Egypt: Al-Jabarti's Chronicle of the French Occupation, 1798*, trans. Shmuel Moreh (Princeton, 1993, originally published: Leiden, 1975.)
Juvaini, ʿAla-ad-Din ʿAta-Malik, *The History of the World-Conqueror*, trans. J. A. Boyle (Seattle, 1997).
Juwayni, Ala-ad-Din ʿAta-Malik, *Ta'rikh-i-Jahan-Gusha*, ed. Mirza Muhammad Qazvini (Leiden, 1912–37).
Juzjani, Minhaj Siraj, *Tabaqat-i-Nasiri*, ed. A. H. Habibi, Vol. 2 (Kabul, 1964–5).
Juzjani, Minhaj Siraj, *Tabakat-i-Nasiri* (*a History of the Muhammedan Dynasties of Asia*), trans. Major H. G. Raverty (Kolkata, 2010).
Kirakos of Gandzakets'i, *Kirakos Gandzakets'i's History of the Armenians*, trans. Robert Bedrosian (New York, 1986).
Kirakos Gaandzakets'i, *History of the Armenians*, trans. Robert Bedrosian, <http://rbedrosian.com/kgtoc.html> (last accessed 12 May 2017).
Kiracos de Gantzac, 'Histoire d'Armenie', in M. Brousset (trans.), *Deux Historiens Arméniens: Kiracos de Gantzax, XIII S., 'Histoire d'Arménie'; Oukhtanès D'Ourha, X S., 'Histoire en trois parties'* (St Petersburg, 1870).
Khwandamir, *Habibu's-Siyar: The History of the Mongols and Genghis Khan*, trans. Wheeler M. Thackston (London, 2012).
Letopis' Po Lavrentievskomu Spisku (St Petersburg, 1872).
'Liao Shih', in Karl A. Wittfogel and Feng Chia Sheng, *History of Chinese Society: Liao 907–1125* (Philadelphia: The American Philosophical Society, 1949).
Al-Maqrizi, Ahmad Ibn ʿAli. *Histoire des Sultans Mamlouks de L'Egypte*, trans. Etienne Quatremere (Paris, 1837, 1845).
Al-Maqrizi, Ahamd Ibn ʿAli, *Kitab al-Suluk li M'arifat fi Dul al-Muluk*, Muhammad Mustafi Ziyadah (ed.) (Cairo, 1956).
Martinez, A. P. (ed. and trans.), 'The Third Portion of the History of Gazan Xan in Rasidu'd-Din's Tarix-e Mobarak-e Gazani', 6 (1986), 41–127.
Master Roger, 'Epistola in miserabile carmen super destructione Regni Hungarie per tartaros facta', trans. Janos M. Bak, Martin Rady, in Janos M. Bak, Martyn Rady and Laszlo Veszpremy (eds), *Anonymous and Master Roger* (Budapest, 2010), 132–227.
Michell, Robert and Nevill Forbes (eds and trans.), *The Chronicle of Novgorod, 1016–1471* (London, 1914).
Mostaert, Antoine and Francis W. Cleaves (eds), *Les Lettres de 1289 et 1305 de ilhan Arghun et Oljeitu a Philippe le Bel* (Cambridge, MA, 1962).
Mussis, Gabriele de, 'Historia de Morbo', in Rosemary Horrox (ed. and trans.), *The Black Death* (Manchester, 1994).
Al-Nasawi, Muhammad ibn Ahmad, *Sirah al-Sultan Jalal al-Din Mankubirti* (Cairo, 1953).

En-Nesawi, Mohammed, *Histoire du Sultan Djelal ed-din Mankobirti*, trans. O. Houdas (Paris, 1895).
Al-Nuwayri, Ahmad ibn ᶜAbd al-Wahhab. *Nihayat al-Arab Fi Funun al-Adab*, ed. Saᶜid ᶜAshur. Cairo: Al-hayat al Misriyyat al-ᶜammat lil-kitab, 1975.
Odoricus de Portu Naonis, 'Relatio de B. Odoricus de Portu Naonis', in P. Anastasius Van Den Wyngaert, *Sinica Franciscana: Itinera et Relationes Fratrum Minorum Saeculi XIII et XIV* (Florence, 1929), 381–495.
Odoric of Pordenone, *The Travels of Friar Odoric*, trans. Henry Yule (Grand Rapids, MI, 2002).
Oljeitu, 'Lettre d'Olejeitu à Phillippe le Bel, datée de 1305', pp. 55–7, in Antoine Mostaert and Francis Woodman Cleaves (eds and trans.), *Les Lettres de 1289 et 1305 des ilkhan Arγun et Oljeitu à Philippe le Bel* (Cambridge, MA, 1962).
Onon, Urgunge (trans.), *The Secret History of the Mongols: The Life and Times of Chinggis Khan* (London, 2001).
Otomo Yoriyasu, 'Organizing Defenses', trans. Thomas D. Conlan, in Thomas D. Conlan, *In Little Need of Divine Intervention* (Ithaca, 1994), 203–4.
Paris, Matthew, *English History*, trans. J. A. Giles (New York, 1968).
Paris, Matthew, *Chronica Majora*, 7 vols, ed. Henry Richards Luard (2012).
Perfecky, George A. (ed. and trans.), *The Hypatian Codex II: The Galician-Volynian Chronicle* (München, 1973).
Plano Carpini, Iohannes de, 'Ystoria Mongalorum', in P. Anastasius Van Den Wyngaert, *Sinica Franciscana: Itinera et Relationes Fratrum Minorum Saeculi XIII et XIV* (Florence, 1929), 27–130.
Plano Carpini, John of, 'History of the Mongols', trans. A Nun of Stanbrook Abbey, in Christopher Dawson, *Mission to Asia* (Toronto, 1980), 3–72.
Polo, Marco, *The Travels of Marco Polo*, trans. Henry Yule and Henri Cordier, ed. Morris Rossabi (New York, 2012).
Polo, Marco, *The Travels*, trans. Nigel Cliff (New York, 2015).
Polo, Marco, *The Travels of Marco Polo*, trans. William Marsden (New York, 2001).
Polo, Marco, *The Travels*, trans. Henry Yule and Henri Cordier (New York, 1993).
Polo, Marco, *The Travels*, trans. R. E. Latham (New York, 1958).
Rachewiltz, Igor de (trans.), *The Secret History of the Mongols: A Mongolian Epic Chronicle of the Thirteenth Century*, 3 vols (Leiden, 2004 and 2013).
Rashiduddin Fazlullah, *Jami'u't-Tawarikh: Compendium of Chronicles*, Vol. 3, *Classical Writings of the Medieval Islamic World: Persian Histories of the Mongol Dynasties*, trans. Wheeler M. Thackston (London, 2012).
Rashiduddin Fazlullah, *The Compendium of Chronicles*, Pt 1–2, trans. W. M. Thackston (Cambridge, MA, 1998).
Rashiduddin Fazlullah, *The Compendium of Chronicles*, Pt 3, trans. W. M. Thackston (Cambridge, MA, 1998).
Rashid al-Din, *Jami' al-tawarikh*, ed. B. Karimi (Tehran: Iqbal, 1983).
Rubruck, William of, 'The Journey of William of Rubruck', trans. A Nun of Stanbrook Abbey, in Christopher Dawson (ed.), *Mission to Asia* (Toronto, 1980), 89–220.
Rubruc, Guillelmus de, 'Itinerarium Willelmi de Rubruc', in P. Anastasius Van Den Wyngaert, *Sinica Franciscana: Itinera et Relationes Fratrum Minorum Saeculi XIII et XIV* (Florence, 1929), 145–332.

Rubruck, William of, *The Mission of Friar William of Rubruck*, trans. Peter Jackson (Indianapolis: Hackett, 2009).
Saint-Quentin, Simon de, *Histoire Des Tartares*, ed. Jean Richard (Paris, 1965).
Sawma, Rabban. *The Monks of Kublai Khan, Emperor of China: Medieval Travels from China through Central Asia to Persia and Beyond*, trans. E. A. Wallis Budge, new introd. by David Morgan (London, 2014).
'Shengwu Qinzheng Lu (Bogda Bagatur Bey-e-Ber Tayilagsan Temdeglel)', in Asaraltu (ed.), *Bogda Bagatur Bey-e-Ber Tayilagsan Temdeglel* (Qayilar, PRC, 1985), 3–95.
Sima Qian, *Records of the Grand Historian: Han Dynasty* II, trans. Burton Watson (New York, 1993).
Skelton, R. A., Thomas Marston and George T. Painter (eds), *The Vinland Map and the Tartar Relation* (New Haven, 1965).
Smpad, *La Chronique Attribuée au Connetable Smbat*, trans. and ed. Gerard Dedeyan (Paris, 1980).
Thomas Agni of Lentini, 'Thomas Agni of Lentini, Papal Legate and Bishop of Bethlehem, to all kings, priests, prelates and nobles (1 March, 1260). Acre', in *LOE*, 153–56.
Thomas of Spalato, *Istorija Archiepiskopov Salony i Splita*, trans. A. I. Solopov, ed. O. A. Akimova (Moscow, 1997).
Thomas of Split, *Historia Salonitanorum atque Spalastinorum pontificum*, Olga Peric (ed.), Damir Karbic, Mirjana Matijevic Sokol, James Ross Sweeney (trans.) (Budapest, 2006).
Togen Eian, 'A Letter Concerning the Mongol Threat', trans. Thomas D. Conlan, in Thomas D. Conlan, *In Little Need of Divine Intervention* (Ithaca, 1994), 201.
Al-'Umari, Ibn Fadl Allah, *Kitab Masalik al-Absar wa Mamalik al-Amsar*, ed. and trans. K. Lech (Wiesbaden, 1968).
Vardan Arewelc'i, 'The Historical Compilation of Vardan Arewelc'i', trans. Robert W. Thomson, *Dumbarton Oaks Papers* 43 (1989), 125–226.
Vartan, 'Les Mongols d'après les historiens arméniens: Extrait de l'histoire universelle de Vartan', ed. and trans. M. Ed Dulaurier, *Journal Asiatique* 13 (1860), 273–315.
Waley, Arthur (trans.), *The Travels of an Alchemist: The Journey of the Taoist ch'ang-ch'un from China to the Hindukush at the Summons of Chingiz Khan recorded by his Disciple Li Chih-ch'ang* (London, 1963).
Yeh-lu Ch'u-Ts'ai, 'The Hsi-yu Lu', trans. Igor de Rachewiltz, *Monumenta Serica* 21 (1962), 1–128.
'*Yuan che*: Notice sur les expeditions en Birmanie faites sous la dynastie des Yuan', in Edouard Huber, 'Etudes indochines: V-La Fin de la dynastie de Pagan', *BEFEO* 9 (1909), 664–79.
'*Yuan Shi* chapter 98', in Ch'i-ch'ing Hsiao, *The Military Establishment of the Yuan Dynasty* (Cambridge, MA, 1978), 72–91.
'*Yuan Shi* chapter 99', in Ch'i-ch'ing Hsiao, *The Military Establishment of the Yuan Dynasty* (Cambridge, MA, 1978), 92–124.
'Yuan tien-chang: Chin Hui-hui mo-sha yang tso su-na', trans. Francis W. Cleaves, *JTS* 16 (1992), 72–3.
Zenkovsky, Serge A. (ed.), *The Nikonian Chronicle*, 5 vols, trans. Serge A. and Betty Jean Zenkovsky (Princeton, 1986).

Zenkovsky, Serge A. *Medieval Russia's Epics, Chronicles, and Tales* (New York, 1974).
Zhao Hong, *Meng-Da Bei-Lu (Polnoe opisanie Mongolo-Tatar)*, trans. N. Ts. Munkuev (Moscow, 1975).

Secondary Sources
Aigle, Denise, *The Mongol Empire between Myth and Reality* (Leiden, 2014).
Alemany, Agusti, *Sources on the Alans: A Critical Companion* (Leiden, 2000).
Allouche, A., 'Teguder's Ultimatum to Qalawun', *IJMES* 22 (1990), 437–46.
Allsen, Thomas T., 'Mongol Census Taking in Rus', 1245–1275', *HUS* 5/i (1981), 32–53.
Allsen, Thomas T., 'The Yuan Dynasty and the Uighurs of Turfan in the 13th Century', in Morris Rossabi (ed.), *China Among Equals* (Berkeley, 1983), 243–79.
Allsen, Thomas T., 'Prelude to the Western Campaigns: Mongol Military Operations in the Volga-Ural Region, 1217–1237', *AEMA* 3 (1983), 5–23.
Allsen, Thomas T., 'The Princes of the Left Hand: An Introduction to the History of the *Ulus* of Orda in the Thirteenth and Early Fourteenth Centuries', *AEMA* 5 (1985), 5–40.
Allsen, Thomas T., 'Guard and Government in the Reign of The Grand Qan Mongke, 1251–1259', *HJAS* 46/ii (1986), 495–521.
Allsen, Thomas T., *Mongol Imperialism: The Policies of the Grand Qan Mongke in China, Russia, and the Islamic Lands, 1251–1259* (Berkeley, 1987).
Allsen, Thomas T., 'Mongolian Princes and Their Merchant Partner 1200–1260', *Asia Major* 3/ii (1989), 83–126.
Allsen, Thomas T., 'Mahmud Yalavac, Maaᶜud Beg, ᶜAli Beg, Bujir', in *ITSOTK* (Wiesbaden, 1993), 122–35.
Allsen, Thomas T. 'The Rise of the Mongolian Empire and Mongolian Rule in North China', in *CHCAR*, 321–413.
Allsen, Thomas T., 'Ever Closer Encounters: The Appropriation of Culture and the Apportionment of Peoples in the Mongol Empire', *Journal of Early Modern History* 1/i (1997), 2–23.
Allsen, Thomas T. *Culture and Conquest in Mongol Eurasia* (New York, 2001).
Allsen, Thomas T., 'Technician Transfers in the Mongolian Empire', *The Central Eurasian Studies Lectures* 2 (Bloomington, IN, 2002).
Allsen, Thomas T., 'A Note on Mongol Imperial Ideology', in *EMLCH* (Bloomington, 2009), 1–9.
Amitai, Reuven, 'Mongol Raids into Palestine (AD 1260–1300)', *JRAS* 2 (1987), 236–55.
Amitai, Reuven, 'Mamluk Espionage among the Mongols and Franks', *Asian and African Studies* 2 (1988), 173–81.
Amitai-Preiss, Reuven, 'In the Aftermath of ᶜAyn Jalut: The Beginnings of the Mamluk–Ilkhanid Cold War', *Al Masaq* 3 (1990), 1–21.
Amitai, Reuven, 'Evidence for the Early Use of the Title Ilkhan among the Mongols', *JRAS* 1 (1991), 353–61.
Amitai-Preiss, Reuven, 'An Exchange of Letters in Arabic Between Abaya Ilkhan and Sultan Baybars (AH 667–AD 1268–9)', *CAJ* 38 (1994), 11–33.
Amitai-Preiss, Reuven, *Mongols and Mamluks: The Mamluk–Ilkhanid War, 1260–1281* (Cambridge, 1995).

Amitai-Preiss, Reuven, 'Sufis and Shamans: Some Remarks on the Islamization of the Mongols in the Ilkhanate', *JESHO* 42/1 (1999), 27–46.

Amitai-Preiss, Reuven and David O. Morgan (eds), *The Mongol Empire and its Legacy* (Leiden, 2001).

Amitai-Preiss, Reuven, 'Mongol Imperial Ideology and the Ilkhanid War against the Mamluks', in *MEL* (Leiden, 2001), 57–72.

Amitai, Reuven, 'The Conversion of Teguder Ilkhan to Islam', *JSAI* 25 (2001), 15–43.

Amitai, Reuven, 'Edward of England and Abagha Ilkhan: A Reexamination of a Failed Attempt at Mongol–Frankish Cooperation', in M. Gervers and J. M. Powell (eds), *Tolerance and Intolerance: Social Conflict in the Age of the Crusades* (Syracuse, NY, 2001), 75–82.

Amitai, Reuven, 'Turko-Mongolian Nomads and the Iqta' System in the Islamic Middle East (ca. 1000–1400)', in Anatoly M. Khazanov and Andre Wink (eds), *Nomads in the Sedentary World* (London, 2001), 152–71.

Amitai, Reuven, 'Whither the Ilkhanid Army? Ghazan's First Campaign into Syria (1299–1300)', in *WIAH*, 221–64.

Amitai, Reuven and Michal Biran (eds), *Mongols, Turks, and Others: Eurasian Nomads and the Sedentary World* (Leiden, 2005)

Amitai, Reuven, 'The Resolution of the Mongol–Mamluk War', in *MTO* (Leiden, 2005), 359–90.

Amitai, Reuven, 'An Arabic Biographical Notice of Kitbugha, the Mongol General Defeated at ʿAyn Jalut', *JSAI* 33 (2007), 219–34.

Amitai, Reuven, *Holy War and Rapprochement: Studies in the Relations between the Mamluk Sultanate and the Mongol Ilkhanate (1260–1335)* (Turnhout, 2013).

Amitai, Reuven, 'Continuity and Change in the Mongol Army of the Ilkhanate', in *MME* (Leiden, 2016), 38–52.

Anderson, Eugene N., *Food and Environment in Early and Medieval China* (Philadelphia, 2014).

Atwood, Christopher P., *Encyclopedia of Mongolia and the Mongol Empire* (New York, 2004).

Atwood, Christopher P., 'Validation by Holiness or Sovereignty: Religious Toleration as Political Theology in the Mongol World Empire of the Thirteenth Century', *IHR* 26/ii (2004), 237–56.

Atwood, Christopher P., 'Titles, Appanages, Marriages, and Officials: A Comparison of Political Forms in The Zungar and Thirteenth-Century Mongol Empires', in David Sneath (ed.), *Imperial Statecraft: Political Forms and Techniques of Governance in Inner Asia, 6th–20th Centuries* (Bellingham, WA, 2006), 207–42. Repr. in David Sneath and Christopher Kaplonski (eds), *The History of Mongolia*, Vol. 2, *Yuan and Late Medieval Period* (Leiden, 2010), 610–34.

Atwood, Christopher P., 'The Sacrificed Brother in the *Secret History of the Mongols*', *MS* 31 (2009), 189–206.

Atwood, Christopher P. 'Pu'a's Boast and Dolqolqu's Death: Historiography of a Hidden Scandal in the Mongol Conquest of the Jin', Conference on Middle Period China, 800–1400, Harvard University, 5–7 June 2014.

Atwood, Christopher P., 'The First Mongol Contacts with the Tibetans', *Revue d'Etudes Tibetaines* 31 (2015), 21–46.

Atwood, Christopher P., 'Alexander, Ja'a Gambo and the Origin of the Jamugha Figure in the *Secret History of the Mongols*', in Terigun [Teligeng 特力更] and Li Jinxiu 李锦绣 (eds), Neilu Ou-Ya lishi wenhua guoji xueshu yantaohui lunwenji 内陆欧亚历史文化国际学术研讨会论文集/*Proceedings of the International Conference on History and Culture of Central Eurasia* (Hohhot, 2015), 161–76.

Atwood, Christopher P., 'How The Secret History of the Mongols was Written', *Mongolica* 49 (2016), 22–53.

Aubin, Jean. 'L'ethnogenese des Qaraunas', *Turcica* 1 (1969), 65–95.

Ayalon, David. 'The Great Yasa of Chingiz Khan. A Reexamination (Part A)', *Studia Islamica* 33 (1971), 97–140.

Bade, David, *Khubilai Khan and the Beautiful Princess of Tumapel* (Ulaanbaatar, 2002).

Bade, David, *Of Palm Wine, Women and War: The Mongolian Naval Expedition to Java in the 13th Century* (Singapore, 2013).

Banzarov, Dorji, 'The Black Faith, or Shamanism Among the Mongols', trans. Jan Nattier and John R. Krueger, *MS* 7 (1981–2), 53–92.

Barfield, Thomas J., *The Perilous Frontier: Nomadic Empires and China, 221 BC to AD 1757* (Cambridge, MA, 1992).

Barthold, W. and Subtelny, M. E., 'Sart', *EI²*.

Barthold, W. and Boyle, J. A., 'Batu', *EI²*.

Beffa, Marie-Lise, 'Les noms dans l'*Histoire secrete des Mongols*', *EM* 27 (1996), 211–20.

Benjamin, Craig (ed.), *The Cambridge World History*, vol. 4, *A World with States, Empires, and Networks, 1200 BCE–900 CE* (Cambridge, 2015).

Berezin, I. N., *Tarchannye jarlyki Tochtamyka, Timur Kuluka i Saadet-Gireja* (Kazan', 1851).

Bihl, M. and A. C. Moule, 'De duabus epistolis Fratrum Minorum Tartariae Aquilonaris an. 1323', *Archivum franciscanum historicum* 16 (1923), 89–112.

Bira, Sh., 'Qubilai Qa'an and 'Phags-pa bLa-ma'', in *MEL* (Leiden, 1999), 240–9.

Bira, Shagdaryn, 'Mongolian Tenggerism and Modern Globalism: A Retrospective Outlook on Globalisation', *IA* 5 (2003), 107–17.

Bira, Shagdaryn, 'Mongolian Tenggerism and Modern Globalism: A Retrospective Outlook on Globalisation, A Lecture Given at the Royal Asiatic Society on 10 October 2002', *JRAS* 14/i (2004), 3–12.

Biran, Michal, *Qaidu and the Rise of the Independent Mongol State in Central Asia* (Richmond, UK, 1997).

Biran, Michal, '"Like a Mighty Wall:" The Armies of the Qara Khitai (1124–1218)', *JSAI* 25 (2001), 44–91.

Biran, Michal, 'The Battle of Herat (1270): A Case of Inter-Mongol Warfare', in *WIAH*, 175–220.

Biran, Michal, 'The Chaghadaids and Islam: The Conversion of Tarmashirin Khan', *JAOS* 122/iv (2002), 742–52.

Biran, Michal, *The Empire of the Qara Khitai in Eurasian History: Between China and the Islamic World* (Cambridge, 2005).

Biran, Michal, *Chinggis Khan* (London, 2007).

Biran, Michal, 'Rulers and City Life in Mongol Central Asia (1220–1370), in David Durand-Guedy (ed.), *Turko-Mongol Rulers, Cities and City Life* (Leiden, 2013), 257–83.

Biran, Michal, 'The Mongol Empire and Inter-Civilizational Exchange', in *The CHW*, vol. 5, *Expanding Webs of Exchange and Conflict* (Cambridge, 2015), 534–58.
Birge, Bettine, *Women, Property, and Confucian reaction in Sung and Yuan China (960–1368)* (Cambridge, 2002).
Black, Jeremy, *Other Pasts, Different Presents, Alternative Futures* (Bloomington, IN 2015).
Borbone, Pier Giorgio, 'Hulegu's Rock-Climbers; A Short-Lived Turkic Word in 13th–14th Century Syriac Historical Writing', in Zhang Dingjing and Abdurishid Yakup (eds), *Studies in Turkic Philology: Festschrift in Honour of the 80th Birthday of Professor Geng Shimin* (Beijing, 2009).
Bold, Bat-Ochir, *Mongolian Nomadic Society: A Reconstruction of the 'Medieval' History of Mongolia* (New York, 2001).
Bosworth, Clifford E., 'Khwarazm', *EI²*.
Bosworth, C. E., 'Khwarazm-Shahs', *EI²*.
Bosworth, Clifford E. *The New Islamic Dynasties: A Chronological and Genealogical Manual* (Edinburgh, 2004).
Boyle, John A. (ed.), *Cambridge History of Iran, vol. 5, The Saljuq and Mongol Periods* (Cambridge, 1968).
Boyle, John A., 'Dynastic and Political History of the Il-Khans', in *CHI*, vol. 5, 303–422.
Boyle, John A., 'The Thirteenth-Century Mongols' Conception of the After Life: The Evidence of their Funerary Practices', *MS* 1 (1974), 5–14.
Boyle, John A., 'The Ismaʿilis and the Mongol Invasion', in Seyyid Hossein Nasr (ed.), *Ismaʿili Contributions to Islamic Culture* (Teheran, 1977), 7–22.
Broadbridge, Anne F., *Kingship and Ideology in the Islamic and Mongol Worlds* (Cambridge, 2008).
Broadbridge, Anne, 'Marriage, Family and Politics: The Ilkhanid–Oirat Connection', *JRAS* 26/i–ii (2016), 121–37.
Brose, Michael C., 'Realism and Idealism in the "*yuanshi*" Chapters on Foreign Relations', *Asia Major*, 3rd series, 19 (2006), 327–47.
Brose, Michael C., *Subjects and Masters: Uyghurs in the Mongol Empire* (Bellingham, WA, 2007).
Buell, Paul D. 'Tribe, Qan, and Ulus in Early Mongol China, Some Prolegomena to Yuan History', Ph.D. dissertation, University of Washington, 1977.
Buell, Paul D., 'The Role of the Sino-Mongolian Frontier Zone in the Rise of Cinggis-Qan', in *SOM* (Bellingham, WA, 1978), 63–76.
Buell, Paul D., 'Sino-Khitan administration in Mongol Bukhara', *JAH* 13/ii (1979), 121–51.
Buell, Paul D., 'Kalmyk Tanggaci People: Thoughts on the Mechanics and Impact of Mongol Expansion', *MS* 6 (1980), 41–59.
Buell, Paul D., 'Early Mongol Expansion into Western Siberia and Turkestan (1207–1219): a Reconstruction', *CAJ* 36 (1992), 1–32.
Buell, Paul D., 'Subotei Ba'atur (1176–1248)', in *ITSOTK* (Wiesbaden, 1993), 13–26.
Buell, Paul D., 'Cinqai', in *ITSOTK* (Wiesbaden, 1993), 95–111.
Buell, Paul D., 'Yeh-lu A-Hai (ca. 1151–ca. 1223), Yeh-lu T'u-Hua (d. 1231)', in *ITSOTK* (Wiesbaden, 1993), 112–21.

Buell, Paul D., 'Saiyid Ajall (1211–1279)', in *ITSOTK* (Wiesbaden, 1993), 466–79.
Buell, Paul D. and Eugene N. Anderson (eds and trans.), *A Soup for the Qan: Chinese Dietary Medicine of the Mongol Era as seen in Hu Szu-Hui's* Yin-Shan Cheng-Yao (London, 2000).
Buell, Paul D., 'Indochina, Vietnamese Nationalism and the Mongols', in *EMLCH*, 21–9.
Buell, Paul D., 'Some Royal Mongol Ladies: Alaqa-beki, Ergene-Qatun and Others', *WHC*, 7/i (February 2010), <http://worldhistoryconnected.press.illinois.edu/7.1/buell.html> (last accessed 7 April 2015).
Cahen, Claude, 'Quelques Textes Négligés Concernant Les Turcomans de Rum au Moment de l'invasion Mongole', *Byzantion* 14 (1939), 131–9.
Cahen, Claude, *Pre-Ottoman Turkey*, trans. J. Jones-Williams (New York, 1968).
Chan, Hok-lam, 'Naqacu the Grand Marshall, a Mongol Warlord in Manchuria during the Yuan–Ming Transition', in *EMLCH* (Bloomington, 2009), 31–46.
Chan, Hok-Lam, 'Chinese Refugees in Annam and Champa at the End of the Sung Dynasty', *JSAH* 7/ii (1966), 1–10.
Ch'en, Paul Heng-chao, *Chinese Legal Tradition Under the Mongols: The Code of 1291 as Reconstructed* (Princeton, 1979).
Ch'en, Yuan, *Western and Central Asians in China Under the Mongols*, paperback edn, trans. Ch'ien Hsing-hai and L. C. Goodrich (Nettetal, 1989).
Ch'i-ch'ing, Hsiao, 'Mid-Yuan Politics', in *CHCAR*, 490–560.
Chiodo, Elisabetta, 'History and Legend: The Nine Paladins of Činggis (Yisun Orlug) According to the 'Great Prayer' (*Yeke očig*)', *UAJ* 13 (1994), 175–225.
Chiodo, Elisabetta, 'Praising Cinggis Qaγan and His Campaigns', *UAJ* 17 (2001/2002), 189–233.
Choi, Charles Q., 'Reign Check: Abundant Rainfall May Have Spurred Expansion of Genghis Khan's Empire', *Scientific American*, 21 March 2012, <http://www.scientificamerican.com/article.cfm?id=abundant-rainfall-may-have-spurred-expansion-of-genghis-khans-empire&page=2> (last accessed 21 August 2013).
Ciociltan, Virgil, *The Mongols and the Black Sea Trade in the Thirteenth and Fourteenth Centuries* (Leiden: Brill, 2012).
Clark, Larry V. and Paul Alexander Draghi (eds), *Aspects of Altaic Civilization II: Proceedings of the XVIII PIAC, June 29–July 5, 1975* (Bloomington, 1978)
Clark, Larry V., 'The Theme of Revenge in *The Secret History of the Mongols*', in *AAC*, 33–57.
Cleaves, Francis Woodman. 'The Historicity of the Baljuna Covenant', *HJAS* 18/iii (1955), 357–421.
Cleaves, Francis W., 'The Rescript of Qubilai Prohibiting the Slaughtering of Animals by Slitting the Throat', *Journal of Turkish Studies* 16 (1992), 69–89.
Clements, Jonathan, *A Brief History of Khubilai Khan: Lord of Xanadu, Emperor of China* (Philadelphia, 2010).
Da-Feng, Qu, 'A Study of Jebe's Expedition to Tung Ching', *AOASH* 51 (1998), 171–7.
Dafeng, Qu, 'On the Qusiqul Army and the Tamaci Army', *CAJ* 42/ii (2001), 266–72.
Dardess, John, 'Shun-Ti and the End of Yuan Rule in China', in *CHCAR*, 561–686.
Dashdondog, Bayarsaikhan, *The Mongols and the Armenians (1220–1335)* (Leiden, 2011).

Davis, Richard L. 'The Reign of Li-tsung (1224–1264)', in *CHCSD*, 839–912.
Davis, Richard L., 'The Reign of Tu-Tsung and His Successors to 1279', in *CHCSD*, 913–62.
De Nicola, Bruno, 'The Queen of the Chaghatayids: Orghīna Khatun and the Rule of Central Asia', *JRAS* 26 (2016), 107–20.
De Nicola, Bruno and Charles Melville (eds), *The Mongol's Middle East: Continuity and Transformation in Ilkhanid Iran* (Leiden, 2016).
De Nicola, Bruno, *Women in Mongol Iran: The Khatuns, 1206–1335* (Edinburgh, 2017).
Dechant, John, 'Depictions of the Islamization of the Mongols in the *Manāqib al-ʿĀrifīn* and the Foundation of the Mawlawī Community', *Mawlana Rumi Review* 2 (2011), 135–64.
Delgado, James P., *Khubilai Khan's Lost Fleet: In Search of a Legendary Fleet* (Berkeley, 2008).
DeWeese, Devin, *Islam and Native Religion in the Golden Horde* (University Park, PA, 1994).
DeWeese, Devin '"Stuck in the Throat of Chingīz Khān:" Envisioning the Mongol Conquests in Some Sufi Accounts from the 14th to 17th Centuries', in Judith Pfeiffer and Sholeh A. Quinn (eds), *History and Historiography of Post-Mongol Central Asia and the Middle East* (Wiesbaden, 2006), 23–60.
DeWeese, Devin, 'Islamization in the Mongol Empire', in *CHIA*, 120–34.
DeWeese, Devin, 'Toktamish', *EI²*.
Di Cosmo, Nicola (ed.), *Warfare in Inner Asian History (500–1800)* (Leiden, 2002).
Di Cosmo, Nicola, *Ancient China and its Enemies: The Rise of Nomadic Power in East Asian History* (New York, 2002).
Di Cosmo, Nicola, Allen J. Frank and Peter B. Golden (eds), *Cambridge History of Inner Asia: The Chinggisid Age* (Cambridge, 2009).
Dimnik, Martin, 'The Siege of Chernigov in 1235', *Medieval Studies* 41 (1979), 387–403.
Dumas, Dominique, 'The Mongols and Buddhism in 1368–1578: Facts–Stereotypes–Prejudices', *UAJ* 19 (2005), 167–221.
Dunnell, Ruth, 'The Hsi Hsia', in Herbert Franke and Denis Twitchett (eds), *CHCAR*, 154–214.
Dunnell, Ruth. *Chinggis Khan* (New York, 2010).
Elverskog, Johan, *Buddhism and Islam on the Silk Road* (Philadelphia, 2010).
Endicott-West, Elizabeth, *Mongolian Rule in China: Local Administration in the Yuan Dynasty* (Cambridge, MA, 1989).
Endicott-West, Elizabeth, 'Merchant Associations in Yuan China: The Ortogh', *Asia Major* 3, no. 2 (1989), 127–53.
Endicott-West, Elizabeth, 'The Yuan Government and Society', in *CHCAR*, 608–25.
Fedorov-Davydov, A., *The Silk Road and the Cities of the Golden Horde*, ed. Jeanine Davis Kimball, trans. Alexander Nymark (Berkeley, 2001).
Fennell, John, *The Crisis of Medieval Russia 1200–1304* (New York, 1983).
Fitzhugh, William, Morris Rossabi and William Honeychurch (eds), *Genghis Khan and the Mongol Empire* (Washington, DC, 2009).
Fleet, Kate (ed.), *Cambridge History of Turkey, vol. 1, Byzantium to Turkey 1071–1453* (Cambridge, 2009).

Fletcher, Joseph F., 'The Mongols: Ecological and Social Perspectives', *HJAS* 46/i (1986), 11–50.
Fletcher, Joseph F., 'Turco-Mongolian Monarchic Tradition in the Ottoman Empire', *HUS* 3/iv (1979–1980), 236–51.
Foltz, Richard, *Spirituality in the Land of the Noble* (London, 2004).
Foltz, Richard, *Religions of Iran from Prehistory to the Present* (London, 2013).
Franke, Herbert and Denis Twitchett (eds), *The Cambridge History of China, vol. 6, Alien Regimes and Border States, 907–1368* (Cambridge, 1994).
Franke, Herbert, 'The Chin dynasty', in *CHCAR*, 215–320.
Franke, Herbert, 'The Forest Peoples of Manchuria: Kitans and Jurchen', in *CHEIA*, 400–23.
Franke, Herbert, 'Ahmad (?–1282)', in *ITSOTK*, 538–57.
Franke, Herbert, 'Sangha (?–1291)', in *ITSOTK*, 558–83.
Frazer, James G., *The Golden Bough*, abridged edn (New York, 1950).
Galstyan, A. G., 'The Conquest of Armenia by the Mongol Armies', *The Armenian Review* 27 (1975), 356–77.
Goitein, Shelomo Dov, 'Glimpses from the Cairo Geniza on Naval Warfare in the Mediterranean and on the Mongol Invasion', *Studi Orientalistici in honore di Levi Della Vida 1* (1956), 393–408.
Golden, Peter B., 'The Peoples of the Russian Forest Belt', in *CHEIA*, 229–55.
Golden, Peter B., 'Tatars', *EI²*.
Golden, Peter B., 'The Karakhanids and Early Islam', in *CHEIA*, 343–70.
Golden, Peter B., *An Introduction to the History of the Turkic Peoples: Ethnogenesis and State-Formation in Medieval and Early Modern Eurasia and the Middle East* (Wiesbaden, 1992).
Golden, Peter B., 'The World of the Rasulid Hexaglot', in Peter B. Golden (ed.), *The King's Dictionary The Rasulid Hexaglot*, trans. Tibor Halasi-Kun, Peter B. Golden, Louis Ligeti and Edmund Schutz (Leiden, 2000), 1–24.
Gommans, Jos, 'Warhorse and Post-nomadic Empire in Asia, c. 1000–1800', *Journal of Global History* 2 (2002), 1–21.
Gongor, 'The Twelve Tumen of the Aglag Khuree Khalkha Mongols', in David Sneath and Christopher Kaplonski (eds), *The History of Mongolia, Vol. 2, Yuan and Late Medieval Period* (Leiden, 2010), 508–21.
Halperin, Charles J., *Russia and the Golden Horde: The Mongol Impact on Medieval Russian History* (Bloomington, 1987).
Halperin, Charles J., *The Tatar Yoke: The Image of the Mongols in Medieval Russia* (Bloomington, 1985, 2009).
Halperin, Charles J. *Russia and the Mongols: Slavs and the Steppe in Medieval and Early Modern Russia* (Bucharest, 2007).
Halperin, Charles J., 'Ivan IV and Chinggis Khan', in Charles J. Halperin, *Russia and the Mongols: Slavs and the Steppe in Medieval and Early Modern Russia* (Bucharest, 2007), 277–97.
Hassan, Mona, *Longing for the Lost Caliphate: A Transregional History* (Princeton, 2016).
Haw, Stephen G., *Marco Polo's China: A Venetian in the realm of Khubilai Khan* (New York, 2006).
Haw, Stephen G., 'Cathayan Arrows and Meteors: The Origins of Chinese Rocketry', *Journal of Chinese Military History* 2 (2013), 28–42.

Heissig, Walther, *The Religions of Mongolia*, trans. Geoffrey Samuel (Berkeley, 1980).
Henthorn, W. E., *Korea: The Mongol Invasions* (Leiden, 1963).
Herman, John E., 'The Mongol Conquest of Dali: The Failed Second Front', in *WIAH* (Leiden, 2002), 295–334.
Hesse, Klaus, 'On the History of Mongolian Shamanism in Anthropological Perspective'. *Anthropos* 82/iv (1987), 403–13.
Heywood, C. J., 'Filling the Black Hole: The Emergence of the Bithynian Atamanates', in K. Cicek, et al. (eds), *The Great Ottoman–Turkish Civilisation* vol. 1 (Istanbul, 2000), 107–15.
Hirotoshi, Shimo, 'Two Important Persian Sources on the Mongol Empire', *EM* 27 (1996), 221–4.
Hodgson, Marshall G. S. *The Order of the Assassins* (New York, 1955).
Hodgson, Marshall G. S. *The Venture of Islam, vol. 3, The Gunpowder Empires and Modern Times* (Chicago, 1977).
Hope, Michael, 'The Transmission of Authority through the Quriltais of the Early Mongol Empire and the Ilkhanate of Iran (1227–1335)', *MS* 35 (2012), 87–116.
Hope, Michael, *Power, Politics, and Tradition in the Mongol Empire and the Ilkhanate of Iran* (Oxford, 2016).
Houston, G. W., 'An Overview of Nestorians in Inner Asia', *CAJ* 24/i (1980), 60–8.
Huber, Edouard, 'Etudes indochines: V. – La Fin de la Dynastie de Pagan', *BEFEO* 9 (1909), 633–80.
Humphreys, R. S., *From Saladin to the Mongols: The Ayyubids of Damascus 1192–1260* (Albany, 1977).
Hyistendahl, Maria, 'Roots of Empire', *Science* 337/6102 (28 September 2012), 1596–9, doi: *10.1126/science.337.6102.1596* (last accessed 21 August 2013).
Imber, Colin, *The Ottoman Empire* (London, 2002).
Jackson, Peter, 'The Dissolution of the Mongol Empire', *CAJ* 22 (1978), 186–244.
Jackson, Peter, 'The Crisis in the Holy Land in 1260', *English Historical Review* 95 (1980), 481– 513.
Jackson, Peter (ed.), *Cambridge History of Iran, vol. 6, The Timurid and Safavid Periods* (Cambridge, 1986).
Jackson, Peter, 'The Crusade Against the Mongols (1241)', *The Journal of Ecclesiastical History* 42/1 (1991), 1–18.
Jackson, Peter, *The Delhi Sultanate: A Political and Military History* (Cambridge, 1999).
Jackson, Peter, 'From Ulus to Khanate: The Making of the Mongol States, c. 1220–1290', in *MEL*, 12–38.
Jackson, Peter, *The Mongols and the West* (Harlow, UK, 2005).
Jackson, Peter, 'The Mongols and the Faith of the Conquered', in *MTO*, 245–90.
Jackson, Peter, 'Medieval Christendom's Encounter with the Alien', in *TIWBME*, 31–54.
Jackson, Peter, 'The Testimony of the Russian "Archbishop" Peter Concerning the Mongols (1244/5): Precious Intelligence or Timely Disinformation?', *JRAS* 26/i–ii (2016), 65–77.
Jackson, Peter, 'Batu b. Jochi b. Chinggis Khan', *EI³*.
Jackson, Peter, *The Mongols and the Islamic World: From Conquest to Conversion* (New Haven, 2017).
Jagchid, Sechin, 'Mongolia and the West', *EM* 27 (1996), 183–97.

Jagchid, Sechin, 'Patterns of Trade and Conflict Between China and the Nomadic Peoples of Mongolia', in Sechin Jagchid (ed.), *Essays in Mongolian Studies* (Provo, UT, 1987), 3–20.

Jamal, Nadia Eboo, *Surviving the Mongols: Nizari Quhistani and the Continuity of Ismaili Tradition in Persia* (London, 2002).

Jamsran, L., 'The Crisis of the Forty and the Four', in David Sneath and Christopher Kaplonski (eds), *The History of Mongolia*, vol. 2, *Yuan and Late Medieval Period* (Leiden, 2010), 497–507.

Jenkins, Gareth, 'A Note on Climatic Cycles and The Rise of Chingis Khan', *CAJ* 18 (1974), 217–26.

Jessee, Scott and Anatoly Isaenko, 'The Military Effectiveness of Alan Mercenaries in Byzantium, 1301–1306', *Journal of Medieval Military History* 11 (2013), 107–32.

Khan, Iqtidar Alam, 'Coming of Gunpowder to the Islamic World and North India: Spotlight on the role of the Mongols', *JAH* 30/i (1996), 27–45.

Khowaiter, A. A., *Baibars the First: His Endeavours and Achievements* (London, 1978).

Kim, Hodong, 'The Early History of the Moghul Nomads: The Legacy of the Chaghatai Khanate', in *MEL*, 290–318.

Kim, Hodong, 'A Reappraisal of Guyug Khan', in *MTO*, 309–38.

Kim, Hodong, 'The Unity of the Mongol Empire and Continental Exchanges Over Eurasia', *Journal of Central Eurasian Studies* 1 (2009), 15–42.

Kim, Hodong, 'Was "Da Yuan" a Chinese Dynasty?', *JSYS* 45 (2015), 279–305.

Kim, Hyun Jin. *The Huns* (London, 2016).

Kolbas, Judith, *The Mongols in Iran: Chingiz Khan to Uljaytu 1220–1309* (London, 2006).

Kolbas, Judith, Timothy May and Vlastimil Novak, *Anatolian Early 14th Century Coin Hoard* (Prague, 2011).

Kolbas, Judith, 'Historical Epic as Mongol Propaganda? Juwayni's Motifs and Motives', in *MME*, 155–71.

Komaroff, Linda and Stefano Carboni (eds), *The Legacy of Genghis Khan* (New York, 2003).

Komaroff, Linda (ed.), *Beyond the Legacy of Genghis Khan* (Leiden, 2006).

Колодзейчик, Дариуш, Попытки восстановления монгольской традиции в Крымском ханстве начала XVII века: байса, Тат ве Тавгач », *Золотоо рдынское Обозрение* 4/i (2015), 91–101.

Krawulsky, Dorothea, *The Mongol Ilkhans and Their Vizier Rashid al-Din* (Frankfurt, 2011).

K'uan-chung, Huang, 'Mountain Fortress Defence: The Experience of the Southern Sung and Korea in Resisting the Mongol Invasion', in Hans Van de Ven (ed.), *Warfare in Chinese History* (Leiden, 2000), 222–51.

Kwanten, Luc. 'The Career of Muqali: A Reassessment'. *The Bulletin of Sung and Yüan Studies* 14 (1978), 31–8.

Lambton, Ann K. S. 'Mongol Fiscal Administration in Persia', *Studia Islamica* 64 (1986), 79–99.

Lambton, Ann K. S., *Continuity and Change in Medieval Persia: Aspects of Administrative, Economic and Social History, 11th–14th Century* (Albany, 1988).

Lambton, Ann K. S., 'The *Athar wa ahya*' of Rashid al-Din Fadl Allah Hamadani and His Contribution as an Agronomist, Arboriculturist and Horticulturalist', *MEL* (Leiden, 1999), 126–54.
Lane, George, *Early Mongol Rule in Thirteenth-Century Iran: A Persian Renaissance* (New York, 2003).
Lewisohn, Leonard, 'Overview: Iranian Islam and Persianate Sufism', in Leonard Lewisohn (ed.), *The Legacy of Medieval Persian Sufism* (London, 1992), 11–43.
Lewisohn, Leonard, *Beyond Faith and Infidelity: The Sufi Poetry and Teachings of Mahmud Shabistari* (Surrey, 1995).
Lindner, Rudi, 'What Was a Nomadic Tribe?', *Comparative Studies in Society and History* 24/iv (1982), 689–711.
Lippard, Bruce G. 'The Mongols and Byzantium, 1243–1341'. Ph.D. dissertation, Department of Uralic and Altaic Studies, Indiana University, 1983.
Mackerras, Colin, 'The Uighurs', *CHIA*, 317–42.
Madden, Thomas F., *The Concise History of the Crusades*, 3rd Student Edn (Lanham, MD, 2014).
Maiorov, Alexander V., 'The Mongol Invasion of South Rus' in 1239–1240s: Controversial and Unresolved Questions', *Journal of Slavic Military Studies* 29/iii (2016), 473–99.
Manz, Beatrice Forbes, 'Tamerlane and the Symbolism of Sovereignty', *Iranian Studies* 21 (1988), 105–22.
Manz, Beatrice Forbes, *The Rise and Rule of Tamerlane* (Cambridge, 1991).
Manz, Beatrice Forbes, 'The Rule of Infidels: The Mongols and the Islamic world', in David O. Morgan and Anthony Reid (eds), *NCHI*, v3, *The Eastern Islamic World Eleventh to Eighteenth Centuries* (Cambridge, 2010), 128–68.
Manz, Beatrice Forbes, 'The Mongol Empire as an Adaptation of the Mongol Empire', *JRAS* 26/i–ii (2016), 281–92.
Minorsky, Vladimir, 'Caucasia III: The Alan Capital Magas and the Mongol Campaigns', *BSOAS* 16 (1952), 215–38.
Martin, H. Desmond, *The Rise of Chingis Khan and His Conquest of North China* (Baltimore, 1950).
Martin, Janet. 'The Land of Darkness and the Golden Horde: the Fur Trade Under the Mongols XIII–XIVth Centuries', *CMRS* 19/iv (1978), 401–21.
Martinez, A. P., 'The Third Portion of the History of Gazan Xan in Rasidu'd-Din's *Tarix-e Mobarak-e Gazani*', *AEMA* 6 (1986), 41–127.
Martinez, A. P., 'Some Notes on the Il-Xanid Army', *AEMA* 6 (1986), 129–242.
Marshall, Robert, *Storm from the East: From Genghis Khan to Khubilai Khan* (Berkeley, 1993).
Маслюженко, Д.Н., 'Тюрко-монгольские традиции в «государстве кочевых узбеков» хана Абу-л-Хайра', *Золотоордынское Обозрение* 2/iii (2014), 121–38.
May, Timothy, "The Mechanics of Conquest and Governance: The Rise and Expansion of the Mongol Empire, 1185–1265", Ph.D. thesis, University of Wisconsin-Madison, 2004.
May, Timothy, 'Nokhod to Noyad: Chinggis Khan's Social Revolution', *Mongolica* 19 (2006), 296–308.
May, Timothy, 'Jamuqa and the Education of Chinggis Khan', *Acta Mongolica* 6 (2006), 273–86.

May, Timothy, 'A Mongol–Ismaili Alliance? Thoughts on the Mongols and Assassins', *JRAS* 14 (2006), 231–9.
May, Timothy, *The Mongol Art of War: Chinggis Khan and the Mongol Military System* (Barnsley, UK, 2007 and Yardley, PA, 2007).
May, Timothy, *Culture and Customs of Mongolia* (Westport, CT, 2009).
May, Timothy, *The Mongol Conquests in World History* (London, 2012).
May, Timothy, 'Livestock and Warfare: Livestock Herding as Warfare in the Mongol Empire', paper presented at the Central Eurasian Studies Society Conference, 3–6 October 2013, The University of Wisconsin-Madison, Madison, Wisconsin.
May, Timothy, 'Spitting Blood: Medieval Mongol Medical Practices', in Larissa Tracy and Kelly DeVries (eds), *'His Brest Tobrosten': Wounds and Wound Repair in Medieval Culture* (Leiden, 2015), 175–93.
May, Timothy, 'Converting the Khan: Christian Missionaries and the Mongol Empire', *WHC* 12/ii (2015), <http://worldhistoryconnected.press.illinois.edu/12.2/forum_may.html>
May, Timothy, The Mongol Art of War and the Tsunami strategy', in Roman Hautala et al. (eds), *Золотоордынская цивилизация. Научный ежегодник*, Выпуск 8 (Казань, 2015), 31–7.
May, Timothy, 'Color Symbolism in the Turko-Mongolian World, in Sungshin Kim (ed.), *The Use of Color in History, Politics, and Art* (Dahlonega, GA, 2016), 51–78.
May, Timothy, 'Commercial Queens: Mongolian Khatuns and the Silk Road', *JRAS* 26 (2106), 89–106.
May, Timothy, 'Mongol Conquest Strategy in the Middle East', in *MME*, 13–37.
May, Timothy, Ил-хаант улс ба Афганистан', pp. 299–325, trans. D. Tod and D. Bayarsaikhan, in Dashdondog Bayarsaikhan and Christopher P. Atwood (eds), *ИЛ-ХААДЫН СУДЛАЛ ШИНЭ ХАНДЛАГА ӨГҮҮЛЛИЙН ЭМХЭТГЭЛ* (Ulaanbaatar, 2016).
May, Timothy, 'Grand Strategy in the Mongol Empire', *Acta Historica Mongolici* 16 (2017), 78–105.
May, Timothy, 'The Mongols as the Scourge of God in the Islamic World', in Robert Gleave and István T. Kristó-Nagy (eds), *Violence in Islamic Thought from the Mongols to European Imperialism* (Edinburgh, 2018).
Melville, Charles, 'Padshah-i Islam: The Conversion of Sultan Mahmud Ghazan Khan', *Pembroke Papers* 1 (1990), 159–77.
Melville, Charles, '"The Year of the Elephant" Mamluk–Mongol Rivalry in the Hejaz in the Reign of Abu Saʿid (1317–1335)', *Studia Iranica* 21 (1992), 197–214.
Melville, Charles, '"Sometimes by the Sword, Sometimes by the Dagger": The Role of the Isma'ilis in Mamluk–Mongol Relations in the 8th/14th Century', in Farhad Daftary (ed.), *Medieval Isma'ili History and Thought* (Cambridge, 1996), 247–63.
Melville, Charles, 'Abu Saʿid and the Revolt of the Amirs in 1319', in Denise Aigle (ed.), *L'Iran Face à La Domination Mongole* (Tehran, 1997), 89–120.
Melville, Charles, 'The Ilkhan Oljeitu's Conquest of Gilan (1307): Rumor and Reality', in *MEL*, 73–125.
Melville, Charles, 'The Keshig in Iran: The Survival of the Royal Mongol Household', in *BLGK*, 135–64.
Melville, Charles, 'Anatolia under the Mongols', in *CHT*, v1, 51–101.

Menache, Sophia, 'Tartars, Jews, Saracens and the Jewish–Mongol "Plot" of 1241', *History* 81 (1996), 319–42. Repr. in *TIWBME* (Burlington, VT, 2010).
Meserve, Ruth, 'An Historical Perspective of Mongol Horse Training, Care and Management: Selected Texts', Ph.D. dissertation, Department of Uralic and Altaic Studies, Indiana University, 1987.
Meserve, Ruth, 'Central Eurasian Nomadic Technology: Hobbles', *UAJ* 23 (2009), 160–74.
Meyvaert, Paul, 'An Unknown Letter of Hulagu, Il-Khan of Persia, to King Louis IX of France', *Viator* 9 (1980), 245–61.
Mirgaleev, I. M., 'Succession to the Throne in the Golden Horde: Replacement of the Batuids by the Tuqai-Timurids', *GHR* 5/ii (2017), 344–51.
Miyawaki, Junko, 'The Legitimacy of Khanship Among the Oyirad (Kalmyk) Tribes in Relation to the Chinggisid Principle', in *MEL*, 319–31.
Moffett, Samuel Hugh, *A History of Christianity in Asia*, vol. 1 (San Francisco, 1992).
Momen, Moojan, *An Introduction of Shi^{c}i Islam* (New Haven, 1985).
Morgan, David, 'The Mongol Armies in Persia', *Der Islam* 56 (1979), 80–96.
Morgan, David, 'Who Ran the Mongol Empire?', *JRAS* 114/ii (1982), 124–36.
Morgan, David, 'The Mongols and the Eastern Mediterranean', *Mediterranean Historical Review* 4/i (1989), 198–211.
Morgan, David, 'Mongol or Persian: The Government of Ilkhanid Iran', *HMEIR* 3 (1996), 62–76.
Morgan, David, 'Reflections on Mongol Communications in the Ilkhanate', in Carole Hillenbrand (ed.), *Studies in Honour of Clifford Edmund Bosworth*, Vol. II (Leiden: Brill, 2000), 375–85.
Morgan, David. *The Mongols*, 2nd edn (Malden, MA, 2007).
Morgan, David, 'Persian as a *lingua franca* in the Mongol Empire', in B. Spooner and W. L. Hanaway (eds), *Literacy in the Persianate World: Writing and the Social Order* (Philadelphia, 2012), 160–70.
Morgan, D. O., 'Oldjeytu', *EI^2*.
Morgan, David O. 'The Empire of Tamerlane: An Unsuccessful Re-run of the Mongol Empire?', in J. R. Maddicott and D. M. Palliser (eds), *The Medieval State: Essays Presented to James Campbell* (London, 2000), 233–41.
Moses, Larry W., 'A Theoretical Approach to the Process of Inner Asian Confederation', *EM* 5 (1974), 113–22.
Moses, Larry W., 'Triplicated Triplets: The Number Nine in the Secret History of the Mongols', *Asian Folklore Studies* 42 (1986), 287–94.
Mote, F. W. *Imperial China, 900–1800* (Cambridge, MA, 2003).
Mott, Christopher, *The Formless Empire: A Short History of Diplomacy and Warfare in Central Asia* (Yardley, PA, 2015).
Nicolle, David, *The Mongol Warlords* (Poole, UK, 1990).
Okada, Hidehiro, 'Origins of the Dorben Oyirad', *UAJ* 7 (1987), 181–211.
Ostrowski, Donald, 'Why did the Metropolitan Move from Kiev to Vladimir in the Thirteenth Century?', *California Slavic Studies* 16 (1993), 83–101.
Ostrowski, Donald, 'The *Tamma* and the Dual-administrative Structure of the Mongol Empire', *BSOAS* 61 (1998), 262–77.
Ostrowski, Donald, *Muscovy and the Mongols: Cross-cultural Influences on the Steppe Frontier, 1304–1589* (Cambridge, 2002).

Ostrowski, Donald, 'The Galician-Volynian Chronicle, the *Life of Alexander Nevskii* and the Thirteenth-Century Military Tale', *Palaeoslavica* 15/ii (2007), 307–24.

Ostrowski, Donald, 'The Tatar Campaign of 1252', *Palaeoslavica* 17/ii (2009), 46–64.

Ostrowksi, Donald, ' Simeon Bekbulatovich's Remarkable Career as Tatar Khan, Grand Prince of Rus', and Monastic Elder', *Russian History* 39/iii (2013), 269–99.

Peacock, A. C. S., *The Great Seljuk Empire* (Edinburgh, 2015).

Pelliot, Paul, *Les Mongols et la Papaute* (Paris, 1923).

Petrushevsky, I. P., 'Socio-economic Condition of Iran Under the Il-Khans', in *CHI*, v5, 483–537.

Pfeiffer, Judith, 'Conversion Versions: Sultan Oljeytu's Conversion to Shi'ism (709/1309) in Muslim Narrative Sources', *MS* 22 (1999), 35–68.

Pogossian, Zaroui, 'Armenians, Mongols and the End of Times: An Overview of 13th Century Sources', in *CDMP* (Wiesbaden, 2012),

Pow, Stephen, 'The Last Campaign and Death of Jebe Noyan', *JRAS* 27/i (2016), 31–51.

Prazniak, Roxanne, 'Tabriz on the Silk Roads: Thirteenth-Century Eurasian Cultural Connections', *Asian Review of World Histories* 1/ii (2013), 169–88.

Rachewiltz, Igor de, 'Personnel and Personalities in North China in the Early Mongol Period', *JESHO* 9 (1966), 88–144.

Rachewiltz, Igor de, 'Some Remarks on the Ideological Foundations of Chingis Khan's Empire', *PFEH* 7 (1973), 21–36.

Rachewiltz, Igor de, 'The title Činggis Qan/Qaɣan re-examined', in W. Heissig and K. Sagaster (eds), *Gedanke und Wirkung. Festschrift zum 90. Gerburtstag von Nikolaus Poppe* (Wiesbaden, 1989), 281–98.

Rachewiltz, Igor de, Hok-Lam Chan, Hsaio Ch'i-ch'ing and Peter W. Geier (eds), *In the Service of the Khan: Eminent Personalities of the Early Mongol-Yüan Period* (Wiesbaden, 1993).

Rachewiltz, Igor de, 'Muqali (1170–1223), Bōl (1197–1220), Tas (1212–1239), An-T'ung (1245–1293)', in *ITSOTK* (Wiesbaden, 1993), 3–12.

Rachewiltz, Igor de, 'Yeh-lu Ch'u-ts'ai, Yeh-lu Chu, Yeh-lu Hsi-liang', in *ITSOTK* (Wiesbaden, 1993), 136–75.

Rachewiltz, Igor de, 'The name of the Mongols in Asia and Europe: A reappraisal', *EM* 27 (1996), 199–210.

Raphael, Kate, 'Mongol Siege Warfare on the Banks of the Euphrates and the Question of Gunpowder (1260–1312)', *JRAS* 19/iii (2009), 355–70.

Ratchnevsky, Paul, 'Sigi-Qutuqu, ein Mongolisher Gefolgsmann Im 12.–13. Jahrundert', *CAJ* 10/ii (1965), 87–120.

Ratchnevksy, Paul, *Genghis Khan: His Life and Legacy*, trans. Thomas Nivison Haining (Cambridge, MA, 1992).

Ravalde, Esther, 'Shams al-Din Juwayni, Vizier and Patron: Mediation between Ruler and Ruled in the Ilkhanate', in *MME*, 55–78.

Richard, Jean, 'La conversion de Berke et les debuts de l'islamisation de la Horde d'Or', *Revue des Etudes Islamique* 35 (1967), 173–84.

Richard, Jean, 'The Mongols and the Franks', *JAH* 3 (1969), 45–58.

Richard, Jean, 'Les Causes des Victoires Mongoles d'après les Historiens Occidentaux du XIIIe Siècle', *CAJ* 23 (1979), 104–17.

Richard, Jean, 'Sur un passage de Simon de Saint-Quentin: Le costume, signe de soumission dans le monde mongol', *EM* 27 (1996), 229–34.
Robinson, David M., *Empire's Twilight: Northeast Asia Under the Mongols* (Cambridge, MA, 2009).
Roemer, H. R., 'The Jalayirids, Muzaffarids and Sarbadars', in *CHI*, vol. 6, 1–41.
Rogers, Greg S., 'An Examination of Historians' Explanations for the Mongol Withdrawal from East Central Europe', *East European Quarterly* 30 (1996), 3–26.
Rossabi, Morris, *Khubilai Khan: His Life and Times* (Berkeley, 1988). Repr. 2009.
Rowell, S. C., *Lithuania Ascending: A Pagan Empire within East-Central Europe, 1295–1345* (Cambridge, 1994).
Rybatzki, Volker, Alessandra Pozzi, Peter W. Geier and John R. Krueger (eds), *The Early Mongols, Language, Culture and History* (Bloomington, 2009)
Sasaki, Randall J. *The Origins of the Lost Fleet of the Mongol Empire* (College Station, TX, 2015).
Satoko, Shimo. 'Three manuscripts of the Mongol History of *Jami' al-Tawarikh*', *EM* 27 (1996), 225–8.
Saunders, J. J., *The History of the Mongol Conquest* (Philadelphia, 1971).
Saunders, J. J., 'The Mongol Defeat at Ain Jalut and the Restoration of the Greek Empire', in J. J. Saunders (ed.), *Muslims and Mongols: Essays on Medieval Asia* (Christchurch, NZ, 1977), 67–76.
Schamiloglu, Uli, 'The Qaraci Beys of the Later Golden Horde: Notes on the Organization of the Mongol World Empire', *AEMA* 4 (1984), 283–97.
Schamiloglu, Uli, 'The *Umdet Ul-Ahbar* and the Turkic Narrative Sources for the Golden Horde and the Later Golden Horde', in Hasan B. Paksoy (ed.), *Central Asian Monuments* (Istanbul, 1992), 81–93.
Schamiloglu, Uli, 'Preliminary Remarks on the Role of the Disease in the History of the Golden Horde', *CAS* 12 (1993), 447–57.
Schamiloglu, Uli, 'The Islamic High Culture of the Golden Horde', in Andras J. E. Bodrogligeti (ed.), *The Golden Cycle* (Sahibqiran, 2002), 200–15.
Schurmann, H. F., *Economic Structure of the Yuan Dynasty* (Cambridge, 1956).
Schurmann, H. F., 'Mongolian Tributary Practices of the Thirteenth Century', *HJAS* 19 (1956), 304–89.
Shkoliar, S. A., *Kitaiskaia doognestrel'naia artilleriia* (Moscow, 1980), 251–2.
Shiraiwa, Kazuhiko, 'Inju in the Jami' al-Tavarikh of Rashid al-Din', *AOASH* 42 (1988), 371–6.
Schwarz, Henry G. (ed.), *Studies on Mongolia: Proceedings of the First North American Conference on Mongolian Studies* (Bellingham, WA, 1978)
Moshe Sharon, *Black Banners from the East, vol. 2, Revolt: The Social and Military Aspects of the 'Abbasid Revolution* (Jerusalem, 1990).
Shimo, Hirotoshi, 'The Qaraunas in the Historical Materials of the Ilkhanate', *The Memoirs of the Toyo Bunko* 33 (1977), 131–81.
Silverstein, Adam J., *Postal Systems in the Pre-Modern Islamic World* (Cambridge, 2007).
Sinor, Denis, 'On Mongol Strategy', in Ch'en Chieh-hsien (ed.), *Proceedings of the Fourth East Asian Altaistic Conference* (Taipei, China, December 1971), 238–49.

Sinor, Denis, 'Horse and Pasture in Inner Asian History', *Oriens Extremus* 19 (1972), 171–84.
Sinor, Denis, 'The Inner Asian Warriors', *JAOS* 101/ii (1981), 133–44.
Sinor, Denis (ed.), *The Cambridge History of Early Inner Asia* (Cambridge, 1990).
Sinor, Denis (ed.), *Aspects of Altaic Civilization III* (Bloomington, IN, 1990).
Skaff, Jonathan Karam, *Sui-Tang China and Its Turko-Mongol Neighbors: Culture, Power, and Connections, 580–800* (New York, 2012).
Smith, John Masson Jr, 'Mongol and Nomadic Taxation', *HJAS* 30 (1970), 46–85.
Smith, John Masson Jr, 'Mongol Manpower and Persian Population', *JESHO* 18/iii (1975), 271–99.
Smith, John Masson, Jr, 'Demographic Considerations in Mongol Siege Warfare', *Archivum Ottomanicum* 13 (1993–4), 329–35.
Smith, John Masson, Jr, 'Mongol Society and Military in the Middle East: Antecedents and Adaptations', in Yaacov Lev (ed.), *War and Society in the Eastern Mediterranean, 7th–15th Centuries* (Leiden, 1996), 249–66.
Smith, John Masson Jr, 'The Nomads' Armament: Home-made Weaponry', in Michael Gerver and Wayne Schlepp (eds), *Religion, Customary Law, and Nomadic Technology* (Toronto, 2000), 51–61.
Smith, John Masson, Jr, 'Mongol Nomadism and Middle Eastern Geography: Qishlaqs and Tumens', in *MEL*, 39–56.
Smith, John Masson, Jr, 'Hulegu Moves West: High Living and Heartbreak on the Road to Baghdad', in *BLGK*, 111–35.
Sneath, David, *The Headless State: Kinship Society, and Misrepresentation of Nomadic Inner Asia* (New York, 2007).
Sneath, David and Christopher Klaponski (eds), *History of Mongolia*, 3 vols (Leiden, 2010).
Somogyi, Joseph De, 'Adh-Dhahabi's "Ta'rikh al-Islam" as an Authority on the Mongol Invasion of the Caliphate', *JRAS* 4 (1936), 595–604.
Tabuldin, Gizat, *Vsemirnaya Genealogiya Chingizidov* (Kokshetau, Kazazkhstan, 2012).
Thorau, Peter, 'The Battle of 'Ayn Jalut: a Re-examination', in P. W. Edbury, *Crusade and Settlement* (Cardiff, 1985), 236–41.
Thorau, Peter, *The Lion of Egypt: Sultan Baybars I and the Near East in the Thirteenth Century*, trans. P. M. Holt (London, 1992).
Togan, Isenbike, *Flexibility and Limitation in Steppe Formations: The Kerait Khanate and Chinggis Khan* (Leiden, 1998).
Togan, Isenbike, 'Otichigin's Place in the Transformation from Family to Dynasty', *CEMA* (Wiesbaden, 2016), 407–23.
Tubach, Jurgen, Sophia G. Vashalomidze and Manfred Zimmer (eds), *Caucasus during the Mongol Period – Der Kaukasus in der Mongolenzeit* (Wiesbaden, 2012).
Twitchett, Denis and Paul Jakov Smith (eds), *The Cambridge History of China*, vol. 5, Part One: *The Sung Dynasty and Its Precursors, 907–1279* (Cambridge, 2009).
Tyerman, Christopher, *God's War: A New History of the Crusades* (Cambridge, MA, 2006).
Urban, William, *The Teutonic Knights: A Military History* (London, 2003).

Vasary, Istvan, 'The Origin of the Institution of Basqaqs', *AOH* 32 (1978), 201–6.
Vasary, Istvan, 'The Golden Horde Term Daruga and Its Survival in Russia', *AOH* 30 (1976), 187–97.
Vasary, Istvan, '"History and Legend" in Berke Khan's Conversion to Islam', in *AAC3* (Bloomington, IN, 1990), 230–52.
Vasary, Istvan, 'Mongolian Impact on the Terminology of the Documents of the Golden Horde', *AOH* 48 (1995), 479–85.
Vasary, Istvan, *Cumans and Tatars: Oriental Military in the Pre-Ottoman Balkans, 1185–1365* (New York, 2005).
Vasary, Istvan, 'Oriental Languages of the *Codex Cumanicus*', in F. Schmider and P. Schreiner (eds), *Il codice cumanico e il suo mondo* (Rome, 2005), 104–24.
Vasary, Istvan, *Turks, Tatars and Russians in the 13th–16th Centuries* (Burlington, VT, 2007).
Vasary, Istvan, 'The Jochid Realm: The Western Steppe and Eastern Europe', in *CHIA*, 67–85.
Vasary, Istvan, 'The Tatar Factor in the Formation of Msucovy's Political Culture', in Reuven Amitai and Michal Biran (eds), *Nomads as Agents of Cultural Change* (Honolulu, 2015), 252–70.
Waterson, James, *Defending Heaven: China's Mongol Wars 1209–1370* (London, 2013).
Weatherford, Jack, *Genghis Khan and the Making of the Modern World* (New York, 2004).
Werner, Cynthia, 'Bride Abduction in Post-Soviet Central Asia: Marking a Shift Towards Patriarchy through Local Discourses of Shame and Tradition', *Journal of Royal Anthropological Institute* 15 (2009), 314–31.
Werner, Cynthia, 'Women, Marriage, and the Nation-State: The Rise of Nonconsensual Bride Kidnapping in Post-Soviet Kazakhstan', in Pauline Jones Luong (ed.), *Transformations of Central Asian States: From Soviet Rule to Independence* (Ithaca, NY, 2004), 59–89.
Wing, Patrick. *The Jalayirids: Dynastic State Formation in the Mongol Middle East* (Edinburgh, 2016).
Woods, J. E. 'A Note on the Mongol Capture of Isfahan', *JNES* 36 (1977), 49–51.
Wylie, Turrell V., 'The First Mongol Conquest of Tibet Reinterpreted', *HJAS* 37/i (1977), 103–33.
Wright, David C., 'Navies in the Mongol Yuan Conquest of Southern Song China, 1274–1279', *MS* 29 (2007), 207–16.
Yamada, Nakaba, *Ghenko: The Mongol Invasion of Japan* (London, 1916).
Yingsheng, Liu, 'War and Peace between the Yuan Dynasty and the Chaghadaid Khanate (1312–1323)', in *MTO*, 339–58.
Zhao, George Qingzhi, *Marriage as Political Strategy and Cultural Expression: Mongolian Royal Marriages from World Empire to Yuan Dynasty* (New York, 2008).
Zimonyi, Istvan and Osman Karatay (eds), *Central Eurasia in the Middle Ages: Studies in Honour of Peter B. Golden* (Wiesbaden, 2016).

Newspaper Articles
'Foreign minister says extreme weather "draining" Mongolia', BBC Monitoring Asia Pacific – Political Supplied by BBC Worldwide Monitoring (Monday 18 January 2010): 579 words. LexisNexis Academic, Web (last accessed 9 January 2015).

'Red Cross launches appeal to help Mongolian herders', BBC Monitoring Asia Pacific – Political Supplied by BBC Worldwide Monitoring (Monday 18 January 2010): 784 words. LexisNexis Academic, Web (last accessed 9 January 2015).

'UNICEF delivers freeze aid for Mongolian children', BBC Monitoring Asia Pacific – Political Supplied by BBC Worldwide Monitoring (Tuesday 2 March 2010): 427 words. LexisNexis Academic, Web (last accessed 9 January 2015).

CERNETIG, MIRO. 'Famine stalks Mongolian steppes; a half million nomads on brink of starvation', *The Globe and Mail* (Canada) (Monday 10 April 2000): 1,402 words. LexisNexis Academic, Web (last accessed 9 January 2015).

Index

Abaqa, Ilkhan, 185, 224, 226, 231–4, 238, 265–6, 287, 290, 340–1, 355, 361, 368–9
Abbasid Caliphate, 56, 75, 108, 121, 140, 162, 165–6, 168, 174, 178–9, 252, 256, 258, 276, 285, 324, 369
Abd al-Rahman, 124, 127, 142–3
Abdullah, Jochid Khan, 356, 364
Abu Bakr, Ilkhanid engineer, 185
Abu Said, Ilkhan, 250–6, 299, 314, 341, 355, 361, 369
Abulustayn, battle of, 233
Accursed, 324
Achmath, 206; *see also* Fanakati, Ahmad
Acre, 72, 167, 238
administration
  basqaq, 83, 88–91, 283, 298, 370, 372; *see also shahna*
  bureaucracy, 84, 99–100, 104, 118, 124, 148, 151–2, 182, 190, 205, 212–14, 225, 231, 237, 250, 252–3, 260
  bureaucrat, 74, 148, 220, 222, 233
  daruga, 90–1, 283, 298, 373
  daruqaci, 90
  divan, 231, 233, 240, 245, 283
  Diwan, 237, 334, 373
Adriatic Sea, 116
advisor, 55, 57, 61, 69, 101, 141, 143, 146, 188–9, 193, 198, 202, 241, 264, 283, 290, 332
Afghanistan, 15, 47, 59, 61, 63–4, 97, 99, 106, 108, 225–7, 229, 232, 248, 267, 271–2, 277, 295, 367; *see also* Balkh; Ghur; Herat
Africa, 169, 301
afterlife, 13, 70, 96
agricultural, 8, 86, 155
agriculturalists, 223
agriculture, 2–3, 84, 245, 247, 273, 317
Ahl al-Kitab, 244
Ahmad, 205–8, 218, 221, 234–6, 240, 253, 283, 309, 319, 355–6, 361, 363, 371

ailment
  Bieber Fever, 300; *see also* disease
  blindness, 183
  blithering, 134
  buboes, 301
  Bubonic Plague, 300–1; *see also* disease
  diarrhoea, 249
  disease, 200, 231, 300–1
  dysentery, 63
  obesity, 217, 296
  rheumatism, 132
  smallpox, 300; *see also* disease
  Spanish Flu, 300
airagh, 8, 14, 33, 158, 189, 312, 372
Aixue, 220
Ajlun, siege of, 167
Aju Noyan, 185
Akanc, Grigor of, 79, 108, 162, 166, 180, 228, 233, 317
Akhtuba River, 288
al-Dajjal, 322, 333, 335; *see also* antichrist
al-Nasir Muhammad, Mamluk sultan, 254–5, 313–14
al-Nasir Yusuf, Ayyubid sultan, 166–7
Ala Qamaq, 132
Ala Tagh, 239
Alamut, siege of, 165
Alan, 19–20, 26, 108, 112, 123, 151, 191, 288–9, 292, 306, 310, 345, 350; *see also* Asud
Alan Goa, 19–20, 151, 350
Alaqa Beki, 50–1, 77, 149, 204, 259, 359
Alaqush Digid Quri, 42, 50–1, 77
Alashan Desert, 2
alba, 85, 155, 372; *see also* taxation
albatu, 85; *see also* taxation
alchemists, 230
Alchi, 77; *see also guregen*
alcohol, 104
alcoholism, 97
alDajjal, 334; *see also* antichrist
Aleppo, 127, 166

399

Alghu, Chaghatayid Khan, 172–3, 259–4, 266–7, 270, 277, 357, 368
alginchi, 81, 372
Algirdas, Lithuanian ruler, 306
Ali Bahahdar, 166Ali, Imam and Caliph, 242, 247, 332, 348
alliance, 12, 18, 23, 35, 45, 50–1, 54, 58, 77, 98, 106–7, 110, 112–13, 144, 152, 163, 229, 232, 238, 261, 271, 285–6, 289, 295–6, 298, 305, 308, 310–11, 314, 318, 323, 345, 365, 375
Almaliq, 45, 59, 202, 258, 260, 262, 267, 270–4, 276
Altai Mountains, 1–2, 15, 44–5, 59, 77, 92, 174, 257, 261, 269, 271
Altaic, 6
Altalun, daughter of Chinggis Khan, 133; *see also* Altun, daughter of Chinggis Khan
Altan Khan, 327; *see also* Jin Empire
Altan Otchigin, 31, 36–7
altan urugh, 39, 44, 67–8, 70, 78, 92, 131, 146, 148, 153–4, 187, 205, 211, 217, 222, 233, 237, 239, 287, 305, 312, 341, 345, 372, 375–6
Altun, daughter of Chinggis Khan, 51, 359
Ambaghai Khan, 18–19, 24–5, 33–4, 49, 70, 327
ambassador, 50, 113, 238, 246
amber, 282
Amu Darya, 15, 63–4, 97, 106, 121, 159, 232, 236, 257, 261, 264–5
Amur River, 2, 174
Ananda, 211, 216–17, 221–2, 278, 360
Anatolia, 122, 166, 231, 238–9, 241, 292, 306, 308, 369
Anbarchi, 239
anda, 28–31, 38, 264, 372
Andalusia, 298
Andijan, 258
Andronikos III Palailogos, Byzantine Emperor, 312
animals
　ass, 65, 248, 327
　camel, 4–6, 8, 42, 48–9, 52, 61, 136–7
　deer, 8, 20
　donkey, 19, 235, 247–8, 327
　elephant, 62, 199–200, 251, 254
　falcon, 23, 48
　fleas, 301
　goats, 5
　horse, 5–8, 10, 14, 19, 26–8, 32–3, 38, 40, 47, 50, 53, 63–5, 80, 82, 91, 96, 104–5, 112, 117, 154, 173, 178, 194, 200–1, 203, 215, 229, 245, 286, 307, 329
　khainag, 5
　lion, 167, 234, 271, 279
　mare, 6–8, 14, 28, 372, 374; *see also* horse
　marmot, 8, 301
　ox, 5, 8, 31, 178, 281
　pigeon, 165, 225
　pigs, 180
　reindeer, 10
　stallions, 6
　wolf, 141
　yak, 5, 82
Ankara, 228, 369
Annam, 200–2, 209, 218, 366; *see also* Dai Viet; Vietnam; Vietnamese
Anti-Christ, 74, 322
antihalal, 219
Antioch, 162, 166, 179, 228, 231; *see also* Bohemund VI, Prince; Tripoli
Antung, 207–8
apocalyptic, 73–4, 117, 179, 226, 315, 317, 322–3, 335
apocryphal, 24, 71, 150, 323, 331
appanage, 84, 92, 125, 205, 221, 226, 229, 237, 241, 257, 261, 270, 272, 282, 291
Aq Orda, 276, 281–3, 304, 349
Aq Saray, battle of, 163, 369
Aqa Bulghai, 152
Aqtaji, 292
Arab, 73, 180, 191, 223, 276, 322
Arabia, 226
Arabian, 56, 75, 121, 168, 174
Arabic, 83, 88, 153, 217, 238, 321, 372
arable, 227, 245
Aragibala, 213, 355, 367
Aral Sea, 15, 46, 56, 75, 121, 168, 174, 228, 262, 280–1, 310
arban, 372
archaeology, 165, 282, 288
archery, 163, 197
architect, 40, 99, 189
architectural, 247
Arghun, 35, 125, 127, 131, 153, 234–9, 241, 252, 295, 338, 355, 361, 369
Arghun Aqa, 125, 127, 131, 152–3, 237
Argutai, 346
Ariq Boke, 139, 170–5, 181, 183, 188, 251, 259–61, 263–4, 295, 338, 340, 345, 354, 359, 366, 368
Ariq Bokeids, 340, 345
aristocracy, 19, 21, 31, 34, 37, 39, 44, 47, 78, 188, 190, 339, 375–6
armada, 198; *see also* navy
Armenia, 107–8, 118, 160, 179, 224, 228, 243, 369; *see also* Armenian
Armenian, 107, 151–2, 162, 166–7, 180, 192, 223–4, 230, 244, 246, 287, 310, 317

armour, 136, 162, 199, 225, 249
Arpa Khan, 251–2
Arran, 56, 75, 107, 121, 168, 226, 229, 239
arrowheads, 81, 162
artillery, 111, 169
artisans
    blacksmiths, 7, 278
    silversmith, 158
artists, 246–7
arts, 30, 128, 230, 246–7
Arugtai, 345
Aryun, 210, 249; *see also* Arghun
Asan Khan, Jochid ruler, 302
Asan the Sartaq, 42–3, 302
Asha Gambu, 64
Ashari, 178
assassination, 160, 207, 212, 251, 302
Assassins, 106, 129, 160, 163–4, 369; *see also* Nizari
assimilation, 171, 195, 228, 281, 337
Astrakhan, 281, 288, 309, 337, 349–50
Astrakhanate, 342
Asud, 345; *see also* Alan
Asutai, 170
atabeg, 128, 145–6, 237, 372
Atamanates, 292
Attila, 317
autonomy, 16, 92, 149, 153, 159, 195, 227, 233, 240, 286, 289, 341
avenue, 253, 338, 347–8
Awliya, Nizam al-Din, 331; *see also* Chisti
ʿAyn Jalut, battle of, 167, 169, 225, 330, 369
Ayurbarwada, Yuan Emperor, 211–13, 217, 338, 354, 360, 367
Ayushiridara, Yuan Emperor, 216, 355
Ayyubids, 56, 75, 107, 121, 162, 166–9, 323
Azerbaijan, 107, 118, 127, 226, 229, 286, 298–9, 302, 306–8, 311, 347, 369, 371
Aziz, Jochid Khan, 302, 356, 364

Baba Tukles, 296–7
bacterium, 301; *see also* disease
Badakhshan, 60
Badr al-Din Lu'lu, 225
Baghdad, 75, 95, 121, 150, 162, 165–6, 168, 178–9, 225–6, 228–9, 233, 235, 243–4, 251–2, 295, 308, 329, 369
Baghdad, siege of, 165–6, 179
Baghdadi, Majd al Din Ahmad ibn ʿUmar, 319; *see also* Sufi
Bai Shibu, 51; *see also* Buyan-Shiban
Baidar, 109, 113, 115, 363
Baidu, 239, 241–2, 355, 361, 369
Baiju, 122, 146, 163, 166, 363, 369
bailo, 206, 283

Bakhshi, 243, 362
Bakufu, 196–7
Balaghai, 229
Baljuna Covenant, 37, 39, 43, 372
Baljuntu, 43
Balkans, 113, 289, 292
Balkh, 228, 262, 319
Baltic Sea, 117, 305
banditry, 182, 214, 216
baptised, 113, 247, 298, 312
Bar Sawma, 238
Baraq, Chaghatayid Khan, 232, 263–6, 277, 356–7, 363, 368
Bashkirs, 110
bastinado, 127, 145; *see also* torture
Batu, Jochid Khan, 109–13, 115–17, 122–3, 125–7, 130–3, 135, 137, 142, 144, 146–7, 149, 171, 176, 180, 229, 282, 284, 286, 288, 293, 295, 298, 302, 340, 346, 355, 364, 370
Batuid, 302, 340
Bayalun Khatun, 312–313
Bayan Khan, Jochid khan, 268, 296
Bayan Merkit, 214–15, 344, 366
Bayan Noyan, 185–6, 203, 209, 268, 344, 366
Baybars, Mamluk Sultan, 153, 166–7, 169, 225, 231, 233, 238, 286, 289–90, 311
bazaaris, 240
bazaars, 240
Begich Noyan, 303
Begtutmish, 38, 70, 149
behead, 146, 169, 331; *see also* executions
Beijing, 175
Bekbulatovich, Symeon, 350
Bekhter, 22, 25–6
Bela IV, Hungarian King, 113, 115–16
Belarus, 305
Belgutei, 22, 26, 28, 30, 33, 137, 203
Bengal, 56, 75, 121, 168, 174, 202
Berdibeg, 302–3, 305, 356, 364, 370
Berke, 109, 112, 126, 135, 142, 149, 171–3, 175–7, 217, 222, 229, 231–2, 261–4, 284–9, 291–3, 301–2, 310–11, 314, 340, 348, 355, 364, 370
Berkecher, 284, 364
Beshbaliq, 89, 202, 267
Bethlehem, 167
beyliks, 308
bichigchi, 55, 83, 152; *see also* administration
bileg, 71
Biqaʾ Valley, 167
bishop, 12, 167
bishoprics, 12
Bithynian, 292
Bo'orchu, 28, 77

Boddhisattva, 16
Bodonchar, 19–20, 23
bodyguard, 40, 69, 78, 84, 152, 190, 213, 374; *see also* keshig
Bohemia, 114
Bohemund VI, Prince, 12, 26, 162; *see also* Antioch; Tripoli
Böl, 55
Bolat, Jochid khan, 302, 356, 364
Bolod, 356; *see also* Pulad, Jochid Khan
Bolod Chingsang, 173, 246
boqta, 132, 372
Boraqchin Khatun, 229, 361–2
Borjigid, 19–20, 23–5, 31, 33–6
Boroqul, 57–8
Borte, 24, 28–31, 35, 43, 51, 77, 95, 359, 365
Botoqui Tarqun, 57–8; *see also* QoriTumed
Boyaoha, 50–1
braided, 79; *see also* hairstyle
braids, 225; *see also* hairstyle
bride abduction, 20, 22, 29
Buchier, William, 158; *see also* silversmith
Buda, 115
Budashiri Khatun, 214
Buddhism, 15–17, 60, 71, 101, 103, 118–19, 125, 128, 141, 143, 156–8, 187, 189, 193, 204–5, 208, 212–13, 216–17, 219–25, 228, 230–1, 234, 238, 242–4, 247, 272–4, 276, 286, 297, 310, 312, 323, 333, 337, 346
Bukhara, 62, 73, 83, 228, 232, 258, 262, 264, 266, 270, 274–5, 315–16, 324, 326–7, 331, 333, 335, 368
Bukhara, Chinggis Khan sack of, 62, 73, 324, 326–7, 331
Bukhara, Ilkhanid sacking, 368
Bukhari, Maulana al-Din, 220
Bulgaria, 113, 116, 280, 288–91
Bulgarian, 288–9
Bulghar, 15–16, 108, 110, 118, 168, 262, 280–2, 284, 310, 370
Bulgharia, 15
Buluqan Khatun, 211, 217
Bunyashir, Northern Yuan khan, 345
Buqatu Salji, 19–20
Buqu Noyan, 237
Buqu Qadagi, 19–20
Buri, 123, 146–7, 270, 363
Burma, 199, 366–7
Buyan-Shiban, 51; *see also* Bai Shibu
Buzan, Chaghatayid khan, 273, 357, 363
Byzantine, 12, 289, 291–2, 312
Byzantium, 292

Cairo, 169, 228, 313
calendar, 220, 318
Caliph, 140, 162, 165–6, 179, 256, 285–6, 313, 320, 329, 331
Caliphal, 311
caliphate, 56, 75, 108, 121, 165, 168, 174, 180, 252, 256, 276, 313, 369
cangue, 26–7, 235
caravan, 15, 60–2, 101, 105, 227, 246, 257, 260, 270, 274, 323–4, 367
caravaneer, 99, 219
caravanserais, 288
Carpathian Mountains, 113, 115
carrion, 103
cartloads, 100, 172
cashmere, 5
Caspian Sea, 15, 56, 58, 63, 75, 108, 110, 112, 121, 168, 174, 248, 282, 309, 373
catapults, 111, 166; *see also* artillery; trebuchet
Catholicus, 220, 224, 244; *see also* Nestorian
Caucasus Mountains, 280, 284, 286, 308
Censorate, 190
census, 79–80, 83, 85, 89–91, 152–3, 155–6, 161, 179, 266, 272, 285, 366, 368, 370
centralisation, 1, 84, 93, 131, 153–4, 156, 272, 341, 344, 349
Cha'ur, 37, 271, 274, 362–3
Chabi Khatun, 170, 185, 189, 199, 203, 205, 209, 360, 366
Chaghadai, 51, 62, 69–70, 92, 94, 102–3, 105, 109, 113, 119, 122–3, 126, 129, 131, 134–5, 146–7, 149, 176, 257, 259, 263, 277, 357, 363, 368
Chaghadaid, 270–4
Chaghatay, 275, 337, 340, 357
Chaghatayid, 125, 131, 133–6, 144, 146–7, 149, 153, 159–60, 170, 172–6, 202, 209–10, 224, 226–8, 231–2, 248–9, 257–67, 269–79, 296–7, 300, 304, 307, 336–7, 339, 343–4, 346–9, 354, 359, 363, 368
chainmail, 249
Chakirmaut, battle of, 38, 44, 47, 365
chamberlain, 99; *see also* administration
Champa, 200–2, 366
chancelleries, 308; *see also* chancellor
chancellor, 55, 125, 127, 146, 152, 207–8, 214–15, 218, 366; *see also* administration
Changchun Zi, 72, 99, 125; *see also* Daoism; Daoist
Changshi, Chaghatayid khan, 273, 357, 363
Changzhou, 186
chao, 103, 192–3, 240–1, 299, 372
Chapar, Ogodeid Khan, 269–71, 296, 362
Chaqa Khatun, 48

Chechiyegen, 51, 258, 359
Chechnya, 112
cherik, 161
Chernigov, 112, 306
*chete*s, 275
Chichek Khatun, 284
Chigu, 77
Chila'un, 46, 364
Chiledu, 20–1
China, 1–2, 9, 15–17, 42–3, 48–56, 61, 67, 72, 75, 78–9, 83–9, 91, 93, 95, 98, 120–1, 124, 127, 131, 143, 146–7, 152–5, 157, 160–1, 168–9, 174–5, 181–2, 185, 187, 189, 191, 194–5, 197, 202, 210, 214–16, 219–20, 240, 257–8, 262, 309, 338, 344–5, 366–7, 375
Chinggis Khan, 18–19, 21, 23–5, 27, 29–33, 35, 37, 39–55, 57–73, 75–8, 82–3, 88–9, 91–2, 94–9, 101–106, 118–20, 125–7, 132–3, 135–7, 144–5, 147, 149–50, 152, 156, 159, 170, 177, 180, 187, 194, 203, 213, 217, 229, 246, 248, 258, 267, 275, 280, 285, 297, 306, 310, 315–17, 320, 323–4, 326–332, 335–6, 339, 341–3, 345, 347–51, 354, 359, 365–7, 372, 375
Chinggisid, 31, 61, 84, 86, 90–2, 109, 122, 126, 131–3, 136, 146–7, 151–4, 160, 226, 233–4, 239, 252, 255, 264, 273, 277, 289, 291, 303–4, 306–7, 310, 313–14, 329, 336–51, 355, 373, 375–6
chingsang, 185, 246, 372
chingxiang, 185, 372
Chinqai, 99, 104, 125, 127, 132, 134–5, 137, 146, 151–2
Chinqai Balghasun, city, 99
Chin Temur, 90
Chisti, 331–2; *see also* Sufism
Choban, 248, 250–2, 254, 334, 341, 369
Chobanids, 256, 302
Chongqing, 169, 202
Chongyol, King of Koryo, 197
Chormaqan, 90, 97, 106–8, 112, 122, 129, 248, 368–9
Chotan, 28
Christianity
  Catholics, 274
  Christendom, 10, 117, 317–18, 323, 333
  Christians, 15, 71, 118, 127, 141, 143, 156–7, 160, 179–80, 187, 207, 213, 217, 219, 223, 228, 272–4, 297, 300, 310, 316–18, 329, 332–3, 337
  churches, 112, 118, 224, 228, 243–4, 297
  Jacobite, 224
  Monophysite, 223–4, 317

Nestorian, 10, 12, 50, 71, 152, 157, 203, 217, 219–20, 223–4, 228, 234, 238, 244, 276, 310, 337
Orthodox, 16, 118, 220, 224, 284, 287–8, 310, 337
Chu River, battle of, 58
Cilicia, 56, 75, 121, 160, 162, 168, 179–80, 224, 228, 231
Circassians, 112
clan, 10, 19, 21, 25, 28, 31–2, 34–6, 40
climate, 2–5, 53, 147, 185, 200–1, 337, 347
coinage, 155, 238, 240, 246
communication, 33, 55, 105, 118, 165, 174, 204, 232, 258
concubine, 182, 195, 206, 269, 289, 361–2
Confucian, 143, 156–8, 182–3, 188–90, 205, 212–15, 217–18, 220, 222, 367
Confucius, 188, 222
Constantinople, 12, 228, 281, 312, 333–4
Copernicus, 230
coronation, 131, 134, 160, 340
counterfactual, 216, 221, 252
Crimea, 281, 284, 292–3, 297–8, 304–5, 309, 337
Crimean, 282, 342, 350, 371
crimes, 96, 125, 192–3, 206, 326
crisis, 52, 68, 76, 118, 126, 182, 217, 231, 235, 240–1, 302, 346
Croatia, 116
cronyism, 206, 214
crucifixion, 169; *see also* torture
Crusade, 64, 95, 108, 117, 167, 169, 238, 318, 329, 368
Cumans, 113, 289–92

Daghestan, 112
Dai Viet, 200–2; *see also* Annam
Daidu, 175, 189, 192, 202–3, 210–11, 213, 219–20, 258, 265, 267–8
Dalan, 31–2, 36, 365
Dalan-baljut, battle of, 31–2, 365
Dalan-Nemurges, battle of, 36, 365
dalay, 92–3, 95, 372
Dali, 159, 161, 200, 202, 366
daluhuachi, 83, 88; *see also darugachi*.
Damascus, 166–7, 228, 244, 322, 369
Daniil of Kiev, 112
Danishmend, 357, 363
Danube River, 75, 121, 289
Dao, 201
Daoism, 72, 158–9, 189
Daoist, 72, 99, 101, 118–19, 125, 143, 156–8, 187, 205
Dar al-Islam, 42, 71, 74, 180, 252, 281, 311, 315, 322–4, 326, 335

Darduqul-Soqor, 57; see also QoriTumed
Daritai, 36–7
daruqachi, 72, 83–4, 86, 88–91, 106, 125, 166, 188, 190, 193, 233, 235, 283, 298, 373
Dasht-i Kipchak, 58, 108–9, 117–18, 123, 280–1, 373
Datong, 50
Dayan Khan, Batu-Mongke, 346
Dayir, 97, 106, 108, 229, 267, 367
decrees, 83, 104, 128, 138, 145, 151–2
deel, 195
dehydration, 250
Delhi, Sultanate of, 56, 71, 75, 106, 120–1, 142, 168, 174–5, 222, 226, 262, 271–2, 324, 347
dendrology, 3
Derbend, 229, 281, 308
Deshou, 211
Dharmabala, 360
Dhu al-Qarnayn, 323–4, 332
Digi, 77
Dilshad Khatun, 251
Dimashq Khwaja, 251
Ding Dachuan, 183
Dingjia, battle of, 185, 366
diplomacy, 31, 33, 58, 61, 65, 71, 73, 99, 142, 197, 201, 216, 223, 232, 238, 241, 251, 254, 293, 296, 300, 327
dirhems, 254
Dissolution of Mongol Empire, 93–4, 159, 171, 223, 226, 229, 257–8, 260, 285, 291–2, 304, 329, 336, 338–9, 341–2, 346, 350–1, 368–70
distinction, 133, 143, 183, 215, 218, 221, 342
Dmitri Donskoi, 303–5, 371
Dmitri of Tver', 299
Dnieper River, 56, 75, 121, 168, 174, 281, 291, 316
Dobun Mergen, 20
Dokuz Khatun, 228, 230–1, 286, 361
Dolqolqu, 98
Don River, 111, 281, 289, 291
Dorbei Doqshin, 57, 63
Dore Temur, Chaghatayid khan, 272–3, 357, 363
dowry, 43, 92, 313
drunkard, 69
drunken, 33
drunkenness, 118
Du'a, Chaghatayid khan, 258, 266–7, 269–70, 273, 296, 357, 368
Dughlat, 274–5, 278, 343–4, 349
Durlukin, 19–21, 23, 31
dushakha, 235; see also cangue

Duzong, 183
dyke, 48, 166, 215

edict, 73, 90, 138, 218–19, 243
Edigu, 308–9, 341–2, 356, 371
Egypt, 107, 166–7, 228, 261, 293, 324, 347
Eid al-Adha, 218
election, 125, 127, 134–6, 138, 170, 235
Eljigidei, 129, 146, 272, 357, 363
embezzling, 206, 208, 221, 233, 299
Emil River, 95, 132, 257, 261–2
emissary, 72, 139, 165, 169, 196, 205, 232, 266, 318
emperor, 9, 16, 19, 33, 52–5, 71, 98, 117, 138, 145, 150, 172, 182–3, 186–9, 195–6, 212–13, 216, 222, 245, 289, 294, 312, 317, 327, 329, 344–5, 351, 359–60, 365, 367, 374
empress, 185–6, 203, 211, 214
England, 117, 238
Englishman, 117
enslaved, 198
enthrone, 96, 135, 164, 172, 176, 231, 271, 278, 367
envoy, 43, 58, 61, 71–2, 99, 106, 127, 138–9, 145, 154, 184–5, 196–7, 201, 238, 258–9, 264, 293, 329, 366
epidemics, 300; see also disease
Erdene Zuu, 100–1, 104
Erdenebileg, 40
erected, 12, 231, 288
Ergene, 149, 204, 258–9
Ergune River, 42
ErkeQara, 32
Esen, 346
Esen-Boqa, Chaghatayid khan, 271
espionage, 61, 248
Etugen, 13, 373
eunuchs, 182
Euphrates, 239
exams, civil service, 212, 367
executions, 14, 193, 208
exile, 28, 147, 193, 214–15
exogamy, 2123
exorcise, 14
explosives, 197
Ezhou, siege of, 162, 170, 183

Fakhr al-Mulk, 152, 154
falconer, 136–7
famine, 52–4, 215, 260
Fanakat, 60
Fanakati, Ahmad, 205, 218, 283
Fancheng, 184–5, 366
faqih, 313, 373

Fars, 56, 121, 168, 228
Fatima, 124, 127, 140, 143, 333
Fatima bint Qays, 333
Ferghana, 153, 277
fiefs, 245
fiscal, 82, 86–7, 91, 93, 131, 152–3, 182–3, 207–8, 210, 215, 231, 240–1, 260, 272, 370
flayed, 206
fleet, 184–6, 197–8, 200–1, 301
flocks, 3, 7, 39, 78, 136, 173
forests, 10, 12, 16, 18, 57, 111, 187, 301, 373
fortifications, 53, 61, 107, 113, 161, 184, 293, 300
Franciscans, 127, 139, 157–8; *see also* Plano Carpini, John of; Rubruck, William of
Frankish, 238
fratricide, 213, 367
fraud, 230, 277
friar, 127, 139, 157–8, 219, 221; *see also* Franciscans
frontiers, 80, 82, 106, 161, 226–7, 238, 257, 268, 276, 328
fur, 16, 42–3, 45, 110, 155, 280, 282

Gaikhatu,Ilkhan, 237, 239–41, 338, 355, 369
Gansu, 9, 17, 55
garrison, 9, 48, 52, 62, 66, 91, 225, 268
Gaza, battle of, 167, 169
Gdansk, 281
generals, 31, 34, 63, 68, 108, 117, 152, 161, 165, 170, 182–4, 197, 216, 226, 235–6, 241, 267, 305, 344
Genoa, 287, 292, 301
genocidal, 36, 66, 119
Genoese, 292–3, 299–301, 304–5, 370
Georgia, 107–8, 112, 118, 179, 224, 228, 243, 369
Georgian, 108, 112, 166–7, 223–4, 230, 244, 310
ger, 4, 8, 21, 29, 68, 80, 136, 189, 373; *see also* yurt.
gerege, 128–30, 154, 204, 373; *see also* paiza; passport
Ghazan, Ilkhan, 221, 237, 241–8, 250, 253, 256, 278, 292–3, 295, 297, 310, 338, 347–8, 355, 361, 369
Ghazna, 106, 228, 262, 272, 367
Ghur, 56, 75, 106, 168, 367
Ghurid Empire, 15, 324, 367
Gilan, 228, 248
globalisation, 97, 119, 328
globalism, 97, 119, 328
Gobi, 2, 9, 16, 44, 49, 373
Gobi Desert, 2, 9, 16, 44

gods, 13, 375
Gog, 317, 322, 332–3, 335
Gok Turks, 1, 118, 276
gold, 45, 53, 105, 128–9, 132, 154, 182, 189, 374
gout, 123, 132, 160
governance, 84, 87, 91, 93, 187, 212, 231, 260, 264, 283, 327
government, 22, 55, 78, 83–4, 86–9, 91–3, 95, 105, 118, 124, 131, 134, 153–5, 159, 182–3, 187–91, 195–6, 204–7, 209–10, 212, 214–15, 217–18, 223–4, 227, 229, 231, 233–4, 237–8, 240, 246, 252, 258, 272, 276, 283, 328, 337–8, 372–3
governor, 57, 60–2, 72, 78, 81, 83–4, 88, 90, 150, 152, 178, 191, 216, 218, 221, 229, 237, 271–2, 277, 302, 372–3, 375–6
grain, 7–8, 45, 183
grapes, 234
Grigor, 79, 108, 162, 166–7, 180, 228, 233, 317
Guangzhou, 202, 219
Guchulug, 41, 44–6, 50, 58–60, 73, 83, 323, 330, 367
gunpowder, 165
guregen, 77, 306, 343, 348, 373
Guyuk, 86, 122–3, 125–35, 137–44, 146–7, 149–50, 152–3, 156, 159, 173, 257–9, 266, 328, 338, 340, 354, 361–2, 366

hadith, 145, 319, 322, 333–5, 373
Hailar River, 2
hairstyle, 79, 119–20
Hajj, 218, 250, 334
Hakata Bay, 196–8, 202
halal, 102–3, 118–19, 177, 205–6, 218
Hamadan, 232
Hanbali, 224, 374; *see also madhhab*
Hangzhou, 186, 192, 202, 219
Hanifi, 224, 247, 297, 301, 374
Hanren, 191, 373
Hanseatic League, 117
Hasan the Sartaq, 42–3; *see also* Asan the Sartaq
headdress, 14, 132, 372
heaven, 20, 55, 96, 130, 141, 182–4, 188, 204, 324–5, 328–30, 344, 375
Hebei, 54
Hebrew, 318, 333
Hejaz, 251, 254
Heqin treaties, 53
Herat, 228, 232, 248, 251, 262, 265, 349, 368
heresy, 10, 12, 165, 178
Hezhou, 162
Hilla, 179, 228

Hindu Kush Mountains, 63, 99
Ho'elun, 20–6, 28–9, 31, 150
Hoelun, 350
Hoi-yin Irgen, 44–5, 57, 61, 63, 65, 67, 76–7, 97, 366, 373
Homs, 244
Huanghe River, 2, 48, 202, 215
Hulegu, 131, 133, 139, 147, 149–50, 153, 159–60, 162–7, 169–74, 178–80, 185, 223–34, 236, 256, 258–63, 285–7, 295, 311, 328–30, 340, 355, 357, 361, 369
Huleguids, 251, 311, 340
Hungarians, 113, 115
Hungary, 56, 75, 113, 115–17, 121, 123, 158, 162, 168, 174, 284, 288–9, 370
Huns, 79
Husayn, 304
hyperinflation, 182–3

Ibaqa, 38
Ibn al-Alqami, 165–6, 178
Ibn al-Athir, 73–4, 85, 321–5, 330, 335
Ibn Battuta, 219–20, 254, 277, 298, 312
Ibn Kafraj Bughra, 73
Ibn Taymiyya, 322
ideology, 77, 96–7, 118, 159, 171, 195, 223, 235, 251, 253–5, 258, 285–7, 290, 299, 310–12, 314, 317, 328–9, 334, 346–7
Idiqut, 51, 89, 148, 178
Idolaters, 157, 312
Ikires, 51
Ili River, 15, 132, 173–4, 202, 261, 264, 273
Ilkhan, 153, 210, 221, 223, 230–1, 233–9, 247–52, 255, 264–6, 275, 287, 290, 292, 295, 311, 314, 341, 347, 359, 361, 368–9
Ilkhanate, 153, 188, 216, 220, 223, 225–9, 231–7, 239, 241–7, 249–53, 255, 257, 259, 262, 265, 270–1, 277, 281, 283, 285–8, 293, 295–9, 307, 310, 312, 336–9, 341, 346–8, 354–5, 369–70
Ilkhanid, 35–6, 44, 51, 78, 150, 224, 226–7, 229–32, 236, 238–9, 242, 244–5, 249–50, 252–3, 255–6, 258, 261, 266, 268, 271, 285–7, 289–90, 293, 295, 298, 302, 305–6, 310–11, 320, 322, 329, 334, 340, 342–3, 347–8, 368
illegitimacy, 172, 235, 289, 303, 374
Iltumish, 106
Ilyas, 275, 304, 343, 349, 363
imam, 141–2, 255
imperialism, 84–7, 147–50, 152–5, 159, 178–9, 244
Inalchuq, 60
India, 63–4, 97, 106, 165, 219, 226, 272, 347

Indochina, 200–1
Indonesia, 195, 201
infidel, 15, 71, 73, 117, 156, 175–6, 180, 223, 252, 255, 286–7, 311, 313, 319, 321, 323, 335
inju, 92–3, 372–3, 375
instability, 103, 122, 151, 156, 167, 211, 273, 279, 287
interregnum, 128, 140, 151
iqta 245, 373
Iran, 15, 59, 78, 85, 90, 106–8, 118, 120, 131, 146, 148, 153, 159, 163–5, 225, 227–31, 234, 239–40, 243–5, 247, 250–2, 255, 257, 259, 276, 286, 295, 307, 311, 340, 348, 368
Iraq, 108, 166, 179, 247, 254, 308
Iraq al-Arabi, 108
Irenjin, 250
irgen, 16, 44–5, 56–7, 61, 63, 65, 67, 76–7, 97, 328, 330, 365–6, 373, 375
Irinchinbal, 214, 355, 360
irrigation, 48, 227, 245
Irtysh, 45–6, 58, 76, 149, 202, 269, 280, 367; *see also* Irtysh River, battle of
Irtysh River, battle of, 45–6
Isfahan, 107, 228, 333–4
Ishaqiyya, 349
Ishmaelites, 317
Islam
  madrasa, 140, 254–5, 288, 312, 374
  mosque, 101, 118, 120, 140, 244, 255, 273, 288, 297, 312, 315–16, 330, 374
  Shia, 143, 165, 178–9, 230, 242, 255–6, 369
  Sunni, 165, 178–9, 242, 247, 253, 256, 274, 348, 374
Islamic, 15, 30, 42, 58, 71, 73–4, 84, 102–4, 118, 128, 147, 155–6, 172, 176, 179, 207, 216, 221–4, 230, 235–6, 242–3, 245, 251–3, 255–6, 270, 275–9, 283, 285, 297, 299, 302, 310–15, 319, 323, 325, 327, 331–2, 334, 337, 354, 374–5
Islamicisation, 346
Islamicise, 221
Islamisation, 142, 253, 255, 275–8, 297, 310, 313, 319, 337
Islamise, 275
Ismaili, 106–7, 129, 160, 165, 168, 178, 369; *see also* Nizari
Ismayil, 346
Ismaᶜili, 163
Issyk Kul, 132, 273

jaghun, 373
jahiliyya, 246, 278

Jajirad, 30–1, 34–5
Jalal al-Din Khwarazmshah, 61, 63–4, 97, 106–17, 225, 323, 367
Jalayir, 11, 152, 251
Jalayirid, 256, 302, 306, 308
Jamuqa, 30–8, 44–5, 57, 365, 373
Jand, 296
Janibeg, 299–303, 305, 356, 364, 369–70
Japan, 56, 75, 121, 168, 195–202, 209, 366–7
Japeth, 332
Jaqa Gambu, 32–3, 38
jarga, 110
jarliq, 90, 129, 145, 221, 236, 243, 298–9, 330, 370, 373
jarqu, 234, 373
jarquchi, 77, 83–4, 138, 146–7, 152, 193, 202, 239, 373, 376
Jazira, 56, 75, 108, 121, 168
Jaʿfar, 43, 71–2
Jebe, 36, 58–60, 62–3, 73, 108–9, 367
Jelme, 31
Jerusalem, 107, 167, 169, 226, 228, 232, 244, 314, 324, 369
Jews, 156, 179, 205, 217, 223, 237–8, 252, 318, 333
Jewry, 318
Jia Sidao, 56, 121, 183–5, 366
jihad, 286–287, 289, 311, 329, 348–9
Jin Empire, 9–10, 12, 16, 18–19, 32–3, 38, 44, 47–50, 52–5, 64–5, 68, 71–2, 76, 92, 97–9, 106, 109, 118, 153, 161, 174, 183, 327, 365–6, 373
Jingim, 189–90, 206, 208–9, 211, 213, 360, 366
jizya, 86, 179, 244, 253
Jochi, 30, 37–8, 45, 51, 57–9, 62, 69–70, 90–2, 97, 108–10, 122, 126, 137, 149, 229, 280, 282, 285, 293, 295, 302, 339–40, 355, 359, 364–5
Jochid, 70, 90–2, 109, 122–3, 126, 131–2, 134–5, 144, 146–7, 149, 151–2, 160, 170–2, 174, 176, 202, 217, 222–4, 226–9, 231–2, 237–9, 244, 248–51, 257, 259–62, 264–5, 268, 272, 274, 280–314, 336–8, 340–3, 346–7, 349–50, 355–6, 364, 370
judicial, 77–8
Jumghur, 171, 361
Jurchen, 12, 15–16, 50, 52, 55, 119, 183, 191, 365, 373
jurisprudence, 374
jurist, 207, 313, 373
Jurkin, 32–5, 37

Juwayni, 31, 45, 58–64, 69, 71, 73–4, 84, 88, 90–1, 94–7, 101–3, 106–7, 109–10, 112, 119, 122, 124–8, 130–43, 145–8, 150, 157, 160–1, 165, 176–8, 180, 225–6, 229, 231, 233–4, 237, 285–6, 315, 321, 323–4, 326, 330–3, 335
juyin, 16, 19, 34, 48–50, 365, 373
Juzjani, Minhaj Siraj, 54, 59–64, 71, 73, 107, 109, 119–20, 128, 130, 133, 137, 141–2, 151, 160, 165–6, 175–8, 180, 226, 324–6

Kaaba, 250, 254, 374
Kabul, 63, 228, 262
Kadir Berdi, 309
Kaffa, 282, 292–3, 300–1, 305, 370
kafir, 313
Kaifeng, 54–5, 98, 202, 327, 365
Kalka, battle of, 108–9, 305, 316, 370–1
Kalmyk, 81–3, 346
Kamakura Shogunate, 196
Kammala, 209
Kandahar, 262
Karakhanids, 15, 258, 276–7
Karatay, 91
karez, 227; *see also* irrigation
Kartid, 228, 248, 251, 349
Kashgar, 60, 202, 262, 266–7
Kataki, 274; *see also* Sufism
Kazakhstan, 9, 20, 69, 92, 309
Kazan, 91, 281, 309, 337, 342, 349
Kebek, Chaghatayid khan, 270–2, 277–8, 356–7, 363
Kemkemjiut, 45, 173; *see also* Hoi-yin Irgen
Kereit, 10–12, 17, 28–9, 32–8, 40–1, 44, 47, 99, 152, 365, 372
Kerman, 228
Kertanagara, 201
Kerulen River, 2, 10, 12, 35–6, 95, 99, 133–4, 213
keshig, 69, 78, 80, 84, 95, 97, 136, 152, 190–1, 213, 345, 374
Keshik, 40, 136
Khaghan, 71, 330, 366, 374
Khalaj, 47
Khalkha River, 10, 20, 36, 44
Khangai Mountains, 2, 38
khanqah, 312, 314
Khanship, 346
kharaj, 155, 374
Kharbanda, 247–8
Kharkhorin, 101, 104, 129, 148, 204, 210, 345

khatun, 122–4, 137–8, 140, 147, 149, 151, 211, 217, 225, 228, 230–1, 234, 248, 251–2, 255, 259, 284, 286, 312–14, 341, 361–3, 366, 368, 374
Khazars, 282
Kherlen River, 2
Khidyr, 356, 364
Khinggan Mountains, 1, 10, 12
Khitan, 9, 15–16, 43, 52, 55, 68, 78, 80, 83, 88, 90, 119, 183, 190–1, 323, 372–3
Khizr, 321
Khojand, 264
Khorasan, 319
Khotan, 60, 202, 262–3, 266–7
Khovsgol, 2
Khubilai, 139, 146–7, 153, 157–62, 170–5, 181–212, 214–21, 224, 231–2, 236, 240, 249, 257, 259–68, 270, 273, 283, 295, 338–40, 354, 359–60, 366–8
Khudabanda, 247–8
Khurasan, 63, 70, 86, 97, 106, 125, 127, 152, 226, 235, 237, 241, 248, 271, 322, 333–4, 368
khutba, 254, 374
Khwarazm, 15, 62, 64, 69, 75, 83, 90, 106, 153, 162, 174, 259, 306–7, 310, 314, 319, 327, 331
Khwarazmian Empire, 59–61, 63–4, 69–73, 76, 85, 90, 97, 99, 106–8, 120, 131, 142, 258, 276, 315, 325, 327, 330–1, 367, 369
Khwarazmshah, 59–60, 62–3, 72–3, 88, 97, 106–7, 225, 319–20, 323–4, 326, 331, 367
Khwurshah, 164–5
kidnapping, 20, 22–3
Kiev, 112, 281, 292, 306
kingmaker, 289–90, 302–3, 334, 340–1, 343, 349–50, 370
kinship, 9, 306
Kipchak, 58, 108–13, 117–18, 123, 213, 280–2, 284, 288, 290, 293, 308, 310, 337, 370, 373
Kirghiz, 11, 45, 57
Kirman, 56, 75, 121, 148, 168, 227
kiswa, 250, 374
Kiyad, 19, 21
Kizil Kum Desert, 62
Kochu, 362
Koke Mongke Tenggeri, 102, 226, 330, 375
Koke Orda, 281–2, 304, 307; *see also* Bayan Khan, Jochid khan; Orda Khan; Qonichi; Toqtamysh
Kokejin, 209, 221, 360
Konya, 228

kopeika, 271
Korea, 89, 181, 195–8, 214, 216
Korean, 184, 191, 195–8, 373
Korguz, 125, 269
Koryo, 196–8, 202
Kose Dagh, battle of, 122, 162, 369
Koten, 113, 125, 127, 149, 362
Koxiejie, 136
Krakow, 114, 281
Kubra, Najm al-Din, 320, 323; *see also* Kubrawiyya; Sufi
Kubrawiyya, 274, 319–21, 323; *see also* Sufism
Kufa, 179
Kulikovo, battle of, 303, 305, 371
Kulpa, 302
kumiss, 8, 33, 297, 317, 374; *see also* airagh
Kunduzcha, battle of, 307, 369, 371
Kupalak, 296
Kurdish, 107
Kurds, 223, 225
Kyoto, 196
Kyrgyzstan, 9, 92, 114

Lake Baikal, 1–2, 10–11, 45, 56, 75, 121, 168, 174, 187, 202, 262
Lake Baljuna, 37, 39, 42–3, 372; *see also* Baljuntu
Lake Balkhash, 56, 75, 121, 149, 168, 173–4, 228, 257, 281
lama, 158, 208, 346, 366
lamellar armour, 249; *see also* armour
Laozi, 158
lawgiver, 18, 194
laws, 94, 119, 145, 212, 317
legitimacy, 29, 31, 44, 55, 94–5, 133, 137–8, 150–1, 172, 178, 181, 188, 213, 236, 241–2, 251–2, 256, 268, 277, 290, 296, 302, 306, 308, 310–11, 313–15, 321, 328–9, 339–41, 343–4, 346–7, 374
levirate, 25, 205, 218, 313
Li Anquan, 47–8
Liao Dynasty, 15–16, 23, 83, 98, 365
Liao Empire, 9–10, 183, 365
Liaodong, 55
Liegnitz, battle of, 114–15
Lithuania, 281, 288, 305–6, 308
Lithuanian, 288, 304–5, 309, 371
livestock, 3–5, 8, 28, 31–2, 53–4, 68, 92, 103, 139, 264, 372, 376
Luristan, 240
Lvov, 281

madhhab, 224, 247, 301, 374
Madinah, 334

Magas, 112, 123
Magog, 317, 322, 332–3, 335
mahmal, 254
Mahmud al-Khwarazmi, 72; *see also* Mahmud Yalavach
Mahmud Yalavach, 72–3, 83–6, 89, 99, 104, 123, 125, 128, 131, 143, 153, 155; *see also daruqachi; jarquchi*
Majd al-Mulk Yazdi, 233–5
Mamai, 303–6, 341–3, 356, 370–371
Mamluk, 166–9, 226, 229, 231–3, 235–9, 244, 248–51, 253–5, 275, 282, 285–7, 289–90, 293, 297, 299, 301, 308, 310–11, 313–14, 322, 324, 329–30, 347, 369, 374–5
Mamluk Sultanate, 174, 226, 228, 231, 235, 238, 249, 255, 275, 282, 285, 287, 290, 301, 311, 322, 347, 369, 375
Manchuria, 1, 16, 55, 67, 103, 132, 174, 202–3, 210, 267, 367
Manchurian, 12, 15, 50
Manchus, 16
Mandate of Heaven, 55, 188, 344
Mandukhai Khatun, 346
Manggala, 360
Manggudai, 364
Mangqud, 32
Manichaeans, 157, 276, 337
Maragha, 167, 228–30, 328–9
Maria Khatun, wife of Toqta, 291
Marj al-Suffar, battle of, 245
marriage, 18, 20, 22–3, 25, 37, 50–1, 70, 77, 120, 203, 206, 218, 282, 298, 305, 313–14, 345, 375
martyr, 320
martyrdom, 321
Masʿud Beg, 83, 89, 125, 128, 131, 143, 153, 259–60, 264–5
Mawar, 228
Mawarannahr, 15, 62, 64, 67, 92, 120, 152–3, 264–6, 271–9, 304, 306–7, 337, 343, 357, 367–8
Maxim, Metropolitan of Kiev, 292
Mazandaran, 86, 125, 226, 237
Maʾjuj, 322–3; *see also* Magog
meat, 4, 7–8, 25, 102–3, 317
Mecca, 228, 244, 250, 254, 313, 334
Mediterranean Sea, 42, 165
Mehmet, 302–3
Menggeser, 137–8, 145–7, 152
Mengguren, 374
Mengli Oghul, 126
mercenaries, 107, 113, 292
meritocracy, 78, 339

Merkit, 10–11, 16, 20–3, 29–30, 38–9, 44–7, 58–9, 69, 119, 122, 133, 214, 344, 367
Merv, 12
Messiah, 318
metropolitan, 288, 292; *see also* Maxim, Metropolitan of Kiev; Orthodox
Michael VIII Palaiologos, Byzantine Emperor, 289
Mikhail of Tver, 298–9, 303
minbar, 277, 315–16, 374
miners, 114
Ming Empire, 193, 216, 309, 343, 367
minqan, 39–41, 77–80, 82, 84, 165, 187–8, 282, 374
minting, 238, 245, 273, 302; *see also* coinage
miracle, 230, 278, 334
Missionary, 10, 12, 113, 118, 157, 258, 284, 297, 310, 314, 347
Moge Khatun, 122, 362
Moghulistan, 274–8, 307, 337, 343, 349, 357, 368
Moghuls, 275, 278
Mohi, battle of, 115–16
moneylenders, 155
Mongke Khan, 83–6, 88, 109, 112, 126–7, 133–9, 144–57, 159–71, 173, 175–81, 183, 187–8, 223, 228–9, 257–8, 261, 271, 285–6, 336, 338–40, 342, 354, 359, 361, 366, 368
Mongke-Temur b. Abaqa, 234, 361
Mongke-Temur, Jochid khan, 264, 287–91, 338, 355, 364, 370
Monglik, 32, 150
Mongolia, 1–7, 9–11, 13–18, 22, 28–9, 32–6, 38–9, 41–2, 44–5, 47–51, 53, 55, 57, 59, 61–5, 67–73, 76–7, 79, 92, 95–6, 99–101, 104–5, 117–18, 123, 129, 132, 139–40, 148–9, 158, 162, 170–2, 174–5, 181, 190, 195, 202–4, 210, 213–14, 216, 248–9, 257, 266–8, 274, 334, 338, 343, 345–6, 354, 365, 367, 373
Mongolisation, 337, 345
monk, 79, 99, 119, 125, 141, 157–8, 166, 193, 204, 208, 230, 234, 238, 242, 333, 366
Moscow, 169, 281, 298–9, 303–5, 342, 370
Moses, 2, 22, 99, 178, 302
Mosul, 73, 225, 228–9, 234, 349, 369
Mubarak Shah, Chaghatayid Khan, 149, 258, 260, 263, 272, 277, 357, 363, 368
Mubarakh Khwaja Khan, Jochid Khan, 302
Mughan steppe, 56, 75, 107, 121, 168, 228, 281, 286, 368
Muhammad b. Bolod, Chaghatayid khan, 274, 278, 357

Muhammad II Khwarazmshah, 59–63, 72, 88, 300, 319–20, 323–4, 331; *see also* Khwarazmian Empire; Khwarazmshah
Muhammad Khudabanda, 247; *see also* khudabanda; Oljeitu, Ilkhan
Muhammad, engineer, 185
Muhammad, Prophet, 43, 71–2, 245, 286, 319, 322, 329
Muqali, 55, 61, 64–5, 72, 76–7, 97, 207–8, 327, 366
Muscovy, 291–2, 296, 298–9, 303–4, 309–10, 349–50; *see also* Moscow
museum, 27, 40, 81, 129–30, 162, 186, 204, 210, 249, 331, 345
Mustansir, Abbasid Caliph, 165
Mustasim, Abbasid Caliph, 165
mutton, 8
Muzaffarids, 256
Myanmar, 195, 199

Nablus, 167
Naiman, 10–12, 34–9, 41, 44–7, 50–1, 58, 60, 67, 120, 122, 365, 367
Najaf, 179, 247
Naliqo'a, Chaghatayid khan, 270, 272, 357, 363, 368
Nanren, 191–2, 194, 374
Napoleon, 111, 324
Naqu b. Guyuk, 133–7, 145, 147, 151, 154, 175–6, 362
Naqu Bayan, 28
Narathihapate, King of Pagan, 199–200
nasic, 139; *see also nasij*
nasij, 132, 374
Nasir al-Din, noyan, 199–200, 218, 221
naval warfare, 182, 187, 201–2, 366
navy, 181–2, 184–5, 187, 197, 293, 300
Nawruz, 236–7, 241–2, 244, 253, 302, 341, 356, 364
Naya, 77
Nayan, 203, 213, 267, 296, 367
Negubei, 266, 357
Negudaris, 232, 248, 336; *see also* Neguder; Qarauna
Neguder, 229
nerge, 110–11, 186, 374
Nestorianism, 12, 141; *see also* Christianity
Ningxia, 9, 17
Niru'un, 19
Nishapur, 228
Nizam al-Din Awliya, 331–2; *see also* Chisti; Sufi
Nizari, 106, 129, 160, 163–5, 178; *see also* Ismaili
Noah, 332

nobility, 23, 93, 113, 124, 136, 203, 242, 297
Noghai, 289–96, 303–4, 308–9, 312, 341–2, 349, 364, 370
nokod, 28–32, 34–6, 39, 51, 343, 374
nomadise, 2–5, 10, 16, 31, 45, 58, 99, 123, 189, 230, 258, 288
Nomuqan, 295, 360
Novogorod, 110–11, 280–1
noyad, 68, 91, 132, 146, 166, 172, 231–41, 251, 255, 263, 272, 277–8, 343, 374
noyan, 91, 94, 97, 106, 109, 133–4, 137, 146, 163, 185, 235, 237, 239, 297, 303, 343–4, 374
Nuᶜman, 313–14

Ob River, 56, 75, 168, 174, 202, 262, 280–1
Odoric, Friar, 202, 219, 221; *see also* Franciscans
Oghul Qaimish, khatun, 85, 131–5, 137–40, 143–8, 150–1, 153–5, 354, 359, 366; *see also* regent
Oghuz, 276, 337
Ogodei Khan, 51, 62, 66, 69–71, 76, 83, 85–6, 88–90, 92, 94–105, 107, 109, 111, 113, 115, 117–26, 128, 131–7, 139–40, 144, 149–51, 153, 156, 159, 173–4, 176–7, 194, 212, 229, 257, 260, 262, 267, 270, 281, 328, 331, 339, 354, 362–3, 366
Ogodeid, 133–6, 144, 146–9, 152–3, 160, 170, 176, 202, 209–10, 257–63, 265, 267, 269–75, 277, 279, 281, 295–6, 336–7, 339, 345, 357, 362, 368
Oirat, 11, 45, 51, 57–8, 258, 345–6, 349
Oljai, 361
Oljei, 234
Oljeitu, Ilkhan, 209–12, 214, 217, 221–2, 246–50, 253, 256, 268–9, 338, 344, 348, 354–5, 360–1, 367, 369; *see also* Kharbanda; khudabanda; Muhammad Khudabanda
Olqunu'ud, 20–1, 23
Onggirad, 11, 20, 23, 28, 35, 51, 77, 86
Onggud, 11, 38, 42, 50–1, 77, 99
Onon Mountains, 2
Onon River, 2, 11–12, 31–2, 35–6, 99, 133–4, 202
Orda Khan, 110, 126, 131, 268, 282, 295, 340, 364; *see also* Aq Orda; Koke Orda
ordinances, 94, 96, 180
ordo, 28, 95, 112, 131–3, 137–8, 151, 154, 255, 258, 276, 283–4, 340, 374
Orghana khatun, 147, 149, 258–60, 263, 266, 357, 363, 368

Orkhon River, 2, 10, 28–9, 95, 99–100, 118, 257, 334
ortoq, 124, 142, 153–5, 208
Orug Khatun, 248, 361, 363
Orus b. Qaidu, 269–71, 362
Otchigin, 31, 50, 68–9, 77, 94–5, 99, 126–7, 131–2, 137, 203, 338
Otrar, 60–2, 70, 262, 296, 309, 323–5, 327, 330, 367
Ottomans, 68, 91, 95, 220, 222, 224, 308, 369
Oyirad, 346
Ozbeg, Jochid Khan, 293, 296–9, 301, 305, 312–14, 342, 355, 364, 370

pagans, 113, 331
paiza, 128–30, 154, 204, 374; *see also gerege*
Pakistan, 15, 61
palace, 100, 186, 189, 211–12, 217, 280, 288, 304, 374; *see also ordo*
Palaiologos dynasty, 289, 312
Palestine, 169, 238, 318
Papacy, 117, 127, 167
Parable of the Arrows, 20, 26, 151, 350
Paris, Matthew, 332
Parthian shot, 41
Parvane, 233, 319
Parwan, battle of, 63
passport, 104–5, 128, 130, 154, 373–4; *see also paiza, gerege*
pastoral, 2–5, 9, 12, 15–16, 45, 79, 102, 210, 282, 373
pastoral nomadism, 2–3, 27–9, 40, 45
pastoralists, 223
pasture, 3, 5, 8, 10, 22, 31, 39, 43, 45–6, 54, 80–1, 91, 107, 111, 117, 123, 132, 136, 161, 163, 167, 199, 239, 245, 260, 262, 264, 270, 287–8, 299, 307, 332
patrimony, 45, 66, 86, 91–3, 123, 149, 171, 239, 282, 295, 375
Pax Mongolica, 210, 246, 249, 270, 293–4, 296, 298, 367–70
peasants, 107, 113, 226–7, 245
Pechenegs, 111
Pereiaslavl, 112
persecution, religious, 12, 60, 73, 118–19, 140–1, 143, 147, 179–80, 187, 208, 218, 244, 253, 274, 278, 318–20
Persia, 12, 85, 87, 92–3, 165, 167, 328
Persian, 63, 78, 83, 85, 87–8, 91, 100, 139–40, 152, 165, 175, 191, 208, 217, 235, 246, 248, 282–3, 285, 287, 290, 296, 316, 319, 321, 337–8, 372
Persianate, 87, 290, 319
Pest, 115

Phagspa lama, 158, 204, 208, 366
Phagspa script, 204, 294, 345
Pharisees, 333
Phillip IV, king of France, 249
pirates, 194, 196
plague, 273, 299–301, 367–70; *see also* ailment
Plano Carpini, John of, 89, 127–8, 131
Poland, 113–14, 116–17, 281, 288, 305, 370
Polo, Marco, 66, 166, 172, 185, 187, 190–2, 206–7, 216–17, 219, 283, 295
Poltava, battle of, 306, 371
Pontic Steppe, 58, 93, 113, 373
postal system, 104, 118, 267, 373; *see also yam*
primogeniture, 68, 133, 173, 338
propaganda, 54, 178, 180, 184, 242, 255
prophecy, 57, 318, 320–1, 329–31, 333–5
Prussia, 113, 305
Pskov, 281
Pulad, Jochid Khan, 309, 356, 363
punishments, 193
Pusan, 196

Qa'an, 71, 76, 80, 84–5, 89, 92, 94, 98, 103, 126, 128, 131, 134–7, 144–5, 148, 150, 152–4, 156–8, 187, 190, 195, 203, 205–6, 209–13, 221, 223, 231–3, 249, 257, 263, 265, 268–9, 271, 286, 317, 342, 366; *see also* Khaghan
Qabul khan, 12, 19–20, 24
Qachi'un, 22
Qadagi, 19–20
Qadan, 109, 112–13, 115–16, 134, 363
Qadaq, 127, 137, 146, 364
Qadaqadin, 138
qadi, 157, 160
Qaidu, 68, 95, 149, 173–5, 198, 202–3, 209–10, 213, 219, 221, 257–8, 260–71, 295–6, 339, 357, 362, 367–8
Qaishan, Yuan emperor, 211–13, 269–71, 338, 354, 360, 367
Qajaru, 25
Qalawun, Mamluk sultan, 236, 290, 311–12
Qalqajit Sands, battle of, 37, 365
Qamar al-Din, 307, 343–4, 357
qams, 134, 139; *see also* shamans
qanat, 227; *see also* irrigation; *karez*
Qangli, 46, 58–9, 280
Qara Khitai, 9–10, 15, 17, 32, 45–6, 50, 58–61, 67, 73, 83, 88, 257, 276, 323, 330, 367, 373
Qara Qada, battle of, 269, 362
Qara Qocho, 267
Qara Qoyunlu, 308
Qarabalghasun, 99–100
Qarachar, 295, 362, 364

qarachu, 39, 78, 147, 233, 235–8, 240–1, 252, 256, 272–3, 282–3, 303–5, 307, 312, 336–51, 355, 370, 375
Qarajang, 159, 200, 218; *see also* Dali; Yunnan
Qaraqorum, 99–101, 104, 118, 123, 129, 148, 156–7, 172–4, 202–3, 210, 230, 258, 260, 262, 265, 267–9, 288, 345, 366
Qarauna, 81, 232, 248, 271–2, 275, 336–7
Qarluq, 45, 56, 59, 61, 276, 330
Qarshi, 272
Qasar, 22, 26, 55, 137
Qatwan Steppe, battle of, 15; *see also* Sanjar, Seljuk sultan; Yelu Dashi
Qatwan, Peace of, 264–5, 269, 367–8
Qayaliq, 149, 260, 262, 276, 296
Qazan, Chaghatayid khan, 274–5, 357, 363
Qazghan, 275, 304, 344, 368
Qazvin, 160
Qidyr, 302
Qing Empire, 9, 27, 193
Qipchaq, 264
Qo'aqchin, 29–30
Qobuk, 95
Qobuq, 257
Qojin, 51
qol, 95, 99
Qonggirad, 23
Qongqotad, 32
Qonichi, Jochid khan, 295–6, 364; *see also* Koke Orda
Qonqurt, 361
qorchi, 97; *see also* keshig
Qorchi, 31, 57–8, 77, 97; *see also* prophecy
QoriTumed, 57–8; *see also* Hoi-yin Irgen
Qorolas, 37
Qoshila, Yuan emperor, 213, 355, 360, 367
Quanzhou, 202
qubchur, 85–6, 155, 179, 375
qubi, 92–3, 154, 264, 372, 375
Qubilai Khan, Yuan Emperor, 77, 205
Qucha, 36–7
quda, 50, 77, 345, 375
Qudu, 122
Quduqa, 57–8
Quhistan, 106, 121, 160, 163–4, 168, 369
Quli b. Orda, 229, 295, 357, 363–4
Qulpa, 356, 364
quriltai, 25, 32–4, 39–40, 57, 68, 70, 76–8, 80, 91, 94–5, 109, 117, 122–3, 125–9, 131–8, 144–6, 149, 151, 159, 170–2, 175, 177–8, 185, 189, 209, 213, 231, 233–4, 241, 261, 265, 295, 341, 365–6, 375
Qurumshi b. Orda, 295, 364
Qutlugh Temur, noyan, 297

Qutui Khatun, 234–5, 259, 361
Qutula Khan, 19–20, 24–5, 31, 33, 365
Qutulun khatun, 269–70
Qutuz, Mamluk sultan, 167, 169

Rabban Sawma, 238
Raden Vijaya, 201–2
Ramadan, 138, 157, 218, 242
Rashid al-Din, 19, 32, 69, 71, 92, 119, 132, 134–5, 138–41, 145–7, 150, 156, 170–3, 177, 180, 203, 206–8, 217–18, 220–1, 225, 230, 234, 239, 242–3, 245–7, 250, 263–4, 277–8, 283, 295–6, 326–7, 335, 351, 369
rebellion, 8, 38, 48–52, 55, 57, 60–1, 63–4, 76, 89, 93, 113, 132, 137, 159, 163, 188, 201, 203, 207–8, 212, 214, 216, 232, 235, 237–41, 250–2, 266–7, 273, 284, 289, 299, 328, 367, 369
regency, 77, 85, 95, 122, 128, 132, 134, 144, 154, 211, 259–60
regent, 50, 68, 76–7, 95, 99, 122–5, 127, 129, 131–5, 137–9, 141, 143–4, 149–51, 156, 170, 258, 345–6, 354, 357, 359, 363, 366, 368–9, 375
regicide, 167, 241, 341
Riazan, 111
roads, 73, 112, 219, 230
Rome, 290
Rostov, 111, 281, 287
Rubruck, William of, 79, 100–1, 114, 137, 139, 142, 146, 151, 157–8, 164, 176–7, 284, 310; *see also* Franciscans
Rumi, 319–20
Rus', 16, 56, 75, 79, 86, 90, 108, 110–13, 117–18, 121, 152, 155, 168, 174, 191, 280, 284–5, 287–8, 291, 293, 299, 303, 305, 310, 314, 316–17, 337, 350, 370
Russia, 2, 84, 89–91, 147, 283, 285, 287, 298, 303–4, 309, 316, 349
Russian, 89–91, 111, 115, 271, 280, 282–5, 287–8, 291, 298–9, 301, 304–5, 308–9, 337, 350, 373

S'ad al-Daula, 237–8, 252
Sa-skya Pandita, 125
sable, 28–9, 42–3
Safavids, 256
Sahib Diwan, 233, 237, 240, 245, 283
Salghurids, 227
Salindi, Uighur ruler, 148; *see also* Uighurstan
Samanids, 258, 276
Samarqand, 62, 88, 228, 258, 262, 264, 270, 281, 346
samurai, 196–7

Sangha, 208, 217, 219, 221
Sanjar, Seljuk sultan, 15, 367
Sarai, 123, 262, 281–2, 284, 287–8, 292–3, 295, 298–9, 302, 306, 308, 312, 314, 337, 371
Sarbadars, 256
Sarban, 266, 362–3
Sartaghtai, 295
Sartaq Khan, Jochid khan, 171, 286, 310, 340, 355, 364
Sassanid, 12
Satan, 335
Sati Beg khatun, 251–2
sayyid, 43, 199, 218, 221, 348–9, 356, 375
Sayyid Ajall, 93, 199, 218, 221
scourge, 324–6, 328, 330, 332, 335
scribe, 55, 137, 152; *see also bichigchi*
secretariat, 87, 152–3, 159, 190, 193, 209, 211–12, 260
secretaries, 83; *see also bichigchi*
sedentary, 1, 7–9, 32, 47–8, 66, 79, 84–7, 89, 91, 93, 103–5, 109, 119, 145, 154–5, 171, 175, 245, 258, 272–5, 284, 291, 300, 307, 313, 337
Selenge River, 2, 10, 148, 202
Seljuks, 15, 91, 122, 162–3, 174, 258, 313, 319, 323, 367, 369
Semirech'e, 277
Semuren, 191–3, 212–13, 215, 218, 375
Senggum b. Toghril, 34, 37, 39, 41, 44, 47
Serbia, 291
Shadibeg, Jochid khan, 309, 356
Shafaiyya, 224, 247; *see also madhhab*
shahna, 83, 88, 90–1, 375; *see also basqaq*
shamanic, 12–16, 70, 102, 134
shamanist, 70, 273–4, 286, 300, 337
shamans, 13–14, 98, 134, 137, 139–40, 234, 253, 255, 296, 329
Shandong, 188, 366
Shangdu, 185, 189, 202–3, 213
Shansi, 54
shariaᶜat, 177, 180, 192, 222, 224, 255, 273, 297, 301, 311, 313, 319, 348–9
Shayban, 110, 282, 302, 340
Shaybanids, 309
Shaykh Hasan the Jalayir, 251
Shevkal, 299
Shidebala, 212–13, 354, 360, 367
Shigi Qutuqu, 63, 77, 85
shihna, 91; *see also basqaq*
Shilemun Bitikchi, 135, 137; *see also bichigchi*
Shingqor, 364
Shiraz, 227–8
Shiremun, 125, 135–8, 145–6, 175–6
Shirindari, 211

Shogunate, 196
shulen, 8, 375
Siberia, 1, 10, 12, 42, 45, 58, 97, 173–4, 280, 309
Siberian, 10, 16, 59, 110, 280, 282, 373
Sibir, 309, 337, 342
Sichuan, 161, 183–4
Sighnaq, 302
Silesia, 113
Silk Road, 17, 42, 101, 219, 257, 308
sinicisation, 218, 265
sinicised, 267, 344
Sinjar, 225
Sistan, 56, 75, 121, 168, 228
Sivas, 228
slicing, 193; *see also* punishments
Smolensk, 281
Sogetu, 200–1
Soldaia, 297
Soqatai, 25
Soqor, 57
sorcery, 139, 143, 229, 234
Sorqan Shira, 26–8, 35
Sorqoqtani, 37, 70, 130, 132–3, 135–6, 138–9, 144, 149–52, 170, 218, 359
soul, 14–15, 70, 375
Soviet, 20, 91
Spalato, 115116
spying, 61, 71–2, 190
steppe, 1–3, 5–6, 8–10, 12–13, 15–19, 23–4, 28, 32–4, 38, 41, 44–9, 53, 58, 67–8, 79, 85, 87, 93, 97, 102, 108–13, 123, 126, 171–2, 175, 187, 189, 203, 210, 212–14, 257–8, 260, 264, 268–70, 272, 276, 280–2, 284, 286, 288, 300–1, 303, 307–10, 317, 323, 337, 342, 349, 367–8, 370, 373, 376
strangulation, 193; *see also* executions
Subedei, 31, 58–9, 61–3, 65, 97–8, 108–110, 112–13, 115–17, 123, 130, 160, 185
Suchigil, 21–2, 24–5, 29–30
Sudak, 281–2
Sufi, 224, 242, 253, 255, 274, 276, 284, 290, 296, 313–15, 319–21, 323, 331–2, 334, 348–9
Sufism
  Afaqiyya, 349
  Malawi, 319
  Mawlawiyya, 319–20
  Naqshbandiyya, 274, 349
suicide, 146, 187
sulde, 70, 375
Suldus, 26, 35
Sultaniyya, 228, 247, 369
sunna, 71, 335, 375

Suzdal, 111, 281, 292
suzerain, 10, 36, 46, 266, 294, 307, 328
Sword Brethern, 288
synagogues, 243; *see also* Jews
Syr Darya, 15, 60, 62, 71, 165, 174, 202, 228, 262–4, 272, 276, 296, 307
Syria, 107, 166–7, 169, 179, 225, 228, 232, 236–7, 244, 253, 306, 308, 347
Syriac, 166, 230

taboo, 14, 22, 32, 138
Tabriz, 228–30, 239–40, 243, 246–7, 250, 258, 262, 281, 299, 302, 369–70
Taghachar, 161
Taichar, 31
Taichu, 34
Taimaz, 106–7
taishi, 345–6, 360, 375
Tajikistan, 9, 59
Takshin, 361
Talas, 257, 262–4, 281
talisman, 234
Tamerlane, 252, 275, 304, 306–7, 339, 341, 343, 357, 368–71
tamgha, 105, 136, 141, 155, 294, 345, 375; *see also* taxation
tammachi, 80, 82, 84, 90–1, 93, 146, 238–9, 375
Tana, 281, 293, 300–1, 308, 370; *see also* Venetian; Venice
Tang Empire, 12, 44, 53–4, 182–3, 257
Tangqut, 364
Tangut, 17, 47–8, 52, 55, 64–6, 69, 76, 109, 152, 186, 191, 217, 373; *see also* Xi Xia
taqiyya, 278; *see also* Shia
Taraghai, 361
Targi, 211–12, 360
Tarim Basin, 47, 121, 152, 168, 174, 202, 268
tariqa, 224, 274, 349, 375; *see also* Sufism
Tarmashirin, Chaghatayid khan, 271–4, 277–8, 357, 363, 368
Tarqun, 57–8
Tartar, 91, 218, 318, 333
Tashkent, 262
Tatar, 10–12, 18–20, 22–4, 33–7, 40, 44, 113, 283, 285, 287, 289–92, 316, 321, 333–4, 349–50, 364–5, 371
Taunal, 146
taxation
    qalan, 86, 155
    tariff, 375
    taxfarming, 142
    toll, 93, 198, 301
Tayichiud, 11–12, 18–19, 24–9, 31, 35
Teb Tenggeri, 150, 329–31

Teguder, 234–6, 242, 253, 311, 355, 361, 369
Tekish, 323
temperature, 2, 4
temple, 72, 101, 118, 157, 189, 212, 218, 225, 243–4
Temuge, 22, 50, 69, 77, 94, 99, 126–7, 131–2, 203, 338
Temujin, 18, 20, 22–39, 42–4, 48, 327, 330, 354, 365, 372
Temulun, 22
Temur Qutlugh, Jochid Khan, 307–9, 356, 364
Temur-i Leng, 304, 339, 357; *see also* Tamerlane
tenggeri, 13, 96–7, 102, 109, 113, 118, 150, 159, 226, 328–31, 375
Tenggerism, 97, 119, 159, 328–9, 347–8
Terek River, 308–9, 371
Teutonic Knights, 113–14, 288, 305
Thailand, 209, 367
Thessaly, 289
Tibet, 56, 75, 120–1, 125, 159, 168, 174, 202, 204, 208, 216, 267
Tiflis, 108, 228, 281, 287
Tigris, 61, 225, 228
timar, 245
Timur, 275, 279, 304–9, 339, 343–4, 348, 357, 368–9, 371; *see also* Temur-i Leng, Tamerlane
Timurids, 337, 349; *see also* Tamerlane
Tinibeg, 299, 356, 364, 370
Tirmidh, 262
tithe, 85, 93
Tiumen, 309
Tobol, 281
Tobolsk, 309
Tode-Mongke, Jochid Khan, 290–1, 295, 311, 338, 355, 364, 370
Toghon Temur, Yuan emperor, 214–16, 219, 344–5, 355, 367
Toghril Ong Khan, 10, 28–38, 43–4, 230, 365
Toghto, 215
Toghus, 216, 355
tolerance, religious, 72, 120, 140, 204–5, 213, 217, 228, 238, 277, 310, 312
toleration, religious, 60, 73, 97, 102–3, 118–19, 140, 156–7, 179, 224, 243
Tolui, 37, 51–2, 63, 68–70, 77, 92, 94–5, 97–8, 109, 126, 133, 144, 150, 152, 170, 228, 339, 354
Toluid, 94–5, 134–6, 139, 144–5, 147–55, 157, 159–61, 163, 165, 167, 169, 171, 173, 175, 177–9, 189, 233, 251, 257, 260–1, 263, 273, 339
Tolun Cherbi, 109

tonsure, 79; *see also* hairstyle
Toqa-Temur, 147, 302, 304
Toqashi, 147
Toqta, 291–4, 296–7, 300, 312–13, 340, 363–4, 370
Toqtamysh, 304–9, 340, 342–3, 356, 364, 368371
Toqtoa, 46, 355, 364
Toquchar, 50, 59
Toquz, 235
Toregene Khatun, 85, 122–8, 131–2, 136, 138–40, 142–4, 150–1, 153, 155, 260, 354, 359, 362, 366; *see also* regent
Tort Aba, 88; *see also* shahna
torture, 127, 225, 235, 244, 327
Torzhok, 111
toyin, 141; *see also* tuin
traders, 16–17
trampled, 140, 146, 166; *see also* executions
Transcaucasia, 106–8, 163, 250, 323
treason, 138, 193
Trebizond, 56, 75, 121, 224, 228
trebuchet, 165, 185, 197, 300; *see also* artillery
tribute, 16, 48–9, 51, 53, 66, 82, 85–6, 97, 107, 110, 127, 148, 160, 162, 180, 195–6, 199–202, 209, 272, 275, 285, 303–4, 327, 365
trigonometry, 230
Tripoli, 162; *see also* Antioch; Bohemund VI, Prince
tsunami, 161
tuft, 79; *see also* hairstyle
tuin, 141
Tukel, 294
Tula River, 2, 10, 40, 65; *see also* Tuul River
Tulunbay, 313–14
Tumapel, 201
tumed, 57–8, 77–9, 99, 113, 272, 289, 309, 346, 375
Tumelun, 51, 77
TumenVladimir, 281
Tungusic, 16
tuq, 25, 70, 82, 213–14, 268, 355, 360
Tuqa, 43, 268
Turanshah, 166
turban, 216, 326, 367
Turco-Mongolian, 91, 95
Turfan, 15, 89, 202, 262
Turkestan, 58, 83, 86, 88, 120, 152–3, 159, 260, 272, 320
Turkicisation, 281, 337–8
Turkmen, 239
Turkmenistan, 12, 59

Turko-Mongol, 10, 53–4, 68, 245, 258, 280, 338
Tusi, 230
Tutar, 229
Tuul River, 2, 10, 40; *see also* Tula River
Tver, 281, 298–9, 303
Tverian, 299
typhoon, 198

Ugra River, battle of the, 309, 371
Uighur, 1, 9, 15, 44–5, 51, 53, 56, 59, 61, 71, 78, 87–9, 99–100, 118, 124, 148, 152, 178, 191, 262, 267, 276, 290, 330, 333, 337–8, 367; *see also* Uighurstan
Uighur Empire, 9, 44, 124; *see also* Uighur
Uighurstan, 15, 45, 67, 89, 153, 202, 257, 262–3, 267–8
Ukraine, 305
ulema, 224, 247–8, 255, 299, 314, 334
ultimogeniture, 68, 95, 133, 338
Umayyad, 324, 331
Urgench, 62, 106, 228, 262, 281, 314
Uriyangqadai, 160–1, 200
Uru'ud, 32, 304–5
Urungtash, 170
Uzbek, 250–1, 271, 274
Uzbekistan, 9, 59

Venetian, 191, 293, 299–301, 304, 370
Venice, 287, 301
Viceregent, 206
viceroy, 50–1, 84, 90, 153, 159, 223, 304
Vienna, 116
Vietnam, 195, 200–1, 366
Vietnamese, 200–1
virgins, 54, 72
vizier, 83, 150, 152, 165–6, 178, 208, 218, 225, 229, 231, 234, 246–7, 250, 263, 283
Vladimir, 111, 292, 303
Vlastimil, 238
Volga, 15, 58, 75, 97–8, 108–10, 123, 174, 281–2, 284, 288, 309–10, 340–1

wafidiyya, 287, 375
wagon, 21, 29, 115, 136
weather, 53, 245, 341
wethers, 42
wheat, 282
widow, 25, 70, 114, 132, 144, 149, 229, 346
wife-collecting, 58
winter, 2, 5–6, 8, 48, 76, 111, 260, 288, 307
witch, 138–40
witchcraft, 127

women, 8, 20, 22–3, 57, 70, 74, 79, 96–7, 136, 139, 147, 151, 165, 195, 202, 206–7, 234, 251–2, 255, 259, 276, 312, 340, 372

Xi Xia, 9–10, 17, 32, 37, 39, 44, 47–9, 52, 56, 64–8, 71–2, 75–6, 93, 121, 125, 149, 159, 168, 174, 292, 327, 363–6
Xianbei, 1
Xiangyang, 184–5, 196, 202, 366
Xiangzong, 327
Xinjiang, 9, 92, 203, 266
Xiongnu, 1, 3, 53, 79, 257, 276, 282
Xuanzong, 52, 55, 71, 327

Yaik River, 262, 281
Yaishan, battle of, 186–7, 197, 200, 366
Yalavach, Mahmud, 72–3, 83–6, 89, 99, 104, 123, 125, 127–8, 131, 143, 153, 155, 276
yam, 104–5, 373
Yangichar, 270, 362
Yangzhou, 186, 191, 202
Yangzi, 162, 170, 202
Yanikant, 71
Yanjing, 72
Yarkands, 262
yarligh, 150; *see also* jarliq
Yarmouth, 117
yasa, 94–5, 102–3, 119, 135, 144–5, 150, 176–8, 180, 191–2, 222, 233, 255, 267, 271, 273–4, 277, 287, 297, 301, 311, 313, 317, 347–8, 363, 375
yasaq, 150, 351
Yasaviyya, 274, 349
yasun, 39, 376
Yazd, 239
Ya'juj, 322–3
Yedi Qunan, battle of, 35

Yeke Monggol Ulus, 39–42, 67, 71, 73–4, 76–7, 88, 92, 94, 118–20, 156, 179, 181, 188, 191, 223, 226–7, 230, 233, 259, 265, 272, 290, 312, 330, 339, 341–2, 345–6, 354, 359, 366
Yellow River, 2; *see also* Huanghe River
Yelu Ahai, 43
Yelu Chucai, 55, 60–1, 65, 85–6, 99, 104, 123–4
Yelu Dashi, 15, 367
Yemen, 254
Yenisei River, 45, 202, 268
Yersinia pestis, 301; *see also* Bubonic Plague
Yesu Mongke, Chaghatayid Khan, 126, 131, 135, 146–8, 258, 357, 363
Yesudar, 361
Yesugei, 19–30, 32, 70, 365
Yesun, 147, 213–14, 273, 354, 357, 360, 363, 367
Yesunjin, 361
Yijing, 188
yogurt, 7
Yoshmut, 226, 231, 287, 361
yosun, 71, 94, 102, 135, 144–5, 150, 178, 180, 277, 347–8, 376
Yuanzhang, 216
Yunnan, 160, 199–202, 217–18, 221
Yunnei, 50
Yuri, 297–9, 370
yurt, 4, 7, 20–1, 136, 288, 376; *see also* ger

Zayton, 202, 219
Zhang Dehui, 190
Zhongdu, 52, 54–5, 72–3, 327, 365
zhud, 53–4, 260, 376
Zhungar, 257, 282, 349
Zhungaria, 173, 257, 264
Zolotaia Orda, 280
Zoroastrian, 12, 156, 223, 276

EU representative:
Easy Access System Europe
Mustamäe tee 50, 10621 Tallinn, Estonia
Gpsr.requests@easproject.com